WRITING COACH

Online

INTERACTIVE WHITEBOARD READY!

To preview Texas Writing Coach Online, follow these easy steps:

1. Go to www.pearsonschool.com/txwritingcoach

2. Click on "Preview Writing Coach Online."

3. Log into the demo site using provided username and password.

Access online demonstrations of the following student resources:

 Interactive Writing Coach™ for paragraph and essay scoring

 Online Journal for writing notes, ideas, and drafts

 Interactive Graphic Organizers for help planning your writing

 Videos on effective writing strategies

 Interactive Models of Mentor Texts and Student Models with audio

 Resources for additional support and information

- Student Edition eText
- Texas All-in-One Workbook eText

- Grammar Tutorials
- Grammar Practice

 DIMENSION ™ Powered By PEARSON

Video game to help you master grammar

www.PearsonSchool.com/DimensionL

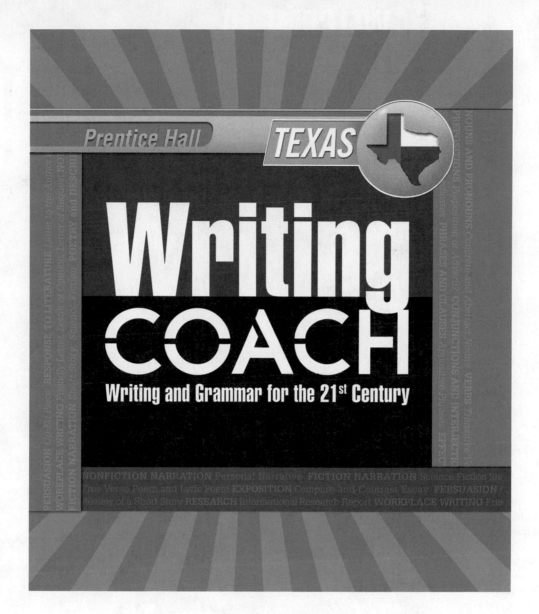

Prentice Hall

TEXAS

Writing COACH

Writing and Grammar for the 21st Century

PEARSON

Upper Saddle River, New Jersey
Boston, Massachusetts
Chandler, Arizona
Glenview, Illinois

WRITING COACH

PEARSON

0-13-252986-6

978-0-13-252986-0

3 4 5 6 7 8 9 10 V052 14 13 12 11

WELCOME TO Writing COACH

Seven Great Reasons to Learn to Write Well

1 Writing is hard, but hard is **rewarding**.

2 Writing helps you **sort things out**.

3 Writing helps you **persuade** others.

4 Writing makes you a **better reader**.

5 Writing makes you **smarter**.

6 Writing helps you get into and through **college**.

7 Writing **prepares you** for the world of work.

AUTHORS

The contributing authors guided the direction and philosophy of *Prentice Hall Writing Coach*. Working with the development team, they helped to build the pedagogical integrity of the program and to ensure its relevance for today's teachers and students.

Program Authors

Jeff Anderson

Jeff Anderson has worked with struggling writers and readers for almost 20 years. His works integrate grammar and editing instruction into the processes of reading and writing. Anderson has written articles in NCTE's *Voices from the Middle, English Journal*, and *Educational Leadership.* Anderson won the NCTE Paul and Kate Farmer Award for his *English Journal* article on teaching grammar in context. He has published two books, *Mechanically Inclined: Building Grammar, Usage, and Style into Writer's Workshop* and *Everyday Editing: Inviting Students to Develop Skill and Craft in Writer's Workshop* as well as a DVD, *The Craft of Grammar.*

Grammar gives me a powerful lens through which to look at my writing. It gives me the freedom to say things exactly the way I want to say them.

Kelly Gallagher

Kelly Gallagher is a full-time English teacher at Magnolia High School in Anaheim, California. He is the former co-director of the South Basin Writing Project at California State University, Long Beach. Gallagher is the author of *Reading Reasons: Motivational Mini-Lessons for Middle and High School, Deeper Reading: Comprehending Challenging Texts 4–12, Teaching Adolescent Writers,* and *Readicide.* He is also featured in the video series, *Building Adolescent Readers.* With a focus on adolescent literacy, Gallagher provides training to educators on a local, national and international level. Gallagher was awarded the Secondary Award of Classroom Excellence from the California Association of Teachers of English—the state's top English teacher honor.

The best swimmers swim the most; the best writers write the most. There's only one way to become a good writer: write!

Contributing Authors

Evelyn Arroyo

Evelyn Arroyo is the author of **A+RISE,** Research-based Instructional Strategies for ELLs (English Language Learners). Her work focuses on closing the achievement gap for minority students and English language learners. Through her publications and presentations, Arroyo provides advice, encouragement, and practical success strategies to help teachers reach their ELL students.

Your rich, colorful cultural life experiences are unique and can easily be painted through words. These experiences define who you are today, and writing is one way to begin capturing your history. Become a risk-taker and fall in love with yourself through your own words.

When you're learning a new language, writing in that language takes effort. The effort pays off big time, though. Writing helps us generate ideas, solve problems, figure out how the language works, and, above all, allows us to express ourselves.

Jim Cummins, Ph.D.

Jim Cummins is a Professor in the Modern Language Centre at the University of Toronto. A well-known educator, lecturer, and author, Cummins focuses his research on bilingual education and the academic achievement of culturally diverse students. He is the author of numerous publications, including **Negotiating Identities: Education for Empowerment in a Diverse Society.**

Grant Wiggins, Ed.D.

Grant Wiggins is the President of Authentic Education. He earned his Ed.D. from Harvard University. Wiggins consults with schools, districts, and state education departments; organizes conferences and workshops; and develops resources on curricular change. He is the co-author, with Jay McTighe, of **Understanding By Design,** the award-winning text published by ASCD.

I hated writing as a student—and my grades showed it. I grew up to be a writer, though. What changed? I began to think I had something to say. That's ultimately why you write: to find out what you are really thinking, really feeling, really believing.

Concepts of grammar can sharpen your reading, communication, and even your reasoning, so I have championed its practice in my classes and in my businesses. Even adults are quick to recognize that a refresher in grammar makes them keener— and more marketable.

Gary Forlini

Gary Forlini is managing partner of the School Growth initiative **Brinkman—Forlini—Williams,** which trains school administrators and teachers in Classroom Instruction and Management. His recent works include the book **Help Teachers Engage Students** and the data system **ObserverTab** for district administrators, **Class Acts: Every Teacher's Guide To Activate Learning**, and the initiative's workshop **Grammar for Teachers**.

WRITING

Writing without grammar only goes so far. Grammar and writing work together. To write well, grammar skills give me great tools.

CORE WRITING CHAPTERS

WRITING COACH
Online
www.TXWritingcoach.com

Interactive Writing Coach™

Interactive Graphic Organizer

Interactive Model

Online Journal

Resources

Video

GRAMMAR

GRAMMAR GAME PLAN

Find It FIX IT **20** Major Grammatical Errors and How to Fix Them

> Grammar without writing is only a collection of rules, but when these rules are put into action as I write, the puzzle comes together.

CORE GRAMMAR CHAPTERS

STUDENT RESOURCES

 Texas Essential Knowledge and Skills

Handbooks

Glossaries

WRITING COACH

Online

- Grammar Tutorials
- Grammar Practice
- Grammar Games

www.TXWritingcoach.com

Writing COACH | How to Use This Program

This program is organized into two distinct sections: one for WRITING and one for GRAMMAR.

In the **WRITING** section, you'll learn strategies, traits, and skills that will help you become a better writer.

In the **GRAMMAR** section, you'll learn the rules and conventions of grammar, usage, and mechanics.

What DIGITAL writing and grammar resources are available?

The Writing Coach Online boxes will indicate opportunities to use online tools.

In **Writing,** use the **Interactive Writing Coach™** in two ways to get personalized guidance and support for your writing.

- Paragraph Feedback and
- Essay Scorer

WRITING COACH

Online
www.TXWritingCoach.com

Interactive Writing Coach™
- Choosing from the Topic Bank gives you access to the Interactive Writing Coach™.
- Submit your writing and receive instant personalized feedback and guidance as you draft, revise, and edit your writing.

WRITING COACH

Online
www.TXWritingCoach.com

Grammar Tutorials
Brush up on your grammar skills with these animated videos.

Grammar Practice
Practice your grammar skills with Writing Coach Online.

Grammar Games
Test your knowledge of grammar in this fast-paced interactive video game.

In **Grammar,** view grammar tutorials, practice your grammar skills, and play grammar video games.

What will you find in the WRITING section?

Writing Genre

Each chapter introduces a different **writing genre.**

Learn about the key characteristics of the **genre** before you start writing.

Focus on a single form of the genre with the **Feature Assignment**.

Writing Coach Online

- View the **Word Bank** words in the eText glossary, and hear them pronounced in both English and Spanish.

- Use your **Online Journal** to record your answers and ideas as you respond to *Try It!* activities.

Mentor Text and Student Model

The **Mentor Text** and **Student Model** provide examples of the genre featured in each chapter.

Writing Coach Online

- Use the **Interactive Model** to mark the text with Reader's and Writer's Response Symbols.

- Listen to an audio recording of the **Mentor Text** or **Student Model.**

Use the **Mentor Text** to see how a professional crafted a piece of writing.

Review the **Student Model** as a guide for composing your own piece.

The **Topic Bank** provides prompts for the **Feature Assignment.**

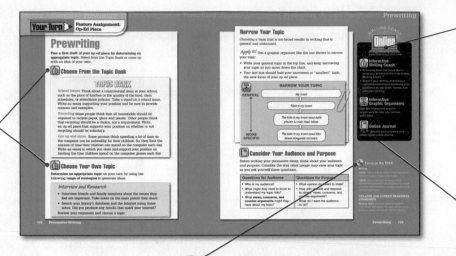

Choose from a bank of topics, or follow steps to find an idea of your own.

Notice the **TEKS** and **College and Career Readiness Standards** that appear throughout each lesson.

Writing Coach Online

- As you narrow your topic, get the right type of support! You'll find three different forms of graphic organizers— one model, one with step-by-step guidance, and one that is blank for you to complete.

- Use *Try It!* ideas to practice new skills. Use *Apply It!* activities as you work on your own writing.

Outline for Success

Whether you are working on your essay drafts online or with a pen and paper, an **Outline for Success** can get you started.

Consult this **outline** for a quick visual specific to the writing task assigned in each chapter.

Follow the bulleted suggestions for each part of your draft, and you'll be on your way to success.

Writing Coach Online

- Start with just a paragraph and build up to your essay draft, or if you are ready, go straight to submitting your essay. The choice is yours!

You can use the **Revision RADaR** strategy as a guide
for making changes to improve your draft.

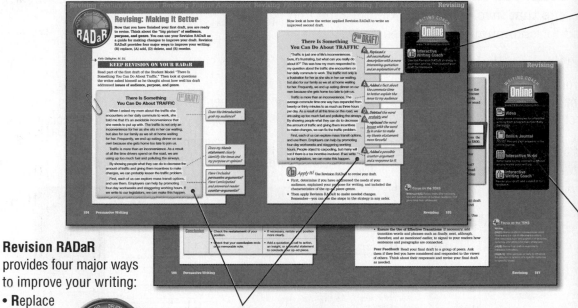

Revision RADaR
provides four major ways
to improve your writing:

- **R**eplace
- **A**dd
- **D**elete
- **R**eorder

Check out these example drafts to
see how to apply **Revision RADaR.**

In the editing stage, **What Do You Notice?** and
Mentor Text help you zoom in on powerful sentences.

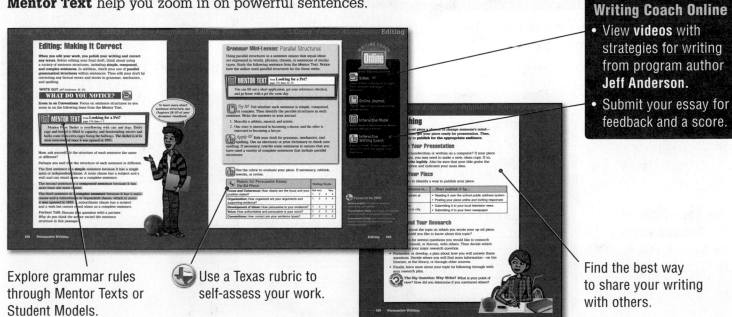

Explore grammar rules
through Mentor Texts or
Student Models.

Use a Texas rubric to
self-assess your work.

Find the best way
to share your writing
with others.

How do end-of-chapter features help you apply what you've learned?

21st Century Learning

In **Make Your Writing Count** and **Writing for Media** you will work on innovative assignments that involve the 21st Century life and career skills you'll need for communicating successfully.

Make Your Writing Count
Work collaboratively on project-based assignments and share what you have learned with others. Projects include:

- Debates
- TV Talk Shows
- News Reports

Writing for Media
Complete an assignment on your own by exploring media forms, and then developing your own content. Projects include:

- Blogs
- Storyboards
- Documentary Scripts
- Multimedia Presentations

Test Prep

The **Writing for Assessment** pages help you prepare for important standardized tests.

SAT/PSAT PREP ACT Notice these icons that emphasize the types of writing you'll find on high-stakes tests.

Use **The ABCDs of On-Demand Writing** for a quick, memorable strategy for success.

Writing Coach Online
Submit your essay for feedback and a score.

Be on the lookout for star icons that highlight the types of writing you'll find on Texas state tests.

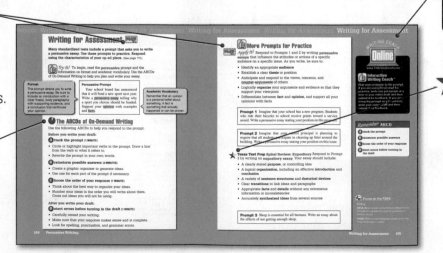

What will you find in the GRAMMAR section?

Grammar Game Plan

The **Find It/Fix It** reference guide helps you fix the **20** most common errors in student writing.

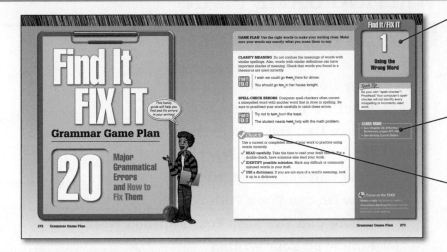

Study each of the 20 common errors and their corrections, which are clearly explained on each page.

Follow cross-references to more instruction in the grammar chapters.

Review the **Check It** features for strategies to help you avoid these errors.

Grammar Chapters

Each grammar chapter begins with a **What Do You Notice?** feature and **Mentor Text.**

Use the **Mentor Text** to help you zoom in on powerful sentences. It showcases the correct use of written language conventions.

Writing Coach Online
The **Writing Coach Online** digital experience for Grammar helps you focus on just the lessons and practice you need.

Use the grammar section as a quick reference handbook. Each **grammar rule** is highlighted and numbered.

 Try **Practice** pages and **Texas Test Warm-Ups** to help you check your progress.

WRITING

WRITING GAME PLAN

CONTENTS

WRITING COACH

Online

www.TXWritingcoach.com

All content available online

- Interactive Writing Coach™
- Interactive Graphic Organizer
- Interactive Models
- Online Journal
- Resources
- Video

WRITING

Connect to the Big Questions

- **What do you think?**
  What do our accomplishments say about us?

- **Why write?**
  What should we put in and leave out to be accurate and honest?

Connect to the Big Questions

- **What do you think?**
  How do challenges help us grow?

- **Why write?**
  What can fiction do better than nonfiction?

www.TXWritingcoach.com

All content available online

- Interactive Writing Coach™
- Interactive Graphic Organizer
- Interactive Models
- Online Journal
- Resources
- Video

WRITING

Focus on the TEKS
Writing (15) Write literary texts to express ideas and feelings about real or imagined people, events, and ideas.

COLLEGE AND CAREER READINESS STANDARDS

College and Career Readiness Standards appear on pages in each chapter.

Connect to the Big Questions

• **What do you think?**
When is a picture better than words?

• **Why write?**
How does one best convey feelings through words on a page?

Focus on the TEKS
Writing (17) Write expository and procedural or work-related texts to communicate ideas and information to specific audiences for specific purposes.

COLLEGE AND CAREER READINESS STANDARDS
College and Career Readiness Standards appear on pages in each chapter.

Connect to the Big Questions

• **What do you think?**
Is newer always better?

• **Why write?**
What should we tell and what should we describe to make information clear?

WRITING COACH
Online
www.TXWritingcoach.com

All content available online

• Interactive Writing Coach™
• Interactive Graphic Organizer
• Interactive Models
• Online Journal
• Resources
• Video

WRITING

Focus on the TEKS
Writing (18) Write persuasive texts to influence the attitudes or actions of a specific audience on specific issues.

COLLEGE AND CAREER READINESS STANDARDS

College and Career Readiness Standards appear on pages in each chapter.

Connect to the Big Questions

• **What do you think?**

Which do you think is more important and why—the community's right to ensure that students are not distracted by cell phones or the individual student's right to use a cell phone?

• **Why write?**

What is your point of view? How will you know if you've convinced others?

Focus on the TEKS
Writing (17) Write expository and procedural or work-related texts to communicate ideas and information to specific audiences for specific purposes.

COLLEGE AND CAREER READINESS STANDARDS

College and Career Readiness Standards appear on pages in each chapter.

Connect to the Big Questions

• **What do you think?**
  What do readers bring to a text that writers may not?

• **Why write?**
  What should you write about to make others interested in a text?

www.TXWritingcoach.com

All content available online
• Interactive Writing Coach™
• Interactive Graphic Organizer
• Interactive Models
• Online Journal
• Resources
• Video

WRITING

Focus on the TEKS
Research

(22) Ask open-ended research questions and develop a plan for answering them.
(23) Determine, locate, and explore the full range of relevant sources addressing a research question and systematically record the gathered information.
(24) Clarify research questions and evaluate and synthesize collected information.
(25) Organize and present ideas and information according to the purpose of the research and their audience.

COLLEGE AND CAREER READINESS STANDARDS

College and Career Readiness Standards appear on pages in each chapter.

Connect to the Big Questions

- **What do you think?**
  What kinds of scientific discoveries affect our lives the most?

- **Why write?**
  Do you understand your subject well enough to write about it? How will you find out what all the facts are?

Connect to the
Big Questions

- **What do you think?**
  What is the best way
  to share information?

- **Why write?**
  What do daily
  workplace
  communications
  require of format,
  content, and style?

www.TXWritingcoach.com

All content available online
- Interactive Writing Coach™
- Interactive Graphic Organizer
- Interactive Models
- Online Journal
- Resources
- Video

GRAMMAR GAME PLAN

Find It/Fix It
The 20 Errors

GRAMMAR

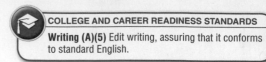

COLLEGE AND CAREER READINESS STANDARDS
Writing (A)(5) Edit writing, assuring that it conforms to standard English.

> **Focus on the TEKS**
> **Conventions (19)** Understand the function of and use the conventions of academic language when speaking and writing.

WRITING COACH

Online

www.TXWritingcoach.com

All content available online
- Grammar Tutorials
- Grammar Practice
- Grammar Games

GRAMMAR

Focus on the TEKS
Conventions (19) Understand the function of and use the conventions of academic language when speaking and writing.

Focus on the TEKS Conventions (19) Understand the function of and use the conventions of academic language when speaking and writing.

Focus on the TEKS Conventions
(19) Understand the function of and use the conventions of academic language when speaking and writing.
(20) Write legibly and use appropriate capitalization and punctuation conventions in compositions.

WRITING COACH

Online
www.TXWritingcoach.com

All content available online
• Grammar Tutorials
• Grammar Practice
• Grammar Games

GRAMMAR
USAGE

 COLLEGE AND CAREER READINESS STANDARDS
Writing (A)(5) Edit writing, assuring that it conforms to standard English.

Focus on the TEKS
Conventions (19) Understand the function of and use the conventions of academic language when speaking and writing.

Focus on the TEKS
Conventions (19) Understand the function of and use the conventions of academic language when speaking and writing.

MECHANICS

**Focus on the TEKS
Conventions (20)** Write
legibly and use appropriate
capitalization and punctuation
conventions in compositions.

WRITING COACH

Online

www.TXWritingcoach.com

All content available online
- Grammar Tutorials
- Grammar Practice
- Grammar Games

GRAMMAR

COLLEGE AND CAREER READINESS STANDARDS

Writing (A)(5) Edit writing, assuring that it conforms to standard English.

WRITING COACH

Online

www.TXWritingcoach.com

All content available online
- Grammar Tutorials
- Grammar Practice
- Grammar Games

STUDENT RESOURCES

ADDITIONAL PRACTICE

 TEXAS WRITING COACH ALL-IN-ONE
- Texas Test Practice
- Texas Reading Rubrics
- Texas Writing Rubrics
- Grammar Practice

NONFICTION NARRATION Personal Narrative FICTION NARRATION Scie
EXPOSITION Compare-and-Contrast Essay PERSUASION Op-Ed Piece RESPO
WORKPLACE WRITING Friendly Letter, Letter of Opinion, Letter of Request NO
hort Story POETRY and DESCRIPTION Free Verse Poem and Lyric Poem EX
ITERATURE Review of a Short Story RESEARCH Informational Research Repor
ION NARRATION Personal Narrative FICTION NARRATION Science Ficti
ION Compare-and-Contrast Essay PERSUASION Op-Ed Piece RESPONSE T
LACE WRITING Friendly Letter, Letter of Opinion, Letter of Request NONFICT
tory POETRY and DESCRIPTION Free Verse Poem and Lyric Poem EXPOSI

Writing

YOU, THE WRITER

Why Do You Write?

Writing well is one of the most important life skills you can develop. Being a good writer can help you achieve success in school and beyond. Most likely, you write for many reasons. You write:

To Share

You probably often write to **share** your experiences with others. Writing can be an easy way to **reach out** to people and connect with them.

To Persuade People

Writing can also be an effective way to **persuade** people to consider your opinions. For example, you may find it's easier to convince someone of your point of view when you've effectively organized your thoughts in an essay or a letter.

To Inform

Another reason to write is to **inform**. Perhaps you want to tell an audience how you built your computer network or how you finally got your e-mail to function properly.

To Enjoy

Personal fullfillment is another important motivation for writing, since writing enables you **to express** your thoughts and feelings. In addition, writing can also help you recall an event, or let you escape from everyday life.

Fortunately, writing well is a skill you can learn and one that you can continue to improve and polish. This program will help you improve your writing skills and give you useful information about the many types of writing.

What Do You Write?

Writing is already an important part of your everyday life. Each day is full of opportunities to write, allowing you to capture, express, think through and share your thoughts and feelings, and demonstrate what you know. Here are some ways you might write.

- Recording thoughts in a journal
- Texting friends or posting on social networking sites
- E-mailing thank-you notes to relatives
- Creating lists of things to do or things you like
- Writing research reports, nonfiction accounts, fiction stories, and essays in school

How Can You Find Ideas?

The good news is that ideas are all around you. You just need to be aware of the rich resources that are available.

By Observing

Observing is a good way to start to find ideas. Did you see anything interesting on your way to school? Was there something unusual about the video game you played last night?

By Reading

Reading is another useful option—look through newspaper articles and editorials, magazines, blogs, and Web sites. Perhaps you read something that surprised you or really made you feel concerned. Those are exactly the subjects that can lead to the ideas you want to write about.

By Watching

Watching is another way to get ideas—watch online videos or television programs, for example.

WRITING COACH

www.TXWritingCoach.com

Online Journal

Try It! Record your notes, answers, and ideas in the online journal. You can also record and save your answers and ideas on pop-up sticky notes in the eText.

" Writer to Writer "

I write when I want to be heard or connect. Writing lets me be a vital part of my community and reach outside it as well. All the while, I get to be me—my unique self.

—Jeff Anderson

How Can You Keep Track of Ideas?

You may sometimes think of great writing ideas in the middle of the night or on the way to math class. These strategies can help you remember those ideas.

Start an Idea Notebook or a Digital Idea File

Reserving a small **notebook** to record ideas can be very valuable. Just writing the essence of an idea, as it comes to you, can later help you develop a topic or essay. A **digital idea file** is exactly the same thing—but it's recorded on your computer, cell phone, or other electronic device.

Keep a Personal Journal

Many people find that keeping a **journal** of their thoughts is helpful. Then, when it's time to select an idea, they can flip through their journal and pick up on the best gems they wrote—sometimes from long ago.

Maintain a Learning Log

A **learning log** is just what it sounds like—a place to record information you have learned, which could be anything from methods of solving equations to computer shortcuts. Writing about something in a learning log might later inspire you to conduct further research on the same topic.

Free Write

Some individuals find that if they just let go and write whatever comes to mind, they eventually produce excellent ideas. **Free writing** requires being relaxed and unstructured. This kind of writing does not require complete sentences, correct spelling, or proper grammar. Whatever ends up on the paper or on the computer screen is fine. Later, the writer can go back and tease out the best ideas.

How Can You Get Started?

Every writer is different, so it makes sense that all writers should try out techniques that might work well for them. Regardless of your writing style, these suggestions should help you get started.

Get Comfortable

It's important to find and create an environment that encourages your writing process. Choose a spot where you'll find it easy to concentrate. Some writers prefer quiet. Others prefer to work in a room with music playing softly.

Have Your Materials Ready

Before starting to write, gather all the background materials you need to get started, including your notes, free writing, reader's journal, and portfolio. Make sure you also have writing tools, such as a pen and paper or a computer.

Spend Time Wisely

Budgeting your available writing time is a wise strategy. Depending on your writing goal, you may want to sketch out your time on a calendar, estimating how long to devote to each stage of the writing process. Then, you can assign deadlines to each part. If you find a particular stage takes longer than you estimated, simply adjust your schedule to ensure that you finish on time.

◄ October ►						
SUNDAY	MONDAY	TUESDAY	WEDNESDAY	THURSDAY	FRIDAY	SATURDAY
		1 Start Research	2 Finish Research	3 Write Outline	4	5
6	7	8 Finish First Draft	9 Finish Revising	10 Finish Proof-reading	11	12
13	14 DUE DATE	15	16	17	18	19
20	21	22	23	24	25	26
27	28	29	30	31		

How Do You Work With Others?

If you think of writing as a solitary activity, think again. Working with others can be a key part of the writing process.

Brainstorming

Brainstorming works when everyone in a group feels free to suggest ideas, whether they seem commonplace or brilliant.

Cooperative Writing

Cooperative writing is a process in which each member of a group concentrates on a different part of an assignment. Then, the group members come together to discuss their ideas and write drafts.

Peer Feedback

Peer feedback comes from classmates who have read your writing and offered suggestions for improvements. When commenting, it's important to provide constructive, or helpful, criticism.

21st Century Learning

Collaborate and Discuss

In **collaborative writing,** each group member takes a role on a writing project. The goal is to work and rework the writing until all members feel they have produced the best result.

Possible Roles in a Collaborative Writing Project

LEADER
Initiates the discussion by clearly expressing group goals and moderates discussions

FACILITATOR
Works to move the discussion forward and clarify ideas

COMPROMISER
Works to find practical solutions to differences of opinion

LISTENER
Actively listens and serves to recall details that were discussed

Using Technology

Technology allows collaboration to occur in ways that were previously unthinkable.

- By working together on the Internet, students around the world have infinite opportunities to collaborate online on a wide range of projects.

- Collaboration can range from projects that foster community cooperation, such as how to improve debates during local elections, to those that increase global awareness, such as focusing on how to encourage more recycling.

- Being able to log in and to contribute to media, such as journals, blogs, and social networks, allows you to connect globally, express your views in writing, and join a world-wide conversation.

Where Can You Keep Your Finished Work?

A **portfolio,** or growing collection of your work, is valuable for many reasons. It can serve as a research bank of ideas and as a record of how your writing is improving. You can create a portfolio on a computer or in a folder or notebook. You'll learn more about managing a portfolio in chapter 3.

A **Reader's Journal,** in which you record quotes and ideas from your reading, can also be used to store original ideas. Your journal can be housed on a computer or in a notebook.

Reflect on Your Writing

Analyzing, making inferences, and drawing conclusions about how you find ideas can help you become a better, more effective writer. Find out more about how you write by asking yourself questions like these:

- Which strategies have I found most effective for finding good ideas for writing?

- What pieces of writing represent my best work and my weakest work? What do the pieces in each group have in common?

With a partner, talk about your collaborative writing experiences. Be sure to share your responses to such questions as these: What project did you work on as a collaborative effort? What did you learn that you might not have discovered if you were developing a writing project by yourself?

TYPES *of* WRITING

Genres and Forms

Genres are types, or categories, of writing.

- Each genre has a specific **purpose,** or goal. For example, the purpose of persuasive writing is to convince readers to agree with the writer's point of view.
- Each genre has specific **characteristics.** Short stories, for example, have characters, a setting, and a plot.

In this chapter, you will be introduced to several genres: nonfiction narratives, fiction narratives, poetry and descriptive writing, expository writing, persuasive writing, responses to literature, and workplace writing.

Forms are subcategories of genres that contain all the characteristics of the genre plus some unique characteristics of their own. For example, a mystery is a form of short story. In addition to plot, characters, and setting, it has a mystery to be solved.

Selecting Genres

In some writing situations, you may need to select the correct genre for conveying your intended meaning.

- To **entertain,** you may choose to write a short story or a humorous essay.
- To **describe** an emotion, writing a poem may be best.
- To **persuade** someone to your point of view, you may want to write a persuasive essay or editorial.

Each genre has unique strengths and weaknesses, and your specific goals will help you decide which is best.

Nonfiction Narration

Nonfiction narratives are any kind of literary text that tells a story about real people, events, and ideas. This genre of writing can take a number of different forms but includes well-developed conflict and resolution, interesting and believable characters, and a range of literary strategies, such as dialogue and suspense. Examples include Jean Fritz's "mk" and Annie Dillard's "An American Childhood."

Personal Narratives

Personal narratives tell true stories about events in a writer's life. These types of writing are also called **autobiographical essays.** The stories may tell about an experience or relationship that is important to the writer, who is the main character. They have a clearly defined focus and communicate the reasons for actions and consequences.

Biographical Narratives

In a **biographical narrative,** the writer shares facts about someone else's life. The writer may describe an important period, experience, or relationship in that other person's life, but presents the information from his or her own perspective.

Blogs

Blogs are online journals that may include autobiographical narratives, reflections, opinions, and other types of comments. They may also reflect genres other than nonfiction such as expository writing, and they may include other media, such as photos, music, or video.

Diary and Journal Entries

Writers record their personal thoughts, feelings, and experiences in **diaries** or **journals**. Writers sometimes keep diaries and journals for many years and then analyze how they reacted to various events over time.

Eyewitness Accounts

Eyewitness accounts are nonfiction writing that focus on historical or other important events. The writer is the narrator and shares his or her thoughts about the event. However, the writer is not the main focus of the writing.

Memoirs

Memoirs usually focus on meaningful scenes from writers' lives. These scenes often reflect on moments of a significant decision or personal discovery. For example, many modern U.S. presidents have written memoirs after they have left office. These memoirs help the public gain a better understanding of the decisions they made while in office.

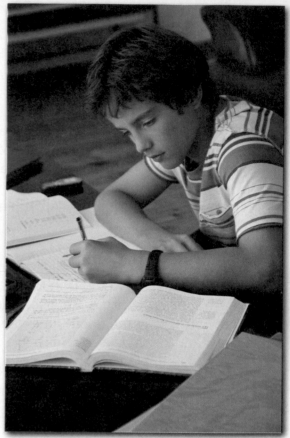

Reflective Essays

Reflective essays present personal experiences, either events that happened to the writers themselves or that they learned about from others. They generally focus on sharing observations and insights they had while thinking about those experiences. Reflective essays often appear as features in magazines and newspapers.

Try It! With a small group, discuss which of the narrative nonfiction forms would be the best choice for each of these purposes. For each, identify two ideas you would expect the writing to address. Discuss your ideas and report your decisions.

- To tell about seeing a championship kite-flying tournament
- To write about one of the first astronauts to walk in space
- To record personal thoughts about a favorite teacher

Fiction Narration

Fiction narratives are literary texts that tell a story about imagined people, events, and ideas. They contain elements such as characters, a setting, a sequence of events, and often, a theme. As with nonfiction narratives, this genre can take many different forms, but most forms include well-developed **conflict** and **resolution.** They also include **interesting and believable elements** and a range of **literary strategies,** such as dialogue and suspense. Examples include Cynthia Rylant's "Papa's Parrot" and Lucille Clifton's "The Luckiest Time of All."

Realistic Fiction

Realistic fiction portrays invented characters and events in everyday situations. Because the focus is on everyday life, realistic fiction often presents problems that many people face and solutions they devise to solve them.

Fantasy Stories

Fantasy stories stretch the imagination and take readers to unreal worlds. Animals may talk, people may fly, or characters may have superhuman powers. Good fantasy stories manage to keep the fantastic elements believable.

Historical Fiction

Historical fiction is about imaginary people living in real places and times in history. Usually, the main characters are fictional people who know and interact with famous people and participate in important historical events.

Mystery Stories

Mystery stories present unexplained or strange events that characters try to solve. These stories are often packed full of suspense and surprises. Some characters in mystery stories, such as Sherlock Holmes, have become so famous that many people think of them as real people.

Myths and Legends

Myths and **legends** are traditional stories, told in cultures around the world. They were created to explain natural events that people could not otherwise explain or understand. They may, for example, tell about the origin of fire or thunder. Many myths and legends include gods, goddesses, and heroes who perform superhuman actions.

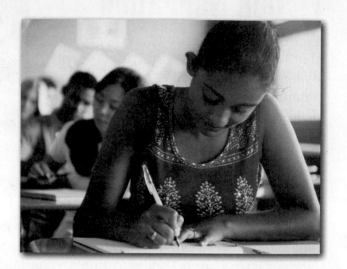

Science Fiction

Science fiction stories tell about real and imagined developments in science and technology and their effects on the way people think and live. Space travel, robots, and life in the future are popular topics in science fiction.

Tall Tales

You can tell a **tall tale** from other story types because it tells about larger-than-life characters in realistic settings. These characters can perform amazing acts of strength and bravery. One very famous hero of tall tales is Pecos Bill, who could ride just about anything—even a tornado!

Try It! Think about what you've read about narrative fiction and narrative nonfiction genres. Then, discuss in a group which **genre** would be best if you were planning a first draft and had these purposes in mind. Select the correct genre for conveying your intended meaning to your audiences. Then, identify two or three ideas that you would expect to include in a first draft. Be sure to explain your choices.

- To tell about a Texas rancher who can lasso lightning
- To share a true story about a famous person
- To tell the story of your most exciting day at school

Poetry and Description

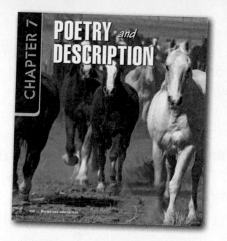

Poetry and other kinds of descriptive literature express ideas and feelings about real or imagined people, events, and ideas. They use rhythm, rhyme, precise language, and sensory details—words that appeal to the senses—to create vivid images. In addition, they use figurative language—writing that means something beyond what the words actually say—to express ideas in new, fresh, and interesting ways.

Structural elements, such as line length and stanzas, also help the poet express ideas and set a mood. Some examples of poetry include Naomi Shihab Nye's "The Rider" and Nikki Giovanni's "Winter."

Ballad

A **ballad** is a form of lyric poetry that expresses the poet's emotions toward someone or something. Ballads rhyme, and some have refrains that repeat after each stanza, which makes them easy to translate into songs.

In many places, traditional folk ballads were passed down as oral poems or songs and then later written. Some ballads tell about cultural heroes. Other ballads tell sad stories or make fun of certain events.

Free Verse

Free verse is poetry that has no regular rhyme, rhythm, or form. Instead, a free verse poem captures the patterns of natural speech. The poet writes in whatever form seems to fit the ideas best. A free verse poem can have almost anything as its subject.

Partner Talk

Think about an example of fiction that you've especially enjoyed reading. Then, choose a partner and report your choices to each other. Be sure to explain what made the fiction piece so enjoyable, interesting, or exciting.

 Focus on the TEKS

Writing (14)(A) Plan a first draft by selecting the correct genre for conveying the intended meaning to an audience.

Prose Poem

A **prose poem** shares many of the features of other poetry, but it takes the form of prose, or non-verse writing. Therefore, a prose poem may look like a short story on a page.

Sonnet

The **sonnet** is a form of rhyming lyric poetry with set rules. It is 14 lines long and usually follows a rhythm scheme called iambic pentameter. Each line has ten syllables and every other syllable is accented.

Haiku

Haiku is a form of non-rhyming poetry that was first developed in Japan hundreds of years ago. Typically, the first line has seven syllables, the second line has five syllables, and the third line has seven syllables. Haiku poets often write about nature and use vivid visual images.

Other Descriptive Writing

Descriptive writing includes descriptive essays, travel writing, and definition essays.

- **Descriptive essays** often use words that involve the senses to create a clear picture of a subject.
- A **travel essay** uses sensory words to describe a place.
- A **definition essay** can draw on a writer's emotional experience to describe something abstract, like friendship or happiness.

  Description can be used in other types of writing. For example, a short story may include strong description.

Try It! Now that you've learned more about poetry and description, discuss which specific **genre** would be best for each of these purposes. Select the correct genre for conveying your intended meaning to your audiences. Then, identify two or three types of information that you would want to include in a first draft. Be ready to explain your thinking.

- To tell about a trip to a beach in Mexico
- To describe a drop of rain
- To tell the story of a character who lives in the wilderness

Exposition

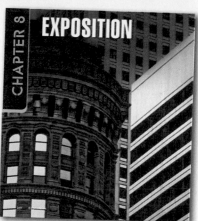

Exposition is writing that seeks to communicate ideas and information. It relies on facts to inform or explain.

- Effective expository writing includes effective introductory paragraphs, body paragraphs, and concluding paragraphs.
- In addition, good expository writing uses a variety of sentence structures and rhetorical devices—deliberate uses of language for specific effects.

Examples of expository writing include Ruwanthi Vigilant's "Houston's Chinatown" and Larry Lunxer's "Mongoose on the Loose."

Analytical Essay

An **analytical essay** explores a topic by supplying relevant information in the form of facts, examples, reasons, and valid inferences to support the writer's claims.

- An **introductory paragraph** presents a thesis statement, the main point to be developed.
- The **body of the essay** provides facts about the topic, using a variety of sentence structures and transitions.
- The **concluding paragraph** sums up ideas.

Compare-and-Contrast Essay

A **compare-and-contrast** essay explores similarities and differences between two or more things for a specific purpose. As with other expository essays, the compare-and-contrast essay offers clear, factual details about the subject.

Cause-and-Effect Essay

A **cause-and-effect essay** traces the results of an event or describes the reasons an event happened. It is clearly organized and gives precise examples that support the relationship between the cause and effect.

Choose a different partner this time. Discuss a poem that you've read in class. Share your thoughts about the poem and describe what made the piece successful.

 Focus on the TEKS

Writing (14)(A) Plan a first draft by selecting the correct genre for conveying the intended meaning to an audience.

Classification Essay

In a **classification essay,** a writer organizes a subject into categories and explains the category into which an item falls.

- An effective classification essay **sorts** its subjects—things or ideas—into several categories.

- It then offers **examples** that fall into each category. For example, a classification essay about video games might discuss three types of video games—action, adventure, and arcade.

- The essay might conclude with a statement about how the items classified are different or about how they are similar.

Problem-Solution Essay

A **problem-solution essay** presents a problem and then offers solutions to that problem. This type of essay may contain opinions, like a persuasive essay, but it is meant to explain rather than persuade.

- An effective problem-solution essay presents a clear statement of the problem, including a summary of its causes and effects.

- Then, it proposes at least one realistic solution and uses facts, statistics, or expert testimony to support the solution.

- The essay should be clearly organized, so that the relationship between the problem and the solution is obvious.

Pro-Con Essay

A **pro-con essay** examines arguments for and against an idea or topic.

- It has a topic that has two sides or points of view. For example, you might choose the following as a topic: Is it right to keep animals in zoos?

- Then, you would develop an essay that tells why it's good to keep animals in zoos, as well as why it's harmful to keep animals in zoos.

- It's important to be sure to give a clear analysis of the topic.

Newspaper and Magazine Articles

Newspaper and **magazine articles** offer information about news and events. They are typically factual and do not include the writer's opinions. They often provide an analysis of events and give readers background information on a topic. Some articles may also reflect genres other than the analytical essay, such as an editorial that aims to persuade.

Internet Articles

Articles on the **Internet** can supply relevant information about a topic.

- They are often like newspaper or magazine articles but may include shorter sentences and paragraphs. In addition, they include more visuals, such as charts and bulleted lists. They may also reflect genres other than analytical essays.

- It's always wise to consider the source when reading Internet articles because only the most reputable sources should be trusted to present correct facts.

On-Demand Writing

Because essay questions often appear on school tests, knowing how to write to **test prompts**, especially under time limits, is an important skill.

Test prompts provide a clear topic with directions about what should be addressed. The effective response to an essay demonstrates not only an understanding of academic content but also good writing skills.

Try It! Think about what you've learned about expository writing and consider the other genres you've discussed. Then, discuss in a group which **genre** would be best if you were planning a first draft with these purposes in mind. Select the correct genre for conveying your intended meaning to your audiences. Then, identify two or three key ideas that you would want to include in a first draft. Be sure to explain your choices.

- To weigh the benefits of two kinds of pets
- To imagine what life would be like on the moon

Share your experiences with writing expository essays with a partner. Talk about strategies that worked well for you, as well as those that weren't as successful. Be sure to include your analysis of why certain strategies worked better than others.

Focus on the TEKS

Writing (14)(A) Plan a first draft by selecting the correct genre for conveying the intended meaning to an audience.

Persuasion

Persuasive writing aims to influence the attitudes or actions of a specific audience on specific issues. A strong persuasive text is logically organized and clearly describes the issue. It also provides precise and relevant evidence that supports a clear thesis statement. Persuasive writing may contain diagrams, graphs, or charts. These visuals can help to convince the reader. Examples include Barbara Jordan's "All Together Now" and Louis L'Amour's "The Eternal Frontier."

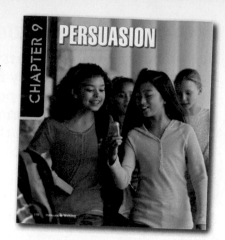

Persuasive Essays or Argumentative Essays

A **persuasive essay** or **argumentative essay** uses logic and reasoning to persuade readers to adopt a certain point of view or to take action. A strong persuasive essay starts with a clear thesis statement and provides supporting arguments based on evidence. It also anticipates readers' counter-arguments and responds to them as well.

Persuasive Speeches

Persuasive speeches are presented aloud and aim to win an audience's support for a policy, position, or action. These speeches often appeal to emotion and reason to convince an audience. Speakers sometimes change their script in order to address each specific audience's concerns.

Editorials

Editorials state the opinion of the editors and publishers of news organizations. Editorials usually present an opinion about a current issue, starting with a clear thesis statement and then offering strong supporting evidence.

Op-Ed Pieces

An **op-ed, or opposite-editorial, piece** is an essay that tries to convince readers to agree with the writer's views on an issue. The writer may not work for the publication and is often an expert on the issue or has an interesting point of view.

Letters to the Editor

Readers write **letters to editors** at print and Internet publications to express opinions in response to previously published articles. A good letter to the editor gives an accurate and honest representation of the writer's views.

Reviews

Reviews evaluate items and activities, such as books, movies, plays, and music, from the writer's point of view. A review often states opinions on the quality of an item or activity and supports those opinions with examples, facts, and other evidence.

Advertisements

Advertisements in all media—from print to online sites to highway billboards—are paid announcements that try to convince people to buy something or do something. Good advertisements use a hook to grab your attention and support their claims. They contain vivid, persuasive language and multimedia techniques, such as music, to appeal to a specific audience.

Propaganda

Propaganda uses emotional appeals and often biased, false, or misleading information to persuade people to think or act in a certain way. Propaganda may tap into people's strongest emotions by generating fear or attacking their ideas of loyalty or patriotism. Because propaganda appears to be objective, it is wise to be aware of the ways it can manipulate people's opinions and actions.

Try It! Think about what you have learned about exposition, description, and persuasion. Form a group to discuss and draw conclusions about which **genres** would be best if you were planning a first draft with each of these intentions in mind. Select the correct genre for conveying your intended meaning to your audiences. Then, identify two or three types of information that you would want to include in a first draft.

- To explain how an event happened
- To describe a beautiful landscape
- To encourage teens to buy teeth-whitening toothpaste

Partner Talk

Share your experiences with various types of persuasive texts with a partner. Talk about the types of persuasive text that you think are most effective, honest, and fair. Be sure to explain your thinking.

Focus on the TEKS

Writing (14)(A) Plan a first draft by selecting the correct genre for conveying the intended meaning to an audience.

Responses to Literature

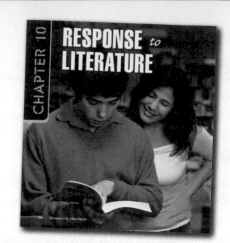

Responses to literature analyze and interpret an author's work. They use clear **thesis statements** and **evidence from the text using embedded quotations to support the writer's ideas.** They also evaluate how well authors have accomplished their goals. Effective responses to literature extend beyond literal analysis to evaluate and discuss how and why the text is effective or not effective.

Critical Reviews

Critical reviews evaluate books, plays, poetry, and other literary works. Reviews present the writer's opinions and support them with specific examples. The responses may analyze the aesthetic effects of an author's use of language in addition to responding to the content of the writing.

Compare-and-Contrast Essays

Compare-and-contrast essays explore similarities and differences between two or more works of literature. These essays provide relevant evidence to support the writer's opinions.

Letters to Authors

Readers write **letters to authors** to share their feelings and thoughts about a work of literature directly.

Blog Comments

Blog comments on an author's Web site or book retailer pages let readers share their ideas about a work. Readers express their opinions and give interpretations of what an author's work means.

Try It! As a group, decide which **genre** would be most appropriate if you were planning a first draft for each of these purposes. Select the correct genre for conveying your intended meaning to your audiences. Then, identify two or three key questions that you would want to answer in a first draft.

- To tell an author why you think her book is excellent
- To write an opinion about a newspaper article
- To imagine how a certain landform came to be

> **Partner Talk**
>
> Interview your partner about his or her experiences writing interpretative responses. Be sure to ask questions such as these:
>
> - How did you support your opinion of the author's work?
> - How did you choose evidence, such as quotes, to support your analysis or opinion?

Research Writing

Research writing is based on factual information from outside sources. Research reports organize and present ideas and information. They present evidence in support of a clear thesis statement.

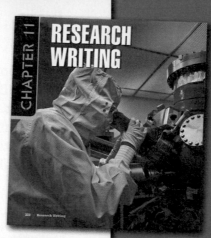

Research Reports and Documented Essays

Research reports and **documented essays** present information and analysis about a topic that the writer has studied. Start with a clear thesis statement. Research reports often include graphics and illustrations. Documented essays are less formal research writing that show the source of every fact, quote, or borrowed idea in parentheses.

Experiment Journals and Lab Reports

Experiment journals and **lab reports** focus on the purposes, procedures, and results of a lab experiment. They often follow a strict format that includes dates and specific observation notes.

Statistical Analysis Reports

A **statistical analysis report** presents numerical data. Writers of this type of report must explain how they gathered their information, analyze their data, tell what significance the findings may have, and explain how these findings support their thesis.

Annotated Bibliographies

An **annotated bibliography** lists the research sources a writer used. It includes the title, author, publication date, publisher, and brief notes that describe and evaluate the source.

Try It! Discuss which kinds of reports you might write if you were planning a first draft for these purposes. **Select the correct form** for conveying your intended meaning to your audiences. Then, identify two or three key questions that you would want to answer in a first draft. Explain your choices.

- To accompany a project you plan to enter in a science fair
- To write about a poll taken to predict the results of an election

Share with a partner the kinds of research writing you've done in school. Explain which projects you've enjoyed and why.

 Focus on the TEKS

Writing (14)(A) Plan a first draft by selecting the correct genre for conveying the intended meaning to an audience.

Workplace Writing

Workplace writing is writing done on the job or as part of a job, often in an office setting. It usually communicates details about a particular job or work project. This type of writing features organized and accurately conveyed information and should include reader-friendly formatting techniques, such as clearly defined sections and enough blank space for easy reading.

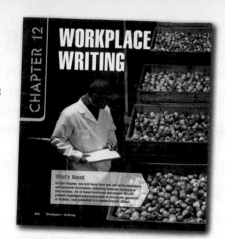

Business Letters and Friendly Letters

A **business letter** is a formal letter written to, from, or within a business. It can be written to make requests or to express concerns or approval. For example, you might write to a company to ask about job opportunities. Business letters follow a specific format that includes an address, date, formal greeting, and closing.

In contrast, a **friendly letter** is a form of correspondence written to communicate between family, friends, or acquaintances. For example, you might write a thank-you note for a gift.

Memos

Memos are short documents usually written from one member of an organization to another or to a group. They are an important means of communicating information within an organization.

E-mails

E-mail is an abbreviation for "electronic mail" and is a form of electronic memo. Because it can be transmitted quickly allowing for instant long-distance communication, e-mail is a very common form of communication that uses a computer and software to send messages.

Forms

Forms are types of workplace writing that ask for specific information to be completed in a particular format. Examples include applications, emergency contact information forms, and tax forms.

Instructions

Instructions are used to explain how to complete a task or procedure. They provide clear, step-by-step guidelines. For example, recipes and user manuals are forms of instructions.

Project Plans

Project plans are short documents usually written from one member of an organization to another. They outline a project's goals and objectives and may include specific details about how certain steps of a project should be achieved.

Résumés

A **résumé** is an overview of a person's experience and qualifications for a job. This document lists a person's job skills and work history. Résumés can also feature information about a person's education.

College Applications

College applications are documents that ask for personal information and details about someone's educational background. College administrators use this information to decide whether or not to accept a student.

Job Applications

Job applications are similar to résumés in that they require a person to list work experience and educational background. Most employers will require a completed job application as part of the hiring process.

Try It! As a group, discuss which form of workplace writing would be best for each of these purposes. Select the correct form for conveying your intended meaning to your audiences. Identify two or three types of information you would expect to include in a first draft.

- To inform the company that made your cell phone that it does not work properly
- To prepare information about your qualifications for a job search
- To create a plan for your group assignment in science class

Partner Talk

Share with a partner your experience with workplace and procedural writing. For example, have you ever written instructions, created a résumé, or completed a job application? What do you find are particular challenges with this type of writing?

Writing for Media

The world of communication has changed significantly in recent years. In addition to writing for print media such as magazines and books, writers also write for a variety of other **media,** in forms such as:

- Scripts for screenplays, video games, and documentaries
- Storyboards for graphic novels and advertisements
- Packaging for every kind of product
- Web sites and blogs

Scripts

Scripts are written for various media, such as documentaries, theater productions, speeches, and audio programs. Movies, television shows, and video games also have scripts.

- A good script focuses on a clearly expressed or implied **theme** and has a specific **purpose.**
- It also contains interesting details, which contribute to a definite **mood or tone.**
- A good script also includes a clear **setting,** **dialogue,** and well-developed **action**.

Blogs

Blogs address just about every purpose and interest. For example, there are blogs about local issues, pets, or food.

Advertisements

Advertisements are designed to persuade someone to buy a product or service. Advertisements use images, words, and music to support their message. Writers write the content of advertisements. In addition, they may help create music and design the sound and the images in the ad.

Creating Multimedia Projects

A **multimedia project** or presentation uses sound, video, and other media to convey a point or entertain an audience. No matter what type of project you choose as your own multimedia project, it is important to follow these steps:

- Decide on the project's **purpose** and your target **audience**.
- Choose **media** that will effectively convey your **message**.
- **Plan** your presentation. Will you work alone or with a partner or group? If you work with others, how you will assign the tasks?
- What **equipment** will you need? Will you produce artwork, record audio, and take photographs? Should you produce a storyboard to show the sequence of details in your presentation? Be sure to allow enough time to produce the text and all the other elements in your project.
- Keep the **writing process** in mind. There should be working and reworking along the way.
- **Assess** the progress of the project as you work. Ask questions, such as: Does my project incorporate appropriate writing genres? Will the presentation interest my audience? Have I kept my purpose in mind?
- **Rehearse!** Before presenting your project, be sure to do several "practice runs" to weed out and correct any errors.
- Keep an electronic record of your presentation for future reference.
- After your presentation, have others assess the project. Their critique will help you to do an even better job next time!

Partner Talk

Share with a partner your experience with writing for media or multimedia projects. Have you created a Web site or contributed to one? Have you had to complete multimedia projects for a class assignment or for a personal project on which you worked? Talk about how writing for media presents different challenges from more traditional writing and how you have dealt with those challenges.

Reflect on Your Writing

Learning more about the different types of writing can help you focus on the characteristics of each type so you can keep improving your own writing. Think about what you've learned in Chapter 2 as you answer these questions:

- What type of writing most interests you?
- What type of writing do you think is most useful? Why?

THE WRITING PROCESS

Writing Traits

Good writing has specific qualities, or traits. In this chapter you will learn about these traits and how to use rubrics to evaluate them. You will also learn how to apply traits during the stages of the writing process.

Focus and Coherence

What ties your piece together?

A piece that is focused and coherent stays on topic and makes it easy for your reader to understand the content. The topic must be clear and supported by well-chosen details. You will also want to include words, phrases, or sentences that help explain the connection among ideas.

Organization

What is the plan for your paper?

A well-organized paper has an obvious plan. You will want to make sure that your ideas move from sentence to sentence and paragraph to paragraph in a logical way. For example, elements in a story often appear in an order that makes sense. Some expository writing presents ideas in order of importance.

Development of Ideas

How do you say what you have to say?

Ideas should be clearly defined and developed logically. You will want to make sure that you have details that help develop and support each idea. You will also want to make sure that you make interesting connections between ideas. Including factual details may also help you convey your ideas.

Voice

What does your writing sound like?

Voice is the combination of word choice and personal writing style that makes your writing unique. Voice connects a reader to the writer. It can show your personality or "take" on a story. Using unique words and phrases will help you create your voice.

Conventions

How do you apply grammar rules?

Conventions are all the rules you have ever learned! Using correct spelling, capitalization, punctuation, grammar, usage, and sentence structure makes it easy for your reader to understand your ideas.

Overview of Writing Traits	
Focus and Coherence	• Focused on topic • Well-chosen details • Smooth transitions
Organization	• Obvious plan • Clear sequence • Strong transitions
Development of Ideas	• Depth of thought • Connections between ideas • Unique perspective
Voice	• Effective word choice • Attention to style
Conventions	• Proper spelling and capitalization • Correct punctuation, grammar, usage, and sentence structure

WRITING COACH Online

www.TXWritingCoach.com

Online Journal

Try It! Record your answers and ideas in the online journal. You can also record and save your answers and ideas on pop-up sticky notes in the eText.

" Writer to Writer "

Good writing is a symphony of traits—all coming together to make the paper sing.

—Kelly Gallagher

COLLEGE AND CAREER READINESS STANDARDS

Writing (1)(A)(4) Recognize the importance of revision as the key to effective writing.

Writing (1)(A)(5) Edit writing for proper voice, tense, and syntax.

Rubrics and How To Use Them

You can use rubrics to evaluate the traits of your writing. A rubric allows you to score your writing on a scale in different categories. You will use a four-point rubric like this to help evaluate your writing in chapters 5–12.

Writing Traits	Rating Scale
Focus and Coherence: How clearly related are the ideas in the piece? Does it have a sense of completeness?	Not very Very 1 2 3 4
Organization: How logically is your piece organized? Do your transitions, or movements from idea to idea, make sense?	1 2 3 4
Development of Ideas: How well do you develop and make connections between ideas?	1 2 3 4
Voice: How authentic and original is your voice?	1 2 3 4
Conventions: How correct is your punctuation? Your capitalization? Your spelling?	1 2 3 4

Each trait to be assessed appears in the first column. The rating scale appears in the second column. The higher your score, the better you accomplished exhibiting each trait in your writing.

Using a Rubric on Your Own

A rubric can be a big help in assessing your writing while it is still in process. Imagine you've just started writing a piece of narrative fiction. You know that narrative fiction should have characters, a setting, and a conflict and resolution. You might use a rubric to make sure your story has all the necessary elements. You can check

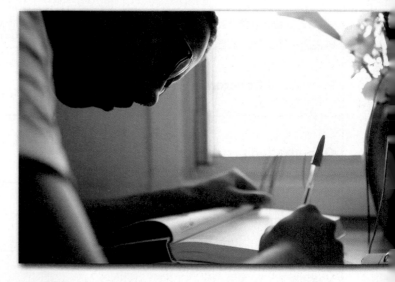

the rubric again as you write to make sure you are on track. For example, you may use the rubric and decide that you have not developed the conflict and its resolution well. You can go back and revise to improve your writing and get a better score.

Narrative Fiction Elements	Rating Scale			
	Not very		Very	
Interesting characters	1	2	3	4
Believable setting	1	2	3	4
Literary strategies	1	2	3	4
Well-developed conflict	1	2	3	4
Well-developed resolution	1	2	3	4

 Try It! If you checked your story against the rubric and rated yourself mostly 1s and 2s, what actions might you want to take next?

Using a Rubric With a Partner

In some cases, building your own rubric can help you ensure that your writing will meet your expectations. For example, if your class has an assignment to write a poem, you and a partner might decide to construct a rubric to check one another's work. A rubric like the one shown here can help point out whether you should make any changes. Extra lines allow room for you to add other criteria.

Poetry Elements	Rating Scale			
	Not very		Very	
Good sensory details	1	2	3	4
Colorful adjectives	1	2	3	4
	1	2	3	4
	1	2	3	4
	1	2	3	4

 Try It! What other elements might you add to the rubric?

Using a Rubric in a Group

It is also helpful to use a rubric in a group. That way you can get input on your writing from many people at the same time. If the group members' ratings of your piece are similar, you will probably have an easy time deciding whether to make changes. If the responses vary significantly, you might want to discuss the results with the group. Then, analyze what led to the differing opinions and make careful judgments about what changes you make.

WRITING COACH

Online

www.TXWritingCoach.com

Online Journal

Try It! Record your answers and ideas in the online journal. You can also record and save your answers and ideas on pop-up sticky notes in the eText.

What Is the Writing Process?

The five steps in the writing process are prewriting, drafting, revising, editing, and publishing. Writing is a process because your idea goes through a series of changes or stages before the product is finished.

Study the diagram to see how moving through the writing process can work. Remember, you can go back to a stage in the process. It does not always have to occur in order.

Prewriting

In prewriting, you will:
- Explore ideas
- Choose a purpose and an audience
- Gather details
- Sequence ideas

Drafting

In drafting, you will:
- Put ideas down
- Develop a thesis or controlling idea
- Structure ideas in a sustained way

Revising

In revising, you will:
- Re-read draft to see what works and what does not
- Use a rubric to evaluate
- Analyze what you want to change or improve
- Make changes

Editing

In the editing phase, you will:
- Check the accuracy of facts
- Correct errors in spelling, grammar, usage, and mechanics

Publishing

In publishing, you will:
- Produce a final polished copy of your writing
- Share your writing

Why Use the Writing Process?

Writing involves careful thinking, which means you will make changes as you write. Even professional writers don't just write their thoughts and call it a finished work of art. They use a process. For example, some writers keep going back to the revising stage many times, while others feel they can do the revision in just one step. It is up to each writer to develop the style that works best to produce the best results.

You might find that the writing process works best for you when you keep these tips in mind:

- Remember that the five steps in the writing process are equally important.
- Think about your audience as you plan your paper and develop your writing.
- Make sure you remember your topic and stick to your specific purpose as you write.
- Give your writing some time to "rest." Sometimes it can be good to work on a piece, walk away, and look at it later, with a fresh eye and mind.

The following pages will describe in more detail how to use each stage of the writing process to improve your writing.

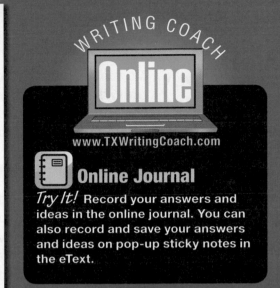

WRITING COACH

Online

www.TXWritingCoach.com

Online Journal

Try It! Record your answers and ideas in the online journal. You can also record and save your answers and ideas on pop-up sticky notes in the eText.

❝ Writer to Writer ❞

Writing process gives us the freedom to write like mad, tinker like an engineer, evaluate like a judge—playing different roles at different stages. Most importantly it gives us the freedom to get our words out of our heads and into the world.

—Jeff Anderson

Prewriting

Prewriting

Drafting

Revising

Editing

Publishing

No matter what kind of writing you do, planning during the prewriting stage is crucial. During prewriting, you determine the topic of your writing, its purpose, and its specific audience. Then, you narrow the topic and gather details.

Determining the Purpose and Audience

What Is Your Purpose?

To be sure your writing communicates your ideas clearly, it is important to clarify why you are writing. Consider what you want your audience to take away from your writing. You may want to entertain them, or you may want to warn them about something. Even when you write an entry in a private journal, you're writing for an audience—you!

Who Is Your Audience?

Think about the people who will read your work and consider what they may already know about your topic. Being able to identify this group and their needs will let you be sure you are providing the right level of information.

Choosing a Topic

Here are just a few of the many techniques you can use to determine an appropriate topic.

- **Brainstorm**
  You can brainstorm by yourself, with a partner, or with a group. Just jot down ideas as they arise, and don't rule out anything. When brainstorming in a group, one person's idea often "piggy-backs" on another.

- **Make a Mind Map**
  A mind map is a quick drawing you sketch as ideas come to you. The mind map can take any form. The important thing is to write quick notes as they come to you and then to draw lines to connect relationships among the ideas.

- **Interview**

  A fun way to find a writing topic is to conduct an interview. You might start by writing interview questions for yourself or someone else. Questions that start with *what, when, why, how,* and *who* are most effective. For example, you might ask, "When was the last time you laughed really hard?" "What made you laugh?" Then, conduct the interview and discover the answers.

- **Review Resources and Discuss Ideas**

  You can review resources, such as books, magazines, newspapers, and digital articles, to get ideas. Discussing your initial ideas with a partner can spark even more ideas.

Narrowing Your Topic

Once you have settled on a topic idea you really like, it may seem too broad to tackle. How can you narrow your topic?

- **Use Graphic Organizers**

  A graphic organizer can help narrow a topic that's too broad. For example, you might choose "Animals" as a topic. You might make your topics smaller and smaller until you narrow the topic to "The Habitat of Emperor Penguins."

Narrow Your Topic

GENERAL

Animal habitats

↓

Antarctic animals

↓

Penguins in the Antarctic

↓

The habitat of Emperor penguins

MORE SPECIFIC

WRITING COACH

Online

www.TXWritingCoach.com

Online Journal

Try It! Record your answers and ideas in the online journal. You can also record and save your answers and ideas on pop-up sticky notes in the eText.

❝ Writer to Writer ❞

Put something down. Anything. Then, magic will happen.

—Jeff Anderson

Prewriting

Drafting

Revising

Editing

Publishing

Prewriting (continued)

- **Use Resource Materials**
  The resource materials you use to find information can also help you narrow a broad topic. Look up your subject online in an encyclopedia or newspaper archive. Scan the resources as you look for specific subtopics to pursue.

Gather Details

After you decide on a topic, you will want to explore and develop your ideas. You might start by looking through online resources again, talking with people who are knowledgeable about your topic, and writing everything you already know about the topic. It will be helpful to gather a variety of details. Look at these types:

- Facts
- Statistics
- Personal observations
- Expert opinions

- Examples
- Descriptions
- Quotations
- Opposing viewpoints

After you have narrowed your topic and gathered details, you will begin to plan your piece. During this part of prewriting, you will develop your essay's thesis or controlling idea—its main point.

As you plan your piece, you can use a graphic organizer. Specific kinds of graphic organizers can help structure specific kinds of writing. For example, a pro-con chart like this one can clarify the reasons for and against an idea.

Pro	Con
Adding funds to the school music budget would allow more students to learn to play instruments.	Giving more money to the music department would mean other programs would get less money.
Research shows that music helps the brain become more flexible.	Other programs, such as sports, are important in keeping students physically healthy.
Band members could stop selling gift-wrap materials at holiday time.	The school board has already approved the current budget allocations.

Drafting

In the drafting stage, you get your ideas down. You may consult an outline or your prewriting notes as you build your first draft.

Prewriting

Drafting

Revising

Editing

Publishing

WRITING COACH

Online

www.TXWritingCoach.com

Online Journal

Try It! Record your answers and ideas in the online journal. You can also record and save your answers and ideas on pop-up sticky notes in the eText.

The Introduction

Most genres should have a strong introduction that immediately grabs the reader's attention and includes the thesis. Even stories and poems need a "hook" to grab interest.

Try It! Which of these first sentences are strong openers? Read these examples of first sentences. Decide which ones are most interesting to you. Explain why they grab your attention. Then, explain why the others are weak.

- Have you ever wondered what it would be like to wake up one morning to find you're someone else?
- There are many ways to paint a room.
- Autumn is a beautiful season.
- On Sunday, we went to the store.
- When I woke up that morning, I had no idea that it would be the best day of my life.

The Body

The body of a paper develops the main idea and details that elaborate on and support the thesis. These details may include interesting facts, examples, statistics, anecdotes or stories, quotations, personal feelings, and sensory descriptions.

The Conclusion

The conclusion typically restates the thesis and summarizes the most important concepts of a paper.

Revising: Making It Better

Prewriting

Drafting

Revising

Editing

Publishing

No one gets every single thing right in a first draft. In fact, most people require more than two drafts to achieve their best writing and thinking. When you have finished your first draft, you're ready to revise.

Revising means "re-seeing." In revising, you look again to see if you can find ways to improve style, word choice, figurative language, sentence variety, and subtlety of meaning. As always, check how well you've addressed the issues of purpose, audience, and genre. Carefully analyze what you'd want to change and then go ahead and do it. Here are some helpful hints on starting the revision stage of the writing process.

Take a Break

Do not begin to revise immediately after you finish a draft. Take some time away from your paper. Get a glass of water, take a walk, or listen to some music. You may even want to wait a day to look at what you've written. When you come back, you will be better able to assess the strengths and weaknesses of your work.

Put Yourself in the Place of the Reader

Take off your writer's hat and put on your reader's hat. Do your best to pretend that you're reading someone else's work and see how it looks to that other person. Look for ideas that might be confusing and consider the questions that a reader might have. By reading the piece with an objective eye, you may find items you'd want to fix and improve.

Read Aloud to Yourself

It may feel strange to read aloud to yourself, but it can be an effective technique. It allows you to hear the flow of words, find errors, and hear where you might improve the work by smoothing out transitions between paragraphs or sections. Of course, if you're more comfortable reading your work aloud to someone else, that works, too.

Share Your Work to Get Feedback

Your friends or family members can help you by reading and reacting to your writing. Ask them whether you've clearly expressed your ideas. Encourage them to tell you which parts were most and least interesting and why. Try to find out if they have any questions about your topic that were not answered. Then, evaluate their input and decide what will make your writing better.

Use a Rubric

A rubric might be just what you need to pinpoint weaknesses in your work. You may want to think about the core parts of the work and rate them on a scale. If you come up short, you'll have a better idea about the kinds of things to improve. You might also use a rubric to invite peer review and input.

WRITING COACH

Online

www.TXWritingCoach.com

Online Journal

Try It! Record your answers and ideas in the online journal. You can also record and save your answers and ideas on pop-up sticky notes in the eText.

Partner Talk

After a group revision session, talk with a partner to analyze each other's feelings on how the session went. Discuss such issues as these: Did the group adhere to the ground rules? What suggestions could you and your partner make to improve the next session?

21st Century Learning

Collaborate and Discuss

When presenting and sharing drafts in the revision stage with a small group, it may be wise to set some ground rules. That way, the group is more likely to help each other analyze their work and make thoughtful changes that result in true improvements.

Here are some suggestions for reviewing drafts as a group:

- Cover the names on papers the group will review to keep the work anonymous.
- Print out copies for everyone in the group.
- Show respect for all group members and their writing.
- Be sure all critiques include positive comments.
- While it is fine to suggest ways to improve the work, present comments in a positive, helpful way. No insults are allowed!
- Plan for a second reading with additional input after the writer has followed selected suggestions.

Revision RADaR

The Revision RADaR strategy, which you will use throughout this book, is an effective tool in helping you conduct a focused revision of your work.

Prewriting

Drafting

Revising

Editing

Publishing

You can use your Revision RADaR to revise your writing. The letters **R**, **A**, **D**, and **R** will help you remember to **r**eplace, **a**dd, **d**elete, and **r**eorder.

To understand more about the Revision RADaR strategy, study the following chart.

R	A	D and	R
Replace . . .	**Add . . .**	**Delete . . .**	**Reorder . . .**
• Words that are not specific • Words that are overused • Sentences that are unclear	• New information • Descriptive adjectives and adverbs • Rhetorical or literary devices	• Unrelated ideas • Sentences that sound good, but do not make sense • Repeated words or phrases • Unnecessary details	• So most important points are last • To make better sense or to flow better • So details support main ideas

R Replace

You can strengthen a text by replacing words that are not specific, words that are overused, and sentences that are unclear. Take a look at this before and after model.

BEFORE
I kicked the soccer ball hard into the goal.

AFTER
With amazing power, I slammed the soccer ball into the goal.

Apply It! **How did the writer replace the overused word** *kicked*? **What other replacement do you see? How did it improve the text?**

Add

You can add new information, descriptive adjectives and adverbs, and rhetorical or literary devices to make your piece more powerful. Study this before and after model.

BEFORE
I was happy when I won the award.

AFTER
I was beyond thrilled when I won the Science Fair award.

Apply It! **How did the second sentence make you feel, compared with the first? Explain. What information was added to the second sentence?**

 Delete

Sometimes taking words out of a text can improve clarity. Analyze this before and after model.

BEFORE
I knew the test would be difficult, so I should have studied harder for the test before the test day.

AFTER
I knew the test would be difficult, so I should have studied harder for it.

Apply It! **Describe the revision you see. How did taking out unnecessary repetition of the word *test* help the sentences flow more naturally?**

 Reorder

When you reorder, you can make sentences flow more logically.

BEFORE
Today, I have band practice, but yesterday I didn't.

AFTER
I didn't have band practice yesterday, but today I do.

Apply It! **Which of the models flows more logically? Why?**

WRITING COACH

Online

www.TXWritingCoach.com

Online Journal

Try It! Record your answers and ideas in the online journal. You can also record and save your answers and ideas on pop-up sticky notes in the eText.

USING TECHNOLOGY

Most word processing programs have a built-in thesaurus tool. You can use the thesaurus to find descriptive words that can often substitute for weaker, overused words.

Revision RADaR (continued)

Prewriting
Drafting
Revising
Editing
Publishing

Read the first draft of the Student Model—a review of the novel *End Game.* Think about how you might use your Revision RADaR to improve the text in a second draft.

Kelly Gallagher, M. Ed.

KEEP REVISION ON YOUR RADAR

End Game Fails to Thrill 1ST DRAFT

I like detective stories. So when my favorite writer, Mary O'Reilly, published a new detective novel, I bought it. Unfortunately, the novel, *End Game,* was incredibly disappointing.

In the story, an online video gamer disappears. A detective, Katherine, tries to track down the missing man through gaming Web sites. But here's where O'Reilly really messed up. It's clear that she didn't research the technology involved in online gaming. For example: "Katherine waited while her dial-up modem connected her to the virtual world."

The cheesy and ridiculous dialogue made my reading experience even worse. The errors in the book were bad enough! For example, the suspect says to Katherine, "I'm gonna get you, copper!" Now, this is the year 2010. A modern-day criminal would never use such outdated, silly lines. Instead of making the story exciting, the dialogue made it laughably bad.

O'Reilly has written many great books. My favorites were *On the High Seas* and *Danger in Denver.* They were great. I loved them! But I think it's time for O'Reilly to put down her pen. She clearly doesn't have what it takes any more to be a great writer. And as for *End Game*…don't waste your money!

Is my introduction interesting? Does it grab my readers' attention?

Have I fully analyzed and explained my examples from the text?

Is my information logically ordered?

Is my information relevant to the thesis? Have I included only necessary information?

After writing a draft, the student asked questions like these:

- What could I **replace**?
- What could I **add**?
- What words might I **delete**?
- Should I **reorder** anything?

The student writer created this second draft.

End Game Fails to Thrill

The suspense and high-paced action in detective stories are so thrilling! I simply can't get enough of these books. So when my favorite writer, Mary O'Reilly, published a new detective novel, I ran to the store to buy my copy. Unfortunately, the novel, *End Game,* was incredibly disappointing.

R *Replaced dull first line with a more engaging opening.*

In the story, an online video gamer disappears. A detective, Katherine, tries to track down the missing man through gaming Web sites. But here's where O'Reilly really messed up. It's clear that she didn't research the technology involved in online gaming. For example: "Katherine waited while her dial-up modem connected her to the virtual world." Dial-up modems aren't fast enough to do serious online gaming!

A *Added a sentence to better explain to my audience why the information from the text was incorrect.*

Although the errors in the book were bad enough, the cheesy and ridiculous dialogue made my reading experience even worse. For example, the suspect says to Katherine, "I'm gonna get you, copper!" Now, this is the year 2010. A modern-day criminal would never use such outdated, silly lines. Instead of making the story exciting, the dialogue made it laughably bad.

R *Reordered text so that the information about the errors connected the ideas in the second and third paragraphs.*

I think it's time for O'Reilly to put down her pen. She clearly doesn't have what it takes any more to be a great writer. And as for *End Game*…don't waste your money!

D *Deleted unnecessary information.*

Try It! What other words did the writer replace? Add? Delete? Reorder?

WRITING COACH

Online

www.TXWritingCoach.com

Online Journal

Try It! Record your answers and ideas in the online journal. You can also record and save your answers and ideas on pop-up sticky notes in the eText.

Partner Talk

Work with a partner to come up with a list of words that describe detective stories. For example, you might use "high-paced action" or "thrilling." Then discuss the value of using more specific words in your writing.

Editing: Making It Correct

Prewriting

Drafting

Revising

Editing

Publishing

Editing is the process of checking the accuracy of facts and correcting errors in spelling, grammar, usage, and mechanics. Using a checklist like the one shown here can help ensure you've done a thorough job of editing.

Editing Checklist

Task	Ask Yourself
Check your facts and spelling	❑ Have I checked that my facts are correct? ❑ Have I used spell check or a dictionary to check any words I'm not sure are spelled correctly?
Check your grammar	❑ Have I written any run-on sentences? ❑ Have I used the correct verbs and verb tenses? ❑ Do my pronouns match their antecedents, or nouns they replace?
Check your usage	❑ Have I used the correct form of irregular verbs? ❑ Have I used object pronouns, such as *me*, *him*, *her*, *us*, and *them* only after verbs or prepositions? ❑ Have I used subject pronouns, such as *I*, *he*, *she*, *we*, and *they* correctly—usually as subjects?
Check for proper use of mechanics	❑ Have I used correct punctuation? ❑ Does each sentence have the correct end mark? ❑ Have I used apostrophes in nouns but not in pronouns to show possession? ❑ Have I used quotation marks around words from another source? ❑ Have I used correct capitalization? ❑ Does each sentence begin with a capital letter? ❑ Do the names of specific people and places begin with a capital letter?

Using Proofreading Marks

Professional editors use a set of proofreading marks to indicate changes in a text. Here is a chart of some of the more common proofreading marks.

	Proofreader's Marks
(b.f.)	boldface
⌐	break text start new line
(caps)	capital letter
⊂	clos e up
e	deletes
⌒/	insert ∧ word
⌄/	insert∧comma
=/	insert∧hyphen
+/	insert let er
⊙/	insert period
(ital)	italic type
(stet)	let stand as is
(l.f.)	**lightface**
(l.c.)	Lower case letter
⌐	move left
⌐	move right
¶	new paragraph
(rom)	*roman type*
	run text up
(sp)	spell out whole word
	transpose

USING TECHNOLOGY

Many word processing programs have automatic spelling and grammar checks. While these tools can be helpful, be sure to pay attention to any suggestions they offer. That's because sometimes inappropriate substitutes are inserted automatically!

Editing: Making It Correct (continued)

WRITE GUY *Jeff Anderson, M. Ed.*

WHAT DO YOU NOTICE?

Using an editing checklist is a great way to check for correct grammar. However, using a checklist is not enough to make your writing grammatically correct. A checklist tells you what to look for, but not how to correct mistakes you find. To do that, you need to develop and apply your knowledge of grammar.

Looking closely at good writing is one way to expand your grammar know-how. The *What Do You Notice?* feature that appears throughout this book will help you zoom in on passages that use grammar correctly and effectively.

As you read this passage, from "Jobs for Kids," zoom in on the sentences in the passage.

I have a paper route. After school, I deliver newspapers on my bike to my neighbors. I love this job because I get exercise, and I get to be outside.

Now, ask yourself: *What do you notice about the sentences in this passage?*

Maybe you noticed that the writer uses sentences of varying lengths and with different structures.

After asking a question that draws your attention to the grammar in the passage, the *What Do You Notice?* feature provides information on a particular grammar topic. For example, following the passage and question, you might read about simple and complex sentences, which are both used in the passage.

The *What Do You Notice?* feature will show you how grammar works in actual writing. It will help you learn how to make your writing correct.

Prewriting

Drafting

Revising

Editing

Publishing

WRITING COACH

Online

www.TXWritingCoach.com

Online Journal

Try It! Record your answers and ideas in the online journal. You can also record and save your answers and ideas on pop-up sticky notes in the eText.

Jobs for Kids

I like having my own money. That way, I can buy things I want and can also save money for my future. But here's the problem: How can we, as kids, make money? There are many types of jobs for kids, but each job has pluses and minuses.

I have a paper route. After school, I deliver newspapers on my bike to my neighbors. I love this job because I get exercise, and I get to be outside. This job isn't for everyone, though. Some kids have a lot of after-school activities, so they don't go straight home. Because papers have to be delivered on time, this can be challenging.

A friend of mine babysits because she has fun with and loves taking care of children. To be a babysitter, you have to find out if your state has a law about how old you have to be before you can babysit. You also have to be a patient, responsible person who is good with children. Finally, it helps to know first-aid, just in case a child gets injured.

My brother does yard work for neighbors. He rakes leaves, weeds gardens, and mows lawns. He loves to be outside and doesn't mind getting dirty. However, there are certain safety issues involved. For example, you have to know how to handle a lawnmower properly and wear protective gear.

What type of job is right for you? What are your interests? Get creative, and start making some money!

" Writer to Writer "

If I wonder how to write any kind of writing, I look at models—well-written examples of the kind of writing I want to do. Models are the greatest how-to lesson I have ever discovered.

—Jeff Anderson

Try It! Read "Jobs for Kids." Then, zoom in on two more passages. Write a response to each question in your journal.

1. What do you notice about the pronouns (*you, he*) in the fourth paragraph?

2. How does the writer use transitions, such as the word *finally*, to connect ideas in the third paragraph?

Publishing

Prewriting

Drafting

Revising

Editing

Publishing

When you publish, you produce a final copy of your work and present it to an audience. When publishing you'll need to decide which form will best reach your audience, exhibit your ideas, show your creativity, and accomplish your main purpose.

To start assessing the optimal way to publish your work, you might ask yourself these questions:

- What do I hope to accomplish by sharing my work with others?
- Should I publish in print form? Give an oral presentation? Publish in print form and give an oral presentation?
- Should I publish online, in traditional print, or both?
- What specific forms are available to choose from?

The answers to most of these questions will most likely link to your purpose for writing and your audience. Some choices seem obvious. For example, if you've written a piece to contribute to a blog, you'll definitely want to send it electronically.

Each publishing form will present different challenges and opportunities and each will demand different forms of preparation. For example, you may need to prepare presentation slides for a speech, or you may want to select music and images if you will be posting a video podcast online.

Ways to Publish

There are many ways to publish your writing. This chart shows some of several opportunities you can pursue to publish your work.

Genre	Publishing Opportunities	
Narration: Nonfiction	• Blogs • Book manuscript • Audio recording	• Private diary or journal entries • Electronic slide show
Narration: Fiction	• Book manuscript • Film	• Audio recording • Oral reading to a group
Poetry and Description	• Bound collection • Visual display	• Audio recording • Oral reading to a group
Exposition and Persuasion	• Print or online article • Web site • Slide show • Visual display	• Film • Audio recording • Oral reading or speech
Response to Literature	• Print or online letters • Visual displays	• Blogs • Slide show
Research Writing	• Traditional paper • Print and online experiment journals	• Multimedia presentation

Reflect on Your Writing

Think about what you learned in Chapter 3 as you answer these questions:

- What did you learn about the writing process?
- What steps in the writing process do you already use in your writing?
- Which stage do you think is the most fun? Which one may be most challenging for you? Explain.

WRITING COACH

Online

www.TXWritingCoach.com

Online Journal

Try It! Record your answers and ideas in the online journal. You can also record and save your answers and ideas on pop-up sticky notes in the eText.

Partner Talk

Discuss the chart on this page with a partner. If there are ways to publish that neither of you has ever tried, talk about how you might go about experimenting with those forms.

SENTENCES, PARAGRAPHS, *and* COMPOSITIONS

Good writers know that strong sentences and paragraphs help to construct effective compositions. Chapter 4 will help you use these building blocks to structure and style excellent writing. It will also present ways to use rhetorical and literary devices and online tools to strengthen your writing.

The Building Blocks: Sentences and Paragraphs

A **sentence** is a group of words with two main parts: a subject and a predicate. Together, these parts express a complete thought.

A **paragraph** is built from a group of sentences that share a common idea and work together to express that idea clearly. The start of a new paragraph has visual clues—either an indent of several spaces in the first line or an extra line of space above it.

In a good piece of writing, each paragraph supports, develops, or explains the main idea of the whole work. Of course, the traits of effective writing—focus and coherence, organization, ideas, voice, and conventions—appear in each paragraph as well.

Writing Strong Sentences

To write strong paragraphs, you need strong sentences. While it may be your habit to write using a single style of sentences, adding variety will help make your writing more interesting. Combining sentences, using compound elements, forming compound sentences, and using subordination all may help you make your sentences stronger, clearer, or more varied.

Combine Sentences

Putting information from one sentence into another can make a more powerful sentence.

BEFORE	Basketball is a fun game. It takes a lot of skill and practice.
AFTER	Basketball, which takes a lot of skill and practice, is a fun game.

Use Compound Elements

You can form compound subjects, verbs, or objects to help the flow.

BEFORE	Students enjoy many different hobbies. Some play sports. Some write poetry. Some paint.
AFTER	Students enjoy many different hobbies, such as playing sports, writing poetry, and painting.

Form Compound Sentences

You can combine two sentences into a compound sentence.

BEFORE	Some people enjoy skateboarding. It can be a dangerous hobby.
AFTER	Some people enjoy skateboarding, but it can be a dangerous hobby.

Use Subordination

Combine two related sentences by rewriting the less important one as a subordinate clause.

BEFORE	Horseback riding allows you to be outside in the fresh air. That is good for you.
AFTER	Horseback riding allows you be outside in the fresh air, which is good for you.

WRITING COACH

Online

www.TXWritingCoach.com

Online Journal

Try It! Record your answers and ideas in the online journal. You can also record and save your answers on pop-up sticky notes in the eText.

LEARN MORE

For more on sentence combining see Chapter 20.

Writing Strong Paragraphs

If all the sentences in a paragraph reflect the main idea and work together to express that idea clearly, the result will be a strong paragraph.

Express Your Main Idea With a Clear Topic Sentence

A **topic sentence** summarizes the main idea of a paragraph. It may appear at the beginning, middle, or end of a paragraph. It may even be unstated. When the topic sentence comes at the beginning of a paragraph, it introduces the main idea and leads the reader naturally to the sentences that follow it. When it appears at the end of a paragraph, it can draw a conclusion or summarize what came before it. If the topic sentence is unstated, the rest of the paragraph must be very clearly developed, so the reader can understand the main idea from the other sentences.

Think about the topic sentence as you read this paragraph.

> There is no question that computer skills are necessary to have today. Without these skills, it will be difficult to get a college degree and find a good job. Most assignments in college must be done on a computer. Much research in college is done on the Internet, and many libraries have switched from a paper card catalog to a digital catalog. In addition, many companies won't hire someone who has no computer skills. After all, if you can't send e-mails and create important documents in word processing programs, how will you be able to properly do many jobs?

 Try It! Look back at the sample paragraph to answer these questions.

1. What is the topic sentence?
2. Does the topic sentence introduce the main idea or draw a final conclusion? Explain.
3. What makes this topic sentence strong?

Write Effective Supporting Sentences

A clear topic sentence is a good start, but it needs to be accompanied by good details that support the paragraph's main idea. Your supporting sentences might tell interesting facts, describe events, or give examples. In addition, the supporting sentences should also provide a smooth transition, so that the paragraph reads clearly and logically.

Think about the topic sentences and supporting details as you read this paragraph.

Owning a dog can be hard work, but it is well worth it! A dog owner must be very responsible and take good care of her pet. She has to feed and walk the dog every day and bathe it regularly. Every dog also needs a lot of play time with its owner! All of this takes a great deal of time and energy. However, a dog can be your best friend. It will love you and protect you, and sometimes make you laugh! Plus, what could be better than snuggling up with a sweet, loving dog?

 Try It! Look at the paragraph and answer these questions.

1. What is the topic sentence of the paragraph?

2. Do you think it's an effective topic sentence? Why or why not?

3. What supporting details does the writer provide?

4. If you were the writer, what other supporting details might you add to strengthen the paragraph?

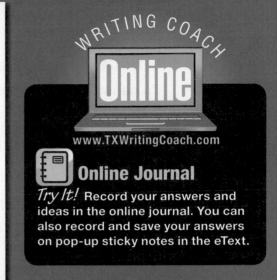

www.TXWritingCoach.com

Online Journal

Try It! Record your answers and ideas in the online journal. You can also record and save your answers on pop-up sticky notes in the eText.

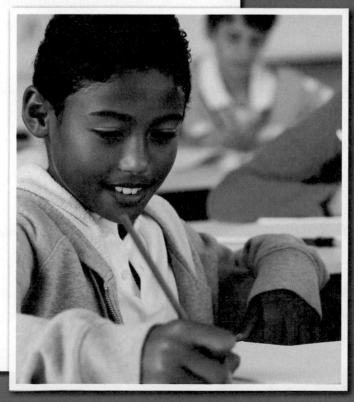

Include a Variety of Sentence Lengths, Structures, and Beginnings

To be interesting, a paragraph should include sentences of different lengths, types, and beginnings. Similarly, if every sentence has the same structure—for example, article, adjective, noun, verb—the paragraph may sound boring or dry.

21st Century Learning

Collaborate and Discuss

With a group, study this writing sample.

> On the night of the school concert, I didn't think I'd survive my stage fright. My hands felt cold and clammy, and a lump was stuck in my throat. A trickle of sweat slipped between my shoulder blades and down my back. I was so nervous! As the band began playing the opening notes of the first song and I stepped up to the microphone, the glare of the bright lights blinded me. I closed my eyes, took a deep breath, and belted out the song without even thinking. When the song was over, the audience responded with deafening applause. I had done it!

Discuss these questions about the paragraph.

1. What is the topic sentence? How does it draw in the reader?

2. What details support the topic sentence in each paragraph?

3. Point out some examples of varying sentence lengths and beginnings.

4. What examples can you find of sentences with a variety of sentence structures?

Partner Talk

Work with a partner to take another look at the writing sample on this page. Talk about what you think the writer did well. Then, discuss what might make the paragraph even stronger.

USING TECHNOLOGY

It's often better to use the tab key, rather than the space bar, to indent a paragraph. Using the tab key helps to ensure that the indents in all paragraphs will be uniform.

Composing Your Piece

You've learned that the building blocks of writing are strong sentences and paragraphs. Now it's time to use those building blocks to construct a composition. While the types of writing vary, most types have a definite structure with clearly defined parts.

The Parts of a Composition

Writers put together and arrange sentences and paragraphs to develop ideas in the clearest way possible in a composition. Some types of writing, such as poetry and advertisements, follow unique rules and may not have sentences and paragraphs that follow a standard structure. However, as you learned in Chapter 3, most compositions have three main sections: an introduction, a body, and a conclusion.

I. Introduction

The introduction of a composition introduces the focus of the composition, usually in a thesis statement. The introduction should engage the reader's interest, with such elements as a question, an unusual fact, or a surprising scene.

II. Body

Just as supporting statements develop the ideas of a topic sentence, the body of a composition develops the thesis statement and main idea. It provides details that help expand on the thesis statement. The paragraphs in the body are arranged in a logical order.

III. Conclusion

As the word implies, the conclusion of a composition concludes or ends a piece of writing. A good way to ensure the reader will remember your thesis statement is to restate it or summarize it in the conclusion. When restating the thesis, it's usually most effective to recast it in other words. Quotations and recommendations are other ways to conclude a composition with memorable impact. The conclusion should provide a parting insight or reinforce the importance of the main idea.

> **"Writer to Writer"**
>
> **Strong, varied sentences and unified paragraphs are the building blocks of effective writing.**
>
> **—Kelly Gallagher**

Rhetorical and Literary Devices

Like any builders, good writers have a set of tools, or devices, at their fingertips to make their writing interesting, engaging, and effective. Writers can use the rhetorical devices of language and their effects to strengthen the power of their style. This section presents some tools you can store in your own writing toolbox to develop effective compositions.

Sound Devices

Sound devices, which create a musical or emotional effect, are most often used in poetry. The most common sound devices include these:

- **Alliteration** is the repetition of consonant sounds at the beginning of words that are close to one another.

  Example: The sweet sound of singing swam in the breeze.

- **Assonance** is the repetition of vowel sounds in words that are close to one another.

  Example: We see shells on the beach, by the sea.

- **Consonance** is the repetition of consonants within or at the end of words.

  Example: The doctor checked the sick patient at three o'clock.

Structural Devices

Structural devices determine the way a piece of writing is organized. Rhyme and meter are most often used to structure poetry, as are stanzas and many other structural devices.

- **Rhyme** is the repetition of sounds at the ends of words. Certain poetry forms have specific rhyme schemes.
- **Meter** is the rhythmical pattern of a poem, determined by the stressed syllables in a line.
- **Visual elements**, such as stanzas, line breaks, line length, fonts, readability, and white space, help determine how a piece of writing is read and interpreted. These elements can also affect the emotional response to a piece.

Other Major Devices

You can use these devices in many forms of writing. They help writers express ideas clearly and engage their readers.

Device	Example
Figurative language is writing that means something beyond what the words actually say. Common forms of figurative language include these: • A **simile** compares two things using the words *like* or *as*. • A **metaphor** compares two things by mentioning one thing as if it is something else. It does not use *like* or *as*. • **Personification** gives human characteristics to a non-human object.	 *His voice sounded like nails on a chalkboard.* *The trapeze artist was a bird in flight.* *The sun smiled down on us.*
Hyperbole is exaggeration used for effect.	*I felt stronger than a superhero!*
Irony is a contradiction between what happens and what is expected.	In a famous story, a wife cuts her hair to buy her husband a watch fob, and he sells his watch to buy her a brush.
Paradox is a statement that contains elements that seem contradictory, but could be true.	Mother Teresa said, "…if you love until it hurts, there can be no more hurt, only more love."
An **oxymoron** is word or phrase that seems to contradict itself.	The movie was seriously funny!
Symbolism is an object that stands for something else.	The American flag is often considered a symbol of freedom.
An **allegory** is a narrative that has a meaning other than what literally appears.	Some say the story of the sinking ship is an allegory for the effects of pride.
Repetition (or tautology) occurs when content is repeated—sometimes needlessly—for effect.	The band's song was loud, loud and far too long.

WRITING COACH

Online

www.TXWritingCoach.com

Online Journal

Try It! Record your answers and ideas in the online journal. You can also record and save your answers on pop-up sticky notes in the eText.

USING TECHNOLOGY

Most word processing programs have a built-in thesaurus tool. You can use the thesaurus to find descriptive words that can often substitute for weaker, overused words.

Partner Talk

There are many online tools that can help you strengthen your writing. For example, you can search for examples of figurative language and sound devices. Then you can model your own writing after the samples. Just be sure that you don't plagiarize or copy the written work of others.

Using Writing Traits to Develop an Effective Composition

You read about rubrics and traits in Chapter 3. Now it's time to look at how they function in good writing.

Focus and Coherence

A composition with strong focus and coherence shows clear relationships between ideas, and rarely shifts from one idea to the next. The composition has a sense of completeness.

Organization

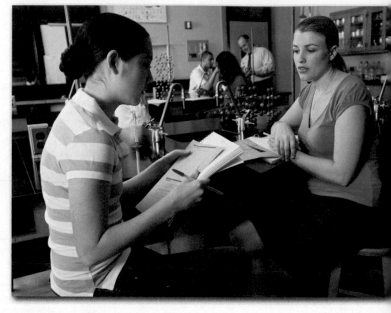

A well-organized composition flows easily from sentence to sentence and paragraph to paragraph. Its organization shows a smooth progression of thought. The paper also avoids wordiness and needless repetition.

Think about focus, coherence, and organization as you read this paragraph.

> At first, Chris didn't like the idea of being on the school newspaper staff. He loved the school paper, but he wasn't sure he wanted to give up his free time after school. Then, Mr. Gadlin, the teacher who helped to run the newspaper, convinced Chris. First, Mr. Gadlin explained that the newspaper needed excellent writers like Chris. Next, he told Chris that without more staffers, the newspaper wouldn't survive. Chris didn't want the newspaper to disappear. So, after much thought, Chris decided to join the staff... and he ended up having a fantastic time doing it!

Try It! Answer the question about the paragraph.

1. Which sequence words help the paragraph flow logically from one sentence to the next?

Development of Ideas

In an excellent piece of writing, every word choice shows that the writer has thought about how to develop ideas clearly.

As you read the sample, think about how it develops its ideas.

Achoo!

Achoo! The common cold, while not usually life threatening, can be a major downer. Who wants to be home and in bed with a runny nose, cough, and sore throat? It happens more often than people like to think, though. According to the Mayo Clinic, students can get as many as six to ten colds a year! If you understand the causes of the common cold and take precautions, you can successfully avoid catching a cold.

A common cold is caused by a virus. Many different viruses could be responsible for your runny nose, but all of them have one thing in common: they're very contagious, which means they get passed along from person to person. A common-cold virus can spread in the air when a sick person coughs, sneezes, or even talks. It can also spread on objects.

Avoiding a cold is fairly easy, if you follow some simple rules. Wash your hands often. Make sure your family keeps doorknobs and countertops clean. Don't share drinking glasses or silverware. Most importantly, if it's possible, avoid being around sick people entirely. If you do happen to catch a cold, sneeze or cough into your elbow, not into your hand, to help keep your cold from spreading to others. No one likes to be sick!

Try It! Think about ideas in the writing sample as you answer these questions.

1. What devices did the writer use to engage the reader in the first paragraph?

2. Which words helped the writer make good connections between ideas in the piece?

3. The passage stresses ways to avoid catching a cold. Find examples of word choice that help reinforce this goal.

WRITING COACH

Online

www.TXWritingCoach.com

Online Journal

Try It! Record your answers and ideas in the online journal. You can also record and save your answers on pop-up sticky notes in the eText.

Partner Talk

Analyze the composition about colds with a partner. Discuss how well it might score on each trait—organization, focus and coherence, and development of ideas—from ineffective (1), to somewhat effective (2), to generally effective (3), to highly effective (4).

Voice

Voice is the tone and perspective that each writer brings to a text. A truly successful paper helps that individuality shine through.

Read the writing sample. Think about voice as you read.

My parents told me that we were going to have a new addition to our family. Yep, that's right—I was going to get a baby brother. I thought my life would never be the same again.

Soon, baby gear started filling up our spare bedroom. Mom painted animals on the walls. She put little locks on all of our cabinets. It all looked so weird. I felt like our house had been taken over. Then, it was time for my parents to leave for China to pick up my new baby brother.

I'll never forget the day my parents got home with 4-month-old Liang. I was sitting on the couch, waiting for them. My stomach was doing flip-flops. Then Mom and Dad walked through the door, carrying this little bundle wrapped in a blanket. Mom sat on the couch with me and introduced me to my new brother. I expected him to totally freak out— to scream and cry. Instead, he just looked up at me with his big, brown eyes and smiled. His tiny hand reached out and grabbed my finger. He had a pretty strong grip!

In the end, I'd been right: my life would never be the same again…but in a good way. I found out that while babies are sometimes loud, smelly, and drooly, all of that stuff didn't matter. I loved my little brother, and I couldn't wait till he grew up, so I could teach him how to use that strong grip to hold a football!

 Try It! Consider the writer's voice as you answer these questions.

1. How would you describe the writer's tone— his attitude toward his subject? Explain.

2. Is the writer's style formal or informal? How do you know?

Conventions

If a piece of writing reflects a good command of spelling, capitalization, punctuation, grammar, usage, and sentence structure, it is much more likely to communicate clearly to readers.

Pay attention to spelling, capitalization, punctuation, grammar, usage, and sentence structure in the first paragraph of a draft.

1ST DRAFT

If your an action-movie fan, you have to run—not walk— to see *Welcome to Mars!* This movie is non-stop action, from start to finish. Me and my friend were blown away by the battle scenes, special effects, and suspense.

The movie has a great message, too: Understanding can lead to peace. In one very tense moment, the lead scientist on Mars is captured by aliens. I was so sure they would kill her! Instead, she stayed with them, learning their language and to learn their ways of life. This led to peace between the humans and the aliens.

Now, read this section of the reviewer's second draft.

2ND DRAFT

If you're an action-movie fan, you have to run—not walk— to see *Welcome to Mars!* This movie is non-stop action, from start to finish. My friend and I were blown away by the battle scenes, special effects, and suspense.

The movie has a great message, too: Understanding can lead to peace. In one very tense moment, the lead scientist on Mars is captured by aliens. I was so sure they would kill her! Instead, she stayed with them, learning their language and their ways of life. This led to peace between the humans and the aliens.

Try It! Answer these questions about both drafts.

1. What errors in convention did the writer correct in the second draft?
2. Why would some people find the second paragraph easier to read?

WRITING COACH

Online

www.TXWritingCoach.com

Online Journal

Try It! Record your answers and ideas in the online journal. You can also record and save your answers on pop-up sticky notes in the eText.

Using Interactive Writing Coach

As you learned in Chapter 3, you can use rubrics and your Revision RADaR to check how well your paragraphs and essays read. With Writing Coach, you also have another tool available to evaluate your work: the Interactive Writing Coach.

The Interactive Writing Coach is a program that you can use anywhere that you have Internet access. Interactive Writing Coach functions like your own personal writing tutor. It gives you personalized feedback on your work.

The Interactive Writing Coach has two parts: **Paragraph Feedback** and **Essay Scorer**.

- Paragraph Feedback gives you feedback on individual paragraphs as you write. It looks at the structure of sentences and paragraphs and gives you information about specific details, such as sentence variety and length.

- Essay Scorer looks at your whole essay and gives you a score and feedback on your entire piece of writing. It will tell you how well your essay reflects the traits of good writing.

This chart shows just a few questions that Paragraph Feedback and Essay Scorer will answer about your writing. The following pages explain Paragraph Feedback and Essay Scorer in more detail.

Sentences	• Are sentences varied in length? • Do sentences have varied beginnings? • Which sentences have too many ideas? • Are adjectives clear and precise? • Is the sentence grammatically correct? • Is all spelling correct in the sentence?
Paragraphs	• Does the paragraph support its topic? • Does the paragraph use transitions? • Does the paragraph contain the right amount of ideas and information?
Compositions	• Does the essay reflect characteristics of the genre? • Does it demonstrate the traits of good writing? • Is the main idea clear? • Is the main idea well supported? • Is the essay cohesive—does it hold together?

Interactive Writing Coach and the Writing Process

You can begin to use Essay Scorer during the drafting section of the writing process. It is best to complete a full draft of your essay before submitting to Essay Scorer. (While you are drafting individual paragraphs, you may want to use Paragraph Feedback.) Keep in mind, however, that your draft does not need to be perfect or polished before you submit to Essay Scorer. You will be able to use feedback from Essay Scorer to revise your draft many times. This chart shows how you might use the Interactive Writing Coach and incorporate Essay Scorer into your writing process.

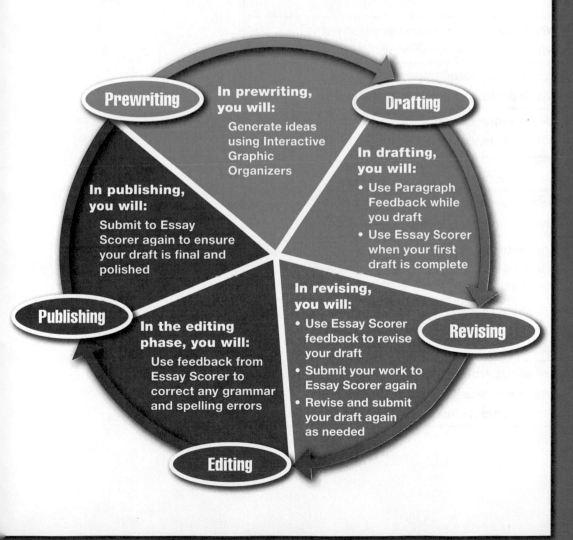

Prewriting

In prewriting, you will:
Generate ideas using Interactive Graphic Organizers

Drafting

In drafting, you will:
- Use Paragraph Feedback while you draft
- Use Essay Scorer when your first draft is complete

In publishing, you will:
Submit to Essay Scorer again to ensure your draft is final and polished

Publishing

In the editing phase, you will:
Use feedback from Essay Scorer to correct any grammar and spelling errors

In revising, you will:
- Use Essay Scorer feedback to revise your draft
- Submit your work to Essay Scorer again
- Revise and submit your draft again as needed

Revising

Editing

Paragraph Feedback With Interactive Writing Coach

Paragraph Feedback assesses the ideas and topic support for each paragraph you write. You can enter your work into Paragraph Feedback one paragraph at a time. This makes it easy to work on individual paragraphs and get new feedback as you revise each one. Here are some things that Paragraph Feedback will be able to tell you.

Overall Paragraph Support	• Does the paragraph support the main idea? • Which sentences do not support the main idea?
Transitions	• Which sentences contain transition words? • Which words are transition words?
Ideas	• How well are ideas presented? • Which sentences have too many ideas?
Sentence Length and Variety	• Which sentences are short, medium, and long? • Which sentences could be longer or shorter for better sense or variety? • Are sentences varied?
Sentence Beginnings	• How do sentences begin? • Are sentence beginnings varied?
Sentence Structure	• Are sentence structures varied? • Are there too many sentences with similar structures?
Vague Adjectives	• Are any adjectives vague or unclear? • Where are adjectives in sentences and paragraphs?
Language Variety	• Are words repeated? • Where are repeated words located? • How can word choice be improved?

Essay Scoring With Interactive Writing Coach

Essay Scorer assesses your essay. It looks at the essay as a whole, and it also evaluates individual paragraphs, sentences, and words. Essay Scorer will help you evaluate the following traits.

WRITING COACH

Online

www.TXWritingCoach.com

Interactive Writing Coach™

Interactive Writing Coach provides support and guidance to help you improve your writing skills.
- Select a topic to write about from the Topic Bank.
- Use the interactive graphic organizers to narrow your topic.
- Go to Writing Coach Online and submit your work, paragraph by paragraph or as a complete draft.
- Receive immediate, personalized feedback as you write, revise, and edit your work.

Focus and Coherence	• Is the topic clear and well stated? • Do the introduction, body, and conclusion work together? • Do ideas flow logically?
Organization	• Is the organization logical? • Is the introduction clear? • Is the conclusion clear? • What transitions are used and are they effective?
Development of Ideas	• Is the main idea clearly stated? • Is the main idea supported by details? • Are supporting ideas well explained? • Are sentences complete and correct?
Voice	• Does the tone match the topic, audience, and purpose? • Does the tone grab the reader's interest? • Does the tone connect with the audience? • Are sentences varied?
Conventions	• Is spelling correct? • Is capitalization used properly? • Is all punctuation (ending, internal, apostrophes) accurate? • Do subjects and verbs agree? • Are pronouns used correctly? • Are adjectives and adverbs used correctly? • Are plurals formed correctly? • Are commonly confused words used correctly?

Whenever you see the Interactive Writing Coach icon you can go to Writing Coach Online and submit your writing, either paragraph by paragraph or as a complete draft, for personalized feedback and scoring.

CHAPTER 5

NONFICTION NARRATION

What Do You Remember?

Why are accomplishments important? What might make accomplishments interesting to other people?

To tell a story about an accomplishment, you will need to remember details of the experience. Using vivid details to describe an accomplishment will make the story more interesting to others.

Try It! Think about a recent accomplishment. Consider these questions as you participate in an extended discussion with a partner. Take turns expressing your ideas and feelings.

- What led up to the accomplishment?
- What challenges did you face?
- What did you see, smell, touch, feel, and hear during the experience?

Review the list you made, and then think about how you would include these details when telling someone about your accomplishment.

What's Ahead

In this chapter, you will review two strong examples of a personal narrative: a Mentor Text and a Student Model. Then, using the examples as guidance, you will write a personal narrative of your own.

WRITING COACH

Online

www.TXWritingCoach.com

 Online Journal

Try It! Record your answers and ideas in the online journal.

You can also record and save your answers and ideas on pop-up sticky notes in the eText.

 Connect to the Big Questions

Discuss these questions with your partner:

1 What do you think? What do our accomplishments say about us?

2 Why write? What should we put in and leave out to be accurate and honest?

 Focus on the TEKS

Writing (16)(A) Write about personal experiences.

NARRATIVE NONFICTION

In this chapter, you will explore a special type of narrative nonfiction: the personal narrative. A personal narrative is a true story in which YOU are the leading character. By writing personal narratives, you can tell readers about yourself and your life. You can entertain them—and maybe make them think, too!

You will develop your personal narrative by taking it through each of the steps of the writing process: prewriting, drafting, revising, editing, and publishing. You will also have an opportunity to create a letter or e-mail about a personal event. To preview the criteria for how your personal narrative will be evaluated, see the rubric on page 83.

Narrative Nonfiction: Personal Narrative

An effective narrative nonfiction essay has these characteristics:

- A **clearly defined focus** that shows why this narrative is worth sharing

- A **sequence of events in chronological, or time, order**

- Details that **communicate the importance of or reason for actions and/or consequences**

- A **plot line with a conflict and resolution**, or a clear problem and its solution, to make the narrative complete and interesting

- **Specific details and quotations**, or dialogue, to help readers imagine characters' actions, gestures, and expressions

- Effective sentence structure and correct **spelling, grammar, and usage**

A personal narrative also includes:

- A focus on yourself, the writer, as the main character

- Vivid images and feelings to help readers experience the setting, characters, and action as you did

Other Forms of Narrative Nonfiction

In addition to a personal narrative, there are other forms of narrative nonfiction, including:

Biographical narratives are stories that share facts about someone else's life.

Blogs are comments that writers share in online forums. They may include personal narratives, opinions, and other types of comments. Blogs often invite other writers to respond online, too. They usually are not thought of as "permanent" writing.

Diary entries, which are highly personal, include experiences, thoughts, and feelings. The audience, however, is private, unless writers choose to share the diary entries.

Narrative essays use personal narratives to illustrate or support a main idea.

Memoirs focus on an important person or event from the writer's own life. Book-length memoirs by famous people are often quite popular.

Reflective essays present personal experiences—events that happened to the writers or that the writers learned about from others. Reflective essays stand out because they do more than tell a story: They also share the writers' thoughts about those experiences. Reflective essays often appear as features in magazines and newspapers.

Try It! For each audience and purpose described, choose a form, such as a blog, diary entry, or reflective essay, that is appropriate for conveying your intended meaning to the audience. Explain your choices.

- To tell online friends a funny story about yourself
- To remind yourself, for the future, about what happened today at your grandmother's birthday party
- To tell and share your feelings about a storm

WORD BANK

People often use these basic and content-based vocabulary words when they talk about narrative nonfiction writing. Work with a partner. Take turns writing each word in a sentence. If you are unsure of the meaning of a word, use the Glossary or a dictionary to check the definition.

conflict	image
consequences	personal
focus	resolution

MENTOR TEXT

Personal Narrative

Learn From Experience

 Read the personal narrative on pages 68–69. As you read, take notes to develop your understanding of basic sight and English vocabulary. Then, read the numbered notes in the margins to learn about how the author presented his ideas.

Answer the *Try It!* questions online or in your notebook.

---

❶ The **focus** is clearly defined from the start. A clear focus helps readers anticipate what the narrative will be about and builds interest in reading it.

Try It! What is the focus of the narrative? Write a sentence telling what you think.

❷ The author describes the events that led up to the **conflict,** or trouble, that he experienced.

Try It! What is the conflict? What reason does the author give for not handing over the paddle?

❸ The author gives **details** to describe how the conflict came to a head.

Try It! Which adjectives and verbs in this section help you picture the high point of the conflict?

Extension Find an example of a personal narrative to compare with this one. What insights about life does each offer?

From
The Pigman & Me

by Paul Zindel

❶ When trouble came to me, it didn't involve anybody I thought it would. It involved the nice, normal, smart boy by the name of John Quinn. Life does that to us a lot. Just when we think something awful's going to happen one way,
5 it throws you a curve and the something awful happens another way. This happened on the first Friday, during gym period, when we were allowed to play games in the school yard. **❷** A boy by the name of Richard Cahill, who lived near an old linoleum factory, asked me if I'd like to play
10 paddle ball with him, and I said, "Yes." Some of the kids played softball, some played warball, and there were a few other games where you could sign out equipment and do what you wanted. What I didn't know was that you were allowed to sign out the paddles for only fifteen minutes per
15 period so more kids could get a chance to use them. I just didn't happen to know that little rule, and Richard Cahill didn't think to tell me about it. Richard was getting a drink from the water fountain when John Quinn came up to me and told me I had to give him my paddle.
20 "No," I said, being a little paranoid about being the new kid and thinking everyone was going to try to take advantage of me.

"Look, you have to give it to me," John Quinn insisted.
❸ That was when I did something berserk. I was so
25 wound up and frightened that I didn't think, and I struck out at him with my right fist. I had forgotten I was holding the paddle, and it smacked into his face, giving him an instant black eye. John was shocked. I was shocked. Richard Cahill came running back and he was shocked.

WRITING COACH

Online

www.TXWritingCoach.com

Interactive Model

Listen to an audio recording of the Mentor Text in the eText. You can refer back to the Mentor Text whenever you need support in developing your own writing.

Online Journal

Try It! Answer the questions about the Mentor Text in the online journal.

30 ❹ "What's going on here?" Mr. Trellis, the gym teacher, growled.

"He hit me with the paddle," John moaned, holding his eye. He was red as a beet, as Little Frankfurter, Conehead, Moose, and lots of the others gathered around.

35 "He tried to take the paddle away from me!" I complained.

"His time was up," John said.

Mr. Trellis set me wise to the rules as he took John over to a supply locker and pulled out a first-aid kit.

"I'm sorry," I said, over and over again.

40 ❺ Then the bell rang, and all John Quinn whispered to me was that he was going to get even. He didn't say it like a nasty rotten kid, just more like an all-American boy who knew he'd have to regain his dignity about having to walk around school with a black eye. Before the end of school,

45 Jennifer came running up to me in the halls and told me John Quinn had announced to everyone he was going to exact revenge on me after school on Monday. That was the note of disaster my first week at school ended on, and I was terrified because I didn't know how to fight. I had

50 never even been in a fight. What had happened was all an accident. It really was.

❹ The author uses dialogue to explain the **resolution,** or outcome, of the conflict here.

Try It! What is the effect of using dialogue to describe the resolution? What insights into the characters does the dialogue give you?

❺ The author finishes describing the **resolution** here.

Try It! What are the consequences, or results, of the author hitting John Quinn with a paddle?

COLLEGE AND CAREER READINESS STANDARDS

Reading (D)(1) Describe insights gained about oneself, others, or the world from reading specific texts.

STUDENT MODEL
Personal Narrative

With a small group, take turns reading the Student Model aloud. Look for techniques the writer uses to draw you, the reader, into the story. Also look for evidence that supports your ideas.

 Use a Reader's Eye

Now, reread the Student Model. On your copy of the Student Model, use the Reader's Response Symbols to react to what you read.

Reader's Response Symbols

+ **I like where this is going.**

– **This isn't clear to me.**

? **What will happen next?**

! **Wow! That is really cool/weird/ interesting!**

 Partner Talk

Participate in an extended discussion with a partner. Express your opinions and share your responses to the Student Model. Discuss what you each thought was the main point of the narrative and why.

Alone in the SPOTLIGHT

by Mark Walker Williams

Have you ever had that nightmare—the one where everyone is staring at you? That nightmare came true for me!

I was in third grade. My school was preparing
5   a show for Independence Day, and my class was going to sing "This Is My Country." Mr. Lee, the music teacher, helped us learn the song. When I sang it at home, my parents were impressed.

"Wonderful!" cried Mom.

10   Dad added, "I can't wait to hear you sing on Friday afternoon."

"You won't be able to hear just me," I said, "but my class sounds great."

For the rest of that week, my class rehearsed
15   our song in the auditorium. We practiced marching onto the risers without tripping. And we practiced standing still without fainting. Then we practiced marching off the stage while singing the chorus two final times. A color guard was going to carry
20   flags onto the stage while we did that. If we could keep from crashing into each other, it would look good. Otherwise, it would be a disaster.

We made mistakes at first, and we joked about each one. Even when we got better, though,
25   I scowled. Someone still might mess up!

The big day came. I sat with my class, but I turned and waved at Mom, Dad, Aunt Miriam,

1

and Grandpa just before the program began. Grandpa grinned and gave me a "thumbs
30 up." I needed that because I was nervous!

The first- and second-graders did a good job. Then it was our turn.

As we sang, my nervousness disappeared. I was inspired—so inspired that I didn't notice
35 my classmates marching off the stage, and I didn't notice the color guard marching onto the stage. I didn't notice the end of the music, either. I just stood there and kept singing!

Finally, Mr. Lee came onto the stage and got my
40 attention. When I walked off with him, I felt like a complete fool.

Afterward, my family met me at my classroom. Before I could apologize, Grandpa exclaimed, "Mark, you were terrific!" Mom, Dad, and Aunt
45 Miriam agreed. They completely ignored my mistake!

"Come on," said Mom as she helped me put on my jacket. "Let's all sing that song while we walk to the bus stop." And we did!

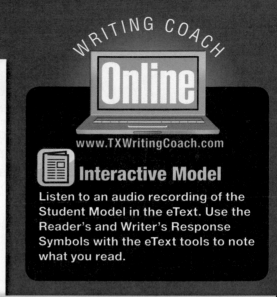

WRITING COACH

Online
www.TXWritingCoach.com

Interactive Model

Listen to an audio recording of the Student Model in the eText. Use the Reader's and Writer's Response Symbols with the eText tools to note what you read.

Use a Writer's Eye

Now evaluate the narrative as a writer. On your copy of the Student Model, use the Writer's Response Symbols to react to what you read. Identify places where the student writer uses characteristics of an effective personal narrative.

Writer's Response Symbols

E.S. Engaging story

C.R. Clear, well-developed conflict and resolution

B.C. Believable characters

S.D. Specific and vivid details

COLLEGE AND CAREER READINESS STANDARDS

Reading (C)(2) Analyze themes, structures, and elements of myths, traditional narratives, and classical and contemporary literature.

2

Your Turn **Feature Assignment:**
Personal Narrative

Prewriting

Plan a first draft of your personal narrative by choosing a topic based on your experience. You may select from the Topic Bank or come up with an idea of your own.

 ## Choose From the Topic Bank

TOPIC BANK

I Was There! Think of a memorable event you have attended. It might be a sporting event, a concert, a field trip, a theatrical performance, or even a family reunion. Write a personal narrative in which you describe the event and explain why it was so special.

It's a Group Thing Think about a group you belong to. It could be an informal group of friends or a more formal group, like a sports team or a school club. Write a personal narrative that describes your group and tells about an event that involved you and your group.

First Contact Think of a friend and how you two met. Write a personal narrative that describes how you and your friend met and explains why you became friends.

 ## Choose Your Own Topic

Determine an appropriate topic on your own by using the following **range of strategies** to generate ideas.

Question and Remember

- List some questions that people might ask about you. Which questions could you answer in a personal narrative?

- Ask family members what they remember about your early childhood. Look for story ideas in their answers.

- Remember something that you have done—something that made you happy. How could you show why you took that action and what the results were?

Review your responses and choose a topic.

Narrow Your Topic

If your topic is too broad, readers might not understand why you are writing. Choose a topic that gives your personal narrative a clearly defined focus.

Apply It! Use a graphic organizer like the one shown to narrow your topic.

- Write the main topic of your story in the top box. Move down the chart, row by row, narrowing your topic.
- Your last box should hold the main focus of your plot.

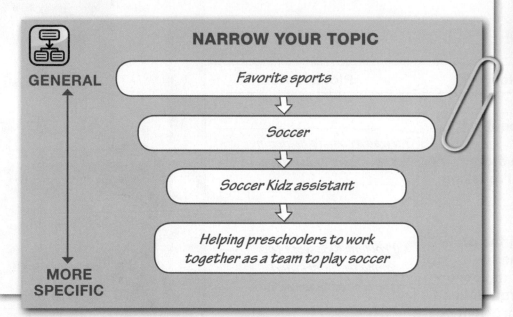

NARROW YOUR TOPIC

GENERAL

Favorite sports

Soccer

Soccer Kidz assistant

Helping preschoolers to work together as a team to play soccer

MORE SPECIFIC

 ## Consider Your Audience

Before writing, think about your audience and purpose. Consider how your writing conveys the intended meaning to this audience. Consider the views of the other as you ask these questions.

Questions for Audience	Questions for Purpose
• Who are the people in my audience? What should I tell them about myself? • What background information will my audience need?	• Why am I writing this personal narrative? What do I want to show, explain, or teach? • What point will this story make?

Record your answers in your writing journal.

WRITING COACH

Online

www.TXWritingCoach.com

Interactive Writing Coach™

- Choosing from the Topic Bank gives you access to the Interactive Writing Coach™.
- Submit your writing and receive instant personalized feedback and guidance as you draft, revise, and edit your writing.

 Interactive Graphic Organizers

Use the interactive graphic organizers to help you narrow your topic.

Online Journal

Try It! Record your answers and ideas in the online journal.

 Focus on the TEKS

Writing (14)(A) Plan a first draft by determining appropriate topics through a range of strategies.

Plan Your Piece

You will use a graphic organizer like the one shown to define your focus, gather details, and plan your piece. When it is complete, you will be ready to write your first draft.

Define Your Focus Your narrative should have **a clearly defined focus**. Complete a chart that uses chronological order to show a conflict and resolution. Include details that show the **importance of or reason for actions** in the narrative, as well as their **consequences**.

Develop Your Personal Narrative

Part of Story	Plot Events
BEGINNING • **A few details about who I am** • **The topic of the story** • **Hint about why I'm telling the story**	• _____ • *I was a coach's helper in the Soccer Kidz league.* • _____
MIDDLE • **Action revealing the problem (conflict) and the reason(s) that it happened** • **Specific details/quotations about how the problem got worse and why it needed to be solved**	• <u>*Problem:*</u> *Kids were too young to understand the idea of teamwork.* • _____ • _____
END • **Action that ended the problem (resolution)** • **The consequences of that action**	• <u>*Solution:*</u> *Had kids think of the game as if acting out a story.* • _____

SETTING: Soccer field at Lincoln Park

CHARACTERS: Me, Coach Tyler, Julia, Enrique,
_____ , _____

Gather Details

To bring their personal narratives to life, writers usually focus on these literary elements.

- **Characters:** *"Josh," Coach Tyler said, "I want you to be my helper for my Soccer Kidz team this summer. Can you handle preschoolers?" "You bet!" I shouted. "I'll be great with them!"*

- **Setting:** *The sun warmed the green field as the kids arrived on Saturday morning. When I waved, they ran across the grass to me.*

- **Plot:** *Despite my instructions, the kids swarmed all over the field. Everyone tried to kick the ball at once. How could we win a game, or even score a goal, if I couldn't get them to understand teamwork?*

Good writers are careful to present **a clearly defined focus**. They also use specific details and vivid images to bring their narratives to life.

Try It! Read the Student Model excerpt. Which details help readers understand some of the characters in this personal narrative?

STUDENT MODEL from **Alone in the Spotlight**
pages 70–71; lines 26–30

> The big day came. I sat with my class, but I turned and waved at Mom, Dad, Aunt Miriam, and Grandpa just before the program began. Grandpa grinned and gave me a "thumbs up." I needed that because I was nervous!

Apply It! Review the elements that narrative writers often use. Decide how your planned story details will make those elements clear.

- Choose details that will help readers zero in on your focus and communicate your purpose for writing.

- Select details that show why events happen, why they are important, and what their outcomes are.

- Add each detail to the correct part of your graphic organizer.

WRITING COACH

Online

www.TXWritingCoach.com

Interactive Graphic Organizers

Use the interactive graphic organizers to help you create a plan for your writing.

Interactive Model

Refer back to the Interactive Model in the eText as you plan your writing.

 Focus on the TEKS

Writing (16)(A) Write a personal narrative that has a clearly defined focus and communicates the importance of or reason for actions and/or consequences.

Drafting

During the drafting stage, you will start to write your ideas for your personal narrative. You will follow an outline that provides an **organizational strategy**, or plan, that will help you build on ideas to write a **focused, organized, and coherent** personal narrative—one in which all the ideas work together.

The Organization of a Nonfiction Narrative

The chart shows an organizational strategy for a nonfiction narrative. Look back at how the Mentor Text follows this organizational strategy. Then, use this chart to help you outline your draft.

Outline for Success

I. Beginning

See Mentor Text, p. 68.

- Clearly defined focus
- Details about the writer

Grab Your Reader

- A personal narrative should focus on a specific series of events.
- Personal details help focus the topic, establish the setting, and set the scene for the conflict to come.

II. Middle

See Mentor Text, pp. 68–69.

- Plot line with a conflict
- Importance of or reasons for actions
- Specific details about characters' movement, expressions, and gestures

Develop Your Plot

- The plot line is usually in chronological order.
- The conflict, or problem, is what gets readers interested in your narrative. It may affect one, some, or all of the characters.
- Specific details about the characters, setting, and action help readers feel as though they are part of the story.

III. End

See Mentor Text, p. 69.

- Resolution
- Consequences of actions

Wrap It Up

- The resolution of a story tells how the problem was solved or events ended it.
- Ending your narrative with a quotation or detail that makes the resolution clear helps sum up the story for the reader.

👍 Start Your Draft

Use this checklist to help you complete your draft. Use the graphic organizer that shows the beginning, middle, and end of your narrative, and the Outline for Success as guides.

While drafting, aim at writing your ideas, not on making your writing perfect. Remember, you will have the chance to improve your draft when you revise and edit.

√ Start by drafting an attention-getting **opening** sentence.

√ Continue your **beginning** by focusing on the topic and connecting with readers in a way that makes them want to keep reading. Make sure your narrative has a clearly defined **focus**.

√ Use chronological order to develop the **middle** of your personal narrative. Present a series of plot events that show **reasons for actions and the consequences** of those actions.

√ Keep the narrative interesting by including vivid images and specific **details** about the characters, setting, and action.

√ At the **end** of your narrative, show the **resolution**—how the conflict worked out.

√ Finish in a way that shows the importance of actions and their **consequences** in the narrative.

WRITING COACH

Online
www.TXWritingCoach.com

📰 **Interactive Model**

Outline for Success View pop-ups of Mentor Text selections referenced in the Outline for Success.

👍 **Interactive Writing Coach™**

Use the Interactive Writing Coach to receive the level of support you need:
• Write one paragraph at a time and submit each one for immediate, detailed feedback.
• Write your entire first draft and submit it for immediate, personalized feedback.

🤠 **Focus on the TEKS**

Writing

(14)(B) Develop drafts by choosing an appropriate organizational strategy and building on ideas to create a focused, organized, and coherent piece of writing.

(16)(A) Write a personal narrative that has a clearly defined focus and communicates the importance of or reason for actions and/or consequences.

Revising: Making It Better

Now that you have finished your first draft, you are ready to revise. Think about the "big picture" of **audience**, **purpose**, and **genre**. You can use the Revision RADaR strategy as a guide for making changes to improve your draft. Revision RADaR provides four major ways to improve your writing: (R) replace, (A) add, (D) delete, and (R) reorder.

Kelly Gallagher, M. Ed.

KEEP REVISION ON YOUR RADaR

Read part of the first draft of the Student Model "Alone in the Spotlight." Then, look at questions the writer asked himself as he thought about how well his draft **addressed issues of audience, purpose, and genre**.

Alone in the Spotlight

We made mistakes at first, and we joked about each one. Even when we got better, though, I scowled.

The big day came. I sat with my class, but I turned and waved at Mom, Dad, Aunt Miriam, and Grandpa. The first- and second-graders did a good job. Then it was our turn. Grandpa grinned and gave me a "thumbs up." I needed that because I was nervous!

As we sang, my nervousness disappeared. I felt fabulous! I was inspired—so inspired that I didn't notice my classmates marching off the stage, and I didn't notice the color guard.

Finally, Mr. Lee came onto the stage and got my attention. When I walked off with him, I felt like a complete fool.

Afterward, my family met me at my classroom. Before I could apologize, Grandpa exclaimed, "Mark, you were terrific!" Mom, Dad, and Aunt Miriam agreed. They actually sounded happy!

> *A narrative should show reasons for actions. Will readers know why I scowled?*

> *These details aren't quite the way I remember them. Will the **sequence** be clear to my **audience**?*

> *Does "I felt fabulous" help my **purpose**, or do readers already understand that? Also, my **purpose** here is to be funny. Do I have enough funny details?*

> *A **resolution** is an important part of writing in this **genre**. Does my resolution tell about the outcome?*

Now look at how the writer applied Revision RADaR to write an improved second draft.

Alone in the SPOTLIGHT

2ND DRAFT

We made mistakes at first, and we joked about each one. Even when we got better, though, I scowled. Someone still might mess up!

 A *Added a sentence to show a reason for an action*

The big day came. I sat with my class, but I turned and waved at Mom, Dad, Aunt Miriam, and Grandpa just before the program began. Grandpa grinned and gave me a "thumbs up." I needed that because I was nervous!

R *Reordered and* **A** *added details to make the sequence of events clear*

The first- and second-graders did a good job. Then it was our turn.

As we sang, my nervousness disappeared. I was inspired—so inspired that I didn't notice my classmates marching off the stage, and I didn't notice the color guard marching onto the stage. I didn't notice the end of the music, either. I just stood there and kept singing!

D *Deleted a sentence that I don't need* **A** *and added two sentences to make the moment funnier*

Finally, Mr. Lee came onto the stage and got my attention. When I walked off with him, I felt like a complete fool.

Afterward, my family met me at my classroom. Before I could apologize, Grandpa exclaimed, "Mark, you were terrific!" Mom, Dad, and Aunt Miriam agreed. They completely ignored my mistake!

R *Replaced a sentence to make the resolution stronger*

 Apply It! Use your Revision RADaR to revise your draft.

- First, determine if you have included the characteristics of the personal narrative genre.
- Then apply the Revision RADaR strategy to make needed changes. Remember—you can use the steps in the strategy in any order.

Focus on the TEKS

Writing (14)(C) Revise drafts after rethinking how well questions of purpose, audience, and genre have been addressed.

COLLEGE AND CAREER READINESS STANDARDS

Writing (A)(4) Recognize the importance of revision as the key to effective writing. Each draft should refine key ideas and organize them more logically and fluidly, use language more precisely and effectively, and draw the reader to the author's purpose.

Look at the Big Picture

Use the chart to evaluate how well each section of your personal narrative addresses **purpose**, **audience**, and **genre**. When necessary, use the suggestions in the chart to revise your narrative.

Section	Evaluate	Revise
Beginning	• Check the opening sentences of your narrative. Do they get readers' attention?	• Add a question, a quotation, or some other detail that makes readers curious.
	• Consider your **focus**; if it is clearly defined, readers will understand the topic and connect with you as the writer.	• Ask yourself, "Why would I want to read this story?" The answer may help you sharpen your focus.
Middle	• Make sure that the plot of your narrative presents a **conflict**—a problem that readers will understand and care about.	• Add or change details to show why the problem matters to you, the writer and main character. If it matters to you, it should matter to readers.
	• Underline reasons for actions in the narrative. Will readers understand why **characters** do what they do?	• Add a detail that answers the question "Why?" At the same time, keep the plot events moving; don't get off track.
	• Review details about **characters**, setting, and action. Could any images be more vivid, specific, and interesting?	• Add or change details, or images, so that readers can "see," "hear," and so on. Make them feel that they are part of the story!
End	• Make sure that your narrative has a **resolution** that shows how the conflict worked out.	• Add or revise details to show how the problem was solved or how events ended it.
	• Underline **consequences** of actions in the narrative and decide whether readers will understand the **importance** of the actions.	• Add a detail that answers the question "So what?" about the outcome and makes one more connection with your readers.

Focus on Craft: Simple, Compound, and Complex Sentences

Subjects and predicates of sentences work together to express ideas. In a **simple sentence**, one subject and one predicate express one idea. In a **compound sentence**, two or more subject-predicate pairs express two or more equal ideas. In a **complex sentence**, two or more subject-predicate pairs express two or more ideas, but one idea is more important than any other. Mixing sentence structures can keep your writing interesting. Think about sentence structures as you read the following sentences from the Student Model.

 STUDENT MODEL from **Alone in the Spotlight** page 70; lines 23–25

> We made mistakes at first, and we joked about each one. Even when we got better, though, I scowled. Someone still might mess up!

Try It! Now, ask yourself these questions:

- Which sentence is simple? Compound? Complex? Explain.
- Would the first sentence be better if it read "We made mistakes at first. We joked about each one"? Explain.

Fine-Tune Your Draft

Apply It! Use the revision suggestions to prepare your final draft **after thinking how well questions of purpose, audience, and genre have been addressed**.

- **Ensure Simple, Compound, and Complex Sentences** Raise the interest level by using a variety of sentence structures.
- **Ensure Vivid Images** Help readers feel a part of your narrative. Add or revise details so that readers can easily imagine the setting, characters, and action.

Teacher Feedback Read your final draft to your teacher. Ask if your personal narrative has **a clearly defined focus**. Think about your teacher's response and revise your final draft as needed.

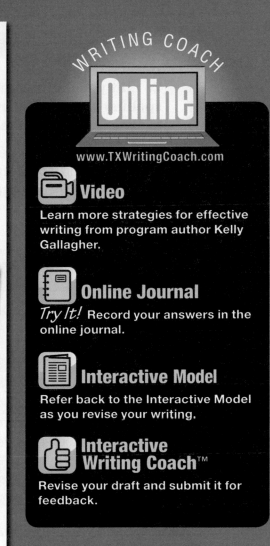

WRITING COACH

Online

www.TXWritingCoach.com

Video
Learn more strategies for effective writing from program author Kelly Gallagher.

Online Journal
Try It! Record your answers in the online journal.

Interactive Model
Refer back to the Interactive Model as you revise your writing.

Interactive Writing Coach™
Revise your draft and submit it for feedback.

Focus on the TEKS

Writing

(14)(C) Revise drafts to ensure vivid images and use of simple, compound, and complex sentences after rethinking how well questions of purpose, audience, and genre have been addressed.

(14)(E) Revise final draft in response to feedback from teacher.

(16)(A) Write a personal narrative that has a clearly defined focus and communicates the importance of or reason for actions and/or consequences.

Editing: Making It Correct

To edit your work, read your draft carefully to correct errors in spelling and grammar. It can be helpful to read your draft aloud to listen for where the writing needs correction.

As you edit, make sure that you have used a **consistent verb tense**, and did not shift to another tense without a reason. Then edit your final draft for errors in **grammar, mechanics, and spelling**.

WRITE GUY *Jeff Anderson, M. Ed.*

WHAT DO YOU NOTICE?

Zoom in on Conventions Focus on verb tenses as you zoom in on these lines from the Mentor Text.

> To learn more about verb tenses, see Chapter 14 of your Grammar Handbook.

 MENTOR TEXT from **The Pigman & Me**
pages 68–69; lines 17–19, 46–47

> Richard was getting a drink from the water fountain when John Quinn came up to me and told me I had to give him my paddle....
> John Quinn had announced to everyone he was going to exact revenge on me after school on Monday.

Now, ask yourself: *When did the events in each sentence occur?*

Perhaps you said that both sentences show actions that happened in the past. A **progressive tense** verb shows that an action is or was happening for a period of time. Progressive tense verbs consist of a form of the helping verb *be*, such as *is, are, was,* or *were*, with the present participle of the main verb, which ends in *-ing*. The past progressive tense "was getting" shows the action Richard was completing for a period of time.

A **perfect tense** verb refers to an action that has been completed. Perfect tense verbs consist of a form of the helping verb *have*, such as *had, have,* or *has*, with the past participle of the main verb, which for regular verbs ends in *-ed* or *-d*. The past perfect tense "had announced" refers to an action that John Quinn completed.

Grammar Mini-Lesson: Consistent Tenses

To learn more, see page 284.

Usually, you use one verb tense for consistency. Sometimes, though, you must change tense to show a sequence of events. **Consistent verb tense** is especially important in sentences with more than one action and clause. "He *has been* to Europe, and he *will go* to Asia." Notice how the past tense is used consistently in the Mentor Text.

 MENTOR TEXT from **The Pigman & Me**
page 68; lines 24–26

I was so <u>wound</u> up and <u>frightened</u> that I <u>didn't</u> think, and I <u>struck</u> out at him with my right fist.

Try It! Rewrite these simple, compound, and complex sentences so that they use **perfect or progressive tenses** consistently, and shift tenses only to make the sequence clear. Write the answers in your journal.

1. Mom attended every softball game and cheers us on. (simple)
2. Brad left the team in March, but he play with us for three years. (compound)
3. I practice soccer when a ball hit me in the head. (complex)

 Apply It! Edit your draft for **grammar, mechanics, capitalization, and spelling**. Check that you have used perfect and progressive verb tenses correctly. Where needed, apply consistent tenses to verbs.

Use the rubric to evaluate your narrative. If necessary, rethink, rewrite, or revise.

Rubric for Narrative Nonfiction: Personal Narrative	Rating Scale			
	Not very		Very	
Focus and Coherence: Does your narrative have a single important event?	1	2	3	4
Organization: How logically organized is your sequence of events?	1	2	3	4
Development of Ideas: How well do you build on each idea to create coherence?	1	2	3	4
Voice: How authentic and engaging is your voice?	1	2	3	4
Conventions: How correct is your verb tense?	1	2	3	4

WRITING COACH

www.TXWritingCoach.com

 Video
Learn effective editing techniques from program author Jeff Anderson.

 Online Journal
Try It! Record your answers in the online journal.

 Interactive Model
Refer back to the Interactive Model as you edit your writing.

 Interactive Writing Coach™
Edit your draft. Check it against the rubric and then submit it for feedback.

Focus on the TEKS

Writing (14)(D) Edit drafts for grammar, mechanics, and spelling.

Conventions

(19)(A) Identify, use, and understand verbs (perfect and progressive tenses).

(19)(C) Use a variety of complete sentences (e.g., simple, compound, complex) that include consistent tenses.

(20)(A) Use conventions of capitalization.

COLLEGE AND CAREER READINESS STANDARDS

Writing (A)(5) Edit writing for proper voice, tense, and syntax, assuring that it conforms to standard English when appropriate.

Publishing

Get your personal narrative ready for presentation. Then, choose a way to **publish it for the appropriate audience.**

Wrap Up Your Presentation

Is your narrative handwritten? If so, you may need to make a new, clean copy. If so, be sure to **write legibly**. Also be sure that your title grabs the reader's attention and indicates the topic of your narrative.

Publish Your Piece

Use the chart to identify a way to publish your personal narrative.

If your audience is...	...then publish it by...
Students or adults at school	• Sharing it in a small-group "read-around" • Presenting it as a humorous reading, if appropriate, in a school talent show
People outside of your school	• Sending it in a letter or e-mail to someone else who played a part in the narrative • Posting it on a blog • Submitting it to an online magazine for young people

 ## Reflect on Your Writing

Now that you are done with your personal narrative, read it over and use your writing journal to answer these questions. Use specific details to describe and explain your reflections. Increase the specificity of your details based on the type of information requested.

- Which part of your narrative do you feel is strongest? Why?

- Is there anything about the narrative that you still want to work on? If so, how will you deal with it?

- Now that you have written this piece of narrative nonfiction, what might you try writing next? Explain.

 The Big Question: Why Write? What did you decide to put in or leave out to be accurate and honest?

Manage Your Portfolio You may wish to include your published personal narrative in your writing portfolio. If so, consider what this narrative reveals about your writing and your growth as a writer.

MAKE YOUR WRITING COUNT

Bring Your Personal Narrative to Life in a Script

A **personal narrative** provides a window into a writer's past. Many movies are biopics—filmed stories based on real personal narratives. Write your own biopic by turning a personal narrative into a script to be acted out or filmed.

Work productively in teams to prepare a script called "A Day in the Life" by assigning roles and giving one another feedback as you plan, write, and rehearse your script. Present your script live or as a video.

Here's your action plan.

1. Choose group roles and set objectives.

2. Review your personal narratives. Choose one that tells an interesting story about a day in the writer's life.

3. Look online for model scripts, and follow the model for script format.

4. Create a script based on your narrative by doing the following:

   - Breaking the narrative into separate scenes
   - Including dialogue to convey a clear and distinct perspective
   - Providing stage directions that tell actors how to gesture

5. Assign group members to act out the script in a dramatic reading. Record the reading on video, or present it live to the class. You might also consider using an online movie-making tool.

Listening and Speaking While rehearsing the script, give each other feedback on vocal expression or gestures that would enhance the presentation. Use specific details to describe and explain your ideas. Increase the specificity of your details based on the type of information you are delivering. When presenting the script, remember to incorporate your peers' feedback. Give each audience member a copy of the script to follow along with, and ask for comments on the script and its presentation.

WRITING COACH

Online

www.TXWritingCoach.com

Online Journal

Reflect on Your Writing Record your answers and ideas in the online journal.

Resource

Link to resources on 21st Century Learning for help in creating a group project.

Focus on the TEKS

Writing (14)(C) Revise final draft in response to feedback from peers.

(14)(E) Publish written work for appropriate audiences.

(20) Write legibly.

COLLEGE AND CAREER READINESS STANDARDS

Speaking (B)(3) Plan and deliver focused and coherent presentations that convey clear and distinct perspectives and demonstrate solid reasoning.

Listening (B)(1) Listen critically and respond appropriately to presentations.

Your Turn ▶ **Writing for Media:**
Event Letter

Event Letter

An **event letter** is a letter or e-mail that recounts, or tells a story about, an event that you want to share—an event in which you had a major part. Your writing will tell a story about yourself, so your task will be much like writing a personal narrative. It will not be exactly the same, however. Because the writing takes the form of a letter, its tone will be a little more casual and will sound more like a friendly conversation.

Try It! Read this part of an event letter. Then, answer these questions. Record your answers in your journal.

1. How can you tell that this event letter is being sent as an e-mail?

2. Who is the **audience** for the letter? How did the writer engage the reader?

3. What is the topic or **focus** of the letter? How can you tell that it is a clearly defined focus?

4. What do you think is the **purpose** of the letter?

5. An event letter tells a story, so review what you know about the **plot** of this story. Who are the characters? What is the setting? What conflict does the writer face, and what do you think the resolution might be?

6. Think about the way that the writer expresses himself. How would you describe the **mood** or tone of the letter? Explain.

Extension Find another example of an event letter, and compare it with this one.

From: Marcus <marcfrye@happywriters.com>
Subject: **What a Story!**
Date: April 14, 2011 7:22:03 PM EDT
To: Tomas <texastomas97@friendsring.com>

Hi, Tomas,

Remember how I told you I was going to take care of a puppy? Well I did. Last week I took care of my Aunt Darlene's Chihuahua puppy Goliath. I was pretty excited at first, since I've always wanted a puppy.

Aunt Darlene dropped Goliath off in his crate along with two whole pages of instructions. As soon as she left, Goliath started to whine. He really seemed to miss Aunt Darlene. I was able to quiet him down by playing with him.

Aunt Darlene's list told me exactly what I had to do to take care of Goliath. I had to feed him twice a day, walk him once, and play fetch with him. I also had to let him outside to use the bathroom four times a day. Doing all of these things took up a lot of time, but the hardest thing was making sure he did not chew everything. One day, he got one of my socks and chewed a hole in it. Another day, he pulled my shoelaces out of my shoe.

I mostly enjoyed taking care of Goliath, but it made me wonder if I really want a puppy of my own. It's sure a lot of work!

Create an Event Letter

Follow these steps to create your own event letter. To plan your event letter, review the graphic organizers on R24–R27 and choose one that suits your needs.

Prewriting

- Identify your target audience. Think about who will read your letter. Will they understand your story?

- Select a topic that you want to share. You might want to share a funny story, or an experience that was out of the ordinary.

- Think about what you want to tell your audience, and make sure that you focus on a single event.

- List or map out the plot of the narrative—its beginning, middle, and end.

- Fill in the details; for example, note things that you or other characters said and how you felt as the action was happening.

Drafting

- Use chronological order to recount the event.

- Write a narrative that tells your personal story and includes details that explain the reasons for actions. You may also want to hint at their importance. Don't forget to reveal consequences.

- Remember to connect to the person who will read the event letter. Think of details or comments that your audience will appreciate.

Revising and Editing

- Review your draft to ensure that your narrative is complete and interesting. Look for specific words and vivid images.

- Review the tone of the letter. If necessary, make changes to give it a more friendly tone.

- Check that spelling, grammar, and mechanics are correct.

Publishing

If you are mailing the letter, create a clean copy and then mail it. If you are sending it as an e-mail, make sure that the recipient's address is correct before you hit SEND. You also may want to attach a photo related to the event.

www.TXWritingCoach.com

 Online Journal

Try It! Record your answers in the online journal.

 Interactive Graphic Organizers

Choose from a variety of graphic organizers to plan and develop your project.

Partner Talk

Before you start drafting, explain your event letter to a partner. Ask for feedback about your plan. For example, are you telling the story completely? In a friendly way?

 Focus on the TEKS

Writing (16)(A) Write a personal narrative that has a clearly defined focus and communicates the importance of or reason for actions and/or consequences.

Writing for Assessment

Many standardized tests include a prompt that asks you to write a personal narrative. Use these prompts to practice. Your compositions should have the same characteristics as your personal narrative. (See page 66.)

 Try It! Read the prompt and the information on format and academic vocabulary. Then, write a **personal narrative** using the ABCDs of On-Demand Writing.

Format

The prompt directs you to write a *personal narrative*. Make sure that you keep a clearly defined focus through your narrative's beginning, middle, and end.

Narrative Prompt

What is the best trip you ever took? Think about what made that trip "best" and then write a personal narrative to share the story. Be sure to include a beginning, a middle, and an end.

Academic Vocabulary

Remember that the *beginning*, *middle*, and *end* make a story. Be sure to include all three parts in your personal narrative.

The ABCDs of On-Demand Writing

Use the following ABCDs to help you respond to the prompt.

Before you write your draft:

A ttack the prompt [1 MINUTE]

- Circle or highlight important verbs in the prompt. Draw a line from the verb to what it refers to.
- Rewrite the prompt in your own words.

B rainstorm possible answers [4 MINUTES]

- Create a graphic organizer to generate ideas.
- Use one for each part of the prompt if necessary.

C hoose the order of your response [1 MINUTE]

- Think about the best way to organize your ideas.
- Number your ideas in the order you will write about them. Cross out ideas you will not be using.

After you write your draft:

D etect errors before turning in the draft [1 MINUTE]

- Carefully reread your writing.
- Make sure that your response makes sense and is complete.
- Look for spelling, punctuation, and grammar errors.

More Prompts for Practice

Apply It! **Texas Test Prep** Respond to Prompts 1 and 2 by writing **personal narratives** with **a clearly defined focus**. As you write, be sure to:

- Identify an appropriate audience for your intended purpose
- Use a graphic organizer, such as a beginning-middle-end organizer, to organize and structure your ideas
- Explain **the importance of or reason for your actions and their consequences**

Prompt 1 How far back can you remember? Think about your earliest childhood memory. Then, write a personal narrative to tell the story of what happened to you at that memorable moment.

Prompt 2 Recall a time when you gave a very special gift to someone. In a personal narrative, recount that event. Show why you chose that gift and how the person who received the gift reacted to it.

More Strategies for Writing for Assessment

- Consider several possible topics and quickly list details that you might use in your response. Then, choose the topic for which you have the strongest ideas.
- If you do not understand any words in the prompt, use context clues to determine the meaning of the unknown words.
- Be sure to follow the ABCDs for writing to a prompt. Planning is an important part of writing. Don't just start writing right away.
- Make sure to reread your piece after you have completed it. This will give you time to find and correct errors. If you are in a timed situation, be sure to leave enough time for this step.

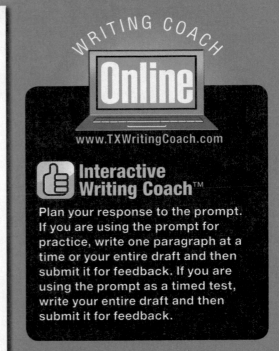

WRITING COACH

Online

www.TXWritingCoach.com

Interactive Writing Coach™

Plan your response to the prompt. If you are using the prompt for practice, write one paragraph at a time or your entire draft and then submit it for feedback. If you are using the prompt as a timed test, write your entire draft and then submit it for feedback.

Remember **ABCD**

Attack the prompt

Brainstorm possible answers

Choose the order of your response

Detect errors before turning in the draft

 Focus on the TEKS

Writing

(16)(A) Write a personal narrative that has a clearly defined focus and communicates the importance of or reason for actions and/or consequences.

CHAPTER 6

FICTION NARRATION

What's the Story?

What is happening in the photograph? What story can you tell about what happened shortly before this photograph was taken?

Many stories have realistic settings. Believable details about setting, such as a mountain bike trail in a forest, help get the reader interested and add to the story. Conflict is also important. Conflict is a challenge or problem the main character faces.

Try It! Think about what might have happened in the moments before the photograph was taken. Write notes about what the biker was doing.

Consider these questions as you participate in an extended discussion with a partner. Take turns expressing your ideas and feelings.

- Why is this person riding through the forest?
- What is this person's challenge?
- How do you think this person feels?

Review your notes. Use your notes to tell a story about the biker. Be sure to use details to make your story believable.

What's Ahead

In this chapter, you will review two strong examples of a fiction story: a Mentor Text and a Student Model. Then, using the examples as guidance, you will write a fiction story of your own.

WRITING COACH

www.TXWritingCoach.com

Online Journal

Try It! Record your answers and ideas in the online journal.

You can also record and save your answers and ideas on pop-up sticky notes in the eText.

Connect to the Big Questions

Discuss these questions with your partner:

1 What do you think? How do challenges help us grow?

2 Why write? What can fiction do better than non-fiction?

 Focus on the TEKS

Writing (15)(A) Write literary texts to express ideas and feelings about real or imagined people, events, and ideas.

SHORT STORY

In this chapter, you will write a short story, or a series of events that have a beginning, middle, and end. You will also explore a special type of literary text called science fiction. A science fiction short story focuses on real or imagined developments in science and technology and their effects on the way people think and live. Space travel, robots, and life in the future are popular topics for science fiction.

You will develop a science fiction story by taking it through each of the steps of the writing process: prewriting, drafting, revising, editing, and publishing. You will also have an opportunity to write a dramatic scene. To preview the criteria for how your science fiction story will be evaluated, see the rubric on page 111.

FEATURE ASSIGNMENT
Short Story: Science Fiction

An effective imaginative short story has these characteristics:

- **A specific, believable setting** created through the use of **sensory details**

- **An engaging plot**, or storyline, with **well-paced action** that **holds reader interest**

- One or more **well-developed, interesting characters**

- A **range of literary strategies and devices**, such as flashback and foreshadowing, to enhance the **style** and **tone**, or attitude

- **Effective sentence structure** and correct spelling, grammar, and usage

A science fiction story also includes:

- A **setting** with more advanced technology than existed when the story was written

- An action-packed **plot** with a **conflict**, or problem, between people's needs and technology, or between people from Earth and aliens

- A **theme** about the relationship between humans and science

Other Forms of Short Stories

In addition to science fiction, there are other forms of short stories, including:

Fantasy stories stretch the imagination and take readers to unreal worlds. Animals may talk, people may fly, or characters may have superhuman powers.

Historical fiction tells about imaginary people living in real places and times in history. Usually, the main characters are fictional people who know and interact with famous people in history and participate in important historical events.

Mystery stories focus on unexplained or strange events that one of the characters tries to solve. These stories are often full of suspense and surprises.

Myths and legends are traditional stories that different cultures have told to explain natural events, human nature, or the origins of things. They often include gods and goddesses from ancient times and heroes who do superhuman things.

Realistic fiction portrays invented characters and events in everyday life that most readers would find familiar.

Tall tales are about larger-than-life characters in realistic settings. The main character typically solves a problem or reaches a goal by doing something wild and fantastic that normal people could never do.

Try It! For each audience and purpose described, choose a story form, such as a fantasy story, mystery, or realistic fiction, that is appropriate for conveying your intended meaning to the audience. Explain your choices.

- To describe how a mystery was solved
- To show how a fictional teen deals with a problem
- To catch the imagination of young children

WRITING COACH

Online

www.TXWritingCoach.com

📁 **Resource**

Word Bank Listen to English and Spanish pronunciations of new words in the eText glossary.

📓 **Online Journal**

Try It! Record your answers and ideas in the online journal.

 WORD BANK

People often use these words when talking about short stories. Work with a partner. Take turns saying each word aloud. If you are unsure of the meaning of a word, use the Glossary or a dictionary to check the definition. Then, write a sentence using each word.

develop	style
imagery	theme
sensory	tone

COLLEGE AND CAREER READINESS STANDARDS

Reading (B)(3) Use reference guides to confirm the meanings of new words or concepts.

MENTOR TEXT Science Fiction

Learn From Experience

 Read the science fiction story on pages 94–97. As you read, take notes to develop your understanding of basic sight and English vocabulary. Then, read the numbered notes in the margins to learn about how the author presented her ideas.

Answer the *Try It!* questions online or in your notebook.

---

❶ The introduction identifies the main **character** and creates a believable **setting.**

Try It! Who is the main character in this story? What details does the author use to set the scene of the story?

❷ Words such as *chatter, rustling, sighing,* and *sharp calls* are all **sensory details.**

Try It! To which of the five senses do these details appeal? Why might the author be stressing this particular sense in the story?

❸ Here, and throughout the story, the author uses a consistent **point of view.**

Try It! From which point of view is the story told: first person or third person? How can you tell?

Extension Find another science fiction story, and compare it with this one. How is the language similar? How is it different?

Traveler

by Barbara Davis

❶ "Here!" Luis shouted. "We can camp here. It's perfect!" His three friends trudged into the forest clearing. Luis had found a beautiful, grassy area ringed with tall pines and oaks. The boys could see the sun shining off the
5 surface of a small lake not too far from where they stood. After carrying heavy backpacks through miles and miles of forest trails, they relished the idea of a swim in cool water.

Joel groaned as he swung his backpack off his shoulders. He dropped down on the grass and wiped the sweat from
10 his face with the bottom of his T-shirt. "Looks great to me. Plenty of dry wood to start a fire, rocks for a fire ring, a place to swim—I vote we set up camp."

Soon, the four were busy setting up tents and hanging their food in trees to discourage bears. "How about you guys
15 finish up here, and I'll go collect firewood?" Luis suggested. Since finding firewood meant even more walking around in the forest, the other boys readily agreed.

❷ As Luis headed into the forest, the boys' campsite chatter faded from his hearing. Instead, Luis heard the
20 light breeze rustling the leaves in the trees. The tall pines sounded like they were sighing. Every once in awhile, he heard the sharp calls of unseen crows. The bushes rustled with the passage of some kind of small animal. At least Luis *hoped* it was a small animal and not a bear.

25 **❸** Listening to all the forest sounds, Luis lost track of time. Eventually, the increasing weight of the firewood sack he had tied around his shoulder let him know it was time to start making his way back to camp. He had gone much farther into the forest than he had intended. He
30 wasn't worried, though. There wasn't a trail yet that Luis couldn't follow. Shifting the weight of the firewood to a more comfortable position, Luis started to take a step back along the way he had come. Suddenly, a voice said, "Not that way!"

35   Luis was so surprised, he almost dropped the firewood. He whipped his head around to see who had spoken. No one was there. He carefully scanned the area around him. Nothing. Luis wasn't the type of kid to imagine voices but, obviously, he had imagined this one. Shrugging off the
40   mystery, he once again started down the trail.
     ❹ "You *really* don't want to go that way." Same voice. This time Luis was sure it wasn't just his imagination.
     His heart beating just a little bit faster, Luis asked, "Who are you? Where are you?" At first, there was no response.
45   Then, Luis heard the tree leaves just above his head start to rustle. He peered closely into the tree, but still couldn't see anything. He focused his eyes even harder. There! He saw something. It looked like a really skinny kid straddling the lowest branch.
50   The kid seemed to be wearing some type of camouflage clothing that allowed him to blend in with the surrounding leaves. If Luis took his eyes off the kid for even a second, the kid blended right back into the tree. ❹ "Ah! You can finally see me. Took you long enough."
55   Now that Luis could see that it was just a kid, he felt foolish for having been slightly scared. "Yeah, I can see you. Why are you telling me not to go this way? This is the way back to my campsite."
     The kid in the tree just smiled. He said, "Maybe. But you
60   still don't want to go that way."
     The bundle of wood was getting heavier by the minute, and Luis didn't feel like playing a game of riddles. Part of him wanted to know who the kid was and what he was doing there in the middle of the forest. The other part of
65   him wanted to get back to the campsite. The second part won out. Luis said, "Yeah, okay. Whatever." With that, he turned and continued down the path. When he looked over his shoulder, all he could see were the leaves of the tree. No kid. Luis shook his head and kept going.
70   ❺ He wasn't sure when he noticed that the forest had grown still. No breeze, no birds, no sounds at all. It was as if the forest was holding its breath. The sun was still shining in streaks along the path, causing the air to shimmer. In the

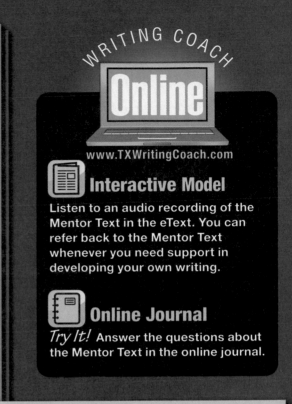

WRITING COACH

Online

www.TXWritingCoach.com

Interactive Model

Listen to an audio recording of the Mentor Text in the eText. You can refer back to the Mentor Text whenever you need support in developing your own writing.

Online Journal

Try It! Answer the questions about the Mentor Text in the online journal.

❹ **Dialogue** helps develop the story and reveal the characters' motivations.

Try It! How does the dialogue help to move the story forward? What do Luis's lines tell you about him?

❺ Here, the author uses **suspense,** which adds interest to the story.

Try It! How does suspense keep readers engaged in a story?

6 The author again uses **sensory details** to describe the scene's setting.

Try It! To which of the five senses do these details appeal? Which details in this passage help you to feel as if you are there, witnessing the action?

7 **Descriptive details** about a character can be a subtle way of saying something about the character's personality.

Try It! What do you think the author is trying to convey about the creature in describing its small, sharp teeth?

8 Further **dialogue** gives more information about the characters and their motives.

Try It! What does the dialogue reveal about the two main characters in this story? What does their conversation reveal about the differences in the times and cultures in which they live?

9 **Action words** can move a story along by changing the pace. In this paragraph, the author uses words such as *burst, panting,* and *skidded* to create a feeling of urgency.

Try It! What other words in the story convey a strong sense of action?

time it took Luis to wonder at how odd the shafts of light looked, he had passed through one of them. When he did, the first thing he realized was that the forest was no longer silent.

It took a moment for him to recognize the sound of water crashing down on rocks. A waterfall? That was impossible. Luis knew for a fact that there were no waterfalls in the forest he and his friends had hiked through. After a few more steps, though, it was clear that he was wrong. **6** There, in all its rushing power was the highest waterfall Luis had ever seen. Even more amazing were the things flying in the air, diving into and out of the frothing water and laughing with the fun of it all. Skinny kids with bat-like wings? Luis's mouth hung open in disbelief. As if that weren't enough, he heard the now-familiar voice: "I told you not to go that way."

This time it was much easier to see the kid because he was standing right next to Luis. Except Luis could now see that it wasn't really a kid at all. With his pointy nose and chin, he almost looked like a cross between a human and a fox. He didn't have fur, though, and his arms and legs were as skinny as twigs. He also had that bizarre quality of looking as if he was constantly blending into and out of his surroundings. Although Luis had a million questions in his brain, none of them were making it to his mouth. For once, "cool as a cucumber in a crisis" Luis was speechless.

7 The creature smiled at Luis. Up close, those teeth were small and sharp. **8** "You're not dreaming. You haven't fallen and conked your head on a stone or anything like that. What you *have* done is pass through one of our portals."

"Portals?" Luis whispered.

"Doorways. Places where we can step between worlds. I'm a Traveler. I travel to other times and other worlds. In Earth years, I'm from about 500 years in the future, and I like this time in your world quite a bit. It's similar to my world. Lots of trees, water. Many of the other places I visit are quite different. Fire, extreme heat, dust. Not so much fun."

The creature smiled again, but it wasn't a pleasant smile. "The thing is, though, we really don't like visitors to *our* world." Luis didn't see what came next, but he felt it—a

hard shove against his chest. The next thing he knew, he
was sitting on the forest trail looking up at the sunlight. In
seconds, he dumped his load of wood and ran as fast as he
could back to the campsite.

9 He burst out of the forest, wide-eyed and panting.
Brad, Tran, and Joel were still pitching the tents and looked
up in surprise. Luis skidded into the clearing ready to sputter
about what he'd just seen, but he stopped himself. What was
he going to say to his friends? They would think he was
crazy. His reputation as a practical, not-easily-fooled kind
of guy would be ruined. Luis shook his head. He wasn't
going to say a word.

"Hey, Luis! What's up? Why are you running? Where's the
wood?" Brad and Tran's questions tumbled over each other.

"Nothing. It's nothing. I just thought I heard a bear and
got a little spooked." Luis replied. "I must have dropped the
load of wood. I'll go back and get it."

10 Joel hadn't said anything at all. He gave Luis an odd
look and said, "I'll go back with you and give you a hand."
Luis was too shaken to protest so he just nodded his head.
As the two friends walked back into the forest, Joel said,
"So, you met a Traveler, huh?"

WRITING COACH

Online

www.TXWritingCoach.com

Interactive Model

Listen to an audio recording of the
Mentor Text in the eText. You can
refer back to the Mentor Text
whenever you need support in
developing your own writing.

Online Journal

Try It! Answer the questions about
the Mentor Text in the online journal.

10 The story's **resolution** contains a device
called a **teaser**. Teasers are sometimes used to
suggest there is more to the story than what is
specifically written.

Try It! What teaser does the author
use? How does it make the story more
interesting?

**COLLEGE AND CAREER READINESS
STANDARDS**

Reading (C)(3) Analyze works of literature for
what they suggest about the historical period
and cultural contexts in which they were written.

Reading (C)(4) Analyze and compare the use
of language in literary works from a variety of
world cultures.

STUDENT MODEL — Science Fiction

 ## Use a Reader's Eye

Now, reread the Student Model. On your copy of the Student Model, use the Reader's Response Symbols to react to what you read.

Reader's Response Symbols

+ **This is a good description.**

- **This isn't clear to me.**

! **This is really cool/weird/interesting!**

? **What will happen next?**

 ### Partner Talk

Express your ideas and feelings about the Student Model with a partner. Discuss what you thought did and didn't work in the story.

Be Careful Where You Wish For

by Linda Radner

Sandy's IDP/D woke her up on time, of course. She carefully checked the top of her earlobe. Yes! It was there! Now she was one of the first to have the latest application for her Internal Daily Planner/
5   Doer (IDP/D). Her IDP/D made sure she was always where she was supposed to be on time. This new app would take her wherever she wished to go!

Sandy found her brother Joe in the kitchen, stirring steamy oatmeal. He was kind of an anti-
10 techno-geek who liked to do things on his own.

"Hey Sis, how's that new app working for you?" Joe asked a little meanly. "Is it living up to the commercials' promises?"

"Haven't tried it yet," Sandy yawned. "But
15 wait: I'd like to have breakfast in the yard." Nothing happened. Then Sandy remembered the new app's default check. She tapped her forehead to confirm her wish.

FLASH! Sandy was freezing in the yard
20 in a storm. Icy rain ran down her neck. She thought about her toasty warm kitchen, tapped her forehead, and FLASH! She was immediately back at the kitchen table.

Joe was laughing. "What happens if
25 you're whisked away in the middle of a class like a crumb off a table?"

"Don't be ridiculous! This app is foolproof. All the commercials say so." Sandy's first class was math. She was already chilled from her soaking

1

30 breakfast. As class started, Sandy looked out the window, wishing she was someplace sunny and warm. But she knew she had to be in school. So she leaned her forehead on her fist and tried to listen.

35 FLASH! She dropped into a desert of bright sun and hot sand. Dripping with sweat, Sandy thought about the cool lake where they swam each summer. As she wiped the sweat off her face, FLASH! and SPLASH! she landed in the middle of the freezing lake. Shivering and out of breath,

40 Sandy wished herself back in her warm kitchen.

Nothing. The app had failed. Her IDP/D took over and dropped her, like a soaked sponge, back in school where she was supposed to be. There she stayed, cold and dripping, until the last bell.

45 After school she walked to the accessories store and had the new app removed. Back at home, Joe had already heard all about her adventure. "So, how did the new toy work out?" he teased.

"Just fine!" Sandy answered. "But I'm

50 going to wait for the new and improved version before I try it again!"

www.TXWritingCoach.com

Interactive Model

Listen to an audio recording of the Student Model in the eText. Use the Reader's and Writer's Response Symbols with the eText tools to note what you read.

Use a Writer's Eye

Now, evaluate the piece as a writer. On your copy of the Student Model, use the Writer's Response Symbols to react to what you read.

Writer's Response Symbols
R.D. Realistic and believable dialogue
S.D. Vivid sensory details that create imagery and suggest mood
W.C. Well-developed, interesting characters
E.S. Engaging story

COLLEGE AND CAREER READINESS STANDARDS

Reading (A)(10) Identify and analyze how an author's use of language appeals to the senses, creates imagery, and suggests mood.

2

Student Model   99

Your Turn

Prewriting

Plan a first draft of your science fiction story by determining an appropriate topic. You can select from the Topic Bank or come up with an idea of your own.

Choose From the Topic Bank

TOPIC BANK

Living on the Moon Imagine living with other Earthlings in a colony on the moon. Where would you live? What would you eat? Write a science fiction story about your experiences.

New Technology Imagine an amazing technological breakthrough. Write a story about the invention and its effects on a group of characters.

The Alien and the Earthling Two characters—one human and one alien—become friends. Write a short story that explains how they meet and how their friendship grows.

Choose Your Own Topic

Determine an appropriate topic on your own by using the following **range of strategies** to generate ideas.

Research and Discuss

- Skim books or Web sites about the universe to find topics that spark your interest. Take notes on the topics that interest you.

- Research some technology you know well. What's ahead for this technology? How might people use it in the future?

- With a group, discuss some ways science could help, or harm, the world. Brainstorm for a list of possibilities. Monitor spoken language by asking follow-up questions to confirm your understanding.

Review your responses and choose a topic.

Narrow Your Topic

Narrowing the topic of your story will help you focus your thinking to write a compelling story.

Apply It! Use a graphic organizer like the one shown to narrow your topic.

- Write the main topic of your story in the top box. Move down the chart, narrowing your topic.
- Your last box should hold the main focus of your plot.

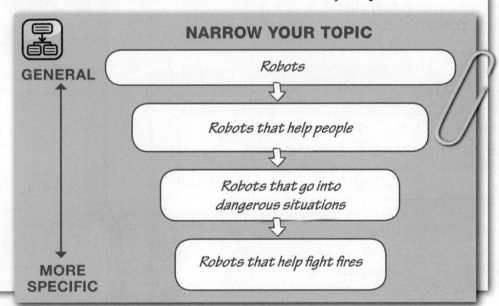

NARROW YOUR TOPIC

GENERAL

Robots

↓

Robots that help people

↓

Robots that go into dangerous situations

↓

Robots that help fight fires

MORE SPECIFIC

Consider Your Audience and Purpose

Before writing, think about your audience and purpose. Consider how the form you selected conveys the intended meaning to this audience. Consider the views of others as you ask these questions.

Questions for Audience	Questions for Purpose
• Who is my audience? • What kinds of story lines will my audience find interesting? • What will my audience need to know about science or technology to understand my science fiction story?	• Why am I writing the story? Do I want to entertain readers, make them think, or scare them? • What literary strategies and devices can I use to enhance the style and tone?

Record your answers in your writing journal.

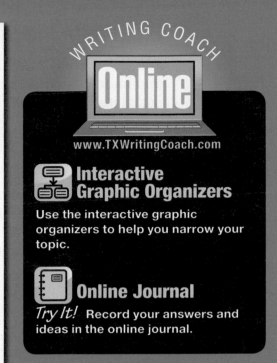

Online

www.TXWritingCoach.com

Interactive Graphic Organizers

Use the interactive graphic organizers to help you narrow your topic.

Online Journal

Try It! Record your answers and ideas in the online journal.

Focus on the TEKS

Writing (14)(A) Plan a first draft by determining appropriate topics through a range of strategies.

COLLEGE AND CAREER READINESS STANDARDS

Writing (A)(1) Determine effective approaches, forms, and rhetorical techniques that demonstrate understanding of the writer's purpose and audience.

Plan Your Piece

You will use the graphic organizer to identify your central idea and main character, plan a plot, and identify details. When it is complete, you will be ready to write your first draft.

Develop an Engaging Story Line Use sensory details to create **a specific, believable setting, and interesting characters** as part of a story line that engages your audience.

Organize Your Science Fiction Story Use a graphic organizer to plan **a plot with well-paced action** that sustains, or holds, readers' interest by building toward a climax and includes a beginning, middle, and end.

Develop Your Science Fiction Story	
Main character and the way he/she/it reflects future technology or scientific knowledge	*Robot FF172 is a robot designed to help firefighters by going into dangerous situations to protect human lives.*
Beginning • **A specific, believable setting** • **Interesting characters** • **A conflict, problem, or goal**	• *The story takes place in a small city.* • *Robot FF172 is the leader of a team of robots specifically developed to fight fires.* • *The human firefighters aren't sure they can trust FF172 or the other robots.*
Middle • **Events that build suspense about the conflict** • **Characters' thoughts and actions** • **The climax, the point of highest tension in the main conflict**	
End • **How the conflict is resolved** • **Wrap-up the theme, showing something about the relationship between humans and technological innovations**	• *After FF172 saves a human firefighter's life, the other humans begin to trust the robots.*

Gather Details

To make the audience want to keep reading, develop interesting characters and a believable setting through the use of **sensory details.** Use details that appeal to the senses of:

- **Sight:** *Snow-white foam blanketed the fire.*
- **Sound:** *The clanging fire alarm rang in our ears.*
- **Taste:** *I craved the fresh, crisp taste of an apple.*
- **Smell:** *The pungent smell of smoke stuck to her clothes.*
- **Touch:** *Water splashed against his skin, cooling his face.*

Writers also use a **range of literary strategies and devices to enhance the style and tone** of a story.

- **Flashback:** *The chief remembered the time before they had robots: Every firefighter at the station went into the danger zone.*
- **Foreshadowing:** *Tran laughed, "You mean someday you might save my life? Right."*
- **Suspense:** *The beam crashed down and blocked the doorway.*

Try It! Read the Student Model excerpt and identify which kinds of details and devices the author uses.

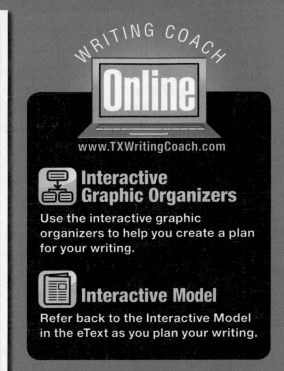

WRITING COACH

Online
www.TXWritingCoach.com

Interactive Graphic Organizers
Use the interactive graphic organizers to help you create a plan for your writing.

Interactive Model
Refer back to the Interactive Model in the eText as you plan your writing.

STUDENT MODEL from **Be Careful Where You Wish For** page 98; lines 19–26

FLASH! Sandy was freezing in the yard in a storm. Icy rain ran down her neck. She thought about her toasty warm kitchen, tapped her forehead, and FLASH! She was immediately back at the kitchen table.

Joe was laughing. "What happens if you're whisked away in the middle of a class like a crumb off a table?"

Apply It! Review the types of details and literary strategies a short story writer can use. Then, include at least one sensory detail and literary strategy or device for each story section.

- Plan to include flashback and foreshadowing **to enhance the style and tone of your story**.
- Be sure to **use sensory details that help create a realistic setting** or help build suspense.

 Focus on the TEKS

Writing (15)(A) Write an imaginative story that sustains reader interest and includes an engaging story line.

Drafting

During the drafting stage, you will start to write your ideas for your science fiction story. You will follow an outline that provides an **organizational strategy** that will help you build on ideas to write a **focused, organized, and coherent** science fiction story.

The Organization of a Short Story

The chart shows an organizational strategy for an imaginative short story. Look back at how the Mentor Text follows this organizational strategy. Then, use this chart to help you outline your draft.

Outline for Success

Beginning

See Mentor Text, p. 94.

- Setting and characters
- Conflict or problem introduced

Middle

See Mentor Text, pp. 94-97.

- Plot with well-paced action, foreshadowing, and flashbacks
- Events that develop the conflict and theme
- Climax

End

See Mentor Text, p. 97.

- Resolution
- Summary of theme

Set the Scene

- The setting of a story is the place and time that it happens. Settings and characters come alive with the use of sensory details.
- The conflict of a story is a problem or struggle. This struggle can be between outside forces, such as humans and technology, or between conflicting emotions within a character.

Build Suspense

- Plots gain momentum as each event intensifies the conflict. Foreshadowing hints at what will happen later. Flashbacks interrupt the sequence of events to show something that happened earlier.
- The theme of a story is its central idea.
- The climax of a story is the point at which the conflict reaches a crisis and suspense is at its highest.

Wrap It Up

- The resolution of a story tells how the conflict was resolved.
- The summary of theme can be shown with character dialogue, an action, or a general statement.

Start Your Draft

Use this checklist to help you complete your draft. Use the graphic organizer that shows the beginning, middle, and end, as well as the Outline for Success as guides.

While drafting, aim at writing your ideas, not on making your writing perfect. Remember, you will have the chance to improve your draft when you revise and edit.

√ Start by drafting the opening of your imaginative story. Describe the setting and characters. Include specific details that will **sustain reader interest.**

√ Set up the **conflict,** or problem, to come.

√ Create a specific, **believable setting** and an engaging story line by building curiosity or suspense. Use vivid words and **sensory details** to help readers experience what the characters experience.

√ Create and develop **interesting characters** who respond to each situation based on their individual personalities.

√ Keep the action moving at a good **pace** and focused on the conflict. Describe events in time order, building to the climax.

√ Try to use a **range of literary strategies** and devices, such as foreshadowing and flashbacks, to enhance the style and tone of your writing.

√ Finish by describing how the conflict is resolved or the problem is **solved** and by showing how the character's ideas or feelings have changed as a result of the story events.

WRITING COACH

Online

Interactive Model

Outline for Success Refer back to Mentor Text in the eText as you write your draft.

 Focus on the TEKS

Writing

(14)(B) Develop drafts by choosing an appropriate organizational strategy and building on ideas to create a focused, organized, and coherent piece of writing.

(15)(A) Write an imaginative story that sustains reader interest and includes well-paced action and an engaging story line.

Revising: Making It Better

Now that you have finished your first draft, you are ready to revise. Think about the "big picture" of **audience, purpose, and genre.** You can use the Revision RADaR strategy as a guide for making changes to improve your draft. Revision RADaR provides four major ways to improve your writing: (R) replace, (A) add, (D) delete, and (R) reorder.

Kelly Gallagher, M. Ed.

KEEP REVISION ON YOUR RADAR

Read part of the first draft of the Student Model "Be Careful Where You Wish For." Then look at questions the writer asked herself as she thought about how well her draft addressed issues of **audience, purpose, and genre.**

Be Careful Where You Wish For

Sandy's IDP/D woke her up on time, of course. She carefully checked the top of her earlobe. She felt the new application for her Internal Daily Planner/Doer (IDP/D). Her IDP/D made sure she was always where she was supposed to be on time. This new app would take her wherever she wished to go!

Sandy found her brother Joe in the kitchen, stirring steamy oatmeal. He was kind of an anti-techno-geek who liked to do things on his own.

"Good morning, Sandy," Joe said. "How is your new IDP/D application? Is it as great as you hoped?"

"Haven't tried it yet," Sandy yawned. "I'm still too sleepy to think. But wait: I'd like to have breakfast in the yard." Nothing happened. Then Sandy tapped her forehead.

FLASH! Sandy was freezing in the yard in a storm. She had remembered the new app's default check. She had to tap her forehead to confirm her wish.

> *Does my opening introduce an interesting main character?*

> *Does my **dialogue** help develop the story and enhance the tone?*

> *Are my events arranged in chronological order?*

Now look at how the writer applied Revision RADaR to write an improved second draft.

Be Careful Where You Wish For

 2ND DRAFT

Sandy's IDP/D woke her up on time, of course. She carefully checked the top of her earlobe. Yes! It was there! Now she was one of the first to have latest application for her Internal Daily Planner/ Doer (IDP/D). Her IDP/D made sure she was always where she was supposed to be on time. This new app would take her wherever she wished to go!

A *Added details describing Sandy's attitude toward her new app to better develop her character*

Sandy found her brother Joe in the kitchen, stirring steamy oatmeal. He was kind of an anti-techno-geek who liked to do things on his own.

"Hey Sis, how's that new app working for you?" Joe asked a little meanly. "Is it living up to the commercials' promises?"

R *Replaced boring dialogue with realistic dialogue that reflects characters' attitudes and tone*

"Haven't tried it yet," Sandy yawned. "But wait: I'd like to have breakfast in the yard." Nothing happened. Then Sandy remembered the new app's default check. She tapped her forehead to confirm her wish.

D *Deleted the unnecessary words I'm still too sleepy to think*

FLASH! Sandy was freezing in the yard in a storm.

R *Reordered sentences to keep events in chronological order*

Apply It! Use your Revision RADaR to revise your draft.

- First, determine if you have engaged your audience, created a specific setting, developed interesting characters, and made the conflict or problem clear.
- Then apply the Revision RADaR strategy to make needed changes. Remember—you can use the steps in the strategy in any order.

 Focus on the TEKS

Writing (14)(C) Revise drafts after rethinking how well questions of purpose, audience, and genre have been addressed.

COLLEGE AND CAREER READINESS STANDARDS

Writing (A)(4) Recognize the importance of revision as the key to effective writing. Each draft should refine key ideas and organize them more logically and fluidly, use language more precisely and effectively, and draw the reader to the author's purpose.

Look at the Big Picture

Use the chart and your analytical skills to evaluate how well each section of your short story addresses **purpose**, **audience**, and **genre**. When necessary, use the suggestions in the chart to revise your story.

Section	Evaluate	Revise
Beginning	• Check the **opening**. Does it introduce an engaging story line? Will it grab readers' attention and make them want to read more?	• Include details about a character, the setting, or the culture that lets readers know this is science fiction. Use precise word choice and vivid images.
	• Make sure that the **conflict** or problem has been introduced.	• Include dialogue, action, and characters' thoughts to help set up the conflict.
	• Check that the **setting** is specific and believable and the characters are realistic and interesting.	• Use sensory and other details to specifically and believably describe the characters, their surroundings, and the technology they use.
Middle	• Check that the **action** is well-paced and the **plot** coherent.	• Present events in time order leading up to the climax.
	• Number in order the **events** that build suspense. Make sure they all build to the **climax**.	• Reorder details as necessary to better build suspense. Take out or replace details that don't contribute to building the story.
	• Use **literary strategies** and **devices** to reinforce the **style** and **tone** of your story.	• Add elements like foreshadowing and flashback to help create suspense.
Conclusion	• Check that **loose ends** of the story are tied up.	• Add details that answer questions such as *What happened then? How did the characters think or act after the climax?*
	• Make sure you sum up the **theme**.	• Add dialogue, events, or a character's thoughts to show how the story illustrates the theme.

Focus on Craft: Internal and External Coherence

Coherence in a piece of writing means that all the parts fit together, support the central idea, and make sense. In a paragraph with **internal coherence**, the sentences follow one another in logical order and all support the central idea of that paragraph. In a composition with **external coherence**, the paragraphs all fit together logically and support the central idea of the story as a whole.

Think about internal and external coherence as you read the excerpt from the Student Model.

 STUDENT MODEL from **Be Careful Where You Wish For** page 99; lines 34–40

> FLASH! She dropped into a desert of bright sun and hot sand. Dripping with sweat, Sandy thought about the cool lake where they swam each summer. As she wiped the sweat off her face, FLASH! and SPLASH! she landed in the middle of the freezing lake. Shivering and out of breath, Sandy wished herself back in her warm kitchen.

Try It! Now, ask yourself these questions. Record your answers in your journal.

- What is the topic—or central idea—of this paragraph?
- How does each sentence support the central idea? Explain.

Fine-Tune Your Draft

Apply It! Use the revision suggestions to prepare your final draft.

- **Ensure Internal and External Coherence** Make sure that ideas, sentences, and paragraphs are organized in a logical sequence and that they flow easily.
- **Ensure Vivid Images** Substitute vivid images for vague or boring words and phrases. For example, change *waited nervously* to *drummed her fingers nervously on the table.*
- **Ensure Consistent Point of View** Make sure that the same person, or voice, tells the whole story.

Peer Feedback Read your final draft to a group of peers. Ask if you have **sustained their interest**. Think about their responses and revise your final draft as needed.

WRITING COACH

Online

www.TXWritingCoach.com

Online Journal

Try It! Record your answers in the online journal.

Interactive Model

Refer back to the Interactive Model as you revise your writing.

Revise Your Draft for Precise Word Choice

As you revise your short story, look for places where you can change a word to be more precise. Find vague verbs like *said*, *walked*, or *saw* and commonly used words like *nice*, *good*, *fun*, or *happy*, and then choose more specific language to convey your exact meaning and create vivid images.

Common word choice:

She walked across the room.

More precise word choice:

She trudged across the room in anger. She glided across the room happily. She bounced across the room excitedly.

 Focus on the TEKS

Writing

(14)(C) Revise drafts to ensure vivid images, consistent point of view, and internal and external coherence after rethinking how well questions of purpose, audience, and genre have been addressed.

(14)(E) Revise final draft in response to feedback from peers.

(15)(A) Write an imaginative story that sustains reader interest and includes well-paced action and an engaging story line.

Editing: Making It Correct

Editing your draft means polishing your work and correcting errors. You may want to read through your work several times, looking for different errors and issues each time.

Before editing your draft, review any pronouns you have used in your writing. Each pronoun must have a clear antecedent, or a clearly stated person, place, or thing that the pronoun later replaces. For example, look at these sentences: *Karen and Walter missed the bus. They were late for school.* The pronoun *they* clearly refers to Karen and Walter. Now look at these sentences: *I am going away for the weekend with my family. It should be fun!* The antecedent for *it* is unclear. The second sentence could be corrected this way: *The trip should be fun!*

WRITE GUY *Jeff Anderson, M. Ed.*

WHAT DO YOU NOTICE?

Zoom in on Conventions Focus on the use of pronouns as you read these sentences from the Student Model.

 STUDENT MODEL from **Be Careful Where You Wish For** page 99; lines 34–37

> She dropped into a desert of bright sun and hot sand. Dripping with sweat, Sandy thought about the cool lake where they swam each summer.

To learn more about pronouns, see Chapter 23 of your Grammar Handbook.

Now, ask yourself: Which sentence contains a vague pronoun reference?

Perhaps you chose the second sentence, which contains a vague pronoun reference. It is unclear to whom the pronoun *they* is referring. To correct this vague pronoun reference, the sentence would read: *Dripping with sweat, Sandy thought about the cool lake where she and her family swam each summer.* In this sentence, the antecedent *she* is clear and the vague pronoun *they* is replaced by the specific noun *family*.

It is important to make the antecedents of your pronouns clear when you write. If you have vague pronoun references in your writing, your readers may be confused. Because of this, they will be less likely to want to continue reading your work.

Grammar Mini-Lesson: Antecedents

To learn more, see Chapter 13.

A **pronoun** is a word that stands for or replaces a noun or another pronoun. The noun that is being replaced is called the **antecedent**. Often, the antecedent can be identified correctly because it appears in a sentence before the pronoun does. Notice how the use of pronouns and antecedents in the Student Model helps keep the writing coherent.

 STUDENT MODEL from **Be Careful Where You Wish For** page 98; lines 1–7

> Sandy's IDP/D woke her up on time, of course. She carefully checked the top of her earlobe…. This new app would take her wherever she wished to go!

Try It! Underline each pronoun and identify its antecedent. If the antecedent is unclear, rewrite to clarify the pronoun-antecedent relationship. Write the answers in your journal.

1. Lorenzo gave Rob his book, and then he studied Chapter 3. *(compound sentence)*

2. Rob turned in the report that he completed the night before. *(complex sentence)*

Apply It! Edit your draft for **grammar, mechanics, capitalization, and spelling.** If necessary, rewrite some complex sentences, making sure you have used **relative pronouns** with **correctly identified antecedents.**

Use the rubric to evaluate your piece. If necessary, rethink, rewrite, or revise.

Rubric for Short Story: Science Fiction	Rating Scale			
	Not very			Very
Focus and Coherence: How well have you developed your characters and plot?	1	2	3	4
Organization: How clearly organized is the sequence of events?	1	2	3	4
Development of Ideas: How well do the dialogue and setting support the plot?	1	2	3	4
Voice: How effective is your word choice in creating tone and style?	1	2	3	4
Conventions: How correct are your pronouns?	1	2	3	4

WRITING COACH

Online

www.TXWritingCoach.com

 Video
Learn effective editing techniques from program author Jeff Anderson.

 Online Journal
Try It! Record your answers in the online journal.

 Interactive Model
Refer back to the Interactive Model as you edit your writing.

Focus on the TEKS

Writing (14)(D) Edit drafts for grammar, mechanics, and spelling.

Conventions

(19)(A) Identify, use, and understand relative pronouns.

(19)(C) Use a variety of complete sentences (e.g., simple, compound, complex) that include correctly identified antecedents.

(20)(A) Use conventions of capitalization.

(21)(A) Spell correctly, including using various resources to determine and check correct spellings.

Publishing

Get your science fiction story ready to present. Then choose a way to **publish your work for an appropriate audience**.

Wrap Up Your Presentation

Is your story handwritten or written on a computer? If you use a computer, be sure to choose a readable font. The purpose of publishing is to share your writing with readers, which means you must choose a plain, easy-to-read font.

Publish Your Piece

Use this chart to identify a way to publish your written work.

If your audience is...	...then publish it by...
A group of science fiction book or movie fans	• Reading it aloud, then holding a question-answer session about the technology in your story's "world" • Posting the story online and inviting comments
Other students in your class	• Submitting it to a class anthology or Web site of science fiction • Producing it as a graphic novel

Reflect on Your Writing

Now that you are done with your science fiction story, read it over and use your writing journal to answer these questions. Use specific details to describe and explain your reflections. Increase the specificity of your details based on the type of information requested.

- What did you enjoy about writing the story? Why?
- Are there any parts of the story with which you struggled? If so, what did you learn from the process?
- Do you think you will try writing fiction again? Explain.

The Big Question: Why Write? What can fiction do better than non-fiction?

Manage Your Portfolio You may wish to include your published science fiction story in your writing portfolio. If so, consider what this piece reveals about your writing and your growth as a writer.

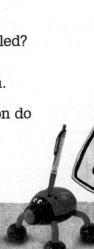

MAKE YOUR WRITING COUNT

Make a Sci-Fi Film Trailer

Science fiction writing has long been a favorite genre for movie producers. Create a **trailer**—a film advertisement shown in movie theaters—for an imaginary film based on your science fiction story.

With a group, produce your trailer as a **multimedia presentation,** blending text, graphics, sound, and other media. As you work, be open and responsive to all of your group members' opinions and perspectives. Present your trailer in a live performance, or video-record it.

Here's your action plan.

1. Choose roles, such as writer, artist, actor, narrator, and director.

2. Review your group's sci-fi stories. Choose one with great action.

3. Find examples of trailers online. Note what elements are especially strong.

4. Create a storyboard, or a series of sketches showing the visual elements of each scene. Your storyboard should:

   - Introduce the main characters and setting

   - Hint at the main conflict without giving away the ending

   - Build excitement about the movie, perhaps through energetic music or rapidly paced shots

   - Show the title of the movie

5. Rehearse and then present the trailer for your class. Record your efforts on video using available technology, if possible.

Listening and Speaking Work as a team to improvise any dialogue or voice-over narration required in the storyboard. Then, use the storyboard to rehearse the dialogue and action. Give each other feedback during and after rehearsal. Present your trailer in a live performance, or video-record it, keeping the feedback in mind.

 WRITING COACH

Online

www.TXWritingCoach.com

Online Journal

Reflect on Your Writing Record your answers and ideas in the online journal.

Resource

Link to resources on 21st Century Learning for help in creating a group project.

Focus on the TEKS

Writing

(14)(E) Publish written work for appropriate audiences.

(17)(D) Produce a multimedia presentation involving text and graphics using available technology.

Your Turn ▷ **Writing for Media: Dramatic Scene**

Dramatic Scene

A **dramatic scene** is a story written to be performed by actors on stage or on film. The purpose of a dramatic scene is generally to entertain, but some contain a message, or theme, the writer wants to convey. Dramatic scenes are written as scripts, with lines for each character and stage directions telling actors how to speak and move. Like other stories, they have a setting, characters, plot, and well-paced action.

Try It! Study the example of a dramatic scene. Then, answer these questions. Record your answers in your journal.

1. At what **audience** is this scene most likely aimed?

2. Is the **story line** of "Power Label" engaging? Explain why or why not.

3. What is the **purpose** of "Power Label"?

4. How would you describe the **pace of events**?

5. Which **character** is most interesting to you? Why?

Extension Find another example of a dramatic scene, and compare it with this one.

Power Label

[*Two friends standing in a kitchen. Friend 1 is holding a large box, like a cereal box, reading its label and looking dreamy.*]

FRIEND 1. [reads excitedly from box label] "Crunchy golden goodness. Power packed in every bite!"

FRIEND 2. [slouching in a chair] Yeah, sounds good.

FRIEND 1. [continues reading, getting more excited] "All the fuel a body needs for a healthy day."

FRIEND 2. [sits up straighter, leans toward Friend 1] Yeah, that could help some, but...

FRIEND 1. [interrupts Friend 2] We have to try this now! Just think how good we'd feel! How strong we'd be! [starts wildly tearing the box to open it, but has trouble getting it open]

FRIEND 2. [stands, walks over to Friend 1] Here, give it to me. Cool down!

FRIEND 1. [hands over the box, but bounces up and down excitedly] Hurry, hurry. I'm so anxious to try it!

FRIEND 2. [gently pushes Friend 1 into a chair; shakes his head] Dude, no food. We're droids, remember? Solar packs, no stomachs? Chill!

FRIEND 1. [head in hands, sadly] But it looks so good....

Create a Dramatic Scene

Follow these steps to create your own dramatic scene. Review the graphic organizers on pages R24–R27, and choose one that suits your needs.

Prewriting

- Identify and narrow a topic, then identify the target audience for your scene. Determine the purpose for writing to this specific audience.
- Create characters and a setting for your scene. When those are in place, outline the story line: the beginning, middle, and end of your scene.

Drafting

- Use a script form to draft your scene. Write an opening that grabs your audience.
- Introduce the characters and create a specific, believable setting.
- Develop an engaging story line with well-paced action through the beginning, middle, and end.
- Write dialogue that gives each of your characters a unique "voice," or way of talking, that characterizes him, her, or it.

Revising and Editing

- Review your draft to make sure events are organized logically. Make sure the conflict, or problem, is clear.
- Use the Revision RADaR strategy to improve your draft.
- Check that spelling, grammar, and mechanics are correct.

Publishing

- Read through your scene with classmates, and then rehearse the scene and perform it for the class with actors and a narrator.
- You may want to record your performance using video. You can also use available technology, such as multimedia software, to add text, graphics, and sound to create a short film from the recording.

www.TXWritingCoach.com

 Online Journal

Try It! Record your answers in the online journal.

 Interactive Graphic Organizers

Choose from a variety of graphic organizers to plan and develop your project.

 Partner Talk

Before you start drafting, explain your dramatic scene to a partner. Use specific details to describe and explain your ideas. Increase the specificity of your details based on the type of information you are delivering. Ask questions about your ideas and plan. For example, will your story hold readers' interest?

 Focus on the TEKS

Writing (17)(D) Produce a multimedia presentation involving text and graphics using available technology.

Writing for Assessment

Some prompts ask you to write an imaginative work. Use these prompts to practice. Respond using the characteristics of your science fiction story. (See page 92.)

Try It! To begin, read the **short story** prompt and the information on format and academic vocabulary. Then use the ABCDs of On-Demand Writing to help you plan and write your short story.

Format

The prompt asks you to write a *short story*. Be sure to start with a beginning that grabs readers' attention and introduces the characters and conflict.

Short Story Prompt

Write a short story about a spaceship crash. Be sure to develop an engaging story line. Use dialogue, foreshadowing and other literary devices in your story.

Academic Vocabulary

Remember, *dialogue* is the conversation between two or more characters in a work of literature. *Foreshadowing* is an author's use of clues about something that will happen later in the story.

The ABCDs of On-Demand Writing

Use the following ABCDs to help you respond to the prompt.

Before you write your draft:

Attack the prompt [1 MINUTE]

- Circle or highlight important verbs in the prompt. Draw a line from the verb to what it refers to.
- Rewrite the prompt in your own words.

Brainstorm possible answers [4 MINUTES]

- Create a graphic organizer to generate ideas.
- Use one for each part of the prompt if necessary.

Choose the order of your response [1 MINUTE]

- Think about the best way to organize your ideas.
- Number your ideas in the order you will write about them. Cross out ideas you will not be using.

After you write your draft:

Detect errors before turning in the draft [1 MINUTE]

- Carefully reread your writing.
- Make sure that your response makes sense and is complete.
- Look for spelling, punctuation, and grammar errors.

More Prompts for Practice

Apply It! **Texas Test Prep** Respond to Prompts 1 and 2 by writing **imaginative short stories** with **engaging story lines** that **sustain the reader's interest**.

- Identify an appropriate audience
- Establish a clear plot focus
- Develop logical and well-paced action
- Create a specific, believable setting through the use of sensory details
- Use **literary strategies and devices** to enhance your **style and tone**

Prompt 1 Write a short story about a character who has an unusual job in the year 2500. Develop an engaging story with a cohesive plot through beginning, middle, and end. Include a believable setting and interesting characters.

Prompt 2 Write a short story about a group of aliens who come to Earth to try and save our planet from an asteroid that is hurtling toward Earth. Develop a story line that retains readers' interest throughout the story.

 Texas Test Prep **Spiral Review: Narrative** Respond to Prompt 3 by writing a **personal narrative**. Make sure your narrative reflects all of the characteristics described on page 66, including **a clearly defined focus** and **explanations of the importance of or reasons for actions and their consquences.**

Prompt 3 Think about a time when you succeeded in doing something that was difficult. Write an appealing narrative that describes what you tried to do and how you succeeded in that attempt. Tell how you felt about your success and describe any other results of your actions.

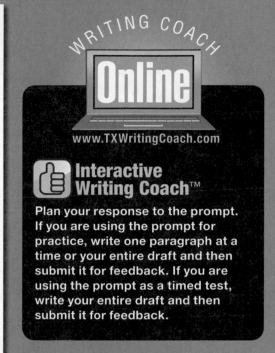

WRITING COACH

Online

www.TXWritingCoach.com

Interactive Writing Coach™

Plan your response to the prompt. If you are using the prompt for practice, write one paragraph at a time or your entire draft and then submit it for feedback. If you are using the prompt as a timed test, write your entire draft and then submit it for feedback.

Remember **ABCD**

Attack the prompt

Brainstorm possible answers

Choose the order of your response

Detect errors before turning in the draft

Focus on the TEKS

Writing

(15)(A) Write an imaginative story that sustains reader interest and includes well-paced action and an engaging story line.

(16)(A) Write a personal narrative that has a clearly defined focus and communicates the importance of or reasons for actions and/or consequences.

POETRY *and* DESCRIPTION

What Do You See?

People see different things when they look at something. Some people may look at this photograph and see a group of horses. Others may look at it and see strength or beauty.

People also use different words to describe what they see. Words can be a powerful way to capture a moment or feeling.

Try It! Take a few minutes to list what you see in the photograph. Remember, you might describe the actual image or you might describe how it makes you feel.

Consider these questions as you participate in an extended discussion with a partner. Take turns expressing your ideas and feelings.

- What details do you see in the photograph?
- What emotions does this photograph make you feel?
- What might you feel if you saw these horses?
- What do the horses mean to you?

Review the list you made. Use your list to describe to a partner what you see in this photograph.

What's Ahead

In this chapter, you will review some strong examples of poems: Mentor Texts and Student Models. Then, using the examples as guidance, you will write a poem of your own.

WRITING COACH

Online

www.TXWritingCoach.com

Online Journal

Try It! Record your answers and ideas in the online journal.

You can also record and save your answers and ideas on pop-up sticky notes in the eText.

Connect to the Big Questions

Discuss these questions with your partner:

1 What do you think? When is a picture better than words?

2 Why write? How does one best convey feeling through words on a page?

Focus on the TEKS

Writing (15)(B) Write literary texts to express ideas and feelings about real or imagined people, events, and ideas.

POETRY AND DESCRIPTION

In this chapter, you will focus on writing a poem. Poetry uses imaginative language, rhythm, and sometimes rhyme to express ideas and feelings in a few strokes. Every single word in a poem has meaning. Therefore, poets look for words that are exact, colorful, and striking to hear. Graphic elements, such as the placement of words and line breaks, are also important in poetry. Description is central to poetry, as it is to most other kinds of writing. Sensory details and vivid language help readers see, hear, smell, taste, or feel something through words.

You will develop a free verse or lyric poem by taking it through each stage of the writing process: prewriting, drafting, revising, editing, and publishing. To preview the criteria for how your poem will be evaluated, see the rubric on page 137. You will also have an opportunity to use your descriptive skills to create an entry describing your hometown for an online travel site.

FEATURE ASSIGNMENT

Poem

An effective poem includes these characteristics and **poetic techniques:**

- A clear **topic, theme,** or **controlling idea**

- **Structural elements,** such as rhyme and meter

- **Figurative language,** such as comparisons that convey mood by pointing out similarities between things that do not seem the same

- **Sensory details** and **imagery** that allow the reader to see, smell, hear, taste, and feel what the poet describes

- **Sound devices** that create a musical or emotional effect

A lyric poem also has these characteristics:

- A strong focus on the poet's feelings about a person, place, thing, or event

- No specific form. Lyric poems can use rhyme and meter or can be free verse.

A free verse poem also has these characteristics:

- Language meant to reflect the patterns of natural speech

- No specific rhyme pattern or meter

- No specific length

Forms of Poetry and Description

There are many forms of poetry and description, including:

Ballads are poems that tell a story and are often meant to be sung. Ballads have a regular rhyme pattern and meter, or "beat." Most ballads repeat words or phrases.

Descriptive essays use precise images and details to help readers imagine a person, place, thing, or event. Like all essays, they include an introduction, body, and conclusion.

Free verse is poetry that imitates the rhythms of everyday speech. Freed of set rhythm and rhyme patterns, free verse uses figurative language and sound devices to convey ideas and feelings.

Haiku are three-line poems first developed in Japan. The first and last lines have five syllables, and the middle line has seven syllables. Haiku are usually about nature.

Lyric poems are poems expressing the speaker's feelings about a certain person, place, thing, or event. Lyric poems can use rhyme and meter or can be free verse.

Prose poems look like prose, or regular text you might find in a story or essay, but use poetic techniques to create a memorable description of a person, place, thing, or event.

Sonnets are 14-line poems with a regular meter and rhyme. One type, the English sonnet, is made up of three four-line stanzas and a final couplet, or two rhyming lines. In each stanza, alternating lines rhyme.

Try It! For each audience and purpose described, choose a form, such as a ballad, lyric poem, or prose poem, that is appropriate for conveying your intended meaning to the audience. Explain your choices.

- To tell classmates about the adventures of your elderly great-uncle, a former test pilot
- To share your feelings with the general public about the first leaves in spring
- To honor your school team's championship with a song

WORD BANK

People often use these basic and content-based vocabulary words when they talk about poetry. Work with a partner. Take turns saying each word aloud. Then, write one sentence using each word. If you are unsure of the meaning of a word, use the Glossary or a dictionary to check the definition.

emotion	stanza
line	symbol
meter	verse

MENTOR TEXT

Free Verse and Lyric Poems

Learn From Experience

 After reading the free verse and lyric poems on pages 122–123, read the numbered notes in the margins to learn about how the poets presented their ideas.

Answer the *Try It!* questions online or in your notebook.

---

❶ The poem is written in free verse divided into two-line stanzas. This **graphic element** helps characterize the speaker in the poem.

Try It! How do you think the speaker sounds? How do the short stanzas help characterize the speaker as an alien from outer space?

❷ The poet uses **figurative language** to convey the alien's interpretation of what it sees.

Try It! What two things are being compared? What does the alien think it sees? What does it actually see?

❸ The last stanza helps reveal the alien's **feelings** about what it sees.

Try It! How does the alien feel about the "people" it sees? How can you tell?

Extension Find other examples of poems to compare with these. Evalute the ways that literal and figurative language affect readers' perceptions.

Southbound on the Freeway

by May Swenson

❶ A tourist came in from Orbitville,
parked in the air, and said:

The creatures of this star
are made of metal and glass.

5 Through the transparent parts
you can see their guts.

Their feet are round and roll
on diagrams or long

measuring tapes, dark
10 with white lines.

They have four eyes.
The two in back are red.

❷ Sometimes you can see a five-eyed
one, with a red eye turning

15 on the top of his head.
He must be special—

The others respect him
and go slow

when he passes, winding
20 among them from behind.

They all hiss as they glide,
like inches, down the marked

❸ tapes. Those soft shapes,
shadowy inside

25 the hard bodies—are they
their guts or their brains?

December Leaves

by Kaye Starbird

The fallen leaves are cornflakes
❹ That fill the lawn's wide dish,
And night and noon
The wind's a spoon
5   That stirs them with a swish.

❺ The sky's a silver sifter,
A-sifting white and slow,
That gently shakes
On crisp brown flakes
10   The sugar known as snow.

WRITING COACH

Online
www.TXWritingCoach.com

Interactive Model
Listen to an audio recording of the Mentor Text in the eText. You can refer back to the Mentor Text whenever you need support in developing your own writing.

Online Journal
Try It! Answer the questions about the Mentor Text in the online journal.

❹ This lyric poem has a set **rhyme scheme** and a regular "beat," or **meter.** Read the stanza aloud to hear the rhymes and the beat.

Try It! Read the second stanza. Is the rhyme scheme the same as that in the first stanza? Explain.

❺ Like the first stanza, the second stanza contains **figurative language.** The metaphor in the stanza compares snow falling to a sifter sifting sugar.

Try It! What are the "crisp brown flakes" in the second stanza?

COLLEGE AND CAREER READINESS STANDARDS

Reading (A)(7) Evaluate the use of both literal and figurative language to inform and shape the perceptions of readers.

STUDENT MODEL
Free Verse and Lyric Poems

With a small group, take turns reading the Student Models aloud. As you read, note the structures and elements of poetry. You may want to take a look at the Poet's Toolbox on page 129. Ask yourself how the poetic language informs and shapes your understanding of the poems.

 Use a Reader's Eye

Now, reread the Student Models. On your copies of the Student Models, use the Reader's Response Symbols to react to what you read.

> **Reader's Response Symbols**
>
> **+** I can picture this.
>
> **–** This image could be stronger.
>
> **?** I wonder what this means.
>
> **!** This is cool!

Participate in an extended discussion with a partner. Express your opinions and share your responses to the Student Model. On what do you agree? How do your feelings about the poems differ?

Grandma's Cupboard

A Free Verse Poem by Jonathan Williamson

Some of Grandma's furniture
lives at our house now.

My favorite is a tall wooden cupboard.
It is golden oak, soft and worn,
5   and it is very,
very old.

It takes me back to Grandma's.
I open its glass doors,
and it smells like her living room
10 a thousand miles away,
with someone else living in it now.

Now, at my own house, in my own living room,
I open the old cupboard doors,
I take a deep breath,
15 and WHOOSH!
I am back in Grandma's house once more.
The cupboard says,
"Welcome back! Good to see you!"

1

Sweet Harmony

A Lyric Poem by Clara Montgomery

It's hard to be sad when you sing,
(It might be a deep-breathing thing),
You open your mouth,
And your rib cage goes south,
5   And your heart feels as grand as a king.

The best is to sing with a friend
And melt your tones to a blend.
It's not "you"—it's not "me"—
It's a glorious "WE!"
10 Such sweet harmony never should end!

2

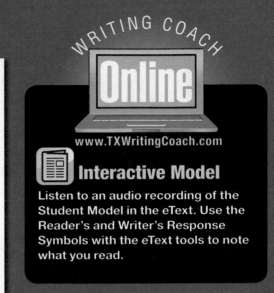

WRITING COACH

Online
www.TXWritingCoach.com

Interactive Model
Listen to an audio recording of the Student Model in the eText. Use the Reader's and Writer's Response Symbols with the eText tools to note what you read.

Use a Writer's Eye

Now, evaluate the poems as a writer. On your copies of the Student Models, use the Writer's Response Symbols to react to what you read. Identify places where the student writers use characteristics of an effective poem.

Writer's Response Symbols

R.R. Rhythm or rhyme fits poem's form

S.D. Effective use of sound devices

F.L. Figurative language conveys a mood

I.D. Images and details appeal to senses

Your Turn ▶ **Feature Assignment:
Free Verse or Lyric Poem**

Prewriting

Plan a first draft of your poem by deciding which form of poem
you want to write—a free verse, lyric, or other type of poem—
and then **determining an appropriate topic.** Select a topic
from the Topic Bank or come up with an idea of your own.

Choose From the Topic Bank

TOPIC BANK

Amazing Place Write a poem to describe the most exciting, most
enjoyable, or weirdest place you have ever visited.

Favorite Thing Write a poem about your most prized possession.
Describe the object and tell why it is so important to you.

My Hero Write a poem about a person you consider to be a hero.
Describe that person and explain why you admire him or her. Be
detailed and specific.

Choose Your Own Topic

Determine an appropriate topic on your own by using the
following **range of strategies** to generate ideas.

Brainstorm, List, and Read

- Work with a partner to brainstorm for categories of places,
  things, and people to write about, such as historical sites,
  electronic gadgets, famous people, and so on.

- List specific places, things, and people matching those
  categories. Circle the topics that interest you most.

- Look through a literature book or poetry collection from
  American, European, and world literature to get ideas from
  topics published poets chose.

Review your responses and choose a topic.

Narrow Your Topic

Narrowing your topic will help you find vivid details to create a well-crafted poem.

Apply It! Use a graphic organizer like the one shown to narrow your topic.

- Write your general topic in the top box, and keep narrowing your topic as you move down the chart.
- Your last box should hold your narrowest or "smallest" topic, the new focus of your poem.

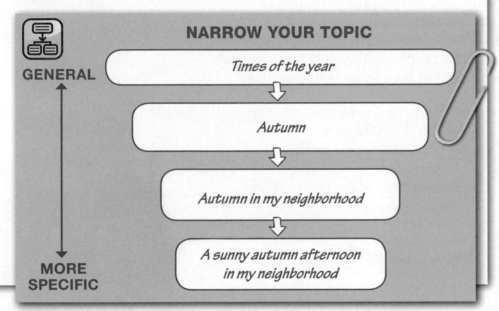

NARROW YOUR TOPIC

GENERAL

Times of the year

Autumn

Autumn in my neighborhood

A sunny autumn afternoon in my neighborhood

MORE SPECIFIC

Consider Your Audience and Purpose

Before writing, think about your audience and purpose. Consider how others may see things as you ask yourself these questions.

Questions for Audience	Questions for Purpose
• Who will read my poem? My teacher? My classmates? A family member? Someone else? • What will my readers need to know to understand my poem? • What form of poetry would best convey my meaning to them?	• Why am I writing? Do I want to entertain my readers by making them laugh? Do I want them to see and feel what I saw and felt? • What kinds of **poetic techniques,** such as **figurative language** and **graphic elements,** will help me fulfill my purpose?

Record your answers in your writing journal.

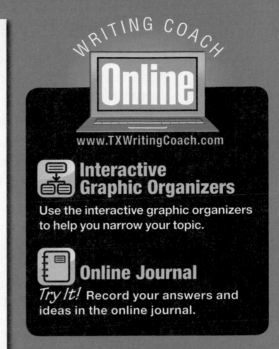

WRITING COACH

Online

www.TXWritingCoach.com

Interactive Graphic Organizers

Use the interactive graphic organizers to help you narrow your topic.

Online Journal

Try It! Record your answers and ideas in the online journal.

Focus on the TEKS

Writing

(14)(A) Plan a first draft by determining appropriate topics through a range of strategies.

(15)(B) Write a poem using poetic techniques, figurative language, and graphic elements.

COLLEGE AND CAREER READINESS STANDARDS

Reading (C)(1) Read a wide variety of texts from American, European, and world literatures.

Plan Your Piece

You will use a graphic organizer like the one shown to develop your ideas and details. When it is complete, you will be ready to write your first draft.

Develop a Topic, Theme, or Controlling Idea To focus your poem, review your notes and write a clear statement of your topic, theme, or controlling idea in the center of a web diagram like the one shown. Name the most important idea or feeling you want to communicate.

Develop Ideas and Details Use the graphic organizer to identify ideas, feelings, and sensory details—details for sights, sounds, tastes, smells, and touch—related to your topic, theme, or controlling idea. Write whatever comes to you. Then, evaluate your ideas. Underline the ones that best fulfill your purpose.

Develop Your Ideas

Sounds
- *Someone playing piano*
- *Children playing*
-

Smells and Tastes
- *Barbecue*
- *Leaves burning*
-

Sights
- *Yellow leaves dancing on the wind*
- *Clear blue sky*
-

Topic, Theme, or Controlling Idea
I love walking through my neighborhood on a sunny autumn day.

Emotions and Feelings
- *Thoughtful*
- *Relaxed and content*
-

Touch
- *My dog's smooth leash*
- *The roughness of my neighbor's wooden fence*

Poet's Toolbox

Poets use a variety of techniques and literary devices to convey ideas, create images, and appeal to readers' emotions. Here are some techniques you might use in your poem.

Figurative Language is writing that means something beyond what the words actually say.	
Simile: comparison using *like* or *as*	*The leaves danced on the wind like birds in flight.*
Metaphor: comparison made by saying that one thing is something else	*The tree's bright red and orange leaves were a fire in the sky.*
Personification: human characteristics applied to non-human objects	*The leaves danced on the wind.*
Symbols add depth and insight to poetry.	
An object that stands for something else	The bright colors of the autumn leaves could symbolize joy.
Sound Devices create a musical or emotional effect.	
Alliteration: repetition of consonant sounds at the beginning of nearby words	*Ch*ildren *ch*arged into piles of leaves on that *ch*illy afternoon.*
Assonance: repetition of vowel sounds in nearby words	*Leaves r*a*ced gr*a*cefully aw*a*y on the wind.*
Consonance: repetition of consonants in the middle or at the end of words	*The brow**n**, falle**n** leaves had all blow**n** away.*
Structural Elements help build the framework for poetic language.	
Rhyme: repetition of sounds at the ends of lines of poetry	Jack-o'-lanterns on **porches** Burned brightly, like **torches.**
Meter: rhythmical pattern of a poem. It is determined by stressed syllables in a line. Some forms of poetry have specific patterns of stressed syllables.	*The **brown**, fallen **leaves** had **all** blown **away**.* (Stressed syllables in poetry are marked with a ´, while unstressed syllables are marked with a ˘.)
Graphic Elements position the words on the page.	
Arrangement of words on a page	capital letters, line spacing, and line breaks

 Apply It! Review the ideas and details you added to your prewriting graphic organizer.

- Decide what techniques from the Poet's Toolbox you would like to use in your poem.
- Keep in mind that some poetic techniques must be used in specific forms, while other techniques are optional.
- The drafting stage is a good time to try out various techniques.

WRITING COACH

Online

www.TXWritingCoach.com

Interactive Graphic Organizers

Use the interactive graphic organizers to help you create a plan for your writing.

Interactive Model

Refer back to the Interactive Model in the eText as you plan your writing.

Focus on the TEKS

Writing (15)(B) Write a poem using poetic techniques, figurative language, and graphic elements.

Drafting

During the drafting stage, you will start to write your ideas for a free verse, lyric, or other form of poem. You will **build on the ideas** you developed in prewriting, **choosing an organizational strategy appropriate** for free verse or lyric poetry.

Drafting a Free Verse Poem or Lyric Poem

Each poetic form has specific characteristics. You will write a **focused, organized, and coherent poem** using these characteristics, the techniques from the Poet's Toolbox, and the ideas, feelings, and sensory details you developed in your graphic organizer.

These charts show the characteristics of the free verse and lyric forms. Review the characteristics. Then, answer the questions in the right column as you draft your poem.

Free Verse Characteristics	Questions to Answer While Drafting
• Number of lines varies • Number of stanzas varies • No meter is used; follows natural patterns of speech • Rhyme is not often used • Poetic techniques used • Feelings or emotions conveyed • Vivid descriptions presented	• How long do I want my poem to be? **Tip:** You don't have to decide an exact number of stanzas and lines. • What sound devices will I use? • What poetic techniques will I use? • What feelings or emotions will I express? • How will I make my descriptions vivid?

Lyric Poem Characteristics	Questions to Answer While Drafting
• Number of lines varies • Stanzas may be used, but they are not required • Rhyme scheme may be used, but it is not required • Meter (regular rhythm) may be used, but it is not required • Poetic techniques used • Feelings or emotions conveyed • Vivid descriptions presented	• How many lines will I write? Will I use stanzas? • Do I want to use rhyme? If so, what words will I rhyme in each stanza? **Tip:** Consult a rhyming dictionary and thesaurus to find the right words. • Do I want to use a regular meter? If so, what rhythm? **Tip:** Read aloud as you write to hear the rhythm. Use a dictionary to see how words are divided into syllables. • What sound devices will I use? • What other poetic techniques will I use? • What feelings or emotions will I express? • How will I make my descriptions vivid?

Start Your Draft

Writing poetry is different than creating most other genres. It is more open. Use the graphic organizer that shows your topic, ideas, and sensory details, and the Poet's Toolbox as guides, but be open to experimenting with your draft.

Remember, the most important part of drafting is just getting your ideas in writing. You can always go back and refine your writing when you revise and edit.

Before You Write

√ Choose the **poetic form** you want to use—free verse poem, lyric poem, or another poetic form.

√ Review the **poetic traditions** of your poetic form that are listed in Drafting a Free Verse Poem or Lyric Poem. Make sure you use these characteristics when you write your draft.

√ State or imply the **theme, topic,** or **controlling idea.** It does not have to be apparent in each line, but should be clear in the poem as a whole.

√ Include your ideas from prewriting. If a feeling, emotion, sensory detail, or other idea does not seem to work, you may decide not to keep it in your poem.

While You Write

√ Use **poetic techniques** to support your ideas. If a technique does not seem to work, try another.

√ Use **figurative language,** such as similes, metaphors, and personification, in your poem. Figurative language will keep your writing interesting.

√ Use **sensory details** in your poem, to make your poem come alive to your readers.

√ Use **graphic elements,** such as line and stanza breaks, to signal changes in ideas.

WRITING COACH

Online

www.TXWritingCoach.com

Interactive Model

Refer back to the Mentor Text in the eText as you write your draft.

 Focus on the TEKS

Writing

(14)(B) Develop drafts by choosing an appropriate organizational strategy and building on ideas to create a focused, organized, and coherent piece of writing.

(15)(B) Write a poem using poetic techniques, figurative language, and graphic elements.

Revising: Making It Better

Now that you have finished your first draft, you are ready to revise. Think about the "big picture" of **audience, purpose, and genre.** You can use your Revision RADaR as a guide for making changes to improve your draft. Revision RADaR provides four major ways to improve your writing: (R) replace, (A) add, (D) delete, and (R) reorder.

Kelly Gallagher, M. Ed.

KEEP REVISION ON YOUR RADaR

Read part of the first draft of the Student Model "Grandma's Cupboard." Then look at questions the writer asked himself as he thought about how well his draft **addressed issues of audience, purpose, and genre.**

Grandma's Cupboard

We have a tall wooden cupboard in our living room
and it is very,
very old.
We got it from my Grandmother's house.

I open its glass doors,
and it smells like her living room,
 a thousand miles away,
with someone else living in it now.

*Did I state or hint at my **central idea** or feeling?*

*Does this **image** help my audience picture what I'm writing about?*

*Do these lines reflect the patterns of **natural speech?***

Now look at how the writer applied Revision RADaR to write an improved second draft.

Grandma's Cupboard

Some of Grandma's furniture
lives at our house now.

D **R** *Deleted the first line and **replaced** it with a line that makes the Grandma connection— my central idea— right away*

My favorite is a tall wooden cupboard
It is golden oak, soft and worn,
and it is very,
very old.

A *Added sensory images of the cupboard to help people see it*

It takes me back to Grandma's.
I open its glass doors,
and it smells like her living room,
a thousand miles away,
with someone else living in it now.

R *Replaced a line to sound more natural and to establish the idea of being reminded of Grandma's house*

Apply It! Use your Revision RADaR to revise your draft.

- First, determine whether you have addressed the needs of your audience and purpose, and included the characteristics of a free verse or lyric poem.

- Next, consider whether you have used **poetic techniques,** such as **vivid images, figurative language,** and **graphic elements,** effectively to express your ideas and feelings. Think about whether or not your word choices are precise.

- Then apply your Revision RADaR to make needed changes. Remember—you can use the steps in Revision RADaR in any order.

Focus on the TEKS

Writing

(14)(C) Revise drafts to ensure precise word choice and vivid images after rethinking how well questions of purpose, audience, and genre have been addressed.

(15)(B) Write a poem using poetic techniques, figurative language, and graphic elements.

Look at the Big Picture

Use the chart and your analytical skills to evaluate how well each section of your poem **addresses purpose, audience, and genre.** When necessary, use the suggestions in the chart to revise your poem.

	Evaluate	Revise
Topic and Sensory Details	• Make sure your controlling idea or **theme** is clear in the poem.	• Think about the most important idea or feeling you want to convey. If needed, add a statement of theme.
	• Check that your **sensory details** all support the controlling idea or theme.	• Replace sensory details that do not support the controlling idea with new details that help paint a clearer picture.
Structural Devices	• Look at the way the poem looks on the page. Make sure you have used **graphic elements,** such as line breaks and white space, effectively.	• Reorder line breaks to group like ideas together or to jar the reader by breaking them apart.
	• Check that your **stanzas** are the length you want.	• Add or delete lines and replace and reorder words to improve the poem's flow.
Poetic Techniques	• Make sure your **figurative language** and word choices help convey your meaning and purpose to your audience.	• Replace boring or vague words with figurative language, vivid words, and sensory details.
	• Pay attention to the sound quality of your draft. Read aloud to check that your **sound devices** are effective and sound correct.	• Use a dictionary or thesaurus to find words to create better assonance or alliteration.

Focus on Craft: Vivid Images

Vivid images are word pictures that appeal to the senses. They help readers see, hear, smell, taste, and feel what the writer is describing. The best images are fresh and precise—and often unexpected. Carefully chosen images can also create the mood of a description. Consider the difference between "hot, stinging sand" and "soft, drifting sand."

Think about vivid images and precise word choice as you read these lines from the Student Model.

STUDENT MODEL from **Grandma's Cupboard,** page 124, lines 4–6

> It is golden oak, soft and worn,
>
> and it is very,
>
> very old.

Try It! Now, ask yourself these questions:

- How do you feel about the cupboard when it is described as "golden oak, soft and worn"?
- How would your feelings about it change if it were described as "brown, old, and scratched" instead?

Fine-Tune Your Draft

Apply It! Use the revision suggestions to prepare your final draft after rethinking how well questions of purpose, audience, and genre have been addressed.

- **Improve Poetic Techniques** Make precise **word choices** and use **figurative language** to create **vivid images** in your poem. Replace words and phrases that do not help convey your meaning or enhance the poem's mood.
- **Fine-tune Graphic Elements** Make sure that the line and stanza breaks keep your meaning clear.

Teacher or Family Feedback Read your poem aloud to your teacher or a family member. Think about the feedback you receive and revise your final draft as needed.

Revise Your Draft for Precise Word Choice The images in your poem are built from words. The more precise, or specific and accurate, your words are, the more vivid your images will be. Read these examples, and determine which presents a more vivid image and why.

First Draft:	Smelling nice, pretty flowers Grow near the path
Revision:	Drooping with fragrance, heavy blossoms Hang over the path

You probably decided that the revision presented a more vivid image than the first draft. You may have realized that word choice made the difference. The phrase *drooping with fragrance* is more precise than the phrase *smelling nice*. It creates a clear picture of how the flowers look and smell. The phrase *hang over* is more precise than *grow near*. It helps you picture exactly how the flowers look.

As you revise your draft, test your word choices. Replace vague words such as *nice*, *good*, *old*, *bad*, *pretty*, and *sad* with more precise words such as *warm*, *enchanting*, *noble*, *decaying*, *fearsome*, and *moody*.

 Focus on the TEKS

Writing

(14)(C) Revise drafts to ensure precise word choice and vivid images after rethinking how well questions of purpose, audience, and genre have been addressed.

(14)(E) Revise final draft in response to feedback from teacher.

(15)(B) Write a poem using poetic techniques, figurative language, and graphic elements.

Editing: Making It Correct

Use the editing process to polish your work and correct errors. It is often helpful to work with a partner when editing your drafts.

As you edit your work, think about the **placement of modifiers,** such as adjectives, adverbs, **adjectival phrases, and adverbial phrases**. Then, edit your final draft for any errors in **grammar, mechanics, and spelling.**

WRITE GUY *Jeff Anderson, M. Ed.*

WHAT DO YOU NOTICE?

Zoom in on Conventions Focus on the location of modifiers as you zoom in on these lines from the Mentor Text.

> **MENTOR TEXT** from **Southbound on the Freeway**
> page 122; lines 7, 13–14
>
> Their feet are round...
> Sometimes you can see a five-eyed
> one, with a red eye...

Now, ask yourself: *Which* **modifiers** *make the description more vivid?*

You may have noticed the adjectives *round, five-eyed,* and *red.* Adjectives are usually placed immediately before or after the noun they modify. In the poem, *red* modifies *eye,* and *five-eyed* modifies *one.* Some adjectives are separated from their noun by a linking verb. For example, the verb *are* separates *feet* from its modifier *round.*

Adverbs often occur immediately before or after the words they modify. However, adverbs can also be placed away from the words they modify. In the poem, the adverb *Sometimes* is placed at the beginning of the sentence, away from *can see,* the verb it modifies.

Partner Talk Discuss this question with a partner:
How does the placement of modifiers affect the rhythm of the poem?

> To learn more about modifiers, see Chapter 15 of your Grammar Handbook.

Grammar Mini-Lesson: Phrases as Modifiers

To learn more, see Chapter 19.

An **adjectival phrase** is a prepositional phrase used as an adjective to modify a noun or a pronoun. An **adverbial phrase** is a prepositional phrase used as an adverb to modify a verb, an adjective, or another adverb. Notice the adjectival and adverbial phrases in the Mentor Text.

 MENTOR TEXT from **Southbound on the Freeway**
page 122; lines 3–4

> The creatures of this star
> are made of metal and glass.

Of this star is an adjectival phrase that modifies the noun *creatures*. *Of metal and glass* is an adverbial phrase that modifies the verb *made*.

 Try It! Identify the adjectival or adverbial phrase in the **simple sentences** below. Write the answers in your journal.

1. He was reading in very dim light.
2. Sue went to the library by the school.

Apply It! Edit your draft for grammar, punctuation, capitalization, and spelling errors. Be sure to use correctly placed modifiers, including adjectival and adverbial phrases.

 WRITING COACH

Online

www.TXWritingCoach.com

 Video
Learn effective editing techniques from program author Jeff Anderson.

Online Journal
Try It! Record your answers in the online journal.

 Interactive Model
Refer back to the Interactive Model as you edit your writing.

Use the rubric to evaluate your poem. If necessary, rethink, rewrite, or revise.

Rubric for Poetry: Free Verse or Lyric Poem	Rating Scale			
	Not very			Very
Focus and Coherence: How well is your poem's subject or controlling idea defined?	1	2	3	4
Organization: How organized are your ideas?	1	2	3	4
Development of Ideas: How well do your ideas develop the specific focus of the poem?	1	2	3	4
Voice: How effectively do you use figurative language and poetic techniques to create a unique voice?	1	2	3	4
Conventions: How correct is your punctuation? Your capitalization? Your spelling?	1	2	3	4

 Focus on the TEKS

Writing (14)(D) Edit drafts for grammar, mechanics, and spelling.

Conventions

(19)(A) Identify, use, and understand adverbial and adjectival phrases.

(19)(C) Use a variety of complete sentences (e.g., simple, compound, complex) that include properly placed modifiers.

(20)(A) Use conventions of capitalization.

Publishing

Publish your poem! First, get your poem ready for presentation. Then, choose a way to publish your work for appropriate audiences.

Wrap Up Your Presentation

If your poem is handwritten, you may need to make a new, clean copy. If so, be sure to **write legibly.** Also make sure your title grabs the reader's attention and indicates your poem's topic.

Publish Your Piece

Use this chart to help you find a way to publish your poem.

If your audience is...	...then publish it by...
Members of your family	• Printing it with family photos or your own drawings and making keepsake copies • Memorizing it and reciting it on a special occasion
Teachers and classmates at your school	• Submitting it to the school newspaper • Posting it on an arts Web site for other students to see

 ## Reflect on Your Writing

Now that you are done with your poem, read it over and use your writing journal to answer these questions.

- Which parts of your final product are especially strong? Why?

- How does knowing how to write a poem help you appreciate other poets' work? Explain.

- Compare your poem to another piece of writing that expresses a similar theme. As you evaluate what the works have in common, consider ways you might learn from both pieces.

 The Big Question: Why Write? How does one best convey feeling through words on a page?

Manage Your Portfolio You may wish to include your published poem in your writing portfolio. If so, consider what this piece reveals about your writing and your growth as a writer.

21st Century Learning

MAKE YOUR WRITING COUNT

Share Poetic Vision Using Graphics and Text

Poetry uses its carefully chosen words to create vivid images in the mind. Help others "see" poetic images by producing a **collection of images** inspired by a classmate's poem.

Work in a group to select a group members' poem and discuss its imagery. Then, brainstorm for ways to illustrate these images using photos, drawings, or other graphic media. Each group member should contribute by preparing or finding appropriate images. The group can then compile text and graphics into a printed photo album or **multimedia presentation.**

Here's your action plan.

1. With your group, read through your peers' poems. Choose one that contains strong "word pictures" or expresses a particular mood or emotion.

2. Work individually to create or find an illustration based on the central image or mood of the poem.

3. Look online for free, downloadable images.

4. Share your illustrations with your group. As a group:
   - Create captions for each image
   - Talk about why different people come up with different illustrations for the same poem

5. Publish the images and poem in a print or electronic multimedia slideshow. Many Web sites offer free photo-album software for creating slide shows.

6. Present your photo album by circulating it among the class groups, by having groups take turns viewing the slideshow on a computer, or by posting it online.

Listening and Speaking After viewing each group's photo album or slideshow, discuss it within your group. Take turns delivering feedback about each of the other groups' work.

WRITING COACH

Online

www.TXWritingCoach.com

Online Journal

Reflect on Your Writing Record your answers and ideas in the online journal.

Resource

Link to resources on 21st Century Learning for help in creating a group project.

Focus on the TEKS

Writing

(14)(E) Publish written work for appropriate audiences.

(17)(D) Produce a multimedia presentation involving text and graphics using available technology.

(20) Write legibly.

COLLEGE AND CAREER READINESS STANDARDS

Reading (A)(6) Analyze imagery in literary texts.

Listening (B)(3) Listen actively and effectively in group discussions.

**Writing for Media:
Travel Writing**

Travel Writing

Travel writing is a type of descriptive writing that focuses on a particular place. The aim of a travel writer is to present useful and interesting information about a location for audiences who are thinking of visiting it. Travel writing includes helpful facts about a place—its location and geography, climate, population, transportation, hotels, restaurants, and so on. Travel writing also features colorful details about local attractions so that readers can get a feeling for the place and choose specific spots to tour.

When you understand the purpose and elements of travel writing, you can make good judgments when you read about other places in print media or online.

Try It! Study the text in the travel writing sample. Then, answer these questions. Record your answers in your journal.

1. What particular **place** is the writer describing?

2. What seems to be the writer's overall **feeling** about this place?

3. Good travel writing includes **specific details** in the description of the place. What specific details are included in this sample of travel writing?

4. Travel writing usually includes **reasons** to visit a place. What reasons do you find in this?

5. To what kind of specific **audience** would this example of travel writing appeal?

Extension Find another example of a travel writing, and compare it with this one.

Austin, Texas, "Bats" a Million

Every evening at dusk, nearly two million bats swoop, flutter, and generally darken the skies around Austin's Congress Avenue Bridge. The nocturnal critters took up residence under the bridge after it was rebuilt in 1980, and the spot has since become a wildly popular haunt for bats and tourists alike.

The Congress Avenue bats form the largest urban bat colony on the planet. Thousands of human tourists flock to the bridge every night to watch the bats emerge on their nightly hunt for insects and other goodies.

Several tour boats offer special views of the nightly bat flight from the river. These tours cost only $8–$10. An annual Labor Day festival called Batfest celebrates the colony with live music, crafts, and, of course, a bat costume contest. But whenever you come to town, a visit to Austin would not be complete without spending some time hanging out (so to speak) at the Congress Avenue Bridge.

Create a Travel Blog

Follow these steps to create your own blog entry describing your hometown for an online travel site. To plan your blog entry, review the graphic organizers on pages R24–R27 and choose one that suits your purpose.

Prewriting

- Identify the place to be described, your town.

- Identify a specific audience and consider its needs and interests. Plan questions about the place that will appeal to your readers.

- Write notes on the details you want to include in your travel writing. Answer these questions as you think about details to include: What are the main attractions of the place? Who in your audience would be most likely to visit it? What does your audience need to know in order to plan a visit?

Drafting

- Format the travel writing as a blog entry.

- First, write a title identifying your town. Then, present your travel information, with interesting and helpful details and strong images. Keep your information clear, specific, and accurate.

- As you write, aim for a lively, colorful style to appeal to your audience. Use a conversational tone and humor appropriate to blog writing.

- Select pictures to include with your blog entry.

Revising and Editing

- Review your draft to ensure that the description is logically organized and the details and images are specific.

- Take out details that do not serve your purpose or that might confuse the reader.

- Check that spelling, grammar, and mechanics are correct.

Publishing

Use the information from your travel blog as the basis for a multimedia presentation. Use some of the text from your writing, as well as photos and other graphics you can find or create. Then, present it to the class.

WRITING COACH

www.TXWritingCoach.com

Online Journal

Try It! **Record your answers in the online journal.**

Interactive Graphic Organizers

Choose from a variety of graphic organizers to plan and develop your project.

Partner Talk

Before you start drafting, describe the place to a partner or small group as your blog writer would. Make sure your description is specific and detailed, and ask for feedback about it. For example, does it sound appealing?

 Focus on the TEKS

Writing (17)(D) Produce a multimedia presentation involving text and graphics using available technology.

COLLEGE AND CAREER READINESS STANDARDS

Speaking (B)(2) Participate actively and effectively in group discussions.

Writing for Assessment

Writing a good poem can take a lot of practice. You can use these prompts to do just that—practice writing poems. Your responses should include the characteristics on page 120.

Try It! To begin, read the prompt and the information on format and academic vocabulary. Use the ABCDs of On-Demand Writing to help you plan and write your **poem**.

Format
The prompt directs you to write a *poem.* Develop your topic by choosing details that convey your main idea.

Poetry Prompt
Think about a tree you have often seen—perhaps one near your home or school. Write a poem describing that tree and your feelings about it. Choose a poetic form and use poetic techniques.

Academic Vocabulary
Remember that *poetic techniques* are the tools poets use to convey their ideas. Each poem has a specific *poetic form*, such as the lyric or free verse poem.

The ABCDs of On-Demand Writing

Use the following ABCDs to help you respond to the prompt.

Before you write your draft:

A ttack the prompt [1 MINUTE]

- Circle or highlight important verbs in the prompt. Draw a line from the verb to what it refers to.
- Rewrite the prompt in your own words.

B rainstorm possible answers [4 MINUTES]

- Create a graphic organizer to generate ideas.
- Use one for each part of the prompt if necessary.

C hoose the order of your response [1 MINUTE]

- Think about the best way to organize your ideas.
- Number your ideas in the order you will write about them. Cross out ideas you will not be using.

After you write your draft:

D etect errors before turning in the draft [1 MINUTE]

- Carefully reread your writing.
- Make sure that your response makes sense and is complete.
- Look for spelling, punctuation, and grammar errors.

More Prompts for Practice

Apply It! Respond to Prompt 1 by writing a **poem** that uses poetic techniques, figurative language, and graphic elements. Be sure to:

- Identify your audience and choose from a variety of **poetic forms** and use **graphic elements,** such as line breaks and stanzas appropriate to your chosen form
- Establish a clear topic, theme, or **controlling idea**
- Use **poetic techniques** and **figurative language** to develop ideas

> **Prompt 1** Poets often get inspiration from their surroundings. Look outside your window right now and think about what you see. Write a poem about something you notice outside your window.

  Texas Test Prep Spiral Review: Narrative If you choose to write a **personal narrative** in response to Prompt 2, make sure your story reflects the characteristics described on page 66.

> **Prompt 2** Write a personal narrative about something funny or interesting that happened when you took a trip somewhere. The place could be another state or country, or somewhere close to home.

Spiral Review: Imaginative Short Story If you choose to write a **short story** in response to Prompt 3, be sure that your story reflects the characteristics described on page 92. Your writing should express your ideas and feelings about the real or imagined people, events, and ideas that you describe. In addition, be sure to:

- Sustain **reader interest**
- Develop an **engaging story line** with **interesting characters, well-paced action** and a well-developed conflict that is resolved
- Use **sensory details** to present a specific, believable **setting**
- Use a range of **literary strategies** and **devices** to enhance the **style** and **tone** of the story

> **Prompt 3** Write a serious or humorous short story about a misunderstanding between friends. Make the misunderstanding the main conflict, and be sure that plot events center around it.

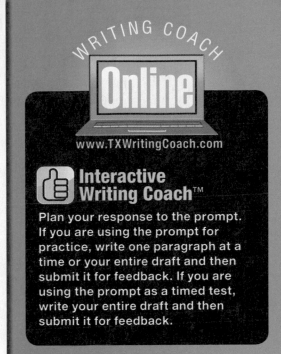

WRITING COACH

Online

www.TXWritingCoach.com

Interactive Writing Coach™

Plan your response to the prompt. If you are using the prompt for practice, write one paragraph at a time or your entire draft and then submit it for feedback. If you are using the prompt as a timed test, write your entire draft and then submit it for feedback.

Remember **ABCD**

Attack the prompt

Brainstorm possible answers

Choose the order of your response

Detect errors before turning in the draft

Focus on the TEKS

Writing

(15)(A-B) Write literary texts to express ideas and feelings about real or imagined people, events, and ideas.

(16)(A) Write a personal narrative that has a clearly defined focus.

CHAPTER 8

EXPOSITION

How Can You Explain This?

What do you know about old and new buildings? What ideas and information about buildings could you share with others?

Information can be presented in many ways. For example, you can compare two things, you can discuss causes and effects, or you can present a problem and a solution.

Try It! How could you compare these two buildings? Take notes as you consider these questions. Then participate in an extended discussion with a partner. Review the ideas you wrote. Then, discuss your comparison. Take turns expressing your ideas and feelings.

- How are these two buildings similar?
- How are these two buildings different?
- What details would you use to describe the buildings?

What's Ahead

In this chapter, you will review two strong examples of an analytical essay: a Mentor Text and a Student Model. Then, using the examples as guides, you will write an expository essay in the compare and contrast form.

WRITING COACH

Online

www.TXWritingCoach.com

Online Journal

Try It! Record your answers and ideas in the online journal.

You can also record and save your answers and ideas on pop-up sticky notes in the eText.

Connect to the Big Questions

Discuss these questions with your partner:

1 What do you think? Is newer always better?

2 Why write? What should we tell and what should we describe to make information clear?

Focus on the TEKS

Writng (17)(A) Write expository and procedural or work-related texts to communicate ideas and information to specific audiences for specific purposes.

EXPOSITORY ESSAY

An expository essay explains a topic by providing facts, quotations, and other details about it. In this chapter, you will learn to write a type of expository essay known as a compare-and-contrast essay. A compare-and-contrast essay provides details about similarities and differences between two or more aspects of a broader topic. For instance, it may examine the similarities and differences between two or more historical events or two or more aspects of nature. It may show how two or more people, places, objects, or experiences are alike or how they are different.

You will develop your compare-and-contrast essay by taking it through each of the steps of the writing process: prewriting, drafting, revising, editing, and publishing. You will also have an opportunity to write a technical newsletter. To preview the criteria for how your compare-and-contrast essay will be evaluated, see the rubric on page 163.

FEATURE ASSIGNMENT

Expository Essay: Compare-and-Contrast Essay

An effective expository essay has these characteristics:

- A **specific topic** about which the essay conveys information

- An **effective introduction** and **conclusion**

- A **clearly stated purpose** and **controlling idea, or thesis**

- **Clear, logical organization** that supports the controlling idea or thesis

- A **variety of transitions** to link details, ideas, and paragraphs

- A **variety of sentence structures** and **rhetorical devices**, such as analogies and rhetorical questions, that help express ideas clearly

- **Facts, quotations**, and **other details** that support the explanations

- **No** unnecessary or **extraneous information** or **inconsistencies**, or facts that do not match

- Ideas that are **accurately synthesized** from **several sources**

A compare-and-contrast essay also includes:

- A **thesis** about **two or more aspects of a broader topic**

- An examination of the **similarities** and **differences** between the two aspects

Other Forms of Expository Essays

In addition to a compare-and-contrast essay, there are other forms of expository essays, including:

Cause-and-effect essays trace the results of an event or the reasons an event happened.

Classification essays organize a subject into categories or explain the category into which an item falls.

Newspaper and magazine articles in print or published on the Internet supply relevant information about a particular topic by analyzing the topic's elements. They may also reflect genres other than expository essays (for example, persuasive writing or narrative nonfiction writing).

Pro-con essays examine the arguments for and against a particular action or decision.

Problem-solution essays identify a problem and explain one or more ways to solve it.

Try It! For each audience and purpose described, choose a form, such as a pro-con essay or a problem-solution essay, that is appropriate for conveying your intended meaning to your audience. Explain your choices.

- To describe the results of a volcanic eruption to students in your science class
- To explain to a friend who is interested in nutrition the categories in which different foods are grouped
- To provide shoppers with an idea of the benefits and drawbacks of a particular product

MENTOR TEXT

Learn From Experience

 After reading the expository essay on pages 148–149, read the numbered notes in the margins to learn about how the author presented her ideas. Later you will read a Student Model, which shares these characteristics and also has the characteristics of a compare-and-contrast essay.

Answer the *Try It!* questions online or in your notebook.

---

1 The introduction has a clearly stated **controlling idea.** The introduction also **grabs readers' interest** by suggesting a comparison between bees and humans.

Try It! What is the **controlling idea** of this essay? What comparison is the author suggesting between bees and humans?

2 A **quotation** from an expert **supports** the controlling idea and sets up the explanations to come.

Try It! How do you know Shaowu Zhang is an expert in bee behavior? What does quoting an expert add to the essay?

3 The author uses a **variety of sentence structures** to explain effectively what Zhang and his team trained the honeybees to do.

Try It! Rewrite this paragraph using only simple sentences. How easy is your version to follow? What other differences do you notice when comparing the two versions?

Brainy Bees Know Two from Three

by Liz Savage

1 One, two, three. . . That's how high you could count if you were a bee. A new study found that honeybees can recognize a pattern based only on the number of elements in it.

5   If the bees learn to recognize three blue dots, then later they can find three yellow stars, three yellow lemons or three purple blobs. For such tiny creatures, that's a big deal.

    Many animals—pigeons, raccoons, dolphins, even salamanders—have shown off their numerical abilities in 10 research experiments. But few studies have ever examined invertebrates, like honeybees.

    Honeybees are pretty clever. They can tell which items are similar to each other and which are different. They can even count the landmarks they pass on the way to get their 15 food. **2** "I have been studying honeybees since 1980, and I am often surprised by our experimental results. The bee is smart," says Shaowu Zhang at the Australian National University in Canberra.

3 Zhang and his team trained about 20 honeybees 20 to fly through a tunnel and into a hole that was marked with either two or three blue dots. On the other side, bees found a chamber with two exits. Each exit was marked with a pattern, either two or three blue dots. If the bees remembered the first pattern and picked the matching 25 hole, the one with the right number of dots, they received a sugary treat. By repeating this training, the bees learned that if they matched the pattern, they would get a reward.

    The honeybees may not think about counting "one, two, three" the same way we do. But the bees got their sugar 30 snack about 70 percent of the time. This confirmed for the

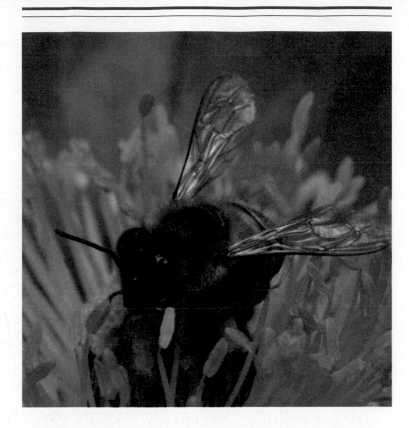

WRITING COACH

Online

www.TXWritingCoach.com

Interactive Model

Listen to an audio recording of the Mentor Text in the eText. You can refer back to the Mentor Text whenever you need support in developing your own writing.

Online Journal

Try It! Answer the questions about the Mentor Text in the online journal.

researchers that the bees were able to detect "sameness," which earlier studies had suggested.

❹ Then the tests got harder. The scientists wanted to see whether the bees could apply that matching rule to new
35 patterns. The bees might have to match two blue dots to two yellow lemons and later on, three green leaves to three yellow stars. Even in these more difficult tests, the bees could tell the difference between two objects and three.

❹ When they were trained to learn a pattern with
40 three items, the bees could distinguish between three and four items, but couldn't do the reverse. Given a four-item pattern, the bees could not tell the difference between four and three. Four was too much to keep track of.

❺ Before you decide bees are dumb, you should know
45 that memory studies have suggested that the number of items a person can consciously remember at any one time is around—four.

❹ The author uses **transitions** to link the sentences in **logical order.**

> *Try It!* How do the transitions help you understand the order in which the events occurred?

❺ The author concludes by **synthesizing information** from other studies to show an unexpected **similarity** between bees and humans.

> *Try It!* What is the similarity between bees and humans? How does this concluding information affect the way you think about bees?

Extension Find another example of an expository essay, and compare it with this one.

STUDENT MODEL

Compare-and-Contrast Essay

With a small group, take turns reading this Student Model aloud. Identify the different characteristics that are being compared or contrasted, and decide if the comparisons and contrasts are clear.

Use a Reader's Eye

Now, reread the Student Model. On your copy of the Student Model, use the Reader's Response Symbols to react to what you read.

Reader's Response Symbols

+ Aha! That makes sense to me.

− This isn't clear to me.

? I have a question about this.

! Wow! That is cool/weird/ interesting.

Participate in an extended discussion with a partner. Express your opinions and share your responses to the Student Model. Discuss the essay's main purpose and likely audience, as well as whether or not it seems appropriate for that purpose and audience.

Canines in the WILD

by Eliot Rayburn

Last summer, my family visited Yellowstone National Park. One morning we saw some animals in the distance. "Look, coyotes!" my sister exclaimed. But a forest ranger told us they weren't coyotes—they were wolves.

5　　My sister's mistake was a common one. Coyotes and wolves have many similarities, even though they are different animals.

Both coyotes and wolves are members of the canine, or dog, family. Their faces are both doglike
10　in appearance and triangular in shape. They are also similar in coloring. Usually their fur is grayish brown, though it can also be rusty, yellowish, white, or black. Wolves have thicker fur than coyotes do, and a coyote's nose and ears are pointier than a
15　wolf's. Still, these differences are rather small.

The biggest difference in appearance is one of size. A full-grown coyote is only about 20 inches tall; a wolf can be nearly twice that tall. A wolf weighs more, too. Some wolves can weigh as much as 80 pounds. In contrast,
20　most coyotes weigh from 20 to 30 pounds. Nevertheless, the size difference won't always help you tell the difference between wolves and coyotes. As the forest ranger at Yellowstone explained, "It's easy to confuse a full-grown coyote with a younger, smaller wolf."

25　　In terms of behavior, wolves and coyotes have many differences. Wolves usually hunt in packs, while coyotes hunt in pairs. Wolves often hunt large animals, like deer and elk. Since coyotes are smaller, they usually go after smaller animals, like mice and

1

---

30 rabbits. And coyotes aren't fussy eaters—they will also eat insects, fruits, vegetables, and even garbage!

Wolves have trouble surviving in places where a lot of people live. In the United States, wolves are a protected species, which means they are in danger
35 of becoming extinct. Coyotes, on the other hand, have an incredible talent for adapting. There are coyotes living right in the middle of Los Angeles! Coyotes can be found in the East, too. They began traveling east on the interstate highway system when
40 it was completed in the 1950s. Now they are fairly common in places like rural New England, where wolves once roamed but are no longer found.

Thus, while coyotes and wolves look alike, their behaviors and situations are different.
45 Wolves are growing rarer and rarer. Coyotes, on the other hand, are thriving.

Wolf

Coyote

WRITING COACH

Online

www.TXWritingCoach.com

Interactive Model

Listen to an audio recording of the Student Model in the eText. Use the Reader's and Writer's Response Symbols with the eText tools to note what you read.

Use a Writer's Eye

Now evaluate the Student Model as a writer. On your copy of the Student Model, use the Writer's Response Symbols to react to what you read. Identify places where the student writer uses the characteristics of an effective compare-and-contrast essay.

Writer's Response Symbols

C.T. Clearly stated thesis

I.C. Effective introduction and conclusion

R.D. Good use of rhetorical devices

S.E. Effective supporting evidence

2

Your Turn > Feature Assignment:
Compare-and-Contrast Essay

Prewriting

Plan a first draft of your compare-and-contrast essay. Select from the Topic Bank or come up with an idea of your own.

 ## Choose From the Topic Bank

TOPIC BANK

Film Adaptations It's fascinating to think about how screenwriters make a movie from a book. Think of a book that has been made into a movie. Write a compare-and-contrast essay that explains what is similar and what is different about the two. Be sure to discuss which one you enjoyed more and why.

Methods of Communication People communicate with each other in different ways. Some people prefer to talk to each other face-to-face, while others prefer the telephone, e-mail, texting, or the Internet. Write an essay comparing and contrasting talking to someone face-to-face with telephoning, texting, e-mailing, or using the Internet.

Subjects Think about the subjects you are learning in school. You probably have a favorite subject and a subject that you don't like as well or that is more difficult for you. Write an essay in which you compare and contrast your favorite class or subject with another class or subject that you may not like as well.

 ## Choose Your Own Topic

Determine a topic on your own by using these ideas.

Associate and Synthesize

- With a partner, play a game of word association in which one of you names something and the other names something that is either the opposite or closely related. After listing your associations, choose one pair to explore in a compare-and-contrast essay.

- List a broad category, such as sports or music. Then, list your favorite type in that category—for example, your favorite type of music might be jazz. Brainstorm for other types in the same category to compare.

Review your responses and choose a topic.

Narrow Your Topic

Some topics are too broad to cover in a compare-and-contrast essay. By narrowing your topic, you can focus on specific similarities and differences.

Apply It! Use a graphic organizer like the one shown to narrow your topic to a manageable size.

- Write your general topic in the top box, and keep narrowing your topic as you move down the chart.
- Your last box should hold your narrowest topic, which will be the new focus of your compare-and-contrast essay.

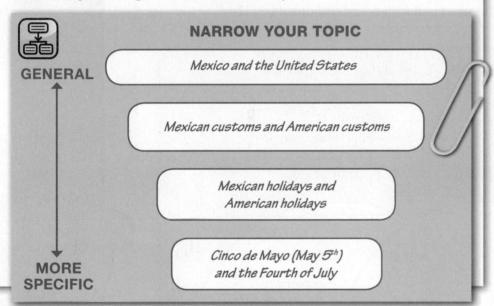

NARROW YOUR TOPIC

GENERAL

Mexico and the United States

Mexican customs and American customs

Mexican holidays and American holidays

Cinco de Mayo (May 5ᵗʰ) and the Fourth of July

MORE SPECIFIC

 ## Consider Your Audience and Purpose

Before writing, think about your audience and purpose. Consider how the form you selected conveys the intended meaning to this audience. Consider the views of others as you ask these questions.

Questions for Audience	Questions for Purpose
• Who is my audience? • Is my audience familiar with my topic? • What questions might my audience have about my topic?	• How might I make the comparisons and contrasts clear to my audience? • What main point about all my comparisons and contrasts do I want to make in my thesis?

Record your answers in your writing journal.

Plan Your Essay

You will use the graphic organizer to state your thesis and identify details that show how your topics are alike and different. When it is complete, you will be ready to write your first draft.

Develop a Clear Thesis Look over your ideas to help you develop a clear thesis, or controlling idea. Your thesis should make a general statement about the similarities and differences in your essay. List it at the top of a graphic organizer like this one.

Logically Organize Your Details Ask yourself how the two aspects of your topic are alike and how they are different. Synthesize the information by listing the details, similarities, and differences in the appropriate sections of the graphic organizer.

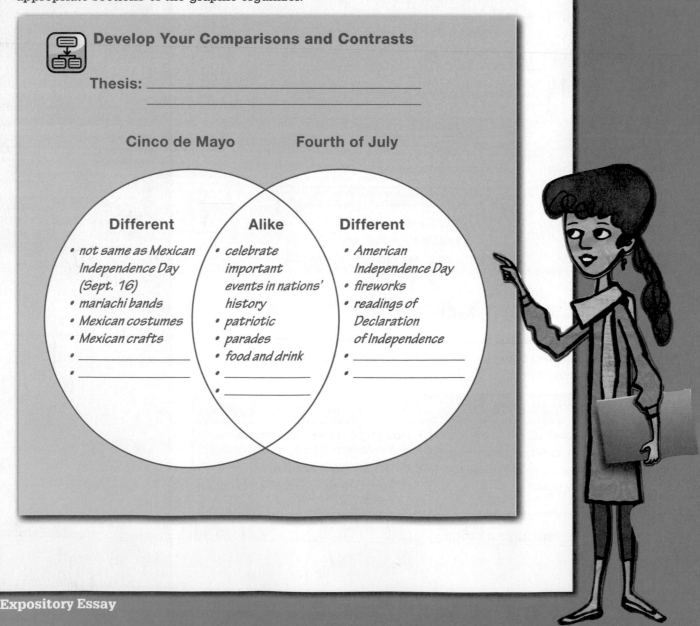

Develop Your Comparisons and Contrasts

Thesis: _____
_____

Cinco de Mayo   Fourth of July

Different
- not same as Mexican Independence Day (Sept. 16)
- mariachi bands
- Mexican costumes
- Mexican crafts
- _____
- _____

Alike
- celebrate important events in nations' history
- patriotic
- parades
- food and drink
- _____
- _____

Different
- American Independence Day
- fireworks
- readings of Declaration of Independence
- _____
- _____

Gather Details

When explaining similarities and differences, writers use some or all of these categories of details. Look at these examples.

- **Facts:** *Cinco de Mayo commemorates a Mexican victory against the French in the Battle of Puebla in 1862.*

- **Quotations:** *"Our annual Cinco de Mayo Festival celebrates the Mexican cultural heritage of many area residents."—Sonia Verdugo, Chairwoman, Cinco de Mayo Festival of Martina, Colorado*

- **Examples:** *Tacos are among the Mexican foods served at Cinco de Mayo celebrations.*

- **Personal Experiences:** *In the Cinco de Mayo parade I saw last year, most people on the floats wore traditional Mexican clothing.*

Try It! Read this Student Model excerpt. Then, identify and take notes about which kinds of details the author used to support his ideas.

STUDENT MODEL from **Canines in the Wild**
page 150; lines 19–24

> In contrast, most coyotes weigh from 20 to 30 pounds. Nevertheless, the size difference won't always help you tell the difference between wolves and coyotes. As the forest ranger at Yellowstone explained, "It's easy to confuse a full-grown coyote with a younger, smaller wolf."

Apply It! Review the types of support an expository essay can use. Think about the different types you might use in discussing the similarities and differences that support your thesis. Also consider which details might be useful for an **effective introduction or conclusion** to your essay.

- Decide which details best support your purpose as stated in your thesis. Eliminate details that do not seem tightly related or relevant, or change your thesis to take them into account.

- Review your notes to find similarities. Then, **synthesize** your information and identify any **inconsistencies.** Do more research, if necessary, to clear up the inconsistencies.

- Identify one or two details that could help make your **introduction or conclusion more effective.** Sometimes a quotation or a personal experience can help capture reader attention in your introduction or make your conclusion more memorable.

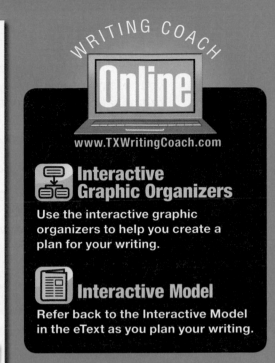

WRITING COACH

Online

www.TXWritingCoach.com

Interactive Graphic Organizers

Use the interactive graphic organizers to help you create a plan for your writing.

Interactive Model

Refer back to the Interactive Model in the eText as you plan your writing.

Focus on the TEKS

Writing

(14)(A) Plan a first draft by developing a thesis or controlling idea.

(17)(A) Write a multi-paragraph essay that presents effective introductions and concluding paragraphs and contains a clearly stated purpose or controlling idea.

COLLEGE AND CAREER READINESS STANDARDS

Writing(A)(3) Evaluate relevance, quality, sufficiency, and depth of preliminary ideas and information, organize material generated, and formulate a thesis.

Drafting

During the drafting stage, you will start to write your ideas for your essay. You will follow an outline that provides an appropriate **organizational strategy** that will help you build on ideas to write a **focused, organized,** and **coherent** compare-and-contrast essay.

The Organization of a Compare-and-Contrast Essay

The chart provides an organizing structure for a compare-and-contrast essay. As you adapt it for your particular compare-and-contrast essay, be sure to keep in mind your audience and purpose.

Outline for Success

I. Introduction

See Mentor Text, p. 148.

- Attention-grabbing opening
- Thesis that states what you are comparing and contrasting

II. Body

See Mentor Text, pp. 148–149.

- **Points of comparison and contrast**

  Point-by-Point
  - Point 1: Topic A and B
  - Point 2: Topic A and B
  - Point 3: Topic A and B

- **Logical organization of points**

  Block Organization
  - Topic A: Points 1, 2, and 3
  - Topic B: Points 1, 2, and 3

III. Conclusion

See Mentor Text, p. 149.

- Restatement of thesis
- Memorable ending

Grab Your Reader

- An interesting opening captures the reader's attention with a quotation, a personal experience, or another strong detail.
- A thesis is a general statement about the two or more aspects that you are comparing and contrasting.

Compare and Contrast

- Each point of comparison and contrast is supported with evidence that explains your points and informs your reader.
- A clear organizational structure helps readers follow your ideas easily. A point-by-point or block organization structure is a good way to structure your ideas. Block organization works best if you have only one or two points of comparison. Point-by-point is used when you have several points of comparison.

Wrap It Up

- A strong conclusion restates the thesis and briefly summarizes your points of comparison and contrast.
- Analogies or rhetorical questions—questions that make the reader think or emphasize a point—help make your ideas memorable.

Start Your Draft

Use this checklist to help you complete your draft. Use the graphic organizer that shows your comparisons and contrasts, and the Outline for Success as guides.

While drafting, aim at writing your ideas, not on making your writing perfect. Remember, you will have the chance to improve your draft when you revise and edit.

√ Start with **opening** sentences that capture your reader's interest and introduce the topic for comparison and contrast.

√ Continue building an **effective** introduction by including a thesis that states your controlling idea about the similarities and differences you will be discussing.

√ Develop the **body** of your compare-and-contrast essay by providing similarities and differences that support your **thesis.**

√ **Synthesize,** or blend together, ideas and information from several sources.

√ Logically organize your essay by including specific facts and details that support your main idea. Make sure to avoid **extraneous,** or unnecessary, information and inconsistencies.

√ Be sure to use **transitions** to link sentences and paragraphs and to make your comparisons and contrasts clear.

√ Use an appropriate **organizing structure** such as point-by-point organization, discussing each similarity and difference one at a time, or block organization, discussing all the qualities of one thing before moving on to the other.

√ Use a variety of different **sentence structures,** such as short or long and simple or complex to keep your writing lively and interesting.

√ End with an effective **conclusion** that restates your thesis in an interesting way and uses a variety of **rhetorical devices** to help your audience see the importance of your topic.

WRITING COACH

Online

www.TXWritingCoach.com

Interactive Model

Outline for Success View pop-ups of Mentor Text selections referenced in the Outline for Success.

 Interactive Writing Coach™

Use the Interactive Writing Coach to receive the level of support you need:
• Write one paragraph at a time and submit each one for immediate, detailed feedback.
• Write your entire first draft and submit it for immediate, personalized feedback.

Focus on the TEKS

Writing

(14)(B) Develop drafts by choosing an appropriate organizational strategy and building on ideas to create a focused, organized, and coherent piece of writing.

(17)(A) Write a multi-paragraph essay that presents effective introductions and concluding paragraphs and contains a clearly stated purpose or controlling idea.

Revising: Making It Better

Now that you have finished your first draft, you are ready to revise. Think about the "big picture" of **audience, purpose,** and **genre.** You can use the Revision RADaR strategy as a guide for making changes to improve your draft. Revision RADaR provides four major ways to improve your writing: (R) replace, (A) add, (D) delete, and (R) reorder.

Kelly Gallagher, M. Ed.

KEEP REVISION ON YOUR RADaR

Read part of the first draft of the Student Model "Canines in the Wild." Then, look at questions the writer asked himself as he thought about how well his draft **addressed issues of audience, purpose, and genre.**

Canines in the Wild

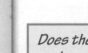 1ST DRAFT

It's easy to mix up wolves and coyotes. Lots of people can't tell the difference, especially from a distance. My sister mixed them up last summer. Her mistake is a common one.

Both coyotes and wolves are members of the canine, or dog, family. The word *coyote* comes from a Native American word. The two animals' faces have a similar dog-like appearance and triangular shape. They are also similar in coloring. Usually their fur is grayish brown. It can be rusty or yellowish. It can also be white or black. Wolves have thicker fur than coyotes do. And a coyote's nose and ears are pointier than a wolf's. Still, these differences are rather small.

The biggest difference in appearance is one of size. A full-grown coyote is only about 20 inches tall; a wolf can be nearly twice that tall. A wolf weighs more, too. Some wolves can weigh as much as 80 pounds.

Does the introduction grab my audience and clearly state my thesis?

Is this detail relevant to the comparisons and contrasts, or is it extraneous information?

How can I vary sentence structures to avoid so many short, choppy sentences?

Now look at how the writer applied Revision RADaR to write an improved second draft.

Canines in the WILD

Last summer, my family visited Yellowstone National Park. One morning we saw some animals in the distance. "Look, coyotes!" my sister exclaimed. But a forest ranger told us they weren't coyotes—they were wolves.

My sister's mistake was a common one. Coyotes and wolves have many similarities, even though they are different animals.

Both coyotes and wolves are members of the canine, or dog, family. Their faces are both doglike in appearance and triangular in shape. They are also similar in coloring. Usually their fur is grayish brown, though it can also be rusty, yellowish, white, or black. Wolves have thicker fur than coyotes do, and a coyote's nose and ears are pointier than a wolf's. Still, these differences are rather small.

The biggest difference in appearance is one of size. A full-grown coyote is only about 20 inches tall; a wolf can be nearly twice that tall. A wolf weighs more, too. Some wolves can weigh as much as 80 pounds.

R **A** *Replaced a more personal anecdote to make the introduction more effective, and added a thesis that makes a clear statement about my topic*

D *Deleted extraneous information not relevant to the comparisons and contrasts I am making*

R *Reordered sentences by combining them to vary sentence structures*

www.TXWritingCoach.com

Interactive Writing Coach™

Use the Revision RADaR strategy in your own writing. Then submit your paragraph or draft for feedback.

 Apply It! Use your Revision RADaR to revise your draft.

- Include all the appropriate characteristics of the expository essay genre.
- Keep your audience and purpose in mind. Make sure that your introduction is effective, interesting, and presents a clearly stated thesis.
- Exchange drafts with a partner. Listen as your partner provides direction for how to improve your work.
- Then, apply the Revision RADaR strategy to make needed changes. Remember—you can use the steps in the strategy in any order.

 Focus on the TEKS

Writing (14)(C) Revise drafts after rethinking how well questions of purpose, audience, and genre have been addressed.

COLLEGE AND CAREER READINESS STANDARDS

Writing (A)(4) Recognize the importance of revision as the key to effective writing.

Look at the Big Picture

Use the chart and your analytical skills to evaluate how well each section of your compare-and-contrast essay addresses **purpose, audience**, and **genre**. When necessary, use the suggestions in the chart to revise your essay.

Section	Evaluate	Revise
Introduction	• Make sure your **opening** grabs readers' attention.	• Use a quotation, a question, or another strong detail to make your introduction effective.
	• Be sure your **thesis** clearly states the two or more aspects of your topic that you are comparing and contrasting.	• Complete and answer these questions to help form a thesis: In general, *how are _____ and _____ (or _____, _____, and _____) alike, and how are they different?* *Why does it matter?*
Body	• Check that you clearly identify **comparisons** and contrasts.	• Add transitions such as *similarly* and *in contrast* to make your ideas clear.
	• Check that your source information is **synthesized** from several sources.	• Combine similar ideas from separate sources to avoid repetition.
	• Check that you have **organized** your comparisons and contrasts in a logical and coherent way.	• Discuss each similarity or difference one at a time, or discuss all the qualities of first one thing and then the other.
	• Check that your **facts** and details are appropriate. Avoid extraneous information or inconsistencies that do not support your thesis.	• Delete details that are not relevant to your thesis or explanations. Confirm that your information is correct and remove any errors or inconsistencies.
	• Check that you have used a variety of **sentence structures.**	• Break or combine sentences to vary their structures.
Conclusion	• Check that you have restated your thesis and summed up **main ideas.**	• Rewrite to sum up all your main points and only your main points.
	• Make sure that your essay ends on a **memorable** note.	• Add rhetorical devices, such as analogies, comparisons, or rhetorical questions, to make your conclusion more effective. Help your audience see why your subject is meaningful.

Focus on Craft: Effective Transitions

Your writing will be smoother if you use clear **transitions**, words and phrases that show the connections between ideas. Transitions that indicate a comparison include *similarly, likewise, in the same way,* and *once again.* Transitions that indicate a contrast include *although, in contrast, on the other hand,* and *however.*

Look for a transition as you read these sentences from the Student Model.

 STUDENT MODEL from **Canines in the Wild**
page 151; lines 33–36

> In the United States, wolves are a protected species, which means they are in danger of becoming extinct. Coyotes, on the other hand, have an incredible talent for adapting.

 Try It! Now, ask yourself these questions. Record your answers in your journal.

- What relationship does the transition *on the other hand* signal?
- Would the relationship between ideas in these sentences be different if the transition *similarly* replaced the current transition? Why or why not?

Fine-Tune Your Draft

Apply It! Use these revision suggestions to prepare your final draft after rethinking how well questions of purpose, audience, and genre have been addressed.

- **Choose Effective Transitions to Convey Meaning** To ensure your ideas flow logically, use transitions between sentences and between paragraphs. Use transitions to clarify relationships between points and to be certain that you have a consistent point of view.
- **Ensure Internal and External Coherence** To present a cohesive essay within each section and as a whole, make sure that ideas, sentences, and paragraphs are organized in a logical sequence and that they flow easily.
- **Check Consistent Point of View** Make sure that the entire essay uses the same person, or voice, consistently. For example, avoid switching from first-person "I" to third-person "she."

Teacher Feedback After submitting your final draft for teacher review, **revise it in response to feedback from your teacher.**

 Focus on the TEKS

Writing

(14)(C) Revise drafts to ensure consistent point of view; internal and external coherence; and the use of effective transitions after rethinking how well questions of purpose, audience, and genre have been addressed.

(14)(E) Revise final draft in response to feedback from teacher.

(17)(A) Write a multi-paragraph essay that presents effective introductions and concluding paragraphs and contains a clearly stated purpose or controlling idea.

Editing: Making It Correct

Use the editing process to polish your work and correct errors. It is often helpful to work with a partner when editing your drafts.

As you edit, think about whether or not you have used **transitions** effectively. A transition is a word or phrase that creates a clear relationship between ideas. Then, edit your final draft for any factual errors and errors in **grammar, mechanics, and spelling**.

WRITE GUY *Jeff Anderson, M. Ed.*

WHAT DO YOU NOTICE?

Zoom in on Conventions Focus on transitions as you zoom in on these sentences from the Student Model.

> **STUDENT MODEL** from **Canines in the Wild**
> page 151; lines 33–36, 43–44
>
> In the United States, wolves are a protected species, which means they are in danger of becoming extinct. Coyotes, on the other hand, have an incredible talent for adapting....
>
> Thus, while coyotes and wolves look alike, their behaviors and situations are different.

Now, ask yourself: *Which words and phrases create a relationship between ideas?*

Perhaps you identified the transition *on the other hand,* which makes clear the relationship of contrast between the first two sentences in the passage.

The transition *Thus* makes clear the cause-and-effect relationship between the last paragraph and the paragraphs that came before it.

Partner Talk Discuss this question with a partner: *What other transitions could the Student Model author have used to express the same relationships?*

> To learn more about phrases and clauses, see Chapter 19 of your Grammar Handbook.

Grammar Mini-Lesson: Using Commas

To learn more, see Chapter 25.

Introductory words, phrases, and clauses should usually be set off from the rest of the sentence by a comma. This rule includes transitions. Notice how commas set off a one-word transition and a transitional phrase in the Student Model.

 STUDENT MODEL from **Canines in the Wild**
page 150; lines 19–22

> In contrast, most coyotes weigh from 20 to 30 pounds. Nevertheless, the size difference won't always help you tell the difference between wolves and coyotes.

 Try It! Identify an introductory word, phrase, and clause in this passage. Then, identify which of these are transitions. Write the passage and add any commas that are needed.

On Tuesday Zoe apologized to her sister for missing her birthday. After her sister accepted her apology Zoe felt relieved and happy. Later she offered to throw her sister a party.

Apply It! **Edit your draft for grammar, punctuation, capitalization, and spelling errors.** Capitalize words correctly and use a dictionary or other resource to check spelling. Be sure to use transitions for **coherence** between sentences and paragraphs. Also, use commas after introductory words, phrases, and clauses, including transitions.

Use the rubric to evaluate your essay. If necessary, rethink, rewrite, or revise.

Rubric for Expository Writing: Compare-and-Contrast Essay	**Rating Scale**			
Focus and Coherence: How well do you explain the similarities and differences of your topic?	Not very 1	2	3	Very 4
Organization: How well are your ideas organized?	1	2	3	4
Development of Ideas: How well do you use details, such as facts and examples, to support your ideas?	1	2	3	4
Voice: How well have you engaged your reader?	1	2	3	4
Conventions: How correct are your commas with transitions?	1	2	3	4

 WRITING COACH

Online

www.TXWritingCoach.com

 Video

Learn effective editing techniques from program author Jeff Anderson.

 Online Journal

Try It! Record your answers in the online journal.

 Interactive Model

Refer back to the Interactive Model as you edit your writing.

 Interactive Writing Coach™

Edit your draft. Check it against the rubric and then submit it for feedback.

 Focus on the TEKS

Writing (14)(D) Edit drafts for grammar, mechanics, and spelling.

Conventions

(19)(A) Identify, use, and understand transitions for sentence to sentence or paragraph to paragraph coherence.

(20)(B) Recognize and use commas after introductory words, phrases, and clauses.

(21)(A) Spell correctly, including using various resources to determine and check correct spellings.

COLLEGE AND CAREER READINESS STANDARDS

Writing (A)(5) Edit writing for proper voice, tense, and syntax, assuring that it conforms to standard English when appropriate.

Publishing

Get your compare-and-contrast essay ready for presentation so you can share what you learned with others. Then, choose a way to **publish it for the appropriate audience**.

Wrap Up Your Presentation

To get your essay ready, you may need to make a new, clean copy. Be sure to add images of the items you're comparing to help readers see the similarities and differences. Finally, make sure that your title grabs the reader's attention and indicates your essay's topic.

Publish Your Essay

Use the chart to identify a way to publish your essay.

If your audience is...	...then publish it by...
Classmates and others at your school	• Submitting it to a school newspaper or magazine • Creating a podcast for classmates to hear
Your local community	• Submitting it to a local print or online newspaper • Reading and discussing it on local public-access TV
The larger community	• Posting it online and inviting responses • Entering it in a regional or national essay contest

 Extend Your Research

Think more about the topic on which you wrote your compare-and-contrast essay. What else would you like to know about this topic? As you write your ideas, use specific details to describe and explain. Increase the specificity of your details based on the type of information you are recording.

- Brainstorm for several questions you would like to research and then consult, or discuss, with others.

- Formulate, or develop, a plan about how you will answer these questions. Decide where you will find more information—on the Internet, at the library, or through other sources.

- Finally, learn more about your topic by following through with your research plan.

 The Big Question: Why Write? What should we tell and what should we describe to make information clear?

MAKE YOUR WRITING COUNT

Entertain Audiences With a Humorous Skit

Compare-and-contrast essays identify similarities and differences between two people, things, or issues. In another context, points of contrast can be emphasized for humor. In fact, comedians often use differences as the basis for skits. Use humor to communicate the message of one of your compare-and-contrast essays.

Produce a **humorous skit** inspired by the differences explored in a compare-and-contrast essay. Develop interesting characters representing the two people, items, or issues analyzed in one of your peers' essays. Perform the skit live or video-record it.

WRITING COACH

Online

www.TXWritingCoach.com

Online Journal

Extend Your Research Record your answers and ideas in the online journal.

Resource

Link to resources on 21st Century Learning for help in creating a group project.

Here's your action plan.

1. Choose roles, including writer, director, performer, and prop master.

2. With your group, evaluate your peers' compare-and-contrast essays. Choose one that compares items or ideas that are easily represented—and that might lend themselves to comedy.

3. View comical skits online. Then, write a skit that portrays each item or idea as a character.

   - Write funny dialogue for each character.
   - Make sure that similarities and differences are clear. Exaggeration may help enhance the humor.
   - Assign two group members to play the parts.
   - Work as a team to rehearse the skit, using costumes and props.
   - If possible, perform and record the skit using a video camera.

4. Present the skit to the class or school either live or as a video. Consider posting the video online.

Listening and Speaking Listen actively as your group writes the skit together. Take turns making suggestions for adding humor during the planning and rehearsal stages. During the performance, keep your peers' feedback in mind. Work as a team to entertain and inform your audience. Listen for feedback.

 Focus on the TEKS

Writing

(14)(E) Publish written work for appropriate audiences.

(15)(A) (iv) Write an imaginative story that develops interesting characters.

(22)(A) Brainstorm, consult with others, decide upon a topic, and formulate a major research question to address the major research topic.

COLLEGE AND CAREER READINESS STANDARDS

Listening (B)(3) Listen actively and effectively in group discussions.

**Writing for Media:
Technical Newsletter**

Technical Newsletter

A **technical newsletter** gives information about the latest advances in electronics or other technologies. It often compares and contrasts new developments or products to help readers make informed decisions. Newsletters are often e-mailed or sent as direct-mail, or mail sent to a specific target audience. Many technical newsletters are geared to audiences of subscribers who are already familiar with the technical field. Others are aimed at more general audiences who need to make a purchase or research new developments in the field.

Try It! Study this sample technical newsletter. Then, answer the five questions about it. Record your answers in your journal.

1. What topic does the newsletter address? Restate the **controlling idea** in your own words.

2. Describe the newsletter's **audience**—are they general readers ready to buy, or "techies" familiar with the topic? Cite details to explain your answer.

3. List the main **similarities** and **differences** that the newsletter points out.

4. Does the newsletter **use point-by-point** or **block organization?** Does the organization help make the similarities and differences clear to you? Why or why not?

5. What **transitions** help make the similarities and differences clearer?

Extension Find another example of a technical newsletter, and compare it with this one.

 TECHNO-TIPS

MP3 Players

An MP3 player is a pocket-sized electronic device that stores and plays back music or other audio files. There are two basic kinds: hard-drive-based MP3 players and flash-based MP3 players. Each has its benefits and drawbacks.

Hard-drive-based MP3 players, sometimes called hard-disk players, have the most gigabytes. This means they have more storage space for your music collection. In fact, some hard-drive-based players can store as many as 40,000 songs. In terms of cost, you get the most storage space for your money with one of these players. However, you also get the largest and heaviest MP3 player. Micro-hard-drive-based MP3 players are a smaller and lighter version, but they also have less storage space. They also do not solve the biggest problem of all hard-drive-based players: Sudden movements cause them to skip. Thus, hard-drive-based players are impractical to use while jogging, running, or working out.

Flash-based MP3 players, sometimes called flash-memory players, are the original MP3 design. They are smaller and lighter than other players, and they do not skip. Their storage space, however, is fairly small. Depending on the model, it ranges from as few as 10 to as many as 8,000 songs. Also, per unit of storage space, flash-based players cost more than their hard-drive-based cousins. Moreover, they can be harder to operate, especially if they have lots of special features.

Create a Technical Newsletter

Follow these steps to create a technical newsletter for a specific audience. To plan your newsletter, review the graphic organizers on pages R24–R27 and choose one that suits your needs.

Prewriting

- Choose a technology that you might like to research. For example, you might choose video games, cell phones, or cameras.
- Determine your audience and purpose. Will you be updating an already informed audience or teaching a more general audience?
- After doing research, decide on two aspects of the topic that you will compare and contrast.
- List the similarities and differences that you would like to discuss.
- Develop a controlling idea that makes a general statement about the similarities and differences.

Drafting

- Begin with a paragraph that identifies your topic. Include a thesis about the two aspects of the topic you will discuss.
- Discuss similarities and differences using block or point-by-point organization. Include graphic elements, such as subheadings or boldfaced text, to help organize your ideas.
- Use correct terminology in discussing the topic. If your audience is new to the topic, include definitions or explanations of unfamiliar terms.
- Use clear transitions to show comparisons, contrasts, and other relationships.
- Give your newsletter a catchy title that identifies its content.

Revising and Editing

- Check that your information is accurate and uses correct terminology.
- Make sure that your information is logically organized and will be clear to your particular audience.
- Remove any details that are not relevant to your purpose.

Publishing

Create your own technical Web site and post your newsletter as a multimedia presentation. Use available technology to add text and graphics to the Web site and your newsletter.

WRITING COACH

Online

www.TXWritingCoach.com

Online Journal

Try It! Record your answers in the online journal.

Interactive Graphic Organizers

Choose from a variety of graphic organizers to plan and develop your project.

Partner Talk

Discuss your topic with a partner. Ask what questions or concerns he or she might have on the topic of your newsletter, and take notes about his or her responses. Consider your partner's responses in deciding on the information to include in your newsletter.

 Focus on the TEKS

Writing (17)(D) Produce a multimedia presentation involving text and graphics using available technology.

Writing for Assessment

Many standardized tests include a prompt that asks you to write an expository essay. You can use the prompts on these pages to practice. Your responses should include most of the same characteristics as your compare-and-contrast essay. (See page 146.)

 Try It! To begin, read the **expository** prompt and the information on format and academic vocabulary. Then write an essay by following the instructions shown in the ABCDs of On-Demand Writing.

Format
The prompt directs you to write a compare-and-contrast *expository essay*. Include an introduction, body paragraphs with similarities and differences, and a conclusion.

Expository Prompt
Write an expository essay that compares and contrasts two different kinds of household pets. Discuss similarities and differences of owning each pet and the work involved in caring for each.

Academic Vocabulary
Remember that *similarities* are elements that are alike; *differences* are elements that are not alike.

The ABCDs of On-Demand Writing

Use the following ABCDs to help you respond to the prompt.

Before you write your draft:

Attack the prompt [1 MINUTE]

- Circle or highlight important verbs in the prompt. Draw a line from the verb to what it refers to.
- Rewrite the prompt in your own words.

Brainstorm possible answers [4 MINUTES]

- Create a graphic organizer to generate ideas.
- Use one for each part of the prompt if necessary.

Choose the order of your response [1 MINUTE]

- Think about the best way to organize your ideas.
- Number your ideas in the order you will write about them. Cross out ideas you will not be using.

After you write your draft:

Detect errors before turning in the draft [1 MINUTE]

- Carefully reread your writing.
- Make sure that your response makes sense and is complete.
- Look for spelling, punctuation, and grammar errors.

More Prompts for Practice

Apply It! **Texas Test Prep** Respond to Prompts 1 and 2 by writing **expository essays**. As you write, be sure to:

- Grab readers' attention with an **effective introductory paragraph** that states a **clear purpose** and end with a memorable **concluding paragraph**
- Use a **variety of sentence structures, rhetorical devices, and transitions** to help make your writing cohesive and interesting
- Use a variety of examples and details to support your ideas. Accurately **synthesize ideas** into a cohesive whole
- For your body, choose a logical **organizing structure appropriate to your facts and details**
- Include **relevant information** with **no inconsistencies**. Remove any extraneous information

> **Prompt 1** Soccer vs. football? Swimming vs. track? Choose two sports, and write an essay comparing and contrasting them. Be sure that you explain the similarities and differences in a way that would be clear to someone unfamiliar with the sport.

> **Prompt 2** Write a compare-and-contrast essay in which you discuss the similarities and differences between two foods you enjoy. Focus on their nutritional benefits as well as their taste. You might also consider other qualities, such as the cost or ease of preparation.

Spiral Review: Poetry Respond to Prompt 3 by writing a **poem**. Make sure your poem reflects all of the characteristics described on page 120, including:

- **Poetic techniques**
- **Figurative language**
- **Graphic elements**

> **Prompt 3** Think about your school. What are your favorite things about your school? What are the best things that have happened there? Write a poem expressing your ideas and feelings about your school.

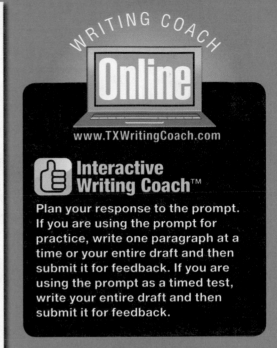

WRITING COACH

Online

www.TXWritingCoach.com

Interactive Writing Coach™

Plan your response to the prompt. If you are using the prompt for practice, write one paragraph at a time or your entire draft and then submit it for feedback. If you are using the prompt as a timed test, write your entire draft and then submit it for feedback.

Remember ABCD

Attack the prompt

Brainstorm possible answers

Choose the order of your response

Detect errors before turning in the draft

Focus on the TEKS

Writing

(17)(A) Write a multi-paragraph essay that presents effective introductions and concluding paragraphs and contains a clearly stated purpose or controlling idea.

(15)(B) Write a poem using poetic techniques, figurative language, and graphic elements.

COLLEGE AND CAREER READINESS STANDARDS

Reading (B)(1) Identify new words and concepts acquired through study of the relationships to other words and concepts.

PERSUASION

What Do You Think?

Should students be allowed to use cell phones in school? This is an issue that people debate. Some schools forbid students to carry and use cell phones; other schools allow cell phones.

Maybe you already have an opinion on student cell phone use. Or perhaps you want to learn more about the issue before taking a position. In either case, one day you might want to convince someone to share your opinion. When you use words to convince people to think or act in a certain way, you are using persuasion.

Try It! Take a few minutes to list reasons why students should and should not be allowed to use cell phones in school.

Consider these questions as you work on your list.

- What do students use their cell phones for in school?
- What useful purposes could cell phones serve in the classroom?
- How could cell phone use in school affect learning?
- Is having a cell phone in school a safety issue? Why?

Review the list you made, and then choose a position on the issue. **Plan a draft by developing a clear thesis or controlling idea** that states your position. Then find a partner, and take turns expressing your thesis ideas to one another.

What's Ahead

In this chapter, you will review two strong examples of a persuasive essay: a Mentor Text and a Student Model. Then, using the examples as guidance, you will write a persuasive essay of your own.

WRITING COACH

Online

www.TXWritingCoach.com

 Online Journal

Try It! Record your answers and ideas in the online journal.

You can also record and save your answers and ideas on pop-up sticky notes in the eText.

Connect to the Big Questions

Discuss these questions with your partner:

1 What do you think? Which do you think is more important and why— the community's right to ensure that students are not distracted by cell phones or the individual student's right to use a cell phone?

2 Why write? What is your point of view? How will you know if you have convinced others?

COLLEGE AND CAREER READINESS STANDARDS

Listening (B)(2) Listen actively and effectively in one-on-one communication situations.

PERSUASIVE WRITING

Persuasion is writing that is meant to convince readers to agree with the writer's opinion. In this chapter, you will explore a special type of persuasive essay, the op-ed piece. An op-ed piece appears in a newspaper or magazine. The term *op-ed* is abbreviated from "opposite editorial" because op-ed pieces were traditionally printed opposite the editorial. An editorial is an unsigned piece of writing that represents the view of a newspaper or magazine as a whole. An op-ed is a signed piece of writing that represents the view of an individual columnist or writer.

You will develop the op-ed piece by taking it through each of the steps of the writing process: prewriting, drafting, revising, editing, and publishing. You will also have an opportunity to create an advertisement. To preview the criteria for how your op-ed piece will be evaluated, see the rubric on page 189.

FEATURE ASSIGNMENT
Persuasive Essay: Op-Ed Piece

An effective persuasive essay has these characteristics:

- A **lead** that introduces the topic or issue and captures readers' interest

- A **clear thesis statement** that tells the writer's opinion

- **Persuasive arguments** that are organized in logical order

- **Evidence that is logically organized** so that it supports the writer's opinion. Evidence may include examples, facts, statistics, and expert opinions.

- Responses to readers' **concerns and counter-arguments**

- **Effective sentence structure** and correct spelling, grammar, and usage

- A **conclusion** that restates your position and ends on a memorable note

- **A natural but authoritative voice** that appeals to both reason and emotion

An effective op-ed piece also includes:

- A response to a **current event** or **topic**

- A **tight focus** on a single event

- A **call to action**

Other Forms of Persuasive Writing

In addition to an op-ed piece, there are other forms of persuasive writing, including:

Advertisements are paid announcements that try to convince people to do or buy something.

Editorials state the opinion of the editors and publishers of news organizations. Editorials are usually about current issues and appear in newspapers, magazines, or on television, radio, or the Internet.

Letters to the editor are written by readers who express an opinion in response to an article that has been published in a newspaper or magazine.

Persuasive essays use logic and reasoning to persuade readers to adopt a certain action or point of view.

Persuasive speeches aim at winning an audience's support for a policy, position, or action.

Propaganda uses emotional appeals and often biased, false, or misleading information to persuade people to think or act in a certain way. Propaganda is often about political issues.

Reviews evaluate items and activities such as books and movies. A review often states an opinion on whether people should spend time and money on the item or activity.

Try It! For each audience and purpose described, choose a form, such as a speech, letter, or review, that is appropriate for conveying your intended meaning to the audience. Explain your choices.

- To disagree with an editorial in your local newspaper
- To convince classmates to read a book that you enjoyed
- To encourage listeners of a radio station to buy tickets to an upcoming concert

MENTOR TEXT | Op-Ed Piece

Learn From Experience

 Read the op-ed piece on pages 174–175. As you read, take notes to develop your understanding of basic sight and English vocabulary. Then, read the numbered notes in the margins to learn about how the author presented her ideas.

Answer the *Try It!* questions online or in your journal.

---

1 The author wrote a description of an animal shelter to introduce the issue: the overcrowding at an animal shelter. The detailed description is an effective **lead** that captures the reader's attention.

Try It! Which adjectives did the author use in the first three sentences to help readers create a strong visual image of an animal shelter?

2 The **thesis** presents the author's main message and persuasive argument by naming the issue and stating the author's viewpoint.

Try It! Does the author establish a clear thesis or position? What issue or problem does she describe, and what solution does she suggest?

3 The author offers three **persuasive arguments** for the need for people to adopt pets from shelters.

Try It! Based on these arguments and the author's purpose, who would you say is her targeted audience? Explain.

Extension Find another example of an op-ed piece, and compare it with this one.

Looking for a Pet?
Look No Further Than Maiden Point Shelter

by Cindy Trumbore

---

1 Maiden Point Shelter is overflowing with cats and dogs. Every cage and kennel is filled to capacity, and heartrending meows and barks come from extra cages lining the hallways. The shelter is at its most overcrowded since it was opened
5 in 1993. **2** There is a simple solution to the overcrowding at Maiden Point Shelter: more people in our area need to adopt pets, rather than buying them. Yet judging from the "designer" pets we see on the streets of our town, the public seems strangely unconvinced of this fact.

10 There are two main reasons for the problem, according to Biz Raleigh, the director. First, we had a mild winter, so more cats were outside. As a result, there are more litters of kittens now. There is another surprising reason, however, for the overcrowding. Raleigh has noticed a direct link between
15 the number of mortgage foreclosures in our area, and the number of pets that get brought to the shelter. When people lose their homes, they are often forced to find housing that doesn't allow pets. **3** In fact, Raleigh says that in the past six months, Maiden Point received nearly 200 cats and dogs
20 alone. That's a 100% increase over the previous six months.

"We're at the point where we'll have to start putting unadoptable animals down to make room for the ones with a better chance," Raleigh says, sighing. "I really don't know why people looking for a pet don't come here first." **3** She
25 points out that pets from pet stores have often been raised in unclean, unhealthy, crowded conditions, especially dogs from so-called "puppy mills." In contrast, the shelter pets are spayed and neutered, and treated for problems such as heartworm and fleas, before they are adopted out.

30 **3** People especially need to open their minds to adopting older pets, she says. Some people assume that when they get an older pet, they will have to "undo" the bad habits it

learned from a previous owner. However, Raleigh says
that just the opposite can be true. **4** "An older pet is often
35 much more used to small children and is housebroken
compared to a kitten or puppy," she says.

If you have never owned a pet, consider getting one from
Maiden Point. There are many benefits, starting with your
health. A study done at the State University of New York at
40 Buffalo in 2001 found that dog and cat owners with high
blood pressure who were in stressful job situations had
lower increases in pressure than people without pets.

There is a very practical reason to consider adopting
from the Maiden Shelter. A "designer" dog or cat can easily
45 cost $500 to $800. At Maiden Point, says Raleigh, for a
mere $100 you can get a cat or dog that is already spayed
or neutered, a month's supply of pet food, a safety collar or
flea collar, and a free check-up with a veterinarian. In case
you have your heart set on a certain breed, Raleigh says that
50 many popular breeds, such as labs, beagles, and Siamese
cats, occasionally turn up at the shelter.

5 So if you're pet-shopping, make Maiden Point Shelter
(555-555-2000 or www.maidenpointshelter.org) your first
stop. You can fill out a short application, get your references
55 checked, and go home with a pet the same day. The shelter
is open weekdays from 9:00 to 5:30 p.m. and Saturdays
from 10:00 a.m. through 3:00. The pet you save will reward
you with many years of love, gratitude, and good health.

4 The author describes the benefits of owning
older pets. These details provide answers to reader
counter-arguments about adopting older animals.

Try It! The author uses a quotation
to address reader counter-arguments.
Do you think stating someone's exact
words might help to convince the
reader? Why or why not?

5 In her **conclusion,** the author includes a
clear call to action by inviting readers to help
solve the problem.

Try It! Why do you think the author
included a telephone number and Web
site in her call to action?

**COLLEGE AND CAREER READINESS
STANDARDS**

Reading (A)(9) Identify and analyze the
audience, purpose, and message of an
informational or persuasive text.

STUDENT MODEL Op-Ed Piece

With a small group, take turns reading the Student Model aloud. As you read, practice newly acquired vocabulary by correctly producing the word's sound. Ask yourself if you find the writer's arguments convincing. Identify the evidence that the writer uses to support his ideas.

Use a Reader's Eye

Now, reread the Student Model. On your copy of the Student Model, use the Reader's Response Symbols to react to what you read.

Reader's Response Symbols

+ **I strongly agree with this.**

− **I strongly disagree with this.**

? **I have a question about this.**

! **Wow! That is cool/weird/ interesting.**

Collaborate with a partner to express your opinions and share your responses to the Student Model. Take notes and discuss responses that were the same for both of you, and that were different.

There Is Something You Can Do About TRAFFIC

by Xander Johnson

"Traffic is just one of life's inconveniences. Sure, it's frustrating, but what can you really do about it?" This was how my mom responded to my question about the traffic she encounters on
5   her daily commute to work. The traffic not only is a frustration for her as she sits in her car waiting, but also for our family as we sit at home waiting for her. Frequently, we end up eating dinner on our own because she gets home too late to join us.

10   Traffic is more than an inconvenience. According to the Department of Transportation, the average commute time one way has expanded from twenty or thirty minutes to as much as three hours per day. As a result of all this time on the road, we are
15   using up too much fuel and polluting the airways. By showing people what they can do to decrease the amount of traffic and giving them incentives to make changes, we can fix the traffic problem.

First, each of us can explore mass transit options,
20   and use them. Employers can help by promoting four-day workweeks and staggering work hours. People object to carpooling, but many will not if there is a tax incentive involved. If we write to our legislators, we can make this happen.

25   Finally, once we are on those traffic-snarled freeways, we can practice simple courtesy, allowing cars in when they clearly need to enter. Department

1

of Transportation studies of so-called "synchronicity" show that a courteous approach keeps traffic
30 flowing faster than fighting for position. As a final step, we should provide financial incentives for people who choose to live close enough to their work that they can commute on foot or by bicycle.

Next time you are sitting in a traffic jam, remember
35 that it not only affects the people on the road. Traffic keeps people from their families and creates more stress. It also creates more stress on the environment. Each of us has to ask ourselves what we can do to solve this problem. We need to make these changes.
40 My mom has started taking the train home from work. She gets home earlier, and now the time that used to be spent in traffic is spent at home with us.

WRITING COACH

Online

www.TXWritingCoach.com

Interactive Model

Listen to an audio recording of the Student Model in the eText. Use the Reader's and Writer's Response Symbols with the eText tools to note what you read.

Use a Writer's Eye

Now evaluate the piece as a writer. On your copies of the Student Models, use the Writer's Response Symbols to react to what you read. Identify places where the student writer uses characteristics of an effective op-ed piece.

Writer's Response Symbols

C.T.   **Clearly stated thesis**

P.A.   **Strong persuasive arguments**

S.E.   **Effective and credible supporting evidence**

C.A.   **Good responses to readers' counter-arguments**

COLLEGE AND CAREER READINESS STANDARDS

Reading (A)(5) Analyze the presentation of information and the strength and quality of evidence used by the author, and judge the coherence and logic of the presentation and the credibility of the argument.

2

Your Turn > **Feature Assignment: Op-Ed Piece**

Prewriting

Plan a first draft of your op-ed piece by determining an appropriate topic. Select from the Topic Bank or come up with an idea of your own.

 ## Choose From the Topic Bank

TOPIC BANK

School Issues Think about a controversial issue at your school, such as the price of lunches or the quality of the food, class schedules, or attendance policies. Take a stand on a school issue. Write an essay supporting your position and be sure to provide reasons and examples.

Recycling Some people think that all households should be required to recycle paper, glass and plastic. Other people think that recycling should be a choice, not a requirement. Write an op-ed piece that supports your position on whether or not recycling should be voluntary.

Get up and move. Some parents think spending a lot of time on the computer can be unhealthy for their children. So, they limit the amount of time their children can spend on the computer each day. Write an essay in which you state and support your position on limiting the time children spend playing computer games each day.

 ## Choose Your Own Topic

Determine an appropriate topic on your own by using the following **range of strategies** to generate ideas.

Interview and Research

- Interview friends and family members about the issues they feel are important. Take notes on the main points they share.
- Search your library's database and the Internet using these notes. Did you produce any results that spark your interest?

Review your responses and choose a topic.

Narrow Your Topic

Choosing a topic that is too broad results in writing that is general and unfocused.

Apply It! Use a graphic organizer like the one shown to narrow your topic.

- Write your general topic in the top box, and keep narrowing your topic as you move down the chart.
- Your last box should hold your narrowest or "smallest" topic, the new focus of your op-ed piece.

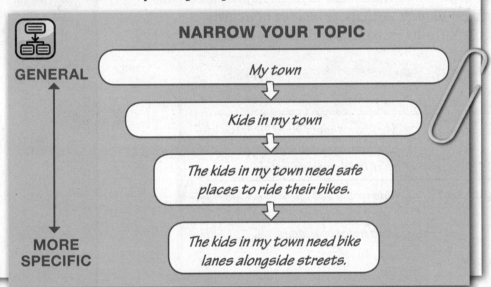

NARROW YOUR TOPIC

GENERAL

My town

Kids in my town

The kids in my town need safe places to ride their bikes.

MORE SPECIFIC

The kids in my town need bike lanes alongside streets.

Consider Your Audience and Purpose

Before writing your persuasive essay, think about your audience and purpose. Consider the way other people may view your topic as you ask yourself these questions.

Questions for Audience	Questions for Purpose
• Who is my audience?	• What opinion do I want to state?
• What might they need to know to understand my topic fully?	• How will I include and respond to others' views, concerns, and counter-arguments?
• What **views, concerns, and counter-arguments** might they have about my topic?	• What do I want the audience to do?

 Focus on the TEKS

Writing

(14)(A) Plan a draft by determining appropriate topics through a range of strategies.

(18)(B) Write a persuasive essay to the appropriate audience that considers the views of others and anticipates reader concerns and counter-arguments.

COLLEGE AND CAREER READINESS STANDARDS

Writing (A)(2) Generate ideas and gather information relevant to the topic and purpose, keeping careful records of outside sources.

Plan Your Piece

You will use a graphic organizer like the one shown to state your thesis, organize your arguments, and identify details. When it is complete, you will be ready to write your first draft.

Develop a Clear Thesis To keep your position and controlling idea clearly before your audience, review your notes and **develop a clear thesis**—one sentence that states your position or sums up your argument. Add your thesis statement to a graphic organizer like the one shown.

Logically Organize Your Arguments Complete the graphic organizer to organize your arguments from least to most important. **Consider the views of others as you anticipate reader concerns and counter-arguments.** Be sure to respond convincingly to each.

DEVELOP YOUR PERSUASIVE ARGUMENTS

Clear Thesis	My town should build bike lanes alongside streets so that kids can ride safely.
First Persuasive Argument	Kids would get more exercise riding their bikes if there were more bike lanes.
Supporting Evidence/ Details	
Second Persuasive Argument	Kids would have fewer bike accidents if there were more bike lanes.
Supporting Evidence/ Details	
Readers' Counter-arguments	Bike lanes make car lanes too narrow.
Response to Counter-arguments	

Gather Details

To provide supporting evidence for their arguments, writers use many kinds of details. Look at these examples:

- **Logical Reasoning:** *There are too many bike accidents in our town. Bike lanes reduce accidents. Therefore, we need more bike lanes.*

- **Statistics:** *After a nearby town built bike lanes, bike accidents were cut in half.*

- **Expert Opinions:** *Public Safety Officer Miller believes that bike lanes will make kids safer.*

- **Personal Observations:** *I feel much safer when I'm biking in a bike lane.*

Good writers are careful to **differentiate between fact and opinion,** supporting their opinions with reliable facts that help prove their points.

- A **fact** is something that actually happened or can be proven.

- An **opinion** is a person's judgment or belief about something.

Try It! Read the Mentor Text excerpt and identify which details the author used to support her argument.

 MENTOR TEXT from **Looking for a Pet?**
page 174; lines 24–29

> She points out that pets from pet stores have often been raised in unclean, unhealthy, crowded conditions, especially dogs from so-called "puppy mills." In contrast, the shelter pets are spayed and neutered, and treated for problems such as heartworm and fleas, before they are adopted out.

 Apply It! Review the types of support a persuasive writer can use. Then identify at least one detail for each of your arguments.

- Review your details to differentiate between fact and opinion. Check that opinions are supported by facts, and record the source of each fact.

- Add these details to your graphic organizer. Be sure to match each detail to the right argument so that your evidence is logically organized to support your viewpoint.

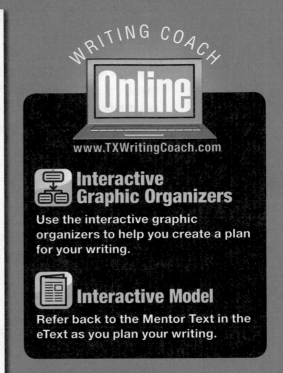

WRITING COACH

Online
www.TXWritingCoach.com

Interactive Graphic Organizers

Use the interactive graphic organizers to help you create a plan for your writing.

Interactive Model

Refer back to the Mentor Text in the eText as you plan your writing.

Focus on the TEKS

Writing

(14)(A) Plan a first draft by developing a thesis or controlling idea.

(18)(A–C) Write persuasive texts to influence the attitudes or actions of a specific audience on specific issues.

COLLEGE AND CAREER READINESS STANDARDS

Writing (A)(3) Evaluate relevance, quality, sufficiency, and depth of preliminary ideas and information, organize material generated, and formulate a thesis.

Drafting

During the drafting stage, you will start to write your ideas for your op-ed piece. You will follow an outline that provides an **organizational strategy** that will help you build on ideas to write a **focused, organized, and coherent** op-ed piece.

The Organization of an Op-Ed Piece

The chart shows an organizational strategy for an op-ed piece. Look back at how the Mentor Text follows this organizational strategy. Then, use this chart to help you outline your draft.

Outline for Success

I. Introduction

See Mentor Text, p. 174.

- Lead
- Clear thesis or position

Grab Your Reader

- A lead is an interesting opening that grabs readers' attention. A lead can ask a question, use an anecdote from your research, present a hypothetical situation, or provide a strong detail.
- A thesis states your position on the issue so that your audience knows what you are supporting.

II. Body

See Mentor Text, pp. 174–175.

- Persuasive arguments
- Logically organized supporting evidence
- Reader concerns and counter-arguments that are proven wrong or shown to be less important than your arguments

Build Your Case

- Writing one paragraph for each argument and its supporting evidence allows readers to easily follow your points. Don't forget to address opposing views.
- Ordering the paragraphs from least to most important will help you build your argument toward the most persuasive point.

III. Conclusion

See Mentor Text, p. 175.

- Restatement of position
- Memorable ending, such as a call to action

Wrap It Up

- Restating your position, echoing the language of your thesis statement, will help cement it in readers' minds.
- Call on your audience to take some kind of action. Make your call to action a concrete suggestion, naming people, places, events, and activities.

Start Your Draft

Use this checklist to help you complete your draft. Use the graphic organizer that shows your thesis, persuasive arguments, and supporting evidence, and the Outline for Success as guides.

While drafting, aim at writing your ideas, not on making your writing perfect. Remember, you will have the chance to improve your draft when you revise and edit.

√ Start by drafting a lead, the opening sentences that grab your readers' attention.

√ Continue to build your **introduction** by telling readers what to expect in the rest of your op-ed piece. Include a clear **thesis** statement.

√ Shape the **body** of your op-ed piece by **logically organizing** your ideas.

√ Develop a focused paragraph for each argument and its supporting evidence.

√ Include paragraphs that consider and respond to other views by answering readers' questions, concerns, and **counter-arguments**.

√ Remember to support opinions with facts and to use **transitional words** such as *first, next,* and *finally* to tie paragraphs together.

√ End with a strong **conclusion** that restates your **position** and leaves readers convinced that your ideas are right.

√ Finish on a powerful note by making a **call to action** or a forceful statement that will leave your audience thinking.

WRITING COACH

Online

www.TXWritingCoach.com

Interactive Model

Outline for Success View pop-ups of Mentor Text selections referenced in the Outline for Success.

Interactive Writing Coach™

Use the Interactive Writing Coach to receive the level of support you need:

• Write one paragraph at a time and submit each one for immediate, detailed feedback.

• Write your entire first draft and submit it for immediate, personalized feedback.

Focus on the TEKS

Writing

(14)(B) Develop drafts by choosing an appropriate organizational strategy and building on ideas to create a focused, organized, and coherent piece of writing.

(18)(A–C) Write persuasive texts to influence the attitudes or actions of a specific audience on specific issues.

Revising: Making It Better

Now that you have finished your first draft, you are ready to revise. Think about the "big picture" of **audience, purpose, and genre**. You can use your Revision RADaR as a guide for making changes to improve your draft. Revision RADaR provides four major ways to improve your writing: (R) replace, (A) add, (D) delete, and (R) reorder.

Kelly Gallagher, M. Ed.

KEEP REVISION ON YOUR RADaR

Read part of the first draft of the Student Model "There Is Something You Can Do About Traffic." Then look at questions the writer asked himself as he thought about how well his draft addressed **issues of audience, purpose, and genre**.

There Is Something You Can Do About TRAFFIC

When I asked my mom about the traffic she encounters on her daily commute to work, she told me that it's an avoidable inconvenience that she needs to put up with. The traffic is not only an inconvenience for her as she sits in her car waiting, but also for our family as we sit at home waiting for her. Frequently, we end up eating dinner on our own because she gets home too late to join us.

Does the introduction grab my audience?

Traffic is more than an inconvenience. As a result of all the time drivers spend on the road, we are using up too much fuel and polluting the airways.

Does my thesis statement clearly identify the issue and my purpose or opinion?

By showing people what they can do to decrease the amount of traffic and giving them incentives to make changes, we can probably lessen the traffic problem.

First, each of us can explore mass transit options, and use them. Employers can help by promoting four-day workweeks and staggering working hours. If we write to our legislators, we can make this happen.

Have I included persuasive arguments? Have I anticipated and answered reader counter-arguments?

Now look at how the writer applied Revision RADaR to write an improved second draft.

There Is Something You Can Do About TRAFFIC

2ND DRAFT

"Traffic is just one of life's inconveniences. Sure, it's frustrating, but what can you really do about it?" This was how my mom responded to my question about the traffic she encounters on her daily commute to work. The traffic not only is a frustration for her as she sits in her car waiting, but also for our family as we sit at home waiting for her. Frequently, we end up eating dinner on our own because she gets home too late to join us.

R *Replaced a dull secondhand description with a more interesting quotation and an explanation of it*

Traffic is more than an inconvenience. The average commute time one way has expanded from twenty or thirty minutes to as much as three hours per day. As a result of all this time on the road, we are using up too much fuel and polluting the airways. By showing people what they can do to decrease the amount of traffic and giving them incentives to make changes, we can fix the traffic problem.

A *Added a fact about the commute time to better explain the issue to my audience*

D *Deleted the word probably and*
R *replaced the word lessen with the word fix in order to make my thesis statement more forceful*

First, each of us can explore mass transit options, and use them. Employers can help by promoting four-day workweeks and staggering working hours. People object to carpooling, but many will not if there is a tax incentive involved. If we write to our legislators, we can make this happen.

A *Added a possible counter-argument and a response to it*

 Apply It! Use Revision RADaR to revise your draft.

- First, determine if you have addressed the needs of your audience, explained your purpose for writing, and included the characteristics of the op-ed piece genre.
- Then apply Revision RADaR to make needed changes. Remember—you can use the steps in the strategy in any order.

 Focus on the TEKS

Writing (14)(C) Revise drafts after rethinking how well questions of purpose, audience, and genre have been addressed.

Look at the Big Picture

Use the chart and your analytical skills to evaluate how well each section of your op-ed piece addresses **purpose, audience, and genre**. When necessary, use the suggestions in the chart to revise your piece.

Section	Evaluate	Revise
Introduction	• Check the **lead**. Will it grab readers' attention and make them want to read more?	• Make your lead more interesting by adding a question, anecdote, quotation, or strong detail.
	• Make sure the **thesis** clearly identifies the issue and states your opinion of it.	• To clearly identify the issue or state your opinion forcefully, turn the thesis statement into a question and answer the question by stating your opinion.
Body	• Check that you have organized your **persuasive arguments** in a logical way that will be clear to your readers.	• Rearrange arguments so that your second strongest argument is first, the weaker arguments are in the middle, and the strongest argument is last.
	• Underline details that offer **supporting evidence**. Draw a line from each detail to the argument it supports.	• Rearrange any detail that is not in the same paragraph as the argument it supports. When necessary, add or take out details.
	• Check that **supporting evidence** includes facts and differentiates between fact and opinion.	• Add facts where needed to strengthen your arguments and back up your opinion.
	• Review reader concerns and **counter-arguments**. Determine if you have anticipated each one.	• Answer each of your readers' likely concerns and counter-arguments with strong details.
Conclusion	• Check the **restatement** of your position.	• If necessary, restate your position more clearly.
	• Check that your **conclusion** ends on a memorable note.	• Add a quotation, a call to action, an insight, or a forceful statement to conclude your op-ed piece.

Focus on Craft: Precise Word Choice

Making **precise word choices** is an effective way to influence the attitudes and actions of your audience on a specific issue. Precise words are more convincing than vague or overly general words. Compare, for example, the vague and precise words in these word pairs: *bad/harmful, hard/backbreaking, nice/gratifying.*

Think about precise word choice as you read the following sentences from the Mentor Text.

 MENTOR TEXT from **Looking for a Pet?**
page 175; lines 43–45

There is a very practical reason to consider adopting from the Maiden Shelter. A "designer" dog or cat can easily cost $500 to $800.

Try It! Now, ask yourself these questions. Record your answers in your journal.

- Does the first sentence sound convincing? Why or why not?
- Would the first sentence be more or less convincing if it read *There is a good reason to consider adopting from the Maiden Shelter?* Explain.

 Fine-Tune Your Draft

Apply It! Use the revision suggestions to prepare your final draft after rethinking how well questions of purpose, audience, and genre have been addressed.

- **Ensure Precise Word Choice** Say exactly what you mean. Use substitutes for words that are vague or imprecise to better describe and explain your points.
- **Ensure the Use of Effective Transitions** If necessary, add transition words and phrases such as *finally, next, although, therefore,* and *as mentioned earlier,* to signal to your readers how sentences and paragraphs are connected.

Peer Feedback Read your final draft to a group of peers. Ask them if they feel you have considered and responded to the views of others. Think about their responses and revise your final draft as needed.

WRITING COACH

Online

www.TXWritingCoach.com

Video
Learn more strategies for effective writing from program author Kelly Gallagher.

Online Journal
Try It! Record your answers in the online journal.

Interactive Model
Refer back to the Interactive Model as you revise your writing.

Interactive Writing Coach™
Revise your draft and submit it for feedback.

Focus on the TEKS

Writing

(14)(C) Revise drafts to ensure precise word choice and the use of effective transitions after rethinking how well questions of purpose, audience, and genre have been addressed.

(14)(E) Revise final draft in response to feedback from peers.

(18)(A-C) Write persuasive texts to influence the attitudes or actions of a specific audience on specific issues.

Editing: Making It Correct

When you edit your work, you polish your writing and correct any errors. Before editing your final draft, think about using a variety of sentence structures, including **simple, compound, and complex sentences.** In addition, check your use of **parallel grammatical structures** within sentences. Then edit your draft by correcting any factual errors and errors in grammar, mechanics, and spelling.

WRITE GUY *Jeff Anderson, M. Ed.*

WHAT DO YOU NOTICE?

Zoom in on Conventions Focus on sentence structures as you zoom in on the following lines from the Mentor Text.

> **MENTOR TEXT** from **Looking for a Pet?**
> page 174; lines 1–5
>
> Maiden Point Shelter is overflowing with cats and dogs. Every cage and kennel is filled to capacity, and heartrending meows and barks come from extra cages lining the hallways. The shelter is at its most overcrowded since it was opened in 1993.

Now, ask yourself: *Is the structure of each sentence the same or different?*

Perhaps you said that the structure of each sentence is different.

The first sentence is a **simple** sentence because it has a single main or independent clause. A main clause has a subject and a verb and can stand alone as a complete sentence.

The second sentence is a **compound sentence** because it has more than one main clause.

The third sentence is a **complex sentence** because it has a main clause and a subordinate or dependent clause, which is *since it was opened in 1993.* A subordinate clause has a subject and a verb but cannot stand alone as a complete sentence.

Partner Talk Discuss this question with a partner: *Why do you think the author varied the sentence structure in this passage?*

> To learn more about sentence structure, see Chapters 18–20 of your Grammar Handbook.

Grammar Mini-Lesson: Parallel Structures

To learn more, see Chapter 20.

Using parallel structures in a sentence means that equal ideas are expressed in words, phrases, clauses, or sentences of similar types. Study the following sentence from the Mentor Text. Notice how the author used parallel structures for the three verbs.

 MENTOR TEXT from **Looking for a Pet?** page 175; lines 54–55

> You can fill out a short application, get your references checked, and go home with a pet the same day.

 Try It! Tell whether each sentence is simple, compound, or complex. Then identify the parallel structures in each sentence. Write the answers in your journal.

1. Marcella is athletic, musical, and artistic.
2. One sister is interested in becoming a doctor, and the other is interested in becoming a lawyer.

Apply It! Edit your draft for grammar, mechanics, and spelling. Use an electronic or print dictionary to check your spelling. If necessary, rewrite some sentences to ensure that you have used a variety of complete sentences that include parallel structures.

Use the rubric to evaluate your piece. If necessary, rethink, rewrite, or revise.

Rubric for Persuasive Essay: Op-Ed Piece	Rating Scale			
	Not very			Very
Focus and Coherence: How clearly are the issue and your position stated?	1	2	3	4
Organization: How organized are your arguments and supporting evidence?	1	2	3	4
Development of Ideas: How persuasive is your evidence?	1	2	3	4
Voice: How authoritative and persuasive is your voice?	1	2	3	4
Conventions: How correct are your sentence types?	1	2	3	4

WRITING COACH
Online
www.TXWritingCoach.com

 Video
Learn effective editing techniques from program author Jeff Anderson.

 Online Journal
Try It! Record your answers in the online journal.

 Interactive Model
Refer back to the Interactive Model as you edit your writing.

 Interactive Writing Coach™
Edit your draft. Check it against the rubric and then submit it for feedback.

 Focus on the TEKS

Writing (14)(D) Edit drafts for grammar, mechanics, and spelling.

Conventions (19)(C) Use a variety of complete sentences that include parallel structures.

Conventions (21)(A) Spell correctly and use various resources to determine and check correct spellings.

Publishing

Give your op-ed piece a chance to change someone's mind—publish it! First, get your piece ready for presentation. Then, choose a way to **publish for the appropriate audience.**

Wrap Up Your Presentation

Is your piece handwritten or written on a computer? If your piece is handwritten, you may need to make a new, clean copy. If so, be sure to **write legibly.** Also be sure that your title grabs the reader's attention and indicates your main idea.

Publish Your Piece

Use the chart to identify a way to publish your piece.

If your audience is...	...then publish it by...
Students or adults at school	• Reading it over the school public address system • Posting your piece online and inviting responses
People in your neighborhood or city	• Submitting it to your local television news • Submitting it to your town newspaper

 Extend Your Research

Think more about the topic on which you wrote your op-ed piece. What else would you like to know about this topic?

- Brainstorm for several questions you would like to research and then consult, or discuss, with others. Then decide which question is your major research question.

- Formulate, or develop, a plan about how you will answer these questions. Decide where you will find more information—on the Internet, at the library, or through other sources.

- Finally, learn more about your topic by following through with your research plan.

 The Big Question: Why Write? What is your point of view? How did you determine if you convinced others?

MAKE YOUR WRITING COUNT

Create a Public Action Day at Your School

An op-ed piece often ends with a call to action that asks readers to do something about an important issue. Help make your school a place where people are organized to take action.

With a group, produce a **multimedia presentation** with text and graphics about the topic of one op-ed piece. Your presentation should use presentation software or a poster to communicate your message clearly using both words and visuals.

Here's your action plan.

1. Set objectives for each group meeting and roles for each member.

2. First, review your peers' op-ed pieces. Choose a few pieces about issues that interest the group. Add a statement to each announcing a "public action" day about the issues.

3. Submit the information to your school and/or local newspaper.

4. Work together to make your presentation. You should include the following in the slideshow or poster display:

   - Words and images that inform people about the issue
   - Several resources such as Web sites and books
   - Persuasive techniques that spark people's interest in the issue
   - A level of formality that is right for the context of your presentation and that will most influence your listener's understanding.

Listening and Speaking With your group, explain why the issue is important and discuss the facts that support your position. Use specific details to describe and explain your ideas. Increase the specificity of your details based on the type of information you are delivering. List questions people may ask. If necessary, do more research on the topic. On Public Action Day, work to convince your audience to support your position.

WRITING COACH

Online

www.TXWritingCoach.com

Online Journal

Extend Your Research Record your research topics and ideas in the online journal.

Resource

Link to resources on 21st Century Learning for help in creating a group project.

Focus on the TEKS

Writing

(14)(E) Publish written work for appropriate audiences.

(17)(D) Produce a multimedia presentation involving text and graphics using available technology.

Conventions (20) Write legibly.

Research (22)(A) Brainstorm, consult with others, decide upon a topic, and formulate a major research question to address the major research topic.

COLLEGE AND CAREER READINESS STANDARDS

Speaking (A)(1) Understand how style and content of spoken language varies in different contexts and influences the listener's understanding.

Your Turn ▶ **Writing for Media: Advertisements**

Advertisements

An **advertisement** is a persuasive message designed to sell a product, service, or viewpoint. Advertisements, or ads, appear in many forms of media. Print ads appear in newspapers and magazines and on signs and billboards. Ads are also broadcast on radio and TV, and posted on the Internet. When you understand advertising techniques used to influence you, you can make better decisions about buying or using a product or service, or adopting a viewpoint.

Try It! Study the picture and the text in the ad. Then, answer these questions. Record your answers in your journal.

1. What **product** is this ad selling?

2. What is the **concept** or main message behind this ad?

3. An ad usually contains a **hook**—a memorable slogan, attention grabbing image, or catchy jingle. What is the hook in this ad?

4. Who is the **target audience** for this ad?

5. An ad makes **claims** about the benefits of the product, service, or viewpoint it is selling. What claims does this ad make?

6. Some ads use celebrity **endorsements** by featuring a well-known person who recommends the product. What well-known person or figure is shown in this ad? How does this person help sell the product?

Extension Find another example of an advertisement, and compare it with this one.

Celebrity Chef Callie says, "Best's Butter makes it better

Create an Advertisement

Follow these steps to create your own ad. To plan your ad, review the graphic organizers on pages R24–R27 and choose one that suits your needs.

Prewriting

- Identify or make up a product or service to advertise.
- As you identify your target audience, anticipate the views and concerns of your audience.
- Choose one of these mediums: a television commercial, or a print or Internet ad.
- Invent a concept or main message for your advertisement, and build this message to create a slogan that provides a hook. Then, list the claims you will make about your product or service.
- List art, music, images, or special effects you will use. Consider using familiar images (a cowboy, a kitten, and so on), situations (a picnic, a day at the beach, and so on), and words or phrases to create your ad.

Drafting

- For a television ad, write a script, the dialogue spoken by actors. Indicate music and special effects in your script.
- For a print or Internet ad, use heads, or words set in larger type, to grab readers. Feature your hook in one or more of the heads. Lay out your ad to achieve an eye-catching look by arranging pictures and text and selecting fonts or type styles for the best effect.

Revising and Editing

Review your draft to ensure that events or ideas are organized logically. Make sure your concept is clearly presented. Take out material that distracts from your message. Check that spelling, grammar, and mechanics are correct.

Publishing

Using text and graphics, make a video recording of your commercial or create a poster for your print or Internet ad. Then, present it to the class.

> **Partner Talk**
>
> Before you start drafting, describe your ad to a partner. Ask for feedback about your plan. For example, is your slogan catchy? Monitor your partner's spoken language by asking follow-up questions to confirm your understanding.

 Focus on the TEKS

Writing (17)(D) Produce a multimedia presentation involving text and graphics using available technology.

Writing for Assessment

Many standardized tests include a prompt that asks you to write a persuasive essay. Use these prompts to practice. Respond using the characteristics of your op-ed piece. (See page 172.)

 Try It! To begin, read the **persuasive** prompt and the information on format and academic vocabulary. Use the ABCDs of On-Demand Writing to help you plan and write your essay.

Format

The prompt directs you to write a *persuasive essay.* Be sure to include an introduction with a clear thesis, body paragraphs with supporting evidence, and a conclusion that reinforces your opinion.

Persuasive Prompt

Your school board has announced that it will fund a new sport next year. Write a persuasive essay telling why a sport you choose should be funded. Support your opinion with examples and facts.

Academic Vocabulary

Remember that an *opinion* is a personal belief about something. A *fact* is something that actually happened or can be proven.

The ABCDs of On-Demand Writing

Use the following ABCDs to help you respond to the prompt.

Before you write your draft:

A ttack the prompt [1 MINUTE]

- Circle or highlight important verbs in the prompt. Draw a line from the verb to what it refers to.
- Rewrite the prompt in your own words.

B rainstorm possible answers [4 MINUTES]

- Create a graphic organizer to generate ideas.
- Use one for each part of the prompt if necessary.

C hoose the order of your response [1 MINUTE]

- Think about the best way to organize your ideas.
- Number your ideas in the order you will write about them. Cross out ideas you will not be using.

After you write your draft:

D etect errors before turning in the draft [1 MINUTE]

- Carefully reread your writing.
- Make sure that your response makes sense and is complete.
- Look for spelling, punctuation, and grammar errors.

More Prompts for Practice

Apply It! Respond to Prompts 1 and 2 by writing **persuasive essays** that influence the attitudes or actions of a specific audience on a specific issue. As you write, be sure to:

- Identify an appropriate **audience**
- Establish a clear **thesis** or position
- Anticipate and respond to the views, concerns, and **counter-arguments** of others
- Logically **organize** your arguments and evidence so that they support your viewpoint
- Differentiate between **fact** and **opinion,** and support all your opinions with facts

> **Prompt 1** Imagine that your school has a new program. Students who ride their bicycles to school receive points toward a service award. Write a persuasive essay stating your position on this program.

> **Prompt 2** Imagine that your school principal is planning to require that all students participate in cleaning up litter around the building. Write a persuasive essay stating your position on this issue.

Texas Test Prep Spiral Review: Expository Respond to Prompt 3 by writing an **expository essay**. Your essay should include:

- A clearly stated **purpose**, or controlling idea
- A logical **organization,** including an effective **introduction** and **conclusion**
- A variety of **sentence structures** and **rhetorical devices**
- Clear **transitions** to link ideas and paragraphs
- Appropriate **facts** and **details** without any extraneous information or inconsistencies
- Accurately **synthesized ideas** from several sources

> **Prompt 3** Sleep is essential for all humans. Write an essay about the effects of not getting enough sleep.

WRITING COACH

Online

www.TXWritingCoach.com

Interactive Writing Coach™

Plan your response to the prompt. If you are using the prompt for practice, write one paragraph at a time or your entire draft and then submit it for feedback. If you are using the prompt as a timed test, write your entire draft and then submit it for feedback

Remember **ABCD**

- **A**ttack the prompt
- **B**rainstorm possible answers
- **C**hoose the order of your response
- **D**etect errors before turning in the draft

 Focus on the TEKS

Writing

(18)(A–C) Write persuasive texts to influence the attitudes or actions of a specific audience on specific issues.

(17)(A) Write a multi-paragraph essay to convey information about a topic.

RESPONSE *to* LITERATURE

What Do You Think?

Authors have purposes for writing. Some authors write to inform. Some write to entertain. Others write to persuade.

Part of being an active reader is analyzing the author's purpose. You think about the author's purpose and find details that show how the author achieves that purpose.

Try It! Think about your favorite book. What do you think the author was trying to communicate by writing this book?

Consider these questions as you participate in an extended discussion with a partner. Take turns expressing your ideas and feelings.

- How did you feel when reading this book?
- How did the author achieve his or her purpose?
- Do you think the author did a good job achieving his or her purpose? Why or why not?
- What details support your answer?

What's Ahead

In this chapter, you will review two strong examples of an interpretative response essay: a Mentor Text and a Student Model. Then, using the examples as guides, you will write an interpretative response essay of your own.

www.TXWritingCoach.com

Online Journal

Try It! Record your answers and ideas in the online journal.

You can also record and save your answers and ideas on pop-up sticky notes in the eText.

Connect to the Big Questions

Discuss these questions with your partner:

1 What do you think? What do readers bring to a text that writers may not?

2 Why write? What should you write about to make others interested in a text?

Focus on the TEKS

Writing (17) Write responses to literary or expository texts that demonstrate the writing skills for multi-paragraph essays and provide sustained evidence from the text using quotations when appropriate.

INTERPRETATIVE RESPONSE

In this chapter, you will explore a special kind of interpretative response, the review of a short story. An interpretative response analyzes an author's work. It often examines story elements, such as theme and plot, as well as features, such as imagery and mood. It discusses what the work communicates to the reader. The reader states his or her opinions about the work and supports those opinions with details from the text.

You will develop your review of a short story by taking it through each of the steps of the writing process: prewriting, drafting, revising, editing, and publishing. You will also have an opportunity to write a movie review. To preview the criteria for how your review of a short story will be evaluated, see the rubric on page 215.

FEATURE ASSIGNMENT

Interpretative Response: Review of a Short Story

An effective interpretative response has these characteristics:

- A strong, interesting **focus or thesis statement**

- **Details** that are focused, organized, and coherent

- A **summary of important features** of the author's work

- **Sustained evidence,** such as examples and quotations from the text to defend and support ideas

- **Ideas and arguments** that demonstrate personal insights, judgments, and understanding of the text

- **Effective sentence structure** and correct spelling, grammar, and usage

A review of a short story also includes:

- an **analysis of story elements,** such as character, plot, setting, and theme

- details about the imagery and mood the author created

- summary of the author's message and overall opinion of the story

Other Forms of Interpretative Response

In addition to a review of a short story, there are other forms of interpretative response, including:

Blog comments on an author's Web site share readers' ideas about an author's work. Readers express their opinions and discuss their understanding of what an author's work means.

Comparison essays explore similarities and differences between two or more works of literature. For example, a comparison essay may compare how main characters in two stories handle a similar problem.

Letters to authors analyze an author's work and explain the reader's response to it. The reader shares with the author of the work his or her thoughts and feelings about the content of the work and about the author's writing style.

Response to literature essays analyze and interpret an author's work. These kinds of essays examine what an author states directly and indirectly and what those statements mean. Response to literature essays also judge how well an author has accomplished what he or she has set out to do.

Try It! For each audience and purpose described, choose a form, such as a letter to an author or a comparison essay, that is appropriate for conveying your intended meaning to the audience. Explain your choices.

- To show a teacher how two novels are alike
- To tell an author how much her poetry meant to you
- To persuade classmates to read a particular book

WRITING COACH Online

www.TXWritingCoach.com

Resource

Word Bank Listen to English and Spanish pronunciations of new words in the eText glossary.

Online Journal

Try It! Record your answers and ideas in the online journal.

WORD BANK

Affixes are word parts used to change the meaning of a root word. For example, the word *write* becomes *prewriting* when the prefix *pre-* and the suffix *-ing* are added to the root word *write*. Work with a partner. Take turns using each word in a sentence. If you are unsure of the meaning of a word, identify any roots or affixes that might help you infer its meaning. If you are still unsure, use the Glossary or a dictionary to check the definition.

analysis	plausible
consider	profound
offensive	reflect

COLLEGE AND CAREER READINESS STANDARDS

Reading (B)(2) Apply knowledge of roots and affixes to infer the meanings of new words.

MENTOR TEXT

Review of a Short Story

Learn From Experience

 After reading the review on pages 200–201, read the numbered notes in the margins to learn how the author presented her ideas.

Answer the *Try It!* questions online or in your notebook.

---

① The **introduction** provides background about Sandra Cisneros.

Try It! What does the reviewer mean when she says that Cisneros grew up "straddling two countries"?

② The reviewer **summarizes** an **important feature** of *The House on Mango Street,* supporting it with a **quotation** from Sandra Cisneros.

Try It! How is each story like a pearl? How is the book as a whole like a necklace?

③ The **thesis statement** provides a strong focus for the review.

Try It! What does the thesis statement reveal about the plot of *The House on Mango Street*?

Extension Find another example of a review of a short story, and compare it with this one.

From Sandra Cisneros: Latina Writer and Activist

by Caryn Mirriam-Goldberg

① Sandra Cisneros was born in Chicago, Illinois, but she was actually born into the traditions, histories, and languages of two countries: the United States and Mexico. Her father was Mexican, and her mother was
5 Mexican American. Her family spoke two languages and frequently journeyed to Mexico for long visits with her father's family. Cisneros grew up straddling two countries, each with its own challenges and gifts, each with its own way of defining Mexicans, Americans, and Mexican
10 Americans. . . .

    Each of the pieces [in Sandra Cisneros's *The House on Mango Street*] tells of the bittersweet life in a Chicago barrio. **②** While each chapter works as a story on its own, each is also part of the larger story. This structure, according to
15 Cisneros, was not an accident. She wanted to write a book that a reader could pick up, open to any chapter, and find a story that made its own sense. "You would understand each story like a little pearl, or you could look at the whole thing like a necklace," says Cisneros. "That's what I always knew
20 from the day that I wrote the first one. I said, "I'm going to do a whole series of these, and it's going to be like this, and it's all connected."

    ③ She succeeded in creating both pearls and a necklace linking them, but she did more than that. She told a story
25 of a girl similar to herself, named Esperanza, who found herself becoming an artist to escape "the trap of the barrio." Cisneros wanted to show people what life in the barrio was like as well as what it was not like. The book stood in sharp contrast to "those people who want to make our barrios look
30 like Sesame Street or some place really warm and beautiful," Cisneros says. At a time when homes like the one she grew up

in were either portrayed as "warm and beautiful" or ignored, Cisneros portrayed how poverty weighs people down, and how people may triumph anyway. . . .

35 Esperanza, a girl who believes in and hopes for a better life in *The House on Mango Street*, lives the everyday challenges of being poor and Mexican. ❹ But through her name, she helps readers see the hope buried under the trash and danger: "In English my name means hope,"
40 Esperanza says. "In Spanish it means too many letters. It means sadness, it means waiting. It is like the number nine. A muddy color. It is the Mexican records my father plays on Sunday mornings when he is shaving, songs like sobbing." Esperanza leads readers through the barrio,
45 always dreaming of a real house, one with stairs, several bathrooms, and a big yard full of trees and grass. She hopes, just like Cisneros hoped, for a house so that "we don't have to pay rent to anybody, or share the yard with the people downstairs, or be careful not to make too much noise, and
50 there isn't a landlord banging on the ceiling with a broom."
❺ Eventually both the fictional Esperanza and the real Cisneros find a home in their own hearts. And they make a promise to return and speak for the family and friends in the barrio they left behind.

WRITING COACH

Online

www.TXWritingCoach.com

Interactive Model

Listen to an audio recording of the Mentor Text in the eText. You can refer back to the Mentor Text whenever you need support in developing your own writing.

Online Journal

Try It! Answer the questions about the Mentor Text in the online journal.

❹ The author provides **relevant evidence** from the book, including a **quotation.**

Try It! How does the evidence support the thesis of the review?

❺ The **conclusion** reveals how Esperanza resolves her conflict.

Try It! Why is an examination of the book's resolution a logical way to end the review?

STUDENT MODEL

With a small group, take turns reading this Student Model aloud. As you read, practice newly acquired vocabulary by correctly producing the word's sound. Look for evidence in the text that supports your understanding of the review.

Use a Reader's Eye

Now, reread the Student Model. On your copy of the Student Model, use the Reader's Response Symbols to react to what you read.

Reader's Response Symbols

+ **I agree with this point.**

− **This isn't clear to me.**

? **I have a question about this.**

! **Well said!**

Partner Talk

Express your opinions, ideas, and feelings about the Student Model to a partner. Take notes on your partner's thoughts and discuss responses that were the same for both of you, as well as responses that were different.

Gary Soto's "Seventh Grade": Something We Can All Relate To

by Stephanie Chang

Have you ever liked someone so much that you tried too hard to get that person's attention? I have, and I bet you have, too. That's exactly what happens in Gary Soto's short story "Seventh

5 Grade." You'll laugh as you read about the things Victor does to get a girl named Teresa to notice him. This story is about what happens when you pretend to be something you are not. The characters in this story sound like people you know.

10 The story takes place on the first day of seventh grade. Victor and his friend Michael are thinking about silly ways, such as making faces, to get girls' attention. Victor has a major crush on Teresa and wants to get her attention.

15 Victor is like other kids our age. He is not sure how to act or what to say. When Teresa first greets him, saying, "Hi, Victor," his cheeks turn red as he says, "Yeah, that's me." He's embarrassed that he said something so silly and

20 gets frustrated. He wonders why he couldn't just say "something nice." This has happened to me too.

Later that day, in French class, the teacher asks if anyone knows French. Victor sees a chance to show off in front of the girl of his dreams. He raises

25 his hand, even though he doesn't know French. Unfortunately for him, the teacher asks him a

1

question in French. The author helps the reader imagine Victor's reaction when he writes: "Great rosebushes of red bloomed on Victor's cheeks."

30   Victor is lucky that Teresa doesn't know French, so he ends up impressing her. The reader knows Victor is thrilled because the "rosebushes" of shame on his cheeks become "bouquets of love"! His cheeks are still red but for another reason.

35   We've all been embarrassed at one time or another, and the author does a great job of showing how that happens. Not all of our embarrassments end on a happy note, but the happy ending of "Seventh Grade" makes you smile. At the same

40   time, you'll clearly see the author's point: you can save yourself a lot of worry and embarrassment if you just be yourself. You'll enjoy this story because it's easy to understand how the characters feel.

WRITING COACH

Online

www.TXWritingCoach.com

Interactive Model

Listen to an audio recording of the Student Model in the eText. Use the Reader's and Writer's Response Symbols with the eText tools to note what you read.

Use a Writer's Eye

Now, evaluate the piece as a writer. On your copy of the Student Model, use the Writer's Response Symbols to react to what you read. Identify places where the student writer uses characteristics of an effective review of a short story.

Writer's Response Symbols	
C.T.	**Clearly stated thesis**
I.A.	**In-depth analysis**
S.E.	**Effective supporting evidence**
E.Q.	**Effective quotations**

2

Your Turn

**Feature Assignment:
Review of a Short Story**

Prewriting

Plan a first draft of your review of a short story **by determining an appropriate topic.** You can select from the Topic Bank or come up with an idea of your own.

 Choose From the Topic Bank

TOPIC BANK

Response to Amy Tan's "Two Kinds" Choose one of the memorable characters in "Two Kinds" by Amy Tan. Write a review of the story in which you discuss the traits that make this character stand out.

Response to Plot Think of a book, short story, essay, or poem that you really liked or disliked. Write a review for your classmates explaining your opinion of the work. Include details to support your point of view.

Response to a Mentor Text Read the excerpt from *The Pigman & Me* by Paul Zindel on page 68. Write a review of the story in which you summarize the conflict between the two characters and discuss the characters' responses.

 Choose Your Own Topic

Determine an appropriate topic on your own by using the following **range of strategies** to generate ideas.

Thought and Discussion

- Discuss a favorite story with friends. Take notes about their ideas and feelings. How are their reactions alike? How do they differ?

- Think about a story that surprised you in some way. Consider the reasons why you were surprised. Compare your reaction with that of another student.

Review your responses and choose a topic.

Narrow Your Topic

If you choose a topic that is too broad, your writing will not have a clear focus.

Apply It! Use a graphic organizer like the one shown to narrow your topic.

- Write your general topic in the first box, and narrow your topic as you move down the chart.
- Your last box should hold your narrowest or "smallest" topic, the new focus of your review of a short story.

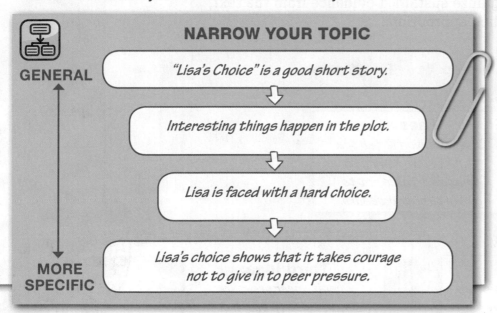

NARROW YOUR TOPIC

GENERAL

"Lisa's Choice" is a good short story.

↓

Interesting things happen in the plot.

↓

Lisa is faced with a hard choice.

↓

MORE SPECIFIC

Lisa's choice shows that it takes courage not to give in to peer pressure.

Consider Your Audience and Purpose

Before writing, think about your audience and purpose. Consider the views of others as you ask yourself these questions.

Questions for Audience	Questions for Purpose
• Who will read my review? My teacher? My classmates?	• What do I want my readers to know about the story?
• What will my audience need to know to understand my opinions?	• What ideas and feelings do I want to convey in my review?
• Is my audience familiar with the selection I will discuss?	• What approches should I use to show I understand the writer's audience and purpose?

Record your answers in your writing journal.

🌟 Focus on the TEKS

Writing (14)(A) Plan a first draft by determining appropriate topics through a range of strategies.

COLLEGE AND CAREER READINESS STANDARDS

Writing (A)(1) Determine effective approaches, forms, and rhetorical techniques that demonstrate understanding of the writer's purpose and audience.

Plan Your Piece

You will use a graphic organizer like the one shown to state your thesis, organize your ideas, and identify details. When it is complete, you will be ready to write your first draft.

Develop Your Thesis Think about your reaction to the short story. State your feelings and thoughts in a **clear thesis**. Add your thesis statement to the graphic organizer.

Logically Organize Your Supporting Evidence Use a graphic organizer to help you organize **sustained evidence from the text, including quotations when appropriate**.

Develop Your Response

Title: Lisa's Choice
Author: Jane Smith

Thesis
Lisa's decision to tell the truth shows how much courage it takes not to give in to peer pressure.

First Idea:
All the other students keep silent about what they saw.

Supporting Evidence:

Third Idea:
Despite peer pressure, Lisa decides to speak out.

Supporting Evidence:

Second Idea:
Peers pressure her to stay silent, and she doubts herself.

Supporting Evidence:

Gather Details

To support their ideas, writers **provide sustained evidence** from the text such as the types of details in these examples:

- **Quotations:** *"I have to do what's right," Lisa said.*
- **Details:** *The classroom was suddenly as silent as a graveyard, and the teacher's eyes followed Lisa like a spotlight.*
- **Examples:** *Jason tried to make a joke, but the other kids were too frightened to laugh.*
- **Relevant Information and Judgments:** *Lisa wasn't trying to be a hero. She didn't even like the accused girl.*
- **Personal Insights:** *The situation described could happen to anyone, in school or out of school.*

Try It! Read the Student Model excerpt and identify the evidence that the author uses to support her ideas.

 STUDENT MODEL from **Gary Soto's "Seventh Grade": Something We Can All Relate To**
page 203; lines 27–34

> The author helps the reader imagine Victor's reaction when he writes: "Great rosebushes of red bloomed on Victor's cheeks."
>
> Victor is lucky that Teresa doesn't know French, so he ends up impressing her. The reader knows Victor is thrilled because the "rosebushes" of shame on his cheeks become "bouquets of love"! His cheeks are still red but for another reason.

Apply It! Review the types of supporting evidence that can be used in a review of a short story. Then identify and write one piece of relevant evidence of each type.

- Review your evidence to make sure it supports your ideas. Be sure to include one or more pieces of each kind of sustained evidence from the text.
- Add your ideas and supporting evidence to your graphic organizer. Remember that your goal is to write a review that is logically organized with appropriate details.
- Be sure to make clear how your evidence supports your thesis.

 Focus on the TEKS

Writing

(14)(A) Plan a first draft by developing a thesis or controlling idea.

(17)(C) Write responses to literary or expository texts that provide sustained evidence from the text using quotations when appropriate.

COLLEGE AND CAREER READINESS STANDARDS

Writing (A)(2) Generate ideas and gather information relevant to the topic and purpose.

Drafting

During the drafting stage, you will start to write your ideas for your review of a short story. You will follow an outline that provides an **organizational strategy** that will help you **build on ideas to write a focused, organized, and coherent** review of a short story.

The Organization of an Interpretative Response

The chart shows an organizational strategy for an interpretative response. Look back at how the Mentor Text follows this organizational strategy. Then, use this chart to help you outline your draft.

Outline for Success

I. Introduction   See Mentor Text, p. 200.

- Strong opening paragraph
- Name of the work and the author
- Clear thesis statement

Grab Your Reader

- An interesting opening can make a strong statement, ask a question, or refer to a character or event in the author's work.
- Both the work about which you are writing and its author should be identified.
- The thesis statement focuses on your overall ideas about the text. The rest of your response will support your thesis.

II. Body   See Mentor Text, pp. 200–201.

- Introduction to and summary of the work
- Evidence from the text
- Analysis of elements
- Personal insights

Develop Your Ideas

- The important features of the work should be briefly summarized.
- Evidence from the text, including quotations and other examples, should support your ideas about the text.
- An analysis of story elements includes your thoughts of character, plot, setting, and theme.
- Your ideas and arguments should show your personal insights and judgments.

III. Conclusion   See Mentor Text, p. 201.

- Restatement of thesis in concluding paragraph
- Explanation of the significance of main points

Wrap It Up

- Briefly restating your thesis in slightly different wording reinforces your point.
- An explanation of the significance of your thesis or main points will leave readers with a clear understanding of your ideas and feelings.

Start Your Draft

Use this checklist to help you complete your draft. Use the graphic organizer that shows your thesis and supporting evidence, and the Outline for Success as guides.

While drafting, aim at writing your ideas, not on making your writing perfect. Remember, you will have the chance to improve your draft when you revise and edit.

√ Start with a strong **opening** that will grab your reader's interest.

√ Your **introduction** should **identify** the story, poem, or other work about which you're writing, as well as the author of the work.

√ Present your thesis statement.

√ The **body** of your review should demonstrate the writing skills for multi-paragraph essays by presenting your **ideas and opinions** in a logical way.

√ Be sure to also include a brief summary of key features of the work.

√ Your ideas and opinions should show your understanding of the text and be supported with **sustained evidence** from the text, including quotations.

√ Include an **analysis** of story elements that relate to your ideas, such as themes or specific plot events.

√ In your **conclusion**, restate or paraphrase your **thesis.**

√ End with a strong **final statement** that clearly expresses your thoughts and feelings about the work.

Interactive Model

Outline for Success View pop-ups of Mentor Text referenced in the Outline for Success.

Interactive Writing Coach™

Use the Interactive Writing Coach to receive the level of support you need:

• Write one paragraph at a time and submit each one for immediate, detailed feedback.

• Write your entire first draft and submit it for immediate, personalized feedback.

 Focus on the TEKS

Writing

(14)(B) Develop drafts by choosing an appropriate organizational strategy and building on ideas to create a focused, organized, and coherent piece of writing.

(17)(C) Write responses to literary or expository texts that provide sustained evidence from the text using quotations when appropriate.

Revising: Making It Better

Now that you have finished your first draft, you are ready to revise. Think about the "big picture" of **audience, purpose, and genre.** You can use the Revision RADaR strategy as a guide for making changes to improve your draft. Revision RADaR provides four ways to improve your writing: (R) replace, (A) add, (D) delete, and (R) reorder.

Kelly Gallagher, M. Ed.

KEEP REVISION ON YOUR RADaR

Read part of the first draft of the Student Model, "Gary Soto's 'Seventh Grade': Something We Can All Relate To." Then look at the questions the writer asked herself as she thought about how well her draft **addressed issues of audience, purpose, and genre.**

Gary Soto's "Seventh Grade": Something We Can All Relate To

Victor is not sure how to act or what to say. When Teresa first greets him, he says something silly. He's embarrassed that he said it and gets frustrated. He wonders why he couldn't just say "something nice."

In French class, the teacher asks if anyone knows French. Victor sees a chance to show off in front of the girl of his dreams. He raises his hand, even though he doesn't know French. Unfortunately for him, the teacher asks him a question in French.

The author shows Victor's embarrassment in this moment by using great imagery. Victor does his best to bluff his way out of the situation, but he fears he has made a fool of himself in front of Teresa. Victor is thrilled. Luckily, Teresa doesn't know French, so she actually *is* impressed.

Have I used supporting details, including quotations from the text? Do my ideas demonstrate insights and understanding of the text?

Have I included transitions to link paragraphs?

Have I used supporting details, such as examples from the text? Are my ideas presented in a logical order?

Now look at how the writer applied Revision RADaR to write an improved second draft.

Gary Soto's "Seventh Grade": Something We Can All Relate To

2ND DRAFT

Like most people our age, though, Victor is not sure how to act or what to say. When Teresa first greets him, saying, "Hi, Victor," he blushes and says, "Yeah, that's me." He's embarrassed that he said something so silly and gets frustrated. He wonders why he couldn't just say "something nice." I know that this has happened to me and my friends many times!

A *Added information to show my understanding of the text*
R *Replaced vague language with quotations from the text*

Later that day, in French class, the teacher asks if anyone knows French. Victor sees a chance to impress the girl of his dreams. He raises his hand, even though he doesn't know French. Unfortunately for him, the teacher asks him a question in French.

A *Added a transition to show that time has gone by and to link the ideas in the two paragraphs*

The author helps the reader imagine Victor's reaction when he writes: "Great rosebushes of red bloomed on Victor's cheeks."

R *Reordered sentences to present information more clearly*

Victor is lucky that Teresa doesn't know French, so he ends up impressing her. The reader knows Victor is thrilled because the "rosebushes" of shame on his cheeks become "bouquets of love"! His cheeks are still red but for another reason.

Apply It! Use your Revision RADaR to revise your draft.

- First, ask yourself: Have I addressed the needs of my audience, made clear my purpose for writing, and included the characteristics of the interpretative response genre?
- Then, apply the Revision RADaR strategy to make needed changes. Remember—you can use the strategy steps in any order.

Focus on the TEKS

Writing (14)(C) Revise drafts after rethinking how well questions of purpose, audience, and genre have been addressed.

Look at the Big Picture

Use the chart and your analytical skills to evaluate how well each section of your review of a short story addresses **purpose, audience, and genre.** When necessary, use the suggestions in the chart to revise your piece.

Section	Evaluate	Revise
Introduction	• Check the **opening.** It should grab readers' interest and make them want to read on.	• Make your opening more interesting by writing a strong first sentence or asking a rhetorical question.
	• Make sure the **thesis** clearly expresses the main idea of your response.	• Does your thesis reflect your thoughts about the story and the controlling idea of your review? If not, rewrite it so that it does.
Body	• Make sure that you have included **sustained evidence** from the text to defend and support ideas.	• Add more supporting evidence as needed. Look for key quotations that support your ideas.
	• Check that you've included ideas and arguments that show personal insights, judgments, and **understanding** of the text.	• Think about the meaning of the story. Add sentences that convey your understanding to readers, if necessary.
	• Make sure you have included an **analysis** of story elements, such as character, plot, setting, and theme.	• Add specific information about story elements to develop and support your main ideas.
	• Check that you have **logically organized** your ideas and supporting evidence. Make sure that you have not included any unnecessary information.	• Reorder text so that sentences and paragraphs are logically organized. Delete information that does not relate to the controlling idea.
Conclusion	• Check the **restatement** of your thesis.	• If necessary, discuss your restatement with a classmate and ask for suggestions.
	• Check that your **conclusion** leaves readers with a clear understanding of your thoughts.	• Add a final statement that sums up how you feel about the work or why it is meaningful to you.

Focus on Craft: Consistent Point of View

Your audience will be confused if you don't have a **consistent point of view** in your review of a short story. Many reviews are written in the first-person point of view, using words such as *I* and *we*. Other reviews are written in the second-person point of view, using *you* and *your*, or in third-person point of view, using *he*, *she*, and *it*.

Think about point of view as you read the following example from the Student Model.

 STUDENT MODEL from **Gary Soto's "Seventh Grade": Something We Can All Relate To** page 202; lines 5–8

> You'll laugh as you read about the things Victor does to get a girl named Teresa to notice him. This story is about what happens when you pretend to be something you are not.

 Try It! Now, ask yourself these questions:

- What point of view does the author of the Student Model use? Why might that be a good choice for a review of a short story?

- Why might a change in point of view confuse the reader?

Fine-Tune Your Draft

Apply It! Use the revision suggestions to prepare your final draft **after rethinking how well questions of purpose, audience, and genre have been addressed.**

- **Use Consistent Point of View** Avoid changing point of view within paragraphs or from one paragraph to the next.

- **Improve Sentence Structure** Break or combine sentences to achieve a variety of sentence structures such as simple, compound, and complex.

Peer Feedback Show your final draft to a group of your peers and ask if your evidence supports your main idea. Listen carefully to their ideas and make revisions as needed.

WRITING COACH
Online
www.TXWritingCoach.com

Video
Learn more strategies for effective writing from program author Kelly Gallagher.

Online Journal
Try It! Record your answers in the online journal.

Interactive Model
Refer back to the Interactive Model as you revise your writing.

Interactive Writing Coach™
Revise your draft and submit it for feedback.

Focus on the TEKS

Writing

(14)(C) Revise drafts for consistent point of view and the use of simple, compound, and complex sentences after rethinking how well questions of purpose, audience, and genre have been addressed.

(14)(E) Revise final draft in response to feedback from peers.

Editing: Making It Correct

Use the editing process to polish your work and correct errors. It is often helpful to work with a partner when editing your drafts.

Before editing, think about how **prepositions and prepositional phrases** may **influence subject-verb agreement.** Also think about the importance of using **consistent tenses** so that readers can follow the order, or sequence, of events. Then, edit your draft by correcting factual errors and errors in **grammar, mechanics, and spelling.** Use a dictionary to check your spelling.

 WRITE GUY *Jeff Anderson, M. Ed.*

WHAT DO YOU NOTICE?

Zoom in on Conventions Focus on subject-verb agreement as you zoom in on this sentence from the Student Model.

To learn more about subject-verb agreement, see Chapter 23 of your Grammar Handbook.

 STUDENT MODEL from **Gary Soto's "Seventh Grade": Something We Can All Relate To**
page 203; lines 32–33

> The "rosebushes" of shame on his cheeks become "bouquets of love"!

Now, ask yourself: *What role does the word "rosebushes" play in the sentence?*

Perhaps you said that "rosebushes" is the subject of the sentence. The verb is *become.* Two prepositional phrases separate the subject and verb: *of shame* and *on his cheeks.*

A prepositional phrase is a group of words that begins with a preposition and contains a noun or pronoun that is the object of the preposition. Subjects and verbs must agree even when they are separated by prepositional phrases, as in the Student Model.

The subject of a sentence is never part of a prepositional phrase. So, neither *shame* nor *cheeks* can be the subject. The plural subject *rosebushes* agrees with the plural verb *become.* A singular subject agrees with a singular verb, for example: *The* rosebush *of shame on his cheek* becomes *"a bouquet of love"!*

Partner Talk Discuss this question with a partner: *How do perpositions and prepositional phrases affect subject-verb agreement?*

Grammar Mini-Lesson: Consistent Tenses

To learn more, see page 284.

Tenses are verb forms that tell if an action takes place in the past, present, or future. It is important to **use tenses consistently** so readers can follow your writing. Sometimes, though, tenses must vary to show sequence, or the order of events. For example: *Last year, he* studied *Spanish, but this year he* studies *French.* Notice how the Student Model author uses present tense verbs consistently to help readers follow the order of events.

 STUDENT MODEL | from **Gary Soto's "Seventh Grade": Something We Can All Relate To**
pages 202–203; lines 23–27

> Victor sees a chance to show off in front of the girl of his dreams. He raises his hand, even though he doesn't know French. Unfortunately for him, the teacher asks him a question in French.

Try It! Complete each sentence using a consistent verb tense. Write the answers in your journal.

1. A box of candies (sat) on the table, and I (know) they are delicious.
2. After we watched the game, we (drive) into town and (eat) dinner.

Apply It! **Edit your draft for grammar, mechanics, and spelling**. Make sure you have used a **variety of complete sentences** that includes consistent tenses. Make sure that **prepositional phrases** do not interrupt **subject-verb agreement**.

Use the rubric to evaluate your piece. If necessary, rethink, rewrite, or revise.

Rubric for Interpretative Response: Review of a Short Story	Rating Scale			
	Not very		Very	
Focus and Coherence: How well does your response present a focused statement about the work?	1	2	3	4
Organization: How clearly organized is your analysis?	1	2	3	4
Development of Ideas: How effectively have you used evidence from the text to support your opinions?	1	2	3	4
Voice: How well have you engaged the reader and sustained his or her interest?	1	2	3	4
Conventions: How correct are your prepositions? Have you used consistent tenses?	1	2	3	4

WRITING COACH

Online

www.TXWritingCoach.com

Video

Learn effective editing techniques from program author Jeff Anderson.

Online Journal

Try It! Record your answers in the online journal.

Interactive Model

Refer back to the Interactive Model as you edit your writing.

Interactive Writing Coach™

Edit your draft. Check it against the rubric and then submit it for feedback.

Focus on the TEKS

Writing (14)(D) Edit drafts for grammar, mechanics, and spelling.

Conventions

(19)(A) Identify, use, and understand prepositions and prepositional phrases and their influence on subject-verb agreement.

(19)(C) Use a variety of complete sentences (e.g., simple, compound, complex) that include consistent tenses.

(21)(A) Spell correctly, including using various resources to determine and check correct spellings.

COLLEGE AND CAREER READINESS STANDARDS

Writing (A)(5) Edit writing for proper voice, tense, and syntax, assuring that it conforms to standard English when appropriate.

Publishing

Share the ideas expressed in your review—publish it! First, get your review ready for presentation. Then, choose a way to **publish it for the appropriate audience.**

Wrap Up Your Presentation

Now that you have finished your draft, add the final details. Include page numbers on each page of your final draft.

Publish Your Review

Use the chart to identify a way to publish your review.

If your audience is...	...then publish it by...
People in your community	• Submitting it to a local newspaper • Creating a multimedia presentation for kids at your local library
Students at school	• Reading it aloud in English class • Posting it online and inviting comments

 Extend Your Research

Think more about the topic of the story on which you wrote your review. What else would you like to know about this topic?

- Brainstorm for several questions you would like to research and then consult, or discuss, with others. Then, decide which question is your major research question.

- Formulate, or develop, a plan about how you will answer the question. Decide where you will find more information—on the Internet, at the library, or through other sources.

- Finally, learn more about your topic by following through with your research plan.

 The Big Question: Why Write? What should you write about to make others interested in a text?

Manage Your Portfolio You may wish to include your published review of a short story in your writing portfolio. If so, consider what this review reveals about your writing and your growth as a writer.

MAKE YOUR WRITING COUNT

Build an Advertisement for a Story of Your Choice

Reviews tell readers whether a story is worth reading. An advertisement for a story encourages readers to want to read it. Catch the attention of potential readers by creating an **advertisement for a story**.

In a group, choose one story review to turn into a **multimedia presentation** of an advertisement. The text of your ad should include the story's title, author, selling points, reviewer comment, and an excerpt. The ad should also include graphics. Create your ad in print or by using available technology.

Here's your action plan.

1. Analyze book ads in newspapers, magazines, or online.

2. With your group, choose a story review to turn into an advertisement. Take notes to refer to as you create the ad.

3. Use catchy phrases, an excerpt, and an image in your ad.

   - Highlight the selling points of the story, including a comment from the review.

   - Choose a short excerpt from the story to attract potential readers.

   - Display the title and author of the story.

4. Create a "cover" for the story (or the book it appears in) to include in the ad.

5. Present your advertisement to the class. If possible, post it on the class Web site.

Listening and Speaking Rehearse the presentation of your advertisement. Although your ad is based on text and graphics, try to bring these elements to life by speaking and gesturing expressively. Listen actively during the presentations of other groups so that you can analyze their ads and give positive feedback.

WRITING COACH

Online

www.TXWritingCoach.com

Online Journal

Extend Your Research Record your answers and ideas in the online journal.

Resource

Link to resources on 21st Century Learning for help in creating a group project.

Focus on the TEKS

Writing

(14)(E) Publish written work for appropriate audiences.

(17)(D) Produce a multimedia presentation involving text and graphics using available technology.

COLLEGE AND CAREER READINESS STANDARDS

Listening (B)(1) Listen critically and respond appropriately to presentations.

Speaking (A)(1) Understand how style and content of spoken language varies in different contexts and influences the listener's understanding.

Writing for Media: Movie Review

21st Century Learning

Movie Review

A **movie review** is an article or essay that discusses a movie, analyzes its story elements, and summarizes important features of the work. Movie reviews appear in newspapers and magazines, on television and radio, and on the Internet. A movie review presents the writer's opinions and supports them with evidence and quotations from the film. Movie reviews may either persuade readers that a film is worthwhile or discourage them from seeing it.

Try It! Study the movie review on this page. Then, answer the questions. Record your answers in your journal.

- What **film** is this movie review about?
- Who made the **movie?**
- What **type** of movie is it?
- What does the **writer** think about the movie? Why does the writer feel this way?
- What **evidence** does the writer use to defend and support his or her ideas and judgment?
- What **story elements** does the writer analyze?
- Would this review **encourage** you to see the movie? Why or why not?

Extension Find another example of a movie review, and compare it with this one.

Karl Johnson's latest sci-fi movie, *Door to Doom*, is his most action-packed film yet. It's also his silliest. Nothing in this movie is believable. The characters are brainless, and the plot makes no sense.

The movie's 16-year-old hero, Dylan, spends the entire movie whining and trying to convince the police that a blue-skinned alien has invaded his neighborhood. He draws this conclusion when he sees a terrifying-looking alien chasing Dylan's neighbor's dog. Despite the missing dog, specks of a strange kind of goo on the ground, and the picture Dylan snaps with his cell phone, no one believes him. "But I saw it happen," he tells the police again and again. "We'll check it out," they always reply, but they don't.

One by one, pets in Dylan's neighborhood vanish. Then his neighbors themselves begin to disappear. Still, the police refuse to investigate. It never occurs to Dylan that he should talk to some other adults or maybe call the newspaper. Instead, he tells only his friend, Jimmy, who suggests that they catch the alien.

From this point on, the plot gets only more ridiculous. Dylan and Jimmy make a series of unsafe decisions and incredibly pointless attempts to catch the alien. Unless you have time and money to waste, the *Door to Doom* is best left unopened.

Write a Movie Review

Follow these steps to write your own movie review. To plan your movie review, review the graphic organizers on pages R24–R27 and choose one that best suits your needs.

Prewriting

- Choose a movie you have recently seen and have strong feelings about—positive *or* negative. Consider why you feel as you do.
- Think about the kind of movie it is, such as a comedy or an adventure film.
- Identify the audience for the movie. Consider not only which people are sure to go see it but also which people *might* see it.
- Think about how to persuade people to see or avoid the movie.
- Consider what evidence from the movie you will use to support your opinion.

Drafting

- Begin with a strong opening. It should grab your readers' interest and express your main idea.
- Write a brief summary. Include an analysis of story elements, such as character and plot. Analyze how the film may have been influenced by myths or literature from a variety of world cultures.
- Defend and support your ideas and opinions with sustained evidence. Include quotations when appropriate.
- End with a strong statement that sums up your feelings.

Revising and Editing

Make sure that your ideas are logically organized and that you support them with details and examples. Be sure you present evidence in a clear and persuasive way. Also be sure to check that spelling, grammar, and mechanics are correct.

Publishing

Post your movie review on a school Web site, and invite classmates to share their opinions. You might also create a multimedia presentation for your class that combines your review with quotes and images from the film.

WRITING COACH

Online
www.TXWritingCoach.com

Online Journal

Try It! Record your answers in the online journal.

Interactive Graphic Organizers

Choose from a variety of graphic organizers to plan and develop your project.

Partner Talk

Before you start drafting, summarize the movie you are reviewing. Then describe and explain your planned movie review to a partner and ask for feedback. For example, you might ask whether you've chosen convincing evidence to support your opinion. Monitor your partner's spoken language by asking follow up questions to confirm your understanding.

 Focus on the TEKS

Writing (17)(D) Produce a multimedia presentation involving text and graphics using available technology.

COLLEGE AND CAREER READINESS STANDARDS

Reading (D)(2) Analyze the influence of myths, folktales, fables, and classical literature from a variety of world cultures on later literature and film.

Writing for Assessment

You may be asked to write to an **interpretative response** prompt. Use the prompts on these pages to practice. Your responses should include the same characteristics as your **review of a short story.** (See page 198.)

 Try It! To begin, read the prompt and the information on format and academic vocabulary. Use the ABCDs of On-Demand Writing to help you write your essay.

Format
The prompt directs you to write an *interpretative response* to a story, book, or poem. Make sure to create a fully developed introduction, body, and conclusion.

Interpretative Response Prompt
Write a critical review interpretative response of a short story, book, or poem you have read. Analyze and evaluate the work. Support your analysis and judgment with specific details, such as examples and quotations from the work.

Academic Vocabulary
Remember that an *analysis* of a story, book, or poem is a study of its elements and parts. Your *judgment* about the work is your opinion of it. Be sure to use key points from the text to support your analysis and opinion.

The ABCDs of On-Demand Writing

Use the following ABCDs to help you respond to the prompt.

Before you write your draft:

A ttack the prompt [1 MINUTE]

- Circle or highlight important verbs in the prompt. Draw a line from the verb to what it refers to.
- Rewrite the prompt in your own words.

B rainstorm possible answers [4 MINUTES]

- Create a graphic organizer to generate ideas.
- Use one for each part of the prompt if necessary.

C hoose the order of your response [1 MINUTE]

- Think about the best way to organize your ideas.
- Number your ideas in the order you will write about them. Cross out ideas you will not be using.

After you write your draft:

D etect errors before turning in the draft [1 MINUTE]

- Carefully reread your writing.
- Make sure that your response makes sense and is complete.
- Look for spelling, punctuation, and grammar errors.

More Prompts for Practice

Apply It! Respond to Prompts 1 and 2 by writing **interpretative responses** that use supporting **evidence from the text**. Be sure to:

- Express the main idea of your response in a clear **thesis statement**
- Summarize **important features of the work**
- Include **sustained evidence from the text to support ideas**
- Use **quotations from the text** when appropriate
- Analyze **story elements,** such as character, plot, and theme

Prompt 1 Many stories have memorable characters. Write an essay that compares and contrasts two characters from two different stories. Support your ideas with details from the texts.

Prompt 2 Most literary works express a theme. For instance, the theme for a work might be "forgiveness is the key to happiness." In an essay, interpret a theme in a short story, book, or poem you have read.

 Spiral Review: Persuasive Respond to Prompt 3 by writing a **persuasive essay** with a **clearly stated thesis or position.** Make sure your persuasive essay has all of the characteristics described on page 172, including:

- A goal to **influence** the attitudes or actions of a specific **audience** about the specific **issue**
- Anticipation of and response to the **concerns, views,** and **counter-arguments** of others
- Logically **organized** arguments and evidence that support a viewpoint
- Distinctions between **fact** and **opinion**

Prompt 3 Write a persuasive essay to convince someone that a particular season of the year is the best. Include types of weather and seasonal activities in your supporting evidence.

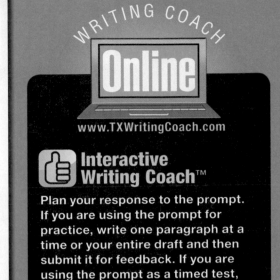

WRITING COACH

Online

www.TXWritingCoach.com

Interactive Writing Coach™

Plan your response to the prompt. If you are using the prompt for practice, write one paragraph at a time or your entire draft and then submit it for feedback. If you are using the prompt as a timed test, write your entire draft and then submit it for feedback.

Remember **ABCD**

Attack the prompt

Brainstorm possible answers

Choose the order of your response

Detect errors before turning in the draft

 Focus on the TEKS

Writing

(17)(C) Write responses to literary or expository texts that provide sustained evidence from the text using quotations when appropriate.

(18)(A-C) Write persuasive texts to influence the attitudes or actions of a specific audience on specific issues.

RESEARCH WRITING

What Do You Want To Know?

How do people find out more information about interesting topics? They do research to gather, organize, and present information.

One of the first steps of research writing is to identify a topic that interests you and then formulate open-ended research questions. Open-ended research questions ask what you want to find out about the topic. For example, if you want to find out more about the scientist in the photograph, you would first decide what you want to know.

Try It! Take a few minutes to brainstorm for some things you want to know about the scientist. Write them in a list.

Consider these questions as you work on your list.

- What do you want to know about the scientist?
- What do you want to know about the protective gear the scientist is wearing?
- What do you want to know about the machine the scientist is using?

Review your list of questions with a partner. Compare lists to determine if any questions overlap or if you can build off each other's ideas. Then, discuss where you would go to research answers to your questions.

What's Ahead

In this chapter, you will review a strong example of an informational research report. Then, using the example as guidance, you will develop your own research plan and write your own informational research report.

WRITING COACH

Online

www.TXWritingCoach.com

 Online Journal

Try It! Record your answers and ideas in the online journal.

You can also record and save your answers and ideas on pop-up sticky notes in the eText.

 Connect to the Big Questions

Discuss these questions with your partner:

1 **What do you think?** What kinds of scientific discoveries affect our lives the most?

2 **Why write?** Do you understand your subject well enough to write about it? How will you find out what all the facts are?

 Focus on the TEKS

(22)(A–B) Ask open-ended research questions and develop a plan for answering them.

(23)(A–E) Determine, locate, and explore the full range of relevant sources addressing a research question.

(24)(A–B) Clarify research questions and evaluate and synthesize collected information.

(25)(A–D) Organize and present ideas and information.

RESEARCH WRITING

Research writing is a way to gather information, and then synthesize, or combine, that information into a report for others to read. In this chapter, you will write an informational research report. Your report will provide information about a topic that interests you. Before you write, you will search for information about your topic in different kinds of sources. You will decide which facts and details to use in your report, and organize your ideas clearly for your audience.

You will develop your informational research report by taking it through each of the steps of the writing process: prewriting, drafting, revising, editing, and publishing. You will also have an opportunity to use your informational research report in an oral report or multimedia presentation involving text and graphics that uses technology available to you. To preview the criteria for how your research report will be evaluated, see the rubric on page 247.

FEATURE ASSIGNMENT

Research Writing: Informational Research Report

An effective informational research report has these characteristics:

- **A clear thesis statement** that explains the **conclusions** of the research and how those conclusions will be supported with evidence

- **Quotations** from—as well as **summaries** or **paraphrases** of—research findings, based on reliable and accurate **primary and secondary sources**

- **Clearly organized evidence,** in the form of relevant facts and details, that explains the topic and the writer's conclusions

- **Graphics,** such as charts, maps, or illustrations, that help explain the research

- Proper **documentation** of sources to show where the writer found information

- Effective sentence structure and **correct spelling, grammar, and usage**

Other Forms of Research Writing

In addition to an informational research report, there are other forms of research writing, including these:

Biographical profiles give specific details about the life and work of a real person. The person may be living or dead, someone famous, or someone familiar to the writer.

Documentaries are filmed reports that focus on a specific topic or issue. These multimedia presentations use spoken and written text as well as photographs, videos, music, and other sound effects.

Historical reports give in-depth information about a past event or situation. These kinds of reports focus on a narrow topic and may discuss causes and effects.

Health reports analyze information and data about new research in health and wellness. A health report might explain new findings about the links between nutrition and health, or the latest news on disease research.

I-Search reports blend informational and personal writing. In an I-search report, you tell the story of your research and investigations, including the dead-ends and small victories, in addition to presenting the results of your research.

Lab reports describe scientific experiments, including observations and conclusions.

Try It! For each research report described, brainstorm for possible topics with others. Then, consult with others to decide on and write a major research question for each topic. As you write, keep your audience and purpose in mind.

- A biographical profile of someone in the news
- A health report about school lunches
- A documentary about a family member for a special occasion

WRITING COACH

Online
www.TXWritingCoach.com

Resource
Word Bank Listen to English and Spanish pronunciations of new words in the eText glossary.

Online Journal
Try It! Record your answers and ideas in the online journal.

WORD BANK

People use these basic and content-based words when they talk about writing that reports information. Work with a partner. Take turns saying and writing each word in a sentence. If you are unsure of the meaning of a word, use the Glossary or a dictionary to check the definition.

authority	research
information	subject
note	support

 Focus on the TEKS

Research (22)(A) Brainstorm, consult with others, decide upon a topic, and formulate a major research question to address the major research topic.

STUDENT MODEL
Informational Research Report

Use a Reader's Eye

Read the Student Model on pages 226–229. On your copy of the Student Model, use the Reader's Response Symbols to react to what you read.

Reader's Response Symbols

√ **OK. I understand this. It's very clearly explained.**

? **I don't follow what the writer is saying here.**

+ **I think the writer needs more details here.**

— **This information doesn't seem relevant.**

! **Wow! That is cool/weird/interesting.**

Learn From Experience

Read the numbered notes as you reread the Student Model to learn about how the writer presented her ideas.

Answer the *Try It!* questions online or in your notebook.

---

❶ The writer uses **proper formatting** for the first page and pagination of research report.

❷ The writer reveals the **research question;** then she reveals her conclusion about it in the **thesis statement.**

Try It! Read the thesis statement. What is the main idea? What research question does it answer? What is the author's purpose?

---

❶ Alvarez 1

❶ Emma Alvarez
Mrs. Davidson
History 7A
13 December 2009

❶ The Cowboy: Myth Versus Reality

Everyone can spot a cowboy a mile away. He is a tall, strong man wearing a big hat, high boots, and bandana. He roams the West on horseback, like a knight of old. He spends most of his time alone except for his
5   best friend—his horse. He is brave, self-reliant, and, above all, free. To many, he represents America itself (Savage 6). ❷ How does this image relate to the real cowboys? The popular image has its roots in the real men who herded cattle for a few decades after the Civil War. However,
10 advertising and popular media reshaped the cowboys' image and smoothed away the less appealing parts of their lives (Savage 9). ❷ This report will show that the popular image of the cowboy is more myth than reality.

The era of the real—that is, working—American cowboy
15 lasted only about twenty-five years, from around 1865 to 1890. It began with the first railroads, which connected the large eastern cities with a few western centers like Chicago, Omaha, and Abilene. At this time, the railroads did not go into Texas cattle country. Cattlemen needed to get their herds to eastern
20 markets, where they would earn much higher prices. So the ranchers hired young men—cowboys—to herd the cattle over hundreds of miles to the nearest railhead. There the animals were loaded onto freight trains going east.

As time passed, however, cowboys were less essential
25 to the cattle industry. Railroads had expanded, so that rail depots were much closer to the cattle ranches. Therefore, long cattle drives every spring and fall were no longer needed. Although some cowboys continued to tend cattle on ranches, by the late 1880s, the era of the working cowboy had wound
30 down (Utley 245). At that point, the cowboy myth began to take over.

Alvarez 2

Before the cowboy myth was created, the cowboy had not been a very popular figure. One person who had seen "real cowboys" remarked that a cowboy is "just a plain bowlegged
35   human who smelled very horsey at times" (Burns). The public saw cowboys as dirty, unruly men—and they often were just that (figure 1). **❸** In 1875, a Wyoming newspaper described a group of "real" cowboys as "rough men with shaggy hair and wild staring eyes in butternut trousers stuffed into great rough
40   boots" (Schultz and Tishler).

In 1884, William F. Cody (known as "Buffalo Bill") began to shine up the cowboy's image:

> **❹** Cody took a six-foot, five-inch Texas cowpuncher named William Levi Taylor and in 1884 introduced
45   him to the audiences of Buffalo Bill's Wild West as Buck Taylor, 'the King of the Cowboys.' Buck Taylor thus became the first bona fide cowboy hero. . . . Cody's careful management of Taylor's career as an entertainer did much to alter the public's perception
50   of cowboys. He portrayed the young Texan as a wistful soul who seemed to be longing to return to the bucolic environs of the Great Plains. Promotional literature assured the public that Taylor, despite his size, was a gentle fellow who liked children (Savage).

55   **❺** In other words, Cody's publicity campaign romanticized and softened the image of the cowboy in order to make his Wild West show more popular. The campaign worked, and the myth

Figure 1. Typical cowboy. Photo taken by D.C.H. Grabill in *Sturgis Dakota Territory* (Washington, DC: Library of Congress; ppmscs 02638; print).

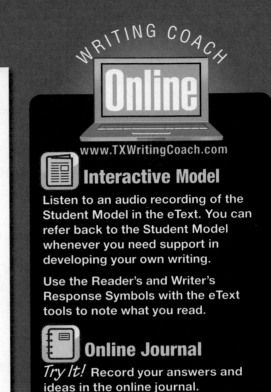

WRITING COACH

Online

www.TXWritingCoach.com

Interactive Model

Listen to an audio recording of the Student Model in the eText. You can refer back to the Student Model whenever you need support in developing your own writing.

Use the Reader's and Writer's Response Symbols with the eText tools to note what you read.

Online Journal

Try It! Record your answers and ideas in the online journal.

❸ This **quotation** gives a firsthand view of nineteenth-century cowboys, **relevant details** provided by an eyewitness who lived among them.

❹ Extended quotations of four lines or more are set off from the text, indented, and not set in quotation marks.

❺ **Evidence** is provided to support the conclusion that the cowboy image was a carefully created myth.

Try It! How does the evidence about Buck Taylor support the writer's thesis statement?

COLLEGE AND CAREER READINESS STANDARDS

Reading (A)(3) Identify explicit and implicit textual information including main ideas and author's purpose.

Informational Research Report (*continued*)

6 **Relevant facts,** in the form of statistics, back up the idea that the cowboys came from varied backgrounds.

Try It! What new ideas about cowboys do these statistics help to support?

7 Here and elsewhere, the writer **summarizes** information she found during her research.

Try It! Do you think this summary helps support the contrast between the cowboy myth and reality? Why or why not?

8 The final paragraph restates the writer's **reason for her conclusion** about the cowboy image, and adds a new thought.

Try It! What new thought does the conclusion add to the report? How does this new thought change your ideas of cowboys?

9 The Works Cited list provides proper **documentation** by listing publication information for each source used to write the report. The **formatting** of the list follows the MLA (Modern Language Association) style manual.

Try It! Study the Works Cited list on page 229. Why is it helpful to readers to list sources in alphabetical order? Why might readers want to know what types of resources—print, Web, and so on—were used?

Extension Review the text features and graphics in this report. How do they help you form an overview and locate information?

of the cowboy was born. The myth soon grew, fed by novels in the nineteenth century. In the twentieth century, the myth was greatly enlarged by movies and television programs (Savage 9–10).

The real cowboy was different in many ways from his myth, beginning with his stature and background. The mythical cowboy is tall. In contrast, Schultz and Tishler say, most actual cowboys were short and slight (though wiry), so as not to weigh down their horses. Like the "King of the Cowboys," the mythical cowboy is Caucasian and a Westerner. **6** However, of the 35,000 men who worked as cowboys between 1865 and 1885, about 25% were African-American; about 12% were Hispanic (Schultz and Tishler).

Many cowboys were not Westerners. They were former Confederate soldiers or sons of Southern families whose properties had been lost in the Civil War. They were also young men from Eastern cities and even Europeans who came west (Burns).

The typical cowboy took up cowpunching in his late teens and left it by the time he turned 30. The salary was relatively low: $30–$40 a month ("Cowboy"). Due to inflation, $40 per month in 1880 would be equal to about $870 in today's money (Officer and Williamson).

The mythical cowboy did not earn much money either, but was seen as a romantic loner who bravely faced down gunslingers. **7** In contrast, the real cowboy led a hard and very boring life, riding for 14 hours a day. He needed his large hat to protect his neck and eyes from the blistering sun and wore a kerchief so that he could breathe during dust storms. Far from being a romantic loner, his life depended on teaming up with his fellow cowboys (figure 2). They had to keep watchful eyes on the cattle, which would often wander away, or, worse, stampede and kill their herders. The cattle, terrain, and weather were all greater threats to real cowboys than gunslingers were. While the cowboy myth celebrates freedom, the actual cowboy was far from

Alvarez 4

Figure 2. Cowboys worked together to herd cattle hundreds of miles. Taken by D.C.H. Grabill in *Sturgis Dakota Territory* (Washington, DC: Library of Congress ppmscs 02628; print).

95 free. He was a hired hand who worked day and night for a rich cattle rancher, and almost every moment of his day was bound over to the animals he herded (Schultz and Tishler).

Like any legendary figure, the mythical cowboy was more heroic and exciting than the reality. ❽ So the cowboy 100 myth, eventually repeated by powerful media like movies and television, blotted out the real cowboy in people's minds. However, this is not to say that the working cowboy vanished completely from the American West. Real cowboys (and cowgirls) tend cattle on ranches to this day, much as their nineteenth-century counterparts did. We just have to look 105 behind the towering myth to see them.

❾ Works Cited

Burns, Ken. "Episode 5: "Cowboys." *The West*. WETA. 2001. Web. 2 Nov. 2009.

"Cowboy." *The New Encyclopedia of the American West*. Ed. Howard R. Lamar. New Haven: Yale UP, 1998. Print.

Officer, Lawrence H. and Samuel H. Williamson. "Six Ways to Compute the Relative Value of a U.S. Dollar Amount, 1774 to Present." *Measuring Worth*. MeasuringWorth, 2009. Web. 2 Nov. 2009.

Savage, William W., Jr. *Cowboy Life: Reconstructing an American Myth*. Norman, Oklahoma: U of Oklahoma P, 1975. Print.

Schultz, Stanley K. and William P. Tishler. "Which 'Old West' and Whose? *American History 102, Lecture 3*. State Historical Society of Wisconsin, 1997. Web. 2 Nov. 2009.

Utley, Robert M., ed. *The Story of the West*. New York: DK Publishing, Inc., 2003. Print.

 Use a Writer's Eye

Now go back to the beginning of the Student Model and evaluate the piece as a writer. On your copy of the Student Model, use the Writer's Response Symbols to react to what you read. Identify places where the student writer uses characteristics of an effective informational research report.

Writer's Response Symbols

T.S.   **Thesis statement**

S.E.   **Supporting evidence**

R.G.   **Relevant graphic**

D.S.   **Proper documentation of sources**

Your Turn

**Feature Assignment:
Informational Research Report**

Prewriting

Begin to plan a first draft by choosing an appropriate topic. You can select from the Topic Bank or come up with one of your own.

 ## Choose From the Topic Bank

TOPIC BANK

Balls, Courts, and Hoops People in other times played many games that share traits with today's sports. Learn about a sport developed by Native Americans or another civilization from the Middle Ages to the twentieth century. What were its origins? How was it played?

Making the Headlines Certain dates in history have special meaning to various localities. What date means a great deal to your community or state? What makes the date important?

What's Living in My Backyard? Our communities host many life forms, from microscopic to human size. Research an ecosystem or microhabitat near your home. Describe this habitat and its organisms. How do these organisms co-exist with human beings?

 ## Choose Your Own Topic

Determine an appropriate topic of your own by using the following range of strategies to generate ideas.

Brainstorm and Browse

- **Consult** with a partner to **brainstorm** for and decide upon a list of topics that interest you.
- **Ask research questions** about your topics. Circle key words and phrases in your questions. Use your key words and phrases to browse your library's reference works and other resources.
- Search the Internet, using the same key words. Work with your partner to help you **decide which topics to research.**
- Review your work and choose a topic.

Formulate Your Research Question

A broad, general topic is almost impossible to research well and cover thoroughly. Plan to do some preliminary research in order to narrow your topic and then formulate a major research question.

Apply It! Use a printed or online graphic organizer like the one shown to narrow your topic.

- Write your general topic in the top box, and keep narrowing your topic with research questions as you move down the chart.
- Your last box should hold your narrowest or "smallest" research question. This will be the focus of your informational research report.

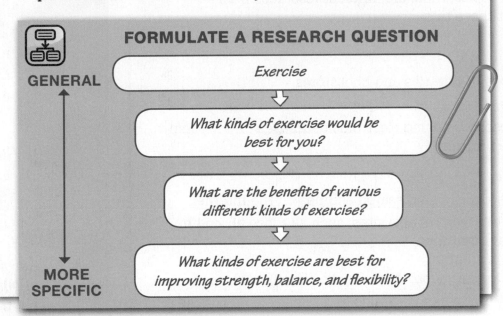

FORMULATE A RESEARCH QUESTION

GENERAL

Exercise

↓

What kinds of exercise would be best for you?

↓

What are the benefits of various different kinds of exercise?

↓

MORE SPECIFIC

What kinds of exercise are best for improving strength, balance, and flexibility?

Consider Your Audiences and Purposes

Before you start researching, think about audiences and purposes. Consider the views of others as you ask yourself these questions.

Questions About Audiences	Questions About Purposes
• Who are my audiences: My teacher? My classmates? Someone else? • What do my audiences need and want to know about the topic for my research report? • What technical terms will I need to explain to my audiences?	• Why am I writing the report: To inform? To make my audiences want to learn more about the topic? • How do I want my audiences to react to my report as they read it? • What is my point of view, or attitude, toward my topic?

Record your answers in your writing journal.

WRITING COACH

www.TXWritingCoach.com

Interactive Writing Coach™

- Choosing from the Topic Bank gives you access to the Interactive Writing Coach™.
- Submit your writing paragraph by paragraph and receive detailed feedback and guidance as you draft, revise, and edit your writing.

Interactive Graphic Organizers

Use the interactive graphic organizers to help you narrow your topic.

Online Journal

Record your answers and ideas in the online journal.

 Focus on the TEKS

Research (22)(A) Brainstorm, consult with others, decide upon a topic, and formulate a major research question to address the major research topic.

COLLEGE AND CAREER READINESS STANDARDS

Research (A)(1-2) Formulate research questions and explore a research topic.

Make a Research Plan

Once you have your research question, you are ready to make a research plan. As part of your plan, you will create a time line for finishing your report. You also will find and evaluate sources of information.

Find Authoritative, Objective Sources For your report, you will need to **compile data,** or gather information, from a variety of sources. Make sure the sources you plan to use are **relevant**— they should be related to the topic you are researching and not out of date. Use a variety of **advanced search strategies** including electronic databases, card catalogues, and search engines to locate your resources. For most topics, there are different resources from which to choose. Look at these tips:

Print Resources

- Find print resources in libraries and bookstores.
- Use encyclopedias, magazines, newspapers, and textbooks.
- Search for print resources using electronic databases or with help from the reference librarian.

Electronic Resources

- Find electronic resources using search engines on the Internet.
- Choose only authoritative, reliable sites, such as those ending in:
    .edu (educational institution)
    .gov (government group)
    .org (not-for-profit organization; these may be biased)
- If you are not sure that a site is reliable and unbiased, do not use it.

Interviews with Experts

- Ask questions of an expert on your topic.
- Set up a short in-person, e-mail, or telephone interview.
- Record the interview and take good notes.

Multimedia Resources

- Watch film or TV documentaries about your topic.
- Listen to podcasts related to the topic.
- Search for relevant photos, diagrams, charts, and graphs.

Evaluate Your Sources Do not assume that all sources of information on your topic are useful, good, or trustworthy. Use the checklist on page 233 to evaluate sources of information you find. The more questions that you can answer with a yes, the more likely you should use the source.

Checklist for Evaluating Sources

Does the source of information:

☐ Contain **relevant** information that answers your research questions?

☐ Provide **facts** and not just unsupported **subjective** opinions?

☐ Give facts and details at a level you can understand?

☐ Tell all sides of a story, so that it is **unbiased**?

☐ Provide **authoritative and accurate** information written or compiled by experts?

☐ Have a recent **publication date**, indicating it is up-to-date?

Distinguish Between Types of Sources As you research, you will discover two kinds of sources: primary sources and secondary sources. Your teacher may require that you use both.

- A **primary source** is an original document you use for a firsthand account or investigation of your topic. For example, population data collected by the parks department is a primary source. Letters, diaries, and speeches are other examples.

- A **secondary source** is research that someone else has conducted and published. For example, a book called *The Birds of Central Texas* is a secondary source. When you use a secondary source, you are using another researcher's point of view on a topic.

Apply It! Create a written **research plan** and timeline with steps you can apply to obtain and evaluate information and to finish your report. After you have done some research in reference works and completed some additional text searches, create and follow a written research plan. List at least four relevant sources, including print and electronic resources, of information that you plan to use.

- Work with your teacher to set deadlines for finishing each step: research, thesis statement, drafting, and final report.

- For each source you plan to use, record full **bibliographic** information in a **standard format**. (See page 236.)

- Use the Checklist for Evaluating Sources to explain whether each of your sources is **reliable and valid**.

- Note whether each source is primary or secondary.

Modify Your Plan After you begin to research and investigate a topic, you may need to **narrow, or broaden, your research question**. If you cannot find answers to a research question, you may decide to refocus, or change the emphasis of, your topic.

WRITING COACH

Online

www.TXWritingCoach.com

Online Journal
Record your answers and ideas in the online journal.

Partner Talk

Review your sources with a partner. Discuss why one source is more useful than another.

Focus on the TEKS

Research

(22)(B) Apply steps for obtaining and evaluating information from a wide variety of sources and create a written plan after preliminary research in reference works and additional text searches.

(23)(A)(C) Determine, locate, and explore the full range of relevant sources addressing a research question and systematically record the information gathered.

(24)(A–B) Clarify research questions and evaluate and synthesize collected information.

COLLEGE AND CAREER READINESS STANDARDS

Research

(A)(3) Refine research topic and devise timeline for completing work.

(B)(1–2) Gather relevant sources and evaluate the validity and reliability of sources.

Collect and Organize Your Data

As you follow your research plan for your informational research report, you will need to use **multiple sources** of information. Notes will help you remember and keep track of your sources and information. Different forms of notes include handwritten notes on note cards, typed notes in an electronic document, and a learning log summarizing what you know and still need to know about your topic.

Keep Track of Multiple Sources You can create a card for each source and give each its own number. **Note the full bibliographic information,** or publishing details for the source, including the author, title, city of publication, publisher, and copyright date. The example shown is from the Student Model. It matches MLA style used in the Works Cited on page 229.

Take Notes When you take notes from a relevant print or electronic source, follow these guidelines.

- Note only **relevant** information—facts and details that get at your research question.

- Look for longer thematic patterns or constructs in the information you investigate. **Categorize** the notes using headings that sum up the **theme** or main idea of each group of notes.

- Be very careful to use your own words. It's all right to use abbreviations and incomplete sentences in your notes.

- If you want to quote someone, enclose the exact words in large quotation marks. If you are taking notes on a computer, you might also boldface the whole quotation. These techniques will remind you that the words are someone else's and not your own.

Apply It! Create numbered source cards for all of your sources. Take notes from each source, creating a different note card for each category of information. Organizing notes by **categories or themes** can help you to make connections between data and to see big ideas. Paraphrase or summarize the information in your own words. If you want to include a direct quotation, carefully copy the original and enclose the quotation in quotation marks.

Source 3

Utley, Robert M., ed. *The Story of the West.* New York: DK Publishing, Inc., 2003. Print.

Notes From Source 3

Cowboys and railroads

- Till about 1880, rr lines were far from cattle ranches, so cowboys had to drive cattle to railheads.

- As rr lines came West, long cattle drives no longer needed.

Avoid Plagiarism

Plagiarism is presenting someone else's words or ideas as your own, without documenting, or identifying, the source of the information. Plagiarism is a serious error with severe consequences. Do not plagiarize.

Careful Note-taking Matters You can plagiarize without meaning to do so. The student who wrote this note card made mistakes. She followed the original source too closely. Also, she didn't include a source number that would link the note card to its source's full publication information.

> The cradle of the range-cattle industry was post-Civil-War Texas, and there livestock dominated the economy, despite depressed conditions of local markets. Little else was available to returning Confederate veterans who sought employment, or to the adolescent sons of men killed in the war.

Original Source

> ### Post-Civil War
> *Post-Civil-War Texas was the cradle of the cattle industry. Livestock dominated the Texas economy, even though local markets were sometimes depressed. Returning Confederate veterans had little employment available to them. This was also true of sons of men killed in the war.*
>
> from *Cowboy Life: Reconstructing an American Myth* by William W. Savage, Jr.

Plagiarized Notes

Partner Talk

Review taking notes with a partner. Explain why each of these is important:

- Citing valid and reliable sources
- Using your own words to summarize ideas
- Making large quotation marks for direct quotations

Monitor your partner's spoken language by asking follow-up questions.

Use these strategies to avoid plagiarism.

- **Paraphrase** When you paraphrase information from a source, restate the writer's idea using your own words. Read a passage, and think about what it means. Then, write it as you might explain it to someone else.

- **Summarize** When you summarize a long passage from a source, briefly state its most important ideas in your own words.

- **Direct Quote** If you use a direct quotation, enclose the writer's exact words in quotation marks, and identify who said it.

 Try It! Look at the plagiarized notes in the example. Highlight the parts to differentiate the lines that are plagiarizing rather than paraphrasing the original. Now, write a new note based on the original source. Do not plagiarize.

Focus on the TEKS

Research (23) (A–D) Determine, locate, and explore the full range of relevant sources addressing a research question and systematically record the information gathered.

COLLEGE AND CAREER READINESS STANDARDS

Research (C)(2) Use source material ethically.

Document Your Sources

When you write a research report, you need to cite all **researched information** that is not common knowledge, and cite it **according to a standard format.**

Works Cited On the Works Cited page at the end of your report, list all the sources that you used. Do not include sources you looked into but did not use. Follow the format shown in a standard style manual, such as that of the Modern Language Association (MLA) or American Psychological Association (APA). Your teacher will tell you which standard format style to use.

Look at the example citations. Use these and the MLA Style for Listing Sources on page R16 as a guide for writing your citations. Pay attention to formatting, including italics, abbreviations, and punctuation.

Book

Author's last name, author's first name followed by the author's middle name or initial (if given). *Full title of book.* City where book was published: Name of publisher, year of publication. Medium of publication.

Slatta, Richard W. *Cowboy: The Illustrated History.* New York: Sterling, 2006. Print.

Magazine Article

Author's last name, author's first name followed by the author's middle name or initial (if given). "Title of article." *Title of magazine* Full date of magazine issue: page numbers or plus sign (+) if the article appears on nonconsecutive pages. Medium of publication.

Draper, Robert. "21st Century Cowboys: Why the Spirit Endures." *National Geographic* Dec. 2007: 114+. Print.

Web Page

Author's last name, author's first name followed by author's middle name or initial (if given) OR compiler, or editor (if given). "Name of page." *Name of Web site.* Name of publisher, institution, or sponsor OR N.p if none given, date of posting OR n.d. if none given. Medium of publication. Date on which you accessed the page.

Officer, Lawrence H. and Samuel H. Williamson. "Six Ways to Compute the Relative Value of a U.S. Dollar Amount, 1774 to Present." *Measuring Worth.* Measuring Worth, 2009. Web. 2 Nov. 2009.

Parenthetical Citations A parenthetical citation refers to a source listed on the Works Cited page. It helps you to **avoid plagiarizing by integrating,** or including, **source information** right in your report. Because a parenthetical citation gives just the author or title and page number, it does not interrupt **the flow ideas.** Here is a parenthetical citation from the Student Model.

 STUDENT MODEL from **"The Cowboy: Myth Versus Reality"** page 227; lines 33–35

> One person who had seen "real cowboys" remarked that a cowboy is "just a plain bowlegged human who smelled very horsey at times" (Burns).

If the name of the author is mentioned in the sentence, only the page number is given in parentheses.

> In contrast, Schultz and Tishler say, most actual cowboys were short and slight (though wiry), so as not to weigh down their horses (2).

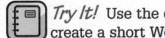 *Try It!* Use the documentation style shown on page 236 to create a short Works Cited page including these sources:

- A Web page called "Rawhide Rodeo Company." The Web site is called rawhiderodeo.com. No information about the author, publisher, or date is available. The writer looked at the page on December 20, 2009.

- An article titled "Calling All Cowboys" by Suzanne Bopp in *National Geographic TRAVELER* magazine. It was published in September 2008 on pages 60–64.

Critique Your Research Process

At every step in the research process, be prepared to adjust or change your research plan. If you can't find enough information, **try broadening your research question.** If you have too much information, you might need to **narrow your question.** In either case, it's important to stick to your **timetable.** If you've found answers to your research question, you're ready to start drafting.

 Apply It! Write an entry on your Works Cited page for every source you used for information in your report. To format your sources correctly, use MLA style or the style your teacher has directed you to use. Confirm that you have researched enough information to begin writing your draft.

WRITING COACH

Online

www.TXWritingCoach.com

Interactive Model

Refer back to the Student Model as you document your sources.

Online Journal

Record your answers and ideas in the online journal.

Partner Talk

Get together with a partner to discuss research sources. Where have you looked for information on your topic? What sources are reliable? How have you been keeping track of the sources you have used? As you speak, practice newly acquired vocabulary by correctly producing the word's sound.

Focus on the TEKS

Research

(23)(C) Record bibliographic information for all notes and sources according to a standard format.

(24)(A) Narrow or broaden the research question, if necessary, based on further research and investigation.

Drafting

During the drafting stage, you will start to write your ideas for your research report. You will write a **clear thesis statement**. You will follow an outline that provides an **organizational strategy** to help you write a **focused, organized, and coherent** research report. As you write your draft or prepare your notes for an oral report, remember to keep your audience in mind.

The Organization of an Informational Research Report

The chart shows an organizational strategy for a research report. Look back at how the Student Model follows this same strategy. Then, create a detailed outline for your research report. Use the template on page R26 to develop your outline. Refer to your Outline for Success as you work.

Outline for Success

I. Introduction

See Student Model, p. 226.

- Lively opening
- Clear thesis statement

II. Body

See Student Model, pp. 226–228.

- Synthesis of information from multiple sources
- Systematic organization of research findings
- Evidence that supports the thesis statement
- Graphics and illustrations to explain concepts

III. Conclusion

See Student Model, p. 229.

- Restatement of thesis
- Memorable ending with a final thought or conclusion

Introduce Your Thesis Statement

- A quotation, story, question, or interesting fact will grab the reader's attention.
- A **clear thesis statement** reflects the major conclusion you have drawn from your research.

Support Your Thesis Statement

- The body of your report synthesizes, or brings together, information to support your **thesis statement**.
- You've grouped your note cards by category, and these categories become major headings in your outline.
- Each paragraph states a major idea and supports it with **evidence,** such as facts, statistics, and examples.
- Photos, charts, diagrams, or other visuals help convey complicated information.

Add a Final Thought

- Your **conclusion** about your topic is restated in the final paragraph.
- You may suggest a new idea or follow-up to the report. In the Student Model, for example, the writer suggests that the reader view a video about contemporary cowboys.

👍 Start Your Draft

To complete your draft, use the checklist. Use your specific thesis statement; your detailed outline that shows your topic sentence and supporting evidence, and your plan for the logical organization of the main ideas; and the Outline for Success as guides.

While drafting, aim at writing your ideas, not on making your writing perfect. Remember, you will have the chance to improve your draft when you revise and edit.

√ Begin your **introduction** with several sentences that catch your reader's attention.

√ End with a clearly worded **thesis statement** based on the **conclusion** you've drawn about your research question.

√ Present your findings in a meaningful format. Develop the **body** of the report one paragraph at a time. Choose only the strongest **supporting evidence** for each **idea**.

√ For each paragraph, draft a **topic sentence** stating the main idea. Each main idea should support your thesis.

√ Marshal the evidence you have collected and organized, then synthesize it to support and explain your topic.

√ Include conclusions you draw from your research. Summarize or paraphrase your research findings in a systematic way that readers can understand. Remember to give relevant, logical reasons for your conclusions.

√ Draft a **concluding paragraph** that restates your thesis. Try to add a final thought to make the ending more memorable or interesting.

WRITING COACH

Online

www.TXWritingCoach.com

📰 **Interactive Model**

Outline for Success View pop-ups of Student Model selections referenced in the Outline for Success.

👍 **Interactive Writing Coach™**

Submit your draft one paragraph at a time and receive immediate, detailed feedback.

Focus on the TEKS

Research (25)(A–C) Organize and present ideas and information according to the purpose of the research and audience.

COLLEGE AND CAREER READINESS STANDARDS

Research (B)(3) Synthesize and organize information effectively.

Provide and Document Evidence

While you are drafting, you will provide **evidence** to support your thesis statement and related claims. Your **claims** are an important part of your **analysis** of your topic. They are your **point of view** or understanding of information connected to you. Be careful to differentiate between your opinions and ideas and those of other people. To do so, **document** the words and ideas of other people when you provide evidence.

Give Facts and Statistics Facts are convincing evidence because they can be proven true. Statistics, or facts stated in numbers, are also convincing when they come from authoritative and up-to-date sources. Document facts and statistics that are not common knowledge or that could not be found in most sources about a topic.

Give Examples Use concrete examples to make abstract or complicated ideas easier to understand. You must identify the source of examples that you found in your research, but you do not need to document examples from your personal experience or observations.

Quote Authorities Direct quotations can be convincing evidence. However, you should not use a quotation when **summarizing** or **paraphrasing** would be just as clear. Weave quotations and citations into the flow of your ideas as shown in this example from the Student Model.

 STUDENT MODEL from **"The Cowboy: Myth Versus Reality"**
page 227; lines 37–40

> In 1875, a Wyoming newspaper described a group of "real" cowboys as "rough men with shaggy hair and wild staring eyes in butternut trousers stuffed into great rough boots" (Schultz and Tishler).

Remember these guidelines:

- Use your own words to identify the expert, integrating quotations and citations into your text to maintain the flow of ideas.
- Separate and inset a quote of four lines or more.
- Use correct punctuation and an accepted format. (See pages 246–247.)
- Follow quotes with a proper parenthetical citation.

Apply It! Draft a paragraph for your research report. Your paragraph should include facts, examples, a quotation, and citation. Remember to correctly format your quotations and citations to avoid interrupting the flow of your ideas.

Use Graphics and Illustrations

Your report can present evidence in graphics and visuals as well as words. For a report on a scientific topic, diagrams, charts, and other types of graphics can help your audience understand your ideas. In other reports, photographs, maps, and other graphics can add valuable concrete detail. Be sure to refer to the graphic (usually called a "figure") in your text. Then, label your visual with a figure or table number, caption, and source citations for the data. Use caution when copying an existing graphic because you will need permission from the copyright holder if you publish your work for use outside school.

- **Photographs** Use a photograph to help your audience picture how something looks. If you insert a photograph in your report, include a caption, or brief sentence explaining what the photo shows.

- **Maps** By providing geographic information visually, maps give your reader a better idea of locations you mention in your report. Always include a legend and a compass rose.

- **Charts, Tables, and Graphs** Create a chart, table, or graph to provide information in a more visual or organized way. Give each a title that tells what it shows. If you include more than one, number them in numerical order. Include a citation for the source of information you used to create the chart, table, or graph.

Ethnicity of Cowboys in the Old West

63% Anglo and other (including Native American) Cowboys

25% African-American Cowboys

12% Mexican and other Hispanic Cowboys

Source: Based on data from Schultz and Tishler

Apply It! Brainstorm for two graphics that you might use to present information in your informational research report in the most meaningful format.

- Be sure to identify the type of information each graphic would explain, find or create the two graphics, and integrate them into your report.

- Remember to give your graphics titles.

- Use a style manual to format graphics and to document your sources.

- Use peer, teacher, or family feedback to check that the quality of your created and researched visuals is appropriate for your report.

Partner Talk

Get together with a partner and participate in an extended discussion to evaluate the graphics that you are considering using. Ask specific questions to enhance your comprehension. Express your opinions and explain to your partner why you have chosen each graphic and how it provides important information for your report.

Focus on the TEKS

Research (25)(C–D) Organize and present ideas and information according to the purpose of the research and audience.

COLLEGE AND CAREER READINESS STANDARDS

Listening

(A)(3) Use a variety of strategies to enhance listening comprehension.

(B)(2) Listen actively and effectively in one-on-one communication situations.

Revising: Making It Better

Now that you have finished your draft, you are ready to revise. Think about the "big picture" of **audience, purpose, and genre**. You can use the Revision RADaR strategy as a guide for making changes to improve your draft. Revision RADaR provides four major ways to improve your writing: (R) replace, (A) add, (D) delete, and (R) reorder.

Kelly Gallagher, M. Ed.

KEEP REVISION ON YOUR RADAR

Read part of the first draft of the Student Model "The Cowboy: Myth Versus Reality." Then, look at the writer's questions about how well her draft addressed issues of audience, purpose, and genre.

1ST DRAFT

The Cowboy: Myth Versus Reality

A cowboy can be spotted from a mile away. He is a tall, strong man in a big hat who rides his horse all over the West. He is brave, self-reliant, and, above all, free. He represents America itself, to many people. (Savage). This report will explore the differences between the popular cowboy image and the real cowboy. How does this image relate to the real cowboys? The popular image has its roots in the real men who herded cattle for a few decades after the Civil War. However, advertising and popular media picked up the cowboy image. (Savage).

*Have I created a lively **opening** that grabs my reader's attention?*

*Is this the best statement of what I plan to do? Should this **thesis statement** come later in the paragraph?*

*Have I used the **appropriate format** to credit my source?*

*Is this **evidence** relevant? Does it support my thesis?*

Now look at how the writer applied Revision RADaR to write an improved second draft.

The Cowboy: Myth Versus Reality

Everyone can spot a cowboy a mile away. He is a tall, strong man wearing a big hat, high boots, and bandana. He roams the West on horseback, like a knight of old. He spends most of his time alone except for his best friend—his horse. He is brave, self-reliant, and, above all, free. To many, he represents America itself. (Savage 6). How does this image relate to the real cowboys? The popular image has its roots in the real men who herded cattle for a few decades after the Civil War. However, advertising and popular media reshaped the cowboys' image and smoothed away the less appealing parts of their lives (Savage 9). This report will show that the popular image of the cowboy is more myth than reality.

D *Added the sentences to make the beginning livelier*

A *Added the page number to make the citation complete*

R *Replaced vague information about the media and popular culture with specific information, paraphrased from a source*

R *Reordered the thesis statement, placing it at the end of the introductory paragraph*

 Apply It! Use your Revision RADaR to revise your draft.

- First, determine whether you have addressed the needs of your audience, stated your thesis, and included the characteristics of an effective research report. Then, check that your ideas make sense within each paragraph and sentence, to track whether your text has **internal coherence.** Also check for **external coherence** by making sure the entire report flows logically.

- Then, apply Revision RADaR to make needed changes. Remember—you can use the steps in the strategy in any order.

 Focus on the TEKS

Writing (14)(C) Revise drafts to ensure internal and external coherence.

Look at the Big Picture

Use the chart and your analytical skills to evaluate how well each section of your research report addresses **purpose, audience, and genre**. When necessary, use the suggestions in the chart to revise your piece.

Section	Evaluate	Revise
Introduction	• Check that the **opening paragraphs** grab readers' attention and make them want to learn more about your topic.	• Add a quotation, anecdote (brief story), or question to make your introduction lively.
	• Make sure you have a **clear thesis statement** that sets forth the major ideas your report will develop.	• Clarify your thesis statement to be sure it identifies the conclusions you have drawn about the topic.
Body	• Make sure each body paragraph develops one main idea and uses **marshalled evidence** to explain the topic.	• Add a topic sentence to each paragraph. Add evidence to support weakly developed paragraphs.
	• Evaluate the **relevance** of the reasons and evidence you use to support your conclusions.	• Take out any details that are not clearly tied to your purposes.
	• Check that information and major ideas are summarized, paraphrased, and organized in a **systematic way**.	• Compare paragraphs to your original outline to make sure similar ideas are categorized by theme or subtopic.
	• Make sure that you have used graphics when a visual can best illustrate the data.	• Convert data into graphics or pick up existing graphics to present your findings in the most meaningful format.
	• Make sure quotations and facts that are not common knowledge are **documented** and **formatted** and do not interrupt the flow of ideas.	• Review your note cards and source cards to confirm the source of each quotation. Add **parenthetical citations** in the correct format and style.
Conclusion	• Check that your final paragraph **restates your thesis**.	• If needed, revise the introduction and conclusion to ensure they agree.
	• Make sure your research report ends with a new **insight**.	• Add a quotation or fact that brings your report to a definite end.
Works Cited/ Bibliography	• Complete your **source list** using the style specified by your teacher.	• Add all documented sources you used in your paper to the Works Cited page.

Focus on Craft: Sentence Variety

Sentences can have different lengths and structures. Some are short and punchy, while others can flow on, connecting several ideas. Sentences can begin in different ways: with a pronoun or noun, with a series of adjectives, or with a prepositional or participial phrase. When you write a research report, try to vary the lengths, structures, and beginnings of your sentences. If you do, your writing will be more interesting to read and will flow more effectively. Look at these sentences from the Student Model.

 STUDENT MODEL from **"The Cowboy: Myth Versus Reality"** page 226; lines 1–7

Everyone can spot a cowboy a mile away. He is a tall, strong man wearing a big hat, high boots, and bandana. He roams the West on horseback, like a knight of old. He spends most of his time alone except for his best friend—his horse. He is brave, self-reliant, and, above all, free. To many, he represents America itself (Savage 6).

 Try It! Now, ask yourself these questions. Record your answers in your journal.

1. Compare the first and second drafts (pages 242–243). Why does the student writer change the structure of the first sentence?

2. Do any sentences in this paragraph begin in the same way? Would you advise the writer to change more sentence beginnings, or is repetition effective here?

Fine-Tune Your Draft

Apply It! Use the revision suggestions to prepare your final draft. Make sure you keep your audience and purpose in mind.

- **Focus on Sentence Variety** Ensure a mix of shorter and longer sentences. Follow a simple sentence with a compound or complex sentence.

- **Use Effective Transitions** Use transitional words and phrases such as *also* and *as a result* to link ideas and connect sentences and paragraphs. Because of the length of your work, you may need transitional sentences or paragraphs to help readers follow your thinking.

Teacher and Family Feedback Share your draft with your teacher or a family member. Carefully review the comments you receive and revise your final draft as needed.

WRITING COACH

Online

www.TXWritingcoach.Com

Online Journal

Try It! Record your answers in the online journal.

Interactive Model

Refer back to the Student Model as you revise your writing.

Interactive Writing Coach™

Revise your draft and submit it paragraph by paragraph for feedback.

 Focus on the TEKS

Writing

(14)(C) Revise drafts to ensure use of simple, compound, and complex sentences and of effective transitions.

(14)(E) Revise final draft in response to feedback from teacher.

Research (25)(A–D) Organize and present ideas and information according to the purpose of the research and audience.

Editing: Making It Correct

Before editing your final draft, you need to make sure you have accurately **paraphrased, summarized, quoted,** and **cited** all researched information. Edit your draft to correctly document sources and format the source material, including quotations. Your teacher can provide guidance on which standard format to follow. Finally, edit your final draft for errors in grammar, mechanics, and spelling.

WRITE GUY *Jeff Anderson, M. Ed.*

WHAT DO YOU NOTICE?

Zoom in on Conventions Focus on quotations as you zoom in on these lines from the Student Model.

> **STUDENT MODEL** from **"The Cowboy: Myth Versus Reality"** page 227; lines 37–40
>
> In 1875, a Wyoming newspaper described a group of "real" cowboys as "rough men with shaggy hair and wild staring eyes in butternut trousers stuffed into great rough boots" (Schultz and Tishler).

Now, ask yourself this question: *How well has the writer integrated the quotation into her paragraph?*

Perhaps you noted that the writer used these helpful techniques to surround the quotation:

- Provided an introductory phrase that tells when the quotation occurred
- Indicated where the quotation originally appeared and what its purpose was
- Told where the quotation was found, using the standard format for parenthetical citations

Partner Talk Discuss this question with a partner: *How easy or hard is it to figure out which words from the Student Model are the student's and which words are not the student's?*

> To learn more about integrating quotations, see Grammar Game Plan Error 18, page 290.

Grammar Mini-Lesson: Punctuation

Punctuating Quotations With Citations Quotations follow some specific rules for punctuation. Study the sentence from the Student Model. Notice how the writer punctuated the quotation with a citation. Notice the period comes after the citation in parentheses.

To learn more, see Chapter 25.

 STUDENT MODEL from **"The Cowboy: Myth Versus Reality"** page 227; lines 33–35

> One person who had seen "real cowboys" remarked that a cowboy is "just a plain bowlegged human who smelled very horsey at times" (Burns).

Try It! Which of these sentences uses correct punctuation for the quotation and for the citation in the parentheses? Write the answers in your journal.

1. Ken Burns and Stephen Ives, the filmmakers, have said "America without the West is unthinkable now." (Episode 5.)

2. Ken Burns and Stephen Ives, the filmmakers, have said, "America without the West is unthinkable now" (Episode 5).

Apply It! Edit your draft for grammar, mechanics, and spelling. If necessary, rewrite sentences to integrate quotations more smoothly into your text to maintain the flow of ideas. Punctuate and cite quotations correctly.

Use the rubric to evaluate your piece. If necessary, rethink, rewrite, or revise.

Rubric for Informational Research Report	Rating Scale			
Focus and Coherence: How specific and clearly expressed is your thesis statement?	Not very 1	2	3	Very 4
Organization: How logical is the progression of your ideas?	1	2	3	4
Development of Ideas: How accurate and thorough is your supporting evidence?	1	2	3	4
Conventions: How correct is the formatting of sources that you used?	1	2	3	4
Voice: How clearly have you expressed your point of view?	1	2	3	4

WRITING COACH

Online

www.TXWritingcoach.Com

Video
Learn effective editing techniques from program author Jeff Anderson.

Online Journal
Try It! Record your answers in the online journal.

Interactive Model
Refer back to the Student Model as you edit your writing.

Interactive Writing Coach™
Edit your draft and check it against the rubric. Submit it paragraph by paragraph for feedback.

 Focus on the TEKS

Research (25)(D) Follow accepted formats for integrating quotations and citations into the written text to maintain a flow of ideas.

Publishing

It is time to share your research report. When you've finished your final draft, publish it for an appropriate audience.

Wrap Up Your Presentation

You teacher may require you to turn in a typed report. Follow the guidelines provided. Create a cover sheet, table of contents, and Works Cited list. Also be sure to add a lively title that indicates the topic of the report.

Publish Your Piece

Use a chart to brainstorm for ways to publish your research report to an appropriate audience. You may decide to circulate or post a written report or share an oral report or multimedia presentation.

If your audience is...	...then publish it by...
Students or teachers at school	• Displaying your report in the library, media center, or other public place • Posting your report on a Web site dedicated to student work
A club with a special interest like science, music, or history	• Giving a talk or doing a multimedia presentation at one of the club's meetings • Submitting your report to the club's newsletter or Web site

 Reflect on Your Writing

Now that you are done with your informational research report, read it over and use your writing journal to answer these questions.

- Which parts of your research report please you the most? Which parts could be improved?
- What will you do differently for your next research report?
- What useful things have you learned about doing research?

 The Big Question: Why Write? Did you understand your subject well enough to write about it? How did you find out what all the facts were?

Manage Your Portfolio You may include your published informational research report in your writing portfolio. If so, consider what this piece reveals about your writing and your growth as a writer.

MAKE YOUR WRITING COUNT

Write a Press Conference Script

Research reports often reveal surprising answers to the questions they pose. Inform your schoolmates about a surprising research report by preparing a **script for a press conference.**

In a press conference, someone with information to share with the press invites journalists to hear that announcement and ask questions. With a group, write a script for a mock press conference about information from a research report. Then, produce a **multimedia presentation.** Your presentation should use text and graphics. Act out your script for classmates, or record it and present it as a podcast.

Here's your action plan.

1. With your group, choose roles such as moderator, one or more experts, and reporters.

2. Select a report from your group that reveals surprising information. Create text, such as a bulleted list of key points, and a supporting graphic to share the news.

3. View a press conference online. Notice how reporters and speakers interact. Pay attention to text and graphics.

4. Plan and write your script.

   - The moderator introduces the experts and topic.
   - The experts give a statement and answer questions, referring to supporting text and graphics.
   - The reporters ask questions and dig for the truth.

5. Practice your presentation. Act out your script for classmates.

6. If presenting a podcast, video-record your press conference and play it for the class.

Listening and Speaking As a group, discuss how to present your script. Memorize the text of the script, and practice your presentation using the graphics. Ask listeners to give feedback on the position and evidence given. Presenters should adjust their content, volume, and pacing accordingly. During the presentation, work to act like participants in a real press conference.

WRITING COACH

Online

www.TXWritingcoach.Com

Online Journal

Reflect on Your Writing Record your answers and ideas in the online journal.

Resource

Link to resources on 21st Century Learning for help in creating a group project.

Focus on the TEKS

Writing (17)(D) Produce a multimedia presentation involving text and graphics using available technology.

COLLEGE AND CAREER READINESS STANDARDS

Listening (A)(1) Analyze and evaluate the effectiveness of a public presentation.

Listening (A)(2) Interpret a speaker's message; identify the position taken and the evidence in support of that position.

Your Turn **Writing For Media: Online Consumer Report**

Online Consumer Report

21st Century Learning

What kinds of applications do various cell phones have? Do some work better than others? Which airlines are the most economical and give the best service? Which commercial dog foods have received the highest recommendations? You can find answers to all your consumer questions by searching the Internet.

In this assignment, you will create your own **online consumer report** about a product or service. You'll follow a research plan as you gather information from multiple sources. Then, you'll put it all together to tell your audience about the pros and cons of various competing products or services. You may provide links from parenthetical citations to a separate Works Cited page.

Try It! Study the excerpt from the online consumer report shown. Then, answer these questions. Record your answers in your journal.

1. What **consumer** product or service is the writer describing?

2. What do you think is the writer's **purpose?** Who do you think is the intended audience?

3. An online consumer report gives **essential information** about a specific product or service, often including statistics about its quality. What information is shown here?

4. Is the writing **subjective,** presenting the writer's opinion, or **objective,** presenting only factual information? How can you tell?

5. What effect does the **photograph** have? What other kinds of visuals would be helpful in this report?

Off to a Flying Start

Airline passengers can sometimes feel like excess baggage. They trudge through long lines at airports. They hover for hours at the gates before they are allowed onto a late-arriving plane. After they squeeze into their seats, they often sit for an hour or more on the tarmac waiting for the plane to take off. The good news is that a relatively new airline, Jet Plane Air, has paid more-than-usual attention to being flyer-friendly.

Jet Plane started flying in 2007, and so far, its "on-time arrival" rate is 82%, which places it near the top among airlines and well above the average of 77%. So far, the airline's in-flight service has received high marks from consumers. Coach passengers have 7% more seating room and legroom than average. *(Jet Plane Air Annual Report, 2009)* Also, passengers in coach receive free meals and free in-flight movies.

Jet Plane Air is not perfect, of course. It schedules fewer flights than larger airlines, although it does fly to most large cities in the U.S. and Canada. It also has no overseas flights. Because it is a new airline, we do not know if Jet Plane Air will maintain its high consumer ratings and excellent flight record. For now, this new airline is off to a flying start. For the latest information, visit the Department of Transportation's Aviation Consumer Protection Division Web site *(Air Consumer on the Web).*

Create an Online Consumer Report

Follow these steps to create your own **online consumer report**. To plan your online consumer report, review the graphic organizers on pages R24–R27 and choose one that suits your needs.

Prewriting

- Consult with others and brainstorm for a list of products and services that you or your family might want to purchase or use in the home or outside the home. When you've finished, circle the topic you have chosen.

- Be sure to identify the target **audience** for your online report. Are you writing to **inform** an audience of teenagers? Families? Parents?

- It's important to create a **research plan** to identify what specific **research question** you will try to answer. You'll need to **gather information** from **a wide variety of sources.** Include steps in your plan for **obtaining and evaluating** information.

- After some preliminary research in reference works and additional texts, create a **written plan** for more specific resources, including print and electronic sources.

- **Evaluate** every source you consider using. Decide whether a source is **reliable** and **valid.** The Internet has the most up-to-date reviews of products and services, but be careful to evaluate review sites for bias.

- **Categorize** your notes to help you see broader patterns. You may need to **broaden or narrow** your research question in order to produce better results. Refine your plan as needed.

- As you take notes, **paraphrase** or **summarize** information. If you use a **direct quotation,** enclose it in big quotation marks to avoid plagiarism. Categorize your notes according to themes or subtopics in order to make connections and see big ideas.

- Find **graphics** and **illustrations** to add to your report. Be sure to record source information for any graphics you intend to use.

- Document your **sources** by making a source card for each source you use. For all notes, record bibliographic information according to a standard format.

WRITING COACH

 Online Journal

Try It! Record your answers in the online journal.

 Interactive Graphic Organizers

Choose from a variety of graphic organizers to plan and develop your project.

Partner Talk

Work with a partner to critique your research plan and research. Discuss:

- The difference between plagiarism and paraphrasing
- The importance of citing valid and reliable sources
- The reasons that one source is more useful than another

 Focus on the TEKS

(22)(A–B) Ask open-ended research questions and develop a plan for answering them.

(23)(A–D) Determine, locate, and explore the full range of relevant sources addressing a research question and systematically record the information gathered.

(24)(A–B) Clarify research questions and evaluate and synthesize collected information.

Your Turn

Online Consumer Report (*continued*)

Drafting

- **Categorize** your notes by subject heading, such as Product Description, Strong Points, Weak Points, or Overall Recommendation. Create an outline based on your subject headings. Then, start writing sentences and paragraphs.

- Present your findings in a **systematic way,** based on your outline and using summarizing or paraphrasing to share your findings. Lively **subheadings** will organize your report and help readers understand the conclusions you have drawn.

- Do not plagiarize. Use your own words, and enclose any direct quotations in quotation marks.

- A good consumer report anticipates the reader's needs and questions about the product or service. Begin with a lively opening that leads up to a **thesis statement** and clearly reveals the **conclusion** you've drawn from your research.

- Marshal the evidence you have collected and organized to **describe** the product or service. Use **graphics** and **illustrations** to present your findings in a meaningful format. Give readers logical and **relevant reasons** for your conclusions.

- Acknowledge your **sources** as needed in context or in a credits section. Avoid interrupting the flow of the report. Use accepted formats for integrating quotations and citations.

Revising

Use Revision RADaR techniques as you review your draft carefully.

- **Replace** general terms with vivid details and unclear explanations with precise ideas.

- **Add** specific details or missing information to support your argument.

- **Delete** information that does not support your thesis or develop your argument.

- **Reorder** sentences and paragraphs to present ideas clearly and logically.

Read aloud your online report to make sure it reads smoothly. Vary sentence lengths. Tie ideas together with transition words.

Editing

Now take the time to check your Online Consumer Report carefully before you post it online. Focus on each sentence and then on each word. Look for these common kinds of errors:

- Errors in subject-verb agreement
- Errors in pronoun usage
- Run-on sentences and sentence fragments
- Spelling and capitalization mistakes
- Omitted punctuation marks
- Improper citations and punctuation of quotations

Publishing

- If your school newspaper has an online version, submit your online consumer report to the editor.
- Search for online forums specializing in the type of product or service that you are writing about, and submit your report as a comment. Some sites specialize in communication technology products, while others provide more general consumer information sites.
- Post your consumer report as a blog entry. Search for one of the Web sites that allow users to create a free blog.
- With your classmates, compile your consumer reports into a Student Consumer Guide. Organize the guide by type of product or service. Print it for classroom display or for your school library.

Extension Find another example of an Online Consumer Report, and compare it with the one you are writing.

WRITING COACH

www.TXWritingcoach.Com

Interactive Graphic Organizers

Choose from a variety of graphic organizers to plan and develop your project.

Partner Talk

Exchange drafts with a partner, and give each other feedback. Ask specific questions to help present an effective product. Is your report logically organized and clearly written? Does it give enough information? Consider your partner's suggestions as you revise your draft.

 Focus on the TEKS

(25)(A–D) Organize and present ideas and information according to the purpose of the research and audience.

COLLEGE AND CAREER READINESS STANDARDS

Reading (A)(8) Compare and analyze how generic features are used across texts.

Research (C)(1) Design and present an effective product.

Writing for Assessment

Some tests include a prompt that asks you to critique a research plan. Use these prompts to practice. In your response, use the characteristics of your informational research report. (See page 224.)

 Try It! Read the prompt carefully, and then create a detailed research plan. Use the ABCDs of On-Demand Writing to help you plan and write your research plan.

Format

Write your *research plan* in the form of an outline. List everything you would do in the order you would do it. Use a main heading, such as *Topic,* and subheadings, for example, *Primary Sources.*

Research Plan Prompt

Write a research plan about a person or event related to an American president. Your plan should include a research topic and question, a list of possible sources, the audience, and the steps you'll take following a timeline. [30 minutes]

Academic Vocabulary

A research plan tells what your major research subject is and what *sources* you will use. It also includes a timeline for researching, drafting, and finalizing your report. One of the most important steps is narrowing your research question for a brief research report.

The ABCDs of On-Demand Writing

Use the following ABCDs to help you respond to the prompt.

Before you write your draft:

A ttack the prompt [1 MINUTE]

- Circle or highlight important verbs in the prompt. Draw a line from the verb to what it refers to.
- Rewrite the prompt in your own words.

B rainstorm possible answers [4 MINUTES]

- Create a graphic organizer to generate ideas.
- Use one for each part of the prompt if necessary.

C hoose the order of your response [1 MINUTE]

- Think about the best way to organize your ideas.
- Number your ideas in the order you will write about them. Cross out ideas you will not be using.

After you write your draft:

D etect errors before turning in the draft [1 MINUTE]

- Carefully reread your writing.
- Look for spelling, punctuation, and grammar errors.
- Make sure that your response makes sense and is complete.

More Prompts for Practice

Apply It! **Critique** the research plan in Prompt 1. In a written response, report on your ideas and make specific suggestions to improve the research plan.

- Does the writer need to broaden or narrow the **research question**? Is it appropriate for the audience and purpose?
- Is the writer planning to find enough sources? Are they varied?
- Does the writer plan to include graphics?
- Does the research plan say anything about evaluating sources?

Prompt 1 Cheryl wrote this research plan. Evaluate her plan to determine what she did well and what needs improvement.

My Topic: I'm going to research the beginning of World War II. My question is, what started the war?

My Research: I'll look for books and old newspaper articles about what triggered the conflict. I'll also search the Internet.

My Writing: Once I have my notes, I can copy them into a draft and then revise it.

Texas Test Prep Spiral Review: Narrative If you choose to respond to Prompt 2, write a **personal narrative**. Make sure your story reflects the characteristics described on page 66.

Prompt 2 Write about a person who has had a major impact on you. This person could be a friend, family member, teacher, or community member. Tell about a significant experience you shared with this person and how it affected you. Use specific details and dialogue.

Spiral Review: Response to Literature If you choose to respond to Prompt 3, write a response to literature. Make sure your response to literature reflects the characteristics on page 198 and includes:

- The writing skills for a **multi-paragraph essay** (See page 146.)
- **Evidence** from the text, including **quotations**
- An analysis of the effects of the author's style or use of literary devices

Prompt 3 Choose an expository or literary text that you feel has an interesting conflict. Write an interpretative response about how the writer created that conflict. Include information about the problem and how it was solved, as well as an analysis of why the conflict was important.

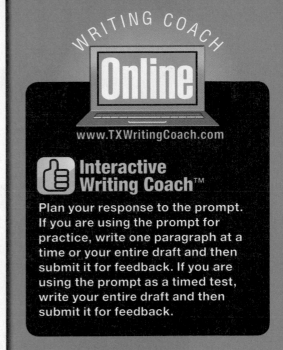

WRITING COACH

Online

www.TXWritingCoach.com

Interactive Writing Coach™

Plan your response to the prompt. If you are using the prompt for practice, write one paragraph at a time or your entire draft and then submit it for feedback. If you are using the prompt as a timed test, write your entire draft and then submit it for feedback.

Remember **ABCD**

Attack the prompt

Brainstorm possible answers

Choose the order of your response

Detect errors before turning in the draft

 Focus on the TEKS

Writing

(16) Write a personal narrative that has a clearly defined focus and includes reflections on decisions, actions, and/or consequences.

(17)(C) Write responses to literary or expository texts.

What's Ahead

In this chapter, you will learn how you can write workplace and practical documents, including business letters and instructions. All of these functional documents should present organized information that is accurately conveyed, or written, and presented in a reader-friendly format.

Characteristics of Writing

Effective workplace and practical writing has these characteristics:

- **Information** that is clear, concise, and focused
- A clear **purpose** and intended **audience**
- **Formal, polite** language
- **Reader-friendly formatting techniques,** such as sufficient white or blank space and clearly defined sections
- Correct **grammar, punctuation,** and **spelling** appropriate to the form of writing

Forms of Writing

Forms of workplace writing include:

Instructions are used to explain how to complete a task or procedure. They are written in a step-by-step format.

Letters of opinion are formal correspondence written to a newspaper, magazine, or other publication. They are written to express an opinion. Letters to the editor are one example of letters of opinion.

Letters of request are formal correspondence written to a business or outside organization. They are written to request information.

Memos are short documents usually written from one member of a group or organization to another or to another group. They assume some background on the topic.

Other forms of practical writing include:

Friendly letters are informal correspondence written to a friend or acquaintance. They can be written for various reasons, including to ask how someone is doing or just to say hello.

 Try It! For each audience and purpose described, select the appropriate form, such as a letter of request, a friendly letter, instructions, or a letter of opinion. Explain your choices.

- To ask for a class schedule from a community center
- To respond to an article in a newspaper

 Connect to the Big Questions

Discuss these questions:

1 What do you think? What is the best way to share information?

2 Why write? What do daily workplace communications require of format, content, and style?

 WORD BANK

These vocabulary words are often used with workplace writing. Use the Glossary or a dictionary to check the definitions.

connection	opinion
introduce	quality

Focus on the TEKS

Writing (17) Write expository and procedural or work-related texts.

STUDENT MODEL **Friendly Letter**

Learn From Experience

 After reading the friendly letter on this page, read the numbered notes in the margin to learn about how the writer presented her ideas. As you read, take notes to develop your understanding of basic sight and English vocabulary.

Try It! Record your answers and ideas in the online journal.

---

1 The friendly letter includes a **date line** and **salutation**. Notice that a comma is placed after the salutation.

2 The writer **clearly explains the reason for writing.**

3 The writer anticipates questions the reader may have and addresses them.

4 The letter ends with an appropriate **closing.** Notice that when a writer sends a friendly letter on paper, he or she signs it.

Try It!

- What is the purpose of this letter? Who is the intended audience?

- Why is it helpful to state a letter's purpose early in the letter?

- How does the writer of the Student Model create a friendly tone?

- What other appropriate closings might the writer have used to end her letter?

---

1 May 18, 2010

Dear Isabel,

I'm excited to hear that you are coming to stay with your aunt this summer. Last year we had so much fun! Will you be staying for the whole month of July like last year?

2 I'm wondering if you want to practice with our local swim team while you're here. Remember what a great time we had at the pool? I've joined the swim team, and I thought you might want to participate in summer practices with me.

3 My mom has already talked to Coach Buckley, and she said it would be fine for you to practice with the team. Think about it and let me know. We have plenty of time, and whatever you decide I know we will have lots of fun this summer. I can't wait to see you!

4 Your friend,

Janine

Feature Assignment: Friendly Letter

Prewriting

- Plan a first draft of your **friendly letter.** You can select from the Topic Bank or come up with an idea of your own.

TOPIC BANK

Reach Out Suppose you have a pen pal who lives in a faraway place. Write a friendly letter to your pen pal, asking what life is like in his or her part of the world.

Good Times Write a friendly letter to a relative, expressing your opinion about a family event you both attended. Include details about the time, place, and purpose of the event.

- Brainstorm for a list of ideas you would like to include in your letter. Consider what **requests for information** you might make.
- Use a telephone directory or online resource to find the accurate contact information for the letter's recipient.

Drafting

- Use reader-friendly formatting techniques, including all the features of an informal letter.
- Use a salutation that matches your relationship with the recipient.
- **Organize the information** so that your purpose is clearly stated.
- Accurately convey information by double-checking your ideas.

Revising and Editing

Before you revise, review your draft to ensure that information is presented accurately and concisely. Ask yourself if the purpose for your letter is clearly identified and addressed.

Publishing

- Print the letter or write it neatly on paper or stationery suitable for the recipient.
- If you plan to e-mail the letter, confirm the correct e-mail address and attach your letter to a message as a Portable Document Format (PDF).

WRITING COACH

Online

www.TXWritingCoach.com

 Interactive Model

Listen to an audio recording of the Student Model.

 Online Journal

Try It! Record your answers and ideas in the online journal.

 Interactive Writing Coach™

Submit your writing and receive personalized feedback and support as you draft, revise, and edit.

 Video

Learn strategies for effective revising and editing from program authors Jeff Anderson and Kelly Gallagher.

Partner Talk

Work with a partner to edit your letter. Ask for feedback on spelling, punctuation, and vocabulary.

 Focus on the TEKS

Writing (17)(B) Write a letter that reflects an opinion, or requests information in a friendly context.

COLLEGE AND CAREER READINESS STANDARDS

Reading (A)(1) Use effective reading strategies to determine a written work's purpose and intended audience.

STUDENT MODEL — Letter of Opinion

Learn From Experience

 After reading the letter of opinion on this page, read the numbered notes in the margin to learn how the writer presented his ideas.

Try It! Record your answers and ideas in the online journal.

---

1 The writer uses conventional business letter formatting, including:

- Writer's address with street, town, state, and zip code
- Date showing day, month, and year
- Recipient's address with full name
- Formal greeting and closing

2 Notice that a colon is placed after the **salutation** of a business letter.

3 The writer states his **opinion** in this **clear thesis statement.**

4 **Facts and details support the point** that the writer is not the only one who thinks kids should have a voice.

5 The writer includes a closing signature along with his typed name, following proper business formatting.

Try It!

- What is the purpose of the letter?
- In your opinion, does the letter fulfill its purpose? Why or why not?

Extension Use the letter's tone to help you distinguish fact from opinion. Write a response that summarizes the issue and responds to the writer's implied attitude.

---

1 Eddie Gates
4307 Windy Circle
Palm Beach Gardens, FL 33418

September 9, 2010

Mr. Maxwell Cooper, Editor
The Downtown Daily
2437 Winston Road
Palm Beach, FL 33480

2 Dear Mr. Cooper:

3 I am very unhappy that the Kids' Review section is being dropped from your newspaper. My parents subscribe to *The Downtown Daily,* and the Kids' Review is the first section I turn to when the newspaper arrives.

The reviews of books, movies, and video games written by kids are interesting to read and give useful information. I think it is important for kids to have a voice in their community, and I know that I am not alone.

4 For example, *Today's News,* in Palm Beach, has a kid's editorial column where young people can give their opinions.

Please do not let kids in our community down. Keep the Kids' Review in *The Downtown Daily.*

Sincerely yours,

5 *Eddie Gates*

Eddie Gates

Feature Assignment: Letter of Opinion

Prewriting

- Plan a first draft of your **letter of opinion**. You can select from the Topic Bank or come up with an idea of your own.

TOPIC BANK

Read All About It! Many students opt to spend their free time playing video games or watching television rather than reading a book for enjoyment. Write a letter to the president of your town's school board about getting students more interested in reading. Offer ideas on how to get students to choose reading over other types of entertainment.

School Days Write a letter to the editor of your school paper, either supporting or opposing its coverage of a school sports team or club. Tell whether the reporting was weak or strong and give reasons for your opinion.

- Brainstorm for a list of things that your letter's recipient will need to know about you and your purpose for writing the letter.
- Find the accurate contact information for the letter's recipient in a telephone directory or online resource.

Drafting

- Use a formal salutation that is suitable for the recipient.
- Include organized information that clearly states your opinion.
- Accurately convey information by double-checking your facts.

Revising and Editing

- Review your draft to ensure **precise word choices.** Check to see if you have clearly expressed your opinion or **registered a complaint** in a business context.

Publishing

- If you plan to mail the letter, print the letter on paper suitable for business correspondence.
- If you plan to e-mail the letter, confirm the correct e-mail address and attach your letter to a message as a PDF.

Partner Talk

Work with a partner to revise your letter. Ask for feedback on the content and organization of the information. Is your opinion clear? Is it well-supported?

 Focus on the TEKS

Writing (17)(B) Write a letter that reflects an opinion or registers a complaint in a business context.

COLLEGE AND CAREER READINESS STANDARDS

Reading (A)(4) Draw and support complex inferences from text.

STUDENT MODEL

Letter of Request

Learn From Experience

 After reading the letter of request on this page, read the numbered notes in the margin to learn about how the writer presented her ideas.

Try It! Record your answers and ideas in the online journal.

---

❶ The writer uses conventional **business letter format,** including writer's address, date, recipient's address, formal salutation, and closing.

❷ The letter begins with a **clear introduction** that expresses the purpose of the letter.

❸ This **request for information** is **clear and focused**. Writers are more likely to get the results they want when their request is clear.

❹ In **formal, polite language,** the writer gives a reasonable deadline for receiving the information.

Try It!

- What impression do you think the writer makes on the reader by using proper business letter format?

- Did the writer include all the information the reader would need to fulfill her request? Explain.

- In your opinion, does the letter fulfill its purpose? Why or why not?

---

❶ Amy Parkland
539 Sunset Road
Western Springs, IL 60558

❶ March 1, 2010

❶ David Nixon, Director
Camp Shady Lanes
2400 Old Oak Lane
Hayward, WI 54843

❶ Dear Mr. Nixon,

❷ I am writing to ask about Camp Shady Lanes' programs for kids ages thirteen and up. My eight-year-old sister attended the camp last summer, and she had a great time. I think I might like to attend the camp this summer if it has programs for older kids like me.

❸ Would you please send me a brochure and any other information about the programs at Camp Shady Lanes? I am in the seventh grade, and I am looking for a camp with a lot of outdoor activities. I especially enjoy swimming and horseback riding. Does the camp offer these?

❹ It would be helpful if I could receive the information by April 15. That way, I can make a decision before the April 30 registration deadline. Thank you for your help!

❶ Sincerely,

Amy Parkland

Amy Parkland

Your Turn

Feature Assignment: Letter of Request

Prewriting

- Plan a first draft of your **letter of request**. You can select from the Topic Bank or come up with an idea of your own.

How It Works Imagine that you have just gotten a new video game or electronic device, but it didn't come with any instructions. Write a letter of request to the company asking it to send you the missing instructions.

Money Back You have purchased an item and now you have changed your mind. Write a letter requesting a refund from the company. Include details about what the item is and why you no longer want it.

- Brainstorm for a list of things that your letter's recipient will need to know about you and your purpose for writing the letter.

- Find the accurate contact information for the letter's recipient in a telephone directory or online resource.

Drafting

- Use reader-friendly formatting techniques, including all of the features of a business letter.

- Organize the information so that the purpose and the request are clearly stated in the letter. Use formal, business language.

- Accurately convey information by double-checking your facts.

Revising and Editing

Review your draft to ensure that information is presented accurately and concisely. Ask yourself if your letter fulfills the purpose: **to request information in a business context.**

Publishing

- If you plan to mail the letter, print the letter on suitable paper.

- If you plan to e-mail the letter, confirm the correct e-mail address and attach your letter to a message as a PDF.

WRITING COACH

Online

www.TXWritingCoach.com

 Interactive Model
Listen to an audio recording of the Student Model.

 Online Journal
Try It! Record your answers and ideas in the online journal.

 Interactive Writing Coach™
Submit your writing and receive personalized feedback and support as you draft, revise, and edit.

 Video
Learn strategies for effective revising and editing from program authors Jeff Anderson and Kelly Gallagher.

 Partner Talk

Read your final draft to a partner. Ask him or her if your request is clearly stated. Monitor your partner's spoken language by asking follow-up questions to confirm your understanding.

 Focus on the TEKS

Writing (17)(B) Write a letter that requests information in a business context.

MAKE YOUR WRITING COUNT

Present a Research Report on Activities for Kids

Letters help people communicate important information to specific audiences. These workplace documents may involve the seeds for activities or ideas that will help classmates learn more. Make a **research report** and presentation to share with your classmates.

With a group, **brainstorm** for several topics from among your work in this chapter. Have a discussion with others and **decide on a topic** that will be helpful to someone thinking about fun activities for kids in and out of school. Work together to **formulate an open-ended research question** that will help you to produce a research report about the topic. Consider topics like joining sports teams, volunteering at local organizations, or planning a family event. Conduct some **preliminary research** in reference works and by searching additional texts to make sure that your question is a good one.

Group members should **consult** one another and **critique the process** as you work, and be prepared to adjust and clarify the research question and process as needed. Remember that a research report should:

- State a specific thesis
- Meet the needs of audience and purpose
- Express a clear point of view
- Provide supporting evidence
- Present ideas in a logical way
- Document sources using correct formatting

Organize a Kids' Fun Day to present your research results to students in your school. Share the information you have gathered in a **multimedia presentation** that uses text and graphics. You may use posters and other displays or an electronic slide show that uses presentation software.

21st Century Learning

Here's your action plan.

1. Research takes time. In a group, make a plan for several group meetings. Set objectives and choose roles for each member.

2. Work together to develop a **written research plan** that includes:

   - Obtaining and evaluating a variety of sources, including a range of **print and electronic sources** as well as data and **quotations from experts**

   - **Categorizing notes by theme** or sub-topic to big ideas

   - Using a standard format to record **bibliographic information** for all notes and sources

   - Checking elements such as publication date and point of view to ensure that your sources are **reliable and valid**

3. Discuss your findings. **Evaluate the sources,** discussing the importance of citing valid and reliable sources. Reject sources that are biased or dated, and explain why they aren't useful. Work together to create a **clear thesis statement**.

4. Outline the report. Assign sections of the outline to each group member. You may need to **narrow or broaden your research question** and research further before you draft.

5. Work together to write a draft by **compiling** collected data and using the **marshalled**—collected and organized—evidence to explain the topic. As a group, discuss the difference between **plagiarism** and **paraphrasing**. Use the proper style for acknowledging sources and for **integrating quotations and citations** without interrupting the flow of ideas.

6. Revise and edit to ensure that the thesis statement is **supported by evidence**. Be sure your report **states relevant reasons for conclusions** and **summarizes** your findings in a systematic way.

7. Finally, add appropriate audio and visuals that help explain the topic and present your findings in a **meaningful format**.

8. Present your report to students, counselors, and teachers.

Listening and Speaking Practice the presentation in front of another group or each other. Listen to questions or comments from the audience to help you make improvements. On Kids' Fun Day, speak clearly and confidently to your audience.

WRITING COACH

Online

www.TXWritingCoach.com

Online Journal
Record your answers and ideas in the online journal.

Resource
Link to resources on 21st Century Learning for help in creating a group project.

 Focus on the TEKS

Research

(22)(A–B) Ask open-ended research questions and develop a plan for answering them.

(23)(A–E) Determine, locate, and explore the full range of relevant sources.

(24)(A–B) Clarify research questions and evaluate and synthesize collected information.

(25)(A–D) Organize and present ideas and information according to the purpose of the research and audience.

COLLEGE AND CAREER READINESS STANDARDS

Listening (B)(1) Listen critically and respond appropriately to presentations.

Reading(A)(11) Identify, analyze, and evaluate similarities and differences in how multiple texts present information.

Your Turn

Writing for Media:
Set of Instructions

21st Century Learning

Set of Instructions

Multimedia presentations are frequently used in schools, in the workplace, at conferences, and online. They are an effective way to present information to a wide audience. Multimedia presentations use a combination of text, images, music, charts, graphics, and animation. They allow people to share information on a variety of topics. A slide show allows the presenter to share only key points in text while giving an oral presentation.

A multimedia presentation is a good way to share a set of instructions. The presenter can provide information to the audience one point at a time, helping the audience to focus. Often, printed versions of the presentation are also given to the audience for reference.

Try It! Study the slides on this page. Then, answer the questions. Record your answers in your journal.

1. How does the **title slide** communicate the purpose of the multimedia presentation?

2. How do the **photos and maps** help the reader follow along?

3. Is the amount of **text** per slide reader-friendly? Explain.

4. What do you think the **presenter** should say as each slide is shown?

Directions from Miller School to Museum

- Head west on Booker St.
- Turn right at Harrington Ave.

N

Harrington Ave.

Booker St.

- Walk .8 of a mile to museum entrance
- Meet on front steps

Extension Find another example of a multimedia presentation, and compare it with this one.

Create a Set of Instructions

Follow these steps to create your own multimedia slide show that features a **set of instructions**. Review the graphic organizers on R24–R27 and choose one that suits your needs.

Prewriting

- Brainstorm for a list of places to which you could provide directions using a slide show.
- Choose the one place you think is best.
- Make a list of the steps involved in the directions.
- Consider the needs of your specific audience. What does the audience already know? What do they need to know?

Drafting

- Divide your directions into slides. Each slide should contain only a small amount of text. This will allow your audience to focus on your **multimedia presentation.**
- Number the steps and order them according to what is done first, second, next, and so on. Include simple maps to show landmarks and stops along the way.
- Write a script for the oral presentation. Organize the information to support the content of each slide.
- Choose colors, backgrounds, **text fonts, and graphics** that will make it easy for your audience to read each slide.

Revising and Editing

- As you revise, review each slide to be sure that its content correctly matches each section of your oral presentation.
- Be sure the design of your slides makes them easy to read.
- Double-check the accuracy of information on your slides.
- Check spelling and grammar.

Publishing

- Present your slide show to your class or another audience. If you use the slide show for multiple presentations, you may need to adjust it for different **audiences and purposes.**
- Speak clearly and allow time for audience questions.

WRITING COACH
Online
www.TXWritingCoach.com

 Online Journal
Try It! **Record your answers and ideas in the online journal.**

 Interactive Graphic Organizers
Use the graphic organizers to plan your multimedia presentation.

 Partner **Talk**

Before publishing, practice your presentation with a partner. Practice newly acquired vocabulary by correctly producing the word's sound.

 Focus on the TEKS

Writing (17)(D) Produce a multimedia presentation involving text and graphics using available technology.

COLLEGE AND CAREER READINESS STANDARDS
Speaking (A)(2) Adjust presentations to particular audiences and purposes.

Writing for Assessment

Many standardized tests include a prompt that asks you to write a procedural text. Use these prompts to practice. Respond using the characteristics of a procedural text. (See pages 266–267.)

 Try It! Read the **procedural text prompt** and the information on the format and academic vocabulary. Use the ABCDs of On-Demand Writing to help you plan and write your procedural text.

Format

The prompt directs you to write a *procedural text*. Describe the purpose of the text in the first section. Be sure to include steps with organized information such as a numbered list or materials list.

Procedural Text Prompt

Your new science lab partner wants to know how to set up for an experiment. He wants written instructions to help him. Write a procedural text that includes stepped-out instructions on how to set up your lab table. [30 minutes]

Academic Vocabulary

A procedural text is a kind of text that tells somebody how to perform a task. *Stepped-out instructions* have numbered lists that provide details in the order they are used.

The ABCDs of On-Demand Writing

Use the following ABCDs to help you respond to the prompt.

Before you write your draft:

A ttack the prompt [1 MINUTE]

- Circle or highlight important verbs in the prompt. Draw a line from the verb to what it refers to.
- Rewrite the prompt in your own words.

B rainstorm possible answers [4 MINUTES]

- Create a graphic organizer to generate ideas.
- Use one for each part of the prompt if necessary.

C hoose the order of your response [1 MINUTE]

- Think about the best way to organize your ideas.
- Number your ideas in the order you will write about them. Cross out ideas you will not be using.

After you write your draft:

D etect errors before turning in the draft [1 MINUTE]

- Carefully reread your writing.
- Make sure that your response makes sense and is complete.
- Look for spelling, punctuation, and grammar errors.

More Prompts for Practice

 Apply It! Respond to Prompt 1 by writing a **procedural text.** As you write, be sure to:

- Consider what your **audience** knows and needs to know
- **Organize** information into steps or paragraphs
- **Define** any terms that your audience may not know

> **Prompt 1** Your mom needs directions from your house to your friend's house. Write a procedural text that includes stepped-out instructions she can follow when she comes to pick you up.

Texas Test Prep Spiral Review: Expository If you choose to respond to Prompt 2, write a compare-and-contrast **expository essay**. Make sure your essay reflects the characteristics described on page 146.

> **Prompt 2** Protecting the environment is an important global concern. However, people have different opinions about what must be done on an everyday basis. Write an expository essay that compares and contrasts two different ways you could choose to help protect the environment in your daily life.

Spiral Review: Research Plan If you choose to respond to Prompt 3, write a **critique of the research plan**. Make sure your critique evaluates all of the characteristics described on page 224. Your critique should determine if the research plan:

- Contains a **narrowed topic** and is appropriate for the **audience**
- Includes enough **primary** and **secondary sources,** and says something about **evaluating** sources

> **Prompt 3** Henri wrote this research plan. Explain what he did well and what needs improvement.
> *My Topic:* I'm interested in comparing real cowboys to cowboys in stories.
> *My Research:* I'm going to search the Internet, talk to the reference librarian, and look for print sources. I know that William H. Cody was a real cowboy, so I'll look for and read books and articles about him.
> *My Drafting:* After a month of research, I will copy my notes to write my draft.

Remember **ABCD**

Attack the prompt

Brainstorm possible answers

Choose the order of your response

Detect errors before turning in the draft

 Focus on the TEKS

Writing (17)(A) Create multi-paragraph essays to convey information about a topic.

Grammar

Find It FIX IT

Grammar Game Plan

This handy guide will help you find and fix errors in your writing!

20 Major Grammatical Errors and How to Fix Them

GAME PLAN Use the right words to make your writing clear. Make sure your words say exactly what you mean them to say.

CLARIFY MEANING Do not confuse the meanings of words with similar spellings. Also, words with similar definitions can have important shades of meaning. Check that words you found in a thesaurus are used correctly.

I wish we could go ~~their~~ ʌ there for dinner.

You should go ~~too~~ ʌ to her house tonight.

SPELL-CHECK ERRORS Computer spell-checkers often correct a misspelled word with another word that is close in spelling. Be sure to proofread your work carefully to catch these errors. In each of the following examples, the word with a strikethrough represents an inappropriate spell-checker correction.

Try not to ~~turn~~ ʌ burn the toast.

The student needs ~~held~~ ʌ help with the math problem.

Check It

Use a current or completed draft of your work to practice using words correctly.

✔ **READ carefully.** Take the time to read your draft closely. For a double-check, have someone else read your work.

✔ **IDENTIFY possible mistakes.** Mark any difficult or commonly misused words in your draft.

✔ **USE a dictionary.** If you are not sure of a word's meaning, look it up in a dictionary.

Tech Tip

Be your own "spell-checker"! Proofread! Your computer's spell-checker will not identify every misspelling or incorrectly used word.

LEARN MORE
- See Chapter 20, Effective Sentences, pages 457–461
- See Writing Coach Online

 Focus on the TEKS

Writing (14)(D) Edit drafts for spelling.

Conventions/Spelling (21) Spell correctly, including using various sources to determine and check correct spelling.

Tech Tip

Remember to add commas to introductory elements that you cut and paste from different parts of a sentence or paragraph.

LEARN MORE

- See Chapter 25, Punctuation, pages 561, 564
- See Writing Coach Online

Focus on the TEKS

Writing (14)(D) Edit drafts for mechanics.

Conventions (20)(B)(i) Use punctuation marks including commas after introductory words, phrases, and clauses.

GAME PLAN Place a comma after the following introductory elements in your work.

WORDS Place a comma after introductory words.

Hello,∧I'm here for the party.

Well,∧it's good to have you.

PHRASES Place a comma after introductory prepositional phrases. If the prepositional phrase has only two words, a comma is not necessary.

Before dinner at 5:00,∧you can wash the tomatoes.

In the evening,∧please remember to take out the trash.

After dinner you should wash the dishes.

CLAUSES Introductory adverbial clauses should be followed by a comma.

When the audience clapped,∧the orchestra stood up to take a bow.

 Check It

Use a current or completed draft of your work to practice placing commas after introductory clauses.

✓ **SCAN your draft.** Look for introductory words, phrases, and clauses.

✓ **IDENTIFY missing commas.** Mark sentence starters that might need a comma.

✓ **USE your textbook.** Check the grammar section of your textbook if you are not sure whether or not to use a comma.

GAME PLAN Provide complete citations for borrowed words and ideas. Use the citation style (such as MLA) that your teacher recommends.

MISSING CITATIONS Cite sources of direct quotes and statistics. Remember–when in doubt, cite the source.

The doctor stated, "This is the most interesting case I've seen"∧(Roberts 12).

Dr. Jones reported that 1 in 10 patients have the disorder∧(Jones 18).

INCOMPLETE CITATIONS Make sure your citations include complete source information. This information will vary depending on the source and the citation style. It often includes the author's name, the source's title, and the page numbers. You may use the shortened version you see here if your paper includes a bibliography where the reader can get the title of the source and the author's first name.

The book has been called "a beautifully written piece" (∧Lynn 8).

An 18 percent increase in sales was reported (Appleton∧72).

Check It

Use a current or completed draft of your work to practice documenting your sources.

✓ **REVIEW your notes.** Look for introductory words, phrases, and clauses.

✓ **USE a style guide.** Check the correct format for your citations in the style guide your teacher recommends.

Tech Tip

When researching for an assignment on the Internet, be sure to use only reputable sources that cite their information. Then, use the correct citation style for Internet sources, which often includes the Web site URL and date visited.

LEARN MORE
- See Chapter 11, Research Writing, pages 234–237
- See Writing Coach Online

 Focus on the TEKS

Research/Organizing and Presenting Ideas (25)(D) Follow accepted formats for integrating quotations and citations into the written text.

4

Vague Pronoun Reference

Tech Tip

It is important to proofread your work after you cut and paste text. You may have inserted vague pronoun references while moving text and making new sentences.

┌─ **LEARN MORE** ─
- See Chapter 6, Fiction Narration, pages 110–111
- See Writing Coach Online

GAME PLAN Create clear pronoun-antecedent relationships to make your writing more accurate and powerful.

VAGUE IDEA Pronouns such as *which, this, that,* and *these* should refer to a specific idea. To avoid a vague reference, try changing a pronoun to an adjective that modifies a specific noun.

Abigail bought her younger brother a baseball and a basketball. That ∧basketball is the one he has been asking for.

UNCLEAR USE OF *IT, THEY,* AND *YOU* Be sure that the pronouns *it, they,* and *you* have a clearly stated antecedent. Replacing the personal pronoun with a specific noun can make a sentence clearer.

My teacher has taught us about World War I and World War II. ~~It~~ ∧World War II will be on the test next week.

The team members asked the coaches ~~if they could~~ ∧to practice the play again.

To make the basketball team, ~~you~~ ∧potential team members must attend every tryout.

✔ **Check It**

Use a current or completed draft of your work to practice identifying vague pronoun references.

✔ **READ** carefully. Read your draft slowly to locate pronouns.

✔ **IDENTIFY** possible errors. Mark any vague pronoun references.

✔ **REVISE** your draft. Rewrite sentences with vague pronoun-antecedent relationships.

 Focus on the TEKS

Writing (14)(D) Edit drafts for grammar.

5

Spelling Error

GAME PLAN Spelling errors can change the meaning of a sentence. Proofread your work after spell-checking to be sure you have used the correct words.

SPELL-CHECK ERRORS Computer spell-checkers often replace misspelled words with others close in spelling but different in meaning. Proofread your work carefully to correct these errors.

Mrs. Douglas likes ~~line~~ pine trees the best.

After the show, my dad ~~grove~~ drove us home.

HOMOPHONES Words that are pronounced the same but have different spellings and meanings are called homophones. Check that you have used the correct homophones to convey your meaning.

Did you say that a ~~be~~ bee stung you?

When we were in the skyscraper, we were ~~hi~~ high above the ground.

✔ Check It

Use a current or completed draft of your work to practice spelling words correctly.

✔ **READ** carefully. Read your draft word by word looking for spelling errors.

✔ **IDENTIFY** possible mistakes. Mark any incorrect words or words that are misspelled.

✔ **USE** a dictionary. If you are not certain how to spell a word or think a homophone has been used incorrectly, check a dictionary.

Tech Tip

Proper nouns are not checked by a computer spell-checker. Proofread to make sure that you have spelled people's names correctly.

LEARN MORE

• See Chapter 20, Effective Sentences, pages 457–461
• See Writing Coach Online

 Focus on the TEKS

Writing (14)(D) Edit drafts for spelling.

Conventions/Spelling (21) Spell correctly, including using various resources to determine and check correct spelling.

6

Punctuation Error With a Quotation

LEARN MORE
- See Chapter 25, Punctuation, pages 577–583
- See Writing Coach Online

GAME PLAN Quotation marks are used to identify direct quotations. Correct punctuation helps to identify quotations and relate them to your work.

DIRECT AND INDIRECT QUOTATIONS A direct quotation is enclosed in quotation marks. Indirect quotations do not need quotation marks.

My mom said, "I'll pick you up from school today."

My mom said that she will pick me up from school.

QUOTATION MARKS WITH OTHER PUNCTUATION When commas or periods end a quotation, the punctuation goes inside the quotation marks. Question marks and exclamation marks go either inside or outside the quotation marks, depending on the sentence structure.

The director said, "Choir tryouts are this Friday."

"I hope I can join the choir!" the girl exclaimed.

Did she say, "I don't think I'll try out for choir"?

 Check It

Use a current or completed draft of your work to practice punctuating quotations correctly.

✓ **READ** carefully. If you used indirect quotations, make sure you did not put them in quotation marks.

✓ **IDENTIFY** direct quotations. Mark each direct quotation in your work. Is each quotation punctuated correctly?

✓ **REVISE** your sentences. Correct all punctuation errors in your quotations.

 Focus on the TEKS

Writing (14)(D) Edit drafts for mechanics.

GAME PLAN Before you insert a comma, think about how your ideas relate to one another. Make sure the comma is necessary.

APPOSITIVES If an appositive is essential to the meaning of a sentence, it is *not* set off by commas.

My friend, Jose, was in charge of making sure everyone in class was on the bus.

PARTICIPIAL PHRASES If a participial phrase is essential to the meaning of a sentence, it should *not* be set off by commas.

The student, standing in the bus aisle, was asked to sit in a seat.

ADJECTIVAL CLAUSES Essential adjectival clauses should *not* be set off by commas.

The bus ride, that took us to the museum, was a short trip.

Check It

Use a current or completed draft of your work to practice correctly punctuating essential elements.

✓ **SCAN** Mentor Texts. Notice how professional writers use commas.

✓ **IDENTIFY** essential elements. Did you incorrectly use commas to indicate these elements?

✓ **REVISE** your sentences. Delete any commas that set off essential elements.

Tech Tip

Remember to add or delete commas as needed when you cut and paste and move text.

LEARN MORE
• See Chapter 25, Punctuation, pages 562–565
• See Writing Coach Online

 Focus on the TEKS

Writing (14)(D) Edit drafts for mechanics.

Conventions (19)(A)(ii-iii) Identify, use, and understand the function of appositive phrases and adjectival phrases and clauses.

8

Unnecessary or Missing Capitalization

Sometimes word processors will automatically capitalize any word that follows a period, even if the period is part of an abbreviation. Proofread carefully for incorrectly capitalized words.

LEARN MORE

• See Chapter 26, Capitalization, pages 608–628
• See Writing Coach Online

 Focus on the TEKS

Writing (14)(D) Edit drafts for mechanics.

Conventions (20)(A) Use conventions of capitalization.

GAME PLAN Follow the rules of capitalization. For example, capitalize proper nouns, the first word of a sentence, and titles of works of art.

PROPER NOUNS Names, geographical locations, and organizations are examples of nouns that should be capitalized.

My sister Jenna lives in Michigan near Lake Huron.

John Fisher works for the Red Cross.

TITLES OF WORKS OF ART The first word and all other key words in the titles of books, poems, stories, plays, paintings, and other works of art are capitalized.

I like to read *Charlotte's Web* to my younger cousins.

I always liked the story "Beauty and the Beast."

✔ Check It

Use a current or completed draft of your work to practice correctly capitalizing words.

✔ **SCAN** your draft. Look for words that are capitalized.

✔ **IDENTIFY** errors in capitalization. Mark words that might be capitalized incorrectly.

✔ **USE** your textbook. Check the grammar section of your textbook if you are not sure if a word should be capitalized.

GAME PLAN Make sure there are no missing words in a text so that your ideas flow smoothly and are clear to readers.

ARTICLES To make sure that ideas flow smoothly, you must proofread your work. A missing word, even a missing article (*a, an, the*), can confuse a reader.

My family is going to ^the band concert at school tonight.

KEY IDEAS When copying and pasting text, you might miss moving a word in a sentence. If that word is part of the main idea of the sentence, your meaning could be lost.

After I rode my bike to school, I realized that I ^forgot my bike lock at home!

I asked the principal if I could store my ^bike inside for the day.

Tech Tip

When cutting and pasting sentences, you may use the same word twice by mistake. Proofread to be sure your sentences read correctly.

LEARN MORE
- See Editing sections in the writing chapters
- See Writing Coach Online

✔ *Check It*

Use a current or completed draft of your work to practice proofreading.

✔ **READ** carefully. Read your draft word by word to make sure that you did not leave out a word.

✔ **IDENTIFY** unclear sentences. Mark any sentences you find that do not make sense. Are they unclear because of a missing word?

✔ **REVISE** your sentences. Add words to your sentences to make the meaning clear.

 Focus on the TEKS

Writing (14)(D) Edit drafts for grammar.

10

Faulty Sentence Structure

Tech Tip

Be careful when you cut one part of a sentence and paste it in another. Remember to check that the new sentence structure is correct.

LEARN MORE
- See Chapter 20, Effective Sentences, pages 462–464
- See Writing Coach Online

 Focus on the TEKS

Writing (14)(D) Edit drafts for grammar.

Conventions (19)(C) Use a variety of complete sentences (e.g., *simple, compound, complex*) that include parallel structures.

GAME PLAN Sentences should express complex ideas clearly. Use parallel, or similar, structures to make your writing clear.

WORDS IN A SERIES Check that the words you use in a series have parallel structure.

When I go on vacation, I like to read, to fish, and ~~biking~~ ∧to bike.

I like baseball because of the running, catching, and ~~to pitch~~ ∧pitching.

COMPARISONS In writing comparisons, be sure to compare a phrase with the same type of phrase. Also, compare a clause with the same type of clause.

She thinks that singing is hard but∧that it is worth the effort.

Billy says the cat is under the bed, but ~~the couch is where his brother thinks he'll find the cat~~ ∧his brother thinks the cat is under the couch.

✓ Check It

Use a current or corrected draft of your work to practice writing using parallel structures.

✓ **SCAN** Mentor Texts. Notice how professional writers present complex ideas.

✓ **IDENTIFY** possible mistakes. Mark any sentences that have faulty parallelism.

✓ **REVISE** your sentences. Rewrite any sentences that do not have correct sentence structure.

GAME PLAN Use commas to set off nonessential elements of sentences.

APPOSITIVE If an appositive is not essential to the meaning of a sentence, it should be set off by commas.

Mrs. Simon,∧<u>Bridget's mom,</u>∧gave me a ride home from school today.

PARTICIPIAL PHRASE A participial phrase not essential to the meaning of a sentence is set off by commas.

Mrs. Simon,∧<u>driving a minivan,</u>∧pulled into my driveway.

ADJECTIVAL CLAUSE Use commas to set off an adjectival clause if it is not essential to the meaning of a sentence.

My mom,∧<u>who had to work late,</u>∧made meatloaf for dinner.

✔ *Check It*

Use a current or completed draft of your work to practice using commas correctly with nonessential elements.

✔ **SCAN** Mentor Texts. Notice how professional writers use commas to set off nonessential elements.

✔ **IDENTIFY** nonessential elements. Did you use commas to indicate these words, phrases, or clauses?

✔ **REVISE** your sentences. Use commas to set off nonessential elements.

Tech Tip

When you cut part of a sentence and paste it to another, be sure to include the correct punctuation. Proofread these sentences carefully.

LEARN MORE
- **See Chapter 25, Punctuation, pages 562–565**
- **See Writing Coach Online**

 Focus on the TEKS

Writing (14)(D) Edit drafts for mechanics.

Conventions (19)(A)(ii-iii) Identify, use, and understand the function of appositive phrases and adjectival phrases and clauses.

12

Unnecessary Shift in Verb Tense

Tech Tip

When you cut text from one section to paste to another, the new sentence may have verbs that are not consistent in tense. Proofread revised sentences to make sure they use consistent tenses.

LEARN MORE
- See Chapter 20, Effective Sentences, pages 466–467
- See Writing Coach Online

Focus on the TEKS

Writing (14)(D) Edit drafts for grammar.

Conventions (19)(C) Use a variety of complete sentences (e.g., *simple, compound, complex*) that include consistent tenses.

GAME PLAN Use consistent verb tenses in your work. Shift tenses only to show that one event comes before or after another.

ACTIONS OCCURRING AT THE SAME TIME Use consistent tenses to show actions that occur at the same time.

I walked to the movie theater, and I ~~watch~~ ∧watched my favorite film.

I dove into the pool, and I ~~swim~~ ∧swam to the other end.

ACTIONS OCCURRING AT DIFFERENT TIMES If actions occur at different times, you can switch from one tense to another. You may use a time word or phrase to show the shift in tense.

Yesterday my family hiked in the forest, but today we ~~swam~~ ∧are swimming in the lake.

I went to school today, but tomorrow, Saturday, I ~~went~~ ∧will go to the mall.

Use a current or completed draft of your work to practice using consistent tenses.

✔ **SCAN** Mentor Texts. Notice how professional writers use consistent tenses within a sentence.

✔ **IDENTIFY** possible mistakes. Mark any unnecessary shift in verb tense within a sentence.

✔ **USE** your textbook. Consult the grammar section of your textbook if you are not sure that have used consistent tenses.

GAME PLAN Use a comma before a coordinating conjunction to separate two or more main clauses in a compound sentence.

MAIN CLAUSES Place a comma before a coordinating conjunction (e.g. *and*, *but*, *or*, *nor*, *yet*, *so*, *for*) in a compound sentence.

Freddie wants to go to the park,ₐbut it is raining.

My aunt is coming to my house for dinner,ₐand she is bringing dessert.

BRIEF CLAUSES The main clauses in some compound sentences are brief and do not need a comma if the meaning is clear.

Mary is 12 years old and Sasha is 14 years old.

SINGLE WORDS Commas should *not* be used to separate single words that are joined by a conjunction.

They brought fruit, and vegetables.

He saw a duck, and goose.

Tech Tip

Be careful when you create a compound sentence by cutting and pasting from different parts of a sentence or paragraph. Remember to include a comma to separate the main clauses.

LEARN MORE
- See Chapter 25, Punctuation, pages 556, 559
- See Writing Coach Online

Use a current or completed draft of your work to practice using commas in compound sentences.

✔ **SCAN** your draft. Look for compound sentences.

✔ **IDENTIFY** missing commas. Mark any compound sentences that should be punctuated with a comma.

✔ **REVISE** your sentences. Add commas before coordinating conjunctions to separate main clauses.

 Focus on the TEKS

Writing (14)(D) Edit drafts for mechanics.

14

Unnecessary or Missing Apostrophe

Tech Tip

Proofread your draft carefully. Not all computer grammar checkers will point out incorrect uses of apostrophes.

LEARN MORE

- See Chapter 22, Using Pronouns, pages 506–509
- See Chapter 25, Punctuation, pages 595–599
- See Writing Coach Online

Focus on the TEKS

Writing (14)(D) Edit drafts for mechanics.

GAME PLAN Use apostrophes correctly to show possession.

SINGULAR NOUNS To show the possessive case of most singular nouns, add an apostrophe and -*s*.

The school**'s**∧talent show was amazing.

PLURAL NOUNS Add an apostrophe to show the possessive case for most plural nouns ending in -*s* or -*es*. For plural nouns that do not end in -*s* or -*es*, add an apostrophe and -*s*.

The students**'**∧chatter was distracting the teacher.

The children**'s**∧clothing store is where my aunt shops for my younger cousin.

POSSESSIVE PRONOUNS Possessive pronouns (e.g. *his, hers, its, our, their*) show possession without the use of an apostrophe. Do not confuse *its* and *it's*. The word *its* shows possession, but the word *it's* means "it is."

~~Hers'~~∧Hers is the car on the left; you can see ~~it's~~∧its dented hood.

✓ Check It

Use a current or completed draft of your work to practice showing possession.

✓ **SCAN** Mentor Texts. Notice when professional writers use apostrophes to indicate possession.

✓ **IDENTIFY** possible mistakes. Mark each apostrophe in your draft. Did you use them correctly to show possession?

✓ **REVISE** your sentences. Make sure to delete any apostrophes you used with possessive pronouns.

GAME PLAN Use correct punctuation to avoid run-on sentences. A run-on sentence is two or more sentences punctuated as if they were a single sentence.

FUSED SENTENCE A fused sentence contains two or more sentences joined with no punctuation. To correct a fused sentence, place a period or an end mark between the main clauses.

My aunt bought her wedding ~~dress it~~ ∧dress. It was made out of lace.

Why did he want to buy a new ~~jacket his~~ ∧jacket? His had hardly been worn.

RUN-ON SENTENCE Place a comma and a coordinating conjunction between main clauses to avoid run-on sentences.

We were going to arrive to the movie on time,∧but my dad got a flat tire on the way to the theater.

Tech Tip

Remember to proofread your work. Not all grammar checkers identify run-on sentences.

LEARN MORE
- See Chapter 20, Effective Sentences, pages 449–452
- See Writing Coach Online

✔ *Check It*

Use a current or completed draft of your work to practice correcting run-on sentences.

✔ **SCAN** your draft. Look for run-on sentences.

✔ **IDENTIFY** missing punctuation. Mark sentences that might need a period or an end mark to separate main clauses.

✔ **REVISE** your sentences. When correcting fused sentences, vary your sentence structure.

 Focus on the TEKS

Writing (14)(D) Edit drafts for mechanics.

GAME PLAN Use correct punctuation to avoid comma splices. A comma splice happens when two or more complete sentences are joined only with a comma.

PERIOD Replace the comma with a period (and capitalize the following word) to separate two complete thoughts.

The blizzard buried my dad's car under a blanket of snow, ~~we~~ ∧. We had to shovel the car out before he could drive to work.

SEMICOLON Replace the comma with a semicolon if the ideas are similar.

Charlie built a sand castle, ∧; the waves knocked it down.

COORDINATING CONJUNCTION A comma splice can be corrected by placing a coordinating conjunction (e.g., *and, or, but, yet, nor*) after the comma.

Clouds started to cover then sun, ∧ and it started to rain.

✓ Check It

Use a current or completed draft of your work to practice correcting comma splices.

✓ **READ** carefully. Take time to read your draft carefully. Have someone else read your work for a double-check.

✓ **IDENTIFY** possible mistakes. Mark any comma splices you find.

✓ **REVISE** your sentences. Fix comma splices in different ways to vary your sentence structure.

Tech Tip

Some grammar checkers will not catch comma splices. Proofread your work carefully to avoid comma splices.

LEARN MORE
- **See Chapter 20, Effective Sentences, pages 449–452**
- **See Chapter 25, Punctuation, pages 556–557**
- **See Writing Coach Online**

 Focus on the TEKS

Writing (14)(D) Edit drafts for mechanics.

Conventions (20)(B)(ii) Use punctuation marks including semicolons.

GAME PLAN Check that pronouns agree with their antecedents in number, person, and gender. When the gender is not specified, the pronoun must still agree in number.

GENDER NEUTRAL ANTECEDENTS When gender is not specific, use *his* or *her* to refer to the singular antecedent.

<u>Each</u> child should be in ~~their~~ ∧his or her bed by 8 p.m.

OR, NOR, AND When two or more singular antecedents are joined by *or* or *nor*, use a singular personal pronoun. Use a plural personal pronoun when two or more antecedents are joined by *and*.

Neither Jerry <u>nor</u> Stu will read the book I gave ~~them~~ ∧him.

Sally <u>and</u> Sue are memorizing ~~her~~ ∧their routine for cheerleading practice.

INDEFINITE PRONOUNS A plural personal pronoun must agree with a plural indefinite pronoun. A singular personal pronoun must agree with a singular indefinite pronoun.

<u>Both</u> of the girls put ~~her~~ ∧their toys away before dinner.

<u>One</u> of the photographers took ~~their~~ ∧his photographs to the studio to get developed.

✓ Check It

Use a current or completed draft of your work to practice pronoun-antecedent agreement.

✔ **READ** carefully. Take time to read your draft carefully. For a double-check, have someone else read your work.

✔ **IDENTIFY** possible mistakes. Mark any pronouns that do not agree with their antecedents in a sentence.

✔ **USE** your textbook. Check the grammar section of your textbook if you are not sure whether your pronouns and antecedents agree.

Tech Tip

Be careful when you cut and paste text from one sentence to another. Check that the pronouns agree with the antecedents in the new sentences you create.

LEARN MORE
- See Chapter 23, Making Words Agree, pages 527–531
- See Writing Coach Online

 Focus on the TEKS

Writing (14)(D) Edit drafts for grammar.

Conventions (19)(C) Use a variety of complete sentences (e.g., *simple, compound, complex*) that include correctly identified antecedents.

18

Poorly Integrated Quotation

Tech Tip

Sometimes you might cut a quote from one sentence and paste it in another. Remember to revise the surrounding sentence to integrate the quote into the text.

LEARN MORE

- See Chapter 25, Punctuation, pages 577–585
- See Writing Coach Online

GAME PLAN Quotations should flow smoothly into the sentence that surrounds them. Add information to explain and link quotes to the rest of your work.

QUOTE IN A SENTENCE Prepare the reader for the information contained in the quote by introducing the quote's idea.

The writer in her book review ʌspoke about the characters in the book: "The main character was brave and loyal" (Jane 2).

Allison says ʌthe author should have included more detail: "The writing was not creative."

QUOTE AS A SENTENCE Place an introductory phrase before or after a quotation that stands alone. In most cases, this phrase should identify the quote's author or speaker.

ʌAccording to Mr. Peters, "The volunteer program is starting again in March" (Wolf 3).

✓ Check It

Use a current or completed draft of your work to practice integrating quotations.

✓ **SCAN Mentor Texts.** Notice how professional writers integrate quotations into their work.

✓ **IDENTIFY quotes.** Mark each quote in your work. Does each quote flow smoothly with the surrounding sentence?

✓ **REVISE your sentences.** Add information as needed to explain and introduce quotes.

 Focus on the TEKS

Research/Organizing and Presenting Ideas (25)(D) Follow accepted formats for integrating quotations into the written text to maintain a flow of ideas.

GAME PLAN Use hyphens correctly in your writing, including with compound words and compound adjectives.

COMPOUND WORDS Hyphens can connect two or more words that are used as one compound word. Some compound words do not require a hyphen. Check a current dictionary if you are not sure about hyphenating a word.

The blue color of my ~~sisterinlaw's~~ sister-in-law's ~~bed-room~~ bedroom is soothing.

My ~~grand-niece~~ grandniece likes to play with a ~~jackinthebox~~ jack-in-the-box.

COMPOUND ADJECTIVES A compound adjective that appears before a noun should be hyphenated. Remember, do not hyphenate a compound proper noun acting as an adjective. Also, do not hyphenate a compound adjective that has a word ending in *-ly*.

The ~~brown eyed~~ brown-eyed girl is my sister.

The ~~friendly-looking~~ friendly looking dog belongs to my neighbor.

My parents enjoy ~~North-Indian~~ North Indian music.

Check It

Use a current or completed draft of your work to practice hyphenating words.

✓ **IDENTIFY** possible errors. Mark any compound adjectives before a noun that are not hyphenated.

✓ **REVISE** your sentences. Add a hyphen to words that should be hyphenated.

✓ **USE** a dictionary. Check a dictionary if you are not sure if a word should be hyphenated.

Tech Tip

The automatic hyphenation setting in word processors causes words at the end of a line of text to hyphenate automatically. Be sure that this setting is turned off when you are writing an essay.

LEARN MORE
- See Chapter 25, Punctuation, pages 589–591
- See Writing Coach Online

 Focus on the TEKS

Writing (14)(D) Edit drafts for mechanics.

Conventions (20)(B)(ii) Use punctuation marks including hyphens.

20

Sentence Fragment

LEARN MORE

- See Chapter 20, Effective Sentences, pages 444–448
- See Writing Coach Online

Focus on the TEKS

Writing (14)(D) Edit drafts for grammar.

Conventions (19)(B) Write complex sentences and differentiate between main versus subordinate clauses.

GAME PLAN Use complete sentences when writing. Make sure you have a subject and a complete verb in each and that each sentence expresses a complete thought.

LACKING A SUBJECT OR VERB A complete sentence must have a subject and a verb.

My grandma is at our house visiting from Arizona. ~~And~~ She always has funny stories!

The cat ˄started to climb the tree.

SUBORDINATE CLAUSE A subordinate clause cannot stand on its own as a complete sentence because it does not express a complete thought.

Joe ate three helpings of salad. ~~After~~ ˄after he had already finished an entire serving of pasta!

My dad waited in front of the school. ~~While~~ ˄while I was finishing a makeup exam.

 Check It

Use a current or completed draft of your work to practice writing complete sentences.

✔ **SCAN** your draft. Look for incomplete sentences.

✔ **IDENTIFY** missing words. Mark sentences that have missing subjects or verbs.

✔ **REVISE** your sentences. Rewrite any sentences that are missing subjects or verbs, or are subordinate clauses standing on their own.

NOUNS *and* PRONOUNS

Using proper nouns, which are always capitalized, can make your writing more specific and informative.

WRITE GUY *Jeff Anderson, M.Ed.*

WHAT DO YOU NOTICE?

See how easy it is to spot the common and proper nouns as you zoom in on these sentences from the story "Papa's Parrot" by Cynthia Rylant.

MENTOR TEXT

The more Mr. Tillian grew to like his parrot, and the more he talked to it instead of people, the more embarrassed Harry became.

Now, ask yourself the following questions:

- Can you explain why the two nouns that begin with the letter *p* in this sentence are both common nouns?
- What are the proper nouns in this sentence?

Parrot and *people* are common nouns because these words could refer to any parrot or any group of people. However, *Mr. Tillian* and *Harry* are proper nouns because they refer to particular people. You can recognize them as proper nouns because they are capitalized.

Grammar for Writers Writers use specific details about people, places, and things to make their stories vivid. Including a mix of common and proper nouns is a good way to do this.

Our principal's first name is Anne. That is a proper noun.

Yes, but it's not proper to call her that.

13.1 Nouns

Nouns are naming words. Words such as *friend*, *sky*, *dog*, *love*, *courage*, and *Seattle* are nouns.

RULE 13.1.1

A **noun** names something.

Most nouns fall into four main groups.

People, Places, Things, and Ideas

The nouns in the chart are grouped under four headings. You may know most of the nouns under the first three headings. You may not have realized that all the words in the fourth group are nouns.

PEOPLE	PLACES	THINGS	IDEAS
veterinarian	Lake Mead	bumblebee	strength
Dr. Robinson	classroom	collar	honesty
Americans	kennel	motorcycle	willingness
leader	Bunker Hill	notebook	obedience

See Practice 13.1A

Concrete and Abstract Nouns

Nouns may be classified as **concrete** or **abstract.** In the chart above, *People*, *Places*, and *Things* are concrete nouns. *Ideas* are abstract nouns.

RULE 13.1.2

A **concrete noun** names something that can be recognized through any of the five senses. An **abstract noun** names something that cannot be recognized through the senses.

CONCRETE NOUNS			
pencil	dog	tractor	river
ABSTRACT NOUNS			
courage	fun	honor	exploration

See Practice 13.1B

Collective Nouns

A few nouns name groups of people or things. A *pack*, for example, is "a group of dogs or other animals that travel together." These nouns are called **collective nouns.**

> A **collective noun** names a group of people or things.

See Practice 13.1C

RULE 13.1.3

COLLECTIVE NOUNS		
club	herd	army
troop	orchestra	committee
class	team	group

Count and Non-count Nouns

Nouns can be grouped as **count** or **non-count** nouns.

> **Count nouns** name things that can be counted. **Non-count nouns** name things that cannot be counted.

RULE 13.1.4

COUNT NOUNS	NON-COUNT NOUNS
orange	thunder
bench	rice
street	equipment

Count nouns can take an article and can be plural.

EXAMPLE   a dog   the dog   four dogs

Non-count nouns do not take an indefinite article (*a* or *an*) and cannot be plural:

EXAMPLES   We had rice in the bowl.
(*not* We had *a* rice in the bowl.)

They need clothing for the business trip.

See Practice 13.1D

(*not* They need clothing*s* for the business trip.)

Read the sentences. Then, write the nouns in each sentence.

EXAMPLE   The leaves fell off the trees and cluttered the sidewalk.

ANSWER   *leaves, trees, sidewalk*

1. Joshua will celebrate his birthday in October.

2. Mr. Grant drives twenty miles to work every day.

3. Sunlight streamed through the window.

4. The Blackstones enjoyed their vacation in the mountains.

5. My brother likes to play tennis.

6. Austin is a popular city to visit.

7. Melissa loves birds, and she has two parakeets.

8. On Thanksgiving Day, we served food at a homeless shelter.

9. Our team scored ten points in the first quarter.

10. Raneesha finished her homework in study hall.

Read the sentences. Then, write the nouns in each sentence, and label each one *concrete* or *abstract*.

EXAMPLE   This magazine has a good article on friendship.

ANSWER   *magazine* — concrete
article — concrete
friendship — abstract

11. The teacher's praise pleased Jonas.

12. Obedience is an important quality in a dog.

13. We marked our yearly growth on a chart.

14. Your courage when facing danger merited this award.

15. People in the United States believe in liberty and justice.

16. Abraham Lincoln was known for his honesty.

17. The fans had great faith in their team.

18. Most students take satisfaction in doing good work.

19. The choir sang in harmony.

20. Those children had a happy childhood.

SPEAKING APPLICATION

With a partner, take turns telling about your favorite place. Your partner should listen for and name three nouns that you use.

WRITING APPLICATION

Use sentence 17 as a model to write three sentences that each contain two concrete nouns and one abstract noun.

PRACTICE 13.1C > Finding Collective Nouns

Read the pairs of nouns. Each pair includes one collective noun. Write the collective noun.

EXAMPLE   teacher, faculty

ANSWER   *faculty*

1. senator, Congress
2. bird, flock
3. team, pitcher
4. student, class
5. army, soldier
6. conductor, orchestra
7. uncle, family
8. committee, member
9. crowd, shopper
10. audience, speaker

PRACTICE 13.1D > Identifying Count and Non-count Nouns

Read the sentences. Then, list the count and non-count nouns. One sentence has only count nouns.

EXAMPLE   The cows shivered in the cold.

ANSWER   *count noun — cows*
          non-count noun — cold

11. My cup of cocoa spilled.
12. We took pictures of the beautiful scenery.
13. Julie left her cellphone on the bus.
14. I will go to the park with you after I finish my homework.
15. Joey rides his bicycle to school in good weather.
16. The children played for hours in the sand.
17. Heavy rain caused flooding in our city.
18. Jazz has been a popular form of music for many years.
19. Lisa's uniform shrank when she washed it in hot water.
20. Loud thunder frightened the dogs in our neighborhood.

SPEAKING APPLICATION

Choose three of the pairs of nouns above. Make up a sentence using each pair and tell your sentences to a partner.

WRITING APPLICATION

Write three sentences and include one of the following in each: a collective noun, a count noun, and a non-count noun.

Recognizing Compound Nouns

Some nouns are made up of two or more words. *Classroom* is a **compound noun** made up of *class* and *room*.

RULE 13.1.5

> A **compound noun** is one noun made by joining two or more words.

Compound nouns are written in three different ways: as single words, as hyphenated words, and as two or more separate words.

COMPOUND NOUNS		
SINGLE WORDS	HYPHENATED WORDS	SEPARATE WORDS
crossbar	by-product	dinner jacket
firefighter	right-hander	pole vault
thunderstorm	middle-distance	pen pal
classroom	mother-in-law	chief justice

See Practice 13.1E

Using Common and Proper Nouns

All nouns can be divided into two large groups: **common nouns** and **proper nouns.**

RULE 13.1.6

> A **common noun** names any one of a class of people, places, things, or ideas. A **proper noun** names a specific person, place, thing, or idea.

Common nouns are not capitalized. Proper nouns are always capitalized.

COMMON NOUNS	PROPER NOUNS
inventor	Alexander Graham Bell
village	Tarrytown
story	"The Tell-Tale Heart"
organization	American Red Cross
idea	Germ Theory of Disease

See Practice 13.1F

PRACTICE 13.1E > Identifying Compound Nouns

Read the sentences. Then, write the compound nouns, and draw a line between the words that make up each compound noun.

EXAMPLE   I was a lifeguard at the beach last summer.

ANSWER   *life | guard*

1. My dog, Ollie, is a great watchdog.

2. Steven's favorite sports are baseball and basketball.

3. Whenever we have a big snowstorm, we light a fire in the fireplace.

4. The fans cheered from the sidelines.

5. We think our middle school is the best in the state!

6. Serena and Robert joined the Air Force.

7. Hector bought the new commemorative stamps at the post office.

8. Charles is very happy with his new wristwatch.

9. Brenda was the winner and Marty was the runner-up in the essay contest.

10. Simon is taking courses to be a motorboat mechanic.

PRACTICE 13.1F > Using Common and Proper Nouns

Read the sentences. Then, rewrite them, replacing the underlined words with proper nouns.

EXAMPLE   Our math teacher gives a lot of homework.

ANSWER   *Mrs. Chen gives a lot of homework.*

11. We watched a movie last weekend.

12. My friend and I like to listen to our favorite band.

13. Our class will be taking a field trip to the state capital.

14. The school nurse will give flu shots next week.

15. My uncle has season tickets to our local basketball team's games.

16. On our summer vacation, we plan to visit two states.

17. We are reading a novel in English class.

18. That doctor works in the emergency room at the hospital.

19. My dad just bought a new car.

20. In two years, we will go to the high school.

SPEAKING APPLICATION

With a partner, take turns stating compound nouns that name occupations. Your partner should notice how the parts create meaning. For example, a *firefighter* is someone who fights fires.

WRITING APPLICATION

Write three sentences describing your town or city. Include at least one proper noun in each sentence.

13.2 Pronouns

Pronouns are words that take the place of nouns. They are used rather than repeating a noun again and again. Pronouns make sentences clearer and more interesting.

WRITING COACH

Online

@www.TXWritingCoach.com

Grammar Tutorials
Brush up on your Grammar skills with these animated videos.

Grammar Practice
Practice your grammar skills with Writing Coach Online.

Grammar Games
Test your knowledge of grammar in this fast-paced interactive video game.

RULE 13.2.1 ▷ **A pronoun is a word that takes the place of a noun or a group of words acting as a noun.**

Imagine, for example, that you are writing about Aunt Bonnie. If you were using only nouns, you might write the following sentence:

WITH NOUNS   Aunt Bonnie was late because **Aunt Bonnie** had waited for **Aunt Bonnie's** books to arrive.

WITH PRONOUNS   Aunt Bonnie was late because **she** had waited for **her** books to arrive.

Sometimes a pronoun takes the place of a noun in the same sentence.

EXAMPLES   My mother ate **her** salad.
pronoun

Many people say eating well has helped **them**.
pronoun

A pronoun can also take the place of a noun used in an earlier sentence.

EXAMPLES   My mother opened her package first. **She** was curious about it.
pronoun

College students must take a language class. **They** can choose from Spanish or Italian.
pronoun

A pronoun may take the place of an entire group of words.

EXAMPLE   Trying to paint can be very hard work. **It** takes practicing on a daily basis.
pronoun

Antecedents of Pronouns

The word or group of words that a pronoun replaces or refers to is called an **antecedent.**

> An **antecedent** is the noun (or group of words acting as a noun) to which a pronoun refers.

Focus on the TEKS

(19)(C) Use a variety of complete sentences (simple, compound, complex) that include correctly identified antecedents.

See TEKS Check

See TEKS Practice

See Practice 13.2A

See Practice 13.2B

EXAMPLES The **police officers** described how **they** did **their** jobs.
antecedent   pronoun   pronoun

Finally, the **police officer** arrived; **he** took control of the problem.
antecedent   pronoun

How Amy was saved is incredible. **It** is an event that she'll speak about often.
antecedent   pronoun

Although **he** was a pastry chef, **Mike** also enjoyed cooking meals.
pronoun   antecedent

Some kinds of pronouns do not have any antecedent.

EXAMPLES **Everyone** in the room knew the truth.
indefinite pronoun

Who broke the antique lamp?
interrogative pronoun

The pronouns *everyone* and *who* do not have a specific antecedent because their meaning is clear without one.

TEKS Check Show that you can use a variety of complete sentences (simple, compound, complex) that include correctly identified antecedents. Write at least three complete sentences that correctly use antecedents. The sentences should be simple, compound, and complex.

TEKS Practice Show that you can use a variety of complete sentences (*simple, compound, complex*) that include correctly identified antecedents by completing the following activities.

PRACTICE 13.2A > Recognizing Pronouns and Antecedents

Read the sentences. Then, write each pronoun and its antecedent.

EXAMPLE   Thomas Edison is known for his many inventions.

ANSWER   *his, Thomas Edison*

1. Todd left his gym bag on the bus.

2. The candidates rehearsed their speeches.

3. While visiting her cousin at the shore, Erica learned to body surf.

4. Jon has trained his dogs to sit, but they don't always obey.

5. The students took out their essays and passed them forward.

6. Danielle and I wanted to help with the celebration, so we baked cookies.

7. Marley misplaced her wallet, but she found it later.

8. When Rachel saw her grandfather, she gave him a hug.

9. As soon as they saw the puppy, the children wanted it.

10. Every region of the country has its special features.

PRACTICE 13.2B > Supplying Pronouns for Antecedents

Read the sentences. Then, write each sentence, filling in the blank with the appropriate pronoun. Correctly identify and underline the antecedent of the pronoun you supply.

EXAMPLE   Jake admitted that ____ was wrong.

ANSWER   <u>Jake</u> admitted that *he* was wrong.

11. Even before the ambulance came into sight, we heard ____ siren.

12. Elizabeth carefully followed the instructions ____ received.

13. After much discussion, the leaders made ____ decision.

14. Morgan was late for ____ first class.

15. Rachel reminded Tyler to bring ____ video games.

16. The band members took ____ places on the field.

17. When the president walked in, everyone welcomed ____.

18. The dog wagged ____ tail.

19. Connor and Mark are planning ____ strategy for the next game.

20. When Laura got home, ____ turned on the television.

SPEAKING APPLICATION

With a partner, take turns describing the situation of a character in a TV program. Name the character, and use at least two pronouns that refer to the character. Your partner should identify the pronouns and the antecedents.

WRITING APPLICATION

Write three sentences that each contain at least one pronoun and an antecedent. Circle each pronoun and draw an arrow to the antecedent. Use simple, compound, and complex complete sentences.

Recognizing Personal Pronouns

The pronouns used most often are **personal pronouns**.

> **Personal pronouns** refer to (1) the person speaking or writing, (2) the person listening or reading, or (3) the topic (person, place, thing, or idea) being discussed or written about.

13.2.3 RULE

The first-person pronouns *I, me, my, mine, we, us, our,* and *ours* refer to the person or persons speaking or writing.

EXAMPLES   **I** like the new magazine layout.

Please give **us** a taste.

The second-person pronouns *you, your,* and *yours* refer to the person or persons spoken or written to.

EXAMPLES   **You** will see it later.

Your dog is barking at me.

The third-person pronouns *he, him, his, she, her, hers, it, its, they, them, their,* and *theirs* refer to the person, place, thing, or idea being spoken or written about.

EXAMPLES   **He** wants to watch the news at 6:00 P.M.

They wrote to the author of the book.

Some personal pronouns show possession. Although they can function as adjectives, they are still identified as personal pronouns because they take the place of possessive nouns.

EXAMPLES   **Heather's** latest novel will be out this February.
                possessive noun

Her picture will be on the back cover.
   possessive pronoun

The chart on the next page presents the personal pronouns.

PERSONAL PRONOUNS		
	SINGULAR	**PLURAL**
First person	I, me, my, mine	we, us, our, ours
Second person	you, your, yours	you, your, yours
Third person	he, him, his, she, her, hers, it, its	they, them, their, theirs

See Practice 13.2C

Reflexive and Intensive Pronouns

The ending -*self* or -*selves* can be added to some pronouns to form **reflexive** or **intensive pronouns.** These two types of pronouns look the same, but they function differently within a sentence.

REFLEXIVE AND INTENSIVE PRONOUNS		
	SINGULAR	**PLURAL**
First person	myself	ourselves
Second person	yourself	yourselves
Third person	himself, herself, itself	themselves

A reflexive pronoun directs the action of the verb toward its subject. Reflexive pronouns point back to a noun or pronoun earlier in the sentence.

A reflexive pronoun is essential to the meaning of a sentence.

REFLEXIVE **Jane** poured **herself** a glass of water.
           noun   reflexive pronoun

           They made **themselves** some turkey sandwiches.
           pronoun   reflexive pronoun

See Practice 13.2D

An intensive pronoun simply adds emphasis to a noun or pronoun in the same sentence.

An intensive pronoun is not essential to the meaning of the sentence.

INTENSIVE The mayor **herself** attended the carnival.

PRACTICE 13.2C	Recognizing Personal Pronouns

Read the sentences. Then, write the personal pronouns in each sentence.

EXAMPLE   I would like to tell you about my experience.

ANSWER   *I, you, my*

1. He did not hear what I said.

2. Alicia said that she is trying out for the swim team.

3. After you complete this form, give it to the instructor.

4. She practices the piano every day.

5. We thought they wanted to go with us.

6. After Mike helped us, we thanked him.

7. Sarah's mother drove them to the skating rink.

8. Did you remember to tell her what time to come?

9. He doesn't speak to me anymore.

10. They could not find my street, but someone gave them directions from their house to mine.

PRACTICE 13.2D	Supplying Reflexive and Intensive Pronouns

Read the sentences. Write the reflexive or intensive pronoun that completes each sentence.

EXAMPLE   The principal made the announcement _____.

ANSWER   *herself*

11. Will you and Jim do all the work _____?

12. I bought _____ a new jacket.

13. She wondered whether she could lift the huge bundle _____.

14. You should be able to complete this project _____.

15. We did not care for the location, but the house _____ was lovely.

16. The students _____ made all the posters.

17. Jason promised _____ he would exercise more often.

18. We planned the entire event _____.

19. Liz sometimes gives _____ pep talks.

20. We _____ were not interested in seeing that exhibit.

SPEAKING APPLICATION

Tell a partner about something you and a friend did recently. Your partner will listen for and name four personal pronouns you use.

WRITING APPLICATION

Write three sentences, using sentences 12, 14, and 16 as models. Replace the nouns and pronouns in those sentences with your own.

Demonstrative Pronouns

Demonstrative pronouns point to people, places, and things, much as you point to them with your finger.

RULE
13.2.6

A **demonstrative pronoun** points to a specific person, place, or thing.

There are two singular and two plural demonstrative pronouns.

DEMONSTRATIVE PRONOUNS			
SINGULAR		PLURAL	
this	that	these	those

This and *these* point to what is near the speaker or writer. *That* and *those* point to what is more distant.

NEAR **This** is where I sleep.

These are my favorite movies of the year.

FAR Is **that** the library across the street?

Those are my books.

See Practice 13.2E

Using Relative Pronouns

Relative pronouns are connecting words.

RULE
13.2.7

A **relative pronoun** begins a subordinate clause and connects it to another idea in the same sentence.

There are five relative pronouns.

RELATIVE PRONOUNS				
that	which	who	whom	whose

The chart on the next page gives examples of relative pronouns connecting subordinate clauses to independent clauses. (See Chapter 19 to find out more about relative pronouns and clauses.)

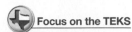 **Focus on the TEKS**

(19)(A)(vi) Identify, use, and understand the function of relative pronouns (e.g., *whose, that, which*) in the context of reading, writing, and speaking.

See TEKS Check

See TEKS Practice

See Practice 13.2F

See Practice 13.2G

See Practice 13.2H

INDEPENDENT CLAUSES	SUBORDINATE CLAUSES
Here is the earring	that Tara lost.
Felix bought our old car,	which needs to be repaired.
She is a painter	who has an unusual talent.
Is this the woman	whom you saw earlier?
She is the one	whose house has a new alarm.
That is the book	that was critiqued yesterday.
Scamper chased the ball	that was under the bed.

Interrogative Pronouns

To interrogate means "to ask questions."

> An **interrogative pronoun** is used to begin a question.

 RULE 13.2.8

All five interrogative pronouns begin with *w*.

INTERROGATIVE PRONOUNS				
what	which	who	whom	whose

Most interrogative pronouns do not have antecedents.

EXAMPLES

What did the teacher say?

Which is the best tutoring center?

Who wants to run a mile with me?

From **whom** will you receive the loan?

See Practice 13.2I

Whose was the best story?

 TEKS Check Show that you can use and understand relative pronouns. With a partner, write three sentences that contain relative pronouns *whose, that,* and *which.* Read the sentences aloud to another pair and ask them to identify the relative pronouns and explain how they are used.

Indefinite Pronouns

An **indefinite pronoun** refers to a person, place, thing, or idea that is not specifically named.

EXAMPLES **Everything** is ready for our trip to Florida.

Everyone wants to see the Harry Potter park.

Anyone can learn to play an instrument.

Something fell out of the closet when I opened the door.

Among its other uses, an indefinite pronoun can function as an adjective or as the subject of a sentence. If it functions as an adjective, it is called an indefinite adjective.

ADJECTIVE **Both** children want to be writers.

SUBJECT **Both** want to be writers.

A few indefinite pronouns can be either singular or plural, depending on their use in the sentence.

INDEFINITE PRONOUNS			
SINGULAR		PLURAL	SINGULAR OR PLURAL
another	much	both	all
anybody	neither	few	any
anyone	nobody	many	more
anything	no one	others	most
each	nothing	several	none
either	one		some
everybody	other		
everyone	somebody		
everything	someone		
little	something		

See Practice 13.2J

TEKS Practice Show that you can identify, use, and understand pronouns, including relative pronouns (e.g. *whose, that, which*), in reading, writing, and speaking by completing the following activities.

PRACTICE 13.2E ⮞ **Identifying Demonstrative Pronouns**

Read the sentences. Then, write the demonstrative pronoun and the noun to which it refers.

EXAMPLE   This is the latest version of the computer.

ANSWER   *this, computer*

1. These are the most comfortable shoes I have ever worn.

2. Of all the pictures, I like those best.

3. This is a new book, and that is an old one.

4. Is that your brother over there?

5. Those are confident students.

6. Is this your final answer?

7. That seems to be the best way to get to the city.

8. Those were the good old days!

9. This is the camera I would like to have.

10. That may be a difficult choice.

PRACTICE 13.2F ⮞ **Supplying Relative Pronouns**

Read the sentences. Then, write the correct relative pronoun (e.g., *whose, that, which*) for each sentence.

EXAMPLE   I know the person _____ lives here.

ANSWER   *who*

11. She planted flowers _____ bloom every spring.

12. It's a popular place _____ kids love.

13. The person _____ answered my questions was very polite.

14. Sondra's outburst, _____ surprised everyone, stopped all conversation.

15. I don't know _____ you're referring to.

16. It was a decision _____ he did not regret.

17. Lee, _____ is very friendly, was the first to greet the new student.

18. We visited the Metropolitan Museum of Art, _____ is on Fifth Avenue in New York.

19. These are the guidelines _____ you must follow.

20. Colin, _____ brother is a star athlete, prefers a quiet life.

SPEAKING APPLICATION

With a partner, take turns identifying and describing items in the classroom. Use relative pronouns (e.g., *whose, that, which*) in your sentences.

WRITING APPLICATION

Write three sentences, and include one of the following relative pronouns in each: *whose, that, which*. Read your sentences aloud to a partner. Have your partner identify each relative pronoun. Then change roles.

TEKS Practice Show that you can identify, use, and understand the function of relative pronouns (e.g., *whose, that, which*) in reading, writing, and speaking by completing the following activities.

PRACTICE 13.2G **Using Relative Pronouns**

For each independent clause, supply a subordinate clause using a relative pronoun. Write the new sentence. Then, read your sentences aloud and have your partner identify the relative pronoun.

EXAMPLE   He is the chemist

ANSWER   *He is the chemist who won the Nobel Prize.*

1. Liz gathered the ingredients
2. The dentist looked at the tooth
3. There is the bike
4. Raphael took the picture
5. Those are the pants
6. Is he the captain
7. Here are the essay topics
8. Bob is the one
9. Wynn wrote the book
10. Tomorrow is the day

PRACTICE 13.2H **Writing With Relative Pronouns**

For each subordinate clause, supply an independent clause to create a complete sentence. Write the new sentence. With a partner, take turns reading your best sentences and discussing why you wrote what you did.

EXAMPLE   which she will bring to the party

ANSWER   *Jenna made a casserole,* which she will bring to the party.

11. who taught me how to swim
12. which needed to be washed
13. that Scott borrowed
14. that Mr. Pizzo bought
15. whom you want on your team
16. whose painting took first prize
17. which has all the latest fashions
18. who trained his dog to dance
19. whom I helped in math class
20. that he buried in the yard

SPEAKING APPLICATION

With a partner, take turns talking about your favorite sports, hobbies, or other interests. Use relative pronouns in your questions and answers and identify them.

WRITING APPLICATION

Write three sentences about an interesting person you know or admire. Use a relative pronoun in each sentence.

Texas Test Warm-Up

DIRECTIONS

Read the introduction and the passage that follows. Then, answer the questions to show that you can identify, use, and understand the function of relative pronouns in reading and writing.

Focus on the TEKS

(19)(A)(vi) Identify, use, and understand the function of relative pronouns (e.g., *whose*, *that*, *which*) in reading, writing, and speaking.

Juana wrote this paragraph about planning the Fall Festival. Read the paragraph and think about the changes you would suggest as a peer editor. When you finish reading, answer the questions that follow.

The Fall Festival

(1) Mrs. Barnes was the teacher who chaired the planning committee and whose classroom was our meeting area. (2) Sal was the one whom suggested we decorate with pumpkins. (3) Allison wanted to offer games and prizes. (4) The games and prizes would appeal to all ages. (5) Darnell insisted on a contest of bobbing for apples, which he said everyone would enjoy. (6) Carla was the volunteer that I assigned to organize hayrides. (7) The next day, I looked over the notes that I took during the meeting. (8) It was clear the fall festival would be a success.

---

1 What change, if any, should be made in sentence 1?

  A Change *who* to **that**

  B Change *who* to **whom**

  C Change *whose* to **whom**

  D Make no change

2 How should sentence 2 be revised?

  F Sal was the one that suggested we decorate with pumpkins.

  G Sal was the one who suggested we decorate with pumpkins.

  H Sal was the one which suggested we decorate with pumpkins.

  J Sal was the one whose suggested we decorate with pumpkins.

3 What is the BEST way to combine sentences 3 and 4?

  A Allison, who would appeal to all ages, wanted to offer games and prizes.

  B Games and prizes whose appeal to all ages, Allison wanted to offer.

  C Which would appeal to all ages, Allison wanted to offer games and prizes.

  D Allison wanted to offer games and prizes that would appeal to all ages.

4 How should sentence 6 be revised?

  F Carla was the volunteer which I assigned to organize hayrides.

  G Carla was the volunteer whose assignment to organize hayrides I gave her.

  H Carla was the volunteer whom I assigned to organize hayrides.

  J Carla was the volunteer that assigning to organize hayrides was clear.

TEKS Practice Show that you can identify, use, and understand pronouns, including relative pronouns, in reading, writing, and speaking by completing the following activities.

PRACTICE 13.2I > **Identifying Interrogative Pronouns**

Read the sentences. Then, write the interrogative pronoun in each sentence.

EXAMPLE   What is your favorite television show?

ANSWER   *What*

1. Who are those people on the stage?
2. What should I do about my lost wallet?
3. Which is the best route to Tulsa?
4. Whose is the nicest outfit?
5. What is her occupation?
6. Who lives in that big house?
7. With whom are you going to the dance?
8. What will happen if I don't follow the directions exactly?
9. Which is worse: being late or not doing your homework?
10. What should we do when we reach the next intersection?

PRACTICE 13.2J > **Supplying Indefinite Pronouns**

Read the sentences. Then, write an appropriate indefinite pronoun for each sentence.

EXAMPLE   _____ was asking about you.

ANSWER   *Someone*

11. _____ likes pizza!
12. _____ of the clerks could help me find what I wanted.
13. _____ of these questions have more than one answer.
14. _____ of my friends are conscientious students.
15. _____ of the vocabulary words are familiar to me.
16. I don't know _____ who would say such a thing.
17. _____ of the monuments will be decorated for the holidays.
18. _____ find the reward worth the risk of the investment.
19. _____ of the bystanders watched the rescue, and _____ tried to help.
20. _____ must be put away before you leave.

SPEAKING APPLICATION

Interview a partner, asking five questions that begin with interrogative pronouns. Your partner should name the interrogative pronouns.

WRITING APPLICATION

Write a brief paragraph describing an incident you observed. Use at least three relative pronouns and indefinite pronouns in your paragraph. You may use the sentences in Practice 13.2J as models.

VERBS

To bring your writing to life, use verbs that describe actions that can be seen and those that cannot be seen.

WRITE GUY *Jeff Anderson, M.Ed.*

WHAT DO YOU NOTICE?

Pinpoint the action verbs as you zoom in on these sentences from the story "The Bear Boy" by Joseph Bruchac.

MENTOR TEXT

> The trackers crept close, hoping to grab the boy and run. But as soon as the mother bear caught their scent, she growled and pushed her cubs and the boy back into the cave.

Now, ask yourself the following questions:

- Which verbs describe actions that you could see or hear?
- How do the verbs *hoping* and *caught* describe a different kind of action?

The verbs *crept*, *grab*, *run*, *growled*, and *pushed* describe actions that could be seen or heard. However, the verbs *hoping* and *caught* describe actions that could not be seen or heard. You could not see the trackers *hoping* because it is something they are feeling. You could not see that the mother bear *caught* the trackers' scent because that action involves her senses.

Grammar for Writers Writers must remember that action is more than just what you do; it is also what you think, feel, and experience. Use verbs to capture every kind of action in your writing.

I want to ace the test on action verbs.

Then you should take action and start studying.

14.1 Action Verbs

Verbs such as *walk, sailed, played, migrate, raced, crossed, learn,* and *arrive* all show some kind of action.

RULE 14.1.1

An **action verb** tells what action someone or something is performing.

EXAMPLES   Mother **carries** the platter.

The train **chugged** into the station.

I **believe** it will rain today.

Heather **remembered** to bring her book.

The verb *carries* explains what Mother did with the platter. The verb *chugged* tells what the train did. The verb *believe* explains my action about the weather. The verb *remembered* explains Heather's action with the book.

Some actions, such as *carries* or *chugged,* can be seen. Some actions, such as *believe* or *remembered,* cannot be seen.

See Practice 14.1A

Using Transitive Verbs

RULE 14.1.2

An action verb is **transitive** if the receiver of the action is named in the sentence. The receiver of the action is called the **object** of the verb.

EXAMPLES   Mrs. Brown **opened** the **door** with great difficulty.
                      verb   object

The bus suddenly **hit** a nearby **tree**.
                      verb   object

In the first example, *opened* is transitive because the object of the verb—*door*—names what Mrs. Brown opened. In the second example, *hit* is transitive because the object of the verb—*tree*—tells what the bus hit.

Using Intransitive Verbs

An action verb is **intransitive** if there is no receiver of the action named in the sentence. An intransitive verb does not have an object.

RULE 14.1.3

EXAMPLES	The class **began**.
	The dog **raced** through the new gate.
	The employees **gathered** in the conference room.
	The fire alarm **rang** at 1:00 P.M.

Some action verbs can be transitive or intransitive. You need to determine if the verb has an object or not.

TRANSITIVE VERB	Kodia **raced Terrence** yesterday.
INTRANSITIVE VERB	Kodia **raced** across the finish line.
TRANSITIVE VERB	The pilot **flew** the **plane**.
INTRANSITIVE VERB	The plane **flew** to Cancun, Mexico.
TRANSITIVE VERB	The guests **rang** the **doorbell**.
INTRANSITIVE VERB	The doorbell **rang** and the dog barked.

See Practice 14.1B

Action Verbs

PRACTICE 14.1A > Finding Action Verbs

Read the sentences. Then, write each action verb.

EXAMPLE   The airplane landed on the ground.

ANSWER   *landed*

1. Alex and a friend hiked up the mountain trail.
2. Hannah played the harp in the talent contest.
3. Kaylee thought she knew the answer.
4. Max expressed his concern to the principal.
5. A tornado rolled across the prairie last week.
6. Devon worries about the future.
7. The chef poured the dressing onto the salad.
8. The crowd cheered wildly when the team scored.
9. My grades in science top those in math.
10. Claire stomped out and slammed the door.

PRACTICE 14.1B > Identifying Transitive and Intransitive Verbs

Read the sentences. Write each verb and label it *transitive* or *intransitive*.

EXAMPLE   Tina wants a summer job.

ANSWER   *wants* — transitive

11. The cruise ship leaves tomorrow.
12. A fierce blizzard hit the Northeast.
13. The work crew never arrives on time.
14. Clouds gathered before the storm.
15. My glasses fell and broke.
16. Some people smile all the time.
17. My mother grows vegetables and flowers in her garden.
18. Good jobs usually require a high school diploma.
19. No one likes people who complain all the time.
20. Advanced math courses provide a challenge for some.

SPEAKING APPLICATION

Tell a partner about a movie you saw recently. Your partner should listen for and name three action verbs.

WRITING APPLICATION

Write two sentences with transitive verbs and two sentences with intransitive verbs.

14.2 Linking Verbs

Some widely used verbs do not show action. They are called **linking verbs**.

A **linking verb** is a verb that connects a subject with a word that describes or identifies it.

EXAMPLES

IDENTIFIES

Kevin **was** a Navy **SEAL**.
subject   linking   predicate
          verb   nominative

IDENTIFIES

The **winners** **were** **Tara and I**.
     subject   linking   predicate
              verb   nominative

DESCRIBES

We **felt** extremely **tired** after our long flight.
subject linking   predicate
        verb   adjective

Recognizing Forms of *Be*

In English, the most common linking verb is *be.* This verb has many forms.

FORMS OF *BE*		
am	can be	has been
are	could be	have been
is	may be	had been
was	might be	could have been
were	must be	may have been
am being	shall be	might have been
are being	should be	must have been
is being	will be	shall have been
was being	would be	should have been
were being		will have been
		would have been

Using Other Linking Verbs

Several other verbs also function as linking verbs. They connect the parts of a sentence in the same way as the forms of *be*. In the sentence below, *shocked* describes *teacher*.

EXAMPLE   The **teacher** **looked** **shocked**.

subject   linking verb   predicate adjective

OTHER LINKING VERBS		
appear	look	sound
become	remain	stay
feel	seem	taste
grow	smell	turn

Action Verb or Linking Verb?

Some verbs can be used either as linking verbs or action verbs.

LINKING   The glass **looked** dirty.
(*Looked* links *glass* and *dirty.*)

ACTION   The host **looked** at the glass.
(The host performed an action.)

LINKING   The crowd **grew** impatient.
(*Grew* links *crowd* and *impatient.*)

ACTION   The farmer **grew** strawberries.
(The farmer performed an action.)

To test whether a verb is a linking verb or an action verb, replace the verb with *is, am,* or *are.* If the sentence still makes sense, then the verb is a linking verb.

EXAMPLE   The crowd **is** impatient.
linking verb

See Practice 14.2A
See Practice 14.2B
See Practice 14.2C
See Practice 14.2D

PRACTICE 14.2A > Identifying Action Verbs and Linking Verbs

Read the sentences. Write the verb in each sentence, and label it either *action* or *linking*.

EXAMPLE   We are optimistic about the outcome.

ANSWER   *are* — linking

1. The couple attended the opening night of the play.
2. Matt Perez will be the captain of the team.
3. I love Van Gogh's painting *Starry Night*.
4. Your idea seems like a good one.
5. Those two women have been friends for years.
6. Robbie chopped wood for the campfire.
7. May I ask you a question?
8. This chili tastes bland.
9. The bell rang at the end of class.
10. The sky became cloudy very quickly.

PRACTICE 14.2B > Using *Be* and Other Linking Verbs

Read the pairs of words below. For each pair of words, write a sentence that uses a linking verb to connect them.

EXAMPLE   trip   adventure

ANSWER   *A trip to Alaska could be an adventure.*

11. soccer   popular
12. contestants   confident
13. Emma   hungry
14. Corey   energetic
15. Louis Sachar   author
16. cellphone   lost
17. Yvonne   president
18. hurricanes   dangerous
19. Oscar   handsome
20. You   winner

SPEAKING APPLICATION

With a partner, take turns describing someone you admire. Use at least two linking and two action verbs. Your partner should identify and label the verbs.

WRITING APPLICATION

Write a short paragraph about some aspect of the weather. In your paragraph, use three different linking verbs.

PRACTICE 14.2C **Identifying Action Verbs and Linking Verbs**

Read the sentences. Then, write the verb or verbs in each sentence, and label them either *action* or *linking*.

EXAMPLE   Oliver grew uneasy as he climbed the front steps of the deserted house.

ANSWER   *grew*— linking; *climbed*— action

1. The factory coughed puffs of steam out of its smokestacks.

2. Harry seemed excited for the chance to play goalie.

3. When a cat is nearby, the neighborhood birds sound the alarm.

4. With Eleanor at the wheel, a drive to school seems terrifying.

5. Maura appeared out of nowhere, and she startled us.

6. When she answered the phone, Maria sounded sleepy.

7. The car must have been towed because today is street cleaning day.

8. Mom tasted the soup; then, she poured it into bowls.

9. Sean threw the ball, and it swooshed into the basket.

10. The spectators became amazed at the elephant's tricks.

PRACTICE 14.2D **Writing With Action and Linking Verbs**

Read the verbs below. For each verb, write a sentence using a form of the verb as indicated below.

EXAMPLE   turned — linking

ANSWER   *At forty years old, his hair turned gray.*

11. be — linking

12. feel — linking

13. smell — linking

14. grow — action

15. sound — action

16. look — action

17. turn — action

18. seem — linking

19. appear — action

20. become — linking

SPEAKING APPLICATION

With a partner, take turns reading the sentences you wrote in Practice 14.2D. Discuss how your sentences are similar and how they are different.

WRITING APPLICATION

Imagine you are exploring another planet. Write a brief paragraph describing this experience. Use four action verbs and four linking verbs in your paragraph.

Texas Test Warm-Up

DIRECTIONS
Read the introduction and the passage that follows. Then, answer the questions to show that you can use and understand the function of linking verbs and action verbs in reading and writing.

Denzel wrote this paragraph describing a dream in which he was a famous lion tamer. Read the paragraph and think about the changes you would suggest as a peer editor. When you finish reading, answer the questions that follow.

The Amazing Denzel

(1) I felt a cold breeze as I approached the lion's cage and unlocked it. (2) The lion sounded asleep, but that was about to change. (3) When the door clanged, he opened one golden eye. (4) As he slowly got to his feet, I seemed increasingly nervous. (5) He might have been able to sense my fear. (6) Fortunately, my pockets contained raw meat. (7) As the lion came toward me, I asked him if he wouldn't mind performing a backflip. (8) He was looking like he was hesitant. (9) I think he was about to do the flip when my alarm went off.

---

1 The meaning of sentence 2 can be clarified by changing the word **sounded** to —

   A became

   B was

   C grew

   D turned

2 The meaning of sentence 4 can be clarified by changing the word **seemed** to —

   F appeared

   G stayed

   H looked

   J became

3 What is the BEST way to rewrite sentence 5?

   A He was seeming to sense my fear.

   B He sensed my fear.

   C He had to have been sensing my fear.

   D He seemed to sense my fear.

4 What is the BEST way to rewrite sentence 8?

   F He felt hesitant.

   G He turned hesitant.

   H He sounded hesitant.

   J He seemed hesitant.

14.3 Helping Verbs

Sometimes, a verb in a sentence is just one word. Often, however, a verb will be made up of several words. This type of verb is called a **verb phrase**.

WRITING COACH

Online
@www.TXWritingCoach.com

Grammar Practice
Practice your grammar skills with Writing Coach Online.

Grammar Games
Test your knowledge of grammar in this fast-paced interactive video game.

RULE 14.3.1

> **Helping verbs** are added before another verb to make a **verb phrase.**

Notice how these helping verbs change the meaning of the verb *open*.

EXAMPLES open   **might have** opened

had opened   **should have** opened

will have opened   **will be** opened

Recognizing Helping Verbs

Forms of *Be* Forms of *be* are often used as helping verbs.

SOME FORMS OF *BE* USED AS HELPING VERBS	
HELPING VERBS	**MAIN VERBS**
am	growing
has been	warned
was being	told
will be	reminded
will have been	waiting
is	opening
was being	trained
should be	written
had been	sent
might have been	played

See Practice 14.3A

Other Helping Verbs Many different verb phrases can be formed using one or more of these helping verbs. The chart below shows just a few.

HELPING VERBS	MAIN VERBS	VERB PHRASES
do	remember	do remember
has	written	has written
would	hope	would hope
shall	see	shall see
can	believe	can believe
could	finish	could finish
may	attempt	may attempt
must have	thought	must have thought
should have	grown	should have grown
might	win	might win
will	jump	will jump
have	planned	have planned
does	want	does want

Sometimes the words in a verb phrase are separated by other words, such as *not* or *certainly*. The parts of the verb phrase in certain types of questions may also be separated.

WORDS SEPARATED

She **could** certainly **have thought** that was hers.

This **has** not **changed** how we feel.

Jeffrey **has** certainly **hit** the most home runs.

The dentist **had** carefully **examined** my teeth.

Did you ever **expect** to be so scared?

When **may** we **open** the envelope?

Did you ever **expect** to see that kind of experiment?

Sophia **must** not **have taken** the car.

Would you ever **want** to go fishing?

See Practice 14.3B

PRACTICE 14.3A > Identifying Helping and Main Verbs

Read the sentences. Write *main verb* if the underlined verb is a main verb. Write *helping verb* if it is a helping verb.

EXAMPLE   Luanne is <u>having</u> a party.

ANSWER   *main verb*

1. The city has <u>built</u> a new basketball court in the park.

2. I <u>will be</u> going right home after school.

3. Has your brother <u>returned</u> yet?

4. The puppy <u>has been</u> barking for an hour.

5. I could have <u>done</u> better if I had tried harder.

6. <u>May</u> I be excused now?

7. The group <u>had been</u> in the gym for a long time.

8. <u>Am</u> I bothering you?

9. We <u>had</u> expected a better performance from the group.

10. The witnesses were being <u>questioned</u> by the police.

PRACTICE 14.3B > Using Verb Phrases

Read the verb phrases. Use each verb phrase in an original sentence.

EXAMPLE   have heard

ANSWER   I *have heard* the good news.

11. has been going

12. have been

13. did get

14. could remember

15. has learned

16. might want

17. is known

18. will have graduated

19. had been produced

20. should be completed

SPEAKING APPLICATION

With a partner, take turns telling about something that didn't go exactly as planned. Your partner should listen for and identify two verb phrases and name the main and helping verbs in the phrases.

WRITING APPLICATION

Write three sentences with verb phrases. Underline the verb phrases in your sentences.

ADJECTIVES and ADVERBS

Enrich your descriptions of people, places, and events by using adjectives and adverbs in your writing.

WRITE GUY *Jeff Anderson, M.Ed.*

WHAT DO YOU NOTICE?

Spot the adjectives and adverbs as you zoom in on these sentences from the story "Zoo" by Edward Hoch.

MENTOR TEXT

> The citizens of Earth clustered around as Professor Hugo's crew quickly collected the waiting dollars, and soon the good Professor himself made an appearance, wearing his many-colored rainbow cape and top hat.

Now, ask yourself the following questions:

- Which adverb modifies the verb *collected*?
- Which adjectives does the author use to describe the cape?

The adverb *quickly* modifies the verb *collected,* creating an image of the speed at which the crew gathered the money. The author uses the adjectives *many-colored* and *rainbow* to modify the noun *cape.* Words such as *rainbow*, which are usually used as nouns, can also be used as adjectives.

Grammar for Writers Use adjectives and adverbs to enrich your writing, but vary how you use them. For example, if you place several adjectives in a row before a noun in one sentence, use fewer or no adjectives in the next sentence.

Which adjective would you use to describe my bike? Speedy or quick?

I would go with flat. Look at your tires!

15.1 Adjectives

Adjectives are words that make language come alive by adding description or information.

WRITING COACH

@www.TXWritingCoach.com

Grammar Tutorials
Brush up on your Grammar skills with these animated videos.

Grammar Practice
Practice your grammar skills with Writing Coach Online.

Grammar Games
Test your knowledge of grammar in this fast-paced interactive video game.

Adjectives help make nouns more specific. For example, *car* is a general word, but a *red two-door car* is more specific. Adjectives such as *red* and *two-door* make nouns and pronouns clearer and more vivid.

RULE 15.1.1

> An **adjective** is a word that describes a noun or pronoun.

Adjectives are often called *modifiers*, because they modify, or change, the meaning of a noun or pronoun. You can use more than one adjective to modify a noun or pronoun. Notice how *shoes* is modified by each set of adjectives below.

EXAMPLES   **old-fashioned** shoes

new **red** shoes

children's **dress** shoes

old **brown** shoes

Adjectives answer several questions about nouns and pronouns. They tell *What kind? Which one? How many?* or *How much?* Numeral adjectives, such as *eleven*, tell exactly how many. In the chart below, notice how adjectives answer these questions.

WHAT KIND?	WHICH ONE?	HOW MANY?	HOW MUCH?
stone house	this judge	two tulips	no time
white paper	each answer	several roses	enough apples
serious argument	those sisters	both brothers	many hobbies
colorful shirts	that student	one car	some birds

Adjective Position An adjective usually comes before the noun it modifies, as do all the adjectives in the chart on the previous page. Sometimes, however, adjectives come after the nouns they modify.

EXAMPLES

MODIFIES

World religions, **complex** and **serious**,
adjective · adjective

are sometimes very confusing.

MODIFIES

The tunnel, **long** and **dark**, frightened us.
noun · adjective · adjective

MODIFIES

Pictures, **bright** and **beautiful**, filled the child's
noun · adjective · adjective

book.

Adjectives that modify pronouns usually come after linking verbs. Sometimes, however, adjectives may come before the pronoun.

AFTER

MODIFIES

He was **quiet** and **contemplative** as he worked.
pronoun · adjective · adjective

MODIFIES

They are **sad** and **mournful**.
pronoun · adjective · adjective

MODIFIES

He is **handsome**.
pronoun · adjective

BEFORE

MODIFIES

Serious and **contemplative**, **she** talked to him.
adjective · adjective · pronoun

MODIFIES

Anxious and **excited**, **she** sat in the movie theater.
adjective · adjective · pronoun

MODIFIES

Quick and **agile**, **they** easily outran the other
adjective · adjective · pronoun

team.

See Practice 15.1A
See Practice 15.1B

PRACTICE 15.1A > Identifying Adjectives

Read the sentences. Then, write each adjective and list the question it answers. (*What kind? Which one? How many? How much?*)

EXAMPLE   We watched two movies last night.

ANSWER   *two* — How many?
            last — Which one?

1. Some people write daily entries in a personal journal.

2. A sudden clap of thunder startled the sleeping dogs.

3. I'll give you five dollars for the antique bottle.

4. Regular exercise contributes to good health.

5. This assignment will take more time.

6. The two explorers ventured into unmapped territory.

7. There is not enough space in that room for the whole group.

8. Several electric cars were on display.

9. Is there any water in that cooler?

10. This organization provides free legal help.

PRACTICE 15.1B > Identifying Adjectives and Words They Modify

Read the sentences. Then, write the adjectives and the words they modify.

EXAMPLE   The timid kitten hid from the noisy visitors.

ANSWER   *timid, kitten*
            noisy, visitors

11. A volcanic eruption frightened the islanders.

12. A model, tall and elegant, strode along the runway.

13. A tiny lizard scurried through the thick undergrowth.

14. These books are heavy!

15. I don't have much change, but I can give you a dollar.

16. An elderly man sat on the shady porch.

17. We have not had any rain for two weeks.

18. The fire department has a new ladder truck.

19. We ate at a Thai restaurant for the first time.

20. Antonio runs two miles every day.

SPEAKING APPLICATION

With a partner, take turns describing your lunch in the cafeteria. Your partner should listen for and name the adjectives and the questions they answer.

WRITING APPLICATION

Use sentences 12, 14, and 19 as models, and write three sentences with different adjectives and nouns.

Articles

Three frequently used adjectives are the words *a*, *an*, and *the*. They are called **articles.** Articles can be **definite** or **indefinite.** Both types indicate that a noun will soon follow.

> ***The*** is a **definite article.** It points to a specific person, place, thing, or idea. ***A*** and ***an*** are **indefinite articles.** They point to any member of a group of similar people, places, things, or ideas.

15.1.2 RULE

DEFINITE	Dr. Kashkin is **the** one to call. (a specific person)
	Go into **the** restaurant. (a specific place)
	I want to learn **the** song. (a specific thing)
INDEFINITE	I want to see **a** movie. (any movie)
	Please take **an** application. (any application)
	You should ask **a** coach for advice. (any coach)

A is used before consonant sounds. *An* is used before vowel sounds. You choose between *a* and *an* based on sound. Some letters are tricky. The letter *h,* a consonant, may sound like either a consonant or a vowel. The letters *o* and *u* are vowels, but they may sometimes sound like consonants.

USING *A* AND *AN*	
***A* WITH CONSONANT SOUNDS**	***AN* WITH VOWEL SOUNDS**
a pink dress	an endangered lion
a happy memory (*h* sound)	an honest president (no *h* sound)
a one-person chair (*w* sound)	an old book (*o* sound)
a union worker (*y* sound)	an uncle (*u* sound)
a truck	an odd shoe
a banana	an apple
a unicorn (*y* sound)	an opponent

See Practice 15.1C

PRACTICE 15.1C > Identifying Definite and Indefinite Articles

Read the sentences. Then, write the articles and label them *definite* or *indefinite*.

EXAMPLE   The travelers boarded a plane to Madrid.

ANSWER   *the* — *definite*
           a — *indefinite*

1. I can't wait to meet the new director.

2. A minute can sometimes seem like an hour.

3. Do you have the time?

4. Mr. Chu was elected to the city council.

5. The students dutifully read the novel.

6. There is an old, rundown car in the driveway.

7. We can spend the afternoon at the beach.

8. A mysterious stranger appeared on the scene.

9. This is an interesting dilemma.

10. The storm caused a huge traffic jam.

SPEAKING APPLICATION

With a partner, take turns describing an item without naming it. Your partner should guess what the item is and name at least five definite and indefinite articles you use.

WRITING APPLICATION

Use sentences 2, 8, and 10 as models, and write three sentences in which you use definite and indefinite articles. Circle the articles and label them *definite* or *indefinite*.

Using Proper Adjectives

A **proper adjective** begins with a capital letter. There are two types of proper adjectives.

> **A proper adjective** is (1) a proper noun used as an adjective or (2) an adjective formed from a proper noun.

A proper noun used as an adjective does *not* change its form. It is merely placed in front of another noun.

PROPER NOUNS	USED AS PROPER ADJECTIVES
Thursday	Thursday afternoon (*Which* afternoon)
Florida	Florida wetlands (*Which* wetlands?)
December	December weather (*What kind* of weather?)

When an adjective is formed from a proper noun, the proper noun will change its form. Notice that endings such as *-n, -ian,* or *-ese* have been added to the proper nouns in the chart below or the spelling has been changed.

PROPER NOUNS	PROPER ADJECTIVES FORMED FROM PROPER NOUNS
America	American history (*Which kind* of history?)
Japan	Japanese cities (*Which* cities?)
Norway	Norwegian legends (*Which* legends?)
Inca	Incan empire (*Which* empire?)
Florida	Floridian sunset (*Which* sunset?)

See Practice 15.1D

Using Nouns as Adjectives

Nouns can sometimes be used as adjectives. A noun used as an adjective usually comes directly before another noun and answers the question *What kind?* or *Which one?*

NOUNS	USED AS ADJECTIVES
shoe	a shoe salesperson (*What kind* of salesperson?)
waterfowl	the waterfowl refuge (*Which* refuge?)
court	a court date (*What kind* of date?)
morning	a morning appointment (*What kind* of appointment?)

Using Compound Adjectives

Adjectives, like nouns, can be compound.

RULE 15.1.4

> A **compound adjective** is made up of more than one word.

Most **compound adjectives** are written as hyphenated words. Some are written as combined words, as in "a *runaway* horse." If you are unsure about how to write a compound adjective, look up the word in a dictionary.

HYPHENATED	COMBINED
a well-known actress	a featherweight boxer
a full-time job	a freshwater lake
snow-covered mountains	a sideways glance
one-sided opinions	heartbreaking news
so-called experts	a nearsighted witness

See Practice 15.1E

PRACTICE 15.1D **Using Proper Adjectives**

Read the sentences. Then, rewrite each sentence to include a proper adjective before the underlined noun.

EXAMPLE My favorite subject is <u>history</u>.

ANSWER *My favorite subject is American history.*

1. Camels are used for travel in the <u>desert</u>.
2. Ana is interested in <u>geography</u>.
3. Rob really enjoys <u>food</u>.
4. The <u>language</u> is easy to learn.
5. We will wear traditional <u>clothing</u> for the play.
6. Bruce wants to study <u>architecture</u>.
7. The Martins visited the <u>ruins</u> on their trip.
8. Ashley dresses in <u>style</u>.
9. When does your <u>class</u> meet?
10. Trina has a <u>pen pal</u>.

PRACTICE 15.1E **Recognizing Nouns Used as Adjectives**

Read the sentences. Write the noun, proper noun, or compound noun used as an adjective. Then, write the noun that the adjective modifies.

EXAMPLE Do you like my new gym clothes?

ANSWER *gym, clothes*

11. Did you get my text message?
12. Elena doesn't like the July heat.
13. Mr. Preston is an expert on shore birds.
14. You may carry the baseball bats.
15. Spencer would like to be an airplane mechanic.
16. Tomorrow, we will follow our usual Friday schedule.
17. I would like to know what the weekend weather will be.
18. Scott spends his free time playing video games.
19. I'll meet you at the tennis court at 3:00.
20. Will you be going to the Valentine's Day dance?

SPEAKING APPLICATION

With a partner, take turns describing a trip you'd like to take. Your partner should listen for and name the nouns used as adjectives and proper adjectives you use.

WRITING APPLICATION

Write three sentences and include one of the following in each: a noun used as an adjective, a proper noun used as an adjective, or a proper adjective.

Using Pronouns as Adjectives

Pronouns, like nouns, can sometimes be used as adjectives.

> **A pronoun becomes an adjective if it modifies a noun.**

EXAMPLES   We see the new puppies on **this** side of the porch.

Which puppies are the females?

In the first example, the demonstrative pronoun *this* modifies *side,* and in the second example, the interrogative pronoun *which* modifies *puppies.*

Using Possessive Nouns and Pronouns as Adjectives

The following personal pronouns are often **possessive adjectives:** *my, your, her, his, its, our,* and *their.* They are adjectives because they come before nouns and answer the question *Which one?* They are pronouns because they have antecedents.

EXAMPLES   The **puppies** wagged **their** tails.
                          antecedent   pronoun

The **school** wants to improve **its** library.
        antecedent   pronoun

In the first example, *their* is an adjective because it modifies *tails.* At the same time, it is a pronoun because it refers to the antecedent *puppies.*

In the second example, *its* is an adjective because it modifies *library.* The word *its* is also a pronoun because it refers to the antecedent *school.*

Note About Possessive Nouns Possessive nouns function as adjectives when they modify a noun.

EXAMPLES   The field is on the **Wongs'** property.

My **dog's** tail wags when I come home.

See Practice 15.1F
See Practice 15.1G

Using Demonstrative Adjectives

This, *that*, *these*, and *those*—the four demonstrative pronouns—can also be **demonstrative adjectives.**

PRONOUN	We heard **that**.
ADJECTIVE	**That** hive is home to many bees.

PRONOUN	Why do you want **these**?
ADJECTIVE	**These** puppies are searching for a chew toy.

Using Interrogative Adjectives

Which, *what*, and *whose*—three of the interrogative pronouns—can be **interrogative adjectives.**

PRONOUN	**Which** do you think she will like?
ADJECTIVE	**Which** puppy do you think he will buy?

PRONOUN	**Whose** is that?
ADJECTIVE	**Whose** cat can that be?

Using Indefinite Adjectives

A number of indefinite pronouns—*both*, *few*, *many*, *each*, *most*, and *all*, among others—can also be used as **indefinite adjectives.**

PRONOUN	I made one of **each**.
ADJECTIVE	**Each** member has a vote.

PRONOUN	I don't have **any**.
ADJECTIVE	Wasn't there **any** soup left?

See Practice 15.1H
See Practice 15.1I

PRACTICE 15.1F > **Recognizing Possessive Nouns and Pronouns Used as Adjectives**

Read the sentences. Then, write the possessive noun or pronoun used as an adjective in each sentence. Some sentences have more than one answer.

EXAMPLE   Ted's canoe almost tipped over.

ANSWER   *Ted's*

1. Chelsea would like a piece of your cake.
2. The doctor's waiting room was crowded.
3. Sasha accidentally stepped on her cat's tail.
4. Our class has its own Web page.
5. The bicycle's tires need air.
6. Harry removed his boots when he came inside.
7. The children came in right away when their mother called them.
8. The team's trophies are in the display case.
9. We had our pictures taken for the yearbook.
10. Mrs. Palumbo buys fresh bread at Maria's bakery.

PRACTICE 15.1G > **Using Possessive Nouns and Pronouns Used as Adjectives**

Read the sentences. Then, rewrite each sentence, completing it with a possessive noun or pronoun used as an adjective.

EXAMPLE   John's dog has a mind of _____ own.

ANSWER   *its*

11. Marco's hard work resulted in _____ success.
12. _____ dress has flowers around its hem.
13. The team's new black and gold uniforms were _____ pride and joy.
14. Ben's grandparents offered to pay for _____ education.
15. After dinner, I took _____ leftovers back to my house.
16. Mrs. Schaffer's computer is _____ link to the rest of the world.
17. My neighbors spend every Saturday in _____ garden.
18. Serena's concentration was broken by _____ bad music.
19. The city's aquarium feeds _____ fish only once a day.
20. On _____ trip, Luis bought a keychain for his brother.

SPEAKING APPLICATION

With a partner, take turns describing something that belongs to another person. Your partner should identify at least one possessive noun and one possessive pronoun used as an adjective.

WRITING APPLICATION

Write a paragraph in which you compare and contrast yourself with a real or imagined brother. Use possessive nouns and pronouns as adjectives to discuss your different tastes and hobbies.

PRACTICE 15.1H	Supplying Demonstrative, Interrogative, and Indefinite Adjectives

Read the sentences. Then, write whether the underlined adjective is demonstrative, interrogative, or indefinite.

EXAMPLE <u>Whose</u> hamster is that running around the yard?

ANSWER *interrogative*

1. <u>Which</u> hamster belongs to the Garcia family?

2. <u>These</u> apples are my favorite.

3. <u>Which</u> apples do you prefer?

4. <u>Some</u> baseball players are switch hitters.

5. <u>What</u> kind of music do you like to listen to?

6. I like <u>most</u> types of music.

7. I didn't have <u>any</u> money left after I bought the book.

8. Is <u>this</u> book the best one in the series?

9. Casey and Samantha are friends with <u>those</u> girls.

10. <u>Whose</u> car should we take to the game?

PRACTICE 15.1I	Identifying Demonstrative, Interrogative, and Indefinite Adjectives

Read the sentences. Then, write the adjective in each sentence and label it *demonstrative*, *interrogative*, or *indefinite*.

EXAMPLE Whose keys are these?

ANSWER *Whose* — interrogative

11. Several students lingered after the game.

12. What difference will five more minutes make?

13. I will turn fourteen this month.

14. Which movie are you going to see?

15. Here are some magazines for you to read.

16. That building is more than two hundred years old.

17. Most children have a natural curiosity.

18. Do you want that CD?

19. These chairs are so comfortable.

20. Whose umbrella did you borrow?

SPEAKING APPLICATION

With a partner, take turns asking each other questions about your favorite movie, television show, and song. The person asking the questions should use interrogative adjectives.

WRITING APPLICATION

Use sentences 11, 12, and 18 in Practice 15.1I as models, and write three sentences in which you use demonstrative, interrogative, and indefinite adjectives. Circle and label the adjectives.

Texas Test Warm-Up

DIRECTIONS
Read the introduction and the passage that follows. Then, answer the questions to show that you can use and understand the function of adjectives in reading and writing.

Jada wrote this paragraph about the school bake sale. Read the paragraph and think about the changes you would suggest as a peer editor. When you finish reading, answer the questions that follow.

The Bake Sale

(1) Our school's bake sale took place last Saturday. (2) These sales raise money for their activities—and they're fun. (3) In this case, the money was going to the art department's supplies. (4) Each student who came had a great time. (5) Students, whose contributions to Saturday sale included pies, cakes, and brownies, showed their enthusiasm for art. (6) There were so many donations; I wasn't sure that student brought what. (7) At the end of the sale, there weren't no items left. (8) That sale was our most successful to date.

1 What change should be made in sentence 2?

A Change *These* to **Which**

B Change *their* to **our**

C Change *their* to **my**

D Change *These* to **That**

2 What change should be made in sentence 5?

F Change *Saturday* to **Saturday's**

G Change *whose* to **which**

H Change *Students* to **Students'**

J Change *their* to **her**

3 The meaning of sentence 6 can be clarified by changing the word *that* to —

A what

B whose

C why

D which

4 How should sentence 7 be revised?

F At the end of the sale, there weren't each items left.

G At the end of the sale, there weren't these items left.

H At the end of the sale, there weren't any items left.

J At the end of the sale, there weren't much items left.

15.2 Adverbs

Adverbs can modify three different parts of speech. They make the meaning of verbs, adjectives, or other adverbs more precise.

RULE 15.2.1

An **adverb** modifies a verb, an adjective, or another adverb.

Although adverbs may modify adjectives and other adverbs, they generally modify verbs.

Using Adverbs That Modify Verbs

Adverbs that modify verbs will answer one of these four questions: *Where? When? In what way? To what extent?* These adverbs are also known as *adverbs of place, adverbs of time, adverbs of manner,* and *adverbs of degree.*

ADVERBS THAT MODIFY VERBS			
WHERE?	**WHEN?**	**IN WHAT WAY?**	**TO WHAT EXTENT?**
push upward	will leave soon	works carefully	hardly ate
fell there	comes daily	speaks well	really surprised
stay nearby	swims often	chews noisily	almost cried
go outside	exhibits yearly	acted willingly	partly finished
is here	report later	walk quietly	nearly won
jump away	come tomorrow	smiled happily	fully agree
drove down	went yesterday	moved gracefully	totally oppose

Negative adverbs, such as *not, never,* and *nowhere,* also modify verbs.

EXAMPLES   Mark **never** **arrived** at the meeting.
                        adverb   verb

She **could** **not** **understand** the essay.
        verb   adverb   verb

The line of questioning **led** **nowhere**.
                                      verb   adverb

See Practice 15.2A

WRITING COACH

Online
@www.TXWritingCoach.com

Grammar Tutorials
Brush up on your Grammar skills with these animated videos.

Grammar Practice
Practice your grammar skills with Writing Coach Online.

Grammar Games
Test your knowledge of grammar in this fast-paced interactive video game.

Using Adverbs That Modify Adjectives

An adverb modifying an adjective answers only one question:
To what extent?

15.2.2

> When adverbs modify adjectives or adverbs, they answer the
> question *To what extent?*

ADVERBS THAT MODIFY ADJECTIVES	
very upset	extremely tall
definitely wrong	not hungry

EXAMPLE   Beaches can be **very** **beautiful**.

The adverb *very* modifies the adjective *beautiful*.

EXAMPLE   The speaker is **extremely** **tall**.

The adverb *extremely* modifies the adjective *tall*.

Adverbs Modifying Other Adverbs

When adverbs modify other adverbs, they again answer the
question *To what extent?*

ADVERBS MODIFYING ADVERBS	
traveled less slowly	move very cautiously
lost too easily	lived almost happily

EXAMPLE   Polar bears are **hardly** **ever** seen in this part of
the park.

The adverb *hardly* modifies the adverb *ever*.

EXAMPLE   When driving, I tire **too** **quickly**.

The adverb *too* modifies the adverb *quickly*.

See Practice 15.2B

PRACTICE 15.2A **Identifying How Adverbs Modify Verbs**

Read the sentences. Write the adverb in each sentence and list the question it answers. (*When? Where? In what way? To what extent?*)

EXAMPLE   Danielle will leave tonight.

ANSWER   *tonight* — When?

1. We have had good success lately.

2. Jared climbed the rock wall slowly and carefully.

3. We hardly noticed the storm brewing.

4. An unhappy customer complained loudly.

5. The coach almost tripped over the equipment on the floor.

6. Tiffany never thought it could happen to her.

7. I need your help now.

8. Ike quietly walked away from the disturbance.

9. Sophia was completely surprised by the remark.

10. Sherwin pulled ahead in the last lap.

PRACTICE 15.2B **Recognizing Adverbs and Words They Modify**

Read the sentences. Write the word that each underlined adverb modifies. Then, write whether that word is a *verb*, an *adjective*, or an *adverb*.

EXAMPLE   The students moved <u>very</u> quickly out of the building during the fire drill.

ANSWER   *quickly* — adverb

11. Ashley looks <u>extremely</u> serious.

12. Dad <u>usually</u> naps after working <u>so</u> hard.

13. Because of the weather, the traffic was moving <u>very</u> slowly.

14. I <u>often</u> walk in the park to think.

15. The mail should be coming <u>soon</u>.

16. Many students thought the assignment was <u>too</u> difficult.

17. Alex slept <u>soundly</u> before the exam.

18. Adam does <u>not</u> want to join our study group.

19. She spoke <u>rather</u> inappropriately.

20. Carson got an <u>exceptionally</u> high grade on his project.

SPEAKING APPLICATION

With a partner, take turns telling about your morning routine of preparing for school. Your partner should listen for and identify at least three adverbs and state how they modify the verbs.

WRITING APPLICATION

Write a brief paragraph in which you praise or criticize a book you've read. Use at least four adverbs. Underline each adverb and draw an arrow to the word it modifies.

Finding Adverbs in Sentences

Adverbs can be found in different places in sentences. The chart below shows examples of possible locations for adverbs. Arrows point to the words that the adverbs modify.

LOCATION OF ADVERBS IN SENTENCES	
LOCATION	**EXAMPLE**
At the beginning of a sentence	Silently, she approached the baby.
At the end of a sentence	She approached the baby silently.
Before a verb	She silently approached the baby.
After a verb	She tiptoed silently toward the baby.
Between parts of a verb phrase	She had silently approached the baby.
Before an adjective	The baby was always quiet.
Before another adverb	The baby cried rather quietly.

Conjunctive adverbs **Conjunctive adverbs** are adverbs that join independent clauses. (See Chapter 17 for more about conjunctive adverbs.)

EXAMPLES   Her car broke down; **therefore** , she missed her
                                      conjunctive adverb
class.

Mike was worried that he would fail; **however** ,
                                                    conjunctive adverb
he passed with flying colors.

See Practice 15.2C

Adverb or Adjective?

Some words can function as adverbs or as adjectives, depending on their use in a sentence.

> If a noun or pronoun is modified by a word, that modifying word is an **adjective.** If a verb, adjective, or adverb is modified by a word, that modifying word is an **adverb.**

An adjective will modify a noun or pronoun and will answer one of the questions *What kind? Which one? How many?* or *How much?*

An adverb will modify a verb, an adjective, or another adverb and will answer one of the questions *Where? When? In what way?* or *To what extent?*

ADVERB MODIFYING VERB	Shopkeepers **work** **hard**. verb adverb When we came to the intersection, we **turned** **left**. verb adverb
ADJECTIVE MODIFYING NOUN	Shopkeepers accomplish **hard** **tasks**. adjective noun Use the **right** **format** for your adjective noun manuscript.

While most words ending in *-ly* are adverbs, some are not. Several adjectives also end in *-ly*. These adjectives are formed by adding *-ly* to nouns.

ADJECTIVES WITH -LY ENDINGS	a **weekly** show a **cuddly** puppy
EXAMPLES	I like movies, but I prefer a **weekly** show. Kodie is different because he's such a **cuddly** puppy.

See Practice 15.2D

PRACTICE 15.2C Locating Adverbs

Read the sentences. Then, write each adverb and the word or words it modifies.

EXAMPLE   His excuse was quite unbelievable.

ANSWER   *quite, unbelievable*

1. Unhappily, the losing team left the field.

2. Camille takes a multivitamin daily.

3. Please move over, so we can all sit comfortably.

4. I have never been so upset as I was then.

5. The student actors performed brilliantly.

6. Most students were thoroughly happy with their report cards.

7. Suddenly, the room went dark!

8. Elisa did not perform well yesterday because she had a headache.

9. You must aim high to achieve success.

10. Karen always greets everyone cheerfully.

PRACTICE 15.2D Recognizing Adverbs and Adjectives

Read the sentences. Then, write whether each underlined word is an *adjective* or an *adverb*.

EXAMPLE   It's been a <u>long</u> time since I've seen him.

ANSWER   *adjective*

11. I arrived at school <u>early</u> this morning.

12. Dad caught the <u>early</u> train to work today.

13. Lianna speaks <u>first</u> in the debate.

14. The player easily scored his <u>first</u> goal.

15. Anna brushed her <u>straight</u> hair.

16. Stand up <u>straight</u>!

17. We had trouble planting vegetables in the <u>hard</u> ground.

18. Hassan and James worked <u>hard</u> on their project.

19. Keep your eyes <u>wide</u> open.

20. The parade route includes all of the <u>wide</u> streets in town.

SPEAKING APPLICATION

With a partner, take turns telling about an exciting event. Use at least three adverbs in different sentence locations. Your partner should identify the adverbs.

WRITING APPLICATION

Use sentences 13 and 14 as models, and write one sentence in which *first* is used as an adjective and one sentence in which *first* is used as an adverb.

PREPOSITIONS

Use prepositions in your writing to illustrate how words are related to each other.

WRITE GUY *Jeff Anderson, M.Ed.*

WHAT DO YOU NOTICE?

Seek out prepositions as you zoom in on this sentence from the essay "Volar: To Fly" by Judith Ortiz Cofer.

MENTOR TEXT

> From up there, over the rooftops, I could see everything, even beyond the few blocks of our barrio; with my X-ray vision I could look inside the homes of people who interested me.

Now, ask yourself the following questions:

- Which prepositions help show the author's physical location as she describes what she sees?
- Which noun is part of the prepositional phrase beginning with *beyond*?

The author uses the prepositions *From* and *over* to convey her location as she observes her surroundings. The preposition *beyond* begins the prepositional phrase *beyond the few blocks*, and the noun included is *blocks*. The phrase that follows, *of our barrio*, is a separate prepositional phrase that begins with *of* and ends with the noun *barrio*.

Grammar for Writers Writers can use prepositions like markers on a map to show where events in a story take place. Prepositions also help show the timing of events.

My list of prepositions was just on my desk. Where did it go?

Let's see ... inside, outside, behind, underneath....

16.1 Prepositions

Prepositions function as connectors, relating one word to another within a sentence.

WRITING COACH

Online

www.TXWritingCoach.com

Prepositions help a speaker or writer express the link between separate items. They can convey information about location, time, or direction or provide details.

Grammar Tutorials
Brush up on your Grammar skills with these animated videos.

Grammar Practice
Practice your grammar skills with Writing Coach Online.

Grammar Games
Test your knowledge of grammar in this fast-paced interactive video game.

RULE 16.1.1

A **preposition** relates the noun or pronoun following it to another word in the sentence.

EXAMPLES

The panda sat **on** the branch **of** the tree.
preposition   noun preposition   noun

The child ran **across** the room and
preposition   noun

hid **underneath** the bed.
preposition   noun

In the first example, the panda sat where? (on the branch) It was on what? (the tree) In the second example, the child ran where? (across the room) The child hid where? (underneath the bed)

FIFTY COMMON PREPOSITIONS				
about	behind	during	off	to
above	below	except	on	toward
across	beneath	for	onto	under
after	beside	from	opposite	underneath
against	besides	in	out	until
along	between	inside	outside	up
among	beyond	into	over	upon
around	but	like	past	with
at	by	near	since	within
before	down	of	through	without

See Practice 16.1A

Compound Prepositions Prepositions consisting of more than one word are called **compound prepositions.** Some of them are listed in the chart below:

COMPOUND PREPOSITIONS		
according to	by means of	instead of
ahead of	in addition to	in view of
apart from	in back of	next to
aside from	in front of	on account of
as of	in place of	on top of
because of	in spite of	out of

Because prepositions have different meanings, using a particular preposition will affect the way other words in a sentence relate to one another. In the first sentence, for example, notice how each preposition changes the relationship between *parade* and *City Hall*.

In this sentence, the preposition changes the relationship between *girls* and *gym*.

See Practice 16.1B

PRACTICE 16.1A ▷ Identifying Prepositions

Read the sentences. Then, write the preposition in each sentence.

EXAMPLE   I will give you an answer by tomorrow.

ANSWER   *by*

1. The price of the leather jacket was reduced.
2. In the mountains, the air is cooler.
3. Josh left his muddy boots outside the door.
4. Lia saw Julie between classes.
5. It appears that the train is on schedule.
6. I found a dollar near the bus stop.
7. Serena felt nervous before the concert.
8. Who is that standing beside Mike?
9. I like stories from Greek mythology.
10. Little Red Riding Hood walked through the forest.

PRACTICE 16.1B ▷ Identifying Compound Prepositions

Read the sentences. Then, write the compound preposition in each sentence.

EXAMPLE   In spite of his good intentions, Rob was late.

ANSWER   *In spite of*

11. School started late on account of the snow.
12. You must turn in your notes in addition to your essay.
13. According to the weather forecast, it will be sunny this week.
14. The principal wants to speak to Sam because of the incident.
15. Your dinner is staying warm on top of the stove.
16. Gayle went to the mall instead of the library.
17. A truck stopped in front of the house.
18. Ike survived by means of his wits.
19. Jessica ate a sandwich in place of a salad.
20. As of today, no one has responded to the ad.

SPEAKING APPLICATION

With a partner, take turns describing the location of another person in the room. Your partner should listen for and name three prepositions that you use.

WRITING APPLICATION

Use sentences 13, 16, and 19 as models, and write three sentences. Use the same prepositions, but change the other words.

Prepositions Used in Sentences

A preposition is never used by itself in a sentence. Instead, it appears as part of a phrase containing one or more other words.

> A **preposition** in a sentence always introduces a **prepositional phrase.**

Prepositional Phrases

A **prepositional phrase** is a group of words that begins with a preposition and ends with a noun or pronoun. The noun or pronoun following the preposition is the **object of the preposition.**

Some prepositional phrases contain just two words—the preposition and its object. Others are longer because they contain modifiers.

EXAMPLES

in soil
preposition object

from the rain **forest**
preposition   object

in place of the older, cracked **phone**
          preposition   object

inside the large, comfortable **car**
preposition   object

with you
preposition object

See Practice 16.1C
See Practice 16.1D
See Practice 16.1F

according to the new **principal**
          preposition   object

Prepositional phrases convey information about location, time, or direction or provide details. (See Chapter 23 to learn about prepositional phrases and their influence on subject–verb agreement.)

Preposition or Adverb?

Some words can be used either as prepositions or as adverbs. The following chart lists some examples. When the word is used as a preposition, it begins a prepositional phrase and is followed by the object of the preposition. If the word has no object, it is probably being used as an adverb.

PREPOSITION OR ADVERB		
above	inside	outside
after	near	past
around	opposite	underneath
before	out	within

PREPOSITION The broken shutter was **outside** the house.

ADVERB The man saw the broken shutter **outside** .

PREPOSITION He appeared **before** the class.

ADVERB He had not heard that **before** .

PREPOSITION The man drove **past** the food store.

ADVERB The car drove **past** quickly.

PREPOSITION He sat **inside** the restaurant.

ADVERB Please go **inside** now.

PREPOSITION The beautician stood **behind** her client.

ADVERB Ann waited **behind** .

PREPOSITION The children waited **near** the playground.

ADVERB I like that the stores are very **near** .

See Practice 16.1E
See Practice 16.1G
See Practice 16.1H

PRACTICE 16.1C **Recognizing Prepositional Phrases**

Read the sentences. Write the prepositional phrase in each sentence, and underline the object of the preposition.

EXAMPLE   This old trunk is covered with dust.

ANSWER   *with dust*

1. The woman in the black coat dropped her purse.

2. Not many people stayed until the end.

3. The golfer hit a ball into the pond.

4. Everyone except Ashley brought lunch.

5. Birds start singing at daybreak.

6. Mrs. Dominguez received a basket of fruit.

7. Keep your papers inside your notebook.

8. He handed the ball to me.

9. We sat around the table discussing the book.

10. That's my brother leaning against the wall.

PRACTICE 16.1D **Distinguishing Prepositions and Prepositional Phrases**

Read the sentences. Write the prepositional phrases. Then, underline the preposition in each phrase.

EXAMPLE   Scrabble is among my favorite games.

ANSWER   *among my favorite games*

11. Two ferries go across that river.

12. There is a fascinating world beneath the ocean.

13. The guests are playing croquet on the lawn.

14. There was a long line outside the theater.

15. The new student is from Alabama.

16. I have a gift for you.

17. You can come through the front door.

18. Your phone fell out of your pocket.

19. Please do not stand in front of the window.

20. We can talk about the schedule later.

SPEAKING APPLICATION

With a partner, take turns describing the location of an object in the room. Use at least two prepositional phrases. Your partner should listen for and identify the prepositional phrases and the objects of each preposition.

WRITING APPLICATION

Write directions to your home from school. Underline the prepositional phrases in your directions.

PRACTICE 16.1E Distinguishing Prepositions and Adverbs

Read the sentences. Label each underlined word *preposition* or *adverb*.

EXAMPLE   Evan left his bicycle <u>outside</u>.

ANSWER   *adverb*

1. Let's go <u>in</u> now.

2. I have not seen Dave <u>around</u> lately.

3. The noise <u>outside</u> the apartment was distracting.

4. I've been to that deli <u>before</u>.

5. My notebook fell <u>behind</u> the desk.

6. We will have to go <u>around</u> the construction site.

7. Set your bundles <u>down</u> onto the table.

8. Dad needs to repair the hole <u>in</u> the fence.

9. We need to be home <u>before</u> 9:00 P.M.

10. Del lives just <u>down</u> the street from me.

PRACTICE 16.1F Supplying Prepositions and Prepositional Phrases

Read the sentences. Then, expand each sentence by adding a prepositional phrase that begins with the preposition in parentheses.

EXAMPLE   You may do your research. (on)

ANSWER   *You may do your research on the Internet.*

11. The tree will be cut down. (by)

12. The ball sailed. (over)

13. Our game was postponed. (with)

14. Malika baked banana bread. (for)

15. Everyone listened intently. (during)

16. Construction will begin soon. (of)

17. The child was crying. (in)

18. I can't go. (without)

19. Why don't you use this pen? (instead of)

20. You need to make up your mind. (prior to)

SPEAKING APPLICATION

With a partner, say a sentence using one of these words: *below, inside*. Your partner should identify whether you used the word as an adverb or a preposition.

WRITING APPLICATION

Write this sentence three times, expanding it with two different prepositional phrases each time: *A student dropped a book*.

PRACTICE 16.1G Distinguishing Prepositions and Adverbs

Read the sentences. Then, label each underlined word *preposition* or *adverb*.

EXAMPLE   The dog chased the squirrel <u>around</u> the yard.

ANSWER   *preposition*

1. Did you remember to put the garbage <u>out</u>?
2. We went <u>out</u> the door quickly.
3. The school is <u>nearby</u> the library.
4. My best friend lives in a house <u>nearby</u>.
5. I had never seen that movie <u>before</u>.
6. We bought our tickets <u>before</u> the movie started.
7. Melinda went <u>inside</u> the house to get her books.
8. Melinda forgot her books <u>inside</u>.
9. I waited for her <u>outside</u> the school.
10. The rain was soaking the flowers <u>outside</u>.

PRACTICE 16.1H Supplying Prepositions and Adverbs

For each word below, write two sentences. In the first sentence, use the word as a preposition. In the second sentence, use the word as an adverb.

EXAMPLE   above

ANSWER   *I placed my suitcase in the bin above my seat.* [preposition]

Look at the helicopter hovering above. [adverb]

11. after
12. around
13. before
14. inside
15. nearby
16. out
17. outside
18. past
19. underneath
20. within

SPEAKING APPLICATION

Take turns with a partner. Choose five of the words in Practice 16.1H. For each word, read aloud one of the sentences you wrote. Your partner should identify whether you used the word as an adverb or as a preposition.

WRITING APPLICATION

Write a paragraph that describes your home or your neighborhood. Use at least three of the following words: *nearby, past, before, after, inside, outside.* Then, underline the word and above it write (p) for preposition or (a) for adverb.

Texas Test Warm-Up

DIRECTIONS

Read the introduction and the passage that follows. Then, answer the questions to show that you can use and understand the function of prepositions and prepositions used as adverbs in reading and writing.

The following paragraph gives directions for making peppermint pull candy. Read the paragraph and think about the changes you would suggest as a peer editor. When you finish reading, answer the questions that follow.

Peppermint Pull Candy

(1) When correctly made, peppermint pull candy will melt. (2) Rub a piece of marble with unsalted butter. (3) Put three drops of peppermint oil on. (4) Boil a mixture of sugar and water on the stove. (5) Use a candy thermometer so you know when the sugar reaches the correct temperature. (6) Once the sugar is ready, pour it over. (7) Let it sit for a few minutes to cool. (8) Then, with both hands, pull the candy. (9) Dip it in food coloring and keep pulling. (10) Finally, stretch it and cut it with scissors.

---

1 What change should be made in sentence 1?

  A Add the adverb **inside** after *made*

  B Add the prepositional phrase **in the comfort of home** after *made*

  C Add the prepositional phrase **in your mouth** after *melt*

  D Add the adverb **before** after *melt*

2 What is the BEST way to rewrite the ideas in sentence 3?

  F Put on three drops of peppermint oil on.

  G Put three drops of peppermint oil.

  H Put three drops of peppermint oil around on.

  J Put three drops of peppermint oil on the marble.

3 What change should be made in sentence 6?

  A Replace the adverb *over* with the prepositional phrase **over the marble**

  B Replace the adverb *over* with the adverb **outside**

  C Replace the adverb *over* with the prepositional phrase **over the floor**

  D Replace the adverb *over* with the adverb **within**

4 The meaning of sentence 10 can be clarified by inserting the adverb **out** —

  F After *stretch*

  G Before *with*

  H Before *stretch*

  J After *it*

CONJUNCTIONS *and* INTERJECTIONS

Use conjunctions when you want to compare and contrast words or ideas in your writing; use interjections to add bursts of emotion.

WRITE GUY *Jeff Anderson, M.Ed.*

WHAT DO YOU NOTICE?

Check for conjunctions as you zoom in on these sentences from the essay "Life Without Gravity" by Robert Zimmerman.

MENTOR TEXT

> Some meals on the space station are eaten with forks and knives, but scooping food with a spoon doesn't work. If the food isn't gooey enough to stick to the spoon, it will float away.

Now, ask yourself the following questions:

- In the first sentence, which conjunction does the author use to show how two things can be used in a similar way?
- In the second sentence, which conjunction introduces a dependent idea?

The coordinating conjunction *and* links the words *forks* and *knives* to show that both tools can be used for eating meals on the space station. The conjunction *but* introduces the contrasting idea that spoons do not work well. In the second sentence, the subordinating conjunction *if* introduces the dependant idea *the food isn't gooey enough to stick to the spoon*. The main idea is *it will float away*.

Grammar for Writers You can use conjunctions to connect two words of the same part of speech or to connect complete sentences to form a new idea.

Conjunctions are important. There are no ifs, ands, or buts about that!

17.1 Conjunctions

Conjunctions are like links in a chain: They help you join words and ideas.

WRITING COACH
Online
@www.TXWritingCoach.com

Grammar Tutorials
Brush up on your Grammar skills with these animated videos.

Grammar Practice
Practice your grammar skills with Writing Coach Online.

Grammar Games
Test your knowledge of grammar in this fast-paced interactive video game.

RULE 17.1.1 > A **conjunction** connects words or groups of words.

Conjunctions fall into three groups: **Coordinating conjunctions, correlative conjunctions,** and **subordinating conjunctions.**

Coordinating Conjunctions

RULE 17.1.2 > **Coordinating conjunctions** connect words of the same kind, such as two or more nouns or verbs. They can also connect larger groups of words, such as prepositional phrases or even complete sentences.

COORDINATING CONJUNCTIONS						
and	but	for	nor	or	so	yet

In the following examples, notice the coordinating conjunctions that connect the highlighted words.

Connecting Nouns	My sister and her friend went to dinner last night to celebrate.
Connecting Verbs	They left for a picnic but forgot the basket.
Connecting Prepositional Phrases	Put the groceries onto the counter or into the refrigerator.
Connecting Two Sentences	The traffic was light, yet we were still late for the meeting.

See Practice 17.1A

Correlative Conjunctions

Correlative conjunctions are *pairs* of words that connect similar kinds of words or groups of words.

CORRELATIVE CONJUNCTIONS		
both . . . and	neither . . . nor	whether . . . or
either . . . or	not only . . . but also	

Notice the correlative conjunctions in the following examples.

Connecting Nouns	Either the train or the bus will take us there.
Connecting Pronouns	Neither they nor I are at fault.
Connecting Verbs	Every night, she both works out and reads.
Connecting Prepositional Phrases	They'll be here—whether on time or late, I can't say.
Connecting Two Clauses	Not only does he cook, but also he cleans!

See Practice 17.1B

Subordinating Conjunctions

Subordinating conjunctions connect two ideas by making one idea dependent on the other.

17.1.3 RULE

FREQUENTLY USED SUBORDINATING CONJUNCTIONS				
after	as soon as	if	though	whenever
although	as though	in order that	till	where
as	because	since	unless	wherever
as if	before	so that	until	while
as long as	even though	than	when	

TEKS Check Show that you can identify, use, and understand the function of subordinating conjunctions. Read a magazine or newspaper article and locate at least five subordinating conjunctions. Explain how each functions in the sentence.

The Dependent Idea The subordinating conjunction always introduces the dependent idea. The subordinating conjunction connects the dependent idea to the main idea.

EXAMPLES I started dinner **after** **she called**.

When **I heard the phone ring**, I jumped.

The examples show that the main idea can come at the beginning or at the end of the sentence. When the dependent idea comes first, it must be separated from the main idea with a comma. If the dependent idea comes second, no comma is necessary.

Conjunctive Adverbs

Conjunctive adverbs are used as conjunctions to connect complete ideas. They are often used as transitions, connecting different ideas by showing comparisons, contrasts, or results. **Transitions** are used in writing to improve the coherence from sentence to sentence and paragraph to paragraph and make your writing smoother.

CONJUNCTIVE ADVERBS			
accordingly	consequently	indeed	otherwise
again	finally	instead	then
also	furthermore	moreover	therefore
besides	however	nevertheless	thus

Notice the punctuation that is used before and after the conjunctive adverb in the following example. (See Chapter 25 for more about punctuation with conjunctive adverbs.)

EXAMPLE That movie was great; **however**, I still prefer the book.

Focus on the TEKS

(19)(A)(vii) Identify, use, and understand the function of subordinating conjunctions (e.g. *because, since*) in reading, writing, and speaking.

See TEKS Check

See TEKS Practice

See Practice 17.1C

See Practice 17.1D

Focus on the TEKS

(19)(A)(iv) Identify, use, and understand the function of conjunctive adverbs (e.g. *consequently, furthermore, indeed*) in reading, writing, and speaking.

(19)(A)(viii) Identify, use, and understand the function of transitions for sentence to sentence and paragraph to paragraph coherence in reading, writing, and speaking.

See TEKS Check

See TEKS Practice

See Practice 17.1E

See Practice 17.1F

TEKS Check Show that you can identify, use, and understand the function of conjunctive adverbs, including transitions. Look though a book you are reading and find at least two conjunctive adverbs and one transition that improves coherence in writing. Explain to a partner the function of the words in the sentences.

PRACTICE 17.1A Supplying Coordinating Conjunctions

Read the sentences. Then, write each sentence, replacing the blank with a coordinating conjunction that makes sense in the sentence.

EXAMPLE   Cats _____ dogs are the most popular house pets.

ANSWER   Cats *and* dogs are the most popular house pets.

1. My sister _____ I do chores after school.

2. The lunch choices are pizza, soup, _____ sandwiches.

3. Billy swept _____ washed the floor.

4. I like science, _____ I prefer math.

5. Chris is inexperienced _____ eager to learn.

6. Mel did not do the assignment, _____ did he come to class.

7. He was late for the bus, _____ he started to run.

8. This tennis racket is light _____ sturdy.

9. We should hurry, _____ the show is about to begin.

10. Laurie has several extracurricular activities, _____ she keeps up her grades.

PRACTICE 17.1B Writing Sentences With Correlative Conjunctions

Write ten sentences, using each of the correlative conjunctions below.

EXAMPLE   whether . . . or

ANSWER   Ellie could not decide *whether* to go to the movies *or* to the mall.

The game will be played *whether* it rains *or* not.

11. both . . . and

12. either . . . or

13. neither . . . nor

14. whether . . . or

15. not only . . . but also

16. both . . . and

17. either . . . or

18. neither . . . nor

19. whether . . . or

20. not only . . . but also

SPEAKING APPLICATION

With a partner, take turns telling about something you saw yesterday or today. Use two coordinating conjunctions in your sentences. Your partner should listen for and name the conjunctions.

WRITING APPLICATION

Write a brief paragraph using two of the correlative conjunction pairs listed above.

PRACTICE 17.1C > **Using Subordinating Conjunctions**

Use the main ideas and subordinating conjunctions below to write complete sentences. With a partner, read your sentences and explain how the subordinating conjunction functions.

EXAMPLE   We will make it to the playoffs (if)

ANSWER   *If we win against the Tigers,* we will make it to the playoffs.

1. I went ahead and made dinner (while)

2. Consider all the options (before)

3. Jasmine hasn't missed a piano lesson (since)

4. Mike brings a good book (whenever)

5. They'll celebrate their anniversary tomorrow (even though)

6. Eugene catches the five o'clock train (unless)

7. I can't go to the movies (because)

8. Mr. Higgins put up a fence (so that)

9. Joan's parents let her play computer games (as long as)

10. The cat will be hiding in the closet (until)

PRACTICE 17.1D > **Writing With Subordinating Conjunctions**

Write complete sentences using the subordinating conjunctions listed. With a partner, read the sentences aloud and explain how the subordinating conjunction functions in each.

EXAMPLE   because

ANSWER   *I'll walk down to the market because we're out of milk.*

11. if

12. whenever

13. since

14. when

15. because

16. unless

17. as soon as

18. before

19. although

20. while

SPEAKING APPLICATION

With a partner, take turns choosing three subordinating conjunctions and using them to talk about your after-school schedules. Your partner should listen for and identify the subordinating conjunctions you use.

WRITING APPLICATION

Write a paragraph about a favorite activity. Use at least three subordinating conjunctions. Read your paragraph to a partner, explaining how the different subordinating conjunctions function.

TEKS Practice Show that you can identify, use, and understand the function of conjunctive adverbs and transitions in reading, writing, and speaking by completing the following activities.

PRACTICE 17.1E > **Using Conjunctive Adverbs in Sentences**

Read the sentences. Then, rewrite each sentence, filling in the blank with a conjunctive adverb. Read each sentence to a partner and explain the function of the conjunctive adverb.

EXAMPLE   I started reading that book; _____, I soon lost interest.

ANSWER   *I started reading that book;* however, *I soon lost interest.*

1. Doctors want people to exercise; _____, many people jog or play sports.
2. Jennifer scored the winning goal in the game; _____, the coach praised her ability.
3. We wanted to play outside after school; _____, it was warm and sunny.
4. I don't want to see that movie; _____, you already saw it last week.
5. Donnie must find his textbook before the test; _____, he will not be prepared.
6. My dad reminds me to turn off the lights; _____, I still forget to do it.
7. Cory thought his jacket was in the car; _____, we did not find it there.
8. Jane ran; _____, she boarded the bus in time.
9. My mom's speech took her all day to write; _____, she worked on it at night.
10. Joaquin likes to write stories; _____, he shares them.

PRACTICE 17.1F > **Using and Writing Conjunctive Adverbs and Transitions**

Read the pairs of sentences. Then, use conjunctive adverbs and transitions to write one new sentence. Read each new sentence to a partner and explain the function of the conjunctive adverbs and the transitions.

EXAMPLE   I have to remind Betsy. She might forget to pick me up.

ANSWER   *I have to remind Betsy;* otherwise, *she might forget to pick me up.*

11. I studied hard. I got an A this semester.
12. Maria babysat five times. She has enough money to buy her mom a present.
13. I enjoyed the first book. I bought the second book.
14. There is a new girl in our lab group. I am no longer the only one.
15. Houston is usually hot in the summer. You should pack light clothing.
16. I practiced basketball a lot. I made the team.
17. We were excited to go to the concert. We were going to see our favorite band.
18. The traffic on the way to the airport was heavy. We missed our flight.
19. Three players on the team were injured in the game. We lost the championship.
20. The play begins in 10 minutes. We ran to our seats.

SPEAKING APPLICATION

With a partner, take turns talking about a book you are reading. Use at least two conjunctive adverbs and one transition. Have your partner identify which ones you used.

WRITING APPLICATION

Write a paragraph about what you did last weekend. Use subordinating conjunctions, conjunctive adverbs, and transitions. Explain to a partner the function of each conjunction.

Texas Test Warm-Up

Focus on the TEKS

(19)(A)(vii) Identify, use, and understand the function of subordinating conjunctions (e.g., *because*, *since*) in reading, writing, and speaking.

(19)(A)(iv) Identify, use, and understand the function of conjunctive adverbs (e.g., *consequently*, *furthermore*, *indeed*) in reading, writing, and speaking.

(19)(A)(viii) Identify, use, and understand the function of transitions for sentence-to-sentence and paragraph-to-paragraph coherence in reading, writing, and speaking.

DIRECTIONS
Read the passage that follows. Then, answer the questions to show that you can identify, use, and understand the function of subordinating conjunctions, conjunctive adverbs, and transitions in reading and writing.

One of Those Days

(1) When I woke up last Tuesday I had a funny feeling it was going to be a bad day. (2) I overslept by 40 minutes. (3) I had to rush to get ready for school. (4) I jumped in the shower, then, I discovered there was no hot water. (5) I put two pieces of bread in the toaster. (6) After that, I went back to my room to make my bed. (7) Suddenly, the smoke detectors in the entire house were going off, my toast had burned. (8) I grabbed a granola bar and ran for the bus. (9) I was five minutes late; however, the bus had just arrived. (10) The driver said, "I'm sorry I'm late. It's one of those days." (11) I answered, "I know what you mean."

1 What change, if any, should be made in sentence 1?

   A Add a comma after *feeling*

   B Add a semicolon after *feeling*

   C Add a comma after *Tuesday*

   D Make no change

2 What is the BEST way to combine sentences 2 and 3?

   F I overslept by 40 minutes; otherwise, I had to rush to get ready for school.

   G I overslept by 40 minutes; nevertheless, I had to rush to get ready for school.

   H I overslept by 40 minutes; therefore, I had to rush to get ready for school.

   J I had to rush to get ready for school; because I overslept by 40 minutes.

3 What change, if any, should be made in sentence 4?

   A Delete the comma after *shower*

   B Change the comma after *shower* to a semicolon

   C Delete the comma after *then*

   D Make no change

4 What is the BEST way to revise sentence 7?

   F Suddenly, the smoke detectors in the entire house were going off because my toast had burned.

   G Suddenly, the smoke detectors in the entire house were going off; consequently, my toast had burned.

   H Suddenly, the smoke detectors in the entire house were going off before my toast had burned.

   J Suddenly, the smoke detectors in the entire house were going off; however, my toast had burned.

17.2 Interjections

The **interjection** is the part of speech that is used the least. Its only use is to express feelings or emotions.

> **An interjection** expresses feeling or emotion and functions independently from the rest of a sentence.

RULE 17.2.1

An interjection has no grammatical relationship to any other word in a sentence. It is, therefore, set off from the rest of the sentence with a comma or an exclamation mark.

Interjections can express different feelings or emotions.

JOY	**Wow!** I can't believe you paid so little.
SURPRISE	**Oh**, I just made plans before you called.
PAIN	**Ouch!** That curling iron is hot.
IMPATIENCE	**Hey!** When are we leaving?
HESITATION	I, **uh**, thought you already knew.

Interjections are used more in speech than in writing. They are informal, rather than formal, expressions. When you do see them in writing, they are often included in dialogue. The following chart lists words often used as interjections.

Focus on the TEKS

(20)(B)(i) Recognize and use punctuation marks including commas after introductory words, phrases, and clauses.

See TEKS Practice

See Practice 17.2A

See Practice 17.2B

INTERJECTIONS			
ah	gosh	nonsense	ugh
aha	great	oh	uh
alas	heavens	oops	um
boy	hey	ouch	well
darn	huh	psst	what
eureka	hurray	shh	whew
fine	my	terrible	wonderful
golly	never	terrific	wow

> **PRACTICE 17.2A** **Identifying Interjections**

Read the sentences. Write the interjection in each sentence. Then, write what emotion the interjection conveys.

EXAMPLE   Wow! Did you see that catch?

ANSWER   *Wow!— surprise*

1. Gosh, I didn't know that.
2. Whew! That was a long walk.
3. Hey! Why did you do that?
4. Oh, no! I can't find my key.
5. Ouch! I stubbed my toe!
6. I, uh, don't really know the answer.
7. Oh, brother, here were go again.
8. Hurray! I knew we would win.
9. Oops! I dropped it again.
10. Terrific! That's great news.

> **PRACTICE 17.2B** **Supplying Interjections**

Read the sentences. Rewrite each sentence, using an appropriate interjection in place of the feeling shown in parentheses. Use a comma or an exclamation mark after each interjection.

EXAMPLE   I forgot my umbrella. (disappointment)

ANSWER   *Darn,* I forgot my umbrella.

11. I just don't believe that. (surprise)
12. She is always late. (impatience)
13. A bee stung me! (pain)
14. I'm so glad you're home safe. (joy)
15. That is a great poster. (surprise)
16. I thought we would never finish. (impatience)
17. Is that all you brought? (impatience)
18. I beg your pardon. (surprise)
19. When did you think it was due? (impatience)
20. I have never seen such ugly colors. (disappointment)

SPEAKING APPLICATION

With a partner, take turns role-playing someone who has just received some news, good or bad. Say your response to the news using an interjection. Your partner should listen for and identify the interjection.

WRITING APPLICATION

Write three sentences, each containing a different interjection. Use a comma or an exclamation mark after each interjection.

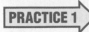 **PRACTICE 1** Writing Sentences With Nouns

Write five sentences, each using one of the following kinds of nouns. Circle those nouns, and underline any other nouns you use.

1. a common noun that names a place
2. a proper noun that names a person
3. a concrete noun
4. a hyphenated compound noun
5. a non-count noun

PRACTICE 2 Identifying Pronouns

Read the sentences. Then, write the pronouns that each sentence contains. Label each pronoun *personal*, *reflexive*, *intensive*, *demonstrative*, *relative*, *interrogative*, or *indefinite*.

1. Tony, who carves wood, made me a spoon.
2. Whose is that?
3. The lifeguard himself said that the pool is open.
4. Everybody enjoyed your fruit salad.
5. Her cat can take care of itself.
6. Has anyone seen this before?
7. Who knows anything about nutrition?
8. Toby, who studied hard, deserved his *A*.
9. My mom sometimes goes to the movies by herself.
10. I myself could never stay up so late.

PRACTICE 3 Using Action and Linking Verbs

Write two sentences for each word below. In the first sentence, use the word as an action verb; in the second sentence, use it as a linking verb.

1. smell
2. look
3. taste
4. feel
5. turn

PRACTICE 4 Identifying Helping Verbs and Main Verbs in Verb Phrases

Read the sentences. Write the complete verb phrase in each sentence. Then, label the parts of each verb phrase *helping* or *main*.

1. The boys have completed all their chores.
2. Betsy's flight will leave at noon.
3. I do not like some of those vegetables.
4. The extra study time has helped me.
5. The task must be finished in one hour.
6. No one can ever remember those song lyrics.
7. I will never again make that mistake.
8. The party has been over since ten o'clock.
9. Did you go to the playground on Monday?
10. She should have dressed in warmer clothing.

Continued on next page ▶

Cumulative Review Chapters 13–17

PRACTICE 5 ▷ Revising Sentences With Adjectives and Adverbs

Read the sentences. Then, rewrite each sentence by adding at least one adjective to modify a noun or a pronoun or one adverb to modify a verb, an adjective, or another adverb.

1. Wendy found her sweater.
2. The girl takes a bus to school.
3. Grandfather snores loudly.
4. A lovely butterfly landed on the flower.
5. The weather was nasty all day.
6. The boat raced through the water.
7. Cows sat in the meadow.
8. She shouted to me from the hallway.
9. The silk shimmered like a rainbow.
10. Have you read a detective story?

PRACTICE 6 ▷ Writing Sentences With Prepositions and Adverbs

Write ten sentences describing different scenes. In your first five sentences, use the prepositional phrases in items 1–5. In your next five sentences, use the words in items 6–10 as adverbs.

1. under the tree branch
2. outside the house
3. before sunrise
4. behind the fence
5. down the chimney
6. under
7. outside
8. before
9. behind
10. down

PRACTICE 7 ▷ Identifying Conjunctions

Read the sentences. Then, identify each underlined word or pair of words as a *coordinating conjunction*, a *subordinating conjunction*, *correlative conjunctions*, or a *conjunctive adverb*.

1. It rained a lot, <u>but</u> we still enjoyed the trip.
2. I laughed <u>because</u> the clown looked so silly.
3. <u>Neither</u> Joshua <u>nor</u> Eric is going to the party.
4. I skipped lunch; <u>nevertheless</u>, I'm not hungry.
5. Alicia <u>and</u> Ellie have joined the Girl Scouts.

PRACTICE 8 ▷ Revising to Include Interjections

Rewrite the following dialogue, adding interjections to help show the speakers' emotions. Use either a comma or an exclamation mark after each interjection.

ELIOT: Did you see the eclipse yesterday?

JANA: I guess I missed it because I had to study.

ELIOT: My brother let me observe the sky through his telescope. It was pretty fantastic.

JANA: I wish I had seen it. I've never seen an eclipse.

ELIOT: I think it will be a long time before there is another eclipse.

JANA: I am so disappointed.

ELIOT: I know. We can research when the next eclipse is expected.

JANA: What a great idea.

BASIC SENTENCE PARTS

Form well-crafted sentences in your writing by pairing carefully chosen subjects and verbs.

WRITE GUY *Jeff Anderson, M.Ed.*

WHAT DO YOU NOTICE?

Zero in on subjects and verbs as you zoom in on these sentences from the essay "The Eternal Frontier" by Louis L'Amour.

MENTOR TEXT

The question I am most often asked is, "Where is the frontier now?" The answer should be obvious. Our frontier lies in outer space.

Now, ask yourself the following questions:

- In the second and third sentences, what are the simple subjects and simple predicates?
- What are the complete subjects and complete predicates in the second and third sentences?

The simple subject in the second sentence is *answer*, and the simple predicate is *should be*. In the third sentence, the simple subject is *frontier*, and the simple predicate is *lies*. The complete subject in the second sentence is *the answer*, and the complete predicate is *should be obvious*. In the third sentence, the complete subject is *our frontier*, and the complete predicate is *lies in outer space*.

Grammar for Writers Make your sentences shorter or longer by working with your subjects and predicates. Think of your simple subject and simple predicate as the starting points of your sentences and build from there.

> In the sentence "History is my favorite subject," history is the simple subject.

> Well, it might be simple for you, but it's complex for me!

18.1 The Basic Sentence

There are many kinds of sentences. Some are short; others are long. Some are simple, and others are more complex. In order to be considered complete, a sentence must have two things: a subject and a verb.

The Two Basic Parts of a Sentence

Every sentence, regardless of its length, must have a subject and a verb.

RULE
18.1.1

A complete **sentence** contains a subject and a verb and expresses a complete thought.

The Subject

A sentence must have a **subject.** Most subjects are nouns or pronouns. The subject is usually, but not always, found near the beginning of the sentence.

RULE
18.1.2

The **subject** of a sentence is the word or group of words that names the person, place, thing, or idea that performs the action or is described. It answers the question *Who?* or *What?* before the verb.

EXAMPLES

The **keys** are lost.

Mr. Levy lost his keys.

He has lost his keys before.

The **keys** are in his pockets.

The noun *keys* is the subject in the first sentence. It tells *what* is lost. In the next sentence, the proper noun *Mr. Levy* tells *who* lost his keys. The pronoun *he* in the third sentence tells *who* lost his keys before. In the last sentence, the noun *keys* tells what are in his pockets.

The Verb

As one of the basic parts of a sentence, the **verb** tells something about the subject.

> The **verb** in a sentence tells what the subject does, what is done to the subject, or what the condition of the subject is.

18.1.3 RULE

EXAMPLES

My dog **won** first place.

The ribbon **was given** at a ceremony.

He **seems** sleepy now.

Won tells what *my dog* did. *Was given* explains what was done with *the ribbon. Seems*, a linking verb, tells something about the condition of *he* by linking the subject to *sleepy.*

See Practice 18.1A

Using Subjects and Verbs to Express Complete Thoughts

Every basic sentence must express a complete thought.

> A sentence is a group of words with a subject and a verb that expresses a complete thought and can stand by itself and still make sense.

18.1.4 RULE

INCOMPLETE THOUGHT

in the closet in the hall

(This group of words cannot stand by itself as a sentence.)

This incomplete thought contains two prepositional phrases. The phrases can become a sentence only after *both* a subject and a verb are added to them.

COMPLETE THOUGHT

The **towels** **are** in the closet in the hall.

subject   verb

(This group of words can stand by itself as a sentence.)

See Practice 18.1B

In grammar, incomplete thoughts are often called **fragments.**

PRACTICE 18.1A > Finding Subject and Verb

Read the sentences. Write the subject and verb of each sentence.

EXAMPLE   The passengers boarded the plane.

ANSWER   *passengers, boarded*

1. We enjoyed a picnic in the park.

2. Winston has two paintings in the exhibit.

3. A skunk wandered through the yard.

4. Huge trucks haul goods across the country.

5. Jane knows who left the note.

6. Kendra has not done her homework yet.

7. The door banged shut behind him.

8. I miss my old neighborhood and school.

9. Where did you get that hat?

10. Marcus fixed the flat tire.

PRACTICE 18.1B > Recognizing Complete Sentences

Read the following groups of words. If a group of words expresses a complete thought, write *complete*. If a group of words expresses an incomplete thought, write *incomplete*.

EXAMPLE   The new store in the mall.

ANSWER   *incomplete*

11. Along a bumpy road.

12. Gloria asked them to be quiet.

13. My new MP3 player on the table.

14. Chloe has never been to Chicago.

15. Destroyed in a wildfire.

16. Randall sings in a band.

17. Finally arrived an hour late.

18. You look happy today.

19. Since I last saw you.

20. Will you please turn out the lights?

SPEAKING APPLICATION

With a partner, take turns talking about today's weather. Your partner should listen for and name three subjects and three verbs in your sentences.

WRITING APPLICATION

Choose three of the incomplete sentences in Practice 18.1B and write them as complete sentences.

18.2 Complete Subjects and Predicates

Have you ever seen tiles laid on a floor? First, a line is drawn in the center of the room. One tile is placed to the left of the line, and another is placed to the right. Then, more tiles are added in the same way: one to the left and one to the right.

Imagine that the first tile on the left is a subject and the first tile on the right is a verb. You would then have a subject and a verb separated by a vertical line, as shown in the example.

EXAMPLE   **Water** | **flowed** .

Now, in the same way that you would add a few more tiles if you were tiling a floor, add a few more words.

EXAMPLE   Cold **water** | **flowed** into the sink.

At this point, you could add still more words.

EXAMPLE   Icy cold **water** | **flowed** into the old metal sink in a steady stream.

The centerline is important in laying tiles. It is just as important in dividing these sentences into two parts. All the words to the left of the line in the preceding examples are part of the **complete subject.** The main noun in the complete subject, *water*, is often called the **simple subject.**

> The **complete subject** of a sentence consists of the subject and any words related to it.

RULE
18.2.1

As in the examples above, the complete subject may be just one word—*water*—or several words—*icy cold water*.

Look at the example sentences again, plus one with new words added.

EXAMPLES   Cold **water** | **flowed** into the sink.

The icy cold **water** | **flowed** into the old metal sink.

Icy cold **water** | **had flowed** into the old metal sink in a steady stream.

All the words to the right of the line in the preceding examples are part of the **complete predicate.** The verb *flowed,* or a verb phrase such as *had flowed,* on the other hand, is often called the **simple predicate.**

See Practice 18.2A

See Practice 18.2A

RULE 18.2.2

The **complete predicate** of a sentence consists of the verb and any words related to it.

As the examples show, a complete predicate may be just the verb itself or the verb and several other words.

Many sentences do not divide so neatly into subject and predicate. Look at the subjects and predicates in the following sentences.

EXAMPLES   **After the game** , our **family** **went out to eat** .

With the snow falling , the **ski team** **began to practice** .

In these sentences, part of the predicate comes *before* the subject, and the rest of the predicate follows the subject.

As you have seen, a complete simple sentence contains a simple subject and a simple predicate. In addition, a complete simple sentence expresses a complete thought.

See Practice 18.2B

PRACTICE 18.2A > **Identifying Complete Subjects and Predicates**

Read the sentences. Rewrite each sentence, and draw a vertical line between the complete subject and the complete predicate. Then, underline the subject once and the verb twice.

EXAMPLE   The Larsons took a train to Washington, D.C.

ANSWER   The *Larsons* | *took* a train to Washington, D.C.

1. Our new television has a very clear picture.

2. Coyotes roam this area at night.

3. The children enjoyed the skateboard ramp in the park.

4. Aidan delivers newspapers every day.

5. Laurie Halse Anderson wrote the novel *Speak*.

6. Reggie is looking for a job after school.

7. Nat and Roseanne did not hear about the changed schedule.

8. The hockey players usually practice early in the morning.

9. My aunt from New York has been visiting us this week.

10. Summer vacation will be here soon.

PRACTICE 18.2B > **Writing Complete Sentences**

Read the items. Each item contains either a complete subject or a complete predicate. Rewrite each item along with the missing part to create complete sentences.

EXAMPLE   _____ are coming with us.

ANSWER   *My cousins from California* are *coming with us.*

11. _____ spread through the forest.

12. The governor of our state _____ .

13. Skills in computer science _____ .

14. _____ rolled off the counter and broke.

15. Three teenage athletes _____ .

16. _____ toppled over.

17. _____ can be prevented.

18. A beautiful rainbow _____ .

19. That car with the dent in its fender _____ .

20. _____ occurs in the summer.

SPEAKING APPLICATION

With a partner, take turns describing one of your hobbies or pastimes using simple sentences. Your partner should listen for and identify the complete subject and predicate in your sentences.

WRITING APPLICATION

Write three sentences about any kind of animal. Draw a vertical line between the complete subject and complete predicate of each sentence.

18.3 Compound Subjects and Compound Verbs

Some sentences have more than one subject. Some have more than one verb.

WRITING COACH

Online

@www.TXWritingCoach.com

Grammar Tutorials
Brush up on your Grammar skills with these animated videos.

Grammar Practice
Practice your grammar skills with Writing Coach Online.

Grammar Games
Test your knowledge of grammar in this fast-paced interactive video game.

Recognizing Compound Subjects

A sentence containing more than one subject is said to have a **compound subject.**

RULE 18.3.1

> A **compound subject** is two or more subjects that have the same verb and are joined by a conjunction such as *and* or *or.*

EXAMPLES

Isabella and Michael **are** popular baby names.
　　　compound subject　　　verb

Birds, rabbits, and other animals **will make**
　　　　　compound subject　　　　　　verb
nests to live in.

Recognizing Compound Verbs

A sentence with two or more verbs is said to have a **compound verb.**

RULE 18.3.2

> A **compound verb** is two or more verbs that have the same subject and are joined by a conjunction such as *and* or *or.*

EXAMPLES

The **team** **may win or lose**.
　　subject　　compound verb

She **reads, edits, and writes** her books.
subject　　　compound verb

Sometimes a sentence will have both a compound subject and a compound verb.

EXAMPLE

Liz and Josh **sang and danced** in
　compound subject　　compound verb
the play.

See Practice 18.3A
See Practice 18.3B

PRACTICE 18.3A > **Recognizing Compound Subjects and Compound Verbs**

Read the sentences. Write the compound subject and/or the compound verb in each sentence.

EXAMPLE   Brad and Tony work for the Recreation Department.

ANSWER   *Brad and Tony*

1. Yolanda designs and sews her own clothes.
2. Oranges, grapefruits, and lemons are citrus fruits.
3. Nina sat in the shade and sipped a cool drink.
4. Either Ollie or Oscar left his sweatshirt here.
5. Nikki wrote a story and posted it on her Web site.
6. Canada, the United States, and Mexico are countries in North America.
7. You may climb the stairs or ride the escalator.
8. Several people in the room coughed and sneezed.
9. We looked for wild strawberries but didn't find any.
10. My friends and I sometimes go to the track and run several laps.

PRACTICE 18.3B > **Combining Sentences With Compound Subjects and Compound Verbs**

Read the sentences. Combine each pair of sentences by using compound subjects or compound verbs.

EXAMPLE   Sylvia aimed the ball carefully. She made a basket.

ANSWER   *Sylvia aimed the ball carefully and made a basket.*

1. This street needs repair. The sidewalk does, too.

2. Jonathan tried out for the team. He made it.

3. I drank a glass of juice. Then, I ran for the school bus.

4. Oil paintings were on sale at the craft fair. Pottery was also on sale.

5. Renee wrote a long letter. She sent it to the editor of the newspaper.

6. Nick mowed the grass. He raked the lawn.

7. The teacher was happy about the test scores. The students were, too.

8. Wind is a renewable energy source. Water is as well.

9. A police officer examined the accident site. She questioned all the witnesses.

10. Tulips grew along the path. Daffodils grew there also.

SPEAKING APPLICATION

With a partner, take turns describing something in your schoolyard. Use a compound subject or a compound verb in one of your sentences. Your partner should listen for and identify the compound.

WRITING APPLICATION

Write two short sentences about what you like to do after school. Then, combine the two short sentences into one longer sentence that has a compound subject and/or compound verb.

18.4 Hard-to-Find Subjects

It can be difficult to identify simple subjects in certain sentences. These sentences do not follow **normal word order** in which the subject comes before the verb. Sometimes the subject will follow the verb or part of a verb phrase. This is called **inverted word order.** Questions are often presented in inverted word order.

WRITING COACH

Online
www.TXWritingCoach.com

Grammar Practice
Practice your grammar skills with Writing Coach Online.

Grammar Games
Test your knowledge of grammar in this fast-paced interactive video game.

NORMAL WORD ORDER   The **meeting** **will begin** at 9:00 A.M. sharp!
                         subject   verb

INVERTED WORD ORDER   When **will** the **meeting** **begin**?
                          verb   subject   verb

Sometimes the subject will not actually be stated in the sentence. It will be understood to be the pronoun *you.* This is often true in sentences that express commands or requests.

The Subject of a Command or Request

When a sentence commands or requests someone to do something, the subject is often unstated.

> The subject of a command or request is understood to be the pronoun *you.*

RULE 18.4.1

COMMANDS OR REQUESTS	HOW THE SENTENCES ARE UNDERSTOOD
Go!	You go!
Start at once.	You start at once.
Please get up.	You please get up.
Heather, write it down.	Heather, you write it down.
Tara, get the confirmation number.	Tara, you get the confirmation number.

See Practice 18.4A

Even though a command or request may begin with the name of the person spoken to, the subject is still understood to be *you.*

Finding Subjects in Questions

Questions are often presented in inverted word order. You will usually find the subject in the middle of the sentence.

> **In questions, the subject often follows the verb.**

RULE 18.4.2

Some questions in inverted word order begin with the words *what*, *whom*, *when*, *where*, *why*, and *how*. Others begin with the verb itself or with a helping verb.

EXAMPLES   How **are** the **muffins** today?

Did **you** **make** them fresh this morning?

Have **you** **found** a basket for them yet?

If you ever have trouble finding the subject in a question, use this trick: Change the question into a statement. The subject will then appear in normal word order before the verb.

QUESTIONS	REWORDED AS STATEMENTS
How **are** you feeling today?	You **are** feeling how today.
What **did** the nurse **say**?	The nurse **did say** what.
Were the newspapers delivered?	The newspapers **were** delivered.
Did she **bring** the newspaper with her?	She **did bring** the newspaper with her.

Not every question is in inverted word order. Some are in normal word order, with the subject before the verb. Questions beginning with *who*, *whose*, or *which* often follow normal word order.

EXAMPLES   **Who** **has** the new car?

Whose new **car** **was** right here?

Which **driver** **should look** at the car?

See Practice 18.4B

PRACTICE 18.4A > **Identifying Subjects in Commands or Requests**

Read the sentences. Write the subject of each sentence.

EXAMPLE   Please bring your own lunch.

ANSWER   *you*

1. Open your books now.
2. Reese, please show me your photos.
3. Pass the ball to Lonnie.
4. Hand me that towel, please.
5. Take the first left after the stoplight.
6. Recharge the battery when it runs down.
7. Do not leave yet.
8. Lou, work with Robert today.
9. Please call me when you get home.
10. Do not forget your gloves.

PRACTICE 18.4B > **Identifying Subjects in Questions**

Read the questions. Write the subject of each question. If you have trouble finding the subject in a question, change the question into a statement.

EXAMPLE   Have you seen Jack today?

ANSWER   *You*

11. Is the report due tomorrow?
12. Did Rosemary enjoy the show?
13. Do you know what prize you won?
14. Does Kerri have an extra pen?
15. Did you bring water for everyone?
16. Would you like me to arrange these chairs?
17. Did Sarah put my folder on my desk?
18. Will we take a field trip?
19. Is she worried about her father?
20. Has everyone had a chance to respond?

SPEAKING APPLICATION

With a partner, take turns explaining how to do a simple task. Your partner should identify the subjects of your sentences.

WRITING APPLICATION

Use sentences 15, 16, and 20 as models and write three sentences of your own. Circle the subjects in your sentences.

Finding the Subject in Sentences Beginning With *There* or *Here*

Sentences beginning with *there* or *here* are usually in inverted word order.

There or **here** is never the subject of a sentence.

There can be used to start a sentence.

SENTENCE STARTER | **There** are two professors from Harvard teaching today.

There and *here* can be used as adverbs at the beginning of sentences. As adverbs, these two words point out *where* and modify the verbs.

ADVERB | **There** goes the town mayor.

Here are the cards from the ceremony.

Be alert to sentences beginning with *there* and *here*. They are probably in inverted word order, with the verb appearing before the subject. If you cannot find the subject, reword the sentence in normal word order. If *there* is just a sentence starter, you can drop it from your reworded sentence.

SENTENCES BEGINNING WITH *THERE* OR *HERE*	REWORDED WITH SUBJECT BEFORE VERB
There is a mistake on the dinner order.	A mistake is on the dinner order.
Here is the correct list of orders.	The correct list of orders is here.

See Practice 18.4C

Finding the Subject in Sentences Inverted for Emphasis

Sometimes a subject is intentionally put after its verb to draw attention to the subject.

> **In some sentences, the subject follows the verb in order to emphasize the subject, or make it stand out.**

RULE 18.4.4

In the following examples, notice how the order of the words builds suspense by leading up to the subject.

EXAMPLES

In the midst of the crowd outside the restaurant **stood** my **parents**.
      verb   subject

Flying above the yard **was** a large red-tailed **hawk**.
verb   verb
subject

Hiding under the warm blanket **was** my little black **puppy**.
verb   verb
subject

You can reword sentences such as these in normal word order to make it easier to find the subject.

INVERTED WORD ORDER	REWORDED WITH SUBJECT BEFORE VERB
In the midst of the crowd outside the restaurant stood my parents.	My parents stood in the midst of the crowd outside the restaurant.
Flying above the yard was a large red-tailed hawk.	A large red-tailed hawk was flying above the yard.
Hiding under the warm blanket was my little black puppy.	My little black puppy was hiding under the blanket.

See Practice 18.4D

PRACTICE 18.4C ▷ Identifying Subjects in Sentences Beginning With *Here* or *There*

Read the sentences. Write the subject of each sentence.

EXAMPLE   Here are the materials you need.

ANSWER   *materials*

1. There are two unread messages in my e-mail.
2. Here comes the coach now.
3. There stood a solitary tree in the field.
4. There goes the last bus without us.
5. Here are a few more players.
6. There is only one right answer.
7. There had been dairy farms in this area.
8. Here lives a famous writer.
9. There are only a few stars out tonight.
10. Here is a map you can follow.

PRACTICE 18.4D ▷ Identifying Subjects in Sentences Inverted for Emphasis

Read the sentences. Write the subject of each sentence.

EXAMPLE   Overhead flew a flock of geese.

ANSWER   *flock*

11. In the middle of the hall hung Grandfather's portrait.
12. Into the office stormed an angry parent.
13. Nowhere will you find better merchandise.
14. Under the porch were two stray kittens.
15. Two blocks from here is the ice cream shop.
16. His good looks he got from his father.
17. All over the yard were broken branches.
18. On these shores landed the first settlers.
19. Down the drain swirled the muddy water.
20. Under no circumstances are you to disturb me!

SPEAKING APPLICATION

With a partner, take turns pointing out two or three things in your classroom using sentences that begin with *Here* or *There*. Your partner should identify the subjects of your sentences.

WRITING APPLICATION

Use sentences 11, 13, and 20 as models, and write three sentences with inverted order of subjects and verbs. Circle the subjects.

18.5 Complements

Often, a subject and verb alone can express a complete thought. For example, *Birds fly* can stand by itself as a sentence, even though it contains only two words, a subject and a verb. Other times, however, the thought begun by a subject and its verb must be completed with other words. For example, *Jacob bought, The waiter told, Our waiter was, Isabella felt,* and *Carolyn won* all contain a subject and verb, but none expresses a complete thought. All these ideas need **complements**.

18.5.1 RULE

> A **complement** is a word or group of words that completes the meaning of a sentence.

Complements are usually nouns, pronouns, or adjectives. They are located right after or very close to the verb. The complements are shown below in blue. The complements answer questions about the subject or verb in order to complete the sentence.

DIFFERENT KINDS OF COMPLEMENTS

Jacob **bought** **dinner**.
subject — verb — complement

The **waiter** **told** **us** the **specials**.
subject — verb — complements

Our **waiter** **was** **impatient**.
subject — verb — complement

Isabella **felt** **happy**.
subject — verb — complement

Carolyn **won** the **game**.
subject — verb — complement

This section will describe three types of complements: **direct objects, indirect objects,** and **subject complements.** All complements add information about the subjects or verbs in the sentence. They paint a clearer picture that helps the reader understand the writer's thoughts.

Recognizing Direct Objects

Direct objects follow action verbs.

A **direct object** is a noun or pronoun that receives the action of a verb.

You can find a direct object by asking *What?* or *Whom?* after an action verb.

EXAMPLES   My younger **sister** **found** the hidden **presents**.
                    subject   verb   direct object

I **called** **Christina** later that day.
subject verb   direct object

My dog **Tinker** **likes** a long **run**
           subject   verb   direct object
in the yard.

Presents, Christina, and *run* are the direct objects of the verbs in the examples. In the first sentence, *presents* answers the question *Found what?* In the second sentence, *Christina* answers the question *Called whom?* In the third sentence, *run* answers the question *Likes what?*

Compound Direct Objects
Like subjects and verbs, direct objects can be compound. That is, one verb can have two or more direct objects.

EXAMPLES   The **baby** **eats** **peas** and other **food**.
                    subject   verb direct object   direct object

The **PTA** **chose** **Mrs. Dorf**,
      subject   verb   direct object

Mrs. Malia, and **Mrs. Niles** to plan the
direct object   direct object
next formal.

See Practice 18.5A
See Practice 18.5B

PRACTICE 18.5A > **Recognizing Direct Objects**

Read the sentences. Write the direct object or the compound direct object in each sentence.

EXAMPLE   Walter Dean Myers has won many awards for his books.

ANSWER   *awards*

1. I usually buy my lunch in the cafeteria.

2. The troop hiked ten miles last week.

3. The rain soaked my jacket.

4. Our teacher showed a film in class.

5. Samantha washed the pots and pans after dinner.

6. Come see the view from here.

7. Tammy saved her money for six months.

8. We brought grapes and apples for snacks.

9. Carole plays both the piano and the flute.

10. Ben asked Joel and me for help.

PRACTICE 18.5B > **Adding Complements**

Read the sentences. Rewrite the sentences, and fill in the blanks with appropriate direct objects. Use both nouns and pronouns.

EXAMPLE   We are reading _____ in English class.

ANSWER   *We are reading Where the Red Fern Grows in English class.*

11. Nadia saved _____ to buy a camera.

12. My family will visit _____ this summer.

13. I asked _____ for a ride home.

14. Our teacher instructed _____ and _____ to hand out the books.

15. We saw _____ , _____ , and a _____ at the fair.

16. Dan met _____ that day.

17. On a clear night, he watches the _____ .

18. Nick designs _____ for a living.

19. I've seen that _____ , but I don't know _____ .

20. Brian put the _____ into the trash can.

SPEAKING APPLICATION

With a partner, take turns telling how a particular sport is played. Your partner should listen for and name at least two direct objects.

WRITING APPLICATION

Use sentences 14 and 15 as models, and write two more sentences with direct objects.

Distinguishing Between Direct Objects, Adverbs, and Objects of Prepositions

Not all action verbs have direct objects. Be careful not to confuse a direct object with an adverb or with the object of a preposition. If you are unsure if a word or phrase is a direct object, ask yourself who or what is receiving the action of the verb.

> **A direct object is never an adverb or the noun or pronoun at the end of a prepositional phrase.**

Compare the following examples. Notice that the action verb *rode* has a direct object in only the first sentence.

EXAMPLES

Dan **rode** his **bike**.
subject   verb   direct object

Dan **rode** **quickly**.
subject   verb   adverb

Dan **rode** **through town**.
subject   verb   prepositional phrase

Each example shows a very common sentence type. The first consists of a subject, a verb, and a direct object. The noun *bike* is the direct object of the verb *rode*.

The second example consists of a subject, a verb, and an adverb. Nothing after the verb in the sentence answers the question *What?* so there is no direct object. *Quickly* modifies the verb and tells *how* Dan rode.

The third example consists of a subject, a verb, and a prepositional phrase. Again, no noun or pronoun answers the question *What?* after the verb. The prepositional phrase tells *where* Dan rode.

Notice also that a single sentence can contain more than one of these three parts.

EXAMPLE

Dan rode his **bike** **quickly**
                direct object   adverb
through town.
prepositional phrase

See Practice 18.5C

Finding Direct Objects in Questions

In normal word order, a direct object follows a verb. In questions that are in inverted word order, however, the direct object often appears before the verb and subject.

> **A direct object in a question will sometimes be found before the verb.**

18.5.4 RULE

In the following chart, questions are paired with sentences reworded in normal word order. Direct objects are highlighted in pink, subjects are highlighted in yellow, and verbs are highlighted in orange. Compare the positions of the direct objects in each.

QUESTIONS	REWORDED IN NORMAL WORD ORDER
What recipes does your grandmother make?	Your grandmother does make what recipes.
What does the baby eat?	The baby does eat what.
Which shoes do you like, the cute flat ones or the fancy boots?	You do like which shoes, the cute flat ones or the fancy boots.
Whom did you meet at the nursery?	You did meet whom at the nursery.

In each of the five questions, the direct object appears before, rather than after, the verb. To locate the direct object in a question, put the sentence into normal word order with the subject appearing before the verb. Then, the direct object will be found in its usual position after the verb.

See Practice 18.5D

PRACTICE 18.5C ▷ Distinguishing Direct Object, Adverb, and Object of a Preposition

Read the sentences. Label each underlined word *DO* for direct object, *ADV* for adverb, and *OP* for object of a preposition.

EXAMPLE   Melissa keeps a parrot in a <u>cage</u>.

ANSWER   *OP*

1. Brad noticed two eggs in the bird's <u>nest</u>.
2. The firefighters responded <u>immediately</u> to the alarm.
3. The art students learned the <u>basics</u> of oil painting.
4. Morgan made a mistake on her math <u>problem</u>.
5. The students sat <u>quietly</u> through the assembly.
6. Phoebe will take Spanish <u>next</u>.
7. Daniel revised and edited his <u>essay</u>.
8. A skater glided smoothly across the <u>ice</u>.
9. Workers removed <u>litter</u> from the roadside.
10. From the top of that hill, you can see for <u>miles</u>.

PRACTICE 18.5D ▷ Finding Direct Objects in Questions

Read the questions. Write the direct object in each question.

EXAMPLE   Which bus do you take?

ANSWER   *bus*

11. What answer did you give to Lucy?
12. How many points did Kevin score?
13. Whom did the team choose as captain?
14. What program should we watch tonight?
15. Whose phone did you borrow?
16. Which shoes do you prefer?
17. What sources did you use for your project?
18. How many books did Tim read?
19. What will you do about your missing keys?
20. Whom did you see there?

SPEAKING APPLICATION

With a partner, take turns talking about something you did yesterday. Your partner should listen for and identify at least one direct object, one adverb, and one object of a preposition.

WRITING APPLICATION

Use sentences 13, 16, and 19 as models, and write three questions. Underline the direct object in each question.

Recognizing Indirect Objects

Sentences with a direct object may also contain another kind of complement, called an **indirect object.** A sentence cannot have an indirect object unless it has a direct object.

> An **indirect object** is a noun or pronoun that comes after an action verb and before a direct object. It names the person or thing to which something is given or for which something is done.

RULE 18.5.5

An indirect object answers the questions *To* or *for whom?* or *To* or *for what?* after an action verb. To find an indirect object, find the direct object first. Then, ask the appropriate question.

EXAMPLE

Tovah's **dad told us** the **story** .
                    indirect object   direct object

(Told *what?* [*story*])
(Told the story *to whom?* [*us*])

Keep in mind the following pattern: *Subject + Verb + Indirect Object + Direct Object.* An indirect object will almost always come between the verb and the direct object in a sentence.

Compound Indirect Objects

Like a subject, verb, or direct object, an indirect object can be compound.

EXAMPLES

Joe gave each **flower and bush** a
subject   verb   compound indirect object

trim .
direct object

(Gave *what?* [*trim*])
(Gave a trim *to what?* [*each flower and bush*])

Dad offered Hannah and me
subject   verb   compound indirect object

dinner and a movie .
compound direct object

(Offered *what?* [*dinner and a movie*])
(Offered dinner and a movie *to whom?* [*Hannah and me*])

See Practice 18.5E

Distinguishing Between Indirect Objects and Objects of Prepositions

Do not confuse an indirect object with the object of a preposition.

RULE 18.5.6

An indirect object never follows the preposition *to* or *for* in a sentence.

Compare the following examples.

EXAMPLES

Grandpa bought **her** a **television**.
indirect   direct object
object

Grandpa bought a **television** for **her**.
            direct object   object of
                                    preposition

In the first example above, *her* is an indirect object. It comes after the verb *bought* and before the direct object *television*. In the second example, *her* is the object of the preposition *for* and follows the direct object *television*.

EXAMPLES

Heather gave **Tara** a **book**.
            indirect   direct
            object   object

Heather gave a **book** to **Tara**.
            direct   object of
            object   preposition

To find the indirect object in the first example above, you must first find the direct object. Ask yourself what Heather gave. She gave a book, so *book* is the direct object. Then, ask yourself to whom Heather gave the book. She gave it to *Tara*, so *Tara* is the indirect object.

Use the same questions in the second example. Again, *book* is the direct object of *gave*; however, *Tara* is no longer the indirect object. Instead, it is the object of the preposition *to*.

See Practice 18.5F

PRACTICE 18.5E ▷ Recognizing Indirect Objects

Read the sentences. Write the indirect object in each sentence.

EXAMPLE   The principal asked Tad some questions.

ANSWER   *Tad*

1. I've already sent her two messages.
2. Carrie fed her cats tuna.
3. Seth made his mother a solemn promise.
4. Please show me your new video game.
5. The boys gave each other a high-five.
6. The baby sitter told the children bedtime stories.
7. Will you lend him a pencil?
8. The business gave the school a donation for new equipment.
9. Our class wrote the author a letter.
10. Many people gave the hurricane victims food and shelter.

PRACTICE 18.5F ▷ Distinguishing Indirect Object and Object of a Preposition

Read the sentences. Write whether the underlined word is an *indirect object* or an *object of a preposition*.

EXAMPLE   Mr. Murphy teaches us social studies.

ANSWER   *indirect object*

11. Phil told Mario the answer.
12. Vanessa wrote her aunt a thank-you note.
13. Do you have any news for us?
14. Let's make ourselves a snack.
15. The teacher explained the assignment to Veronica.
16. Ivy did her research in the library.
17. David passed Brett the ball.
18. Cecilia wanted time for herself.
19. The Chamber of Commerce gives one worthy student a scholarship.
20. Tara whispered a secret to Jocelyn.

SPEAKING APPLICATION

With a partner, tell about a birthday or holiday celebration. Your partner should listen for and name two indirect objects that you use.

WRITING APPLICATION

Rewrite sentences 11, 14, and 19 to include a prepositional phrase.

Subject Complements

Both direct objects and indirect objects are complements used with action verbs. Linking verbs, however, have a different kind of complement called a **subject complement.** Like direct and indirect objects, subject complements add information to a sentence. However, subject complements give readers more information about the subject of the sentence, not the verb.

RULE 18.5.7

A **subject complement** is a noun, pronoun, or adjective that follows a linking verb and provides important details about the subject.

Predicate Nouns and Pronouns
Both nouns and pronouns are sometimes used as subject complements after linking verbs.

RULE 18.5.8

A **predicate noun** or **predicate pronoun** follows a linking verb and renames or identifies the subject of the sentence.

It is easy to recognize predicate nouns and predicate pronouns. The linking verb acts much like an equal sign between the subject and the noun or pronoun that follows the verb. Both the subject and the predicate noun or pronoun refer to the same person or thing.

EXAMPLES

Bonnie **will be** the **head** of our committee.
    subject   verb   predicate noun

(The predicate noun *head* renames the subject *Bonnie.*)

My first **car** **was** a white **convertible**.
      subject verb   predicate noun

(The predicate noun *convertible* identifies the subject *car.*)

The two **winners** **are** **we**.
     subject   verb predicate pronoun

(The predicate pronoun *we* identifies the subject *winners.*)

See Practice 18.5G

Predicate Adjectives

A linking verb can also be followed by a **predicate adjective.**

> **A predicate adjective** follows a linking verb and describes the subject of the sentence.

A predicate adjective is considered part of the complete predicate of a sentence because it comes after a linking verb. In spite of this, a predicate adjective does not modify the words in the predicate. Instead, it describes the noun or pronoun that serves as the subject of the linking verb.

EXAMPLES   The **flight** to Mexico **was long**.
                 subject   verb   predicate adjective

(The predicate adjective *long* describes the subject *flight*.)

The **teacher seemed** very **sensitive**
       subject   verb   predicate adjective
to the needs of her students.

(The predicate adjective *sensitive* describes the subject *teacher*.)

Compound Subject Complements

Like other sentence parts, subject complements can be compound.

> **A compound subject complement** consists of two or more predicate nouns, pronouns, or adjectives joined by a conjunction such as *and* or *or*.

EXAMPLES   My two best **subjects are English and history**.
                            subject   verb   compound predicate noun

The **grass felt warm and wet**.
       subject   verb   compound predicate adjective

See Practice 18.5H
See Practice 18.5I
See Practice 18.5J

The **dessert was ice cream and fruit**.
       subject   verb   compound predicate noun

PRACTICE 18.5G ▶ Identifying Predicate Nouns and Predicate Pronouns

Read the sentences. Write the predicate noun and/or the predicate pronoun in each sentence.

EXAMPLE   Whales are the largest mammals.

ANSWER   *mammals*

1. Gabe's favorite sport is lacrosse.

2. Regina is becoming a good painter.

3. The capital of Texas is Austin.

4. Mr. Hughes has been the director for years.

5. The group leaders are Isabel and she.

6. The best part of camp was the swimming.

7. Jordan will be our representative in the debate.

8. Shakespeare is probably the most famous playwright ever.

9. Amy remains my friend even though she moved away.

10. Your new car should be a hybrid.

PRACTICE 18.5H ▶ Identifying Predicate Adjectives

Read the sentences. Write the predicate adjective or adjectives in each sentence.

EXAMPLE   Robin appears confident about her chances.

ANSWER   *confident*

11. That antique table seems valuable.

12. As the storm continued, the roads became slippery.

13. The character in the black shirt looks suspicious.

14. Thanksgiving dinner was delicious and filling.

15. Laura sounded joyful about the news.

16. You should be thankful for your good health.

17. These plants grow taller every day.

18. This soup tastes so good.

19. The weather for our outing was breezy and warm.

20. Stefan felt better after a break.

SPEAKING APPLICATION

With a partner, make a statement about someone or something. Use a predicate noun or predicate adjective in your statement. Your partner should listen for and name the predicate noun or predicate adjective.

WRITING APPLICATION

Write a short paragraph describing someone or something. Use at least one predicate adjective and one predicate noun or predicate pronoun, and underline them in your paragraph.

PRACTICE 18.5I **Writing With Predicate Nouns, Predicate Pronouns, and Predicate Adjectives**

Read the sentence starters. Then, as indicated in parentheses, write a complete sentence using a predicate noun, predicate pronoun, or predicate adjective.

EXAMPLE   (predicate noun) Mr. Sloan might become

ANSWER   *Mr. Sloan might become the basketball coach.*

1. (predicate noun) The O'Reillys are our

2. (predicate adjective) Sunning themselves on the beach, my parents seemed

3. (predicate noun) Ms. Long could be the best

4. (predicate pronoun) The last person on the bus was

5. (predicate adjective) After dance class, she looked

6. (predicate noun) Last September, Kali became

7. (predicate pronoun) The big winner was

8. (predicate adjective) This chili tastes

9. (predicate adjective) The student council members are

10. (predicate adjective) After the game the team seemed

PRACTICE 18.5J **Writing With Compound Subject Complements**

Read the sentence starters. Then, add a compound subject complement to create a complete sentence.

EXAMPLE   Ice cream, when left out too long, becomes

ANSWER   *Ice cream, when left out too long, becomes warm and runny.*

11. Your speech sounded

12. My grandfather was a

13. To his friends, José seemed

14. Just how I like it, the sandwich is

15. The last two contestants were

16. Her best friend from kindergarten is now

17. After a day of exercising, Darnell is

18. The water looks

19. My two favorite foods are

20. His flight delayed again, Ted grew

SPEAKING APPLICATION

With a partner, take turns discussing sports. Use at least one predicate noun, one predicate pronoun, and one predicate adjective. Your partner should listen for and name the types of subject complements you used.

WRITING APPLICATION

Write a letter recommending a friend for a babysitting job. Use predicate nouns, predicate pronouns, and predicate adjectives. Include at least one compound subject complement.

Texas Test Warm-Up

DIRECTIONS
Read the introduction and the passage that follows. Then, answer the questions to show that you can use and understand the function of subject complements in reading and writing.

Sasha wrote this paragraph about a school event called Battle of the Bands. Read the paragraph and think about the changes you would suggest as a peer editor. When you finish reading, answer the questions that follow.

Battle of the Bands

(1) The Battle of the Bands competition were hosted by my school. (2) It is my favorite school event. (3) This year, the four bands were Union Bay Band, Tim and Cat, Sushi Rocks, and Candyband. (4) Union Bay Band was amazing. (5) Union Bay Band was the best. (6) The members were very talented and energetic. (7) Candyband was the runner-up. (8) I thought their second song was much better than their first. (9) My favorites were Union Bay Band and Sushi Rocks. (10) Overall, it was a great show.

1 What change, if any, should be made in sentence 1?

A Change *were* to **is**

B Add a comma after **competition**

C Add an apostrophe after the *d* in **Bands**

D Make no change

2 What is the BEST way to combine sentences 4 and 5 to create a compound subject complement?

F Union Bay Band was amazing.

G Union Bay Band was the best.

H Union Bay Band was amazing and the best.

J Union Bay Band was the best, and Union Bay Band was amazing.

3 What change, if any, should be made in sentence 6?

A Change *were* to **was**

B Change *and* to **or**

C Add a comma after **were**

D Make no change

4 What change, if any, should be made to sentence 9?

F Change *favorites* to **favorite**

G Change *were* to **was**

H Change *favorites were* to **favorite is**

J Make no change

PHRASES *and* CLAUSES

Knowing how to construct phrases and clauses will help you add information to your sentences and make them more interesting.

WRITE GUY *Jeff Anderson, M.Ed.*

WHAT DO YOU NOTICE?

Search for phrases and clauses as you zoom in on lines from the poem "The Rider" by Naomi Shihab Nye.

MENTOR TEXT

> A boy told me
> if he rollerskated fast enough
> his loneliness couldn't catch up to him,
>
> the best reason I ever heard
> for trying to be a champion.

Now, ask yourself the following questions:

- What makes the entire second line a clause?
- In the third line, what makes the words *to him* a phrase?

The second line is a clause because it is a group of words that has its own subject and verb. The subject is *he* and the verb is *rollerskated*. In the third line, *to him* is a phrase because a phrase is a group of words that does not contain a subject and verb. Phrases are used to add more information to a sentence.

Grammar for Writers Phrases and clauses are an important part of a writer's toolbox. Use them to tell more about the main nouns and verbs in your sentences.

You added some interesting information to your sentences.

It must be a phrase I'm going through.

19.1 Phrases

Sentences are usually built with more than just a subject and a predicate. **Phrases** play an important role in sentences by adding more information.

WRITING COACH

Online

@www.TXWritingCoach.com

Grammar Tutorials
Brush up on your Grammar skills with these animated videos.

Grammar Practice
Practice your grammar skills with Writing Coach Online.

Grammar Games
Test your knowledge of grammar in this fast-paced interactive video game.

RULE 19.1.1

> A **phrase** is a group of words that functions in a sentence as a single part of speech. Phrases do not contain a subject and a verb.

Prepositional Phrases

A **prepositional phrase** has at least two parts, a preposition and a noun or pronoun that is the object of the preposition.

EXAMPLES

near **beaches**
prep   object

around **palm trees**
prep   object

The object of the preposition may be modified by one or more adjectives.

EXAMPLES

near warm sandy **beaches**
prep adj   adj   object

around beautiful tall **palm trees**
prep   adj   adj object

The object may also be a compound, consisting of two or more objects connected by a conjunction such as *and* or *nor*.

EXAMPLES

near warm sandy **beaches** and **lakes**
prep adj   adj   object   object

around beautiful tall **palm trees** and **cacti**
prep   adj   adj   object   object

See Practice 19.1A

In a sentence, some prepositional phrases can act as adjectives that modify a noun or pronoun. Other prepositional phrases can act as adverbs that modify a verb, adjective, or adverb.

Using Prepositional Phrases That Act as Adjectives

A prepositional phrase that acts as an adjective in a sentence is called an **adjective phrase** or **adjectival phrase.**

> An **adjective phrase** or **adjectival phrase** is a prepositional phrase that modifies a noun or pronoun by telling *what kind* or *which one.*

RULE 19.1.2

Unlike one-word adjectives, which usually come before the nouns or pronouns they modify, adjectival phrases usually come after the nouns or pronouns they modify.

ONE-WORD ADJECTIVES	ADJECTIVAL PHRASES
The sandy beach began there.	The beach with two lighthouses began there.
The anxious lifeguard stopped us.	The lifeguard with the anxious face stopped us.

Adjectival phrases answer the same questions as one-word adjectives do. *What kind* of beach began there? *Which* lifeguard stopped us?

USES OF ADJECTIVAL PHRASES	
Modifying a Subject	The sound of the rain scared us.
Modifying a Direct Object	It pounded the roof of the house .

When two adjectival phrases appear in a row, the second phrase may modify the object of the preposition in the first phrase or both phrases may modify the same noun or pronoun.

ADJECTIVAL PHRASES IN A ROW	
Modifying the Object of a Preposition	The gutters on the house in the field filled rapidly.
Modifying the Same Noun	There was a smell of roses in the house .

Focus on the TEKS

(19)(A)(iii) Identify, use, and understand the function of adjectival phrases in the context of reading, writing, and speaking.

See TEKS Check

See TEKS Practice

See Practice 19.1B

See Practice 19.1C

TEKS Check Show that you can identify and understand the function of adjectival phrases. With a partner, find a newspaper or magazine article. Underline any prepositional phrases you can identify. Place a star next to the phrases that function as adjectival phrases. Save your work for a future activity.

Using Prepositional Phrases That Act as Adverbs

A prepositional phrase that acts as an adverb modifies the same parts of speech as a one-word adverb does.

> An **adverbial phrase** or **adverb phrase** is a prepositional phrase that modifies a verb, an adjective, or an adverb. Adverbial phrases point out *where, when, in what way,* or *to what extent.*

Adverbial phrases are used in the same way as one-word adverbs, but they sometimes provide more precise details.

ONE-WORD ADVERBS	ADVERBIAL PHRASES
Bring your shoes here.	Bring your shoes into the garage.
The concert began early.	The concert began at exactly 6:00 P.M.

Adverbial phrases can modify verbs, adjectives, and adverbs.

USES OF ADVERBIAL PHRASES	
Modifying a Verb	Snow fell in heavy clumps. (Fell *in what way?*)
Modifying an Adjective	The day was cold for May. (Cold *in what way?*)
Modifying an Adverb	The snow fell heavily for that time of year. (Heavily *in what way?*)

Adverbial phrases, unlike adjectival phrases, are not always located near the words they modify in a sentence.

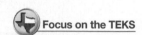

EXAMPLE **During the storm**, people closed up their shops.

Two or more adverbial phrases can also be located in different parts of the sentence and still modify the same word.

EXAMPLE **During the night**, the cold was felt **throughout the house**.

Focus on the TEKS

(19)(A)(iii) Identify, use, and understand the function of adverbial phrases in the context of reading, writing, and speaking.

See TEKS Check

See TEKS Practice

See Practice 19.1D

See Practice 19.1E

See Practice 19.1F

TEKS Check Show that you can identify and understand the function of adverbial phrases. With a partner, review the newspaper or magazine article you worked with previously. Select a prepositional phrase that is not adverbial and rewrite it to make it an adverbial phrase.

TEKS Practice Show that you can identify, use, and understand the function of adjectival phrases in reading, writing, and speaking by completing the following activities.

PRACTICE 19.1A > **Identifying Prepositional Phrases**

Read the sentences. Then, write the prepositional phrase in each sentence, and underline the object of the preposition.

EXAMPLE   That story about wolves was fascinating.

ANSWER   *about wolves*

1. The sound of a harp is very soothing.

2. Please take your feet off the chair.

3. Were you able to find Quentin and Stewart in the crowd?

4. Justin likes to browse through magazines.

5. Rebecca will finish her project by Monday.

6. Elizabeth II is the queen of England.

7. Everyone reads the notices on the board.

8. The train to Chicago was late.

9. Valentina likes all vegetables except eggplant.

10. I do not watch television during the week.

PRACTICE 19.1B > **Identifying Adjectival Phrases**

Read the sentences. Then, write the adjectival phrase in each sentence. One sentence has two adjectival phrases.

EXAMPLE   The leaves on the trees are turning brown.

ANSWER   *on the trees*

11. The head of the committee read the report.

12. The plant near the window is a bamboo.

13. The singer with the deep voice stole the show.

14. Ramona delivered an excellent presentation on colonial cooking.

15. Brandon is wearing a shirt with a school logo.

16. Do you have the solution to this problem?

17. The trail up the mountain is well marked.

18. The photo in the newspaper was not very clear.

19. The girl beside Carla is her sister.

20. The first room on the left in that corridor is the nurse's office.

SPEAKING APPLICATION

With a partner, tell about your neighborhood. Your partner should listen for and name at least one adjectival phrase, one prepositional phrase, and the object of the preposition.

WRITING APPLICATION

Write this sentence twice, adding two different adjectival phrases each time: *Two girls walked into the store.* Explain to a partner how the phrase functions in the sentence.

PRACTICE 19.1C ► Writing Adjectival Phrases

Read each sentence. Rewrite each sentence adding one or more adjectival phrases. Then, read the sentences to a partner who identifies the adjectival phrase.

EXAMPLE   The book was dusty.

ANSWER   *The book **on the top shelf** was dusty.*

1. The fountain is a good place to make wishes.
2. Cindy bought the sparkling earrings.
3. The waiter has arrived.
4. The audience fell silent.
5. Arkee sensed something wrong.
6. The get-well-soon cards piled up.
7. My family is planning a vacation.
8. The flowers look thirsty.
9. Lin's broken arm finally healed.
10. The first bite tasted delicious.

PRACTICE 19.1D ► Identifying Adverbial Phrases

Read the sentences. Then, write the adverbial phrase in each sentence. One sentence has two adverbial phrases.

EXAMPLE   A hawk dived from the tree.

ANSWER   *from the tree*

11. I can help you in a minute.
12. Oliver is very good at chess.
13. Franklin was bored during the recital.
14. Olivia included two graphs in her report.
15. That car parked by the hydrant was ticketed.
16. The winner stepped onto the platform.
17. The kayaker moved steadily across the lake.
18. Lily fastened the necklace around her neck.
19. The dog woke up from his nap with a start.
20. Let's go without further delay.

SPEAKING APPLICATION

With a partner, take turns talking about your favorite pastimes. Use three adjectival and three adverbial phrases. Have your partner listen for and identify the phrases you used.

WRITING APPLICATION

Write a brief description of a movie you have seen or would like to see. Use three adjectival and three adverbial phrases. Read your description to a partner, and discuss the function of each phrase.

TEKS Practice Show that you can identify, use, and understand the function of adjectival and adverbial phrases in reading, writing, and speaking by completing the following activities.

Phrases

PRACTICE 19.1E ▷ Writing Adverbial Phrases

Read the sentences. Then, rewrite the sentences adding an adverbial phrase. Read your new sentences to a partner, who should identify the adverbial phrase.

EXAMPLE   The janitor locked the door.

ANSWER   *The janitor locked the door* **at night.**

1. Hernando read ten novels.
2. The executives presented the proposal.
3. Mr. Trigg checks the mail.
4. I have to write a two-page essay.
5. The tiger waited to pounce.
6. The marching band played.
7. Violet must finish cleaning her room.
8. Principal Caprio inspires trust.
9. The heat penetrated the car.
10. Tony brought donuts.

PRACTICE 19.1F ▷ Writing Adjectival and Adverbial Phrases

Read the sentences. Then, rewrite the sentences by adding adjectival or adverbial phrases, as directed in parentheses.

EXAMPLE   I found your book. (adverbial phrase)

ANSWER   *I found your book* **under the desk.**

11. A lifeguard dived. (adverbial phrase)
12. The cat yawned and walked away. (adjectival phrase)
13. The statue attracts many visitors. (adjectival phrase)
14. Scientists study the moon. (adverbial phrase)
15. Everyone admired Jana's new haircut. (adjectival phrase)
16. The jacket was extremely uncomfortable. (adjectival phrase)
17. We waited. (adverbial phrase)
18. She gave me a bowl. (adjectival phrase)
19. You will find everything you need. (adverbial phrase)
20. Four men moved furniture. (adjectival phrase, adverbial phrase)

SPEAKING APPLICATION

With a partner, take turns describing the location of something. Your partner should listen for and identify at least three adverbial phrases. Together, discuss the function, or purpose, of these phrases in the sentences.

WRITING APPLICATION

Write a paragraph about a television program. Use at least one adjectival and one adverbial phrase. Underline the prepositional phrases, and label them *adjectival* or *adverbial*. Then, explain the purpose of these phrases in your writing.

Focus on the TEKS

(19)(A)(iii) Identify, use, and understand the function of adjectival phrases in reading, writing, and speaking.

(19)(A)(iii) Identify, use, and understand the function of adverbial phrases in reading, writing, and speaking.

 # Texas Test Warm-Up

DIRECTIONS
Read the introduction and the passage that follows. Then, answer the questions to show that you can use and understand the function of adjectival phrases and adverbial phrases in reading and writing.

Sonya wrote the following paragraph about a jazz band called the Hot Five. Read the paragraph and think about the changes you would suggest as a peer editor. When you finish reading, answer the questions that follow.

The Hot Five

(1) My dad took me to see his favorite jazz band, the Hot Five, on Friday night. (2) The small club was packed. (3) The band started with *Nights in Tunisia.* (4) The rhythm seemed to guide the rest of the group. (5) The bass set the rhythm. (6) While his solo, the piano player rearranged the melody to delight. (7) When the trumpet played by itself, the room was quiet. (8) At the break, there was a sense. (9) No one could wait to hear what they would play next.

---

1 How should sentence 2 be revised?

  A The small was packed.

  B The small club was packed with eager listeners.

  C The small in the club was packed.

  D The small club was with the packed.

2 What is the BEST way to combine sentences 4 and 5?

  F The rhythm seemed to guide the rest of the group and the bass.

  G The rhythm, seemed to guide the rest of the group.

  H The rhythm seemed to guide the bass.

  J The rhythm of the bass seemed to guide the rest of the group.

3 What is the BEST way to rewrite the ideas in sentence 6?

  A On his solo, the piano player rearranged the melody to delight.

  B During his solo, the piano player rearranged the melody to the delight of everyone.

  C His solo rearranged the melody to delight.

  D After his solo, the piano player rearranged the melody to delight me.

4 What is the BEST way to revise sentence 8?

  F At the break, there was a sense of excitement in the room.

  G At the break, there was a sense the night was over.

  H At the break, there was a sense of finality.

  J At the break, there was a sense to hear more.

Using Appositives and Appositive Phrases

Appositives, like adjectival phrases, give information about nouns or pronouns.

RULE 19.1.4

> An **appositive** is a noun or pronoun placed after another noun or pronoun to identify, rename, or explain the preceding word.

Appositives are very useful in writing because they give additional information without using many words.

MODIFIES

EXAMPLES　The tour guide **Mr. Torres** led an exciting tour of the London Tower.

MODIFIES

I admire the artist **Vincent Van Gogh**.

Focus on the TEKS

(19)(A)(ii) Identify, use, and understand the function of appositive phrases in the context of reading, writing, and speaking.

See TEKS Check

See TEKS Practice

See Practice 19.1G

See Practice 19.1H

An appositive with its own modifiers creates an **appositive phrase.**

RULE 19.1.5

> An **appositive phrase** is a noun or pronoun with modifiers. It is placed next to a noun or pronoun and adds information or details.

The modifiers in an appositive phrase can be adjectives or adjectival phrases.

EXAMPLES　Aunt Kelly, my **favorite aunt**, writes novels.
　　　　　　　　　　　　　　　adjective　noun

It is a photograph, a **portrait in black and white**.
　　　　　　　　　　　　noun　　　　adj phrase

Appositives and appositive phrases can also be a compound.

EXAMPLE　Athletes, **men** and **women**, played together.
　　　　　　　　　　compound noun

TEKS Check Show that you can identify and understand the function of appositive phrases. Locate three appositive phrases in magazines or newspapers and share your findings with a classmate. Explain how these phrases add meaning to the writing. Then write at least one sentence with an appositive phrase.

TEKS Practice Show that you can identify, use, and understand the function of appositive phrases in reading, writing, and speaking by completing the following activities.

PRACTICE 19.1G > Identifying Appositives and Appositive Phrases

Read the sentences. Then, write the appositive or appositive phrase in each sentence. Explain which word the phrase modifies.

EXAMPLE   My science teacher, Mr. Rodriguez, directed our lab experiments.

ANSWER   *Mr. Rodriguez*

1. We are reading a novel, *Holes* by Louis Sachar, for English class.

2. My brother John has been accepted by the state college.

3. She and Molly, the first ones to arrive, organized the activities.

4. Owen, a sports fan, won tickets to the game.

5. Bianca Wilson, my best friend, is in most of my classes.

6. The magnificent sight, a panoramic view of the valley, took our breath away.

7. Barack Obama, the first African American president, took office on January 20, 2009.

8. The Notables, a local singing group, will perform at the assembly.

9. A member of the audience threw a bouquet, yellow and white roses, to the singer.

10. Janelle, the group's photographer, took pictures everywhere they went.

PRACTICE 19.1H > Combining Sentences With Appositive Phrases

Read the sentences. Combine each pair of sentences by using an appositive phrase.

EXAMPLE   Mrs. Reedy took the band to a competition. She is the director.

ANSWER   *Mrs. Reedy, the director, took the band to a competition.*

11. Isabel finished her assignment early. Her assignment was a report on animal behavior.

12. A car was wrecked. It was a white sedan.

13. Harry's brothers went with him to play basketball. Ron and Sam are his brothers.

14. Vivian enjoys her favorite pastime. Her favorite pastime is solving puzzles.

15. Warren Wilkes is a reporter for *The Daily Times*. He wrote a story on the trial.

16. Elvis Presley was the king of rock-and-roll. He lived in a mansion in Memphis.

17. The child had no fear of the dog. The child was a four-year-old boy.

18. I read a good article in this magazine. The article was "Eating Well for Health."

19. Consuela Carter presented a talk on ecology. She is a professor of earth science.

20. Give your job application to Mr. Haynes. He is the hiring manager.

SPEAKING APPLICATION

In a small group, take turns introducing one another, using one sentence with an appositive phrase in it. The group members should listen for and identify the appositive phrase. As a group, discuss the function or purpose of these appositive phrases.

WRITING APPLICATION

Use your combined sentences 13 and 20 as models, and write two new sentences with appositive phrases. Then, read each sentence aloud and explain the function, or purpose, of these appositive phrases.

Using Verbals and Verbal Phrases

A **verbal** is any verb form that is used in a sentence not as a verb but as another part of speech.

Like verbs, verbals can be modified by an adverb or adverbial phrase. They can also be followed by a complement. A verbal used with a modifier or a complement is called a **verbal phrase.**

Participles

Participles are verb forms with two basic uses. When they are used with helping verbs, they are verbs. When they are used alone to modify nouns or pronouns, they become adjectives.

> A **participle** is a form of a verb that is often used as an adjective.

19.1.6 RULE

Focus on the TEKS

(19)(A)(i) Identify, use, and understand the function of participles in the context of reading, writing, and speaking.

See TEKS Check

See TEKS Practice

See Practice 19.1I

See Practice 19.1J

There are two kinds of participles, **present participles** and **past participles.** Each kind can be recognized by its ending.

All present participles end in *-ing.*

EXAMPLES   talking   doing   eating   wanting

Most past participles end either in *-ed* or in *-d.*

EXAMPLES   opened   jumped   played   moved

Other past participles end in *-n, -t, -en,* or another irregular ending.

EXAMPLES   grown   felt   bought   eaten   held

Both present and past participles can be used in sentences as adjectives. They tell *what kind* or *which one.*

PRESENT PARTICIPLES	PAST PARTICIPLES
She led a walking tour.	Chilled fruit juice is refreshing.
Speaking slowly, he gave us directions.	She was, by then, a grown woman.

TEKS Check Show you can identify, use, and understand the function of participles. Write four sentences, three of which contain participles. Read your sentences aloud to a partner. Have your partner identify the participles in each sentence.

Participle or Verb?

Sometimes, verb phrases (verbs with helping verbs) are confused with participles. A verb phrase always begins with a helping verb. A participle used as an adjective stands by itself and modifies a noun or pronoun.

VERB PHRASES	PARTICIPLES
The bicyclist was racing around the corner.	The racing bicyclist crashed into the tree.
Explorers may have traveled down this road.	The traveled road led to the finish line.

Participial Phrases

A participle can be expanded into a participial phrase by adding a complement or modifier.

RULE 19.1.7

> A **participial phrase** is a present or past participle and its modifiers. The entire phrase acts as an adjective in a sentence.

Participial phrases can be formed by adding an adverb, an adverbial phrase, or a complement to a participle.

EXAMPLES   The teacher, **speaking slowly**, explained the essay requirements.

The well-known instructor, **honored by the award**, began his speech.

The first participial phrase contains the adverb *slowly* added to the participle *speaking*. The second includes the adverbial phrase *by the award* added to the participle *honored*.

A participial phrase can also be placed at the beginning of a sentence. The phrase is usually followed by a comma.

EXAMPLE   **Honored by the award**, the well-known instructor began his speech.

Focus on the TEKS

(19)(A)(i) Identify, use, and understand the function of participles in the context of reading, writing, and speaking.

See TEKS Check

See TEKS Practice

See Practice 19.1K

See Practice 19.1L

 TEKS Check Show that you can identify, use, and understand the function of participles. Write two sentences with verb phrases and two with participle phrases. Exchange sentences with a partner. Read your partner's sentences and identify the participles.

TEKS Practice Show that you can identify, use, and understand the function of participles in reading, speaking, and writing by completing the following activities.

PRACTICE 19.1I ▷ **Identifying Present and Past Participles**

Read the sentences. Then, write the participle in each sentence, and label it *present participle* or *past participle.*

EXAMPLE   We just watched an exciting match.

ANSWER   *exciting — present participle*

1. Mel separated the good pieces of furniture from the damaged ones.

2. Sherlock Holmes solved many baffling mysteries.

3. Lucy put a frozen dinner into the microwave.

4. The gathering clouds made the picnickers finish quickly and leave.

5. Elroy made a running dive for the football.

6. A hushed audience waited for the curtain to rise.

7. The campers ate toasted sandwiches around the fire.

8. A soldier knelt by his fallen comrade.

9. Keep in mind the intended audience for your essay.

10. The rising noise level indicated that everyone was having a good time.

PRACTICE 19.1J ▷ **Distinguishing Verbs and Participles**

Read the sentences. Then, write *verb* or *participle* for the underlined word in each sentence. Explain how each participle or verb functions in the sentence.

EXAMPLE   No one noticed him <u>walking</u> away.

ANSWER   *participle*

11. We had not <u>expected</u> such a large turnout.

12. <u>Coming</u> closer, Fiona grabbed my hand.

13. An unhappy customer was <u>muttering</u> to himself.

14. We avoided the dogs <u>snarling</u> behind the fence.

15. Determined to get a good grade, Jane has been <u>studying</u> hard every night.

16. Has anyone ever <u>stolen</u> your lunch?

17. <u>Stunned</u> by the headlights, the deer just stood in the road.

18. Let's review the vocabulary we <u>studied</u> last week.

19. The river is <u>rising</u> from all the rain.

20. I must have <u>broken</u> it unintentionally.

SPEAKING APPLICATION

With a partner, take turns making up two sentences using these words as participles: *swinging* and *broken.* Take turns telling your sentences to your partner, who should identify what the words modify.

WRITING APPLICATION

Write two sentences using both of these words in each sentence: *dangling* and *crowded.* Use each word once as a participle and once as a verb. Read your sentences aloud to a partner. Have your partner identify which word is a participle and which is a verb.

TEKS Practice Show that you can identify, use, and understand the function of participles in reading, speaking, and writing by completing the following activities.

PRACTICE 19.1K > Identifying Participial Phrases

Read the sentences. Then, write the participial phrase in each sentence. Underline the participle.

EXAMPLE   Everyone was out enjoying the lovely day.

ANSWER   *enjoying the lovely day*

1. Jeffrey sat there, wondering what to do.

2. Cramming her papers into her notebook, Vicki hurried out of the room.

3. The shop, closed for the day, was dark and quiet.

4. Smiling sweetly, the little ballerina danced her part.

5. You can see an osprey sitting on its nest in the bird sanctuary.

6. Waving his arms and shouting, Clay ran after the bus.

7. Pedro, tired after the game, relaxed on the couch.

8. *The Adventures of Huckleberry Finn,* written by Mark Twain, is a classic American novel.

9. Lola rehearsed her oral report, reading it aloud several times.

10. The glove found on the sidewalk was muddy and torn.

PRACTICE 19.1L > Combining Sentences Using Participial Phrases

Read the sentences. Combine each pair of sentences by using a participial phrase. Read the new sentences to a partner. Discuss how the participles function in each sentence.

EXAMPLE   Felicia did not hear the teacher's question. She was lost in a daydream.

ANSWER   *Lost in a daydream, Felicia did not hear the teacher's question.*

11. Mia was speaking very softly. She explained what happened.

12. The gymnasts performed like ballet dancers. They were trained by professionals.

13. The children were squealing excitedly. They played games in the yard.

14. The dog was restrained on a leash. It was unable to chase other dogs.

15. A fire truck sped down the street. Its siren was blasting.

16. Pam was thrilled by her victory. She jumped up and down.

17. Kent finally found his homework paper. It was tucked between the pages of his book.

18. The old letter was difficult to read. It was creased at its folds.

19. Jed was startled by the noise. He sat upright.

20. Eli went over to speak to the girl. The girl was smiling at him.

SPEAKING APPLICATION

With a partner, use one of the sentences in Practice 19.1K as a model, and describe an item. Use at least one participial phrase. Your partner should listen for and identify the participial phrase.

WRITING APPLICATION

Use your combined sentences 12, 15, and 20 as models, and write two new sentences with participial phrases. Read your sentences to a partner. Have your partner identify each participle and explain how it is used in the sentence.

Gerunds

Like present participles, **gerunds** end in -*ing*. While present participles are used as adjectives, gerunds can be used as subjects, direct objects, predicate nouns, and objects of prepositions.

> **A gerund** is a form of a verb that acts as a noun.

RULE 19.1.8

USE OF GERUNDS IN SENTENCES	
Subject	Rebuilding was a good idea.
Direct Object	Amy enjoys drawing.
Predicate Noun	Her favorite activity is running.
Object of a Preposition	Kate never gets tired of reading.

Gerund Phrases

Gerunds can also be part of a phrase.

> **A gerund phrase** is a gerund with modifiers or a complement, all acting together as a noun.

RULE 19.1.9

This chart shows how gerunds are expanded to form gerund phrases.

FORMING GERUND PHRASES	
Gerund With Adjectives	The loud, piercing ringing went on all afternoon.
Gerund With Direct Object	Reading historical fiction has inspired many playwrights.
Gerund With Prepositional Phrase	Her favorite activity is running through the forest.
Gerund With Adverb and Prepositional Phrases	The painter amazed the spectators by painting skillfully with brushes on the window.

See Practice 19.1M
See Practice 19.1N

Infinitives

Infinitives are verb forms that are used as nouns, adjectives, and adverbs. Like participles and gerunds, they can be combined with other words to form phrases.

RULE
19.1.10

> An **infinitive** is a verb form that can be used as a noun, an adjective, or an adverb. The word *to* usually appears before the verb.

EXAMPLES   It is important **to speak**.

He is the one **to see**.

To answer can be difficult sometimes.

Infinitive Phrases

RULE
19.1.11

> An **infinitive phrase** is an infinitive with modifiers or a complement, all acting together as a single part of speech.

EXAMPLES   It is important **to speak quietly**.

It is not polite **to speak loudly in class**.

They want **to tell you a secret**.

An **infinitive phrase** can be used in a sentence as a noun, an adjective, or an adverb. As a noun, an infinitive phrase can function as a subject, an object, or an appositive.

USES OF INFINITIVES	
Used as a Subject	To remain calm is important.
Used as an Object	She tried to remain calm.
Used as an Appositive	The officer's suggestion, to remain calm, had worked.
Used as an Adjective	It was her intention to remain calm.
Used as an Adverb	It isn't always easy to remain calm when you're upset.

See Practice 19.1O
See Practice 19.1P

PRACTICE 19.1M ▷ Identifying Gerund Phrases

Read the sentences. Then, write the gerund phrase from each sentence, and underline the gerund. Remember to include all modifiers with the phrase.

EXAMPLE   Listening to music relaxes me.

ANSWER   *Listening to music*

1. Naomi likes reading historical novels.

2. Forecasting the weather can be a challenge.

3. You might be able to gain an advantage by using strategy.

4. Silas recently tried skateboarding on a ramp.

5. The first step in the assignment is locating appropriate sources.

6. Veronica could not stop laughing at the joke.

7. Annabel and Diana were exhausted from working all afternoon.

8. Winning the match is not everything.

9. The mayor opposed raising the speed limit through town.

10. Playing the drums is Neil's only interest.

PRACTICE 19.1N ▷ Writing Gerunds and Gerund Phrases

Read the sentences. Then, rewrite each sentence, completing it with a gerund or gerund phrase.

EXAMPLE   The team celebrated by _____.

ANSWER   *The team celebrated by singing the school song.*

11. _____ motivates Zelda to earn money after school.

12. Eva's family enjoyed _____ last summer.

13. Duncan sends text messages while _____.

14. Henry Ford is famous for _____.

15. _____ is the way Selena memorizes her lines for the play.

16. A fox escaped its pursuer by _____.

17. _____ builds strength and flexibility.

18. Jason thought he might give _____ a try.

19. _____ was easier than Amy expected.

20. Alonzo's job is _____.

SPEAKING APPLICATION

With a partner, take turns telling about something you like to do. Your partner should listen for and identify a gerund or gerund phrase that you use.

WRITING APPLICATION

Use sentences 12, 13, and 19 as models, and write three sentences with gerunds or gerund phrases.

PRACTICE 19.10 ▷ Identifying Infinitives and Infinitive Phrases

Read the sentences. Then, write the infinitive phrase from each sentence, and underline the infinitive. Also write *noun*, *adjective*, or *adverb* to describe each infinitive phrase.

EXAMPLE   We stopped by the roadside to admire the view.

ANSWER   *to admire the view* — adverb

1. Wade likes to swim in the lake.

2. Mrs. Manning planned to visit the museum.

3. To break that record will be a challenge.

4. That is the best place to go fishing.

5. This poem is easy to understand.

6. The child tried to hide in the closet.

7. It's time to leave for school now.

8. The Wilsons plan to sell their house.

9. The driver swerved to avoid the puddle.

10. Justin's goal is to be a singer in a band.

PRACTICE 19.1P ▷ Writing Infinitives and Infinitive Phrases

Read the sentences. Then, rewrite each sentence, completing it with an infinitive or an infinitive phrase.

EXAMPLE   Kirk still has plenty of work _____.

ANSWER   *Kirk still has plenty of work to finish by tomorrow.*

11. The teacher raised her hands _____.

12. _____ is Martha's plan for this year.

13. Your next book _____ is *Dragonwings*.

14. Judy's role is _____.

15. An assembly _____ will start at 9:00 o'clock.

16. _____ may not be wise.

17. The best way _____ is _____.

18. I think it is best _____.

19. The first person _____ will win a ticket.

20. Ariana got into position _____.

SPEAKING APPLICATION

In a small group, take turns "selling" each other a simple item, such as a pencil or paper clip. The group members should listen for and identify the infinitive phrases you use.

WRITING APPLICATION

Write a short paragraph explaining the purpose of the item you "sold" in the Speaking Application. Use at least two infinitive phrases and underline them.

19.2 Clauses

Clauses are the basic structural unit of a sentence.

A clause is a group of words with its own subject and verb.

RULE 19.2.1

There are two basic kinds of clauses, **main** or **independent clauses** and **subordinate clauses**.

A main or independent clause has a subject and a verb and can stand by itself as a complete sentence.

RULE 19.2.2

As you can see in the examples below, a main clause can be long or short. All main clauses express a complete thought and can stand by themselves as complete sentences.

EXAMPLES

The **girl** **skipped**.
subject · verb

Later that night, **he** **began** reading his book.
subject · verb

A subordinate clause, also known as a dependent clause, has a subject and a verb but cannot stand by itself as a complete sentence. It is only part of a sentence.

RULE 19.2.3

SUBORDINATE CLAUSES

after **she** **presented** her paper
subject · verb

while the **group** **studied**
subject · verb

After reading a subordinate clause, you will still need more information to have a complete sentence.

 TEKS Check Show that you can differentiate between main versus subordinate clauses. Find a paragraph in a magazine or a newspaper. Circle the main clauses you see. Save this paragraph for a future activity.

Subordinate clauses begin with subordinating conjunctions or relative pronouns.

Some subordinate clauses begin with **subordinating conjunctions,** such as *if, since, when, although, after, because,* and *while*. Others begin with **relative pronouns,** such as *who, which,* or *that*. These words are clues that the clause may not be able to stand alone. Notice how the addition of subordinating words changes the meaning of the main clauses in the examples below.

| COMPARING TWO KINDS OF CLAUSES ||
MAIN	SUBORDINATE
She speaks this afternoon.	*when* she speaks this afternoon
The garden has green tomatoes.	*because* the garden has green tomatoes
I planted the cucumbers.	the cucumbers *that* I planted

In order to form a complete thought, a subordinate clause must be combined with a main clause.

EXAMPLES

After she presented her paper, Rachael felt
        subordinate clause   main clause
relaxed.

The board applauded **after Rachael presented**
     main clause   subordinate clause
her paper.

It was Rachael **who was asked to present last**.
   main clause   subordinate clause

When they arrive tonight, the Woods will eat.
    subordinate clause   main clause

 Focus on the TEKS

(19)(B) Differentiate between main versus subordinate clauses.

See TEKS Check

See TEKS Practice

See Practice 19.2A

See Practice 19.2B

 TEKS Check Show that you can differentiate between main versus subordinate clauses. Return to the paragraph you were previously analyzing. Underline any subordinate clauses you see. Determine which main clauses are related to the clauses you underlined.

TEKS Practice Show that you can differentiate between main versus subordinate clauses by completing the following activities.

Clauses

PRACTICE 19.2A **Identifying Main and Subordinate Clauses**

Read the sentences. Then, write the main and subordinate clauses in each sentence, and label them *main clause* or *subordinate clause*.

EXAMPLE   After you left, Maria opened her presents.

ANSWER   *After you left* — subordinate clause
Maria opened her presents — main clause

1. Although they do not always agree, Jake and Chris are best friends.

2. Dino thought about baseball practice as he walked home.

3. Please take out the garbage before you leave.

4. Because my dog is afraid of thunder, he hides under the bed during storms.

5. If you want to come with me, make sure you bring an umbrella.

6. Let's wait here until Stephen arrives.

7. We eat outside when the weather is nice.

8. Let's discuss the plans as we'll be traveling together.

9. Ethan and Grace are ready to leave as soon as the bus arrives.

10. The painting that you bought is hanging in the hallway.

PRACTICE 19.2B **Identifying and Using Main and Subordinate Clauses**

Read the clauses. Write *main clause* or *subordinate clause* for each clause. Then, expand each subordinate clause into a complete complex sentence by adding a main clause.

EXAMPLE   Unless we find the shovel.

ANSWER   *subordinate clause*
We cannot clear away the snow unless we find the shovel.

11. Here is a picture of my cousin.

12. That my mother bought for me.

13. Robots are used in many factories.

14. Although my brother is a talented musician.

15. Our show did not make a profit.

16. When you make up your mind.

17. Two other people waited in the office.

18. As soon as Elizabeth gets home.

19. I just can't decide.

20. Who found Hal's wallet.

SPEAKING APPLICATION

With a partner, take turns selecting two subordinate clauses from the sentences in Practice 19.2A. Add a main clause to each, and then say the sentence.

WRITING APPLICATION

Write two complex sentences that contain both main and subordinate clauses. Underline the subordinate clauses. Explain to a partner how the main and subordinate clauses function in the sentence together.

Adjectival Clauses

A subordinate clause will sometimes act as an adjective in a sentence. An adjectival clause or adjective clause is a dependent clause and cannot stand on its own.

> An **adjectival clause** or **adjective clause** is a subordinate clause that modifies a noun or a pronoun.

Like one-word adjectives and adjectival phrases, **adjectival clauses** tell *what kind* or *which one*.

EXAMPLES

WHAT KIND?

stars **that are bright and glowing**

WHICH ONE?

the country **where I was born**

Recognizing Adjectival Clauses

Most adjectival clauses begin with the words *that*, *which*, *who*, *whom*, and *whose*. Sometimes an adjectival clause begins with a subordinating conjunction, such as *since*, *where*, or *when*. In the chart below, the adjectival clauses are hightlighted in pink.

ADJECTIVAL CLAUSES
The professor **whom I had asked for help** met with me before class. (*Which* professor?)
The charity auction, **which was advertised in the local paper**, is Friday. (*Which* charity auction?)
In the months **since she started working**, Anne has become an accomplished teacher. (*Which* months?)
I hid my jewelry box in the hall closet **on which there is a lock**. (*Which* closet?)
We visited the theme park **that honors cultures around the world**. (*Which* park?)
The theme park **whose rides include teacups** is located in Florida. (*Which* park?)

 Focus on the TEKS

(19)(A)(iii) Identify, use, and understand the function of adjectival clauses in the context of reading, writing, and speaking.

See TEKS Check

See TEKS Practice

See Practice 19.2C

 TEKS Check Show that you can identify, use, and understand adjectival clauses. Read a newspaper or magazine article and list any adjectival clauses you find. Read the sentences to a partner and discuss how the adjectival clauses function in the sentence.

Combining Sentences With Adjectival Clauses

Two sentences can be combined into one sentence by changing one of them into an adjectival clause. Sometimes you will need to add a relative pronoun or subordinating conjunction to make the sentence read correctly. In the sentences below, the adjectival clauses are highlighted in pink.

TWO SENTENCES	COMBINED WITH AN ADJECTIVAL CLAUSE
My English professor has written novels based on fictional stories. My professor is a famous author.	My English professor, who has written novels based on fictional stories, is a famous author.
We visited the Air and Space Museum. The Air and Space Museum is my favorite museum.	We visited the Air and Space Museum, which is my favorite.
We decided to shop at the outlet mall. We usually get the best deals there.	We decided to shop at the outlet mall where we usually get the best deals.
Emma visited her grandparents. Emma's grandparents live in an apartment in New York.	Emma visited her grandparents, who live in an apartment in New York.
Carolyn goes to dance class. Her class is in a ballet studio.	Carolyn goes to dance class that is in a ballet studio.

Focus on the TEKS

(19)(A)(iii) Identify, use, and understand the function of adjectival clauses in the context of reading, writing, and speaking.

See TEKS Check

See TEKS Practice

See Practice 19.2C

See Practice 19.2D

 TEKS Check Show that you can identify, use, and understand adjectival clauses. Write two pairs of sentences. Trade your sentences with a partner. Use adjectival clauses to combine the two sentences into one sentence. Read the new sentences and discuss how the adjectival clause functions.

TEKS Practice Show that you can use, identify, and understand the function of adjectival clauses in reading, writing, and speaking by completing the following activities.

PRACTICE 19.2C > **Identifying Adjectival Clauses**

Read the sentences. Then, write the adjectival clause in each sentence.

EXAMPLE   This is a movie that I will never forget.

ANSWER   *that I will never forget*

1. The men who came in a jeep are repairing the fence now.

2. This is the time of year when people take vacations.

3. Follow these directions, which will take you right to the campground.

4. Thomas Jefferson is the president who is responsible for the Louisiana Purchase.

5. I have a pearl necklace that belonged to my grandmother.

6. The road came to an end, where we had to turn around.

7. Hollywood, which is part of Los Angeles, is a tourist destination.

8. The manager needs someone who will stock the shelves.

9. Christa, whom you met earlier, will also be on the committee.

10. This is the house that my uncle fixed up.

PRACTICE 19.2D > **Combining Sentences Using Adjectival Clauses**

Read the sentences. Combine the pairs of sentences by changing one of them into an adjectival clause. Read the new sentences and discuss how the adjectival clause functions.

EXAMPLE   The runner is being congratulated. She won the race.

ANSWER   *The runner who won the race is being congratulated.*

11. The rain fell for two days. It kept the farmers from planting their crops.

12. I need to write two more sentences. These sentences will support my topic sentence.

13. Many adventurers have climbed Mt. Everest. Mt. Everest is the highest peak in the world.

14. The train leaves at 7:00. It arrives in Washington, D.C., at 11:30.

15. I like to look up information on the Internet. You can find everything there.

16. The woman was upset. Her purse was lost.

17. Here are some sponges. You can use these to wash the car.

18. A mechanic tuned up the car. It had not been running well.

19. David told a story. It made everyone laugh.

20. Alexa is my friend. She made this playlist for me.

SPEAKING APPLICATION

With a partner, summarize a mystery story that you have read or seen on television. Use at least one sentence with an adjectival clause. Your partner should listen for and identify the adjectival clause. Together, discuss the function, or purpose, of the adjectival clause.

WRITING APPLICATION

Use your combined sentences 11, 16, and 19 as models, and write three new sentences with adjectival clauses. Read the sentences and explain how the adjectival clauses function in the sentences.

Adverbial Clauses

Subordinate clauses can also be used as adverbs. Adverbial clauses or adverb clauses are dependent clauses.

> An **adverbial clause** or **adverb clause** is a subordinate clause that modifies a verb, an adjective, or an adverb.

19.2.6 RULE

Adverbial clauses can answer any of the following questions about the words they modify: *Where? When? In what manner? To what extent? Under what conditions?* or *Why?*

ADVERBIAL CLAUSES	
Modifying Verbs	Put the luggage wherever you find an empty closet . (Put *where?*)
	The game will begin after we sing the National Anthem . (Will begin *when?*)
	Amy spoke as if she were very serious . (Spoke *in what manner?*)
	I will go to Greece if you do too . (Will go *under what conditions?*)
Modifying an Adjective	I am tired because I have been working all day . (Tired *why?*)
Modifying an Adverb	She knows more than other teachers do . (More *to what extent?*)

Recognizing Adverbial Clauses

> A **subordinating conjunction** introduces an adverbial clause.

19.2.7 RULE

A **subordinating conjunction** always introduces an adverbial clause. In a sentence, the conjunction will usually appear in one of two places—either at the beginning, when the adverbial clause begins the sentence, or in the middle, connecting the independent clause to the subordinate clause. In the examples on the next page, the subordinating conjunctions are highlighted in purple.

 TEKS Check Show that you can use, identify, and understand adverbial clauses. Write two sentences that each contain an adverbial clause. Read the sentences to a partner and discuss how the adverbial clause functions in the sentence.

EXAMPLES **Because** you slept late, I will prepare breakfast.

I will prepare breakfast **because** you slept late.

Whenever you have a test, I expect you to study.

I expect you to study **whenever** you have a test.

Common Subordinating Conjunctions

Here are the most common subordinating conjunctions. Knowing them can help you recognize adverbial clauses.

COMMON SUBORDINATING CONJUNCTIONS		
after	even though	unless
although	if	until
as	in order that	when
as if	since	whenever
as long as	so that	where
because	than	wherever
before	though	while

Elliptical Adverbial Clauses

In certain adverbial clauses, words are left out. These clauses are said to be elliptical.

RULE 19.2.8

> In an **elliptical adverbial clause,** the verb or the subject and verb are understood rather than stated.

Many elliptical adverbial clauses are introduced by one of two subordinating conjunctions, *as* or *than*. In the following examples, the understood words have been added in parentheses. The first elliptical adverbial clause is missing a verb; the second is missing a subject and a verb.

EXAMPLES My sister can eat as much **as I** (can eat).

I like this movie more **than** (I liked) **that one**.

 TEKS Check Show that you can identify, use, and understand subordinating conjunctions and adverbial clauses. Write three sentences with subordinating conjunctions introducing an adverbial clause. Read the sentences to a partner and have your partner identify each clause.

Focus on the TEKS

(19)(A)(iii) Identify, use, and understand the function of adverbial clauses in the context of reading, writing, and speaking.

(19)(A)(vii) Identify, use, and understand the function of subordinating conjunctions (e.g. *because, since*) in reading, writing, and speaking.

See TEKS Check

See TEKS Practice

See Practice 19.2E

See Practice 19.2F

TEKS Practice Show that you can use, identify, and understand adverbial clauses and subordinating conjunctions in reading, speaking, and writing by completing the following activities.

PRACTICE 19.2E **Identifying Adverbial Clauses and Recognizing Elliptical Adverbial Clauses**

Read the sentences. Then, write the adverbial clauses. For any of the adverbial clauses that are elliptical, add the understood words in parentheses.

EXAMPLE   Isabel likes reading mysteries more than biographies.

ANSWER   *than (she likes reading) biographies*

1. After we took a walk, we stopped for ice cream.

2. Kurt did not give his oral report today because he has laryngitis.

3. Although Maria is not especially tall, she plans to try out for basketball.

4. Driving can be unpleasant when there is a lot of traffic.

5. Brett waited while Alan collected his equipment.

6. You have grown since we last saw you.

7. We can leave as long as you are ready.

8. If you are really interested, talk to Miss Knox.

9. This computer is older than that one.

10. I am not allowed to watch television unless my homework is finished.

PRACTICE 19.2F **Combining Sentences With Adverbial Clauses**

Read the sentences. Combine each pair of sentences by changing one of them into an adverbial clause. Use an appropriate subordinating conjunction, and drop or change words as necessary.

EXAMPLE   Gabe stayed in the car. I ran into the store.

ANSWER   *Gabe stayed in the car while I ran into the store.*

11. Veronica took notes. We made our plans.

12. Jude was not nervous. He stepped onstage.

13. Laura did very well on her science test. She had studied.

14. I will tell you. You must keep it a secret.

15. Robin will rehearse carefully. She will give her presentation.

16. Keith feels much more energetic. He has started jogging.

17. Volunteers put sandbags on the banks. The river overflowed its banks.

18. The garden will dry up. It rains.

19. We worked hard all week. We wanted to have the weekend free.

20. I will call you. I need help.

SPEAKING APPLICATION

With a partner, make up an excuse for being late or for not doing something, using two adverbial clauses. Your partner should listen for and identify the adverbial clauses.

WRITING APPLICATION

Write a few sentences about something you learned in your social studies class. Use at least two adverbial clauses and appropriate subordinating conjunctions. Read your sentences to a partner. Discuss how the adverbial clause and subordinating conjunction function in each sentence.

19.3 Classifying Sentences by Structure

All sentences can be classified according to the number and kinds of clauses they contain.

WRITING COACH

Online

@www.TXWritingCoach.com

Grammar Tutorials

Brush up on your Grammar skills with these animated videos.

Grammar Practice

Practice your grammar skills with Writing Coach Online.

Grammar Games

Test your knowledge of grammar in this fast-paced interactive video game.

The Simple Sentence

The **simple sentence** is the most common type of sentence structure.

RULE 19.3.1

> A **simple sentence** consists of a single independent clause.

Simple sentences vary in length. Some are quite short; others can be several lines long. All simple sentences, however, contain just one subject and one verb. They may also contain adjectives, adverbs, complements, and phrases in different combinations.

Simple sentences can also have various compound parts. They can have a compound subject, a compound verb, or both. Sometimes, they will also have other compound elements, such as a compound direct object or a compound phrase.

All of the following sentences are simple sentences.

TYPES OF SIMPLE SENTENCES	
With One Subject and Verb	The snow fell .
With a Compound Subject	Snow and ice are common.
With a Compound Verb	The window squeaked and shook .
With a Compound Subject and Compound Verb	My brother and sister brought bagels and made coffee for brunch.
With a Compound Direct Object	She opened the flower box and the card . direct object direct object
With a Compound Prepositional Phrase	You can drive from the east coast or from the west . prep phrase prep phrase

A simple sentence never has a subordinate clause, and it never has more than one main or independent clause.

The Compound Sentence

A **compound sentence** is made up of more than one simple sentence.

> **A compound sentence** consists of two or more main or independent clauses.

RULE 19.3.2

In most compound sentences, the main or independent clauses are joined by a comma and a coordinating conjunction (*and, but, for, nor, or, so,* or *yet*). They may also be connected with a semicolon (;) or a colon (:).

EXAMPLES   **Jamie** **ran** a two-day athletic clinic **,** **and** four professional **athletes** **donated** their time.

All of the athletes **spoke** on the first day **;** **one** **was missing** the second day.

See Practice 19.3A
See Practice 19.3B

Notice in both of the preceding examples that there are two separate and complete main clauses, each with its own subject and verb. Like simple sentences, compound sentences never contain subordinate clauses.

The Complex Sentence

Complex sentences contain subordinate clauses, which can be either adjectival clauses or adverbial clauses.

> **A complex sentence** consists of one main or independent clause and one or more subordinate clauses.

RULE 19.3.3

In a complex sentence, the independent clause is often called the **main clause.** The main clause has its own subject and verb, as does each subordinate clause.

In a complex sentence, the main clause can stand alone as a simple sentence. The subordinate clause cannot stand alone as a sentence.

EXAMPLES   **May 14, 1948, is the day** **that Israel became**
                main clause   subordinate clause

a state .

Because this day is so important, **celebrations**
                subordinate clause

of all kinds take place .
                main clause

In some complex sentences, the main clause is split by a subordinate clause that acts as an adjective.

EXAMPLE   **Citizens** , **who have the day off** , **participate in**
                                subordinate clause

exciting activities .

The two parts of the main clause form one main clause: *Citizens participate in exciting activities.*

Focus on the TEKS

(19)(B) Write complex sentences and differentiate between main versus subordinate clauses.

See TEKS Check

See TEKS Practice

See Practice 19.3C

See Practice 19.3D

See Practice 19.3E

See Practice 19.3F

The Compound-Complex Sentence

A **compound-complex sentence,** as the name indicates, contains the elements of both a compound sentence and a complex sentence.

RULE
19.3.4 ▷

> A **compound-complex sentence** consists of two or more main or independent clauses and one or more subordinate clauses.

EXAMPLE   **As he was leaving for work** ,
                        subordinate clause

Andy remembered to take his glasses , but
                        main clause

he forgot the presentation **that he had worked**
                main clause   subordinate clause

on the night before .

 TEKS Check Write three complex sentences. Differentiate between the main clause and the subordinate clause in each sentence.

PRACTICE 19.3A ▷ **Distinguishing Simple and Compound Sentences**

Read the sentences. Then, write *simple* or *compound* for each sentence.

EXAMPLE   Many people now drive fuel-efficient cars.

ANSWER   *simple*

1. Laurel discovered a box of old photos in the back of the closet.

2. Marissa watered the plants and fertilized them.

3. Calcium and vitamin D are important for strong bones, so I drink milk.

4. Evan sent a text message to his girlfriend.

5. Please follow the ushers to your seat, for the show will start soon.

6. This may be your lucky day.

7. Tourists throw coins into the fountain for good luck.

8. George thanked the presenters and sat down.

9. Martin tried to share his ideas with Eugene, but Eugene was not listening.

10. The library hired a new assistant, but I have not met him yet.

PRACTICE 19.3B ▷ **Combining Simple Sentences to Form Compound Sentences**

Read the sentences. Combine the pairs of simple sentences to form compound sentences.

EXAMPLE   The newspaper was delivered this morning. I have not read it yet.

ANSWER   *The newspaper was delivered this morning, but I have not read it yet.*

11. The lilacs will bloom in May. The roses and lilies bloom later.

12. No one answered the phone. I left a voice message.

13. The rain had left puddles. The children splashed through them.

14. A tornado roared through the edge of town. No one was injured.

15. Celeste stepped inside. The room became quiet.

16. Some people have good fortune. Others always struggle with hardships.

17. Martha lowered her head. Tears fell from her eyes.

18. We should hurry. The show will start soon.

19. Bea had a headache. She did not complain.

20. Rosa forgot to turn off the lights. They stayed on all night.

SPEAKING APPLICATION

With a partner, take turns describing an action. Use only simple sentences.

WRITING APPLICATION

Use your compound sentences 11, 12, and 15 as models, and write three new compound sentences.

PRACTICE 19.3C > Recognizing Complex Sentences

Read the sentences. Then, label each sentence *complex* or *not complex*.

EXAMPLE A wave destroyed the sand castle, so the children were sad.

ANSWER *not complex*

1. If you give me the seeds, I will plant them.
2. National park rangers lead natural history tours through the parks.
3. Emily tore the paper in half and gave half to Sue.
4. Our dog was waiting as we pulled into the driveway.
5. Wendy, who has been taking art lessons, showed us a pencil sketch.
6. After she spoke with a counselor, Amber changed her mind.
7. Only the finest musicians play in the symphony orchestra.
8. On a clear night, you can see satellites moving through the sky.
9. Mimi was wearing pants that were too long.
10. The crowd roared when the designated hitter struck out.

PRACTICE 19.3D > Writing Complex Sentences

Read the sentences. Combine each pair of sentences by changing one of them into a subordinating clause. Add or drop words and punctuation as necessary.

EXAMPLE I will cook dinner. Buy some vegetables at the store.

ANSWER *I will cook dinner if you buy some vegetables at the store.*

11. We should pick up Kayla at her house. It is on the left side of the street.
12. My grandparents live in Austin. It is 350 miles away.
13. The car stopped suddenly. It ran out of gas.
14. On Saturday, the temperature reached 102 degrees. It was the third day of the heat wave.
15. I finished the math test before everyone else. It was so easy.
16. Pedro walks his dog three times a day. Pedro is fond of animals.
17. The volleyball players were exhausted. They practiced for four hours.
18. The car accident caused the traffic to come to a complete stop. It started to move again soon.
19. I might vote for Carla. Carla is both smart and fair.
20. I cannot seem to finish this book. This book is long and complicated.

SPEAKING APPLICATION

With a partner, take turns telling about a program you watch on television. Your partner should listen for and identify at least one complex sentence.

WRITING APPLICATION

Write three complex sentences about your favorite holiday. Share your sentences with a partner, and have your partner label the main and subordinate clauses.

TEKS Practice Show that you can write complex sentences and differentiate between main and subordinate clauses by completing the following activities.

PRACTICE 19.3E ▷ Writing Complex Sentences

Read each subordinate clause. Then, write a main clause and unite the main and subordinate clauses into a complex sentence.

EXAMPLE   because his birthday is in July

ANSWER   *Because his birthday is in July, Diego will have his party at a water park.*

1. if you can leave a little earlier
2. who learn a second language at an early age
3. although pet fish need feeding only once a day
4. when my alarm went off
5. that the librarian recommended
6. unless the temperature drops below 50 degrees
7. which will probably win an award
8. while Toby was away at summer camp
9. whose jewelry designs are popular
10. before she left for school

PRACTICE 19.3F ▷ Distinguishing Compound and Complex Sentences

Read the sentences. Then, label each sentence *compound* or *complex*.

EXAMPLE   When Tanya lost her phone, she was very upset.

ANSWER   *complex*

11. The hikers, who had not yet had lunch, were getting hungry.
12. The fog rolled in, and everyone felt cold.
13. Summer will be here before you know it.
14. William likes horror stories, so he has been reading Edgar Allan Poe's short stories.
15. Dorie read about the discovery in the newspaper, where there was a full-page article.
16. Seals and dolphins are sometimes stranded on beaches when the tide goes out.
17. Arlo is very well-informed, so I trust his judgment.
18. Even after we stopped shouting, we could hear the echoes in the mountains.
19. Naomi has agreed to participate, but Luanne is still thinking about it.
20. Nick is so good at chess that no one can beat him.

SPEAKING APPLICATION

With a partner, take turns explaining a process. The process could be directions for how to make something. Your partner should listen for and identify at least two complex sentences. Together discuss the function of the main clause and the subordinate clause in each sentence.

WRITING APPLICATION

Write one compound and one complex sentence. Use these words as the subject and verb in one of the clauses in each sentence: *James rode.*

Classifying Sentences by Structure

 Focus on the TEKS

(19)(B) Write complex sentences and differentiate between main versus subordinate clauses.

 # Texas Test Warm-Up

DIRECTIONS

Read the introduction and the passage that follows. Then, answer the questions to show that you can write complex sentences and differentiate between main versus subordinate clauses in reading and writing.

Hernando wrote this paragraph about his favorite side dish, mashed potatoes. Read the paragraph and think about the changes you would suggest as a peer editor. When you finish reading, answer the questions that follow.

The Best Mashed Potatoes

(1) I love my mom's mashed potatoes. (2) My mom makes the best mashed potatoes I have ever tasted. (3) First, take four large red potatoes that are easy to find in the supermarket. (4) Peel the potatoes. (5) Cut the potatoes, they are already peeled. (6) Place the potatoes in boiling water for 8 minutes. (7) Strain them and add them to a large bowl. (8) Place ¼ cup of lowfat milk and two tablespoons of butter in the large bowl first. (9) Mix the potatoes, milk, and butter with a hand mixer until smooth. (10) Add salt as needed and serve immediately.

---

1 What is the BEST way to combine sentences 1 and 2?

A I love my mom's mashed potatoes, she makes the best mashed potatoes I have ever tasted.

B I love my mom's mashed potatoes, which arc the best I have ever tasted.

C The best mashed potatoes are my mom's, which I have ever tasted.

D The best mashed potatoes which I love are my mom's.

2 What change, if any, should be made in sentence 3?

F Delete the comma after *First*

G Change *that* to **which**

H Change *that* to **which** and add a comma before **which**

J Make no change

3 What is the BEST way to revise sentence 5?

A Peel the potatoes, which have already been cut.

B Cut the potatoes that are peeled.

C Peel the cut potatoes.

D Cut the potatoes, already.

4 What is the BEST way to combine sentences 7 and 8?

F Strain them and add them to a large bowl, which should contain ¼ cup of lowfat milk and two tablespoons of butter.

G Strain them and add them first to a large bowl of ¼ cup of lowfat milk and two tablespoons of butter.

H Strain them and place ¼ cup of lowfat milk and two tablespoons of butter.

J Strain them and add them to a large bowl, place ¼ cup of lowfat milk and two tablespoons of butter in the large bowl first.

EFFECTIVE SENTENCES

Knowing how different types of sentences function will help you construct clear, meaningful ideas in your writing.

WRITE GUY *Jeff Anderson, M.Ed.*

WHAT DO YOU NOTICE?

Keep an eye out for different types of sentences as you zoom in on these sentences from the screenplay *The Monsters Are Due on Maple Street* by Rod Serling.

MENTOR TEXT

> So I've got a car that starts by itself—well, that's a freak thing, I admit it. But does that make me some kind of a criminal or something? I don't know why the car works—it just does!

Now, ask yourself the following questions:

- Which sentence is interrogative? How can you tell?
- What does the end punctuation tell you about the last sentence?

The second sentence is interrogative because it asks a question. You can tell the second sentence is interrogative because there is a question mark at the end of it. The exclamation mark at the end of the last sentence tells you that it is exclamatory. The purpose of an exclamatory sentence is to convey strong emotion.

Grammar for Writers Using a variety of sentences allows writers to make their writing sound lively. Think carefully about which end punctuation mark is most appropriate in each of your sentences. Try not to overuse exclamation marks or they will lose their effect.

How can I tell if a sentence is imperative?

When it's a command. Now, raise your hand before asking a question.

20.1 Classifying the Four Functions of a Sentence

Sentences can be classified according to what they do. Some sentences present facts or information in a direct way, while others pose questions to the reader or listener. Still others present orders or directions. A fourth type of sentence expresses strong emotion.

These four types of sentences are called **declarative, interrogative, imperative,** and **exclamatory.** As well as having a different purpose, each type of sentence is constructed in a different way.

The type of sentence you are writing determines the punctuation mark you use to end the sentence. The three end marks are the **period (.),** the **question mark (?),** and the **exclamation mark (!).**

The **declarative sentence** is the most common type of sentence. It is used to state, or "declare," ideas.

RULE 20.1.1

> **A declarative sentence** states, or declares, an idea and ends with a period.

DECLARATIVE

The cellphone rang.

Cellphones help us keep in touch with our friends and family.

Although cellphones are useful in emergencies, used too often, they can lead people to waste a lot of time.

Interrogative means "asking." An **interrogative sentence** is a question. Interrogative sentences often begin with *who, what, when, why, how,* or *how many.* They end with a question mark.

> **An interrogative sentence** asks a question and ends with a question mark.

INTERROGATIVE   When is band practice going to start?

Where will the concert be held?

What songs are we going to play?

> **An imperative sentence** gives an order, or command, or a direction and ends with either a period or an exclamation mark.

The word *imperative* comes from the Latin word that means "commanding." **Imperative sentences** are commands or directions. Most imperative sentences start with a verb. In this type of sentence, the subject is understood to be *you*.

IMPERATIVE   Take the stairs, not the elevator.

Walk, don't run!

Notice the punctuation at the end of these examples. In the first sentence, the period suggests that a mild command is being given in an ordinary tone of voice. The exclamation mark at the end of the second sentence suggests a strong command, one given in a loud voice.

> **An exclamatory sentence** conveys strong emotion and ends with an exclamation mark.

See Practice 20.1A
See Practice 20.1B
See Practice 20.1C
See Practice 20.1D

Exclaim means "to shout out." **Exclamatory sentences** are used to "shout out" emotions such as happiness, fear, delight, or anger.

EXCLAMATORY   He isn't watching where he's going!

The glass is going to tip over!

PRACTICE 20.1A **Identifying Four Types of Sentences**

Read the sentences. Then, identify each type of sentence by writing *declarative*, *interrogative*, *imperative*, or *exclamatory*.

EXAMPLE   Read the instructions before you begin.

ANSWER   *imperative*

1. Who brought those delicious cookies?

2. Both generals signed the treaty.

3. Ted, take your feet off the chair.

4. We all had such a good time!

5. Do you know where Erin is?

6. Ricardo is interested in entomology, the study of insects.

7. Presidents' Day celebrates the birthdays of Presidents Washington and Lincoln.

8. I forgot my money!

9. Please leave now.

10. Why are you laughing?

PRACTICE 20.1B **Punctuating Four Types of Sentences**

Read the sentences. Then, rewrite each sentence, adding the correct end punctuation.

EXAMPLE   What time does practice start

ANSWER   *What time does practice start?*

11. My subscription to this magazine is about to expire

12. Explain how you arrived at that solution

13. What are you studying in social studies

14. Who is that lurking in the hall

15. Come quickly

16. Cynthia Rylant is a writer whose books I enjoy

17. You look so happy

18. Tell us about your trip

19. What movie did you see last weekend

20. I can't find my notes

SPEAKING APPLICATION

With a small group, carry on a brief dialogue. One person will begin with a question. Each person in the group will continue with a different type of sentence until you have used all types of sentences at least once.

WRITING APPLICATION

Write a brief paragraph in which you use all four types of sentences at least once.

PRACTICE 20.1C > **Writing Four Types of Sentences**

Read the topics. For each topic, write the type of sentence specified in parentheses. Be sure to use the appropriate end punctuation.

EXAMPLE   this door (interrogative)

ANSWER   *Why is this door locked?*

1. the bicycle trail (declarative)

2. the comedian (exclamatory)

3. you (interrogative)

4. you (imperative)

5. the kitchen in our apartment (declarative)

6. a dump truck (declarative)

7. Sam (interrogative)

8. Selena (exclamatory)

9. you (imperative)

10. who (interrogative)

PRACTICE 20.1D > **Revising Four Types of Sentences**

Read the sentences. Rewrite each sentence, changing it to the type of sentence specified in parentheses. Be sure to use the appropriate end punctuation.

EXAMPLE   The rain stopped late in the day. (exclamatory)

ANSWER   *The rain finally stopped!*

11. Audrey is a very talented musician. (exclamatory)

12. Spencer had to wait for two hours. (interrogative)

13. Where will the meeting be held? (declarative)

14. Is Fiona planning to swim today? (declarative)

15. This water is cold. (exclamatory)

16. Will you take this list to the office? (imperative)

17. The fire was started by a careless camper. (interrogative)

18. What has Lisa broken? (declarative)

19. She will walk the dog. (interrogative)

20. I would like you to pay attention. (imperative)

SPEAKING APPLICATION

With a partner, name a type of sentence. Your partner will say that type of sentence and then name a different type for you to say.

WRITING APPLICATION

Write a short conversation between two people. Use each type of sentence at least once in the conversation.

20.2 Combining Sentences

Good writing should include sentences of varying lengths and complexity to create a flow of ideas. One way to achieve sentence variety is to combine sentences to express two or more related ideas or pieces of information in a single sentence.

Look at the example below. Then, look at how the ideas are combined in different ways.

EXAMPLE   I went to the movies. I saw an adventure film.

COMBINED   I went to the movies and saw an adventure film.

I saw an adventure film when I went to the movies.

Combining Sentence Parts

RULE 20.2.1

> Sentences can be combined by using a **compound subject**, a **compound verb**, or a **compound object**.

EXAMPLE   Anne Marie enjoys watching mysteries.
Susan enjoys watching mysteries.

COMPOUND SUBJECT   **Anne Marie** and **Susan** enjoy watching mysteries.

EXAMPLE   Ken sells movie tickets in the evening.
Ken sweeps the theater after the last show.

COMPOUND VERB   Ken **sells** movie tickets in the evening and **sweeps** the theater after the last show.

EXAMPLE   Marta loves romantic comedies.
Marta loves adventure films.

COMPOUND OBJECT   Marta loves romantic **comedies** and adventure **films**.

See Practice 20.2A

Joining Clauses

A **compound sentence** consists of two or more main or independent clauses. (See Chapter 19 for more information about clauses.) Use a compound sentence when combining related ideas of equal weight.

To create a compound sentence, join two main clauses with a comma and a coordinating conjunction. Common conjunctions include *and*, *but*, *nor*, *for*, *so*, *or*, and *yet*. You can also link the two sentences with a semicolon (;) if they are closely related.

> Sentences can be combined by joining two main clauses to create a **compound sentence.**

EXAMPLE	Janice went to a dance recital. She saw several different styles of dance.
COMPOUND SENTENCE	Janice went to a dance recital, and she saw several different styles of dance.
EXAMPLE	Janice enjoyed watching jazz and tap dancing. She particularly liked watching ballet.
COMPOUND SENTENCE	Janice enjoyed watching jazz and tap dancing, but she particularly liked watching ballet.
EXAMPLE	Janice wanted to learn to dance. She asked the teacher for lessons.
COMPOUND SENTENCE	Janice wanted to learn to dance, so she asked the teacher for lessons.
EXAMPLE	Janice goes to dance class. She studies both jazz and tap dancing.
COMPOUND SENTENCE	Janice goes to dance class; she studies both jazz and tap dancing

See Practice 20.2B

Sentences can be combined by changing one of them into a subordinate clause.

A **complex sentence** consists of one **main** or **independent clause** and one or more **subordinate clauses.** (See Chapter 19 for more information about clauses.) Combine sentences into a complex sentence to emphasize that one of the ideas in the sentence depends on the other. A subordinating conjunction will help readers understand the relationship. Common subordinating conjunctions are *after, although, because, before, since,* and *unless.* Generally no punctuation is required when a main and a subordinate clause are combined. When the subordinate clause comes first, a comma is needed. (See Chapter 25 for more information on punctuation.)

EXAMPLE The sky grew dark. The storm clouds blew in.

COMBINED The sky grew dark because the storm clouds blew in.

See Practice 20.2C

RULE 20.2.4

Sentences can be combined by changing one of them into a phrase.

When combining sentences in which one of the sentences simply adds details, change one of the sentences into a **phrase.**

EXAMPLE The Capitol Building is interesting to visit.

It is in Washington, D.C.

COMBINED The Capitol Building in Washington, D.C., is interesting to visit.

EXAMPLE The White House is in Washington, D.C.
The president and his family live there.

COMBINED The White House, where the president and his family live, is in Washington, D.C.

See Practice 20.2D

PRACTICE 20.2A **Combining Sentences Using Compound Subjects, Verbs, and Objects**

Read the sentences. Combine the sentences in each group into a single sentence. Identify each combination as *compound subject, compound verb,* or *compound object.*

EXAMPLE   Leo opened the box. He took out the contents.

ANSWER   *Leo opened the box and took out the contents.* — compound verb

1. Cars filled the lot. Pickup trucks were there.

2. Lia vacuumed the floor. She dusted furniture.

3. The rescue squad was at the accident site in a few minutes. Firefighters were there, too.

4. Quentin delivered two pizzas. He also delivered a large salad.

5. We often see a movie on the weekend. We often go to the mall on the weekend.

6. Hannah found some old letters in the attic. She also found some documents.

7. Mr. Pierce studied law. He also studied math.

8. Lee participated in the swim meet. I did, too.

9. The audience applauded. The audience cheered wildly.

10. We donated blankets to the shelter. We also donated food.

PRACTICE 20.2B **Combining Sentences Using Main Clauses**

Read the sentences. Combine each pair into a compound sentence, using the coordinating conjunction in parentheses. Be sure to use the correct punctuation for compound sentences.

EXAMPLE   I spent an hour on the crossword puzzle. I did not finish it. (but)

ANSWER   *I spent an hour on the crossword puzzle, but I did not finish it.*

11. José likes to cook. He prepares meals. (so)

12. Becky stopped searching. She no longer expected to find her lost bracelet. (for)

13. You could borrow the book from the library. You could buy it. (or)

14. Emily takes piano lessons. She practices an hour a day. (and)

15. Henry VIII was Queen Elizabeth's father. Her mother was Anne Boleyn. (;)

16. Soccer used to be Ryan's favorite sport. Now he prefers basketball. (but)

17. Patrick did not come to the meeting. He did not send in his report. (and)

18. Nelson had hoped to be the first in line for tickets. He did not arrive in time. (but)

19. Miners found gold in California in 1848. Fortune seekers soon flocked there. (and)

20. You can visit Abby in the hospital. You can wait until she comes home. (or)

SPEAKING APPLICATION

With a partner, tell about two people who did something and two things that they did. Use a compound subject and a compound verb. Your partner should listen for and identify them.

WRITING APPLICATION

Use the sentences you wrote for 11, 13, and 18 as models, and write three new compound sentences with the connectors shown in parentheses.

PRACTICE 20.2C **Combining Sentences Using Subordinate Clauses**

Read the sentences. Combine each pair by changing one sentence into a subordinate clause, using the subordinating conjunction in parentheses. Be sure to use the correct punctuation for complex sentences.

EXAMPLE   Dave paced back and forth. He rehearsed his speech. (as)

ANSWER   *Dave paced back and forth as he rehearsed his speech.*

1. The fog clears. The plane will take off. (when)

2. Caleb did his chores early in the day. It would be too hot to work later. (because)

3. Lara cannot play field hockey. Her fracture is healed. (until)

4. Our team has better guards. Central has some good players. (although)

5. Morgan entered the room. The lights went out. (as)

6. Dennis cast his fishing line into the stream. He has caught five fish. (since)

7. You must leave now. I'll walk with you. (if)

8. He worked hard. He did not succeed. (though)

9. The driver pulled to the side of the road. The tire blew out. (when)

10. People do not believe everything Dawn says. Dawn always exaggerates. (because)

PRACTICE 20.2D **Combining Sentences Using Phrases**

Read the sentences. Combine each pair of sentences by changing one into a phrase.

EXAMPLE   Olivia sells pottery. She attends craft fairs.

ANSWER   *Olivia sells pottery at craft fairs.*

11. You can take the subway. It goes from Central to South Station.

12. The book sold out quickly. It was an exciting thriller.

13. Children splashed in the fountain. It was in the park.

14. The rock was very smooth. It had been tossed around by the waves.

15. The watchdog snarled and barked. It barked at the intruder.

16. I found this article. It is about the new school.

17. Alan walked through a dark room. He tripped over some shoes on the floor.

18. People celebrate Thanksgiving. They eat turkey.

19. In some countries, people use camels. Camels are their transportation.

20. Many ponds and valleys were formed. They were formed by glaciers.

SPEAKING APPLICATION

With a partner, take turns talking about something you agree or disagree with. Use subordinating conjunctions. Your partner should listen for and name the conjunctions.

WRITING APPLICATION

Use the sentences you wrote for 11, 12, and 14 as models, and write three new combined sentences. Include phrases in different locations in the sentences.

20.3 Varying Sentences

When you vary the length and form of the sentences you write, you are able to create a rhythm, achieve an effect, or emphasize the connections between ideas.

There are several ways you can introduce variety into the sentences you write.

20.3.1 RULE

> **Varying the length of sentences makes writing lively and interesting to read.**

WRITING COACH

Online

@www.TXWritingCoach.com

Grammar Practice
Practice your grammar skills with Writing Coach Online.

Grammar Games
Test your knowledge of grammar in this fast-paced interactive video game.

Varying Sentence Length

Reading too many long sentences in a row can be just as uninteresting as reading too many short sentences in a row. When you want to emphasize a point or surprise a reader, insert a short, direct sentence to interrupt the flow of several long sentences.

EXAMPLE Veteran's Day is a holiday that is observed in the United States to honor all of those who served in the armed forces in times of war. The holiday has not always been called Veteran's Day. **It was first called Armistice Day.** It is celebrated in most states on November 11.

You can also break some longer sentences into shorter sentences. If the longer sentence contains two or more ideas, you can break up the ideas into separate sentences. However, if a longer sentence contains only one main idea, you should not break it apart.

LONGER SENTENCE Veteran's Day was proclaimed in 1919 by President Wilson to commemorate the ending of World War I.

TWO SENTENCES Veteran's Day was proclaimed in 1919 by President Wilson. It commemorated the ending of World War I.

See Practice 20.3A

Varying Sentence Beginnings

Another way to create variety is by changing from the usual subject–verb order in a sentence.

Sentence beginnings can also be varied by reversing the traditional subject–verb order or starting the sentence with an adverb or a phrase.

EXAMPLES

The **team** **is** **here**.
subject   verb   adverb

Here **is** the **team**.
adverb   verb   subject

The **fullback** **dove** **into the end zone**.
subject   verb   prepositional phrase

Into the end zone **dove** the **fullback**.
prepositional phrase   verb   subject

The **referee** **called** the **play** **quickly**.
subject   verb   direct object   adverb

Quickly, the **referee** **called** the **play**.
adverb   subject   verb   direct object

Another way to vary your sentences is to begin them in different ways. For instance, you can start sentences with different parts of speech.

See Practice 20.3B

WAYS TO VARY SENTENCE BEGINNINGS	
Start with a noun.	Sweaters, surprisingly, are not difficult to knit.
Start with an adverb.	Surprisingly, sweaters are not difficult to knit.
Start with an infinitive.	To knit sweaters is, surprisingly, not difficult.
Start with a gerund.	Knitting sweaters is, surprisingly, not difficult.
Start with a prepositional phrase.	For an accomplished knitter, sweaters are not difficult to make.

PRACTICE 20.3A ▷ Varying Sentence Length

Read the sentences. Rewrite each long compound sentence as two or more shorter sentences.

EXAMPLE   Ivan thought he should do the yard work he had agreed to do or his homework, but instead he decided to spend his Saturday morning riding his bike.

ANSWER   *Ivan thought he should do the yard work he had agreed to do or his homework. Instead, he decided to spend his Saturday morning riding his bike.*

1. If you want to take really good photographs, you could practice a lot or you could take a course or you could learn how to fix up your pictures using a computer program.

2. The doorbell rang, and Erin ran to answer it, and the dog slipped out the open door, so she ran after him.

3. Canada is a very large country with a relatively small population and only a few big cities, but these cities are close to the United States, so American tourists often visit them.

4. It was drizzling, but it was a warm rain, so people were not uncomfortable standing under big umbrellas watching a track meet.

5. Mimi had gone with her mother to an appointment, and then she went shopping with her, but she really wanted to stay home and read her book.

PRACTICE 20.3B ▷ Varying Sentence Beginnings

Read the sentences. Rewrite each sentence, changing the beginning as specified in parentheses. If there are two sentences, combine them, using one of the sentences to help you create the specified beginning.

EXAMPLE   We stopped to get sandwiches on our way home. (Begin with a prepositional phrase.)

ANSWER   *On our way home,* we stopped to get sandwiches.

6. Wendy smiled to herself, remembering the good time she had. (Begin with a participial phrase.)

7. The ice melted slowly. (Begin with an adverb.)

8. The chorus came next onto the stage. (Reverse the subject-verb order.)

9. Rob dropped his notes. It was in the middle of his speech. (Begin with a prepositional phrase.)

10. Mrs. Kane is a bird-watcher. She travels around the country to see different birds. (Begin with an appositive phrase.)

SPEAKING APPLICATION

With a partner, discuss your reasons for dividing one of the long compound sentences in Practice 20.3A into shorter sentences.

WRITING APPLICATION

Use your revised sentences 6–10 as models and write five sentences with varied beginnings.

Practice   443

20.4 Avoiding Sentence Problems

Recognizing problems with sentences will help you avoid and fix any problems in your writing.

Correcting Fragments

Some groups of words—even though they have a capital letter at the beginning and a period at the end—are not complete sentences. They are **fragments.**

RULE **20.4.1**

> A **fragment** is a group of words that does not express a complete thought.

A fragment can be a group of words that includes a possible subject but no verb. A fragment could also be a group of words that includes a possible verb but no subject. It can even be a group of words that contains no subject and no verb. Fragments can be turned into complete sentences by adding a subject, a verb, or both.

FRAGMENTS	COMPLETE SENTENCES
was ready for bed	**I** was ready for bed. (A subject is added.)
the clock on the wall	The clock on the wall **needs** to be reset. (A verb is added.)
in my room	My **jeans are** in my room. (A subject and verb are added.)

See Practice 20.4A

Correcting Phrase Fragments A **phrase fragment** cannot stand alone because it does not have both a subject and a verb.

RULE **20.4.2**

> A **phrase fragment** should not be capitalized and punctuated as if it were a sentence.

A phrase fragment can be corrected in one of two ways: (1) by adding it to a nearby sentence or (2) by adding whatever is needed to make it a complete sentence.

PHRASE FRAGMENT	The circus will begin at 8:00 on Sunday. `in the arena`
ADDED TO OTHER SENTENCE	The circus will begin at 8:00 on Sunday `in the arena`.
PHRASE FRAGMENT	There will be lions and elephants. `and tightrope walkers`
COMPLETE SENTENCES	There will be lions and elephants. There will also be `tightrope walkers`.

CHANGING PHRASE FRAGMENTS INTO SENTENCES	
PHRASE FRAGMENT	**COMPLETE SENTENCE**
into the center ring	The horses galloped `into the center ring`.
cheering the acrobats	The crowd was `cheering the acrobats`.
to see the clowns	The children waited `to see the clowns`.

See Practice 20.4B

Correcting Clause Fragments

All clauses have subjects and verbs, but some cannot stand alone as sentences.

> A **subordinate clause** should not be capitalized and punctuated as if it were a sentence.

RULE 20.4.3

Subordinate clauses do not express complete thoughts. Although a subordinate adjective or adverb clause has a subject and a verb, it cannot stand by itself as a sentence. (See Chapter 19 for more information about subordinate clauses and the words that begin them.)

Like phrase fragments, **clause fragments** can usually be corrected in either of two ways: (1) by attaching the fragment to a nearby sentence or (2) by adding whatever words are needed to turn the fragment into a sentence.

CLAUSE FRAGMENT	I saw the show. **that you described in your last letter**
COMPLETE SENTENCE	I saw the show **that you described in your last letter**.
CLAUSE FRAGMENT	I bought tickets as soon as they went on sale. **because I wanted good seats**
COMPLETE SENTENCE	I bought tickets as soon as they went on sale **because I wanted good seats**.
CLAUSE FRAGMENT	I wanted to sit in the first row. **so I could see everything**
COMPLETE SENTENCE	I wanted to sit in the first row **so I could see everything**.

To change a clause fragment into a sentence by the second method, you must add an independent clause to the fragment.

CHANGING CLAUSE FRAGMENTS INTO SENTENCES	
CLAUSE FRAGMENT	**COMPLETE SENTENCE**
that was ringing	Everyone heard the bell **that was ringing**. The bell **that was ringing** was heard by everyone.
when we got home	Dinner was ready **when we got home**. **When we got home**, dinner was ready.
what we were seeing	I could not believe **what we were seeing**.

See Practice 20.4C
See Practice 20.4D

PRACTICE 20.4A **Recognizing Fragments**

Read the groups of words. Then, write whether each group of words is a *sentence* or a *fragment*.

EXAMPLE   Searching for a lost ship.

ANSWER   *fragment*

1. When Rodney went to Curtis Middle School.

2. Today will be a very important day.

3. Under extreme pressure.

4. Which is a very good deal.

5. A television news reporter on the scene.

6. Walking on an icy pavement can be dangerous.

7. Torn at the edges.

8. By today at noon.

9. Val was not able to take notes because the speaker talked too fast.

10. He did.

PRACTICE 20.4B **Changing Phrase Fragments Into Sentences**

Read the phrase fragments. Then, use each fragment in a sentence.

EXAMPLE   during the week

ANSWER   *Danielle sometimes babysits during the week.*

11. on the computer for two hours

12. aside from that

13. walking by the shore

14. a children's doctor

15. hidden from sight

16. in the waiting room of the hospital

17. the guidance counselor

18. to answer all the questions on the test

19. not on weekends

20. in the sunshine by the window

SPEAKING APPLICATION

With a partner, take turns turning three of the fragments in Practice 20.4A into sentences.

WRITING APPLICATION

Choose two of the fragments in Practice 20.4B, and write two more sentences for each of them.

PRACTICE 20.4C > **Changing Clause Fragments Into Sentences**

Read the clause fragments. Then, use each fragment in a sentence.

EXAMPLE   after the book was published

ANSWER   *After the book was published, the author was famous.*

1. until you told me

2. as if it had been trampled

3. when the nurse left the room

4. wherever you go

5. because the race ended in a tie

6. as the clock struck midnight

7. before the bell rings

8. as you probably know

9. though the motor was running

10. since we last met

PRACTICE 20.4D > **Changing Fragments Into Sentences**

Read the groups of words. If a group of words is a fragment, use it in a sentence. If a group of words is already a sentence, write *sentence*.

EXAMPLE   As Olivia waited.

ANSWER   *As Olivia waited, she thought about what she would say.*

11. On the top shelf in the closet.

12. Before it's too late.

13. Who did all the artwork.

14. An e-mail message came with five attachments.

15. Diving from the rocks.

16. Born on Valentine's Day.

17. Meet me in front of the entrance.

18. Thinking about the problem.

19. His favorite author, Walter Dean Myers.

20. Although it was very cold out.

SPEAKING APPLICATION

With a partner, choose one of the fragments in Practice 20.4C, and use it again in two new sentences. Take turns saying these sentences.

WRITING APPLICATION

Write two more sentences for two fragments in Practice 20.4D.

Run-on Sentences

A fragment is an incomplete sentence. A **run-on,** on the other hand, is two or more complete sentences that are punctuated as though they were one sentence.

A **run-on** is two or more complete sentences that are not properly joined or separated.

20.4.4   RULE

Run-ons are usually the result of carelessness. Check your sentences carefully to see where one sentence ends and the next one begins.

Two Kinds of Run-ons

There are two kinds of run-ons. The first one is made up of two sentences that are run together without any punctuation between them. This is called a **fused sentence.**

The second type of run-on consists of two or more sentences separated by only a comma. This type of run-on is called a **comma splice.**

FUSED SENTENCES	I go to the fair every year I like the crafts.
	Jake practices hard he wants to make the team.
COMMA SPLICE	There will be fireworks on July 4, I like the parade, too.
	Keisha is a great dancer, I love it when she shows me new steps.

See Practice 20.4E

A good way to distinguish between a run-on and a sentence is to read the words aloud. Your ear will tell you whether you have one or two complete thoughts and whether you need to make a complete break between the thoughts.

Three Ways to Correct Run-ons

There are three ways to correct run-on sentences. You can use
end marks, commas and coordinating conjunctions, or semicolons.

Using End Marks

Periods, question marks, and exclamation marks are useful to fix
run-on sentences.

RULE 20.4.5

> **Use an end mark to separate a run-on sentence into two
> sentences.**

Sometimes the best way to correct a run-on is to use an end
mark to split the run-on into two shorter but complete sentences.
End marks help your reader pause and group your ideas more
effectively.

RUN-ON	I have to babysit on the weekends, my brother goes to practice.
CORRECTED	I have to babysit on the weekends. My brother goes to practice.
RUN-ON	Watch out the ball is coming toward you.
CORRECTED	Watch out! The ball is coming toward you.
RUN-ON	Have you bought your tickets I have mine.
CORRECTED	Have you bought your tickets? I have mine.
RUN-ON	What's going on, I can't figure out where I'm supposed to stand.
CORRECTED	What's going on? I can't figure out where I'm supposed to stand.

Using Commas and Coordinating Conjunctions

Sometimes the two parts of a run-on are related and should
be combined into a compound sentence.

> **Use a comma and a coordinating conjunction to combine two independent clauses into a compound sentence.**

RULE 20.4.6

To separate the clauses properly, use both a comma and a coordinating conjunction. The most common coordinating conjunctions are *and, but, or, for, nor,* and *yet.* Before you separate a sentence into parts, though, be sure each part expresses a complete thought.

RUN-ON   May went to the store, she forgot her shopping list.

CORRECTED   May went to the store, but she forgot her shopping list.

RUN-ON   She remembered most of the things she needed, she bought a few extra things.

CORRECTED   She remembered most of the things she needed, and she bought a few extra things.

Using Semicolons
You can sometimes use a semicolon to connect the two parts of a run-on into a correct sentence.

> **Use a semicolon to connect two closely related ideas into one sentence.**

RULE 20.4.7

Use a semicolon only when the ideas in both parts of the sentence are closely related.

RUN-ON   My first class next year starts at 8:00, my last class ends at 3:00.

CORRECTED   My first class next year starts at 8:00; my last class ends at 3:00.

See Practice 20.4F

PRACTICE 20.4E ▷ Recognizing Run-ons

Read the groups of words. Then, write whether each group is a *sentence* or a *run-on*.

EXAMPLE The movie was a fast-paced thriller, Kirk likes thrillers.

ANSWER *run-on*

1. My cousin from San Diego visited me, and we talked until midnight.

2. Callie writes children's stories, she reads them during the library story hour.

3. Mark picked up the newspaper and read the headlines, then he scanned the sports section.

4. In some areas, trees are being destroyed by insects.

5. He wanted to graduate from high school he did.

6. Warren, a careful person, is serious about whatever he does.

7. Benjamin Franklin was a printer, an inventor, a diplomat, and a convention delegate.

8. Some people like to play sports, others prefer to be spectators.

9. Roy waved at me from the stands, I waved back.

10. Abby sent Troy a text message he did not reply.

PRACTICE 20.4F ▷ Correcting Run-ons

Read the sentences. Rewrite each run-on sentence to correct the problem.

EXAMPLE Computers have changed drastically in fifty years, they have become faster and smaller.

ANSWER *Computers have changed drastically in fifty years. They have become faster and smaller.*

11. The sun dropped behind the horizon over the lake, we watched the spectacular sunset.

12. The lobby was filled with teenagers, they wanted to buy tickets to the concert.

13. Caleb likes to read limericks he read some in Edward Lear's *A Book of Nonsense*.

14. Lola graduated from college then she took a job in New York.

15. Firefighters quickly arrived they were able to bring the fire under control.

16. Rock climbing can be exciting but dangerous, rock climbers need to be cautious.

17. First, boil the water then add the rice.

18. Ethan did not like the movie Erica enjoyed it very much.

19. Alec had a good game, he scored two runs and made two outs.

20. Mark Twain created two famous characters these characters are Tom Sawyer and Huckleberry Finn.

SPEAKING APPLICATION

With a partner, identify one sentence and one run-on in Practice 20.4E. Explain why the sentence is correct and the run-on is not.

WRITING APPLICATION

Use sentences 17 and 18 as models, and write a new sentence for each in the same way you corrected them.

Properly Placing Modifiers

If a phrase or clause acting as an adjective or adverb is not placed near the word it modifies, it may seem to modify a different word. Then the sentence may seem unclear or odd.

> **A modifier** should be placed as close as possible to the word it describes.

 20.4.8 RULE

A modifier placed too far away from the word it describes is called a **misplaced modifier.**

MISPLACED MODIFIER

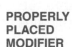 Mark went scuba diving in the lake **with his flippers** .

The misplaced phrase *with his flippers* makes it seem as though the lake has flippers.

PROPERLY PLACED MODIFIER

 With his flippers , Mark went scuba diving in the lake.

Below is a different type of misplaced modifier that is sometimes called a **dangling modifier.** A dangling modifier at the beginning of a sentence causes the sentence to be unclear.

DANGLING MODIFIER

 Sitting on the boat , the sun felt hot.

In this sentence, *sitting on the boat* should modify a person or people. Instead, it incorrectly modifies *sun*.

CORRECTED **Sitting on the boat ,** we felt the hot sun.

TEKS Check Show that you can use a variety of complete sentences (e.g., *simple, compound, complex*) that include properly placed modifiers. From a newspaper, choose one simple sentence, one compound sentence, and one complex sentence and identify the properly placed modifiers. Then, write three of your own sentences and read them aloud to a partner. Your partner should name the modifiers and the words they describe.

TEKS Practice Show that you can use a variety of complete sentences (e.g., *simple, compound, complex*) that include properly placed modifiers by completing the following activities.

PRACTICE 20.4G > **Revising to Correct Misplaced Modifiers**

Read the sentences. Then, rewrite each sentence to correct the underlined misplaced modifier.

EXAMPLE   Simon found a twenty-dollar bill <u>walking home from school</u>.

ANSWER   *Walking home from school, Simon found a twenty-dollar bill.*

1. Hillary has a cat named Tiger <u>with stripes</u>.

2. Glen searched for the hidden clues <u>with a GPS system</u>.

3. <u>Working on my computer</u>, the power went out.

4. We watched seals diving for fish <u>standing on the shore</u>.

5. Victoria reviewed the speech that she would give <u>sitting in the backyard</u>.

6. I watched the squirrels and pigeons <u>eating my lunch in the park</u>.

7. <u>Accompanied by the First Lady</u>, the crowd cheered as the president arrived.

8. <u>Listening to my MP3 player</u>, the work gets done quickly.

9. A black jacket was found by a student <u>with red sleeves</u>.

10. Please summarize what you just read <u>with your book closed</u>.

PRACTICE 20.4H > **Recognizing and Correcting Misplaced Modifiers**

Read the sentences. If a sentence has a misplaced modifier, rewrite the sentence so the modifier is properly placed. If a sentence is correct, write *correct.*

EXAMPLE   With her tail twitching, Audra watched her cat stalk a squirrel.

ANSWER   *Audra watched her cat twitching its tail and stalking a squirrel.*

11. Evan got up early and turned on the television still in his pajamas.

12. Rosa waited for the bus with her friends.

13. Putting on her best clothes, Kate prepared for an interview.

14. A man jumped into the pond to rescue the dog with all his clothes on.

15. Remembering his promise, Luis left early.

16. Because of the rain, Claire walked her dog with an umbrella.

17. On her way home, Victoria stopped at the library.

18. I saw a red-tailed hawk looking through my binoculars.

19. Gil stomped out, slamming the door.

20. I saw my friend Pedro talking to his brother in the hall.

SPEAKING APPLICATION

With a partner, take turns describing your favorite season of the year. Be sure to use a combination of simple, compound, and complex sentences with modifiers. Your partner should identify the modifiers and correct any misplaced modifiers.

WRITING APPLICATION

Write a brief description of one of your favorite meals. Include one simple sentence, one compound sentence, and one complex sentence. Then, discuss your sentences with a partner. Your partner should identify the modifiers and correct any misplaced modifiers.

Avoiding Double Negatives

Negative words, such as *nothing* and *not*, are used to deny or to say *no*. Some people mistakenly use **double negatives**—two negative words—when only one is needed.

> **Avoid writing sentences that contain double negatives.**

20.4.9 RULE

In the following examples, negative words are highlighted. The first sentence in each example contains double negatives. The corrected sentences show two ways to correct each double-negative sentence.

DOUBLE NEGATIVES	Maggie **didn't** invite **nobody**.
CORRECTED SENTENCES	Maggie **didn't** invite anybody.
	Maggie invited **nobody**.
DOUBLE NEGATIVES	I **haven't no** more money.
CORRECTED SENTENCES	I have **no** more money.
	I **haven't** any more money.
DOUBLE NEGATIVES	Jack and Phil **didn't** go **nowhere**.
CORRECTED SENTENCES	Jack and Phil **didn't** go anywhere.
	Jack and Phil went **nowhere**.
DOUBLE NEGATIVES	It seems the sun **doesn't** shine **no** more.
CORRECTED SENTENCES	It seems the sun **doesn't** shine any more.
	It seems the sun shines **no** more.
DOUBLE NEGATIVES	A few rainy days **didn't** bother **no one**.
CORRECTED SENTENCES	A few rainy days **didn't** bother anyone.
	A few rainy days bothered **no one**.

See Practice 20.4I
See Practice 20.4J

PRACTICE 20.4I ⟩ **Using Negatives Correctly**

Read the sentences. Then, write the word in parentheses that makes each sentence negative without creating a double negative.

EXAMPLE   The teacher didn't hear (no one, anyone) answer.

ANSWER   *anyone*

1. Sue doesn't go (anywhere, nowhere) without her phone.

2. Christa said she didn't want (any, no) bread.

3. Jon didn't bring (any, no) money with him.

4. Ollie (can, can't) never remember his locker combination.

5. Nadine didn't bring (anything, nothing) to the party.

6. He never has (no, any) time to help me.

7. Claudia couldn't find her ring (anywhere, nowhere).

8. Tabitha doesn't know (anyone, no one) in that class.

9. By the time we were ready for dessert, there wasn't (any, none) left.

10. Zach claims he didn't do (anything, nothing).

PRACTICE 20.4J ⟩ **Revising to Correct Double Negatives**

Read the sentences. Then, rewrite each sentence to correct the double negative.

EXAMPLE   He didn't want no help with the cleanup.

ANSWER   *He didn't want any help with the cleanup.*

11. There wasn't nowhere to hang up the coats.

12. I didn't get no text message from Liz.

13. Isn't there no one here who can give me directions?

14. The sweatshirt didn't have no hood.

15. I can't find nothing in this closet.

16. That old house hasn't had no paint for years.

17. There isn't no one at the ticket window.

18. Tony didn't remember nothing about the accident.

19. Amber never said nothing to no one.

20. Tonia didn't see nothing in the store that she liked.

SPEAKING APPLICATION

With a partner or small group, take turns telling each other a very brief narrative in which you use the words *no one, nothing,* and *nowhere.* Be sure not to use double negatives.

WRITING APPLICATION

Write three sentences in which you use three of these negative words without creating a double negative: *never, no,* and *none.*

Avoiding Common Usage Problems

This section contains fifteen common usage problems in alphabetical order. Some are expressions that you should avoid in both your speaking and your writing. Others are words that are often confused because of similar spellings or meanings.

(1) accept, except   Do not confuse the spelling of these words. *Accept*, a verb, means "to take what is offered" or "to agree to." *Except*, a preposition, means "leaving out" or "other than."

VERB	Meg **accepted** her award.
PREPOSITION	Everyone was given a raise **except** me.

(2) advice, advise   Do not confuse the spelling of these related words. *Advice*, a noun, means "an opinion." *Advise*, a verb, means "to give an opinion."

NOUN	What **advice** can you give me about studying?
VERB	I **advise** you to study every night.

(3) affect, effect   *Affect*, a verb, means "to influence" or "to cause a change in." *Effect*, usually a noun, means "result."

VERB	The hurricane **affected** the dunes on the beach.
NOUN	The **effects** of hurricanes may be seen for years.

(4) at   Do not use *at* after *where*.

INCORRECT	Does your mother know **where** you're **at**?
CORRECT	Does your mother know **where** you are?

(5) because   Do not use *because* after *the reason*. Eliminate one or the other.

INCORRECT	**The reason** I'm happy is **because** I won the race.
CORRECT	I'm happy **because** I won the race.
	The **reason** I'm happy is **that** I won the race.

(6) beside, besides These two prepositions have different meanings and cannot be interchanged. *Beside* means "at the side of" or "close to." *Besides* means "in addition to."

EXAMPLES   My classroom is **beside** hers on this floor.

No one **besides** us is here in the afternoon.

(7) different from, different than *Different from* is preferred over *different than*.

EXAMPLE   The new buses are **different from** last year's buses.

(8) farther, further *Farther* is used to refer to distance. *Further* means "additional" or "to a greater degree or extent."

EXAMPLES   His house was **farther** than mine.

I will have no **further** communication with you.

(9) in, into *In* refers to position. *Into* suggests motion.

POSITION   My books are **in** my backpack.

MOTION   I put my backpack **into** my locker.

(10) kind of, sort of Do not use *kind of* or *sort of* to mean "rather" or "somewhat."

INCORRECT   I'm **sort of** good at swimming.

CORRECT   I'm **rather** good at swimming.

(11) like *Like*, a preposition, means "similar to" or "in the same way as." It should be followed by an object. Do not use *like* before a subject and a verb. Use *as* or *that* instead.

PREPOSITION   My sister looks **like** our dad.

INCORRECT   This apple doesn't taste **like** it should.

CORRECT   This apple doesn't taste **as** it should.

(12) that, which, who   *That* and *which* refer to things. *Who* refers only to people.

THINGS	People liked the music **that** I played.
PEOPLE	The man **who** played the trumpet is my dad.

(13) their, there, they're   Do not confuse the spelling of these three words. *Their,* a possessive adjective, always modifies a noun. *There* is usually used as a sentence starter or as an adverb. *They're* is a contraction of *they are.*

POSSESSIVE ADJECTIVE	The students lined up for **their** buses.
SENTENCE STARTER	**There** is the Broadway bus.
ADVERB	The bus stop is over **there** .
CONTRACTION	**They're** waiting in the rain.

(14) to, too, two   Do not confuse the spelling of these words. *To* plus a noun creates a prepositional phrase. *To* plus a verb creates an infinitive. *Too* is an adverb and modifies verbs, adjectives, and other adverbs. *Two* is a number.

PREPOSITION	**to** the store	**to** Texas	
INFINITIVE	**to** stand	**to** run	
ADVERB	**too** cloudy	**too** badly	
NUMBER	**two** shoes	**two** shirts	

(15) when, where, why   Do not use *when, where,* or *why* directly after a linking verb such as *is.* Reword the sentence.

INCORRECT	To explore the ruins is **why** we went to Mexico.
CORRECT	We went to Mexico to explore the ruins.
INCORRECT	In the evening is **when** I do my homework.
CORRECT	I do my homework in the evening.

See Practice 20.4K
See Practice 20.4L
See Practice 20.4M
See Practice 20.4N

Read the sentences. Then, write the word in parentheses that best completes each sentence.

EXAMPLE   The hikers went (farther, further) than they had planned.

ANSWER   *farther*

1. The judges have made (there, their) decision.

2. Toby took his equipment (in, into) the locker room.

3. The (affects, effects) of the hurricane are still evident.

4. Everyone has had a turn (accept, except) Lindsay.

5. I could use some (advice, advise) on how to run this machine.

6. Steve introduced his grandfather (that, who) had been a general in the army.

7. Abe's brother wanted (to, too) much money for the bike.

8. Laura needed (farther, further) encouragement to audition for the play.

9. You can place your backpack (beside, besides) the others.

10. Julian is different (from, than) his brother.

Read the sentences. If the underlined word is used correctly, write *correct*. If the word is incorrect, write the correct word.

EXAMPLE   Rick is standing <u>besides</u> Cassie in the picture.

ANSWER   *beside*

11. Poor nutrition can <u>affect</u> your ability in school.

12. Grace is a person <u>that</u> is always willing to help.

13. Jeff walked <u>in</u> the classroom.

14. Eve and Tara worked on <u>they're</u> project after school.

15. I have no <u>further</u> information for you at this time.

16. Gwen's idea is different <u>than</u> Rebecca's.

17. The students <u>who</u> made the banner are seventh graders.

18. Jocelyn offers <u>advise</u>, even if you don't want it.

19. Mark was honored to <u>except</u> the award.

20. Brian wants a game <u>like</u> Leo's.

SPEAKING APPLICATION

With a partner, use the words *advice* and *effect* to tell an observation you have made about people in general. Your partner should check that you have used the words correctly.

WRITING APPLICATION

Write two or three related sentences using all of these words correctly: *accept, advice, their,* and *too*.

PRACTICE 20.4M **Recognizing and Correcting Usage Problems**

Read the sentences. Then, if a sentence has a usage problem, rewrite it to correct the problem. If a sentence is correct, write *correct*.

EXAMPLE   Robin wondered where the meeting was at.

ANSWER   *Robin wondered where the meeting was.*

1. The person who can help you is not here today.

2. A late paper could effect your grade.

3. Luke's goals are different from mine.

4. The Mancinos took there dog with them on vacation.

5. The reason I am late is because the bus broke down.

6. The best time is when everyone else has left and it's quiet.

7. We sat besides the Owens family.

8. People that want respect should give respect.

9. I don't know why you always say that.

10. Archie refused to accept payment for helping Mrs. Holden shovel her walk.

PRACTICE 20.4N **Avoiding Usage Problems**

Read the pairs of words. For each pair of words, write two sentences that are related in meaning.

EXAMPLE   accept, except

ANSWER   *The teacher accepted the papers early. Everyone except Crystal had finished.*

11. besides, beside

12. into, in

13. as, like

14. who, that

15. too, to

16. advice, advise

17. farther, further

18. their, there

19. except, accept

20. effect, affect

SPEAKING APPLICATION

With a partner, choose two of the incorrect sentences in Practice 20.4M, and explain why the usage is incorrect.

WRITING APPLICATION

Write a short paragraph in which you use all of these words correctly: *beside, affect, except,* and *there*.

Using Parallel Structures

Good writers try to present a series of ideas in similar grammatical structures. This way, the ideas read smoothly. If one element in a series is not parallel with the others, the result may be confusing. Parallel structures are important in simple, compound, and complex sentences.

Recognizing the Correct Use of Parallelism
To present a series of ideas of equal importance, you should use parallel grammatical structures.

RULE 20.4.10 >

> **Parallelism** involves presenting equal ideas in words, phrases, clauses, or sentences of similar types.

PARALLEL WORDS	The lost dog looked **scared, dirty,** and **hungry**.
PARALLEL PHRASES	I wanted more than anything to **take him home, give him a bath,** and **feed him**.
PARALLEL CLAUSES	The dog **that you found** and **that you want to bring home** belongs to someone else.
PARALLEL SENTENCES	**We have to find his owner. We have to do the right thing.**

Find It / FIX IT

10

Grammar Game Plan

Correcting Faulty Parallelism
Faulty parallelism occurs when a writer uses unequal grammatical structures to express related ideas. This can cause sentences to sound unbalanced.

RULE 20.4.11 >

> Correct a sentence with faulty parallelism by rewriting it so that each parallel idea is expressed in the same grammatical structure.

Faulty parallelism can involve words, phrases, and clauses in a series or in comparisons.

Nonparallel Words, Phrases, and Clauses in a Series
Always check for parallelism when your writing contains items in
a series.

Correcting Faulty Parallelism in a Series

NONPARALLEL STRUCTURES	Three steps in the writing process are **drafting**, **revision**, and **editing**. gerund noun gerund
CORRECTION	Three steps in the writing process are **drafting**, **revising**, and **editing**. gerund gerund gerund

Nonparallel Words, Phrases, and Clauses in Comparison
In writing comparisons, you generally should compare a phrase
with the same type of phrase. Similarly, you should compare a
clause with the same type of clause.

Correcting Faulty Parallelism in Comparisons

NONPARALLEL STRUCTURES	I think **that drafting is the easiest step**, but
	             noun clause
	
	the most patience is required for revising.
	        independent clause

CORRECTION	I think **that drafting is the easiest step** but
	             noun clause
	
	that revising requires the most patience.
	        noun clause

Focus on the TEKS

(19)(C) Use a variety
of complete sentences
(e.g., simple, compound,
complex) that include
parallel structures.

See TEKS Practice

See Practice 20.4O

See Practice 20.4P

NONPARALLEL STRUCTURES	**Jocelyn** prefers swimming **in cold water** while
	  subject prepositional phrase
	the warm **water** delights her **friends**.
	     subject direct object

CORRECTION	**Jocelyn** prefers swimming **in cold water** while
	  subject prepositional phrase
	her **friends** prefer swimming **in warm water**.
	  subject prepositional phrase

TEKS Practice Show that you can use a variety of complete sentences (e.g., simple, compound, complex) that include parallel structures by completing the following activities.

PRACTICE 20.4O **Using Parallel Structures With Items in a Series**

Read each sentence. Then, rewrite the sentences to correct the faulty parallelism. If the item is correct, then write *correct*. Read your new sentences to a partner. Your partner should identify the parallelism.

EXAMPLE   My mother is an excellent dentist, a great cook, and plays the piano well.

ANSWER   *My mother is an excellent dentist, a great cook, and a good pianist.*

1. I bought two bags of potatoes, three tomatoes that were ripe, and one head of lettuce.

2. I could not wait to use my new surfboard, and visiting my friend, Kelly.

3. The teacher assigned one book report and is giving us a test tomorrow.

4. My hobbies are going to the movies and chess.

5. For your birthday, we can go bowling but no swimming is allowed.

6. Some of my friends think that Ping Pong is not a sport, and that it shouldn't be in the Olympics.

7. Pat likes diving, swimming, and to surf.

8. We will miss the bus and be late for the play.

9. I like to paint, sketch and drawing.

10. My best subject is English, and I am not bad at math and science.

PRACTICE 20.4P **Using Parallel Structures in Comparisons**

Read each sentence. Then, rewrite the sentences to correct the faulty parallelism in comparisons. Read your new sentences to a partner. Your partner should identify the parallel structures.

EXAMPLE   I left school at 4:30 P.M. rather than going home at 3:00 P.M.

ANSWER   *I left school at 4:30 P.M. rather than at 3:00 P.M.*

11. Most people work during the day not night.

12. Shane did the dishes while Joanna cooks.

13. I enjoyed my meal more than Christopher.

14. I am as fond of dogs as much as I like cats.

15. Pia is as good a softball player as basketball is Shania's strength.

16. Because of traffic, my mother arrived at 7:00 P.M. instead of coming home at 5:30 P.M.

17. Juan enjoyed the nonfiction book as much as the science fiction story is his brother's favorite.

18. I prefer waking up late while my sister is an early riser.

19. My sister prefers apples to eating oranges.

20. Geraldo enjoys playing the clarinet as much as guitar appeals to his brother.

SPEAKING APPLICATION

With a partner, take turns talking about your favorite foods. Include at least one simple sentence, one compound sentence, and one complex sentence and use parallel structures. You partner should identify where you have used parallel structures.

WRITING APPLICATION

Write a paragraph about your school subjects. Include one simple, one compound, and one complex sentence. Show parallel structures in a series and in comparison. Read your paragraph. Your partner should identify where you have used parallel structures.

Texas Test Warm-Up

DIRECTIONS

Read the introduction and the passage that follows. Then, answer the questions to show that you can use a variety of complete sentences (e.g., simple, compound, complex) that include parallel structures in reading and writing.

Focus on the TEKS

(19)(C) Use a variety of complete sentences (e.g., simple, compound, complex) that include parallel structures.

Fiona wrote this paragraph about her summer vacation. Read the paragraph and think about the changes you would suggest as a peer editor. When you finish reading, answer the questions that follow.

Summer Fun

(1) This summer, I did many different things and went to lots of places. (2) The first two weeks of the summer break, I went to the swim club, my grandma's house, and the mall was somewhere I spent time, as well. (3) The last two weeks in July, I went away to camp. (4) My favorite camp activities were tennis, arts and crafts, and of course, going to swim. (5) The last Saturday at camp is visiting day, which means that parents come to visit. (6) Friends can also come.

1 What change, if any, should be made in sentence 1?

A *did* to **went**

B *went to* to **did**

C Change *lots of* to **many different**

D Make no change

2 What would be the BEST way to rewrite the ideas in sentence 2?

F The first two weeks of the summer break, I went to the swim club, my grandma's house, and the mall was somewhere I spent time.

G The first two weeks of the summer break, I went to the swim club, to my grandma's house, and to the mall.

H The first two weeks of the summer break, the swim club, my grandma's house, and the mall were somewhere I spent time.

J I went to the swim club and my grandma's house, as well as the mall the first two weeks of summer.

3 What change, if any, should be made in sentence 4?

A Change *going to swim* to **swimming**

B Insert **playing** after *were*

C Insert **making** before *arts*

D Make no change

4 What is the BEST way to combine sentences 5 and 6?

F The last Saturday at camp is visiting day, which means that parents come to visit and that friends can also come.

G The last Saturday at camp is visiting day, which means that parents and friends can come to visit.

H The last Saturday at camp is visiting day, which means that parents come and friends also come to visit.

J The last Saturday at camp, parents and friends come to visit on visiting day.

Using Consistent Tenses

Verbs have a number of different tenses that tell when actions happen. For example, past tense is used for actions that happened in the past. Present tense shows actions that happen in the present or that happen regularly. Future tense is used to show actions that will take place in the future. Switching from one tense to another can be confusing in any type of sentence: simple, compound, and complex.

> **Use consistent verb tenses to show actions that occur during the same period of time.**

INCONSISTENT TENSES

I **went** to the movies, and
past

I **see** my friend waiting for me.
present

CONSISTENT TENSES

I **went** to the movies, and
past

I **saw** my friend waiting for me.
past

The verb *went* sets the action in the past. The other action also occurred in the past.

Using Inconsistent Tenses Correctly

Sometimes, actions take place at different times. In these instances, you may switch from one tense to another. Sometimes you may use a time word or phrase to explain the switch in tense.

EXAMPLE

I **stayed** up really late last night, so now
past

I **am** very sleepy.
present

 Focus on the TEKS

(19)(C) Use a variety of complete sentences (e.g., simple, compound, complex) that include consistent tenses.

See TEKS Practice

See Practice 20.4Q

See Practice 20.4R

TEKS Practice Show that you can use a variety of complete sentences (e.g., simple, compound, complex) that include consistent tenses by completing the following activities.

PRACTICE 20.4Q > Writing Sentences With Consistent Verb Tenses

Read each sentence. Then, rewrite the sentences to correct inconsistent verb tenses. Read your new sentences to a partner. Your partner should identify the consistent verb tenses.

EXAMPLE   Helene goes to the mall and bought a new pair of shoes.

ANSWER   Helene *went* to the mall and bought a new pair of shoes.

1. After I finished my homework, I go outside to shoot baskets with Jamie.

2. Every morning, my mom drops me off at school and then went to work.

3. Ms. Jones taught us about the scientific method and then gives a pop quiz.

4. Even though she apologized before, I was still mad at Kaitlin now.

5. Yesterday, I woke up early so that I have time to finish my report.

6. Did you go to the football game or did you went straight home?

7. The bus driver gets mad when we screamed.

8. I like when my dad came home early and plays baseball with me.

9. I am a good chess player but I was even better at checkers.

10. Lydia was mad at Amy for the mean things Amy says about Mia.

PRACTICE 20.4R > Writing Sentences With Consistent Verb Tenses

Read the verb pairs. Then, write a sentence using each pair in the present, past, or future tense. Read your sentences to a partner. Your partner should identify the consistent tenses.

EXAMPLE   leave, wait

ANSWER   *Because I left my house before my sister, I waited for her on the corner.*

11. study, take

12. remember, be

13. work, play

14. cook, clean

15. enjoy, dislike

16. tell, laugh

17. win, celebrate

18. arrive, depart

19. become, dream

20. sleep, forget

SPEAKING APPLICATION

With a partner, take turns discussing your favorite weekend activities. Include at least one simple sentence, one compound sentence, and one complex sentence. Use consistent tenses in your sentences. Your partner should identify the consistent tenses.

WRITING APPLICATION

Write a paragraph about a recent event in sports, at school, or in your community. Include at least one simple, one compound, and one complex sentence. Use consistent tenses. Read your paragraph to a partner, who should identify the tenses.

Cumulative Review Chapters 18–20

PRACTICE 1 > **Using Complete Subjects and Predicates**

Each item below contains only a complete subject or a complete predicate. Rewrite each item, making a sentence by adding the missing part indicated in parentheses.

1. The supermarket cashier (add a predicate).
2. (add a subject) enjoyed the performance.
3. The television weather forecaster (add a predicate).
4. Was (add a subject) difficult to do?
5. The roller coaster (add a predicate).
6. (add a subject) raced across the room.
7. The new community center (add a predicate).
8. (add a subject) made a huge hole.
9. The boy and his parents (add a predicate).
10. (add a subject) entered another contest.

PRACTICE 2 > **Using Direct Objects**

Rewrite each incomplete sentence, supplying a direct object where indicated in parentheses. You may also include the article *a, an,* or *the* or another modifier along with the direct object.

1. Dogs need (direct object).
2. The children are making (direct object).
3. In the school office, I saw (direct object).
4. Janice paints (direct object) for a living.
5. Barry left (direct object) on the table.
6. He asked (direct object) for change for a dollar.
7. I enjoyed (direct object) at the parade.
8. Last week, Diane met (direct object) in the park.
9. The pilot showed us (direct object).
10. What caused (direct object) on the moon?

PRACTICE 3 > **Identifying Indirect Objects**

Read the sentences. Then, write the indirect object in each sentence. If there is no indirect object, write *none*.

1. The nurse gave the patient an injection.
2. Eddie told us a very funny joke.
3. My mom bought herself a lovely silk blouse.
4. Craig clips coupons for supermarket savings.
5. Don't hand her the scissors the wrong way.
6. The rodeo performer showed us a rope trick.
7. Amy offered her seat to a lady with a baby.
8. We wish you a happy holiday.
9. The police officer asked the driver for her license.
10. Who will give the dog a bath?

PRACTICE 4 > **Identifying Subject Complements**

Read the sentences. Then, write the subject complement in each sentence. Also indicate whether it is a *predicate noun, predicate pronoun,* or *predicate adjective.*

1. The student with the best grades is you.
2. Jack London was a popular adventure writer.
3. The cousins looked happy to see each other.
4. Trina will be the next class president.
5. The drive to Springfield seemed very scenic.
6. Lucia has been the manager for ten years.
7. Of all the skaters, the most graceful one is you.
8. Please do not be late to the concert.
9. That magic show was really something.
10. Are we being careful enough?

Read the sentences. Then, rewrite each sentence, supplying the type of prepositional phrase indicated in parentheses.

1. Paco joined the club. (Add an adjectival phrase.)
2. Lillian tossed a Frisbee. (Add an adverbial phrase.)
3. The noise was loud. (Add an adjectival phrase.)
4. Dad grilled chicken. (Add an adverbial phrase.)
5. Dina rang the bell. (Add an adjectival phrase.)

PRACTICE 6 ▷ Identifying Appositive, Participial, Gerund, and Infinitive Phrases

Read the sentences. Then, write whether the underlined phrase in each sentence is an *appositive phrase*, a *participial phrase*, a *gerund phrase*, or an *infinitive phrase*.

1. We need to buy light bulbs.
2. Alex plans on running the marathon.
3. Scared by the cat, the mouse scampered off.
4. We looked through binoculars to see the spotted owl.
5. The thesaurus, a book of synonyms, is also available online.
6. The figure dashing through the trees seemed like an owl in the fog.
7. An enthusiastic fisherman, Ernest Hemingway lived for a time in Key West.
8. Knitting woolen sweaters is one of my sister's special skills.
9. Packing her suitcase, Audra broke a fingernail.
10. Max plans to become a skiing instructor.

PRACTICE 7 ▷ Recognizing Main and Subordinate Clauses

Read the sentences. Then, write and label the *main clause* and the *subordinate clause* in each sentence.

1. The school bus was late because the traffic on Manning Boulevard was terrible.
2. When the bus neared his stop, Martin rang the bell at the rear door.
3. The state senator, who was first elected more than ten years ago, is running for office again.
4. We will visit Montana in two weeks unless a blizzard prevents the trip.
5. I watched the first episode, which I had seen before.

PRACTICE 8 ▷ Combining Sentences With Subordinate Clauses

Read the sentences. Combine each pair of sentences by turning one into a subordinate clause. Then, underline the subordinate clause, and indicate whether it is an *adjectival clause* or an *adverbial clause.*

1. My cousin is wearing a cast. She broke her leg skating on the ice last week.
2. My brother will be applying to several colleges. He is a junior in high school.
3. I hunted in every closet. I finally found that old family photo album.
4. The department store will open earlier than usual. It has a big sale today.
5. We walked nearly five miles today. My feet are very sore.

Continued on next page ▶

Cumulative Review Chapters 18–20

PRACTICE 9 Writing Sentences

For each item, write the indicated type of sentence, using the words provided.

1. Write a compound sentence using *the inventor* as one of the subjects.

2. Write a declarative sentence using *the elevator* as the subject.

3. Write a complex sentence using *is running* as one of the verbs.

4. Write an exclamatory sentence using the word *marvelous.*

5. Write an imperative sentence using *unlock* as the verb.

PRACTICE 10 Combining Sentences

Read the sentences. Combine each pair of sentences by using compound structures. Indicate whether your sentence contains a *compound subject,* a *compound verb,* or a *compound object,* or whether it is a *compound sentence.*

1. Geraldo waited in the ticket line. Frederica waited there, too.

2. Jacques ordered a turkey sandwich for lunch. He also ordered a salad.

3. The designer selected the fabrics carefully. She also matched them carefully.

4. Fern may have left her keys on the kitchen counter. She may have left her scarf in the car.

5. They were hoping for an experienced baker. The person they finally hired has little experience.

PRACTICE 11 Revising to Correct Fragments and Run-ons

Read each group of words. If it is a fragment, use it in a sentence. If it is a run-on, correct the run-on. If a sentence needs no correction, write *correct.*

1. The groom waiting at the altar.

2. The child was riding on the merry-go-round.

3. I was reading in bed my eyes were closing.

4. When you arrive for the picnic.

5. The movie was awful, I sat through it anyway.

PRACTICE 12 Revising to Correct Common Usage Problems

Read the sentences. Then, rewrite each sentence to correct misplaced modifiers, double negatives, and other usage problems.

1. What does the financial planner advice your family to do?

2. Lack of sufficient daylight during the short winter days effects the mood of some people.

3. Coughing so much, she could speak no farther.

4. Wearing a warm coat, the cold weather did not bother me.

5. I like every vegetable accept cabbage.

6. Madeline didn't see none of her friends at the block party.

7. The reason I left is because I have another appointment.

8. The girls were to tired to do they're homework.

9. Phyllis wore new boots that were apparently too big on her feet.

10. Meteorology is where you study the weather.

USING VERBS

Understanding the different tenses of regular and irregular verbs will help you clearly convey actions in your writing.

WRITE GUY *Jeff Anderson, M.Ed.*

WHAT DO YOU NOTICE?

Lock onto the verbs as you zoom in on these sentences from "Two Kinds," an excerpt from *The Joy Luck Club* by Amy Tan.

MENTOR TEXT

"No!" I said, and I now felt stronger, as if my true self had finally emerged. So this was what had been inside me all along.

Now, ask yourself the following questions:

- What principal part of the verb *emerge* is used in the first sentence?
- What forms of irregular verbs are used in both sentences?

In the first sentence, the principal part of the verb *emerge* is the past participle *emerged*. The verb phrase is formed by combining the past participle *emerged* with the helping verb *had*. The forms of irregular verbs used in these sentences are *said, felt, had, was,* and *been*, which are past or past participial forms of *say, feel, have,* and *be*. They are irregular because their principal parts do not follow the pattern of adding *-ed* or *-d* to the present form to create the past and past participial forms.

Grammar for Writers Knowing how to use the principal parts of a verb correctly allows writers to communicate a time of action or state of being. Watch out for irregular verbs, and be prepared to check that you are using the correct tenses.

How do you keep from getting stuck in the past?

That's easy. Stop using the past tense!

21.1 The Four Principal Parts of Verbs

Verbs have different tenses to express time. The tense of the verb *walk* in the sentence "They *walk* very fast" expresses action in the present. In "They *walked* too far from home," the tense of the verb shows that the action happened in the past. In "They *will walk* home from school," the verb expresses action in the future. These forms of verbs are known as **tenses**.

A verb's **tense** shows the time of the action or state of being that is being described. To use the tenses of a verb correctly, you must know the **principal parts** of the verb.

RULE 21.1.1

> A verb has four **principal parts: the present**, the **present participle**, the **past**, and the **past participle**.

THE FOUR PRINCIPAL PARTS OF *VISIT*			
PRESENT	**PRESENT PARTICIPLE**	**PAST**	**PAST PARTICIPLE**
visit	(am) visiting	visited	(have) visited

The first principal part, called the present, is the form of a verb that is listed in a dictionary. The present participle and the past participle must be combined with helping verbs before they can be used as verbs in sentences. The result will always be a verb phrase.

EXAMPLES He **visits** the library every day.

Jake **was visiting** the library yesterday.

They **visited** the library.

We **have visited** the library in the last three weeks.

The way the past and past participle of a verb are formed shows whether the verb is **regular** or **irregular**.

Using Regular Verbs

Most verbs are **regular,** which means that their past and past participle forms follow a standard, predictable pattern.

> The past and past participle of a **regular verb** are formed by adding **-ed** or **-d** to the present form.

To form the past and past participle of a regular verb such as *chirp* or *hover*, you simply add *-ed* to the present. With regular verbs that already end in *e*—verbs such as *move* and *charge*—you simply add *-d* to the present.

PRINCIPAL PARTS OF REGULAR VERBS			
PRESENT	PRESENT PARTICIPLE	PAST	PAST PARTICIPLE
call	(am) calling	called	(have) called
change	(am) changing	changed	(have) changed
charge	(am) charging	charged	(have) charged
chirp	(am) chirping	chirped	(have) chirped
contain	(am) containing	contained	(have) contained
describe	(am) describing	described	(have) described
fix	(am) fixing	fixed	(have) fixed
hover	(am) hovering	hovered	(have) hovered
jump	(am) jumping	jumped	(have) jumped
lift	(am) lifting	lifted	(have) lifted
look	(am) looking	looked	(have) looked
move	(am) moving	moved	(have) moved
play	(am) playing	played	(have) played
save	(am) saving	saved	(have) saved
serve	(am) serving	served	(have) served
ski	(am) skiing	skied	(have) skied
talk	(am) talking	talked	(have) talked
type	(am) typing	typed	(have) typed
visit	(am) visiting	visited	(have) visited
walk	(am) walking	walked	(have) walked

See Practice 21.1A
See Practice 21.1B

The Four Principal Parts of Verbs

PRACTICE 21.1A **Identifying Principal Parts of Regular Verbs**

Read the sentences. Then, label each underlined verb *present, present participle, past,* or *past participle.*

EXAMPLE   Angie <u>has invited</u> twenty people to her party.

ANSWER   *past participle*

1. The boss <u>ordered</u> all work to stop at once.
2. We <u>missed</u> you at the group meeting today.
3. I <u>presume</u> this is the right place.
4. Alicia <u>was laughing</u> at Joel's joke.
5. No one <u>had noticed</u> that Del was not there.
6. Hugo <u>has attended</u> every rehearsal.
7. Kim <u>is wondering</u> why you said that.
8. Alex <u>did</u> not <u>continue</u> his speech.
9. Tamara <u>has</u> not <u>submitted</u> her report yet.
10. It <u>was raining</u>, but the soccer team <u>practiced</u> anyway.

PRACTICE 21.1B **Supplying the Principal Parts of Regular Verbs**

Read the verbs. Then, write and label the four principal parts of each verb. Use a form of the helping verb *be* with the present participle and a form of the helping verb *have* with the past participle.

EXAMPLE   talk

ANSWER   *talk* — present
          is talking — present participle
          talked — past
          has talked — past participle

11. watch
12. burn
13. complete
14. suggest
15. ski
16. carry
17. work
18. try
19. stop
20. continue

SPEAKING APPLICATION

With a partner, take turns making a statement in which you use two principal parts of one of the verbs in Practice 21.1B. Your partner should identify which principal parts you use.

WRITING APPLICATION

Write several sentences or a brief paragraph in which you use three principal parts of one of these verbs: *disappear, return,* and *discuss.*

Using Irregular Verbs

While most verbs are regular, many very common verbs are **irregular**—their past and past participle forms do not follow a predictable pattern.

> The past and past participle of an **irregular verb** are not formed by adding *-ed* or *-d* to the present tense form.

21.1.3 RULE

IRREGULAR VERBS WITH THE SAME PAST AND PAST PARTICIPLE			
PRESENT	PRESENT PARTICIPLE	PAST	PAST PARTICIPLE
bring	(am) bringing	brought	(have) brought
build	(am) building	built	(have) built
buy	(am) buying	bought	(have) bought
catch	(am) catching	caught	(have) caught
fight	(am) fighting	fought	(have) fought
find	(am) finding	found	(have) found
get	(am) getting	got	(have) got *or* (have) gotten
hold	(am) holding	held	(have) held
lay	(am) laying	laid	(have) laid
lead	(am) leading	led	(have) led
lose	(am) losing	lost	(have) lost
pay	(am) paying	paid	(have) paid
say	(am) saying	said	(have) said
sit	(am) sitting	sat	(have) sat
sleep	(am) sleeping	slept	(have) slept
spin	(am) spinning	spun	(have) spun
stand	(am) standing	stood	(have) stood
stick	(am) sticking	stuck	(have) stuck
swing	(am) swinging	swung	(have) swung
teach	(am) teaching	taught	(have) taught
win	(am) winning	won	(have) won

Check a dictionary whenever you are in doubt about the correct form of an irregular verb.

IRREGULAR VERBS WITH THE SAME PRESENT, PAST, AND PAST PARTICIPLE

PRESENT	PRESENT PARTICIPLE	PAST	PAST PARTICIPLE
bid	(am) bidding	bid	(have) bid
burst	(am) bursting	burst	(have) burst
cost	(am) costing	cost	(have) cost
hurt	(am) hurting	hurt	(have) hurt
put	(am) putting	put	(have) put
set	(am) setting	set	(have) set

IRREGULAR VERBS THAT CHANGE IN OTHER WAYS

PRESENT	PRESENT PARTICIPLE	PAST	PAST PARTICIPLE
arise	(am) arising	arose	(have) arisen
be	(am) being	was	(have) been
bear	(am) bearing	bore	(have) borne
beat	(am) beating	beat	(have) beaten
begin	(am) beginning	began	(have) begun
blow	(am) blowing	blew	(have) blown
break	(am) breaking	broke	(have) broken
choose	(am) choosing	chose	(have) chosen
come	(am) coming	came	(have) come
do	(am) doing	did	(have) done
draw	(am) drawing	drew	(have) drawn
drink	(am) drinking	drank	(have) drunk
drive	(am) driving	drove	(have) driven
eat	(am) eating	ate	(have) eaten
fall	(am) falling	fell	(have) fallen
fly	(am) flying	flew	(have) flown
forget	(am) forgetting	forgot	(have) forgotten
freeze	(am) freezing	froze	(have) frozen

IRREGULAR VERBS THAT CHANGE IN OTHER WAYS (CONTINUED)			
PRESENT	**PRESENT PARTICIPLE**	**PAST**	**PAST PARTICIPLE**
give	(am) giving	gave	(have) given
go	(am) going	went	(have) gone
grow	(am) growing	grew	(have) grown
know	(am) knowing	knew	(have) known
lie	(am) lying	lay	(have) lain
ride	(am) riding	rode	(have) ridden
ring	(am) ringing	rang	(have) rung
rise	(am) rising	rose	(have) risen
run	(am) running	ran	(have) run
see	(am) seeing	saw	(have) seen
shake	(am) shaking	shook	(have) shaken
sing	(am) singing	sang	(have) sung
sink	(am) sinking	sank	(have) sunk
speak	(am) speaking	spoke	(have) spoken
spring	(am) springing	sprang	(have) sprung
strive	(am) striving	strove	(have) striven
swear	(am) swearing	swore	(have) sworn
swim	(am) swimming	swam	(have) swum
take	(am) taking	took	(have) taken
tear	(am) tearing	tore	(have) torn
throw	(am) throwing	threw	(have) thrown
wear	(am) wearing	wore	(have) worn
weave	(am) weaving	wove	(have) woven
write	(am) writing	wrote	(have) written

See Practice 21.1C

See Practice 21.1D

See Practice 21.1E

See Practice 21.1F

As you can see, there are many irregular verbs. For most of these verbs, you should memorize the different forms. Whenever you are not sure of which form of an irregular verb to use, check a dictionary.

PRACTICE 21.1C ▷ **Supplying the Principal Parts of Irregular Verbs**

Read the verbs. Then, write and label the four principal parts of each verb. Use a form of the helping verb *be* with the present participle, and a form of the helping verb *have* with the past participle.

EXAMPLE   fly

ANSWER   *fly* — present

is flying — present participle

flew — past

has flown — past participle

1. go
2. ride
3. tear
4. ring
5. choose
6. draw
7. eat
8. arise
9. hurt
10. wear

PRACTICE 21.1D ▷ **Choosing the Correct Form of Irregular Verbs**

Read the sentences. Then, choose and write the form of the verb in parentheses that correctly completes each sentence.

EXAMPLE   We had (drove, driven) all day.

ANSWER   *driven*

11. The balloon (burst, bursted).
12. Aunt Lucy (bring, brought) us a gift.
13. My grandfather (shook, shaked) the apples off the tree.
14. Some of those trees in the back have (grew, grown) too tall.
15. Diana has (took, taken) piano lessons.
16. The wind (blowed, blew) fiercely all night.
17. The construction workers have already (builded, built) the foundation.
18. Ken (caught, catched) three fish during his fishing expedition.
19. Have you (wrote, written) a thank-you note to your grandmother?
20. Rhondella has (led, leaded) her team to victory.

SPEAKING APPLICATION

With a partner, take turns making a statement in which you use two principal parts of one of the verbs listed in Practice 21.1C. Your partner should identify which principal parts you use.

WRITING APPLICATION

Write three sentences, using different principal parts of these verbs: *know, choose,* and *tell.* You may use any of the sentences in Practice 21.1D as models.

PRACTICE 21.1E > **Using Irregular Verbs**

Read the sentences. Rewrite each sentence, using the form of the verb in parentheses that correctly completes the sentence.

EXAMPLE   Daniel (sing) the lead in last year's musical.

ANSWER   *Daniel sang the lead in last year's musical.*

1. Marty has not (speak) to anyone about her plan.

2. Alexa has (choose) a new ring tone for her phone.

3. The little child has (put) his shoes on the wrong feet.

4. Curtis (pay) the bill for our meal.

5. Who (see) the shooting stars last night?

6. In the 1770s and 1780s, American colonists (fight) for independence.

7. Marya (stand) staring at her feet, trying to think of an answer.

8. The chorus (rise) together when the director (give) the signal.

9. Gary's socks (shrink) in the wash.

10. Ryan (bring) some video games for us to play.

PRACTICE 21.1F > **Revising for Irregular Verbs**

Read the sentences. Then, if the underlined verb is in the correct form, write *correct*. If it is not, rewrite the sentence with the correct verb form.

EXAMPLE   The water in the birdbath had <u>froze</u>.

ANSWER   *The water in the birdbath had frozen.*

11. Abby <u>blowed</u> out the candle before she left the room.

12. Anthony's uncle <u>taught</u> him to play the banjo.

13. Maggie and Jennifer <u>brung</u> sandwiches for the group.

14. We have <u>sat</u> here too long.

15. Colin <u>drank</u> the water.

16. The *Titanic* <u>sunk</u> after hitting an iceberg.

17. That window has been <u>broken</u> twice this year.

18. The boots <u>costed</u> too much, so I did not buy them.

19. Sophie <u>swum</u> across the pond and back today.

20. I <u>seen</u> that movie before.

SPEAKING APPLICATION

With a partner, take turns telling about an event you have observed. Use the past and past participle forms of three of these verbs: *come*, *see*, *stand*, and *speak*.

WRITING APPLICATION

Write three sentences using the past or past participle forms of these verbs: *begin*, *drive*, and *write*. You may use the sentences in Practices 21.1E and 21.1F as models.

21.2 The Six Tenses of Verbs

In English, verbs have six **tenses**: the **present**, the **past**, the **future**, the **present perfect**, the **past perfect**, and the **future perfect**.

WRITING COACH

Online

@www.TXWritingCoach.com

Grammar Practice

Practice your grammar skills with Writing Coach Online.

Grammar Games

Test your knowledge of grammar in this fast-paced interactive video game.

RULE 21.2.1

The tense of a verb shows the time of the action or state of being.

Every tense has both **basic** forms and **progressive** forms.

Identifying the Basic Forms of the Six Tenses

The chart below shows the **basic** forms of the six tenses, using *speak* as an example. The first column gives the name of each tense. The second column gives the basic form of *speak* in all six tenses. The third column gives the principal part needed to form each tense. Only three of the four principal parts are used in the basic forms: the present, the past, and the past participle.

BASIC FORMS OF THE SIX TENSES OF *SPEAK*		
TENSE	**BASIC FORM**	**PRINCIPAL PART USED**
Present	I speak.	Present
Past	I spoke.	Past
Future	I will speak.	Present
Present Perfect	I have spoken.	Past Participle
Past Perfect	I had spoken.	Past Participle
Future Perfect	I will have spoken.	Past Participle

Study the chart carefully. First, learn the names of the tenses. Then, learn the principal parts needed to form them. Notice also that the last four tenses need helping verbs.

As you have already learned, some verbs form their tenses in a regular, predictable pattern. Other verbs use an irregular pattern. *Speak* is an example of an irregular verb.

See Practice 21.2A

Conjugating the Basic Forms of Verbs

A helpful way to become familiar with all the forms of a verb is by **conjugating** it.

> A **conjugation** is a list of the singular and plural forms of a verb in a particular tense.

 21.2.2 RULE

Each tense in a conjugation has six forms that fit with first-, second-, and third-person forms of the personal pronouns. These forms may change for each personal pronoun, and they may change for each tense.

To conjugate any verb, begin by listing its principal parts. For example, the principal parts of the verb *go* are *go, going, went,* and *gone*. The following chart shows the conjugation of all the basic forms of *go* in all six tenses. The forms of the helping verbs may also change for each personal pronoun and tense.

 Focus on the TEKS

(19)(A)(i) Use and understand the function of perfect tense verbs in the context of reading, writing, and speaking.

See TEKS Check

See TEKS Practice

See Practice 21.2B

See Practice 21.2C

See Practice 21.2D

CONJUGATION OF THE BASIC FORMS OF *GO*		
TENSE	**SINGULAR**	**PLURAL**
Present	I go. You go. He, she, or it goes.	We go. You go. They go.
Past	I went. You went. He, she, or it went.	We went. You went. They went.
Future	I will go. You will go. He, she, or it will go.	We will go. You will go. They will go.
Present Perfect	I have gone. You have gone. He, she, or it has gone.	We have gone. You have gone. They have gone.
Past Perfect	I had gone. You had gone. He, she, or it had gone.	We had gone. You had gone. They had gone.
Future Perfect	I will have gone. You will have gone. He, she, or it will have gone.	We will have gone. You will have gone. They will have gone.

TEKS Check Show that you can use and understand the function of perfect tense verbs. Tell a partner three sentences that use the present perfect verb tense. Have your partner restate the sentences using the past perfect or future perfect verb tense.

Conjugating *Be*

The verb *be* is an important verb to know how to conjugate. It is both the most common and the most irregular verb in the English language. You have already seen how to use forms of *be* with the perfect tenses. You will also use the basic forms of *be* when you conjugate the progressive forms of verbs later in this section.

PRINCIPAL PARTS OF *BE*			
PRESENT	**PRESENT PARTICIPLE**	**PAST**	**PAST PARTICIPLE**
be	being	was	been

Once you know the principal parts of *be*, you can conjugate all of the basic forms of *be*.

CONJUGATION OF THE BASIC FORMS OF *BE*		
TENSE	**SINGULAR**	**PLURAL**
Present	I am. You are. He, she, or it is.	We are. You are. They are.
Past	I was. You were. He, she, or it was.	We were. You were. They were.
Future	I will be. You will be. He, she, or it will be.	We will be. You will be. They will be.
Present Perfect	I have been. You have been. He, she, or it has been.	We have been. You have been. They have been.
Past Perfect	I had been. You had been. He, she, or it had been.	We had been. You had been. They had been.
Future Perfect	I will have been. You will have been. He, she, or it will have been.	We will have been. You will have been. They will have been.

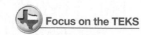 **Focus on the TEKS**

(19)(A)(i) Use and understand the function of perfect tense verbs in the context of reading, writing, and speaking.

See TEKS Check

See TEKS Practice

See Practice 21.2E

See Practice 21.2F

 TEKS Check Show that you can use and understand the function of perfect tense verbs. With a partner, describe your weekend, using the present perfect, past perfect, and future perfect tenses of the verb *be*. Your partner should name the tenses you use.

TEKS Practice Show that you can use and understand the function of perfect tense verbs in the context of reading, writing, and speaking by completing the following activities.

The Six Tenses of Verbs

PRACTICE 21.2A **Identifying Present, Past, and Future Tenses of Verbs**

Read the sentences. Then, label each underlined verb *present*, *past*, or *future*.

EXAMPLE   I <u>will give</u> you an answer later.

ANSWER   *future*

1. <u>May</u> I <u>interrupt</u> you for a moment?

2. Judith <u>squeezed</u> the lemon into her tea.

3. You <u>will enjoy</u> the performance tomorrow.

4. Betsy <u>saves</u> the bottles to recycle.

5. We <u>will remember</u> this day forever.

6. Shyly, Neal <u>smiled</u> at Lizzie.

7. The team <u>hopes</u> for a victory tonight.

8. Kirsten <u>attended</u> a different school last year.

9. Felicia quickly <u>brushed</u> her teeth and <u>left</u> for school.

10. After you read the chapter, you <u>will discuss</u> it in groups.

PRACTICE 21.2B **Identifying Perfect Tenses of Verbs**

Read the sentences. Then, write the verb in each sentence, and label it *present perfect*, *past perfect*, or *future perfect*.

EXAMPLE   The group has chosen James as its spokesperson.

ANSWER   *has chosen* — *present perfect*

11. Everyone had left the cafeteria by 1:00 P.M.

12. I have not seen Will since yesterday.

13. By December, the birds will have migrated south for the winter.

14. Brandon had left his book in the gym after practice.

15. The rain has delayed the opening of the game.

16. By this time tomorrow, I will have completed my research project.

17. Mandy has seen three of the five home games.

18. I have worn my favorite red sweatshirt many times.

19. Beth had thoughtfully marked her draft for revision.

20. How long have you known her?

SPEAKING APPLICATION

With a partner, use the verbs in sentences 4, 5, and 6 to make three statements in which you use present, past, and future tenses. Your partner should identify the verb tense in each statement.

WRITING APPLICATION

Use the perfect verb tenses in sentences 11, 16, and 18, and write three sentences with other verbs in the perfect tense.

PRACTICE 21.2C ▸ Writing Sentences Using the Perfect Tenses of Verbs

Read each present tense verb. Then, write a sentence using the perfect tense indicated in parentheses. Read your sentences to a partner, who should listen for and name the perfect tense verbs.

EXAMPLE   leave (past perfect)

ANSWER   *I had left the house when I realized that I forgot my backpack.*

1. be (present perfect)

2. give (future perfect)

3. allow (past perfect)

4. remember (present perfect)

5. score (future perfect)

6. speak (past perfect)

7. forget (present perfect)

8. go (future perfect)

9. skate (past perfect)

10. cook (present perfect)

PRACTICE 21.2D ▸ Writing Sentences Using the Perfect Tenses of Verbs

Read the sentences. Then, use the subjects and verbs provided to write new sentences using the perfect tense indicated in parentheses. Read your sentences to a partner, who should listen for and name the perfect tense verbs.

EXAMPLE   I am. (present perfect)

ANSWER   I *have been* to Sharon's house many times.

11. She runs. (future perfect)

12. My mother goes. (past perfect)

13. The dog sleeps. (present perfect)

14. The cat plays. (future perfect)

15. I study. (past perfect)

16. Juana forgets. (present perfect)

17. Michael remembers. (future perfect)

18. My father arrives. (past perfect)

19. I enjoy. (present perfect)

20. I prefer. (past perfect)

SPEAKING APPLICATION

With a partner, take turns talking about the actions of a dog or cat. Use perfect tense verbs in at least three sentences. Your partner should listen for and name the perfect tense verbs.

WRITING APPLICATION

Write six sentences about a topic of your choice. In each sentence, use a perfect tense verb. Then, underline and identify the perfect tense verb in each sentence.

TEKS Practice Show that you can use and understand the function of perfect tenses of verbs in the context of reading, writing, and speaking by completing the following activities.

The Six Tenses of Verbs

PRACTICE 21.2E ▷ Forming Verb Tenses

Read the sentences, which are all in the present tense. Then, rewrite each sentence, changing it to the tense indicated in parentheses.

EXAMPLE   The teacher repeats the directions. (future)

ANSWER   *The teacher will repeat the directions.*

1. Tina confides her plan to Rhonda. (past)

2. Ashley hints about a party. (present perfect)

3. Dom insists on paying for my lunch. (past)

4. By 9:00 P.M., the store closes. (future perfect)

5. Karen proposes a solution to the dilemma. (past perfect)

6. No one believes your excuse. (future)

7. Nick works on his project in the library. (past)

8. Hailey sketches the scene on her drawing pad. (future)

9. Noah thinks about the consequences. (past perfect)

10. Amanda performs in the talent show. (present perfect)

PRACTICE 21.2F ▷ Using Verb Tenses Correctly

Read the sentences. Then, write the verb in parentheses that correctly completes each sentence.

EXAMPLE   Starting next week, stores (are, will be) open later for the holidays.

ANSWER   *will be*

11. Joanna (eats, ate) salmon for dinner yesterday.

12. Tony never (imagined, will imagine) that he could win the spelling bee.

13. By next week, the play (has completed, will have completed) its run.

14. I (will meet, have met) you at 5:00 P.M.

15. David (shouts, shouted) with glee when he heard the news.

16. The committee (will discuss, has discussed) your proposal when it meets later this week.

17. Did you get the message I (sent, have sent) this morning?

18. I (will give, have given) you my answer already.

19. Until today, Mark (has, had) perfect attendance.

20. The ticket office (is, was) closed when we went to buy tickets.

SPEAKING APPLICATION

With a partner, take turns talking about jobs or careers that might interest you. In your sentences, use at least three perfect tense verbs. Your partner should listen for and name the perfect tense verbs.

WRITING APPLICATION

Write a paragraph about how you spent your time last summer. Use at least three perfect tense verbs. Read your paragraph to a partner. Your partner should listen for and name the perfect tense verbs.

Focus on the TEKS

(19)(A)(i) Use and understand the function of perfect tense verbs in the context of reading and writing.

Texas Test Warm-Up

DIRECTIONS
Read the introduction and the passage that follows. Then, answer the questions to show that you can use and understand the function of perfect tense verbs in reading and writing.

Nate wrote this paragraph about his dog, Jake. Read the paragraph and think about the changes you would suggest as a peer editor. When you finish reading, answer the questions that follow.

Where Had Jake Gone?

(1) My dog, Jake, had ate breakfast and wanted to go out. (2) I had opened the back door before breakfast because I had know he was going to scratch at the door. (3) I had left the room to make my bed. (4) He must have slipped out. (5) I heard my sister shouting, "Jake, where are you? Come, boy!" (6) Where had Jake gone? (7) After we had searching for 20 minutes, my mom said that we had to go to school, and that she would find him. (8) We reluctantly opened the front door, and there was Jake, wagging his little tail. (9) He had run around the yard to the front door!

---

1 What change, if any, should be made in sentence 1?

  A Change *had ate* to **had eaten**

  B Change *had ate* to **has eaten**

  C Change *wanted* to **has want**

  D Make no change

2 What change, if any, should be made in sentence 2?

  F Change *had opened* to **have opened**

  G Change *had know* to **had known**

  H Change *had know* to **have known**

  J Make no change

3 What is the BEST way to combine sentences 3 and 4?

  A I had left the room to make my bed; he must have slipped out.

  B He must have slipped out; I had left the room to make my bed.

  C Before I leave the room to make my bed, he must slip out.

  D He must have slipped out after I had left the room to make my bed.

4 The meaning of sentence 7 can be clarified by changing the word *searching* to —

  F search

  G searched

  H looking

  J look

Recognizing the Progressive Tense of Verbs

The six tenses of *go* and *be* in their basic forms were shown in the charts earlier in this section. Each of these tenses also has a progressive tense or form. The progressive form describes an event that is in progress. In contrast, the basic forms of a verb describe events that have a definite beginning and end.

> The **progressive tense,** or form, of a verb shows an action or condition that is ongoing.

21.2.3 RULE

All six of the progressive tenses of a verb are made using just one principal part: the present participle. This is the principal part that ends in *-ing*. Then, the correct form of *be* is added to create the progressive tense or form.

Progressive Tenses of *Write*

PROGRESSIVE TENSE = be + present participle

PRESENT   I **am** **writing** in the class.
             be present participle

PAST   I **was** **writing** in class all day.
             be present participle

FUTURE   I **will be** **writing** in class this week.
             be   present participle

PRESENT PERFECT   I **have been** **writing** since I was young.
                    be   present participle

PAST PERFECT   I **had been** **writing** only in class, but now
                 be   present participle
                 I also write at home.

FUTURE PERFECT   I **will have been** **writing** in class for twelve
                   be   present participle
                   years by the time I graduate high school.

⊕ **TEKS Check** Show that you can use and understand the function of progressive tense verbs. Read each sentence on this page aloud to a partner. Work together to write sentences using progressive tense verbs.

Conjugating Progressive Tenses

To create the progressive tenses or forms of a verb, you must know the basic forms of *be*.

> **To conjugate the progressive forms of a verb, add the present participle of the verb to a conjugation of the basic forms of *be*.**

A conjugation of the basic forms of *be* is shown earlier in this section. Compare that conjugation with the following conjugation of the progressive forms of *see*. Notice that, even though the present participle form of the verb does not change, the form of the helping verb does change. It is the form of *be* that tells you whether the action or condition is taking place in the past, present, or future.

CONJUGATION OF THE PROGRESSIVE FORMS OF *SEE*		
TENSE	**SINGULAR**	**PLURAL**
Present Progressive	I am seeing. You are seeing. He, she, or it is seeing.	We are seeing. You are seeing. They are seeing.
Past Progressive	I was seeing. You were seeing. He, she, or it was seeing.	We were seeing. You were seeing. They were seeing.
Future Progressive	I will be seeing. You will be seeing. He, she, or it will be seeing.	We will be seeing. You will be seeing. They will be seeing.
Present Perfect Progressive	I have been seeing. You have been seeing. He, she, or it has been seeing.	We have been seeing. You have been seeing. They have been seeing.
Past Perfect Progressive	I had been seeing. You had been seeing. He, she, or it had been seeing.	We had been seeing. You had been seeing. They had been seeing.
Future Perfect Progressive	I will have been seeing. You will have been seeing. He, she, or it will have been seeing.	We will have been seeing. You will have been seeing. They will have been seeing.

 Focus on the TEKS

(19)(A)(i) Use and understand the function of progressive tense verbs in the context of reading, writing, and speaking.

See TEKS Check

See TEKS Practice

See Practice 21.2G

See Practice 21.2H

TEKS Check Show that you can use and understand the function of progressive tense verbs. Write a description about something you have been studying. Use the progressive tense. Read your description aloud to a partner and discuss the function of the progressive tense verbs you used.

TEKS Practice Show that you can use and understand the function of progressive tense verbs in the context of reading, writing, and speaking by completing the following activities.

PRACTICE 21.2G **Identifying the Progressive Tenses of Verbs**

Read the sentences. Then, write whether the underlined verb tense in each sentence is *present progressive, past progressive, future progressive, present perfect progressive, past perfect progressive,* or *future perfect progressive.*

EXAMPLE   The group <u>was singing</u> on the bus.

ANSWER   *past progressive*

1. Lisa <u>is sitting</u> next to Michael.

2. I <u>had been planning</u> to clean my room today.

3. We <u>have been hoping</u> to see the exhibit at the library.

4. Our guests <u>will be arriving</u> any minute now.

5. By the time we finish, we <u>will have been painting</u> the porch for two days.

6. He <u>was nodding</u> his head in agreement.

7. I <u>had been thinking</u> about you before you called.

8. They <u>are preparing</u> to leave now.

9. Our science class <u>will be studying</u> the solar system soon.

10. I <u>have been spending</u> my money foolishly.

PRACTICE 21.2H **Using Progressive Tenses of Verbs**

Read the sentences. Then, rewrite each sentence using the tense of the verb in parentheses.

EXAMPLE   Eric _____ for a summer job. (*look,* present progressive)

ANSWER   *Eric is looking for a summer job.*

11. I _____ to ask you something. (*mean,* present perfect progressive)

12. The leaves _____ faster than we could rake them. (*fall,* past perfect progressive)

13. I _____ for two hours. (*study,* present perfect progressive)

14. Will you _____ the drama club? (*join,* future progressive)

15. Carson _____ to go to the Grand Canyon. (*plan,* present perfect progressive)

16. Lou and Tom _____ at Todd's silly pun. (*laugh,* past progressive)

17. The track team _____ every day after school. (*run,* present perfect progressive)

18. Your flight _____ soon. (*depart,* future progressive)

19. We _____ to rehearse for the play. (*continue,* present progressive)

20. Vanessa _____ to use the computer. (*wait,* past progressive)

SPEAKING APPLICATION

With a partner, take turns talking about school events. Your partner should listen for and identify two verbs you use in a progressive tense.

WRITING APPLICATION

Write a paragraph about a current event. Use a variety of sentences with progressive tense verbs. Then, exchange papers with a partner. Read your sentences aloud and discuss the purpose of the progressive tense verbs.

Identifying Active and Passive Voice

Just as verbs change tense to show time, they may also change form to show whether or not the subject of the verb is performing an action.

21.2.5

> The **voice** of a verb shows whether or not the subject is performing the action.

In English, most verbs have two **voices: active,** to show that the subject is performing an action, and **passive,** to show that the subject is having an action performed on it.

21.2.6

> A verb is in the **active voice** when its subject performs the action.

ACTIVE VOICE

Mike **plays** the guitar.

Sandra **sang** the song.

In each example above, the subject performs the action, so the verb is said to be in the active voice.

21.2.7

> A verb is in the **passive voice** when its subject does not perform the action.

PASSIVE VOICE

The guitar **is being played** by Mike.

The song **was sung** by Sandra.

In each example above, the person doing the action becomes the object of the preposition *by* and is no longer the subject. Both subjects—*guitar* and *song*—are receivers rather than performers of the action. When the subject is acted upon, the verb is said to be in the passive voice.

See Practice 21.2I

Forming the Tenses of Passive Verbs

A passive verb always has two parts.

> **A passive verb** is always a verb phrase made from a form of *be* plus a past participle.

21.2.8 RULE

The following chart shows a conjugation of the passive forms of the verb *present* with the pronoun *it*.

CONJUGATION OF THE PASSIVE FORMS OF *PRESENT*	
TENSE	**PASSIVE FORM**
Present	It is presented.
Past	It was presented.
Future	It will be presented.
Present Perfect	It has been presented.
Past Perfect	It had been presented.
Future Perfect	It will have been presented.

While there are uses for the passive voice, most writing is more lively when it is in the active voice. Think about how to change each sentence below to the active voice. Follow the pattern in the first two examples.

PASSIVE   It **is marked** on the board.

ACTIVE   We **have marked** it on the board.

PASSIVE   It **was marked** on the board.

ACTIVE   We **marked** it on the board.

PASSIVE   It **will be marked** on the board for the class.

It **has been marked** on the board.

It **had been marked** on the board.

It **will have been marked** on the board.

Using Active and Passive Voices

Each of the two voices has its proper use in English.

Use the active voice whenever possible.

Sentences with active verbs are less wordy and more forceful than those with passive verbs. Compare, for example, the following sentences. Notice the different number of words each sentence needs to report the same information.

ACTIVE   Students **studied** an exam guide.

PASSIVE   An exam guide **was studied** by students.

Although you should aim to use the active voice in most of your writing, there will be times when you will need to use the passive voice.

Use the passive voice to emphasize the receiver of an action rather than the performer of an action.

In the following example, the receiver of the action is the subject *coach*. It is the *team* (the direct object) that is actually performing the action.

EMPHASIS   The coach **was supported** by the team.
ON RECEIVER

The passive voice should also be used when there is no performer of the action.

Use the passive voice to point out the receiver of an action when the performer is unknown or not named in the sentence.

PERFORMER   The new book **was written** sometime
UNKNOWN   last year.

See Practice 21.2J

PRACTICE 21.2I ▷ **Distinguishing Active and Passive Voice**

Read the sentences. Then, write *AV* if the underlined verb is in active voice or *PV* if the verb is in passive voice.

EXAMPLE   The injured player <u>was carried</u> off the field.

ANSWER   *PV*

1. A new delegate <u>was appointed</u> by the governor.

2. A meter maid <u>ticketed</u> the illegally parked car.

3. The principal <u>brought</u> the matter to our attention.

4. The halls of the building <u>had been swept</u> during the night.

5. The new city hall <u>was designed</u> by a local architect.

6. Undoubtedly, the audience <u>will be persuaded</u> by your speech.

7. Deer <u>have eaten</u> the bark on these trees.

8. The contract <u>had been signed</u> by both parties.

9. The chef <u>presented</u> an appetizing meal.

10. The fence <u>had been painted</u> white.

PRACTICE 21.2J ▷ **Revising to Use Active Voice**

Read the sentences. Then, rewrite each sentence that is in passive voice so that it is in active voice. If the sentence is already in active voice, write *active*.

EXAMPLE   The fallen tree has been removed by the landscaper.

ANSWER   *The landscaper removed the fallen tree.*

11. The clerk is wrapping the package.

12. After the performance, the tents were taken down by the circus crew.

13. The principal has not yet told the students about the early dismissal.

14. The dog was walked by Thalia.

15. The coaches are planning next year's schedules.

16. These flowers were arranged by the garden committee.

17. New computers have been purchased by the school.

18. Anne has given an excellent oral report.

19. My seat was taken by someone during intermission.

20. We have been assigned two chapters by Miss Romero.

SPEAKING APPLICATION

With a partner, choose a sentence from Practice 21.2I or 21.2J and say it aloud. If the sentence is in active voice, say it again in passive voice. If it is passive, change it to active. Your partner should do the same for another sentence.

WRITING APPLICATION

Write three sentences about a performance you have seen. Use only active voice.

Moods of Verbs

Verbs in English also use **mood** to describe the status of an action.

RULE **21.2.12**

> There are three moods for English verbs: the **indicative mood,** the **subjunctive mood**, and the **imperative mood.**

The **indicative mood** indicates, or states, something. It is also used to ask questions. The **subjunctive mood** describes a wish or a condition that may be contrary to fact.

INDICATIVE MOOD	SUBJUNCTIVE MOOD
Tim **is** on my team.	I wish Bill **were** on my team too.
Kate **has** a new DVD.	If Susan **had brought** the DVD over, we could have watched it together.
I **would** like to be captain of the team.	If I **were** captain of the hockey team, I would be fair to everyone.

The subjunctive mood can be used to describe situations that are unlikely to happen or not possible. It is often used in clauses that begin with *if* or *that*. In these cases, use the plural form of the verb.

EXAMPLES   If I **were** you, I would run to the store before the snow.
(I am not you, so the situation is not possible.)

John wished that he **were going** to the game this week.
(He is not going until next month, so the situation is not possible.)

The **imperative** mood states a request or command and always uses the present tense. A mild imperative is followed by a period; a strong imperative is followed by an exclamation point.

EXAMPLES   **Call** me when you get home.
Watch out!

Notice that the subject, *you*, is understood but omitted.

See Practice 21.2K
See Practice 21.2L

PRACTICE 21.2K ▷ **Identifying Moods of Verbs**

Read the sentences. Then, write *indicative, subjunctive,* or *imperative* for the mood of the underlined verb in each sentence.

EXAMPLE   If John <u>were</u> here now, what would he think?

ANSWER   *subjunctive*

1. <u>Tell</u> your mother where you are going.
2. Ben <u>went</u> to the soccer game.
3. <u>Listen</u> to this lovely music!
4. I wish I <u>had heard</u> about this earlier.
5. Wade <u>sat</u> next to me at the play.
6. If I <u>were</u> you, I'd study for the quiz.
7. Please <u>stay</u> here for a little while.
8. We <u>went</u> out for a pizza last night.
9. If Jaime <u>were</u> captain, he would be fair.
10. Katherine <u>has</u> an appointment with her orthodontist today.

PRACTICE 21.2L ▷ **Writing Sentences to Express Mood**

Read the verbs. Write sentences using the different moods of verbs as indicated below.

EXAMPLE   were (subjunctive)

ANSWER   *If I were a contestant, I'd win the prize.*

11. turn (imperative)
12. disturbs (indicative)
13. had finished (subjunctive)
14. wanted (indicative)
15. answer (imperative)
16. had been (subjunctive)
17. stop (imperative)
18. were (subjunctive)
19. delivers (indicative)
20. take (imperative)

SPEAKING APPLICATION

Use sentences 1, 5, and 6 as models, and make up sentences of your own using the same moods. Take turns saying your sentences to a partner, who will identify the mood of each sentence.

WRITING APPLICATION

Use sentences 2, 3, and 9 as models, and write three sentences in which you use the same mood as in the model sentences.

21.3 Troublesome Verbs

The following verbs cause problems for many speakers and writers of English. Some of the problems involve using the principal parts of certain verbs. Others involve learning to distinguish between the meanings of certain confusing pairs of verbs.

WRITING COACH

Online

@www.TXWritingCoach.com

Grammar Practice
Practice your grammar skills with Writing Coach Online.

Grammar Games
Test your knowledge of grammar in this fast-paced interactive video game.

(1) ain't   *Ain't* is not considered standard English. Avoid using it in speaking and in writing.

INCORRECT   He **ain't** the first to reach the mountain top.

CORRECT   He **isn't** the first to reach the mountain top.

(2) did, done   Remember that *done* is a past participle and can be used as a verb only with a helping verb such as *have* or *has*. Instead of using *done* without a helping verb, use *did*.

INCORRECT   I already **done** my English homework.

CORRECT   I already **did** my English homework.

I **have** already **done** my English homework.

See Practice 21.3A

(3) dragged, drug   *Drag* is a regular verb. Its principal parts are *drag, dragging, dragged,* and *dragged. Drug* is never correct as the past or past participle of *drag*.

INCORRECT   The dog **drug** the ball across the yard.

CORRECT   The dog **dragged** the ball across the yard.

(4) gone, went   *Gone* is the past participle of *go* and can be used as a verb only with a helping verb such as *have* or *has. Went* is the past of *go* and is never used with a helping verb.

INCORRECT   James and Alice **gone** to the beach.
We **should have went** along with them.

CORRECT   James and Alice **went** (or **have gone**) to the beach.
We **should have gone** along with them.

(5) *have, of* The words *have* and *of* often sound very similar. Be careful not to write *of* when you mean the helping verb *have* or its contraction *'ve*.

INCORRECT	We should **of** waited for Tim.
CORRECT	We should **have** (or **should've**) waited for Tim.

(6) *lay, lie* These verbs look and sound almost alike and have similar meanings. The first step in distinguishing between *lay* and *lie* is to memorize the principal parts of both verbs.

PRINCIPAL PARTS	lay	laying	laid	laid
	lie	lying	lay	lain

Lay usually means "to put (something) down" or "to place (something)." It is almost always followed by a direct object. *Lie* means "to rest in a reclining position" or "to be situated." This verb is used to show the position of a person, place, or thing. *Lie* is never followed by a direct object.

EXAMPLES	The teacher **lays** her chalk on the desk.
	The doctor must **lie** down to rest.

Pay special attention to the past tense of *lay* and *lie*. *Lay* is the past tense of *lie*. The past tense of *lay* is *laid*.

PRESENT TENSE OF *LAY*	I **lay** the mug on the counter.
PAST TENSE OF *LAY*	The painter **laid** his brush on the easel.
PAST TENSE OF *LIE*	The dog **lay** down in his bed.

See Practice 21.3B

(7) *leave, let* *Leave* means "to allow to remain." *Let* means "to permit." Do not reverse the meanings.

INCORRECT	**Leave** me to review the exam.
	Let the answer sheet alone.
CORRECT	**Let** me review the exam.
	Leave the answer sheet alone.

(8) _raise, rise_   _Raise_ can mean "to lift (something) upward," "to build (something)," or "to increase (something)." It is usually followed by a direct object. _Rise_ is not usually followed by a direct object. This verb means "to get up," "to go up," or "to be increased."

| EXAMPLES | **Raise** the blinds so we can see the sun. |
| | The runners must **rise** early to train. |

(9) _saw, seen_   _Seen_ is a past participle and can be used as a verb only with a helping verb such as _have_ or _has_.

| INCORRECT | I **seen** the painting last month. |
| CORRECT | I **saw** the painting last month. |

(10) _says, said_   A common mistake in reporting what someone said is to use _says_ (present tense) rather than _said_ (past tense).

| INCORRECT | The doctor **says** , "It is urgent." |
| CORRECT | The doctor **said** , "It is urgent." |

(11) _set, sit_   The first step in learning to distinguish between _set_ and _sit_ is to become thoroughly familiar with their principal parts.

| PRINCIPAL PARTS | set | setting | set | set |
| | sit | sitting | sat | sat |

Set means "to put (something) in a certain place or position." It is usually followed by a direct object. _Sit_ usually means "to be seated" or "to rest." It is usually not followed by a direct object.

EXAMPLES	She **set** the plate on the table.
	We **have set** the china safely in the cabinet.
	Tyler **sat** in the reclining chair.
	The eagle **has sat** on the branch since morning.

See Practice 21.3C
See Practice 21.3D

| PRACTICE 21.3A ▷ Using *Did* and *Done* | PRACTICE 21.3B ▷ Using *Lay* and *Lie* |

Read the sentences. Then, for each sentence, if *did* or *done* is used correctly, write *correct*. If it is not, write *incorrect*.

EXAMPLE	We done a group activity in class today.
ANSWER	*incorrect*

1. Jeremy has done an excellent job on his science fair project.

2. We did our work quietly in study hall.

3. I done everything you asked.

4. The artist did a sketch before he began to paint.

5. We done a good job.

6. Rolanda did her homework every day.

7. Charles has done his share of the work already.

8. That red car done a U-turn in the middle of the road.

9. Lynn did ten laps in the pool today.

10. Jane and Judie have already done the grocery shopping.

Read the sentences. Then, choose and write the correct form of the verb from the pair in parentheses.

EXAMPLE	The note (lay, lie) unread on the table.
ANSWER	*lay*

11. I would like to (lie, lay) down for a nap.

12. Those magazines have been (lying, laying) on the floor for a week.

13. Isabella was so tired that she (laid, lay) down right after dinner.

14. The cat has (laid, lain) in the sun all afternoon.

15. Mia (laid, lie) out two place settings at the table.

16. Natalie and Kelly (lay, lie) down in the snow and made snow angels.

17. The workers had (laid, lain) the foundation before starting on the wall.

18. (Lay, Lie) out all your notecards on your desk so you can rearrange them.

19. Earlier today, the children (laid, lay) the blocks in a circle.

20. Hal likes to (lie, lay) on the floor and read.

SPEAKING APPLICATION

With a partner, take turns using *did* and *done* in sentences.

WRITING APPLICATION

Write three sentences in which you correctly use different forms of *lay* and *lie*. You may use sentences from Practice 21.3B as models.

Troublesome Verbs

PRACTICE 21.3C ▸ Using *Set* and *Sit*

Read the sentences. Then, choose and write the correct form of the verb from the pair in parentheses.

EXAMPLE   Please (sit, set) your bags on the table.

ANSWER   *set*

1. Rebecca (set, sat) the money on her dresser.

2. We had (set, sat) in the waiting room for almost an hour.

3. Sasha (sat, set) all the chairs in rows.

4. Will you stay and (sit, set) with me for a while?

5. Ray (set, sat) his GPS device on the table.

6. Grandfather (set, sat) his feet on a stool.

7. You can read a book while you're (sitting, setting) on the train.

8. Please (set, sit) down over there.

9. When you put the cookies in the oven, (set, sit) the timer for 10 minutes.

10. Let's (sit, set) in the shade under those trees.

PRACTICE 21.3D ▸ Using Troublesome Verbs

Read the sentences. If the underlined verb is used correctly, write *correct*. If it is not, rewrite the sentence using the correct verb.

EXAMPLE   The girls have <u>went</u> for a walk.

ANSWER   *The girls have gone for a walk.*

11. <u>Let</u> your jacket on the bench while you mow the lawn.

12. Alicia <u>went</u> to basketball camp for a week.

13. I <u>seen</u> Rich at the baseball field yesterday.

14. We probably should <u>of</u> asked for directions.

15. In some yoga positions, you <u>raise</u> your arms above your head.

16. I saw Joey in the hall, and he <u>says</u>, "Help me make a spreadsheet."

17. Kelsey <u>dragged</u> the cursor down the menu to choose the file she wanted.

18. Wyatt <u>isn't</u> here yet.

19. <u>Let</u> the soup cool before you eat it.

20. The temperature <u>raised</u> 10 degrees in the last hour.

SPEAKING APPLICATION

With a partner, take turns describing a favorite activity. Use at least two of the troublesome verbs in Practices 21.3C and 21.3D. Your partner should confirm that you are using the verbs correctly.

WRITING APPLICATION

Write three sentences in which you use these verbs correctly: *raise, seen,* and *should have.*

USING PRONOUNS

Make your writing easy for readers to follow by using pronouns correctly.

WRITE GUY *Jeff Anderson, M.Ed.*

WHAT DO YOU NOTICE?

Focus on the pronouns as you zoom in on these sentences from the book *Angela's Ashes* by Frank McCourt.

MENTOR TEXT

> Patricia says she has two books by her bed. One is a poetry book and that's the one she loves.

Now, ask yourself the following questions:

- In the first sentence, which pronoun shows possession?
- What purpose does the pronoun *she* serve in these sentences?

In the first sentence, the pronoun *her* is possessive because it shows that the bed belongs to Patricia. The pronoun *she,* used in both sentences, refers to *Patricia.* Using *she* helps the author avoid repeating Patricia's name.

Grammar for Writers A writer can use pronouns to create sentences that flow smoothly. Keep an eye out for areas of your writing that could benefit from replacing nouns with pronouns.

Ms. Green is a great teacher. Ms. Green always knows the answer. Ms. Green plays the piano. Ms. Green ...

I get the idea. She can do anything.

22.1 Recognizing Cases of Personal Pronouns

In Chapter 13, you learned that personal pronouns can be arranged in three groups: first person, second person, and third person. Pronouns can also be grouped by their **cases**.

WRITING COACH

Online

@www.TXWritingCoach.com

Grammar Practice
Practice your grammar skills with Writing Coach Online.

Grammar Games
Test your knowledge of grammar in this fast-paced interactive video game.

RULE **22.1.1**

English has three cases: **nominative, objective,** and **possessive.**

The chart below shows the personal pronouns grouped according to the three cases. The case shows whether a pronoun is being used as a subject, an object, or a possessive.

THE THREE CASES OF PERSONAL PRONOUNS	
NOMINATIVE CASE	**USE IN A SENTENCE**
I, we, you, he, she, it, they	subject of a verb predicate pronoun
OBJECTIVE CASE	**USE IN A SENTENCE**
me, us, you, him, her, it, them	indirect object object of a preposition direct object
POSSESSIVE CASE	**USE IN A SENTENCE**
my, mine, our, ours, your, yours, his, her, hers, its, their, theirs	to show ownership

SUBJECT OF A VERB	**We** wanted badly to see the movie.
PREDICATE PRONOUN	The oldest is **she**.
INDIRECT OBJECT	Please give **me** the notebook.
OBJECT OF A PREPOSITION	Please show the diploma to **me**.
DIRECT OBJECT	A soccer ball hit **her** on the head.
TO SHOW OWNERSHIP	That is **my** sweater, not **yours**.

See Practice 22.1A
See Practice 22.1B

PRACTICE 22.1A Identifying Cases of Personal Pronouns

Read the sentences. Then, identify the case of each underlined personal pronoun by writing *nominative*, *objective*, or *possessive*.

EXAMPLE   <u>They</u> used to live on this street.

ANSWER   *nominative*

1. A reporter asked <u>him</u> some questions.
2. Do you know <u>her</u>?
3. <u>She</u> and <u>I</u> are best friends.
4. <u>We</u> try hard to be on time.
5. That sweatshirt on the floor is <u>his</u>.
6. Kerrie watched <u>them</u> through the window.
7. <u>He</u> and Glen are in the computer lab.
8. The manager thanked <u>us</u> for <u>our</u> help.
9. That seat is <u>yours</u>.
10. Kara brought <u>it</u> for <u>me</u>.

PRACTICE 22.1B Identifying Pronoun Cases and Uses

Read the sentences. Write the case of each underlined pronoun. Then, label it *subject of a verb*, *predicate pronoun*, *direct object*, *indirect object*, or *object of a preposition*.

EXAMPLE   <u>She</u> and Tonia led the march.

ANSWER   *nominative, subject of a verb*

11. Please come to the pool with <u>me</u>.
12. <u>They</u> held a bake sale to raise money.
13. Selena waved to <u>them</u> from the window.
14. <u>She</u> did not answer my message.
15. Can you give <u>us</u> some information?
16. The first person to sign up was <u>he</u>.
17. Jay dribbled the ball and passed <u>it</u> to Boyd.
18. <u>We</u> went to the airport in a taxi.
19. Can you lend <u>her</u> your bicycle helmet?
20. The winner was <u>I</u>.

SPEAKING APPLICATION

With a partner, take turns describing one of your friends and telling something about him or her. Your partner should listen for and name the personal pronouns you use.

WRITING APPLICATION

Write a short paragraph about an event in which you participated. Underline your pronouns and identify the case of each.

Practice   503

The Nominative Case

Personal pronouns in the nominative case have two uses.

> Use the **nominative** case for (1) the subject of a verb and (2) a predicate pronoun.

Note that predicate pronouns follow linking verbs. Pronouns that follow linking verbs should be in the nominative case. The linking verbs are highlighted in orange in the examples below.

SUBJECTS   **She** hopes to be in the chorus.

Excitedly, **they** prepared for the show.

PREDICATE PRONOUNS   It **was** **I** who suggested a hike.

The best players **are** **she** and Frank.

Checking for Errors in the Nominative Case
People seldom forget to use the nominative case for a pronoun that is used by itself as a subject. Problems sometimes arise, however, when the pronoun is part of a compound subject.

INCORRECT   Chris and **me** played chess.

CORRECT   Chris and **I** played chess.

To make sure you are using the correct case of the pronoun in a compound subject, isolate the pronoun and the verb in the sentence. *Me played chess* is obviously wrong, so the nominative case *I* should be used instead.

If the sentence is in verb–subject order, rearrange it into subject–verb order, and then isolate the pronoun and verb.

INCORRECT   Are you and **her** going to the park?

REARRANGED   You and **?** are going to the park.

CORRECT   Are you and **she** going to the park?

See Practice 22.1.C
See Practice 22.1.D

The Objective Case

Personal pronouns in the objective case have three uses.

> Use the **objective** case for (1) a direct object, (2) an indirect object, and (3) the object of a preposition.

DIRECT OBJECT	Joe's comment on the play upset **me**.
	The coach lectured **her**.
INDIRECT OBJECT	Tell **her** the plan.
	My friend gave **me** instructions to follow.
OBJECT OF PREPOSITION	Our class president voted for **him**.
	The bees swarmed around **me**.

Checking for Errors in the Objective Case

As with the nominative case, people seldom forget to use the objective case for a pronoun that is used by itself as a direct object, indirect object, or object of a preposition. Problems may arise, however, when the pronoun is part of a compound object.

INCORRECT	The bees swarmed around Patty and **I**.
CORRECT	The bees swarmed around Patty and **me**.

To make sure you are using the correct case of the pronoun in a compound object, use only the pronoun with the rest of the sentence. *The bees swarmed around I* is obviously wrong, so the objective case *me* should be used instead.

If the sentence is in verb–subject order, rearrange it into subject–verb order.

INCORRECT	Did my mother give Alice and **she** an apple?
REARRANGED	My mother gave Alice and **?** an apple.
CORRECT	Did my mother give Alice and **her** an apple?

See Practice 22.1E
See Practice 22.1F

The Possessive Case

Personal pronouns in the possessive case show ownership of one
sort or another.

> Use the **possessive** case of personal pronouns before nouns
> to show possession. In addition, certain personal pronouns
> may also be used by themselves to indicate possession.

BEFORE
NOUNS

The team won **its** race.

Chris held **my** baseball.

BY
THEMSELVES

Is this ruler **yours** or **mine**?

Hers was the best essay.

Checking for Errors in the Possessive Case

Personal pronouns in the possessive case are never written with
an apostrophe because they already show ownership. Keep this in
mind, especially with possessive pronouns that end in *s*.

INCORRECT

This table is **our's**, not **their's**.

CORRECT

This table is **ours**, not **theirs**.

When the pronoun *it* is followed by an apostrophe and an *s*, the
word becomes *it's*, which is a contraction of *it is*. The possessive
pronoun *its* does not have an apostrophe.

CONTRACTION

It's going to snow today.

POSSESSIVE
PRONOUN

The team loves **its** stadium.

To check if you need the contraction *it's* or the possessive
pronoun *its*, substitute *it is* and reread the sentence.

INCORRECT

My jacket has lost **it's** button.

CORRECT

My jacket has lost **its** button.

See Practice 22.1G
See Practice 22.1H

PRACTICE 22.1C > **Identifying Nominative Case Pronouns**

Read the sentences. Write the correct pronoun from the choices in parentheses. Then, label the pronoun *subject of a verb* or *predicate pronoun*.

EXAMPLE   (She, Her) and I went together.

ANSWER   *She — subject of a verb*

1. (They, Them) and the others left early.

2. Have you and (she, her) finished your project?

3. You and (me, I) should start a band.

4. (He, Him) and (me, I) both read the same book.

5. The second- and third-place winners were Ramon and (he, him).

6. The last person to leave was (she, her).

7. (She, Her) and Hugh offered to decorate the gym for the dance.

8. The Bulldogs and (we, us) made it to the finals.

9. The person who called you was (he, him).

10. The culprits in the case were (they, them).

PRACTICE 22.1D > **Writing Sentences Using Nominative Case Pronouns**

Read the sentences. Then, rewrite each sentence, filling in the blank with a nominative case pronoun. Label the pronoun *subject of a verb* or *predicate pronoun*.

EXAMPLE   It was _____ who called Kelly last night.

ANSWER   *It was I who called Kelly last night. — predicate pronoun*

11. Max and _____ are the stars of the play.

12. _____ kids want to see them perform.

13. She and _____ are going to the dress rehearsal.

14. The best character in the play is _____.

15. Do you and _____ want to come with us tonight?

16. It is _____ who has to take care of the younger kids.

17. _____ and Veronica are well behaved.

18. He and _____ also go to bed very early.

19. It was _____ who wanted me to eat dinner at their house.

20. You and _____ have much in common.

SPEAKING APPLICATION

Tell a partner about something you and a friend did. Your partner should identify two pronouns in the nominative case.

WRITING APPLICATION

Write three sentences about a type of physical exercise you enjoy. Include a nominative case pronoun in each sentence. Then, underline each nominative case pronoun.

Read the sentences. Write an objective case pronoun to complete each sentence. Then, label each pronoun *direct object*, *indirect object*, or *object of a preposition*.

EXAMPLE   I asked _____ for directions.

ANSWER   *him* — *direct object*

1. Wayne told _____ his latest joke.

2. Between you and _____, I'd rather not go.

3. You can probably find _____ on the tennis court.

4. Meredith made dinner for Julian and _____.

5. Go with Colleen and _____ to the show.

6. I have some good news for you and _____.

7. Give _____ a turn at bat.

8. A puppy followed _____ to the bus stop.

9. The coach gave Manny and _____ some extra pointers.

10. There was a disagreement between Traci and _____.

Read each objective case pronoun. Then, write a complete sentence using the objective case pronoun. The pronoun should function as a direct object, an indirect object, or an object of a preposition, as indicated in parentheses.

EXAMPLE   Her (object of a preposition)

ANSWER   Her mother spoke to *her* about her behavior.

11. me (direct object)

12. her (indirect object)

13. him and her (object of a preposition)

14. him and me (object of a preposition)

15. them (indirect object)

16. him (direct object)

17. them (direct object)

18. me (indirect object)

19. him (object of a preposition)

20. her and me (object of a preposition)

SPEAKING APPLICATION

With a partner, take turns describing a recent gathering with family or friends. Use at least three objective case pronouns. Your partner should identify and check for correct usage of the objective case pronouns in your statements.

WRITING APPLICATION

Write a brief paragraph about pets. Use at least three objective case pronouns in your paragraph. Then, underline the objective case pronouns and label them *direct object*, *indirect object*, or *object of a preposition*.

PRACTICE 22.1G > **Using Possessive Case Pronouns**

Read the sentences. Write the correct pronoun **from** the choices in parentheses.

EXAMPLE   That equipment is (their's, theirs).

ANSWER   *theirs*

1. (My, Mine) is the green bag.
2. Caleb's notebook is on the table with (your, yours).
3. The choice will be (hers, her's) alone.
4. My shirt is missing one of (its, it's) buttons.
5. If this is Gillian's sweater, then that one is (yours, your's).
6. (Ours, Our's) is the best float in the parade.
7. This car has had (its, it's) problems.
8. Dr. Swenson is (their, theirs) dentist.
9. The large sculpture on the corner table is (her, hers).
10. Here is (my, mine) mother now.

PRACTICE 22.1H > **Supplying Possessive Case Pronouns**

Read each possessive case pronoun. Then, write a complete sentence using the possessive case pronoun.

EXAMPLE   its

ANSWER   *The dog chewed on its toy bone.*

11. our
12. my
13. her
14. its
15. their
16. our
17. your
18. their
19. his
20. yours

SPEAKING APPLICATION

With a partner, take turns making statements about the ownership of items in your classroom. Your partner should identify the possessive case pronouns in your statements and make sure that they were used correctly.

WRITING APPLICATION

Write a brief paragraph about your most prized possession, such as a piece of jewelry or clothing, a book, or a photograph of someone special. Describe the object, using at least three possessive case pronouns.

Texas Test Warm-Up

DIRECTIONS

Read the introduction and the passage that follows. Then, answer the questions to show that you can use and understand the function of nominative, objective, and possessive case pronouns in reading and writing.

Chloe wrote this paragraph about her younger brothers, who are twins. Read the paragraph and think about the changes you would suggest as a peer editor. When you finish reading, answer the questions that follow.

Seeing Double

(1) My younger brothers are identical twins. (2) There names are Zach and Jack. (3) Them and I get along just fine. (4) However, sometimes they work together or alone to play tricks on people. (5) One day, Zach, wearing a blue shirt, asked our uncle for money. (6) He gave Zach a dollar, and Zach walked out. (7) Five minutes later, a boy in a red shirt came in and asked for money. (8) Assuming it was Jack, our uncle handed he a dollar as well. (9) Just then, the real Jack walked into the room. (10) "Hey, I must be seeing double, Zach, give us one dollar back!" exclaimed our uncle.

1 What change, if any, should be made in sentence 2?

  A Change *There* to **Their**

  B Change *are* to **were**

  C Change *and* to **or**

  D Make no change

2 What change, if any, should be made in sentence 3?

  F Change *I* to **me**

  G Change *Them* to **They**

  H Change *Them and I* to **Us all**

  J Make no change

3 What is the BEST way to revise sentence 8?

  A Assuming it was Jack, our uncle handed him a dollar as well.

  B Assuming it was Jack, our uncle handed Jack a dollar as well.

  C Assuming it was him, our uncle handed Jack a dollar as well.

  D Assuming it was him, our uncle handed him a dollar as well.

4 The meaning of sentence 10 can be clarified by changing the word *us* to —

  F my

  G our

  H him

  J me

Cases of *Who* and *Whom* The pronouns *who* and *whom* are often confused. *Who* is a nominative case pronoun, and *whom* is an objective case pronoun. *Who* and *whom* have two common uses in sentences: They can be used in questions or to begin subordinate clauses in complex sentences.

> **Use *who* for the subject of a verb. Use *whom* for (1) the direct object of a verb and (2) the object of a preposition.**

22.1.5 RULE

You will often find *who* used as the subject of a question. *Who* may also be used as the subject of a subordinate clause in a complex sentence.

SUBJECT OF A QUESTION	**Who** scored the most goals?
SUBJECT OF A SUBORDINATE CLAUSE	I admire the player **who** scored the most goals.

The following examples show *whom* used in questions.

DIRECT OBJECT	**Whom** did you see at the dinner?
OBJECT OF PREPOSITION	From **whom** is he getting a new puppy?

Questions that include *whom* are generally in inverted word order, with the verb appearing before the subject. If you reword the first example in subject–verb word order, you will see that *whom* is the direct object of the verb *did see: You did see whom?* In the second example, *whom* is the object of the preposition *from: He is getting the new puppy from whom?*

Subordinate clauses that begin with *whom* can be rearranged to show that the pronoun is a direct object.

EXAMPLE	The substitute teacher was not **whom** I expected.
REARRANGED SUBORDINATE CLAUSE	I expected **whom**.

See Practice 22.1I
See Practice 22.1J

PRACTICE 22.1I > **Using *Who* and *Whom***

Read the sentences. Write the pronoun in parentheses that correctly completes each sentence.

EXAMPLE   (Who, Whom) did you tell first?

ANSWER   *Whom*

1. We wanted to know (who, whom) was there.

2. (Whom, Who) taught you to play a guitar?

3. (Who, Whom) do you think we should nominate?

4. To (whom, who) should I address the letter?

5. (Who, Whom) could possibly want that old thing?

6. I do not know (whom, who) you're referring to.

7. The one (who, whom) gave me this locket is my Aunt Cecile.

8. I don't know (who, whom) I can ask for advice.

9. (Whom, Who) did you hear that from?

10. (Who, Whom) did he pick for the team?

PRACTICE 22.1J > **Revising to Correct *Who* and *Whom***

Read the sentences. Then, if a sentence uses *who* or *whom* incorrectly, rewrite the sentence with the correct pronoun form. If a sentence has no pronoun error, write *correct*.

EXAMPLE   Who did you vote for?

ANSWER   *Whom did you vote for?*

11. Do you know whom is the fastest runner on the team?

12. Portia goes to Dr. Shah, who is an orthodontist.

13. Whom did you sit with at the game?

14. This is my friend Madelyn, who I told you about.

15. Did you see who that was?

16. Who are you looking for?

17. Who forgot to put the lid back onto the jar?

18. Luther is someone who you can always count on.

19. Who is that gift for?

20. Please see whom is at the door.

SPEAKING APPLICATION

With a partner, take turns asking two questions: one beginning with *who* and one beginning with *whom*. Your partner should identify how these pronouns are used in your sentences.

WRITING APPLICATION

Use sentences 2 and 3 as models, and write two questions using *who* and *whom* correctly.

MAKING WORDS AGREE

Making subjects agree with verbs and pronouns agree with the words to which they refer will help your writing flow smoothly.

WRITE GUY *Jeff Anderson, M.Ed.*

WHAT DO YOU NOTICE?

Focus on agreement as you zoom in on these sentences from the essay "Rattlesnake Hunt" by Marjorie Kinnan Rawlings.

MENTOR TEXT

"It is a slow and heavy snake," Ross said. "It lies in wait on a small game trail and strikes the rat or rabbit passing by."

Now, ask yourself the following questions:

- What does the pronoun *it* refer to in these sentences?
- What are the verbs in the second sentence? How can you tell that these verbs agree with the subject?

The pronoun *it* refers to the noun *snake*. *It* agrees with *snake* because both are third person and singular. The second sentence includes a compound verb made of the verbs *lies* and *strikes*. The -*s* ending on both verbs shows they are singular and, therefore, agree with the singular subject *it*.

Grammar for Writers As writers craft sentences, they note whether their subjects are singular, plural, or compound, and choose verbs that match the subjects. As you write sentences, think about the number of each subject before choosing a verb that matches it.

My aunt say I never call her.

Hmm ... my aunt says that, too.

23.1 Subject-Verb Agreement

For a sentence to be correct, its subject and verb must match each other, or agree. Subject–verb agreement has one main rule.

WRITING COACH

Online
@www.TXWritingCoach.com

Grammar Practice
Practice your grammar skills with Writing Coach Online.

Grammar Games
Test your knowledge of grammar in this fast-paced interactive video game.

RULE 23.1.1

> **The subject and verb in a sentence must agree in number.**

In grammar, the concept of **number** is simple. The number of a word can be either **singular** or **plural.** A singular word indicates *one*. A plural word indicates *more than one.* In English, only nouns, pronouns, and verbs have number.

Singular and Plural Subjects

Most of the time, it is easy to tell whether a simple subject, such as a noun or pronoun, is singular or plural. That is because most nouns are made plural by adding *-s* or *-es* to their singular form.

EXAMPLES		
canyon	canyon**s**	
year	year**s**	
bus	bus**es**	
lunch	lunch**es**	

Some nouns form plurals in irregular ways.

EXAMPLES	
woman	**women**
ox	**oxen**
leaf	**leaves**
knife	**knives**

Pronouns also have different forms to indicate singular and plural. For example, the pronouns *I, he, she, it,* and *this* are singular. *We, they,* and *these* are plural. *You, who,* and *some* can be either singular or plural.

Singular and Plural Verbs

Like nouns, verbs have singular and plural forms. Problems involving number in verbs normally involve the third-person forms in the present tense (*she wants, they want*) and certain forms of the verb *be* (*I am, he is* or *was, we are* or *were*).

The chart shows all the basic forms of several different verbs in the present tense.

SINGULAR AND PLURAL VERBS IN THE PRESENT TENSE		
SINGULAR		PLURAL
First and Second Person	Third Person	First, Second, and Third Person
(I, you) send	(he, she, it) sends	(we, you, they) send
(I, you) go	(he, she, it) goes	(we, you, they) go
(I, you) look	(he, she, it) looks	(we, you, they) look
(I, you) dance	(he, she, it) dances	(we, you, they) dance
(I, you) visit	(he, she, it) visits	(we, you, they) visit
(I, you) work	(he, she, it) works	(we, you, they) work
(I, you) run	(he, she, it) runs	(we, you, they) run
(I, you) discuss	(he, she, it) discusses	(we, you, they) discuss
(I, you) vote	(he, she, it) votes	(we, you, they) vote
(I, you) choose	(he, she, it) chooses	(we, you, they) choose
(I, you) learn	(he, she, it) learns	(we, you, they) learn

Notice that the form of the verb changes only in the third-person singular, when an *-s* or *-es* is added to the verb. Unlike nouns, which usually become plural when *-s* or *-es* is added, verbs with *-s* or *-es* added to them are singular.

The helping verb *be* may also indicate whether a verb is singular or plural. The following chart shows only those forms of the verb *be* that are always singular.

FORMS OF THE HELPING VERB *BE* THAT ARE ALWAYS SINGULAR			
am	is	was	has been

Making Verbs Agree With Singular and Plural Subjects

To check subject–verb agreement, determine the number of the subject. Then, make sure the verb has the same number.

SINGULAR SUBJECT AND VERB

Jeff enjoys swimming.

She was at the park earlier today.

PLURAL SUBJECT AND VERB

They enjoy swimming.

Joggers were at the park earlier today.

RULE 23.1.2

> A prepositional phrase that comes between a subject and its verb does not affect subject–verb agreement.

Often, a subject is separated from its verb by a prepositional phrase. In these cases, it is important to remember that the object of a preposition is never the subject of a sentence.

INCORRECT   The **arrival** of the fire trucks **have caused** much excitement at the parade.

CORRECT   The **arrival** of the fire trucks **has caused** much excitement at the parade.

INCORRECT   The **cheers** of the crowd **was heard** outside.

CORRECT   The **cheers** of the crowd **were heard** outside.

In the first example, the subject is *arrival,* not *fire trucks* which is the object of the preposition *of.* Because *arrival* is singular, the singular verb *has caused* must be used. In the second example, the subject is the plural *cheers,* not *crowd*; therefore, it takes the plural verb *were heard.*

Focus on the TEKS

(19)(A)(v) Identify, use, and understand the function of prepositions and prepositional phrases and their influence on subject-verb agreement.

See TEKS Check

See TEKS Practice

See Practice 23.1A

See Practice 23.1B

 TEKS Check Show that you can identify, use, and understand the function of prepositions and prepositional phrases. Write three sentences that use prepositional phrases. Read the sentences to a partner. Have your partner confirm that the subject-verb agreement is correct.

TEKS Practice Show that you can identify, use, and understand the function of prepositions and prepositional phrases and their influence on subject-verb agreement by completing the following activities.

Subject-Verb Agreement

PRACTICE 23.1A **Making Subjects and Verbs Agree**

Read the sentences. Write the verb in parentheses that agrees with the subject. Then, label the subject *singular*, *plural*, or *both*. Be sure to think about prepositional phrases and their influence on subject-verb agreement.

EXAMPLE   Usually, ducks (swim, swims) in this pond.

ANSWER   *swim — plural*

1. You (was, were) early today!

2. Lisa (recognize, recognizes) the backpack as her own.

3. The computers in the lab (is, are) available for use.

4. Where (is, are) my keys?

5. One of these machines (is, are) not working.

6. My teeth (chatter, chatters) in the cold.

7. These boots (cost, costs) too much.

8. Some word problems in math (is, are) challenging.

9. There (is, are) twenty-five students in this room.

10. That bag of pretzels (is, are) not enough.

PRACTICE 23.1B **Revising for Subject-Verb Agreement**

Read the sentences. Then, if a sentence has an error in subject-verb agreement, rewrite the sentence correctly. Read your corrected sentences to your partner and have your partner confirm that the subject-verb agreement is correct. If a sentence has no error, write *correct*.

EXAMPLE   Craters on the moon is visible through telescopes.

ANSWER   *Craters on the moon are visible through telescopes.*

11. The pictures hanging on the wall is dusty.

12. Was you able to find what you needed?

13. Members of the committee are wearing nametags.

14. There's already five people waiting for the door to open.

15. The benches in the garden are wet.

16. The list of winners are posted on the bulletin board.

17. The decision of the judges is final.

18. Here is the groceries you wanted.

19. Where was the playoffs held?

20. One of the guides are able to help you.

SPEAKING APPLICATION

With a partner, take turns summarizing a story or book you read, using the present tense of the verbs and making sure the verbs agree with your subjects. Include a prepositional phrase in at least one of your sentences, and have your partner identify the phrase.

WRITING APPLICATION

Use sentences 4 and 5 as models, and write two sentences, making sure the verbs agree with the subjects. Be sure to think about prepositional phrases and their influence on subject-verb agreement.

Making Verbs Agree With Collective Nouns

Collective nouns—such as *assembly*, *audience*, *class*, *club*, and *committee*—name groups of people or things. Collective nouns are challenging as subjects because they can take either singular or plural verbs. The number of the verb depends on the meaning of the collective noun in the sentence.

RULE 23.1.3

Use a singular verb with a collective noun acting as a single unit. Use a plural verb when the individual members of the group are acting individually.

SINGULAR   The **committee votes** on the topics.

PLURAL   The **committee have split** the responsibilities.

SINGULAR   The dance **class plans** a recital.

PLURAL   The dance **class were pleased** with their individual performances.

SINGULAR   The garden **club grows** vegetables and flowers.

PLURAL   The garden **club have chosen** to plant their favorite vegetables and flowers.

SINGULAR   The scout **troop marches** on Main Street.

PLURAL   The scout **troop have prepared** different sandwiches for lunch.

SINGULAR   The **team cheers** after the game.

PLURAL   The **team scatter** across the playing field.

See Practice 23.1C
See Practice 23.1D

PRACTICE 23.1C > **Making Verbs Agree With Collective Nouns**

Read the sentences. Then, write the verb in parentheses that agrees with the subject.

EXAMPLE   The audience (is, are) waiting for the concert to begin.

ANSWER   *is*

1. The team (arrive, arrives) separately before the game.

2. Our family (try, tries) to eat dinner together every evening.

3. A flock of geese (land, lands) near the river every day.

4. The jury (find, finds) the defendant guilty.

5. The board of directors (don't, doesn't) always agree among themselves.

6. The computer club (discuss, discusses) new applications.

7. A group of older kids (hang, hangs) out in the pizza parlor.

8. The army (need, needs) more volunteers.

9. The flight crew (is, are) attentive to the passengers.

10. The choir (sing, sings) every Sunday.

PRACTICE 23.1D > **Revising for Agreement Between Verbs and Collective Nouns**

Read the sentences. Then, if a sentence has an error in subject-verb agreement, rewrite the sentence correctly. If a sentence has no error, write *correct*.

EXAMPLE   The orchestra give a free concert every year.

ANSWER   *The orchestra gives a free concert every year.*

11. The herd are waiting to be fed.

12. This bunch of radishes look wilted.

13. The navy sail around the world.

14. The faculty has a meeting at 2:30 P.M.

15. The band are rehearsing in separate rooms.

16. The crowd are eager for the candidate to appear.

17. At summer camp, the scout troop learns survival skills.

18. The staff at the fitness center are very helpful.

19. The committee don't always follow the agenda at meetings.

20. The cheerleading squad practices twice a week.

SPEAKING APPLICATION

With a partner, tell about the activities of a group you belong to or know about. Use at least two collective nouns, such as *group*, *team*, and *club*, as subjects in your sentences, and be sure your verbs agree.

WRITING APPLICATION

Write three sentences in the present tense, using these collective nouns as subjects: *crew*, *band*, and *crowd*.

Making Verbs Agree With Compound Subjects

A **compound subject** refers to two or more subjects that share a verb. Compound subjects are connected by conjunctions such as *and, or,* or *nor.*

EXAMPLES   The **museums** and **historical sites** in New York
            └─── compound subject ───┘
            City **attract** many visitors.
                 └ plural verb ┘

            Either **Jamal** or **Catherine** **knows** the way to the
                   └── compound subject ──┘   └ singular
            train station.   verb ┘

            Neither the **Statue of Liberty** nor **Ellis Island**
                        └──────── compound subject ────────┘
            disappoints tourists.
            └ singular
              verb ┘

A number of rules can help you choose the right verb to use with a compound subject.

Compound Subjects Joined by *And*

RULE 23.1.4

When a compound subject is connected by *and*, the verb that follows is usually plural.

EXAMPLE   **Dallas** and **Houston** **are** my favorite Texas cities.
           └─── compound subject ───┘ └ plural verb ┘

There is an exception to this rule: If the parts of a compound subject are thought of as one person or thing, the subject is singular and takes a singular verb.

EXAMPLES   **Bacon and eggs** **is** my favorite breakfast.
            └ compound subject ┘ └ singular
                                   verb ┘

            Cream and sugar **is** in the kitchen.
            └ compound subject ┘ └ singular
                                   verb ┘

Compound Subjects Joined by *Or* or *Nor*

> When two singular subjects are joined by *or* or *nor,* use a singular verb. When two plural subjects are joined by *or* or *nor,* use a plural verb.

23.1.5 RULE

SINGULAR   A **bus** or a **subway** **provides** good
                compound subject   singular
                              verb
            transportation to the city.

PLURAL   Neither **children** nor **adults** **like** to be told what
                       compound subject   plural verb
            to do.

In the first example, *or* joins two singular subjects. Although two vehicles make up the compound subject, the subject does not take a plural verb. Either a bus or a subway provides good transportation, not both of them.

> When a compound subject is made up of one singular and one plural subject joined by *or* or *nor,* the verb agrees with the subject closer to it.

23.1.6 RULE

EXAMPLES   Either the **monuments** or the **White House**
                    plural subject   singular subject
            is closed to visitors today.
            singular verb

            Either the **White House** or the **monuments**
                    singular subject   plural subject
            are closed to visitors today.
            plural verb

See Practice 23.1E

Agreement in Inverted Sentences

In most sentences, the subject comes before the verb. Sometimes, however, this order is turned around, or **inverted.** In other sentences, the helping verb comes before the subject even though the main verb follows the subject.

When a subject comes after the verb, the subject and verb still must agree with each other in number.

EXAMPLE   **Do** the historical **sites** in Philadelphia sound
            plural verb   plural subject
exciting to you?

Sentences Beginning With a Prepositional Phrase
In sentences that begin with a prepositional phrase, the object of the preposition may look like a subject, even though it is not.

EXAMPLE   Along the shore **were** many gray **seagulls**.
                            plural verb   plural subject

In this example, the plural verb *were* agrees with the plural subject *seagulls*. The singular noun *shore* is the object of the preposition *along*.

Sentences Beginning With *There* or *Here*
Sentences beginning with *there* or *here* are almost always in inverted word order.

EXAMPLES   There **were** several **books** about the economy.
                  plural verb   plural subject

            Here **is** the latest **book** about the economy.
            singular verb   singular subject

The contractions *there's* and *here's* both contain the singular verb *is*: *there is* and *here is.* Do not use these contractions as plural subjects.

INCORRECT   Here**'s** the **books** for the library.

CORRECT   Here **are** the **books** for the library.

Questions With Inverted Word Order
Many questions are also written in inverted word order.

EXAMPLE   Where **are** the **books** for the library?
                  plural verb   plural subject

See Practice 23.1F

PRACTICE 23.1E > Making Verbs Agree With Compound Subjects

Read the **sentences**. Then, write the verb in parentheses that agrees with the subject.

EXAMPLE   A book and an apple (is, are) lying on the table.

ANSWER   *are*

1. Either Dad or Mom (make, makes) breakfast every morning.

2. English and math (is, are) my favorite subjects.

3. Neither the baseball bats nor the gloves (was, were) put away.

4. Sarah or her sister (take, takes) the dog for a walk every day.

5. The book and papers (stay, stays) in the locker.

6. Neither the jacket nor the shoes (fit, fits) well.

7. Carrie, Gillian, or Hugh (write, writes) the blog each day.

8. Mrs. Carter and her daughters often (dress, dresses) alike.

9. The chairs and the table (has, have) not been moved in yet.

10. E-mail and text messaging (make, makes) communication almost instantaneous.

PRACTICE 23.1F > Revising for Agreement Between Verbs and Compound Subjects

Read the **sentences**. Then, if a sentence has an error in subject-verb agreement, rewrite the sentence correctly. If a sentence has no error, write *correct*.

EXAMPLE   Neither Billy nor John have arrived yet.

ANSWER   *Neither Billy nor John has arrived yet.*

11. Joe and Ted always comes early.

12. Either Jake or Sophia collects the papers today.

13. Jeff or the dog have tracked mud onto the floor.

14. Milk or lemon is used with tea.

15. Either my watch or that clock are fast.

16. In the center of the park is a playground and a basketball court.

17. Either Regina or Zoe own that scarf.

18. Neither the plumber nor the electrician is here.

19. Eva's positive outlook and her willingness to help wins her many friends.

20. That old barn and farmhouse seems deserted.

SPEAKING APPLICATION

With a **partner**, take turns discussing things in the **classroom**, using sentence 3 as a model. Your partner should check for subject-verb agreement in your sentences.

WRITING APPLICATION

Use sentences 17, 18, and 19 as models, and write three sentences with correct subject-verb agreement.

Verb Agreement With Indefinite Pronouns

Indefinite pronouns refer to people, places, or things in a general way.

23.1.8

> When an **indefinite pronoun** is the subject of a sentence, the verb must agree in number with the pronoun.

INDEFINITE PRONOUNS				
SINGULAR			PLURAL	SINGULAR OR PLURAL
anybody	everyone	nothing	both	all
anyone	everything	one	few	any
anything	much	other	many	more
each	neither	somebody	several	most
either	nobody	someone	others	none
everybody	no one	something		some

Indefinite Pronouns That Are Always Singular

Indefinite pronouns that are always singular take singular verbs. Do not be misled by a prepositional phrase that follows an indefinite pronoun. The singular verb agrees with the indefinite pronoun, not with the object of the preposition.

EXAMPLES

Each of the soccer team uniforms **is** red
singular subject   singular verb
and gold.

Either of the sweaters on the bed **is** warm.
singular subject   singular verb

Everyone in the theater **was** delighted
singular subject   singular verb
by the play.

Each of the boys **takes** guitar lessons.
singular subject   singular verb

Indefinite Pronouns That Are Always Plural
Indefinite pronouns that are always plural are used with plural verbs.

EXAMPLE **Both** of my sisters **are going** to the concert.
plural subject   plural verb

Many of my friends **are coming** to cheer for me at
plural subject   plural verb

my first track meet.

Several have started to research their reports.
plural subject   plural verb

Few are happy with the new uniforms.
plural subject plural verb

Indefinite Pronouns That May Be Either Singular or Plural
Many indefinite pronouns can take either a singular or a plural verb.

> **The number of the indefinite pronoun is the same as the number of its referent, or the noun to which it refers.**

23.1.9
RULE

The indefinite pronoun is singular if the referent is singular. If the referent is plural, the indefinite pronoun is plural.

SINGULAR **Some** of the **juice is** frozen.

PLURAL **Some** of the **oranges are** frozen, too.

In the examples above, *some* is singular when it refers to *juice*, but plural when it refers to *oranges*.

SINGULAR **All** of my **spaghetti is** gone.

PLURAL **All** of these **meatballs are** for you.

See Practice 23.1G
See Practice 23.1H

In these examples, *all* is singular when it refers to *spaghetti*, but plural when it refers to *meatballs*.

PRACTICE 23.1G Making Verbs Agree With Indefinite Pronouns

Read the sentences. Then, write the verb in parentheses that agrees with the subject.

EXAMPLE   Each of the students (was, were) eager to begin.

ANSWER   *was*

1. Nobody (want, wants) to take responsibility.

2. Some of these sandwiches (is, are) vegetarian.

3. Both of my sisters (sing, sings) in the chorus.

4. Everyone in the class (is, are) present today.

5. Anyone (is, are) able to solve that problem.

6. All of the computers (is, are) being used right now.

7. Many of the contestants (has, have) excellent qualifications.

8. If someone (answer, answers) the ad, let me know.

9. Most of the money (has, have) been spent.

10. Neither of the jobs (require, requires) much experience.

PRACTICE 23.1H Revising for Agreement Between Verbs and Indefinite Pronouns

Read the sentences. Then, if a sentence has an error in subject-verb agreement, rewrite the sentence correctly. If a sentence has no error, write *correct*.

EXAMPLE   Neither were willing to concede defeat.

ANSWER   *Neither was willing to concede defeat.*

11. Several of the batteries has to be replaced.

12. Nobody like to be on the losing side.

13. Either are a good title for your story.

14. Many of these used books are in good condition.

15. Some of these poems are pretty good.

16. All of the grapes has been eaten.

17. A few of my friends goes to a different school.

18. Most of the jewelry on display were quite expensive.

19. None of these games are much fun.

20. Any of your drawings are good enough to be exhibited.

SPEAKING APPLICATION

With a partner, tell about something in your class, using sentence 4 as a model. Your partner should listen for and confirm that your verb agrees with your subject.

WRITING APPLICATION

Use sentences 10, 13, and 19 as models, and write three sentences of your own with correct subject-verb agreement.

23.2 Agreement Between Pronouns and Antecedents

Find It / FIX IT

17
Grammar Game Plan

An **antecedent** is the word or words for which a pronoun stands. A pronoun's antecedent may be a noun, a group of words acting as a noun, or even another pronoun. As with subjects and verbs, pronouns should agree with their antecedents.

Making Personal Pronouns and Antecedents Agree

Person tells whether a pronoun refers to the person speaking (first person), the person spoken to (second person), or the person, place, or thing spoken about (third person). **Number** tells whether the pronoun is singular or plural. **Gender** tells whether a third-person-singular antecedent is masculine or feminine.

> **A personal pronoun must agree with its antecedent in person, number, and gender.**

23.2.1 RULE

EXAMPLE   I told **Betsy** to bring a sweater with **her**.

In this example, the pronoun *her* is third person and singular. It agrees with its feminine antecedent, *Betsy*.

Avoiding Shifts in Person
A personal pronoun must have the same person as its antecedent. Otherwise, the meaning of the sentence is unclear.

INCORRECT   The **drivers** know **we** must check the speed limit on local streets.
(Who must check the speed limit? *We* must.)

CORRECT   The **drivers** know **they** must check the speed limit on local streets.
(Who must check the speed limit? *The drivers* must.)

As you can see, a shift in the person of the personal pronoun can make it unclear who is going to check the speed limit.

Avoiding Problems With Number and Gender

Making pronouns and antecedents agree in number and gender can be difficult. Problems may arise when the antecedent is a collective noun, when the antecedent is a compound joined by *or* or *nor,* or when the gender of the antecedent is not known.

Making Pronouns Agree in Number With Collective Nouns
Collective nouns are challenging because they can take either singular or plural pronouns. The number of the pronoun depends on the meaning of the collective noun in the sentence.

RULE 23.2.2

> **Use a singular pronoun to refer to a collective noun that names a group that is acting as a single unit. Use a plural pronoun to refer to a collective noun when the members or parts of a group are acting individually.**

SINGULAR   The **class** **showed** **its** appreciation with applause.

PLURAL   The **class** **voted** for **their** favorite books.

In the first example above, the class is acting as a single unit when it applauds, so the singular pronoun, *its,* refers to *class.* In the second example, each member of the class is voting individually, so the plural pronoun, *their,* refers to *class.*

Making Pronouns Agree in Number With Compound Nouns

RULE 23.2.3

> **Use a singular personal pronoun to refer to two or more singular antecedents joined by *or* or *nor.* Use a plural pronoun with two or more singular antecedents joined by *and.***

Two or more singular antecedents joined by *or* or *nor* must have a singular pronoun, just as they must have a singular verb.

INCORRECT   **Andrew** or **Jeff** will take **their** basketball.

CORRECT   **Andrew** or **Jeff** will take **his** basketball.

CORRECT   **Andrew** and **Jeff** will take **their** basketballs.

Avoiding Problems With Gender

When the gender of a third-person-singular antecedent is not known, you can make the pronoun agree with its antecedent in one of three ways:

(1) Use *he or she, him or her,* or *his or hers.*

(2) Rewrite the sentence so that the antecedent and pronoun are both plural.

(3) Rewrite the sentence to eliminate the pronoun.

Traditionally, the masculine pronouns *he* and *his* have been used to stand for both males and females. Today, using *he or she* and *him or her* is preferred. If any of these corrections seem awkward to you, rewrite the sentence.

Making Personal Pronouns and Indefinite Pronouns Agree

Indefinite pronouns are words such as *each, everybody, either,* and *one.* Pay special attention to the number of a personal pronoun when the antecedent is a singular indefinite pronoun.

> **Use a singular personal pronoun when its antecedent is a singular indefinite pronoun.**

23.2.4 RULE

Do not be misled by a prepositional phrase that follows an indefinite pronoun. The personal pronoun agrees with the indefinite pronoun, not with the object of the preposition.

Focus on the TEKS

(19)(C) Use a variety of complete sentences (e.g., *simple, compound, complex*) that include correctly identified antecedents.

See TEKS Check

See TEKS Practice

See Practice 23.2A

See Practice 23.2B

See Practice 23.2C

See Practice 23.2D

INCORRECT   **One** of the dogs has lost **their** bone.

CORRECT   **One** of the dogs has lost **its** bone.

INCORRECT   **Everyone** in the history class wanted to tell about **their** idea.

CORRECT   **Everyone** in the history class wanted to tell about **his or her** idea.

CORRECT   **All** of the students in the history class told about **their** ideas.

PRACTICE 23.2A > **Using Correct Antecedents**

Read these simple, compound, and complex sentences. Then, rewrite the sentences to correct pronoun-antecedent agreement. Circle the pronoun and underline the antecedent.

EXAMPLE   When we went to the beach, she lent me our sunscreen.

ANSWER   *When we went to the beach, she lent me her sunscreen.*

1. Alex lent us their car that was about to run out of gas.

2. Erin wanted us to meet their friend, who is about to enter our class.

3. After the movie ended, everyone told their impressions.

4. No one wanted to give up their Saturday, so we rescheduled the meeting.

5. The kitten curled up their little body and slept in front of the fire.

6. I lost its CD, so I had to buy her a replacement.

7. Since it stopped raining, we can ride its bikes.

8. Laslo offered to help, but the team preferred to work on their own.

9. Did you forget to bring me our scarf?

10. The students know they must study, and they form our own study groups.

PRACTICE 23.2B > **Writing Sentences With Pronoun-Antecedent Agreement**

Write complete sentences with pronoun-antecedent agreement. Use each subject provided and add the correct pronoun. Write the type of sentence that is indicated in parentheses.

EXAMPLE   Everyone (compound sentence)

ANSWER   *Everyone offered his or her suggestion, and we decided to vote.*

11. The teachers (simple sentence)

12. Each (simple sentence)

13. The musicians (compound sentence)

14. Billy (complex sentence)

15. Everyone (compound sentence)

16. The dog (complex sentence)

17. One (complex sentence)

18. Lisa and Margot (complex sentence)

19. All (compound sentence)

20. The orchestra (simple sentence)

SPEAKING APPLICATION

Use the sentences on this page as models. With a partner, make up one simple, one compound, and one complex sentence. Your partner should check that your pronouns and antecedents agree and then tell you a sentence.

WRITING APPLICATION

Write one simple, one compound, and one complex sentence about your favorite type of music. Read your sentences aloud to a partner. Work with your partner to correct any sentences that have incorrectly identified antecedents.

TEKS Practice Show that you can use a variety of complete sentences (e.g., simple, compound, complex) that include correctly identified antecedents by completing the following activities.

PRACTICE 23.2C ▷ **Revising for Pronoun-Antecedent Agreement**

Read the sentences. Rewrite each sentence choosing the correct pronoun in parentheses. Circle the pronoun and underline the antecedent.

EXAMPLE   Neither Janie nor Maria has returned (their, her) books to the library.

ANSWER   *Neither Janie nor Maria has returned (her) books to the library.*

1. Each boy paid for (their, his) own lunch, and each boy bought a sandwich.

2. If a person asks for directions, please try to help (them, him or her).

3. Everyone should fasten (their, his or her) seat belt.

4. All students choose (their, our) classes.

5. Has Marco or Dina given (their, his or her) oral report yet?

6. If there is time, some of the students may read (their, our) poems aloud.

7. Both Andrew and Arnold were wearing (their, his) new team caps.

8. None of these pencils have (their, his) erasers, and all of them are red.

9. Everyone should cast (his or her, their) vote.

10. Each student has (his or her, their) own goals.

PRACTICE 23.2D ▷ **Writing Sentences With Pronoun-Antecedent Agreement**

Write complete sentences with pronoun-antecedent agreement. Use each subject provided and add the correct pronoun. Write the type of sentence that is indicated in parentheses.

EXAMPLE   The class (complex sentence)

ANSWER   *While the class wrote their reports, the teacher graded test papers.*

11. The group (simple sentence)

12. All (compound sentence)

13. Each (complex sentence)

14. Esther or Briana (simple sentence)

15. Tanya and Victor (complex sentence)

16. Everyone (complex sentence)

17. The community (simple sentence)

18. The voters (compound sentence)

19. The police department (complex sentence)

20. The police officers (simple sentence)

SPEAKING APPLICATION

With a partner, take turns discussing advantages and disadvantages of pets. Using correct pronoun-antecedent agreement, speak in a variety of simple, compound, and complex sentences. Your partner should listen for pronoun-antecedent agreement.

WRITING APPLICATION

Write one simple, one compound, and one complex sentence about a person or group you admire. Be sure to use correct pronoun-antecedent agreement. Have a partner read your sentences aloud and check for agreement.

Focus on the TEKS

(19)(C) Use a variety of complete sentences (e.g., simple, compound, complex) that include correctly identified antecedents.

 # Texas Test Warm-Up

DIRECTIONS
Read the introduction and the passage that follows. Then, answer the questions to show that you can use a variety of complete sentences (e.g., simple, compound, complex) that include correctly identified antecedents in reading and writing.

Mario wrote this paragraph about his favorite teacher. Read the paragraph and think about the changes you would suggest as a peer editor. When you finish reading, answer the questions that follow.

Teacher of the Year

(1) This year, the school will vote for their Teacher of the Year. (2) Everyone in the school is allowed to give their opinion. (3) Most of us believe that Mr. Fernandez, who teaches Spanish and Latin, is the best because he is patient and fun. (4) For example, when the new words in a chapter is hard, Mr. Fernandez draws pictures to help us remember it. (5) Those strategies really work, and they make learning fun. (6) We hope Mr. Fernandez wins the award. (7) Our class agrees that Mr. Fernandez is its Teacher of the Year.

---

1 What change, if any, should be made in sentence 1?

  A Change *their* to **his or her**

  B Change *their* to **its**

  C Change *their* to **your**

  D Make no change

2 What change, if any, should be made in sentence 2?

  F Change *their* to **his or her**

  G Change *their* to **its**

  H Change *their* to **your**

  J Make no change

3 What is the BEST way to revise sentence 4?

  A For example, when the new words in a chapter are hard, Mr. Fernandez draws pictures to help us remember it.

  B For example, when the new words in a chapter is hard, Mr. Fernandez draws pictures to help us remember them.

  C For example, when the new words in a chapter are hard, Mr. Fernandez draws pictures to help us remember them.

  D For example, when the new words in a chapter is hard, Mr. Fernandez draws a picture to help us remember him.

4 The meaning of sentence 7 can be clarified by changing the word *its* to —

  F his or her

  G their

  H our

  J your

USING MODIFIERS

Using adjectives and adverbs to make comparisons will help you create strong images in your writing.

WRITE GUY *Jeff Anderson, M.Ed.*

WHAT DO YOU NOTICE?

Search for modifiers as you zoom in on these sentences from the story "Ribbons" by Laurence Yep.

MENTOR TEXT

> Suddenly I felt as if there were an invisible ribbon binding us, tougher than silk and satin, stronger even than steel; and it joined her to Mom and Mom to me.

Now, ask yourself the following questions:

- Which noun does the adjective *invisible* modify?
- Why does the author add the ending *-er* to the words *tough* and *strong*?

The adjective *invisible* modifies the noun *ribbon*. The author uses the ending *-er* to make the comparative form of the adjectives *tough* and *strong*. *Tougher* compares the ribbon to silk and then to satin, and *stronger* compares the ribbon to steel.

Grammar for Writers Writers use the forms of comparison to create more precise descriptions. Use the different forms of adjectives to paint vivid images for readers.

This is the longest quiz I've ever taken.

Wait until you see tomorrow's quiz! It's even longer.

24.1 Comparisons Using Adjectives and Adverbs

You may recall that adjectives and adverbs are **modifiers**. Adjectives can modify nouns or pronouns. Adverbs can modify verbs, adjectives, or other adverbs. You can use modifiers to make comparisons.

WRITING COACH

Online

@www.TXWritingCoach.com

Grammar Practice

Practice your grammar skills with Writing Coach Online.

Grammar Games

Test your knowledge of grammar in this fast-paced interactive video game.

Three Forms of Comparison

Modifiers change their form when they show comparison. These different forms are called **forms,** or **degrees, of comparison.**

RULE 24.1.1

> Most adjectives and adverbs have three forms, or degrees, of comparison: **positive, comparative,** and **superlative.**

The **positive degree** is used when no comparison is being made. This is the form of a word that is listed in a dictionary. The **comparative degree** is used when two items are being compared. The **superlative degree** is used when three or more items are being compared. When the superlative degree is used, the article *the* is often added.

DEGREE	ADJECTIVE	ADVERB
Positive	The family moved into a large home.	Tom swam fast.
Comparative	Soon, they will need a larger home.	Tom swam faster than Joe.
Superlative	The family is living in the largest home on the street.	Of the three swimmers, Tom is the fastest.

Like verbs, adjectives and adverbs change forms in different ways. Some adjectives and adverbs change in regular ways, or according to predictable patterns. As you can see in the chart above, *large* and *fast* form their comparative and superlative degrees regularly, by adding *-er* and *-est* to their positive form.

Regular Modifiers With One or Two Syllables

Most modifiers are **regular**—their degrees of comparison are formed in predictable ways.

> **Use *-er* or *more* to form the comparative degree and use *-est* or *most* to form the superlative degree of most one- and two-syllable modifiers.**

COMPARATIVE AND SUPERLATIVE DEGREES FORMED WITH *-ER* AND *-EST*		
POSITIVE	COMPARATIVE	SUPERLATIVE
deep	deeper	deepest
fast	faster	fastest
friendly	friendlier	friendliest
narrow	narrower	narrowest
sunny	sunnier	sunniest

Use *more* to form a modifier's comparative degree when adding *-er* sounds awkward. Use *most* to form a modifier's superlative degree when adding *-est* sounds awkward.

COMPARATIVE AND SUPERLATIVE DEGREES FORMED WITH *MORE* AND *MOST*		
POSITIVE	COMPARATIVE	SUPERLATIVE
careful	more careful	most careful
complete	more complete	most complete
handsome	more handsome	most handsome
often	more often	most often
quietly	more quietly	most quietly

More and *most* should not be used when the result sounds awkward, however. If you are not sure which form to use, check a dictionary. Most dictionaries list modifiers formed with *-er* and *-est*.

See Practice 24.1A

Regular Modifiers With Three or More Syllables

Modifiers for words with three or more syllables follow the same rules.

RULE 24.1.3 **Use *more* and *most* to form the comparative and superlative degrees of all modifiers of three or more syllables. Do not use *-er* or *-est* with modifiers of more than two syllables.**

DEGREES OF MODIFIERS WITH THREE OR MORE SYLLABLES		
POSTIVE	COMPARATIVE	SUPERLATIVE
expensive	more expensive	most expensive
flexible	more flexible	most flexible

Adverbs Ending in *-ly*

To modify most adverbs ending in *-ly*, use *more* or *most*.

RULE 24.1.4 **Use *more* to form the comparative degree and *most* to form the superlative degree of most adverbs ending in *-ly*.**

EXAMPLES   slowly, more slowly, most slowly

quietly, more quietly, most quietly

Using *Less* and *Least*

Less and *least* can show decreasing comparisons.

RULE 24.1.5 **Use *less* with a modifier to form the decreasing comparative degree and *least* to form the decreasing superlative degree.**

EXAMPLES   friendly, less friendly, least friendly

quickly, less quickly, least quickly

See Practice 24.1B

PRACTICE 24.1A ▷ **Forming Comparatives and Superlatives of One- and Two-Syllable Modifiers**

Read the modifiers. **Write the** comparative and **superlative** forms of each modifier.

EXAMPLE   quiet

ANSWER   *quieter, quietest*

1. slim

2. rich

3. happy

4. shy

5. helpful

6. soon

7. polite

8. late

9. evenly

10. dirty

PRACTICE 24.1B ▷ **Using Forms of Modifiers**

Read the sentences. Then, write each **sentence,** using the form of the modifier in parentheses.

EXAMPLE   Today is the ____ day of the year! (*hot*, superlative)

ANSWER   *Today is the hottest day of the year!*

11. Damian's ____ brother is starting college in the fall. (*old*, superlative)

12. I thought this book was ____ than the other one I read. (*funny*, comparative)

13. Celia is the ____ of the two skaters. (*graceful*, comparative)

14. Curtis felt ____ after his snack than before. (*energetic*, comparative)

15. Morgan is the ____ reader in our class. (*fast*, superlative)

16. Of all the speakers, Kara gave the ____ presentation. (*thorough*, superlative)

17. The play was ____ than we had expected. (*exciting*, comparative)

18. The sidewalk is ____ on this side of the street. (*safe*, comparative)

19. January and February are usually the ____ months. (*cold*, superlative)

20. This cereal is ____ than I like. (*sweet*, comparative)

SPEAKING APPLICATION

Tell a partner **about a trait** or quality of several people **you know.** Use a comparative **and a** superlative **form of an** adjective in this structure: Jack is **taller than Kim. Dane is the** tallest of all **my friends.**

WRITING APPLICATION

Write a paragraph comparing different versions of a game or song or several episodes of a television program. Use at least one comparative form and one superlative form of each modifier.

Irregular Adjectives and Adverbs

A few adjectives and adverbs are irregular.

Memorize the comparative and superlative forms of adjectives and adverbs that have irregular spellings.

The chart lists the most common irregular modifiers.

DEGREES OF IRREGULAR ADJECTIVES AND ADVERBS		
POSITIVE	COMPARATIVE	SUPERLATIVE
bad (adjective)	worse	worst
badly (adverb)	worse	worst
far (distance)	farther	farthest
far (extent)	further	furthest
good (adjective)	better	best
well (adverb)	better	best
many	more	most
much	more	most

When you are unsure about how a modifier forms its degrees of comparison, check a dictionary.

See Practice 24.1C

Using Comparative and Superlative Degrees

Keep these rules in mind when you use the comparative and superlative degrees.

Use the comparative degree to compare *two* people, places, or things. Use the superlative degree to compare *three or more* people, places, or things.

Usually, you do not need to mention specific numbers when you are making a comparison. Other words in the sentence should help make the meaning clear whether you are comparing two items or three or more items.

EXAMPLES   The coach felt **better** once all the
swimmers were in the locker room on time.

The swim team completed the practice session in
its **best** time this week.

Pay particular attention to the modifiers you use when you are
comparing just two items. Do not use the superlative degree with
fewer than three items.

INCORRECT   Of their two relay races, that one was the **best**.

CORRECT   Of their two relay races, that one was **better**.

INCORRECT   Mark's car was the **fastest** of the two cars.

CORRECT   Mark's car was the **faster** of the two cars.

> Do not make **double comparisons.** Do not use both -*er* and
> *more* to form the comparative degree or both -*est* and *most* to
> form the superlative degree. Also, be sure not to use -*er, more,*
> and *most* with an irregular modifier.

24.1.8 RULE

INCORRECT   She read the story the **most fastest**.

CORRECT   She read the story the **fastest**.

INCORRECT   The snowstorm was **more worse** than any they
had seen in years.

CORRECT   The snowstorm was **worse** than any they had
seen in years.

See Practice 24.1D

PRACTICE 24.1C Forming Comparatives and Superlatives of Irregular Adjectives and Adverbs

Read the modifiers. Write the comparative and superlative forms of each modifier.

EXAMPLE   well (adverb)

ANSWER   *better, best*

1. far (extent)

2. badly (adverb)

3. much

4. bad (adjective)

5. far (distance)

6. good (adjective)

7. many

PRACTICE 24.1D Using Comparatives and Superlatives of Irregular Adjectives and Adverbs

Read the sentences. Then, write each sentence, using the form of the modifier in parentheses.

EXAMPLE   That was the _____ meal I have ever eaten. (*bad*, superlative)

ANSWER   *That was the worst meal I have ever eaten.*

8. This book is _____ than the author's previous one. (*good*, comparative)

9. This is the _____ fun I have had all week! (*much*, superlative)

10. Peter and Matthew had to travel _____ to get here. (*far*, superlative)

11. The storm was _____ than expected. (*bad*, comparative)

12. I have no _____ interest in this subject. (*far*, comparative)

13. Quentin usually does _____ on tests than I do. (*well*, comparative)

14. Who is the _____ artist in the class? (*good*, superlative)

15. Marcus has _____ songs on his playlist than Nelson does. (*many*, comparative)

16. Are you feeling _____ today? (*well*, comparative)

17. The comic performed _____ than the singer. (*good*, comparative)

SPEAKING APPLICATION

Tell a partner about an event. You may exaggerate the details. Use comparative and superlative forms of any of the modifiers above.

WRITING APPLICATION

Write a short paragraph comparing several versions or brands of an item. Use at least one comparative form and one superlative form.

Making Logical Comparisons

In most situations, you will have no problem forming the degrees of modifiers and using them correctly in sentences. Sometimes, however, you may find that the way you have phrased a sentence makes your comparison unclear. You will then need to think about the words you have chosen and revise your sentence, making sure that your comparison is logical.

> **When you make a comparison, be sure you are comparing things that have clear similarities.**

Balanced Comparisons

Most comparisons make a statement or ask a question about the way in which similar things are either alike or different.

EXAMPLE   Is the **Atlantic Ocean** **deeper** than the **Pacific Ocean**?
(Both bodies of water have depths that can be measured and compared.)

Because the sentence compares depth to depth, the comparison is balanced. Problems can occur, however, when a sentence compares dissimilar things. For example, it would be illogical to compare the depth of one ocean to the shape of another ocean. Depth and shape are not similar things and cannot be compared meaningfully.

ILLOGICAL   The stories in my book are longer than your book.
(*Stories* and *book* cannot be logically compared.)

LOGICAL   The stories in my book are longer than the stories in your book.
(Two sets of stories can be logically compared.)

> **Make sure that your sentences compare only similar items.**

An unbalanced comparison is usually the result of carelessness. The writer may have simply left something out. Read the following incorrect sentences carefully.

INCORRECT **Planting grass** is **easier** than a **garden** .

The **number of inlets** on the East Coast is **larger** than the **West Coast** .

In the first sentence, planting grass is mistakenly compared to a garden. In the second sentence, the number of inlets are compared to the West Coast. Both sentences can easily be corrected to make the comparisons balanced.

CORRECT **Planting grass** is **easier** than **planting a garden** .

The **number of inlets** on the East Coast is **larger** than the **number** on the West Coast .

See Practice 24.1E

Other and *Else* in Comparisons

Another common error in writing comparisons is to compare something to itself.

RULE 24.1.11

> When comparing one of a group to the rest of the group, make sure your sentence contains the word *other* or *else.*

Adding *other* or *else* can make a comparison clear. For example, in the second sentence below, because *Edward* is himself a student, he cannot logically be compared to *all students*. He must be compared to *all other students*.

PROBLEM SENTENCES	CORRECTED SENTENCES
At the track meet, my brother sprinted to the finish line before anyone.	At the track meet, my brother sprinted to the finish line before anyone else.
Edward collected more kinds of shells than any student did.	Edward collected more kinds of shells than any other student did.

See Practice 24.1F

PRACTICE 24.1E **Making Balanced Comparisons**

Read the sentences. Rewrite each sentence, correcting the unbalanced comparison.

EXAMPLE   My grade on the second test was better than the first.

ANSWER   *My grade on the second test was better than my grade on the first.*

1. The information on this Web site is more detailed than that one.
2. Ben's scoring record is better than Jason.
3. I like the details in this painting better than Vanessa's.
4. The weather here is as cold as Alaska.
5. There are fewer berries in my basket than yours.
6. The service at Mario's Restaurant is better than Lucky's.
7. I think the articles in this magazine are more interesting than that magazine.
8. Josie's dog is not as obedient as Ingrid.
9. Eddie's video game has better features than Manny.
10. The toddler got more food on the floor than his mouth.

PRACTICE 24.1F **Using *Other* and *Else* to Make Comparisons**

Read the sentences. Rewrite each sentence, adding *other* or *else* to make the comparisons logical.

EXAMPLE   Gabby is faster than anyone on the team.

ANSWER   *Gabby is faster than anyone else on the team.*

11. Dion plays his drum louder than anyone in the band.
12. Jan's outfit is more colorful than anyone's.
13. Tom uses better strategy than any player.
14. Our school has a better debate team than any school in the league.
15. Greg sings better than anyone in the group.
16. Joanne helps out as much as anyone in her family.
17. Maddie's argument is more logical than anyone's.
18. That movie was more exciting than any I have seen lately.
19. Ollie gave a better demonstration than anyone.
20. Alison was more tired than anyone in the group after the long practice.

SPEAKING APPLICATION

With a partner, use your corrected sentence 1 as a model, and make a logical comparison between two items. Your partner should check that your comparison is correct.

WRITING APPLICATION

Use sentences 12, 13, and 14 as models, and write three new sentences making logical comparisons.

24.2 Troublesome Adjectives and Adverbs

The common adjectives and adverbs listed below often cause problems in both speaking and writing.

WRITING COACH

Online

@www.TXWritingCoach.com

Grammar Practice
Practice your grammar skills with Writing Coach Online.

Grammar Games
Test your knowledge of grammar in this fast-paced interactive video game.

(1) bad and badly *Bad* is an adjective. Use it after linking verbs, such as *are, appear, feel, look,* and *sound. Badly* is an adverb. Use it after action verbs, such as *act, behave, do,* and *perform.*

INCORRECT	Marco looked **badly** after the game.
CORRECT	Marco looked **bad** after the game.

INCORRECT	My sister did **bad** on the test.
CORRECT	My sister did **badly** on the test.

(2) good and well *Good* is an adjective. *Well* can be either an adjective or an adverb, depending on its meaning. A common mistake is the use of *good* after an action verb. Use the adverb *well* instead.

INCORRECT	The puppy behaved **good** all day.
	The book is **well**.

CORRECT	The puppy behaved **well** all day.
	The book is **good**.

As adjectives, *good* and *well* have slightly different meanings, which are often confused. *Well* usually refers simply to health.

EXAMPLES	Charlie felt **good** after hockey practice.
	The spaghetti smells **good**.
	That kitten is not **well**.

(3) *fewer and less* Use the adjective *fewer* to answer the question, "How many?" Use the adjective *less* to answer the question, "How much?"

HOW MANY	**fewer** dollars	**fewer** children
HOW MUCH	**less** money	**less** water

(4) *just* When used as an adverb, *just* often means "no more than." When *just* has this meaning, place it right before the word it logically modifies.

INCORRECT	Does he **just** want **one bottle of water**?
CORRECT	Does he want **just** **one bottle of water**?

(5) *only* The position of *only* in a sentence sometimes affects the sentence's entire meaning. Consider the meaning of these sentences.

EXAMPLES

Only he went to the baseball game.
(Nobody else went to the game.)

He **only** went to the baseball game.
(He did nothing else except go to the game.)

He went **only** to the baseball game.
(He went to the baseball game and nowhere else.)

Mistakes involving *only* usually occur when its placement in a sentence makes the meaning unclear.

UNCLEAR

Only follow directions from me.

BETTER

Follow directions **only** from me.
(not from anyone else)

See Practice 24.2A
See Practice 24.2B
See Practice 24.2C
See Practice 24.2D

Follow **only** directions from me.
(nothing but directions)

Troublesome Adjectives and Adverbs

PRACTICE 24.2A ▷ Using *Bad* and *Badly*, *Good* and *Well*

Read the sentences. Write the word in parentheses that correctly completes each sentence.

EXAMPLE My little brother behaves (bad, badly) when he is upset.

ANSWER *badly*

1. Marissa is a (good, well) swimmer.

2. Lee's new job is working out (good, well).

3. Unfortunately, the repair work was done (bad, badly).

4. Casey did (good, well) on his project.

5. This old car is running (bad, badly).

6. Charlotte looks (good, well) in her prom dress.

7. Walt looked (bad, badly) after the race.

8. The weather is looking (good, well) for the picnic.

9. Rosemary is feeling (bad, badly) today.

10. It seemed like a (good, well) idea, but it did not turn out (good, well).

PRACTICE 24.2B ▷ Revising for Troublesome Modifiers

Read the sentences. Rewrite the sentences that contain errors in the use of modifiers. If a sentence has no error, write *correct*.

EXAMPLE Jorge feels well about his decision.

ANSWER *Jorge feels good about his decision.*

11. The patient is feeling good today.

12. The plants looked badly because they had not been watered.

13. Chloe felt bad about her mistake.

14. We all look good in those pictures.

15. Nicole and Arianna danced good in the show.

16. Olivia and Sue work well together.

17. That flutist plays good.

18. Because the event was badly planned, it was not successful.

19. Joshua draws really good.

20. Rachel's intentions were good, but she did not follow through.

SPEAKING APPLICATION

Tell a partner two sentences using *bad* and *badly*. Your partner should say two sentences using *good* and *well*.

WRITING APPLICATION

Write a short paragraph evaluating a movie or television show you have recently seen. Use *bad*, *badly*, *good*, and *well* to describe the plot, the characters, or any other details of the movie or show.

PRACTICE 24.2C > **Writing Sentences Using** *Fewer* or *Less*

Read the sentences. If the underlined word in the sentence is incorrect, rewrite the sentence correctly. If the underlined word in the sentence is correct, write *correct*.

EXAMPLE   I have <u>less</u> quarters than dimes.

ANSWER   *I have* **fewer** *quarters than dimes.*

1. Do you have <u>less</u> money than you had last week?

2. There are <u>less</u> students in my math class than in my science class.

3. We have <u>fewer</u> time left to spend at the pool than I thought.

4. My mother thought the recipe called for <u>fewer</u> eggs than four.

5. The car had <u>less</u> gallons of gas than we needed to get there.

6. The car had <u>less</u> gas than we needed to get there.

7. Is 90 greater than or <u>less</u> than 900?

8. There are <u>less</u> grapes in this bowl than in that one.

9. I bought a small popcorn instead of a large because I wanted <u>fewer</u> popcorn.

10. It is healthier to eat <u>less</u> salty snacks and more fruit each day.

PRACTICE 24.2D > **Writing Sentences Using** *Just* **and** *Only*

Read the sentences below. For each one, write a new sentence using the word *just* or *only* to match the meaning of the sentence given.

EXAMPLE   We are going to this specific movie tonight. (only)

ANSWER   *We are going to* **only** *this movie tonight.*

11. We have the exact amount of milk needed for the recipe. (just)

12. The person from our school at the skating rink was Brian. (only)

13. The teacher said, "Follow instructions from nobody else but me."(only)

14. Zach wants a sandwich for lunch and nothing else. (just)

15. Arlene is the one person who brought a present. (just)

16. Cindy bought oatmeal at the store and nothing else. (only)

17. Cindy was the one person who bought oatmeal at the store. (only)

18. The parents gave the babysitter their cell phone number and no other information. (just)

19. The babysitter was the one person who had the parents' cell phone number. (just)

20. Remember to do the odd-numbered math problems, not the even-numbered ones. (just)

SPEAKING APPLICATION

With a partner, take turns discussing homework or other school projects. Use *fewer, less, just,* and *only* at least once. Your partner should listen for proper use of the words and correct any errors.

WRITING APPLICATION

Write a brief paragraph about a shopping trip you plan to take. Use *fewer, less, just,* and *only* at least once. Exchange paragraphs with a partner. Check for and correct any errors in the paragraph.

Texas Test Warm-Up

DIRECTIONS
Read the introduction and the passage that follows. Then, answer the questions to show that you can use troublesome adjectives and adverbs (e.g., *bad/badly*; *good/well*; *fewer/less*; *just/only*) correctly in reading and writing.

Shanequa wrote this paragraph about her first job as a babysitter. Read the paragraph and think about the changes you would suggest as a peer editor. When you finish reading, answer the questions that follow.

Fewer Than Five

(1) I just completed a course in babysitting, and I think I did pretty good. (2) So, when my neighbor asked me to watch her five children on Friday, I agreed. (3) My neighbor said that she needed only me from 4:00 P.M. until 7:00 P.M. (4) She also said that if she finished her errands in less time, she'd be home earlier. (5) I wish I could say that my first babysitting experience went well, but it went bad. (6) The five kids fought the entire time. (7) I think next time I'll babysit for a family with less children.

1 What change, if any, should be made in sentence 1?

   A Change *good* to **bad**

   B Change *good* to **well**

   C Delete *pretty*

   D Make no change

2 How should sentence 3 be revised?

   F Only my neighbor said that she needed me from 4:00 P.M. until 7:00 P.M.

   G My neighbor said only that she needed only me from 4:00 P.M. until 7:00 P.M.

   H My neighbor said that she needed me only from 4:00 P.M. until 7:00 P.M.

   J My only neighbor said that she needed me from 4:00 P.M. until 7:00 P.M.

3 What change, if any, should be made in sentence 5?

   A Change *well* to **good**

   B Change *well* to **better**

   C Change *bad* to **badly**

   D Make no change

4 What change, if any, should be made in sentence 7?

   F Change *less* to **lesser**

   G Change *less* to **fewer**

   H Change *less* to **just**

   J Make no change

Cumulative Review Chapters 21–24

PRACTICE 1 > Identifying Verb Tenses

Read the sentences. For each sentence, write whether the verb tense is *present*, *past*, *future*, *present perfect*, *past perfect*, or *future perfect*. Also indicate if the verb is *progressive*.

1. Ms. Paloma has worked at the bank for years.

2. My mother is preparing a huge meal for the holidays.

3. The committee will meet tomorrow morning.

4. On June 1, Troy will have been living in San Antonio for exactly five years.

5. Penelope has been designing her own clothing for some time.

6. Restaurants generally throw away their leftovers.

7. My father studied to be a chemical engineer.

8. The standardized test for seventh graders will be starting in half an hour.

9. A dozen swans were floating in the pond.

10. No one else had ever grown anything like Mr. Marshall's hybrid lily.

PRACTICE 2 > Revising to Use Active Voice

Read the sentences. Then, rewrite each passive voice sentence so that it is in active voice. If a sentence is already in active voice, write *active.*

1. The story was written by Shirley Jackson.

2. The best guacamole is prepared by Suzie.

3. The treehouse is in the maple tree by the creek.

4. Mr. Levinson's generous gift to the town was accepted by the mayor in a special ceremony.

5. Anita is flying to Minneapolis tomorrow.

PRACTICE 3 > Using Verbs Correctly

Read the sentences. Then, rewrite the sentences to correct any incorrect verb forms. If a sentence has no errors, write *correct.*

1. Last evening, I drunk a mug of cocoa.

2. I have never flew on that airline.

3. Yesterday morning, Portia lay this funny mouse pad in front of my computer.

4. You should not set in the sun for so many hours.

5. Yesterday at the movies, Peggy says to me, "Popcorn is low in calories."

6. Dad finally done his tax return.

7. The voters have chose a new person to become our state's governor.

8. I seen my cousins from the Philippines for the first time last August.

9. The bucket has apparently sprang a leak.

10. This past winter, the pipes in the old house froze and burst.

PRACTICE 4 > Identifying Pronoun Cases and Uses

Read the sentences. Write whether each underlined pronoun is in the *nominative*, *objective*, or *possessive* case. Then, write whether it is used as a *subject*, a *predicate pronoun*, a *direct object*, an *indirect object*, or the *object of a preposition*.

1. The babysitter sang to <u>her</u> until she fell asleep.

2. The driving instructor gave <u>him</u> a lesson.

3. <u>Hers</u> is the bright blue coat.

4. The quiet music calmed <u>me</u>.

5. The best athletes on the team were Jasper and <u>I</u>.

Continued on next page ▶

Cumulative Review   Chapters 21–24

▷ **Using Pronouns Correctly**

Read the sentences. Then, rewrite the sentences to correct any incorrect pronouns. If a sentence has no errors, write *correct*.

1. Claudia and him exchanged papers.
2. The coyote howled it's long and lonesome cry.
3. Whom did the artist portray in the painting?
4. The best swimmers are Drew and me.
5. The bus driver gave Bridget and I change.
6. Share the dessert between you and he.
7. Viv is the one who the class chose as president.
8. Their's is the last truck on the left.
9. Don't discourage Sonny and she.
10. I have no idea whom that politician is.

PRACTICE 6 ▷ **Revising for Subject–Verb Agreement**

Read the sentences. Then, rewrite the sentences to correct any errors in subject–verb agreement. If a sentence has no errors, write *correct*.

1. Each of the pianists practice for hours.
2. Neither Abe nor he see many movies.
3. A box of mints always sit atop her dresser.
4. The committee quarrels about choosing new members.
5. None of those golfers ride in the cart.
6. Deirdre and Lex enjoy line dancing.
7. Ham and eggs are my favorite breakfast.
8. The lawyer or her associates argues in court.
9. Do the mayor or the governor know the facts?
10. The class has been dismissed for the day.

PRACTICE 7 ▷ **Revising for Pronoun–Antecedent Agreement**

Read the sentences. Then, rewrite the sentences to correct any errors in pronoun–antecedent agreement. If a sentence has no errors, write *correct*.

1. None of the computers lost its memory.
2. Either the cat or the dog lost its collar.
3. Each of the chairs had their upholstery replaced.
4. Natasha has a job at which you input data.
5. In the past, everyone kept their hats in hatboxes.
6. Amelia and Leah wore ribbons in her hair.
7. Neither George nor Pete did their chores.
8. Several of the birds had damage to its wings.
9. Some of the beauticians did his or her own hair.
10. Did everybody know his or her state senator?

PRACTICE 8 ▷ **Using Modifiers Correctly**

Read the sentences. Then, rewrite the sentences to correct any errors involving modifiers. If a sentence has no errors, write *correct*.

1. The stagnant pond smells really badly.
2. I can do nothing farther for you.
3. I am feeling more well than I felt before.
4. Less customers shop here on weekends.
5. Of their three bad songs, this is the baddest.
6. The tour boats only sail in the summer.
7. Tammy is kinder than I am.
8. Beau performed good on the test.
9. In my opinion, robins are prettier than any bird.
10. Is there a guitarist more good than he is?

PUNCTUATION

Using punctuation correctly in your writing will help you present ideas clearly.

WRITE GUY *Jeff Anderson, M.Ed.*

WHAT DO YOU NOTICE?

Look out for punctuation marks as you zoom in on these sentences from "Icarus and Daedalus" by Josephine Preston Peabody.

MENTOR TEXT

> The heat of the sun had melted the wax from his wings; the feathers were falling, one by one, like snowflakes; and there was none to help.

Now, ask yourself the following questions:

- What is the purpose of the commas in this sentence?
- Why does the author use semicolons in this sentence?

The author uses commas to set off the phrase *one by one* from the rest of the sentence. Commas are used because it is a nonessential phrase; if the phrase is taken away, the sentence still makes sense. The author uses semicolons to separate the three main or independent clauses because they are closely related ideas.

Grammar for Writers A writer can use a semicolon to connect closely linked main or independent clauses. Think of a sentence as a chain and the semicolon as a link that joins equal parts into a strong whole.

My favorite fruits are apples and pears and bananas and mangos.

Have you ever tried them with a sprinkling of commas?

25.1 End Marks

End marks signal the end or conclusion of a sentence, word, or phrase. There are three end marks: the **period (.)**, the **question mark (?)**, and the **exclamation mark (!)**.

Using Periods

A **period** indicates the end of a sentence or an abbreviation.

RULE 25.1.1 Use a period to end a **declarative** sentence—a statement of fact, idea, or opinion.

DECLARATIVE SENTENCE   This is a beautiful painting.

RULE 25.1.2 Use a period to end most **imperative** sentences—sentences that give directions or commands.

IMPERATIVE SENTENCE   Finish doing your homework.

RULE 25.1.3 Use a period to end a sentence that contains an **indirect question.**

An **indirect question** restates a question in a declarative sentence. It does not give the speaker's exact words.

INDIRECT QUESTION   Mike asked me if I would go.

RULE 25.1.4 Use a period after most **abbreviations** and **initials**.

ABBREVIATIONS   Mr.   St.   Sen.   in.   Sr.

INITIALS   John F. Kennedy   T. S. Eliot

Note: The abbreviation for *inch, in.,* is the only measurement abbreviation that uses a period after it.

When a sentence ends with an abbreviation that uses a period, do not put a second period at the end.

EXAMPLE   Remember to call John Leary Sr.

Do not use periods with acronyms, words formed with the first or first few letters of a series of words.

EXAMPLES   NATO   North Atlantic Treaty Organization

USA   United States of America

Using Question Marks

A **question mark** follows a word, phrase, or sentence that asks a question.

Use a question mark after an interrogative sentence—one that asks a direct question.

INTERROGATIVE SENTENCES   Do reptiles hatch from eggs ?

What time are you coming ?

Sometimes a single word or brief phrase is used to ask a direct question. This type of question is punctuated as though it were a complete sentence because the words that are left out are easily understood.

Use a question mark after a word or phrase that asks a question.

EXAMPLES   I will meet you before the show. Where ?

Let's meet for brunch. What time ?

See Practice 25.1A

Using Exclamation Marks

Use an exclamation mark to end a word, phrase, or sentence that shows strong emotion.

EXAMPLES

I can't believe I forgot!

I am so happy to see you!

Use an exclamation mark after an imperative sentence that gives a forceful or urgent command.

IMPERATIVE SENTENCE

Watch out for that car!

Don't move!

While imperative sentences containing forceful commands often end with an exclamation mark, mild imperatives should end with a period.

MILD IMPERATIVES

Please stay here.

Bring your sweater with you.

Use an exclamation mark after an interjection that expresses strong emotion.

INTERJECTIONS

Oh no! I lost my keys.

Ouch! That really hurts.

Exclamation marks should not be used too often. Overusing them reduces their emotional effect and makes writing less effective.

See Practice 25.1B

PRACTICE 25.1A > Using Question Marks and Periods

Read the sentences. Rewrite each sentence, adding missing question marks and periods.

EXAMPLE Mr Moroney is the substitute math teacher today

ANSWER *Mr. Moroney is the substitute math teacher today.*

1. When will you return my video game

2. Proofread your final draft carefully

3. Did you watch the inauguration of the president

4. Marci asked if I would go with her to the mall

5. Will Prof J D Snow give another lecture

6. Sgt Sanchez spoke about her experiences overseas

7. Please handle that DVD carefully

8. What exactly does *digital* mean

9. Dr Angela Preston is a veterinarian

10. That old mansion has some furniture from the 1800s

PRACTICE 25.1B > Using Exclamation Marks and Periods

Read the sentences. Rewrite each sentence, adding missing exclamation marks and periods.

EXAMPLE Wow What a great shot

ANSWER *Wow! What a great shot!*

11. Watch your step there

12. Boy, was she angry

13. I thought I would never finish

14. Oh, I forgot my password

15. That is the most beautiful rose I have ever seen

16. Julio has been calling me all afternoon

17. Keep your eye on the ball

18. Please close the door

19. What a brilliant idea

20. We picked up enough trash to fill three bags

SPEAKING APPLICATION

Ask a partner a question. Your partner should answer and ask you a question. Use your voices to indicate the end punctuation.

WRITING APPLICATION

Write a paragraph as if you were giving a play-by-play description of a game or other exciting event. Use appropriate end punctuation.

25.2 Commas

End marks signal a full stop. **Commas** signal a brief pause.
A comma may be used to separate elements in a sentence or to
set off part of a sentence. Include a comma in your writing when
you want your reader to group information in your sentence.

Using Commas in Compound Sentences

A **compound sentence** consists of two or more main or
independent clauses that are joined by a coordinating
conjunction, such as *and, but, for, nor, or, so,* or *yet.*

RULE **25.2.1**

> Use a comma before the conjunction to separate two main or
> independent clauses in a **compound sentence.**

COMPOUND SENTENCE	Children have learned many things by age five **,** but they still may need help getting dressed.

Use a comma before a conjunction only when there are complete
sentences on both sides of the conjunction. If the conjunction joins
single words, phrases, or subordinate clauses, do not use a comma.

SINGLE WORDS	We saw chimpanzees and gorillas.
PHRASES	Edie likes drawing pictures and taking photos.
SUBORDINATE CLAUSES	Choose someone who has experience but who can also follow directions.

In some compound sentences, the main or independent clauses
are very brief, and the meaning is clear. When this occurs, the
comma before the conjunction may be omitted.

EXAMPLE	Christie tried hard but she was unsuccessful.	See Practice 25.2A

Avoiding Comma Splices

A **comma splice** occurs when two or more sentences have been
joined with only a comma between them.

25.2.2 **RULE**

> Avoid **comma splices** by making sure all of your ideas are properly linked.

INCORRECT   The sun was shining brightly, he forgot to bring his sunglasses.

CORRECT   The sun was shining brightly. He forgot to bring his sunglasses.

Using Commas in a Series

Sometimes, a sentence lists a number of single words or groups of words. When three or more of these items are listed, the list is called a **series.** Separate the items in a series with commas.

25.2.3 **RULE**

> Use commas to separate three or more words, phrases, or clauses in a **series.**

A comma follows each of the items except the last one in a series. The conjunction *and* or *or* is added after the last comma.

SERIES OF WORDS   The forest animals included deer, squirrels, skunks, and rabbits.

SERIES OF PHRASES   Her directions sent us across the field, through the woods, and past the farmhouse.

There are two exceptions to this rule. If each item except the last one in a series is followed by a conjunction, do not use commas. Also, do not use a comma to separate groups of words that are considered to be one item.

EXAMPLES   Hana brought apples and peaches and cherries.

    The caterer supplied oil and vinegar, salt and pepper, and bread and butter.

See Practice 25.2B

Using Commas Between Adjectives

Sometimes, two or more adjectives are placed before the noun they describe.

> **Use commas to separate adjectives of equal rank.**

There are two ways to tell whether adjectives in a sentence are of equal rank:

- If the word *and* can be placed between the adjectives without changing the meaning, the adjectives are of equal rank.

- If the order of the adjectives can be changed, they are of equal rank.

EXAMPLE   Bianca made a simple, polite request.

(*A simple and polite request* does not change the sentence's meaning. *A polite, simple request* also does not change the meaning.)

> **Do not use commas to separate adjectives that must appear in a specific order.**

Do not use a comma if adding *and* or changing the order of the adjectives would result in a sentence that makes no sense.

INCORRECT   Some and colorful birds perched on the roof.

INCORRECT   Colorful some birds perched on the roof.

CORRECT   Some colorful birds perched on the roof.

> **Do not use a comma to separate the last adjective in a series from the noun it modifies.**

INCORRECT   We walked on a long, twisting, scenic, road.

CORRECT   We walked on a long, twisting, scenic road.

See Practice 25.2C
See Practice 25.2D

PRACTICE 25.2A ▷ Using Commas in Compound Sentences

Read the sentences. Rewrite each sentence, adding commas where they are needed.

EXAMPLE   Our team played their best yet they still lost the game.

ANSWER   *Our team played their best, yet they still lost the game.*

1. Emma wanted a cat or dog but her mother is allergic to them.

2. Brad searched diligently yet he could not find the socks for his uniform.

3. This pocket watch is valuable to me for it belonged to my grandfather.

4. We needed to earn some money for the club trip so we had a bake sale.

5. Ryan will come here later and he will bring his games.

6. Jessica and Gavin have been working on that puzzle for nearly two hours but they are not finished.

7. The referee blew the whistle and the game stopped.

8. Trina likes yogurt for breakfast but her sister likes toast and juice.

9. The tune kept running through my head yet I could not think of the title.

10. Put the milk back in the refrigerator or it will turn sour.

PRACTICE 25.2B ▷ Using Commas in a Series

Read the sentences. Rewrite each sentence, adding commas as needed.

EXAMPLE   My grandmother knits scarves sweaters and mittens.

ANSWER   *My grandmother knits scarves, sweaters, and mittens.*

11. For lunch, you can choose soup pizza or salad.

12. The hikers tramped over rocks across a stream and into a dark forest.

13. I would like a dog that wags its tail comes when I call and doesn't jump on people.

14. The actors dancers and musicians all came on stage for a bow after the performance.

15. Mrs. Wong bought carrots onions and potatoes for a stew.

16. The parts of a business letter are the date the inside address the greeting the body the closing and the signature.

17. Del grabbed his jacket rushed out the door and ran down the sidewalk.

18. My courses this year are English math science social studies and Spanish.

19. Evan looked on the floor under the table and behind the couch for the remote control.

20. Mercury Venus Mars and Jupiter are the closest planets to Earth.

WRITING APPLICATION

Use sentences 8, 9, and 10 as models and write three compound sentences. Place a comma correctly in each sentence.

WRITING APPLICATION

Complete this sentence with a series: *I have only ten dollars to spend on _____.* Punctuate the series correctly.

PRACTICE 25.2C → Using Commas Between Adjectives

Read the sentences. Rewrite the sentences, adding commas where necessary. If no comma is needed, write *correct*.

EXAMPLE   Giselle is a graceful talented gymnast.

ANSWER   *Giselle is a graceful, talented gymnast.*

1. I have two large apples to share.

2. A rude angry customer complained to the manager.

3. Wild animals have many clever ways of surviving.

4. The hot humid air made us feel listless.

5. That cheese has a strong unpleasant odor.

6. We live in a red brick apartment building.

7. My parents listen to the great old songs by the Beatles.

8. An enthusiastic kind grandfather was telling stories to the children.

9. Charles prefers his sturdy old bicycle to his brother's shiny new one.

10. There were three rotten apples at the bottom of the basket.

PRACTICE 25.2D → Proofreading Sentences for Commas

Read the sentences. Rewrite each sentence, adding commas where they are needed.

EXAMPLE   Anna bought cheese crackers and dips.

ANSWER   *Anna bought cheese, crackers, and dips.*

11. A tall elegant model walked across the stage.

12. Emily created the design for the poster and Roger wrote the text.

13. We wondered who the woman was where she came from, and what she wanted.

14. Sherman usually wears baggy faded jeans but today he is wearing shorts.

15. The children built a great big snowman and they put a hat on its head.

16. You can take a sandwich or you can buy lunch there.

17. Vernon eats only fruits vegetables beans and whole grains.

18. Our dog chased a rabbit across the grass through the flowers and under a fence.

19. I tried to watch that documentary but I didn't enjoy it so I turned it off.

20. Leslie did not like the hot spicy dip.

WRITING APPLICATION

Use the sentences in Practice 25.2C as models and write three sentences. Include two or more adjectives in each to describe something. Use a comma to separate the adjectives, if necessary.

WRITING APPLICATION

Use sentences 13 and 14 as models and write two sentences. Use commas correctly to indicate a series, a compound sentence, and equal adjectives.

Using Commas After Introductory Words, Phrases, and Clauses

When a sentence begins with an introductory word, phrase, or other structures, that word or phrase is usually separated from the rest of the sentence by a comma.

> Use a comma after most introductory words, phrases, or dependent clauses.

25.2.7 RULE

 Focus on the TEKS

(20)(B)(i) Use punctuation marks including commas after introductory words, phrases, and clauses.

See TEKS Check

See TEKS Practice

See Practice 25.2E

KINDS OF INTRODUCTORY MATERIAL	
Introductory Word	Hey, give me your binoculars quickly before the bear moves.
	Dwayne, please bring me my boots and jacket.
	Well, I certainly wasn't prepared for that.
	Shani, where did you go?
Introductory Phrase	To conserve energy, we are lowering the heat.
	With Jaime sick, Ana didn't know how she would finish the poster.
	In the morning, the highway to the city is jammed with cars.
	To visit Sweden, you will need a passport.
Introductory Adverbial Clause	Although it was early, my sister was dressed and waiting for the bus.
	When the raccoons got into the garbage, they made a mess.
	When the dancers took a bow, the audience applauded wildly.

When a prepositional phrase of only two words begins a sentence, a comma is not absolutely necessary.

EXAMPLES   At dawn I slowly opened my eyes.

In June we plan to visit my aunt.

TEKS Check Show that you can use punctuation marks, including commas after introductory words, phrases, and clauses. Write three to four sentences that use correct punctuation marks after introductory words, phrases, and clauses. Discuss the purpose of the correct punctuation with a partner.

Find It/FIX IT

7

Grammar Game Plan

Using Commas With Parenthetical Expressions

A **parenthetical expression** is a word or phrase that is not essential to the meaning of the sentence. These words or phrases generally add extra information to the basic sentence.

RULE

25.2.8

> Use commas to set off **parenthetical expressions** from the rest of the sentence.

Find It/FIX IT

11

Grammar Game Plan

A parenthetical expression in the middle of a sentence needs two commas. A parenthetical expression at the end of a sentence needs only one.

KINDS OF PARENTHETICAL EXPRESSIONS	
Names of People Being Addressed	Listen carefully, Ava, while I tell you how to do it. Please sit down, Brian.
Certain Adverbs	The suitcase, therefore, is quite a bit heavier. I arrived too late to help, however.
Common Expressions	They know she did her best, of course. He is not the best one for the job, in my opinion.
Contrasting Expressions	The award should be theirs, not yours. These shirts, not those, are ready to be packed.

See Practice 25.2F
See Practice 25.2G

Using Commas With Nonessential Expressions

To determine when a phrase or clause should be set off with commas, decide whether the phrase or clause is **essential** or **nonessential** to the meaning of the sentence. Nonessential expressions can be left out without changing the meaning of the sentence.

> Use commas to set off **nonessential** expressions from the main clause. Do not set off **essential** material with commas.

Appositives and Appositive Phrases

Appositives are often set off with commas, but only when their meaning is not essential to the sentence. In the first example below, the appositive *West Side Story* is not set off with commas because it clarifies which movie is being discussed.

ESSENTIAL	The award-winning movie *West Side Story* takes place in New York City.
NONESSENTIAL	*West Side Story*, an award-winning movie, takes place in New York City.

Participial Phrases

Like appositives, participial phrases are set off with commas when their meaning is nonessential. In the first example below, *sitting on the bench* is essential because it tells which woman is the aunt.

ESSENTIAL	The woman sitting on the bench is my aunt.
NONESSENTIAL	Aunt Jane, sitting on the bench, visited us today.

Adjectival Clauses

Adjectival clauses, too, are set off with commas only if they are nonessential. In the second example below, *a new player who could score goals* is nonessential because it adds information about Derek. The main clause in the sentence is about the team welcoming Derek, not about what Derek can do.

ESSENTIAL	The team needed a player who could score goals.
NONESSENTIAL	The team welcomed Derek, who could score goals.

See Practice 25.2H

TEKS Practice Show that you can use punctuation marks, including commas after introductory words, phrases, and clauses, by completing the following activities.

PRACTICE 25.2E **Using Commas After Introductory Words, Phrases, or Clauses**

Read the sentences. Rewrite each sentence, adding the comma needed after the introductory word, phrase, or clause.

EXAMPLE   Actually there's no correct answer to that problem.

ANSWER   *Actually, there's no correct answer to that problem.*

1. Oh I forgot to tell you about the assignment.

2. Without a moment's hesitation he agreed to help.

3. When Tiffany wants to think about something she takes a long walk.

4. No that's not what I meant.

5. Before you go talk to Mr. Cortez.

6. In case of an emergency exit the building at once.

7. As soon as I saw the situation I knew what I had to do.

8. Suddenly a clap of thunder startled everyone.

9. If we do not sell enough tickets we may have to cancel the show.

10. Dad thanks for getting me the concert tickets for my birthday.

PRACTICE 25.2F **Proofreading a Passage for Commas**

Read the paragraph. Rewrite the paragraph, adding commas where they are needed.

EXAMPLE   When Avery wanted to take courses at the museum school he had to submit an application go to an interview and show his three best works. It was a lot to do but he thought it was worth it.

ANSWER   *When Avery wanted to take courses at the museum school, he had to submit an application, go to an interview, and show his three best works. It was a lot to do, but he thought it was worth it.*

Last week Sylvia helped her family prepare to move so they would be ready on moving day. First they went through the closets pulled out clothes they did not wear and put them in large plastic bags so they could donate them. Then they emptied drawers cupboards and bookcases. Before packing they wrapped glasses dishes and other breakable things in paper. Finally everything was neatly packed and the movers loaded their belongings onto a truck. Off they went to their new home.

SPEAKING APPLICATION

Find three sentences in a newspaper or magazine that have introductory words, phrases, and clauses. Read the sentences aloud to a partner, without the commas. Discuss how the commas make the meaning clear.

WRITING APPLICATION

Write a brief narrative paragraph about an event in which you participated. Include introductory words, phrases, and clauses. Use commas correctly in your sentences. Discuss the purpose of the commas with a partner.

PRACTICE 25.2G Using Commas With Parenthetical Expressions

Read the sentences. Rewrite each sentence, adding commas as needed to set off parenthetical expressions.

EXAMPLE   I hope to see you there Jess.

ANSWER   *I hope to see you there, Jess.*

1. Jasmine in my opinion is a very good artist.

2. You can of course change your mind later.

3. I think you should wear your blue shirt not this one.

4. I forgot his birthday however.

5. This is the last envelope thank goodness that I will have to lick.

6. Do you know Gil who won the award?

7. Snakes contrary to popular opinion are not slimy.

8. I really like our new principal don't you?

9. It's only been a week I think since we've been back.

10. These running shoes on the other hand will give you more support.

PRACTICE 25.2H Using Commas With Nonessential Expressions

Read the sentences. Rewrite the sentences, adding commas where necessary. If a sentence is punctuated correctly, write *correct*.

EXAMPLE   This old plate which was just found dates from colonial times.

ANSWER   *This old plate, which was just found, dates from colonial times.*

11. Edward Bloor the author of *Tangerine* lives in Florida.

12. That quotation is from Confucius who was a great Chinese philosopher.

13. George delivered the argument that convinced the listeners.

14. Tara's little brother a persistent troublemaker annoyed us all afternoon.

15. An athlete who practices will perform well.

16. The town hall built in 1920 needs repairing.

17. Any member missing three rehearsals will be dropped from the cast.

18. The Statue of Liberty a gift from France stands on Liberty Island in New York Harbor.

19. Yo-Yo Ma the popular cellist encourages young musicians of all types.

20. Judd the lifeguard teaches swimming.

SPEAKING APPLICATION

Take turns reading sentence 6 aloud with a partner. Explain how it can be misinterpreted without the correct punctuation.

WRITING APPLICATION

Write two sentences, one with a nonessential expression and one with an expression that is essential. Use commas correctly with the nonessential expression.

Using Commas With Dates and Geographical Names

Dates usually have several parts, including months, days, and years. Commas prevent dates from being unclear.

> **When a date is made up of three parts, use a comma after each item, except in the case of a month followed by a day.**

Notice in the examples that commas are not used to set off a month followed by a numeral standing for a day. Commas are used when both the month and the date are used as an appositive to rename a day of the week.

EXAMPLES　On March 12, 1945, my grandfather came to the United States with one small suitcase.

Friday, April 12, was an important date for Marco and his family.

When a date contains only a month and a year, commas are unnecessary.

EXAMPLES　He will visit us in June 2015.

Most of the places we visited in July 2005 were in the Midwest.

> **When a geographical name is made up of a city and a state, use a comma after each item except when the state ends a sentence.**

EXAMPLES　She lived in Dallas, Texas, for several years and then moved to Atlanta, Georgia.

Amma went to Chicago, Illinois, to visit the many museums in the area.

See Practice 25.2I

Using Commas in Numbers

Numbers of one hundred or less and numbers made up of two words (for example, *three thousand*) are generally spelled out in words. Other large numbers (for example, 8,463) are written in numerals. Commas make large numbers easier to read.

> With large numbers of more than three digits, count from the right and add a comma to the left of every third digit to separate it from every fourth digit.

RULE 25.2.12

EXAMPLES

5,897 books

654,298 students

a population of 2,567,365

> Use commas with three or more numbers written in a series.

RULE 25.2.13

EXAMPLES

Fill out pages 23, 24, and 25 completely.

The three winners had 5, 7, and 9 goals during the season.

> Do not use a comma with ZIP Codes, telephone numbers, page numbers, years, serial numbers, or house numbers.

RULE 25.2.14

ZIP CODE	32819
TELEPHONE NUMBER	(407) 472-8543
PAGE NUMBER	on page 3148
YEAR	the year 1949
SERIAL NUMBER	506 486 5787
HOUSE NUMBER	6491 Broad Street

See Practice 25.2J

PRACTICE 25.2I **Using Commas in Dates and Geographical Names**

Read the sentences. Rewrite each sentence, adding commas where they are needed.

EXAMPLE   Dallas Texas is my hometown.

ANSWER   *Dallas, Texas, is my hometown.*

1. My date of birth is May 25 2000.

2. I hope to visit Honolulu Hawaii some day.

3. The company my mother works for has offices in Atlanta Georgia and Chicago Illinois.

4. President John F. Kennedy was assassinated on November 22 1963.

5. My grandmother grew up in Ottawa Canada.

6. We lived in Austin Texas from June 2002 to September 2008.

7. On Friday October 21 my brother will turn fifteen.

8. On July 4 1776 the Declaration of Independence was approved.

9. The first organized baseball game was played on June 19 1846 in Hoboken New Jersey.

10. We drove from Phoenix Arizona to Albuquerque New Mexico in two days.

PRACTICE 25.2J **Using Commas in Numbers**

Rewrite each item, adding commas where needed. If no commas are needed, write *correct*.

EXAMPLE   1250717

ANSWER   *1,250,717*

11. 4067

12. 103000

13. 2982525

14. the year 1950

15. 1600 Pennsylvania Avenue

16. ZIP Code 61620

17. India's population in 2008: 1147995900

18. questions 2 4 5 and 6

19. telephone number (818) 555-8888

20. page 1032

WRITING APPLICATION

Write a sentence in which you give your date of birth. In another sentence, tell the city and state in which you live. If you have also lived somewhere else, write that too. Use commas correctly in your sentences.

WRITING APPLICATION

Search online or in a reference book to find the current population of your state. Use that number in a sentence about your state. Be sure to use commas correctly in the number.

Using Commas With Addresses and in Letters

Commas are also used in addresses, salutations of friendly letters, and closings of friendly or business letters.

> **Use a comma after each item in an address made up of two or more parts.**

25.2.15 RULE

In the following example, commas are placed after the name, street, and city. There is no comma between the state and the ZIP Code.

EXAMPLE   He is writing to John Keen, 137 Adams Street, Reno, Nevada 89509.

Fewer commas are needed when an address is written in a letter or on an envelope.

EXAMPLE   Greg Harrison
92 Essex Avenue
Roselle, New Jersey 07203

> **Use a comma after the salutation in a personal letter and after the closing in all letters.**

25.2.16 RULE

See Practice 25.2K
See Practice 25.2L

SALUTATION   Dear Bill,   **CLOSING**   Yours truly,

Using Commas With Direct Quotations

Commas are also used to separate **direct quotations** from other phrases in a sentence.

> **Use commas to set off a direct quotation from the rest of a sentence.**

25.2.17 RULE

EXAMPLES   Naomi said, "Please wait for me."

"I will," Rosa answered, "if you walk faster."

PRACTICE 25.2K **Using Commas in Addresses and Letters**

Read the items. Rewrite each item, adding commas where needed. If no commas are needed, write *correct*.

EXAMPLE   Very truly yours

ANSWER   *Very truly yours,*

1. Longview TX 75603

2. Dear Mr. Knox

3. 2662 Steele Road

4. With best regards

5. 5109 Greenway Boulevard

6. 25 Prospect Street, Apt. 3

7. Yours sincerely

8. Molly's address is 442 Ocean Avenue 3rd floor Tallahassee Florida 32306.

9. Dear Grandma

10. The Holloways
16 Sunset Avenue
Scottsdale AZ 85250

PRACTICE 25.2L **Revising a Letter by Adding Commas**

Read the letter. Rewrite the letter, adding commas where necessary.

EXAMPLE   Dear Mrs. Juarez

ANSWER   *Dear Mrs. Juarez,*

1421 Mountain Drive
Madison WI 53716

April 21 2010

Dear Aunt Glenda

Thank you very much for the sweater you sent for my birthday. It fits perfectly and you know I love blue! I've already worn it to school and I received three compliments on it. You are so thoughtful to remember me.

Much love
Emily

WRITING APPLICATION

Write this sentence, completing it with your own address: *I live at _____.*

WRITING APPLICATION

Write a letter or note to a relative or friend. Use correct letter form, and use commas as needed.

25.3 Semicolons and Colons

The **semicolon (;)** joins related **independent clauses** and signals a longer pause than a comma. The **colon (:)** is used to introduce lists of items and in other special situations.

Using Semicolons to Join Independent Clauses

Sometimes two **independent clauses** are so closely connected in meaning that they make up a single sentence, rather than two separate sentences.

> Use a **semicolon** to join related **independent clauses** that are not joined by the conjunctions *and, or, nor, for, but, so,* or *yet.*

RULE 25.3.1

INDEPENDENT CLAUSES	Bill enjoys exploring jungle areas.
	His sister is more interested in deserts.
CLAUSES JOINED BY SEMICOLONS	Bill enjoys exploring jungle areas ; his sister is more interested in deserts.

A semicolon should be used only when there is a close relationship between the two independent clauses. If the clauses are not very closely related, they should be written as separate sentences with a period or another end mark to separate them or joined with a coordinating conjunction.

Note that when a sentence contains three or more related independent clauses, they may still be separated with semicolons.

EXAMPLES	Dark clouds rolled in ; the ocean became rough ; the sand began to blow.
	Bea wrote about insects ; Nat wrote about spiders ; Frank wrote about insects and spiders.

Using Semicolons to Join Clauses Separated by Conjunctive Adverbs or Transitional Expressions

Semicolons help writers show how their ideas connect.

RULE 25.3.2

> Use a semicolon to join independent clauses separated by either a **conjunctive adverb** or a **transitional expression.**

CONJUNCTIVE ADVERBS	*also, besides, consequently, first, furthermore, however, indeed, instead, moreover, nevertheless, otherwise, second, then, therefore, thus*
TRANSITIONAL EXPRESSIONS	*as a result, at this time, for instance, in fact, on the other hand, that is*
EXAMPLE	We met Tomas at the concession stand ; otherwise , we would never have found him at the theater.

Remember to place a comma after the conjunctive adverb or transitional expression. The comma sets off the conjunctive adverb or transitional expression, which acts as an introductory expression to the second clause.

Using Semicolons to Avoid Confusion

Sometimes, to avoid confusion, semicolons are used to separate items in a series.

RULE 25.3.3

> Consider the use of semicolons to avoid confusion when items in a series already contain commas.

Place a semicolon after all but the last complete item in a series.

EXAMPLES	The dark country road ; the still , silent forest ; and the sky , black and moonless , encouraged them to head toward home.
	Three important dates for my family are January 1 , 2001 ; April 5 , 2003 ; and May 28 , 2000.

Focus on the TEKS

(20)(B)(ii) Use punctuation marks including semicolons.

See TEKS Check

See TEKS Practice

See Practice 25.3A

See Practice 25.3B

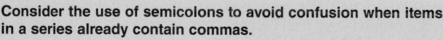**TEKS Check** Show that you can use correct punctuation marks, including semicolons. Write three sentences that use semicolons and read them aloud to a partner. Discuss the purpose of the semicolons.

Using Colons

The **colon (:)** is used to introduce lists of items and in certain special situations.

> **Use a colon after an independent clause to introduce a list of items.**

The independent clause that comes before the colon often includes the words *the following, as follows, these,* or *those.*

EXAMPLE   Manny's family is planning to visit the following cities: Dallas, Fort Worth, and Austin.

Remember to use commas to separate three or more items in a series.

> **In most cases, do not use a colon after a verb, and never use a colon after a preposition.**

INCORRECT   I like to play: football, baseball, and soccer.

CORRECT   I like to play football, baseball, and soccer.

 Focus on the TEKS

(20)(B)(ii) Use punctuation marks including colons.

See TEKS Check

See TEKS Practice

See Practice 25.3C

See Practice 25.3D

> **Use a colon to introduce a long or formal quotation.**

EXAMPLE   The sign clearly states the law: "No motor vehicles allowed beyond this point at any time."

SOME ADDITIONAL USES OF THE COLON	
To Separate Hours and Minutes	8:45 A.M. 10:05 P.M.
After the Salutation in a Business Letter	Dear Sir or Madam: Dear Ms. Langly:
On Warnings and Labels	Notice: Shop is closed for repairs. Note: Please turn off cellphones.

 TEKS Check Show that you can use correct punctuation marks including colons. Write two to three sentences that use colons in different ways. Read your sentences aloud to a partner, and then discuss the purpose of the colons.

TEKS Practice Show that you can use correct punctuation marks, including semicolons, by completing the following activities.

PRACTICE 25.3A ▶ Using Semicolons

Read the sentences. Rewrite each sentence, adding any necessary semicolons.

EXAMPLE   I opened the shades sunlight poured into the room.

ANSWER   *I opened the shades; sunlight poured into the room.*

1. I'll prepare dinner meanwhile, you set the table.

2. Suzanne likes crossword puzzles Kevin prefers chess.

3. Mammals have hair birds have feathers amphibians have neither.

4. The weather forecast was for rain instead, we had sleet.

5. Andrew's alarm did not go off consequently, he was late for school.

6. Please turn on the fan we need some air.

7. Some people are very confident at least, they act that way.

8. In some stores, you can get newspapers and magazines household supplies, such as batteries and cleaners and sandwiches and soups to go.

9. The sky was gray the wind blew the waves crashed on the rocks.

10. Peter can give you some tips he is an excellent tennis player.

PRACTICE 25.3B ▶ Writing Sentences Using Semicolons

Read the sentences below. Then, write new sentences by adding a related independent clause to each sentence provided. Use semicolons correctly in your new sentences.

EXAMPLE   The class was going to end in four minutes.

ANSWER   *The class was going to end in four minutes; therefore, we had only enough time to finish one problem.*

11. I wish I could go to camp this summer.

12. Charlie found a part-time job mowing lawns.

13. We have to hurry if we are going to catch the bus.

14. I prefer pears to apples.

15. Emily brought an umbrella to school today.

16. We should make stir-fry for dinner tonight.

17. Put the laundry in the dresser.

18. The election was very close.

19. My mother said that I could go to your house.

20. We have to walk three more blocks.

WRITING APPLICATION

Work with a partner. Use sentences 2, 3, and 5 in Practice 25.3A as models. Write three sentences of your own. Then, read your sentences to your partner and explain the purpose of each semicolon.

WRITING APPLICATION

Work with a partner. Write one sentence using semicolons in a series. Write one sentence using a semicolon to separate two independent clauses. Have your partner read your sentences aloud, checking for the correct use of semicolons.

TEKS Practice Show that you can use correct punctuation marks, including colons, by completing the following activities.

 Semicolons and Colons

PRACTICE 25.3C Using Colons

Read the sentences. Rewrite each sentence, adding any necessary colons. If no colon is needed, write *correct*.

EXAMPLE   Your appointment is at 915 A.M.

ANSWER   *Your appointment is at 9:15 A.M.*

1. This is what you should do apologize and give her flowers.

2. You must be ready by 6:30 P.M.

3. Warning Hard hats required at this site.

4. Microchips are found in hundreds of common devices telephones, GPS systems, and MP3 players, for example.

5. Margo packed only three things pajamas, a toothbrush, and a change of clothes.

6. So far, I have found only one good source for my report: the author's official Web site.

7. This evening's program is as follows opening remarks at 700, presentations from 715 to 800, closing remarks at 815.

8. Caution Bridge is slippery when wet.

9. Dear Sir or Madam:

10. Put the following ingredients into your salad lettuce, spinach, sliced apples, and dried cranberries.

PRACTICE 25.3D Writing Sentences Using Colons

Read the rules for using colons below. Write a sentence using a colon for each rule. Then, have a partner read your sentences aloud to check for the correct use of colons.

EXAMPLE   to introduce a list of items

ANSWER   *You will need the following supplies for the camping trip: a sleeping bag, a water bottle, a flashlight, and a warm jacket.*

11. to introduce a long or formal quotation

12. to separate hours and minutes

13. after the salutation in a business letter

14. on a warning

15. to introduce a list of items

16. to introduce a long or formal quotation

17. to separate hours and minutes

18. after the salutation in a business letter

19. on a label

20. to introduce a list of items

SPEAKING APPLICATION

With a partner, take turns reading aloud the sentences created in Practice 25.3D. Read the word *colon* whenever there is a colon. Then, discuss which usages of colons are most common.

WRITING APPLICATION

Write three sentences about school. In your sentences, use colons in three different ways. Exchange papers with your partner. Your partner should read your sentences aloud and explain the use of each colon.

Focus on the TEKS

(20)(B)(ii) Use correct punctuation marks, including semicolons and colons.

Texas Test Warm-Up

DIRECTIONS
Read the introduction and the passage that follows. Then, answer the questions to show that you can use correct punctuation, including semicolons and colons, in reading and writing.

Vince wrote this business letter to a potential employer, the owner of a convenience store. Read the letter and think about the changes you would suggest as a peer editor. When you finish reading, answer the questions that follow.

(1) Dear Mrs. Gonzalez;

(2) I am writing to express my interest in working in your store: I would like to own a convenience store some day myself. (3) I work well with others, I am friendly, helpful, and good at working with money. (4) I am also responsible; in fact, people say I'm mature for my age. (5) Please note that I can be flexible about my hours. (6) I will look forward to hearing from you.

(7) Sincerely,
(8) Vince Bradford

---

1 What change, if any, should be made in sentence 1?

  A Change the semicolon to a colon

  B Delete the semicolon

  C Change the semicolon to a comma

  D Make no change

2 What change, if any, should be made in sentence 2?

  F Change the colon to a comma

  G Change the colon to a semicolon

  H Change the period to an exclamation point

  J Make no change

3 What change, if any, should be made in sentence 3?

  A Delete the comma after *others*

  B Change the comma after *others* to a semicolon

  C Change the comma after *others* to a colon

  D Make no change

4 What change, if any, should be made in sentence 4?

  F Change the semicolon to a comma

  G Change the semicolon to a colon

  H Delete the semicolon

  J Make no change

25.4 Quotation Marks, Underlining, and Italics

Quotation marks (" ") set off direct quotations, dialogue, and certain types of titles. Other types of titles may be **underlined** or set in *italics,* a slanted type style.

Using Quotation Marks With Quotations

Quotation marks identify the spoken or written words of others. A **direct quotation** represents a person's exact speech or thoughts. An **indirect quotation** reports the general meaning of what a person said or thought.

Both types of quotations are acceptable when you write. Direct quotations, however, generally result in a livelier writing style.

> **Direct quotations should be enclosed in quotation marks.**

EXAMPLE   Janine said, "Tomorrow we are going hiking."

"Does anyone know the way?" asked Ted.

RULE

25.4.1

> **Indirect quotations do not require quotation marks.**

EXAMPLES   John said that he would feed the fish.

Scott wondered why the coach hadn't called him about rescheduling the game.

RULE

25.4.2

Using Direct Quotations With Introductory, Concluding, and Interrupting Expressions

Commas help you set off introductory information so that your reader understands who is speaking. Writers usually identify a speaker by using words such as *he asked* or *she said* with a quotation. These expressions can introduce, conclude, or interrupt a quotation.

Direct Quotations With Introductory Expressions

Commas are also used to indicate where **introductory expressions** end.

> When an **introductory expression** precedes a direct quotation, place a comma after the introductory expression, and write the quotation as a full sentence.

EXAMPLES   Barney asked the tour guide **,** **"**Is it difficult to identify artifacts?**"**

Dorothy wondered **,** **"**What play will the drama club choose to present this year?**"**

If an introductory expression is very long, set it off with a colon instead of a comma.

EXAMPLE   At the end of the practice, Miguel outlined his goals for the future **:** **"**I would like to increase my speed by the end of the year.**"**

Direct Quotations With Concluding Expressions

Direct quotations may sometimes end with **concluding expressions.**

> When a **concluding expression** follows a direct quotation, write the quotation as a full sentence ending with a comma, question mark, or exclamation mark inside the quotation mark. Then, write the concluding expression. Be sure to use end punctuation to close the sentence.

Concluding expressions are not complete sentences; therefore, they do not begin with capital letters. Notice also that the closing quotation marks are always placed outside the punctuation at the end of direct quotations followed by concluding expressions.

EXAMPLE   **"**I think you would have fun at our camp **!** **"** said Timothy excitedly.

Direct Quotations With Interrupting Expressions

You may use an interrupting expression in a direct quotation, which is also called a **divided quotation.** Interrupting expressions help writers clarify who is speaking and can also break up a long quotation.

> When the direct quotation of one sentence is interrupted, end the first part of the direct quotation with a comma and a quotation mark. Place a comma after the **interrupting expression,** and then use a new set of quotation marks to enclose the rest of the quotation.

RULE 25.4.5

EXAMPLES   "Because the camp is located on a lake," explained Ginnie, "we can go swimming and boating."

"Do you think," interrupted Juana, "that I could learn to water ski?"

Do not capitalize the first word of the second part of the sentence.

> When two sentences in a direct quotation are separated by an **interrupting expression,** end the first quoted sentence with a comma, question mark, or exclamation mark and a quotation mark. Place a period after the interrupter, and then write the second quoted sentence as a full quotation.

RULE 25.4.6

EXAMPLES   "We came face to face with a grizzly bear on one of our hikes," said Juan. "It was scary."

"That must have been amazing!" exclaimed Jenna. "How close did you get to the bear?"

See Practice 25.4A
See Practice 25.4B

PRACTICE 25.4A **Using Quotation Marks With Direct Quotations**

Read the sentences. If the sentence contains a direct quotation, write *D*. If it contains an indirect quotation, write *I*. Then, rewrite each sentence that contains a direct quotation, adding the quotation marks where needed.

EXAMPLE   Jenna reported that no one was injured during the game.

ANSWER   *I*

1. When you come home from school, Mother said, please do your laundry.

2. Martha wanted to know what I did yesterday.

3. I wonder, mused Catherine, whatever happened to our former neighbors.

4. Jamie announced, I feel confident about this test.

5. Abby thought that something was wrong.

6. When is this project due? Jordan asked.

7. Brian told us that he joined the drama club.

8. May I see your tickets? the usher asked.

9. Wendy said that she would join us later.

10. No, Clayton replied, I don't think that's a good idea.

PRACTICE 25.4B **Punctuating With Expressions**

Read the sentences. Rewrite each sentence, adding commas and quotation marks where needed.

EXAMPLE   Where should we begin? Kristen asked.

ANSWER   *"Where should we begin?" Kristen asked.*

11. Please let me see that magazine said Dane.

12. Gregory said I will teach you how to play this game.

13. Juan groaned I think I've misplaced my phone.

14. I would be happy to be your partner! Elisa exclaimed.

15. Let's call Randall Mac suggested. He always has some good ideas.

16. I'm not sure Rick said hesitantly where to go from here.

17. We can park here for an hour Carl noted. Then we'll have to add more money to the parking meter.

18. I want you to notice Steven declared that I have arrived on time today!

19. Maya's text message read See you at lunch.

20. I have just printed my final draft Vinny declared. After I proofread it, I'll hand it in.

SPEAKING APPLICATION

With a partner, take turns reporting direct and indirect conversational remarks. Your partner should tell whether each remark is a direct or an indirect quotation. You may use the examples in Practice 25.4A as models.

WRITING APPLICATION

Write three statements reporting something that you have said or that you have heard someone else say in the last few days. Use expressions (for example, *she said*), and put the speaker's words in quotation marks.

Using Quotation Marks With Other Punctuation Marks

You have seen that a comma or period used with a direct quotation goes inside the final quotation mark. In some cases, however, end marks should be placed outside of quotation marks.

 Find It/ FIX IT

6

Grammar
Game Plan

> **Always place a comma or a period inside the final quotation mark.**

 25.4.7 RULE

EXAMPLES   **"** Our class trip is this Tuesday **,** **"** said Janet **.**

Matthew added **,** **"** We are leaving the school very early by bus **.** **"**

> **Place a question mark or an exclamation mark inside the final quotation mark if the end mark is part of the quotation. Do not use an additional end mark outside the quotation marks.**

25.4.8 RULE

EXAMPLES   Joe asked **,** **"** What animal eats the most leaves **?** **"**

Peter said to Andy **,** **"** Help me get this raccoon out of my car **!** **"**

> **Place a question mark or exclamation mark outside the final quotation mark if the end mark is part of the entire sentence, not part of the quotation.**

 25.4.9 RULE

EXAMPLES   Don't say **,** **"** I doubt that will work **"** **!**

What famous person said **,** **"** We have nothing to fear but fear itself **"** **?**

See Practice 25.4C

Using Single Quotation Marks for Quotations Within Quotations

Double quotation marks are used to enclose the main quotation. The rules for using commas and end marks with **single quotation marks (' ')** are the same as they are with double quotation marks.

Single quotation marks are used to separate a quote that appears inside of another quotation.

> Use **single quotation marks** to set off a quotation within a quotation.

EXAMPLES   "I thought I heard him say , 'I lost my wallet ! ' as he ran off , " said Neil .

Nate said , "Someone yelled , 'Fire ! ' right before we smelled the smoke . "

Punctuating Explanatory Material Within Quotes

Sometimes it is necessary to add information to a quotation that explains the quote more fully. In that case, brackets tell your reader which information came from the original speaker and which came from someone else. (See Section 25.7 for more information on brackets.)

> Use brackets to enclose an explanation located within a quotation to show that the explanation is not part of the original quotation.

EXAMPLE   The mayor said , "The new park is the result of two communities [New City and Hillsdale] working together . "

"We [the citizens of Brookfield] dedicate the new community center to our senior citizens . "

See Practice 25.4D

PRACTICE 25.4C **Using Quotation Marks With Other Punctuation Marks**

Read the sentences. Decide whether the missing punctuation goes inside or outside the quotation marks. Then, rewrite the sentences, adding the proper punctuation for quotations.

EXAMPLE   Who wrote, "Hold fast to dreams"

ANSWER   *Who wrote, "Hold fast to dreams"?*

1. Did I hear someone say, "Let's have ice cream"

2. "Who gave permission to leave" asked the assistant principal.

3. Someone shouted, "Time out"

4. Did she answer, "Not right now, thank you"

5. A new student asked, "Can you direct me to the nurse's office"

6. Did your mother really say, "I'll give you the money if you need it"

7. Milton asked, "Is it too late to apply"

8. "I knew you could do it" my dad exclaimed.

9. Dee wondered, "Where did everyone go"

10. The boating instructor shouted, "Put on your lifejackets"

PRACTICE 25.4D **Punctuating Quotations Within Quotations and Explanatory Material**

Read the sentences. Rewrite each sentence, adding single quotation marks or brackets where needed.

EXAMPLE   Jon said, "I enjoyed reading The Treasure of Lemon Brown."

ANSWER   *Jon said, "I enjoyed reading 'The Treasure of Lemon Brown.'"*

11. "For tomorrow," Mrs. May said, "please read the story Amigo Brothers."

12. Jan asked, "Did he say, I'll help?"

13. Paula asked, "Can anyone recite the poem Sarah Cynthia Sylvia Stout?"

14. "Did she say, I lost my hat?" Mom asked.

15. Lori wondered, "What does Longfellow mean by Each burning deed and thought?"

16. Mr. Metzger said, "I will now recite the poem Casey at the Bat."

17. "Did you hear him say, I've had it?" asked Liz.

18. The music director announced, "Miss Amory will sing Greensleeves, an old folk song."

19. Ron said, "When did you ever hear him Mr. Shah say, I don't want pizza?"

20. Sheila asked, "Does anyone know the words to the second verse of America?"

WRITING APPLICATION

Write three sentences in which you correctly use punctuation inside and outside quotation marks.

WRITING APPLICATION

Write two sentences with quotations within quotations. In your sentences, use single and double quotation marks correctly.

Using Quotation Marks for Dialogue

A conversation between two or more people is called a **dialogue.**
Adding dialogue makes your writing lively because it brings
different points of view into your work. It makes your work sound
like speech, so dialogue makes your reader feel involved in the
scene you describe.

> When you are writing a **dialogue,** indent to begin a new
> paragraph with each change of speaker. Also be sure to add
> quotation marks around a speaker's words. When a new
> speaker is quoted, be sure to indicate the change to your reader
> by adding information that identifies the new speaker.

EXAMPLE

"Will you be going with us on the family trip
again this summer?" Noreen asked her cousin.

Gwen hesitated before answering. "I'm afraid
so. My parents think I enjoy the experience of
traveling with our whole family."

"You fooled me, too," Noreen replied.
"Maybe the trip will be better this year. I think
we're going to places that have large parks. If
we're lucky, we might even be able to go on a
few rides."

"Well, at least it can't be any worse," sighed
Gwen. "On the last trip, we waited in line for one
hour at three different historic homes in one day!"

"I remember those lines," said Noreen.
"Didn't you get sunburned while we were
waiting?"

Notice that each sentence is punctuated according to the rules
discussed earlier in this section.

See Practice 25.4E
See Practice 25.4F

PRACTICE 25.4E › Using Quotation Marks in Dialogue

Read the dialogue. Then, rewrite the dialogue. Use proper spacing for quotations and create additional paragraphs where needed. Be sure to use quotation marks and other punctuation correctly.

EXAMPLE Can I ask you something? Matt asked Angelo. Sure Angelo answered. What?

ANSWER *"Can I ask you something?" Matt asked Angelo.*

"Sure," Angelo answered. "What?"

I would like to learn about forensic science Rose commented. You've been watching too many crime shows laughed Tim. Really Rose said it's fascinating, and I would even consider it as a career. Well there are many colleges that offer courses, but I think they're tough courses. There's a lot of science involved, Tim said. That's all right, I like science Rose replied. You could probably look online to find the requirements and places that offer courses Tim suggested. That's what I'll do Rose concluded.

PRACTICE 25.4F › Revising Dialogue for Punctuation and Paragraphs

Read the dialogue. Then, rewrite the dialogue. Add quotation marks and other punctuation, and begin new paragraphs where needed.

EXAMPLE Hello, my name is Gwendolyn, the new girl said. What's your name? I'm Elizabeth. Nice to meet you.

ANSWER *"Hello, my name is Gwendolyn," the new girl said. "What's your name?"*

"I'm Elizabeth. Nice to meet you."

Justin and Marina walked into the sandwich shop for lunch. When they were seated at a table, a waiter came to take their order. What can I get you the waiter asked. I'll have the tuna salad sandwich with pickles Justin said. I'll have the vegetarian special Marina added. What would you like to drink with that asked the waiter. We'll both have water Marina responded. The waiter said Thank you. I'll bring your orders shortly. Then, he walked away.

SPEAKING APPLICATION

Read the dialogue in Practice 25.4E with a partner, each of you taking the part of one speaker. Read it again after you have revised it. Discuss why the original dialogue is confusing to read and your revised dialogue is easy to read.

WRITING APPLICATION

Write a dialogue in which you have participated, or you can make up a conversation. Use expressions (for example, *he said*, *she replied*), quotation marks, and correct paragraphing.

Using Quotation Marks in Titles

Quotation marks are generally used to set off the titles of shorter works.

RULE 25.4.13 Use **quotation marks** to enclose the titles of short written works and around the title of a work that is mentioned as part of a collection.

WRITTEN WORKS THAT USE QUOTATION MARKS	
Title of a Short Story	"The Gift of the Magi"
Chapter From a Book	"The Test Is in the Tasting" from *No-Work Garden Book*
Title of a Short Poem	"Lucy"
Title of an Article	"How to Build a Birdhouse"
Title Mentioned as Part of a Collection	"Uncle Vanya" in *Eight Great Comedies*

RULE 25.4.14 Use **quotation marks** around the titles of episodes in a television or radio series, songs, and parts of a long musical composition.

ARTISTIC WORKS THAT USE QUOTATION MARKS	
Title of an Episode	"The Nile" from *Cousteau Odyssey*
Title of a Song	"The Best Things in Life Are Free"
Title of a Part of a Long Musical Work	"The Storm" from the *William Tell Overture*

Using Underlining and Italics in Titles

Underlining and **italics** help make titles and other special words and names stand out in your writing. Underlining is used only in handwritten or typewritten material. In printed material, italic (slanted) print is used instead of underlining.

UNDERLINING   <u>The Secret Garden</u>   ITALICS   *The Secret Garden*

Underline or **italicize** the titles of long written works and publications that are published as a single work.

WRITTEN WORKS THAT ARE UNDERLINED OR ITALICIZED	
Title of a Book or Play	*The Giver; West Side Story*
Title of a Long Poem	*The Song of Hiawatha*
Title of a Magazine or Newspaper	*Time; The Washington Post*

Underline or **italicize** the titles of movies, television and radio series, long works of music, and art.

ARTISTIC WORKS THAT ARE UNDERLINED OR ITALICIZED	
Title of a Movie	*Schindler's List*
Title of a Television Series	*Lost*
Title of a Long Work of Music	*The Four Seasons*
Title of a Music Album	*Abbey Road*
Title of a Painting	*Starry Night*
Title of a Sculpture	*Venus de Milo*

Underline or **italicize** the names of individual air, sea, and spacecraft.

EXAMPLES   *Apollo 13*   the USS *Intrepid*

Underline or **italicize** words and letters used as names for themselves and foreign words.

EXAMPLES   How do you spell *Mississippi?*

See Practice 25.4G

See Practice 25.4H

My family uses the toast *santé,* which means "good health" in French.

Quotation Marks, Underlining, and Italics

PRACTICE 25.4G > **Underlining Titles, Names and Words**

Read the sentences. Rewrite each sentence, underlining titles, names, and words where needed. You can use italics if you are typing your answers.

EXAMPLE   I loved Stuart Little when I was younger.

ANSWER   I loved <u>Stuart Little</u> when I was younger.

1. Our class performed The Phantom Tollbooth.

2. Caroline knows all the songs from The Sound of Music.

3. Suzie read Goodnight Moon to the children she was babysitting.

4. Amanda was uncertain of the meaning of amorphous, so she looked it up in Webster's New World Dictionary.

5. My mom reads The Houston Chronicle.

6. We plan to see High School Musical at the theater next month.

7. Chloe really enjoyed the RMS Titanic exhibition at the children's museum.

8. For his biography report, Jethro read Walter Dean Myers's memoir Bad Boy.

9. I can't wait to see The Lion King again.

10. You can see the famous painting George Washington Crossing the Delaware at the Metropolitan Museum of Art.

PRACTICE 25.4H > **Using Underlining and Quotation Marks**

Read the sentences. Rewrite each sentence, enclosing the titles in quotation marks or underlining them. You can use italics if you are typing your answers.

EXAMPLE   The choir sang Oh Shenandoah.

ANSWER   The choir sang "Oh Shenandoah."

11. My mom liked to read Pat the Bunny to me when I was very young.

12. I read an article in Now magazine titled How to Survive a Computer Crash.

13. The concert will end with America the Beautiful.

14. In honor of Black History Month, LaVerne will sing Lift Every Voice and Sing.

15. My little brother's favorite television program is Krazy Kats Cartoons.

16. My friend Jim, who likes technology, reads Future magazine.

17. One of Rodin's famous statues is The Thinker.

18. The Apollo 13 astronauts faced life-threatening challenges in space.

19. Our assignment for tomorrow is to read Laurence Yep's story Ribbons.

20. David memorized and recited The Raven by Edgar Allan Poe.

WRITING APPLICATION

Write several sentences in which you refer to a movie you have seen, a television program you watch, and a book you have read recently. Underline the titles.

WRITING APPLICATION

Make a list of the following: a song that you like, a poem that you have read in language arts, and a magazine with which you are familiar. Punctuate the titles correctly.

25.5 Hyphens

Hyphens (-) are used to combine words and to show a connection between the syllables of words that are broken at the ends of lines.

Find It/ FIX IT

19
Grammar
Game Plan

Using Hyphens in Numbers

Hyphens are used to join compound numbers and fractions.

> Use a **hyphen** when you write two-word numbers from twenty-one through ninety-nine.

RULE 25.5.1

EXAMPLES   twenty - four   fifty - one

> Use a **hyphen** when you use a fraction as an adjective but not when you use a fraction as a noun.

RULE 25.5.2

ADJECTIVE   The class is three - fourths full.

NOUN   Two thirds of the students attended.

Using Hyphens for Prefixes and Suffixes

Many words with common prefixes are no longer hyphenated. The following prefixes are often used before proper nouns: *ante-, anti-, post-, pre-, pro-,* and *un-.* Check a dictionary when you are unsure about using a hyphen.

> Use a **hyphen** after a prefix that is followed by a proper noun or adjective.

RULE 25.5.3

EXAMPLES   post - Revolutionary   mid - April

> Use a **hyphen** in words with the prefixes *all-, ex-,* and *self-* and the suffix *-elect*.

RULE 25.5.4

EXAMPLES   all - powerful   ex - leader

Hyphens   589

Using Hyphens in Compound Words

Compound words are two or more words that must be read together to create a single idea.

Use a **hyphen** to connect two or more nouns that are used as one compound word, unless a dictionary gives a different spelling.

EXAMPLES   son-in-law   great-grandmother

Using Hyphens With Compound Modifiers

Hyphens help your reader group information properly.

Use a hyphen to connect a **compound modifier** that comes before a noun. Do not use a hyphen with a compound modifier that includes a word ending in *-ly* or in a compound proper adjective.

EXAMPLE   The team used a full-court press.

INCORRECT   poorly-written text   South-Asian tourist

CORRECT   poorly written text   South Asian tourist

A hyphen is not necessary when a compound modifier follows the noun it describes.

MODIFIER BEFORE NOUN   The storm moved in an east-to-west direction.

MODIFIER AFTER NOUN   The storm moved in the direction east to west.

However, if a dictionary spells a word with a hyphen, the word must always be hyphenated, even when it follows a noun.

EXAMPLE   The goalie is happy-go-lucky.

 TEKS Check Show that you can use correct punctuation including hyphens. Write directions from your home to your school. Explain to a partner why the hyphens you used are needed.

Focus on the TEKS

(20)(B)(ii) Use correct punctuation marks including hyphens.

See TEKS Check

See TEKS Practice

See Practice 25.5A

See Practice 25.5B

TEKS Practice Show that you can use correct punctuation, including hyphens, by completing the following activities.

Hyphens

PRACTICE 25.5A ▷ Using Hyphens in Numbers and Words

Read the following items. Write each item, adding hyphens where needed. If an item is already correct, write *correct*.

EXAMPLE a world famous star

ANSWER *a world-famous star*

1. mid January temperature
2. sixty six pencils
3. a bench that is well built
4. self respect
5. one third of a cup
6. one hundred people
7. two thirds of the students
8. well known actor
9. post Civil War
10. president elect

PRACTICE 25.5B ▷ Proofreading for Hyphens

Read the sentences. Rewrite each sentence, adding hyphens where needed.

EXAMPLE At the half, our team was ahead by twenty two points.

ANSWER *At the half, our team was ahead by **twenty-two** points.*

11. Success builds self confidence.
12. Red hot embers glowed in the fireplace.
13. The recipe calls for one half teaspoon of cinnamon.
14. In London, we rode on the top level of a double decker bus.
15. My brother in law took me to the movies yesterday.
16. Sometimes, Beau's friends are annoyed by his all knowing attitude.
17. Rubble from a torn down building was strewn over the lot.
18. The ex governor stood on the platform beside the governor elect.
19. Fifty five people attended the fund raiser last night.
20. The adventurers will need an off road vehicle to get to that remote campsite.

SPEAKING APPLICATION

With a partner, brainstorm and list five terms that you use or have seen that are written with a hyphen. Take turns using these terms in phrases or sentences.

WRITING APPLICATION

Write two sentences in which you use words with *self-* or *ex-* as prefixes.

Using Hyphens at the Ends of Lines

Hyphens serve a useful purpose when they are used to divide words at the ends of lines. They should not, however, be used more often than is necessary because they can make reading feel choppy.

> **Avoid dividing words at the end of a line whenever possible. If a word must be divided, always divide it between syllables.**

EXAMPLE   Marcia seems to have taken my advice most seriously and is doing better.

Check a dictionary if you are unsure how a word is divided into syllables. Looking up the word *seriously*, for example, you would find that its syllables are *se-ri-ous-ly*.

> **A hyphen used to divide a word should never be placed at the beginning of the second line. It must be placed at the end of the first line.**

INCORRECT   Julio has taken many photo
-graphs of animals.

CORRECT   Julio has taken many photographs of animals.

Using Hyphens Correctly to Divide Words

One-syllable words cannot be divided.

> **Do *not* divide one-syllable words even if they seem long or sound like words with two syllables.**

INCORRECT   fif-th   brow-se   stra-ight

CORRECT   fifth   browse   straight

Do *not* divide a word so that a single letter stands alone.

25.5.10 RULE

INCORRECT	i-dle	a-lone	ink-y
CORRECT	idle	alone	inky

Also avoid placing *-ed* at the beginning of a new line.

INCORRECT   Our last soccer game of the year was interrupted by lightning.

CORRECT   Our last soccer game of the year was
interrupted by lightning.

Focus on the TEKS

(20)(B)(ii) Use correct
punctuation marks
including hyphens.

See TEKS Check

See TEKS Practice

See Practice 25.5C

See Practice 25.5D

Avoid dividing proper nouns or proper adjectives.

25.5.11 RULE

INCORRECT	Dal-las	Don-ald
CORRECT	Dallas	Donald

Divide a hyphenated word only immediately following the existing hyphen.

25.5.12 RULE

INCORRECT   Students are taking an ever-in-
creasing interest in the environment.

CORRECT   Students are taking an ever-
increasing interest in the environment.

TEKS Practice Show that you can use correct punctuation, including hyphens, by completing the following activities.

PRACTICE 25.5C >	**Using Hyphens to Divide Words**

Read the following words. Rewrite each word. Then, draw vertical lines between syllables that can be divided at the end of a line. Do nothing to words that cannot be divided.

EXAMPLE   vocabulary

ANSWER   *vo|cab|u|lar|y*

1. tornado

2. warned

3. sacrifice

4. special

5. prediction

6. question

7. readjust

8. investigate

9. forgetful

10. collapse

PRACTICE 25.5D >	**Using Hyphens in Words in Sentences**

Read the sentences. If a word has been divided correctly, write *correct*. If not, rewrite the sentence, dividing the word correctly or writing it as one word if it cannot be divided.

EXAMPLE   Many of my friends are in-terested in learning Spanish.

ANSWER   *correct*

11. The water was blue and the sun-light sparkled on the waves.

12. The university students pa-rticipated in a rally.

13. We strolled the streets of our neighbor-hood after dinner.

14. Please tell me if the plumber has call-ed about our broken sink.

15. My mother will be driv-ing us to the concert.

16. A mid-April snowstorm took every-one by surprise.

17. Next week, the school-wide tourn-ament will begin.

18. I believe Stephen was the onl-y player who missed the game.

19. Do you have any specific ques-tions about the quiz instructions?

20. Mrs. Marquez asked us to cir-cle the correct answer.

WRITING APPLICATION

Look at a draft of a piece of writing you have done. Select three words and write them in syllables, showing how you would break them at the end of a line using a hyphen.

WRITING APPLICATION

Use three sentences from Practice 25.5D as models, and write sentences with hyphenated words.

25.6 Apostrophes

The **apostrophe** (') is used to show possession or ownership. It is also used in shortened forms of words called contractions. In a contraction, the apostrophe marks the place where letters have been omitted.

Find It/FIX IT

14

Grammar Game Plan

Using Apostrophes With Possessive Nouns

Apostrophes are used with nouns to show ownership or possession.

> Add an apostrophe and -s to show the possessive case of most singular nouns and plural nouns that do not end in -s or -es.

RULE 25.6.1

EXAMPLES   The doctor**'**s advice included plenty of rest.

The men**'**s store in town is having a huge sale.

Even when a singular noun already ends in -*s*, you can usually add an apostrophe and -*s* to show possession.

EXAMPLE   It was her boss**'**s idea to work longer hours.

In classical or ancient names that end in -*s*, it is common to omit the final -*s* to make pronunciation easier.

EXAMPLE   Ulysses**'** wisdom was well known.

> Add an apostrophe to show the possessive case of plural nouns ending in -s or -es. Do not add an -s.

RULE 25.6.2

EXAMPLE   The bees**'** buzzing was all I could hear.

RULE 25.6.3 Add an apostrophe and *-s* (or just an apostrophe if the word is a plural ending in *-s*) to the last word of a compound noun to form the possessive.

EXAMPLES   the Boy Scouts**'** camping trip

my grandfather**'**s house

See Practice 25.6A

Using Apostrophes With Pronouns

Both indefinite and personal pronouns can show possession.

RULE 25.6.4 Use an apostrophe and *-s* with indefinite pronouns to show possession.

EXAMPLES   anyone**'**s seat   everyone else**'**s name

RULE 25.6.5 Do not use an apostrophe with possessive personal pronouns.

POSSESSIVE PERSONAL PRONOUNS		
	SINGULAR	PLURAL
First Person	my, mine	our, ours
Second Person	your, yours	your, yours
Third Person	his; her, hers; its	their, theirs

Some of these pronouns act as adjectives.

EXAMPLES   The dog carried a ball in its mouth.

Their house is for sale.

Others act as subjects, objects, and subject complements.

EXAMPLES   Mine is the blue jacket.

The red jacket is hers.

See Practice 25.6B

Using Apostrophes With Contractions

Contractions are used in informal speech and writing, especially in dialogue because they create the sound of speech.

> Use an **apostrophe** in a **contraction** to show where one or more letters have been omitted.

COMMON CONTRACTIONS		
Verb + *not*	is not = isn't	cannot = can't
Noun or Pronoun + *will*	I will = I'll	we will = we'll
Noun or Pronoun + *be*	you are = you're	Andy is = Andy's
Noun or Pronoun + *would*	she would = she'd	who would = who'd

> Avoid using contractions in formal speech and writing.

Contractions may be used in dialogue and in informal speech and writing, but they should be avoided in formal usage.

INFORMAL WRITING   What's the latest news?

FORMAL WRITING   What is the latest news?

Using Apostrophes to Create Plurals

Do not use an apostrophe to form plurals, except in specific instances.

> Use an **apostrophe** and *-s* to create the plural form of a letter, numeral, or a word used as a name for itself.   25.6.8   RULE

See Practice 25.6C
See Practice 25.6D

EXAMPLES   Remember your *thank you*'s.

Your *b*'s and *d*'s look alike.

PRACTICE 25.6A > **Using Apostrophes to Show Ownership**

Read each phrase. Write the possessive form of each item.

EXAMPLE   clothing store for men

ANSWER   *men's clothing store*

1. work of the painter

2. hat belonging to Nina

3. apartment where the Maldonados live

4. eyes of a cat

5. the strength of Atlas

6. pizzeria owned by Mario

7. a vacation for a week

8. the soccer team for girls

9. the mitt belonging to the catcher

10. an idea from the brother of Ollie

PRACTICE 25.6B > **Using Apostrophes With Pronouns**

Read the sentences. If all pronouns in a sentence are used correctly, write *correct*. If one or more pronouns are used incorrectly, rewrite the sentence correctly.

EXAMPLE   Her's is the best drawing.

ANSWER   *Hers is the best drawing.*

11. This is someone elses scarf, not mine.

12. We found everyone else's folder but not his.

13. No ones ideas will be ignored.

14. The dog was favoring its left front paw.

15. Everyones support is necessary.

16. The seats in the first row are our's.

17. Someones equipment was left in the gym.

18. The choice will be your's alone.

19. After you read your poem aloud, Julie will read hers.

20. Our writing group shared papers with another group; we read their's and they read ours.

WRITING APPLICATION

Look around the classroom. List five items or characteristics that you see and the possessor of each.

WRITING APPLICATION

Write two or three sentences in which you use *our, ours,* and the possessive form of *someone.*

PRACTICE 25.6C **Using Apostrophes in Contractions**

Read the sentences. Each sentence contains a word group that can be written as a contraction. Write the contractions.

EXAMPLE   That is a very good question.

ANSWER   *That's*

1. I cannot eat another bite!

2. We are planning to go in a group.

3. Kyle will not be here today.

4. Who is still in need of help?

5. I have been working for two days on this essay.

6. It does not matter what you say now.

7. We do not have the resources we need for this job.

8. It is too early to predict the outcome.

9. What will we do next?

10. I would be glad to help you with that.

PRACTICE 25.6D **Proofreading for Apostrophes**

Read the sentences. Rewrite each sentence, adding apostrophes where needed.

EXAMPLE   Mike said he couldnt go to the park today.

ANSWER   *Mike said he couldn't go to the park today.*

11. Its a difficult situation to be in.

12. Why dont you come also?

13. Hes been spending time with a new crowd.

14. I wouldve been here earlier if I had not been stuck in traffic.

15. Shell be right with you.

16. Arent you finished yet?

17. We shouldve thought of that sooner.

18. Alans on his way now.

19. Youre going to need a warm jacket.

20. Wed better hurry if we want to get there on time.

WRITING APPLICATION

Use your rewritten sentences 3, 4, and 5 as models, and write three new sentences with the same subjects and contractions.

WRITING APPLICATION

Use the contractions you wrote for sentences 11, 14, and 16, and write three sentences of your own.

25.7 Parentheses and Brackets

Parentheses and **brackets** enclose explanations or other information that may be omitted from the rest of the sentence without changing its basic meaning or construction.

WRITING COACH

Online

www.TXWritingCoach.com

Grammar Practice

Practice your grammar skills with Writing Coach Online.

Grammar Games

Test your knowledge of grammar in this fast-paced interactive video game.

Parentheses

Parentheses are used to separate information from the rest of a sentence or paragraph.

RULE 25.7.1   Use **parentheses** to set off explanations or other information that is loosely related to the rest of the sentence.

EXAMPLE   James Fenimore Cooper **(**1789–1851**)** was well known for his historical novels.

RULE 25.7.2   A **parenthetical sentence** within another sentence should not begin with a capital letter unless the parenthetical sentence begins with a word that should be capitalized.

EXAMPLE   New puppies **(**my family just bought one**)** require a lot of care and patience.

RULE 25.7.3   A **parenthetical sentence** within another sentence may end with a question mark or exclamation mark if applicable, but it should not end with a period.

INCORRECT   The playoff schedule **(**the league is still working on it**.)** will be available soon **.**

CORRECT   The playoff schedule **(**the league is still working on it**!)** will be available soon **.**

Parenthetical Sentences That Stand on Their Own

Parenthetical sentences add information to another sentence or a paragraph.

> A **parenthetical sentence** that stands on its own should begin with a capital letter and end with an end mark before the closing parenthesis.

25.7.4 RULE

EXAMPLE   The playoff schedule will be available soon **.**

(Can you believe they are still working on it **?)**

Brackets

Brackets have one major use: to enclose a word or words in a quotation that were not spoken by the person or source that is quoted.

> Use **brackets** to enclose an explanation located within a quote to show that the explanation is not part of the original quote.

25.7.5 RULE

EXAMPLE   An eyewitness to the accident said, "This intersection has been a problem since the stop sign was installed **[** in 2001 **]** ."

> Use **brackets** to enclose an explanation that is located within parenthetical text.

25.7.6 RULE

See Practice 25.7A
See Practice 25.7B

EXAMPLE   Abraham Lincoln **(** the sixteenth president of the United States **[** 1861–1865 **])** came from humble origins.

PRACTICE 25.7A > **Using Parentheses and
Brackets**

Read the sentences. Rewrite the sentences,
adding parentheses or brackets where
appropriate.

EXAMPLE   Louisa May Alcott 1832–1888 wrote
Little Women and *Little Men.*

ANSWER   *Louisa May Alcott (1832–1888)
wrote Little Women and Little
Men.*

1. Being late for a movie something I can't stand
doesn't seem to bother some of my friends.

2. The coach finally dismissed the players.
They'd put in three long hours of practice.

3. We hope to climb the highest mountain Mt.
Washington in the Presidential Range.

4. In some states Connecticut, for example, it
is illegal to use a cellphone while driving.

5. After Jennifer's trip to Mexico June 15–25,
she became very interested in Aztec culture.

6. During the solo, someone in the audience
commented, "That student Phoebe Robinson
is a very talented musician."

PRACTICE 25.7B > **Proofreading for Parentheses
and Brackets**

Read the paragraph. Rewrite the paragraph,
adding parentheses or brackets where
appropriate.

EXAMPLE   My great-grandfather wrote, "I
fought in the war World War I as a
young man."

ANSWER   *My great-grandfather wrote,
"I fought in the war [World War I]
as a young man."*

My great-grandfather's diary read, "That
was the year 1917 we entered the war." I had
studied that war World War I in school, so the
diary interested me. He wrote, "We were under
Pershing's command General John J. Pershing.
When we got here France, Pershing wanted to
honor Lafayette." I remembered Lafayette from
studying the American Revolution. The diary
continued, "That day in July July 4, 1917, we had
a parade to his Lafayette's tomb. Pershing's aide
his assistant said, 'Lafayette, we are here!' That
speech cheered up our friends the French." So
many Americans died about 120,000. I'm glad my
great-grandfather he lived to age 85 wasn't one
of them.

WRITING APPLICATION

**Use sentences 1 and 4 as models, and write
two new sentences into which you insert
parenthetical information.**

WRITING APPLICATION

**Write a sentence that includes a quotation with
a comment inserted into the quotation using
brackets.**

25.8 Ellipses and Dashes

An **ellipsis** (. . .) shows where words have been omitted from a quoted passage. It can also mark a pause in dialogue. A **dash** (—) shows a strong, sudden break in thought or speech.

Using the Ellipsis

An **ellipsis** consists of three evenly spaced periods, or ellipsis points, in a row. There is a space before the first ellipsis point, between ellipsis points, and after the last ellipsis point. The plural form of the word *ellipsis* is *ellipses*.

> Use an **ellipsis** to show where words have been omitted from a quoted passage. Including an ellipsis shows the reader that the writer has chosen to omit some information.

25.8.1 RULE

QUOTED PASSAGE	"Four score and seven years ago our fathers brought forth on this continent a new nation conceived in liberty and dedicated to the proposition that all men are created equal." –Abraham Lincoln, *The Gettysburg Address*, November 19, 1863
QUOTED PASSAGE WITH WORDS OMITTED	"Fourscore and seven years ago our fathers brought forth . . . a new nation . . . dedicated to the proposition that all men are created equal."

Ellipses in Advertising

Ellipses are commonly used in ads for movies and other media. When you see an ellipsis in an ad, think about what might have been omitted. You might want to find the original review because the ad might be giving a different impression from what the reviewer intended.

ORIGINAL REVIEW	"I am amazed that anyone would think this movie is exciting or even worth seeing."
AD WORDING	" . . . exciting . . . worth seeing"

RULE 25.8.2

Use an **ellipsis** to mark a pause in a dialogue or speech.

EXAMPLE   "But, in a larger sense, we can not dedicate ... we can not consecrate ... we can not hallow ... this ground."

RULE 25.8.3

It is not necessary to use an **ellipsis** to show an omission at the beginning of material you are quoting. However, if you choose to omit any words *within* material you quote, you must use an ellipsis to show where information has been omitted.

UNNECESSARY   " ... Now we are engaged in a great civil war, testing whether that nation, or any nation, so conceived and so dedicated, can long endure."

CORRECT   "Now we are engaged in a great civil war, testing whether that nation, or any nation so conceived and so dedicated, can long endure."

RULE 25.8.4

Use an **ellipsis** to show an omission, pause, or interruption in the middle of a sentence.

EXAMPLE   "But, in a larger sense, we cannot dedicate ... this ground."

RULE 25.8.5

Use an **ellipsis** and an end mark to show an omission or a pause at the end of a sentence.

EXAMPLE   "I don't know how we are going to get this mess cleaned up. Maybe we could. ... "

If you omit words from a source you are quoting, omit the punctuation that accompanies the words unless it is correct in your sentence.

See Practice 25.8A

Dashes

Like commas and parentheses, **dashes** separate certain words, phrases, or clauses from the rest of the sentence or paragraph. Dashes, however, signal a stronger, more sudden interruption in thought or speech than commas or parentheses. A dash may also take the place of certain words before an explanation.

Use a dash to show a strong, sudden break in thought or speech.

RULE 25.8.6

EXAMPLE I can't believe how quickly we arrived—hey, where are you going?

If the interrupting expression is in the middle of the sentence, use a dash on either side of it to set it off from the rest of the sentence.

EXAMPLE I read a book—it's in the library—about dinosaurs that have been newly discovered.

Use a dash in place of *in other words, namely,* or *that is* before an explanation.

RULE 25.8.7

EXAMPLES Dario reads books for one purpose—to learn.

To come in first in the relay race—this was the team's hope.

Dashes can also be used to set off nonessential appositives or modifiers.

EXAMPLE A team player—someone who will make sacrifices for the good of the team—is what we need.

See Practice 25.8B

PRACTICE 25.8A ▶ **Using Ellipses**

Read the sentences. For each sentence, tell whether ellipses (or ellipsis points) are used to indicate a *pause* or an *omission*.

EXAMPLE   "Well . . . I'm not sure about this," said Luis.

ANSWER   *pause*

1. Wow . . . I don't know how to thank you.

2. In her review, Kate wrote, "This exciting movie kept me on the edge of my seat . . . I can't wait to see it again."

3. Of course, we could always . . . uh . . . try a different tactic.

4. John F. Kennedy said, "Ask not what your country can do for you . . . ."

5. Mom . . . are you sure I can't go to Max's house after I finish my homework?

6. The Preamble to the Constitution reads, "We the people of the United States . . . do ordain and establish this Constitution for the United States of America."

7. Well . . . um . . . let me think about it.

8. The words of Dr. Martin Luther King Jr., "Let freedom ring . . . From every mountainside, let freedom ring," still move us today.

9. Keena . . . are you still there . . . or did you hang up?

10. The last line of "All Summer in a Day" reads, "They unlocked the door . . . and let Margot out."

PRACTICE 25.8B ▶ **Using Dashes**

Read the sentences. Rewrite each sentence, adding dashes where they are needed.

EXAMPLE   Bernard plays several instruments guitar, banjo, and drums.

ANSWER   *Bernard plays several instruments — guitar, banjo, and drums.*

11. There's only one thing I still need to pack for my trip sunscreen.

12. All of the preparations for the dance including the decorations have been made.

13. I would like to present the winner Hector Rodriguez.

14. I already have all of the ingredients for this recipe even the walnuts.

15. Head east on the trail wait, you forgot the map!

16. The money thirty dollars is on the table.

17. The committee announced what they need to get the job done more money, more time, more people.

18. Jonah had only one goal to be the fastest sprinter on the team.

19. My favorite restaurant The Corner Diner is closed for renovations.

20. An Academy Award an Oscar recognizes outstanding work in a motion picture.

SPEAKING APPLICATION

With a partner, read aloud Sentences 7 and 9. Then, together, write a sentence that uses ellipsis points for the same purpose.

WRITING APPLICATION

Copy a passage from a selection in your literature textbook. Leave out a part of the passage, either in the middle or at the end, and use ellipses to show where the omission occurs.

CAPITALIZATION

Understanding the rules of capitalization will help you to craft clear sentences.

WRITE GUY *Jeff Anderson, M.Ed.*

WHAT DO YOU NOTICE?

Locate capital letters as you zoom in on sentences from the folktale "Sun and Moon in a Box," retold by Alfonso Ortiz and Richard Erdoes.

MENTOR TEXT

> "Let us steal the box," said Coyote.
> "No, that would be wrong," said Eagle. "Let us just borrow it."
> When the Kachinas were not looking, Eagle grabbed the box and flew off. Coyote ran after him on the ground.

Now, ask yourself the following questions:

- Why are the words *eagle* and *coyote* capitalized?
- In Eagle's quotation, why are the words *no* and *let* capitalized?

The words *eagle* and *coyote* are usually common nouns, but here they are the names of characters, so they are capitalized as proper nouns. Because Eagle's quotation includes two complete sentences, the first word of each sentence begins with a capital letter.

Grammar for Writers A capital letter not only signals the start of a sentence, but it can also show the beginning of a quotation. When writing dialogue, be sure to follow capitalization rules, so readers can hear your character's words clearly.

What word should be capitalized in this sentence?

What? The word what!

26.1 Using Capitalization

Capital letters are used for the first words in all sentences and in many quotations. They are also used for the word *I*, whatever its position in a sentence.

The Word *I*

RULE **26.1.1**

The pronoun *I* is always capitalized.

EXAMPLE **I** worked for two years as an assistant before **I** received a promotion.

Sentences

One of the most common uses of a capital letter is to signal the beginning of a sentence. The first word in a sentence must begin with a capital letter.

RULE **26.1.2**

Capitalize the first word in declarative, interrogative, imperative, and exclamatory sentences.

DECLARATIVE **S**trong gusts of wind made it very difficult to golf on the course.

INTERROGATIVE **W**ho found the answer to that very difficult question?

IMPERATIVE **T**hink carefully before you answer.

EXCLAMATORY **W**hat an amazing situation this is!

See Practice 26.1A

Sometimes only part of a sentence is written. The rest of the sentence is understood. In these cases, a capital is still needed for the first word.

EXAMPLES **W**here?   **W**ho said?   **S**urely!

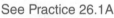
See Practice 26.1B

Quotations

A capital letter also signals the first word in a **direct quotation,** a person's exact words.

RULE 26.1.3

> Capitalize the first word in a quotation if the quotation is a complete sentence.

EXAMPLES

Several people shouted, "**S**top the car!"

"**S**he really wants to see that play," Helen confided.

Randy asked, "**H**as anyone seen my dog?"

RULE 26.1.4

> When a quotation consists of one complete sentence in two parts, only capitalize the first part of the quotation.

EXAMPLES

"**H**ow much longer," asked Bob, "**w**ill this game continue?"

"**P**enguins seem to have no special fear of humans," she said, "**a**nd have approached groups of explorers without hesitation."

RULE 26.1.5

> If a quotation contains more than one sentence, the first word of each sentence begins with a capital.

Focus on the TEKS

(20)(A) Use conventions of capitalization.

See TEKS Practice

See Practice 26.1C

See Practice 26.1D

EXAMPLES

"**P**lease distribute these menus to everyone," said the waiter. "**T**hey show the specials of the day."

"**R**emember to bring your project," said my friend. "**Y**ou will need it for class tomorrow."

PRACTICE 26.1A ▷ Writing Sentences Using Capitalization

Read the sentences. Rewrite each sentence, adding the missing capitalization.

EXAMPLE   i went back to the school to get the book i needed for homework.

ANSWER   *I went back to the school to get the book I needed for homework.*

1. My mother said i could buy the shoes that i saw in the magazine.

2. i want to read another book by that author i like.

3. Because i am the youngest, i often get chores no one else wants.

4. i know that i am my dog's favorite person in the family.

5. i thought i told you that i was going to be late.

6. i played football after i finished my homework.

7. i have to practice the piano every day if i want to improve.

8. i tried out for the school play, and i was chosen for a part.

9. i cannot decide what i want to be when i grow up.

10. i didn't think i would be good at golf, but i am.

PRACTICE 26.1B ▷ Writing Sentences Using Capitalization

Read the sentences. Rewrite each sentence, adding the missing capitals. Then, write if the sentence is declarative, interrogative, imperative, or exclamatory.

EXAMPLE   did you really get the highest grade in the class?

ANSWER   *Did you really get the highest grade in the class? — interrogative*

11. i can't believe it either!

12. ask me the next time you borrow my sweater.

13. it is time to go home now.

14. why can't we stay a little longer?

15. do your homework after dinner.

16. todd wasn't able to fix the computer.

17. i miss you, too!

18. when are you going on your fishing trip?

19. i love your new shoes!

20. aren't they great?

WRITING APPLICATION

Write four sentences using the word *I*. Remember to capitalize each sentence correctly. Exchange sentences with a partner. Check each other's work for correct capitalization.

WRITING APPLICATION

Write a paragraph about your favorite holiday. Use at least one declarative, one interrogative, one imperative, and one exclamatory sentence in your paragraph. Exchange paragraphs with a partner and check for correct capitalization.

TEKS Practice Show that you can use conventions of capitalization by completing the following activities.

Using Capitalization

PRACTICE 26.1C ▷ Supplying Capitalization

Read the sentences. Rewrite each sentence, adding the missing capitals.

EXAMPLE   she and i became good friends.

ANSWER   *She and I became good friends.*

1. my teacher thinks i have a good chance to get the role i want in the play.

2. spencer asked, "where did you get that hat?"

3. what should we do first?

4. will you come with us? why not?

5. who said, "i have but one life to give for my country"?

6. "my favorite color," said kerrie, "is blue."

7. are you going to the rodeo? when?

8. what a great idea that is!

9. "start your research in the library," our teacher told us. "the media specialist will help you find sources."

10. jen asked, "do you have a pencil i may borrow?"

PRACTICE 26.1D ▷ Proofreading for Capitalization

Read the sentences. Rewrite each sentence, correcting any capitalization errors.

EXAMPLE   Which book should i read for my report?

ANSWER   *Which book should I read for my report?*

11. I don't know what i'll wear to the dance.

12. Gail called and said, "i need some help with my math homework. Will you come over soon?"

13. "where," wondered Mrs. Getz, "is my measuring cup?"

14. let me see your artwork.

15. Perry quoted this line from *Hamlet*: "to be, or not to be: that is the question."

16. did you ask Jackie to distribute some of these flyers?

17. "I'll be finished by six o'clock," Dorie said. She added, "may I meet you then?"

18. if you wait a minute, i'll walk with you.

19. Wow! did you see that home run?

20. wait for the signal before you begin.

WRITING APPLICATION

Using sentences 6 and 9 in Practice 26.1C as models, write two new sentences with correct capitalization in quotations.

WRITING APPLICATION

Write a short conversation you had with someone yesterday or today. Check that you have used correct capitalization.

Texas Test Warm-Up

Focus on the TEKS

(20)(A) Use conventions of capitalization.

DIRECTIONS
Read the introduction and the passage that follows. Then, answer the questions to show that you can use and understand the function of conventions of capitalization in reading and writing.

Carmen wrote this paragraph about a weekend trip to her cousin's house. Read the paragraph and think about the changes you would suggest as a peer editor. When you finish reading, answer the questions that follow.

My Cousin Robyn

(1) My cousin robyn and i are close, but we live many miles apart. (2) Robyn lives in Austin, and I live in Houston. (3) I was excited to visit her over a long weekend. (4) "It's hard to believe, Robyn exclaimed when she saw me, "How tall you've gotten." (5) She was right; I have grown over four inches this year. (6) We enjoyed our time together, shopping and eating at a fabulous mexican restaurant. (7) It was sad saying goodbye. (8) "Do you promise," Robyn asked, "to e-mail me the pictures you took?" (9) I sent Robyn the pictures the next day!

---

1 What change, if any, should be made in sentence 1?

  A Change *cousin* to **Cousin**

  B Change *are* to **is**

  C Change *robyn and i* to **Robyn and I**

  D Make no change

2 What is the BEST way to edit sentence 4?

  F "It's hard to believe, Robyn exclaimed when she saw me, "how tall you've gotten."

  G "It's hard to believe," Robyn exclaimed when she saw me, "How tall you've gotten!"

  H "It's hard to believe," Robyn exclaimed when she saw me, "how tall you've gotten!"

  J "It's hard to believe, Robyn exclaimed when she saw me, "how tall you've gotten?"

3 What change, if any, should be made in sentence 6?

  A Change *restaurant* to **Restaurant**

  B Change *mexican* to **Mexican**

  C Change *shopping* to **Shopping**

  D Make no change

4 What change, if any, should be made in sentence 8?

  F Change *to* to **To**

  G Delete the comma after asked

  H Change the question mark to an exclamation mark

  J Make no change

Using Capitalization for Proper Nouns

An important use of capital letters is to show that a word is a **proper noun.** Proper nouns name specific people, places, or things.

> Capitalize all **proper nouns.**

26.1.6 RULE

EXAMPLES	**J**ack **K**ennedy
	Devils **T**ower **N**ational **M**onument
	George **W**ashington **B**ridge
	Sears **T**ower

Names of People

> Capitalize each part of a person's full name, including initials.

26.1.7 RULE

EXAMPLES	**M**ary **L**ynn **S**wanson
	Eric **J. T. W**atson
	L. T. Alworth

When a last name has two parts and the first part is *Mac, Mc, O',* or *St.,* the second part of the last name must also be capitalized.

EXAMPLES	**M**ac**D**onald
	Mc**L**aughlin
	O'Gill
	St. **P**eter

Focus on the TEKS

(20)(A) Use conventions of capitalization.

See TEKS Practice

See Practice 26.1E

For two-part last names that do not begin with *Mac, Mc, O',* or *St.,* the capitalization varies. Check a reliable source, such as a biographical dictionary, for the correct spelling.

Geographical Places

Any specific geographical location listed on a map should be capitalized.

RULE 26.1.8

Capitalize geographical names.

GEOGRAPHICAL NAMES	
Streets	Warren Street, Carlton Avenue, Interstate 10
Cities	Baltimore, London, Memphis, Tokyo
States	Arizona, Florida, Hawaii, Idaho
Nations	Italy, Canada, Kenya, France, Peru, South Korea
Continents	North America, Asia, Africa, Antarctica
Deserts	Sahara, Negev, Mojave
Mountains	Mount Everest, Rocky Mountains
Regions	Great Plains, Appalachian Highlands, Northwest
Islands	Canary Islands, Fiji Islands
Rivers	Mississippi River, Amazon River
Lakes	Lake Michigan, Great Salt Lake, Lake Erie
Bays	Hudson Bay, Baffin Bay, Biscayne Bay
Seas	Black Sea, Mediterranean Sea, North Sea
Oceans	Atlantic Ocean, Arctic Ocean

Regions and Map Directions

Names of regions, such as the South and the Northeast, are capitalized because they refer to a specific geographical location. Map directions that do not refer to a specific geographical location are not capitalized.

RULE 26.1.9

Do not capitalize compass points, such as north, southwest, or east, when they simply refer to direction.

REGION   My uncle lives in the **S**outheast.

DIRECTION   Our car headed **s**outh on River Street.

Specific Events and Time Periods

Capitalize the names of specific events, periods of time, and documents.

26.1.10 RULE

The following chart contains examples of events, periods of time, and documents that require capitalization.

SPECIFIC EVENTS AND TIMES	
Historical Periods	Age of Enlightenment, Middle Ages, the Renaissance
Historical Events	World War II, Boston Tea Party, Battle of Lexington
Documents	Bill of Rights, Treaty of Paris, Declaration of Independence
Days	Wednesday, Saturday
Months	December, October
Holidays	Thanksgiving, Labor Day
Religious Days	Christmas, Passover, Ramadan
Special Events	Fiddlers' Convention, Boston Marathon, Super Bowl

Names of Seasons
The names of the seasons are an exception to this rule.
Even though they name a specific period of time, the seasons of the year are not capitalized unless they are part of a title or an event name.

Focus on the TEKS

(20)(A) Use conventions of capitalization.

See TEKS Check

See TEKS Practice

See Practice 26.1F

SEASONS   A popular activity this **w**inter is skiing.

The students traveled in the **f**all.

TITLE   During a hot **s**pring, I read *The Long **W**inter.*

EVENT   It was so hot at the **S**pring Festival it felt

like **s**ummer.

TEKS Check Show that you can consistently and correctly use conventions of capitalization as you write a paragraph that includes reference to two seasons used in event titles and one holiday.

TEKS Practice Show that you can use conventions of capitalization by completing the following activities.

PRACTICE 26.1E Using Capitalization for Names of People

Read the sentences. Write each name, adding the missing capitals.

EXAMPLE   ina and ivy are twins.

ANSWER   *Ina, Ivy*

1. The mcmullens live next door to us.

2. Our class read a story by edgar allan poe.

3. t. j. gonzales will be the speaker at the assembly.

4. gina deangelo and paul o'connor are both in my social studies class.

5. pete named his dog scottie.

6. May I have a piece of cake, mom?

7. louis l'amour wrote stories and essays about the West.

8. susan b. anthony was an American civil rights leader.

9. Today is grandma's birthday.

10. My full name is julianna claire maria lugo, but my friends call me juli.

PRACTICE 26.1F Using Capitalization for Geographical Places, Specific Events, and Time Periods

Read the sentences. Write the name of each geographical place, specific event, and time period, adding the missing capitals.

EXAMPLE   The colorado river flows through the grand canyon.

ANSWER   *Colorado River, Grand Canyon*

11. My brother lives in tokyo, japan.

12. The panama canal links the caribbean sea with the pacific ocean.

13. Last july, my family visited warsaw, poland.

14. Huck Finn and Jim floated down the mississippi river on a raft.

15. World leaders are trying to resolve the conflicts in the middle east.

16. The Morrisons gave a slide show of their safari in kenya.

17. We visited three new england states: maine, new hampshire, and vermont.

18. My cousin plans to run in the new york city marathon next year.

19. During the middle ages in europe, many towns and cities grew as trade developed.

20. My grandparents sold their house in pennsylvania and moved south.

WRITING APPLICATION

Write your full name and the names of your siblings if you have any. Then, write the names of your teachers and your principal.

WRITING APPLICATION

Write your address, including your city and state. Then, list any bodies of water or mountains in your region.

Specific Groups

Proper nouns that name specific groups also require capitalization.

> **Capitalize the names of various organizations, government bodies, political parties, and nationalities, as well as the languages spoken by different groups.**

EXAMPLES   We made a very generous donation to the **R**ed **C**ross.

My friend Shirley, who speaks **C**hinese fluently, works as a translator.

The **D**epartment of **T**ransportation often issues travel alerts.

The proper nouns shown in the chart are groups with which many people are familiar. All specific groups, however, must be capitalized, even if they are not well known.

SPECIFIC GROUPS	
Clubs	Kiwanis Club Rotary Club
Organizations	National Governors Association National Organization for Women
Institutions	Massachusetts Institute of Technology Smithsonian Institution
Businesses	Simon Chemical Corporation Fido's Favorite Pet Foods
Government Bodies	United States Congress Supreme Court
Political Parties	Democrats Republican Party
Nationalities	Chinese, German Nigerian, Iranian
Languages	English, Spanish Korean, Swahili

Focus on the TEKS

(20)(A) Use conventions of capitalization.

See TEKS Practice

See Practice 26.1G

Religious References

Use capitals for the names of the religions of the world and certain other words related to religion.

RULE

26.1.12

> **Capitalize references to religions, deities, and religious scriptures.**

The following chart presents words related to five of the world's major religions. Next to each religion are examples of some of the related religious words that must be capitalized. Note that the name of each religion is also capitalized.

RELIGIOUS REFERENCES	
Christianity	God, Lord, Father, Holy Spirit, Bible, books of the Bible (Genesis, Deuteronomy, Psalms, and so on)
Judaism	Lord, Father, Prophets, Torah, Talmud, Midrash
Islam	Allah, Prophet, Mohammed, Quran
Hinduism	Brahma, Bhagavad Gita, Vedas
Buddhism	Buddha, Mahayana, Hinayana

Note in the following examples, however, that the words *god* and *goddess* in references to mythology are not capitalized. A god's or goddess's name, however, is capitalized.

EXAMPLES   In Greek mythology, the supreme **g**od was **Z**eus.

The **g**oddess **H**era was the wife of **Z**eus and was the **g**oddess of women.

Specific Places and Items

Monuments, memorials, buildings, celestial bodies, awards, the names of specific vehicles, and trademarked products should be capitalized.

> **Capitalize the names of specific places and items.**

26.1.13 RULE

OTHER SPECIAL PLACES AND ITEMS	
Monuments	Statue of Liberty Washington Monument
Memorials	Winston Churchill Memorial Vietnam Veterans Memorial
Buildings	Houston Museum of Fine Arts Empire State Building the Capitol Building (in Washington, D.C.)
Celestial Bodies (except the moon and sun)	Earth, Milky Way Jupiter, Aries
Awards	Newbery Medal Nobel Peace Prize
Air, Sea, and Space Craft	Spirit of St. Louis Monitor Voyager 2 Metroliner
Trademarked Brands	Krazy Korn Eco-Friendly Cleanser
Names	Zenox Kermit the Frog the Great Houdini

> **Capitalize the names of awards.**

26.1.14 RULE

Notice that *the* is not capitalized in these examples.

Focus on the TEKS

(20)(A) Use conventions of capitalization.

See TEKS Practice

See Practice 26.1H

EXAMPLES	the Emmy Awards
	the Rhodes Scholarship
	the Most Valuable Player Award
	the Purple Heart

Using Capitalization

 TEKS Practice Show that you can use conventions of capitalization by completing the following activities.

PRACTICE 26.1G ▷ **Using Capitalization for Groups and Organizations**

Read the sentences. Write each group or organization, adding the missing capitals.

EXAMPLE   My little brother just joined the cub scouts.

ANSWER   *Cub Scouts*

1. The green valley cyclers go on biking trips every weekend.

2. The international red cross provides local assistance after disasters.

3. The college board sponsors college entrance exams.

4. That case went all the way to the supreme court.

5. Our superintendent graduated from howard university.

6. The girl scouts sell cookies every year.

7. I found local information at the chamber of commerce.

8. You can get new running shoes at sammy's sporting goods.

9. The city council meets every Wednesday.

10. You can take some interesting and unusual courses at northern community college.

PRACTICE 26.1H ▷ **Using Capitalization for Religious References and Specific Items and Places**

Read the sentences. Write each term that should be capitalized, adding the missing capitals.

EXAMPLE   Author Toni Morrison won a nobel prize in literature.

ANSWER   *Nobel Prize in Literature*

11. The planet mars has always fascinated scientists.

12. The Goldbergs host a seder dinner during passover.

13. In Washington, D.C., we visited the vietnam veterans memorial and the capitol.

14. Many muslims make an annual pilgrimage to Mecca, called the hajj.

15. The president travels on *air force one*.

16. I enjoy watching the oscars ceremony.

17. My father took the *acela* train from Providence to New York.

18. yogi's yogurt yummies are my new favorite snack.

19. The bible, the torah, and the qur'an are three major religious texts.

20. The USS *john f. kennedy* aircraft carrier is no longer in operation.

WRITING APPLICATION

Write the names of five organizations or groups in your school and community. Capitalize the names correctly.

WRITING APPLICATION

Write the names of the following:

- a religious event or holiday
- a planet
- your favorite cereal
- a building in your town or city

Using Capitalization for Proper Adjectives

When a proper noun or a form of a proper noun is used to describe another noun, it is called a **proper adjective.** Proper adjectives usually need a capital letter.

> **Capitalize most proper adjectives.**

RULE 26.1.15

In the following examples, notice that both proper nouns and proper adjectives are capitalized. Common nouns that are modified by proper adjectives, however, are not capitalized.

PROPER NOUNS	**W** orld **W** ar II
	M exico
PROPER ADJECTIVES	a **W** orld **W** ar II **b** attleship
	a **M** exican **h** at

The names of some countries and states must be modified to be used as proper adjectives. For example, something from Kenya is Kenyan, someone from Texas is Texan, a chair from Spain is a Spanish chair, and a building in France is a French building.

Brand Names as Adjectives

Trademarked brand names are considered to be proper nouns. If you use a brand name to describe a common noun, the brand name becomes a proper adjective. In this case, capitalize only the proper adjective and not the common noun.

> **Capitalize brand names used as adjectives.**

RULE 26.1.16

Focus on the TEKS

(20)(A) Use conventions of capitalization.

See TEKS Practice

See Practice 26.1I

PROPER NOUN	**F** ruit **G** rains
PROPER ADJECTIVE	**F** ruit **G** rains **c** ereal

Notice that only the proper adjective *Fruit Grains* is capitalized. The word *cereal* is not capitalized because it is a common noun; it is not part of the trademarked name.

Using Capitalization for Titles of People

A person's title shows his or her or relationship to other people. Whether a title is capitalized often depends on how it is used in a sentence.

Social and Professional Titles

Social and professional titles may be written before a person's name or used alone in place of a person's name.

RULE 26.1.17

> **Capitalize the title of a person when the title is followed by the person's name or when it is used in place of a person's name in direct address.**

BEFORE A NAME	**R**everend O'Connor and **D**octor Brennan have arrived.
IN DIRECT ADDRESS	Look, **L**ieutenant, here is the missing clue!

TITLES OF PEOPLE	
Social	Mister, Madam or Madame, Miss, Ms., Sir
Business	Doctor, Professor, Superintendent, Attorney
Religious	Reverend, Father, Rabbi, Bishop, Sister
Military	Private, Ensign, Captain, General, Admiral
Government	President, Senator, Representative, Governor, Mayor, Prince, Queen, King

In most cases, do not capitalize titles that are used alone or that follow a person's name—especially if the title is preceded by the articles *a, an,* or *the.*

EXAMPLES	Roger Simmons, the **d**etective assigned to the case, will call you.
	Tell your **state representative** how you feel about the issue.
	My brother George, who is a **p**rivate in the army, will be home on leave soon.

Government Officials

> Capitalize the titles of government officials when they immediately precede the name of specific officials. If no person is named, these titles should be written in lower case.

26.1.18 RULE

EXAMPLES

Vice **P**resident **B**iden will preside at the meeting.

The club **v**ice **p**resident will preside at the meeting.

Superintendent **W**aller will speak to the students about the quality of education.

The **s**uperintendent of **s**chools is responsible for the quality of education.

Note: Certain honorary titles are always capitalized, even if the title is not used with a proper name or direct address. These titles include the First Lady of the United States, Speaker of the House of Representatives, Queen Mother of England, and the Prince of Wales.

Titles for Family Relationships

> Capitalize titles showing family relationships when the title is used with the person's name or as the person's name—except when the title comes after a possessive noun or pronoun.

26.1.19 RULE

BEFORE A NAME

We respect **A**unt Betsy's opinion.

IN PLACE OF A NAME

Is **G**randfather going?

Focus on the TEKS

(20)(A) Use conventions of capitalization.

See TEKS Practice
See Practice 26.1J

AFTER POSSESSIVES

Jeff's **f**ather is the team doctor.

Notice that the family title *father* used in the last example is not capitalized because it is used after the possessive word *Jeff's*.

PRACTICE 26.1I > **Using Capitalization for Proper Adjectives**

Read the sentences. Write the proper adjectives, adding the correct capitalization.

EXAMPLE   The canadian winters can be quite severe.

ANSWER   *Canadian*

1. The egyptian pyramids are one of the wonders of the world.

2. I saw an exhibit of japanese woodblock prints at the museum.

3. Mary Shelley wrote *Frankenstein*, an early gothic novel.

4. My mother enjoys irish breakfast tea.

5. Ivan was interested in the german sports cars at the auto show.

6. We went to a restaurant for thai food.

7. Bill and Cindy Duquette are dreaming about a caribbean vacation.

8. In 1776, american colonists declared independence from their english rulers.

9. We drink florida orange juice every day.

10. Will you help me study for the spanish test?

PRACTICE 26.1J > **Using Capitalization for Titles of People**

Read the sentences. If the title in each sentence is correctly capitalized, write *correct*. If it is not, rewrite the title correctly.

EXAMPLE   My mother took me to doctor Perez when I had the flu.

ANSWER   *Doctor*

11. In the opening ceremony, Mayor Massey will cut the ribbon and give a speech.

12. All in the court rose as judge Saris entered.

13. The evening news featured an interview with governor Chase.

14. An army recruiter, lieutenant Carson, will be here next week.

15. The ceremony was performed by Reverend Walker.

16. I went on a camping trip with uncle Stan.

17. Perhaps you should write a letter to senator Olson.

18. General Colin Powell later became Secretary of State.

19. My grandma Ginny loves to cook.

20. The library will present a lecture by professor Watkins on green energy.

WRITING APPLICATION

Write three proper adjectives and the nouns they modify. You may use the proper adjectives in the sentences above as models. Capitalize the proper adjectives.

WRITING APPLICATION

Write the title and name of one of your town or city officials, the governor of your state, and one senator and representative from your state.

Using Capitalization for Titles of Works

Capital letters are used for the titles of things such as written works, pieces of art, and school courses.

> **Capitalize the first word and all other key words in the titles of books, newspapers, magazines, short stories, poems, plays, movies, songs, and artworks.**

RULE 26.1.20

Do not capitalize articles (*a, an, the*), prepositions (*of, to*), and conjunctions (*and, but*) that are fewer than four letters long unless they begin a title. Verbs and personal pronouns, no matter how short, are always capitalized in titles.

EXAMPLE "**I**n **E**xile" by Anton Chekhov

> **Capitalize the title of a school course when it is followed by a course number or when it refers to a language. Otherwise, do not capitalize school subjects.**

RULE 26.1.21

EXAMPLES **G**erman **L**iterature 130 **S**cience II

I have **s**cience this morning.

Using Capitalization in Letters

Several parts of friendly and business letters are capitalized.

> **In the heading, capitalize the street, city, state, and month.**

RULE 26.1.22

EXAMPLES **F**irst **S**treet **B**oonton **M**aryland **J**une

> **In the salutation, capitalize the first word, any title, and the name of the person or group mentioned. In the closing, capitalize the first word.**

RULE 26.1.23

Focus on the TEKS

(20)(A) Use conventions of capitalization.

See TEKS Practice

See Practice 26.1K

See Practice 26.1L

SALUTATIONS **M**y **d**ear **J**ustin, **D**ear **A**unt **S**ally,

CLOSINGS **Y**our **n**eighbor, **B**est **w**ishes, **L**ove,

TEKS Practice Show that you can use conventions of capitalization by completing the following activities.

PRACTICE 26.1K **Using Capitalization for Titles of Things**

Read the sentences. Write the titles, adding the correct capitalization.

EXAMPLE   *star wars* has become a classic movie.

ANSWER   *Star Wars*

1. Our teacher gave a dramatic reading of the poem "the highwayman" by Alfred Noyes.

2. Do you know how Tom got people to whitewash the fence in *the adventures of tom sawyer?*

3. Everyone stood when "the star-spangled banner" was played.

4. My dad reads *the wall street journal.*

5. The book *charlie and the chocolate factory* was made into a film.

6. I would like to see the *mona lisa* in the Louvre Museum in Paris.

7. The children in nursery school sang "twinkle, twinkle, little star."

8. Andy used *newsweek* magazine as one of his sources for his report.

9. The poem "a noiseless patient spider" by Walt Whitman is one of my favorites.

10. In 1620, the Pilgrims crossed the Atlantic on the *mayflower.*

PRACTICE 26.1L **Using Capitalization for Titles of Things**

Read the sentences. Rewrite each sentence, adding the missing capitals.

EXAMPLE   I am taking first-year spanish.

ANSWER   *I am taking first-year Spanish.*

11. Today in language arts class, we discussed "all summer in a day."

12. Allie has seen *the lion king* six times.

13. Our class enjoyed Gary Soto's story "seventh grade."

14. Estelle read *kira-kira* for her independent reading report.

15. Laura has been learning to play J. S. Bach's "minuet in g."

16. Vincent Van Gogh's painting *starry night* has inspired many people.

17. Caitlin has done well in algebra I, so next year she'll take algebra II.

18. Jeff faithfully reads *sports illustrated.*

19. My sister is taking chemistry 101 at her college.

20. One of Shakespeare's most popular plays is *the tragedy of romeo and juliet.*

WRITING APPLICATION

Write titles of the following, with correct capitalization:
- a short story you have read
- a book you like
- your favorite movie
- a television program

WRITING APPLICATION

Write statements in which you make an evaluation of each of the following:
- a book or article you have read recently
- a movie or program you have viewed recently

Capitalize titles correctly.

Using Capitalization in Abbreviations, Acronyms, and Initials

An **abbreviation** is a shortened form of a word or phrase. An **acronym** is an abbreviation of a phrase that takes one or more letters from each word in the phrase being abbreviated.

> In general, capitalize **abbreviations, acronyms,** and **initials** if the words or names they stand for are capitalized.

RULE 26.1.24

INITIALS	**A . C .** Black
TITLES	**D** r. Samuel Green **S** r.
ACADEMIC DEGREES	Samuel Green, **M.D.**, Ben Queen, **Ph.D.**
ACRONYMS	**UNICEF** , **ROTC**

Abbreviations for most units of measurement are not capitalized.

EXAMPLES	**i** n. (inches) **t** bsp. (tablespoon)

> Capitalize **abbreviations** that appear in addresses.

RULE 26.1.25

Use a two-letter state abbreviation without periods when the abbreviation is followed by a ZIP code in an address. Capitalize both letters of the state abbreviation.

EXAMPLE	Trenton, **NJ** 08629

> Capitalize **acronyms** that stand for proper nouns, such as businesses, government bodies, and organizations.

RULE 26.1.26

Spell out the name of an organization and include its acronym in parentheses the first time you use it. Use only the acronym in later references.

EXAMPLE	Have you heard of the Food and Drug Administration (**FDA**)? The **FDA** is responsible for protecting the public health.

Focus on the TEKS

(20)(A) Use conventions of capitalization.

See TEKS Practice
See Practice 26.1M
See Practice 26.1N

TEKS Practice Show that you can use conventions of capitalization by completing the following activities.

PRACTICE 26.1M **Using Capitalization for Abbreviations**

Read the items. Rewrite each item, adding capitals as needed. If the item is already correct, write *correct*.

EXAMPLE   Columbia rd.

ANSWER   Columbia *Rd.*

1. Gov. Brown

2. dr. Suarez

3. Atlanta, ga 30301

4. uss *Constitution*

5. Richard Smith jr.

6. one tsp. salt

7. Sixth Ave.

8. maj. Armstrong

9. 146 lake st.

10. 5 ft 2 in.

PRACTICE 26.1N **Using Capitalization for Initials and Acronyms**

Read the sentences. Write the initials and acronyms, adding capitals as needed. If the sentence is correct, write *correct*.

EXAMPLE   Have you read *The Lord of the Rings* trilogy by j.r.r. Tolkien?

ANSWER   *J.R.R.*

11. We visited nasa's Johnson Space Center when we were in Houston.

12. Arthur Kelly, d.v.m., works at the veterinary hospital where we take our dog.

13. The John F. Kennedy Presidential Library and Museum in Boston opened in 1979.

14. Check the SPF before you buy that sunscreen.

15. The ncaa basketball tournament is a popular event every spring.

16. The speed limit on this street is 25 mph.

17. The naacp played an active role in the civil rights movement in the 1960s.

18. My brother's name is Christopher John, but he likes to be called cj.

19. Because she loves animals, Heather volunteers for the aspca.

20. We flew into t. f. Green Airport in Providence, r.i.

SPEAKING APPLICATION

Make up an acronym and use it in a sentence. Share your sentence with a partner, who will guess what the acronym stands for. Explain the acronym if necessary.

WRITING APPLICATION

Address a letter envelope to a relative or acquaintance. Use the person's title and full name, including middle initial. Use abbreviations for the street and state.

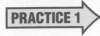

PRACTICE 1 ▷ **Using Periods, Question Marks, and Exclamation Marks**

Read the sentences. Then, rewrite the sentences, adding periods, question marks, and exclamation marks where needed.

1. Ana lives on St Charles Ave in New Orleans

2. Is he coming to the picnic

3. She asked if she left her umbrella here

4. Please set the table for dinner

5. What a brilliant student he is

6. Watch out for the monster

7. On what street is the office located

8. Yikes Did I forget your birthday

9. The stranger knocked on every door Why

10. How excited I am about the concert

PRACTICE 2 ▷ **Using Commas Correctly**

Read the sentences. Then, rewrite the sentences, adding commas where needed. If a sentence is correct as is, write *correct.*

1. To get enough calcium drink plenty of milk.

2. A pencil would work but a pen would be better.

3. The gerbil a small rodent resembles a hamster.

4. Josie said "So Agnes where are you going?"

5. His scarred rugged face showed character.

6. The news is in the paper on television and online.

7. They got those two black dogs in May 2008.

8. We served precisely 1211 meals on July 4 2009.

9. "You did well on the test of course" said Lee.

10. It's at 77 East Adams Street Chicago Illinois 60603.

PRACTICE 3 ▷ **Using Colons, Semicolons, and Quotation Marks**

Read the sentences. Then, rewrite the sentences, using colons, semicolons, and quotation marks where needed. If a sentence is correct as is, write *correct.*

1. Dad likes tennis, however, he likes golf more.

2. Please buy the following milk, eggs, and bread.

3. Who said, Whatever you are, be a good one?

4. Yes, said Mrs. Ross, the class ends at 330.

5. The artist has a new exhibit, I love her work.

6. Caution Do not walk between the subway cars.

7. Marla asked, Did you see my hat anywhere?

8. How I enjoyed the poem The Highwayman!

9. Tomas asked that we turn off our cellphones.

10. Originating in Africa are okra, a plant, gumbo, a stew, and the banjo, a musical instrument.

PRACTICE 4 ▷ **Using Apostrophes Correctly**

Read the sentences. Then, rewrite the sentences, adding or removing apostrophes as needed. If a sentence is correct as is, write *correct.*

1. This is clearly Lucas's work and nobody elses.

2. Jans not here and cant help with Als homework.

3. The dog gnaws on it's bone when its hungry.

4. Most students' grades are A's or B's.

5. The Greek myth described Zeus's anger.

6. My sister Sarahs photo is in the yearbook.

7. I'm shocked that you dont tell her shes right.

8. Hers is the nicest shop on Main Street.

9. Randy would'nt go anywhere on Friday's.

10. Please indicate whats theirs and whats yours.

Continued on next page ▶

Cumulative Review Chapters 25–26

PRACTICE 5 > **Using Underlining (or Italics), Hyphens, Dashes, Parentheses, Brackets, and Ellipses**

Read the sentences. Then, rewrite the sentences, adding underlining (or italics if you type your answers on the computer), hyphens, dashes, brackets, parentheses, and ellipses. If a sentence is correct as is, write *correct*.

1. My brother in law is a self taught tennis player.

2. Who wrote the novel To Kill a Mockingbird?

3. The book is set during World War I 1914–1918.

4. We invited Gretchen she is a new student to come to the tryouts for the school play.

5. The paper published her nicely written letter.

6. In her speech, the mayor said, "He the mayor's son did a great service for our city."

7. Our founders accepted as "unalienable rights . . . Life, Liberty, and the Pursuit of Happiness."

8. The legislature voted on the bill. See page 3 for a list of members' votes column 1.

9. The ship on which Columbus himself sailed was the Santa Maria.

10. Sandra's goal an Olympic medal seemed as distant as ever.

PRACTICE 6 > **Using Correct Capitalization**

Read the sentences. Then, rewrite each sentence, using capital letters where needed.

1. the american revolution formally ended with the signing of the treaty of paris.

2. t. s. eliot, a british author born in america, wrote the poem "the love song of j. alfred prufrock."

3. each spring, grandpa buys good guys fertilizer.

4. author toni morrison has won the nobel prize in literature.

5. visiting the northwest, we saw mount hood.

6. the planet venus is named for the roman goddess venus, whom the greeks called aphrodite.

7. "the last time doctor abis left the usa for a vacation," ingrid said, "was in june of 2007."

8. the high museum of art is just east of interstate 85 at 1280 peachtree street in atlanta, georgia.

9. metro networks monitors traffic conditions in the new york area from atop the empire state building.

10. the current president of the united states belongs to the democratic party.

11. is aunt margie a member of the aarp?

12. We spoke with reverend graves last sunday.

13. "i met ms. lee," said ian, "last summer in iowa."

14. my cousin takes biology 101 at duke university.

15. the vedas are sacred scriptures of hinduism.

PRACTICE 7 > **Writing Sentences With Correct Capitalization**

Read the following items. Then, write a sentence about each item. Be sure to use correct capitalization.

1. a local politician

2. a famous or local zoo

3. your favorite beach or park

4. your favorite movie

5. a novel that you really liked or really disliked

RESOURCES FOR
Writing
COACH

Texas Essential Knowledge and Skills (TEKS)

(1) The English Language Arts and Reading Texas Essential Knowledge and Skills (TEKS) are organized into the following strands: Reading, where students read and understand a wide variety of literary and informational texts; Writing, where students compose a variety of written texts with a clear controlling idea, coherent organization, and sufficient detail; Research, where students are expected to know how to locate a range of relevant sources and evaluate, synthesize, and present ideas and information; Listening and Speaking, where students listen and respond to the ideas of others while contributing their own ideas in conversations and in groups; and Oral and Written Conventions, where students learn how to use the oral and written conventions of the English language in speaking and writing. The standards are cumulative—students will continue to address earlier standards as needed while they attend to standards for their grade. In seventh grade, students will engage in activities that build on their prior knowledge and skills in order to strengthen their reading, writing, and oral language skills. Students should read and write on a daily basis.

(2) For students whose first language is not English, the students' native language serves as a foundation for English language acquisition.

(A) English language learners (ELLs) are acquiring English, learning content in English, and learning to read simultaneously. For this reason, it is imperative that reading instruction should be comprehensive and that students receive instruction in phonemic awareness, phonics, decoding, and word attack skills while simultaneously being taught academic vocabulary and comprehension skills and strategies. Reading instruction that enhances ELL's ability to decode unfamiliar words and to make sense of those words in context will expedite their ability to make sense of what they read and learn from reading. Additionally, developing fluency, spelling, and grammatical conventions of academic language must be done in meaningful contexts and not in isolation.

(B) For ELLs, comprehension of texts requires additional scaffolds to support comprehensible input. ELL students should use the knowledge of their first language (e.g., cognates) to further vocabulary development. Vocabulary needs to be taught in the context of connected discourse so that language is meaningful. ELLs must learn how rhetorical devices in English differ from those in their native language. At the same time English learners are learning in English, the focus is on academic English, concepts, and the language structures specific to the content.

(C) During initial stages of English development, ELLs are expected to meet standards in a second language that many monolingual English speakers find difficult to meet in their native language. However, English language learners' abilities to meet these standards will be influenced by their proficiency in English. While English language learners can analyze, synthesize, and evaluate, their level of English proficiency may impede their ability to demonstrate this knowledge during the initial stages of English language acquisition. It is also critical to understand that ELLs with no previous or with interrupted schooling will require explicit and strategic support as they acquire English and learn to learn in English simultaneously.

(3) To meet Public Education Goal 1 of the Texas Education Code, §4.002, which states, "The students in the public education system will demonstrate exemplary performance in the reading and writing of the English language," students will accomplish the essential knowledge, skills, and student expectations at Grade 7 as described in subsection (b) of this section.

(4) To meet Texas Education Code, §28.002(h), which states, ". . . each school district shall foster the continuation of the tradition of teaching United States and Texas history and the free enterprise system in regular subject matter and in reading courses and in the adoption of textbooks," students will be provided oral and written narratives as well as other informational texts that can help them to become thoughtful, active citizens who appreciate the basic democratic values of our state and nation.

(b) Knowledge and skills.

(14) Writing/Writing Process.
Students use elements of the writing process (planning, drafting, revising, editing, and publishing) to compose text. Students are expected to:

(A) plan a first draft by selecting a genre appropriate for conveying the intended meaning to an audience, determining appropriate topics through a range of strategies (e.g., discussion, background reading, personal interests, interviews), and developing a thesis or controlling idea;

(B) develop drafts by choosing an appropriate organizational strategy (e.g., sequence of events, cause-effect, compare-contrast) and building on ideas to create a focused, organized, and coherent piece of writing;

(C) revise drafts to ensure precise word choice and vivid images; consistent point of view; use of simple, compound, and complex sentences; internal and external coherence; and the use of effective transitions after rethinking how well questions of purpose, audience, and genre have been addressed;

(D) edit drafts for grammar, mechanics, and spelling; and

(E) revise final draft in response to feedback from peers and teacher and publish written work for appropriate audiences.

(15) Writing/Literary Texts.
Students write literary texts to express their ideas and feelings about real or imagined people, events, and ideas. Students are expected to:

(A) write an Imaginative story that:

    (i) sustains reader interest;

    (ii) includes well-paced action and an engaging story line;

    (iii) creates a specific, believable setting through the use of sensory details;

    (iv) develops interesting characters; and

    (v) uses a range of literary strategies and devices to enhance the style and tone; and

(B) write a poem using:

    (i) poetic techniques (e.g., rhyme scheme, meter);

    (ii) figurative language (e.g., personification, idioms, hyperbole); and

    (iii) graphic elements (e.g., word position).

(16) Writing.
Students write about their own experiences. Students are expected to write a personal narrative that has a clearly defined focus and communicates the importance of or reasons for actions and/or consequences.

(17) Writing/Expository and Procedural Texts.
Students write expository and procedural or work-related texts to communicate ideas and information to specific audiences for specific purposes. Students are expected to:

(A) write a multi-paragraph essay to convey information about a topic that:

    (i) presents effective introductions and concluding paragraphs;

    (ii) contains a clearly stated purpose or controlling idea;

    (iii) is logically organized with appropriate facts and details and includes no extraneous information or inconsistencies;

    (iv) accurately synthesizes ideas from several sources; and

> **(v)** uses a variety of sentence structures, rhetorical devices, and transitions to link paragraphs;

(B) write a letter that reflects an opinion, registers a complaint, or requests information in a business or friendly context;

(C) write responses to literary or expository texts that demonstrate the writing skills for multi-paragraph essays and provide sustained evidence from the text using quotations when appropriate; and

(D) produce a multimedia presentation involving text and graphics using available technology.

(18) Writing/Persuasive Texts.
Students write persuasive texts to influence the attitudes or actions of a specific audience on specific issues. Students are expected to write a persuasive essay to the appropriate audience that:

(A) establishes a clear thesis or position;

(B) considers and responds to the views of others and anticipates and answers reader concerns and counter-arguments; and

(C) includes evidence that is logically organized to support the author's viewpoint and that differentiates between fact and opinion.

(19) Oral and Written Conventions/Conventions.
Students understand the function of and use the conventions of academic language when speaking and writing. Students will continue to apply earlier standards with greater complexity. Students are expected to:

(A) identify, use, and understand the function of the following parts of speech in the context of reading, writing, and speaking:

> **(i)** verbs (perfect and progressive tenses) and participles;

> **(ii)** appositive phrases;

> **(iii)** adverbial and adjectival phrases and clauses;

> **(iv)** conjunctive adverbs (e.g., consequently, furthermore, indeed);

> **(v)** prepositions and prepositional phrases and their influence on subject-verb agreement;

> **(vi)** relative pronouns (e.g., whose, that, which);

> **(vii)** subordinating conjunctions (e.g., because, since); and

> **(viii)** transitions for sentence to sentence or paragraph to paragraph coherence;

(B) write complex sentences and differentiate between main versus subordinate clauses; and

(C) use a variety of complete sentences (e.g., simple, compound, complex) that include properly placed modifiers, correctly identified antecedents, parallel structures, and consistent tenses.

(20) Oral and Written Conventions/Handwriting, Capitalization, and Punctuation.
Students write legibly and use appropriate capitalization and punctuation conventions in their compositions. Students are expected to:

(A) use conventions of capitalization; and

(B) recognize and use punctuation marks including:

> **(i)** commas after introductory words, phrases, and clauses; and

> **(ii)** semicolons, colons, and hyphens.

(21) Oral and Written Conventions/Spelling.
Students spell correctly. Students are expected to spell correctly, including using various resources to determine and check correct spellings.

(22) Research/Research Plan.
Students ask open-ended research questions and develop a plan for answering them. Students are expected to:

- **(A)** brainstorm, consult with others, decide upon a topic, and formulate a major research question to address the major research topic; and

- **(B)** apply steps for obtaining and evaluating information from a wide variety of sources and create a written plan after preliminary research in reference works and additional text searches.

(23) Research/Gathering Sources.
Students determine, locate, and explore the full range of relevant sources addressing a research question and systematically record the information they gather. Students are expected to:

- **(A)** follow the research plan to gather information from a range of relevant print and electronic sources using advanced search strategies;

- **(B)** categorize information thematically in order to see the larger constructs inherent in the information;

- **(C)** record bibliographic information (e.g., author, title, page number) for all notes and sources according to a standard format; and

- **(D)** differentiate between paraphrasing and plagiarism and identify the importance of citing valid and reliable sources.

(24) Research/Synthesizing Information.
Students clarify research questions and evaluate and synthesize collected information. Students are expected to:

- **(A)** narrow or broaden the major research question, if necessary, based on further research and investigation; and

- **(B)** utilize elements that demonstrate the reliability and validity of the sources used (e.g., publication date, coverage, language, point of view) and explain why one source is more useful than another.

(25) Research/Organizing and Presenting Ideas.
Students organize and present their ideas and information according to the purpose of the research and their audience. Students are expected to synthesize the research into a written or an oral presentation that:

- **(A)** draws conclusions and summarizes or paraphrases the findings in a systematic way;

- **(B)** marshals evidence to explain the topic and gives relevant reasons for conclusions;

- **(C)** presents the findings in a meaningful format; and

- **(D)** follows accepted formats for integrating quotations and citations into the written text to maintain a flow of ideas.

WRITING FOR
Media

New technology has created many new ways to communicate. Today, it is easy to contribute information to the Internet and send a variety of messages to friends far and near. You can also share your ideas through photos, illustrations, video, and sound recordings.

Writing for Media gives you an overview of some ways you can use today's technology to create, share, and find information. **Here are the topics you will find in this section:**

- **Blogs**
- **Social Networking**
- **Widgets and Feeds**
- **Multimedia Elements**
- **Podcasts**
- **Wikis**

Blogs

A **blog** is a common form of online writing. The word *blog* is a contraction of *Web log*. Most blogs include a series of entries known as posts. The posts appear in a single column and are displayed in reverse chronological order. That means that the most recent post is at the top of the page. As you scroll down, you will find earlier posts.

Blogs have become increasingly popular. Researchers estimate that 75,000 new blogs are launched every day. Blog authors are often called bloggers. They can use their personal sites to share ideas, songs, videos, photos, and other media. People who read blogs can often post their responses with a comments feature found in each new post.

Because blogs are designed so that they are easy to update, bloggers can post new messages as often as they like, often daily. For some people blogs become a public journal or diary in which they share their thoughts about daily events.

Types of Blogs

Not all blogs are the same. Many blogs have a single author, but others are group projects. These are some common types of blog:

- **Personal blogs** often have a general focus. Bloggers post their thoughts on any topic they find interesting in their daily lives.

- **Topical blogs** focus on a specific theme, such as movie reviews, political news, class assignments, or health-care opportunities.

 WEB SAFETY Using the Internet safely means keeping personal information personal. Never include your address (e-mail or physical), last name, or telephone numbers. Avoid mentioning places you go to often.

Never give out passwords you use to access other Web sites and do not respond to e-mails from people you do not know.

Anatomy of a Blog

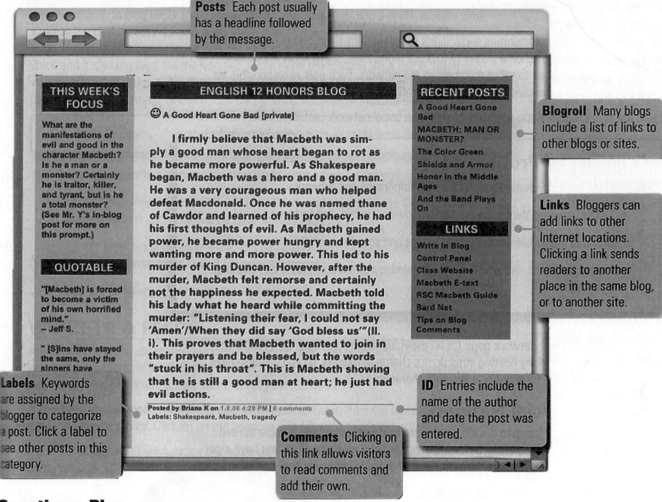

Posts Each post usually has a headline followed by the message.

THIS WEEK'S FOCUS

What are the manifestations of evil and good in the character Macbeth? Is he a man or a monster? Certainly he is traitor, killer, and tyrant, but is he a total monster? (See Mr. Y's in-blog post for more on this prompt.)

QUOTABLE

"[Macbeth] is forced to become a victim of his own horrified mind."
— Jeff S.

" [S]ins have stayed the same, only the sinners have

ENGLISH 12 HONORS BLOG

☺ A Good Heart Gone Bad [private]

 I firmly believe that Macbeth was simply a good man whose heart began to rot as he became more powerful. As Shakespeare began, Macbeth was a hero and a good man. He was a very courageous man who helped defeat Macdonald. Once he was named thane of Cawdor and learned of his prophecy, he had his first thoughts of evil. As Macbeth gained power, he became power hungry and kept wanting more and more power. This led to his murder of King Duncan. However, after the murder, Macbeth felt remorse and certainly not the happiness he expected. Macbeth told his Lady what he heard while committing the murder: "Listening their fear, I could not say 'Amen'/When they did say 'God bless us'"(II. i). This proves that Macbeth wanted to join in their prayers and be blessed, but the words "stuck in his throat". This is Macbeth showing that he is still a good man at heart; he just had evil actions.

Posted by Briana K on 1.8.08 4:29 PM | 6 comments
Labels: Shakespeare, Macbeth, tragedy

RECENT POSTS

A Good Heart Gone Bad
MACBETH: MAN OR MONSTER?
The Color Green
Shields and Armor
Honor in the Middle Ages
And the Band Plays On

LINKS

Write In Blog
Control Panel
Class Website
Macbeth E-text
RSC Macbeth Guide
Bard Net
Tips on Blog Comments

Blogroll Many blogs include a list of links to other blogs or sites.

Links Bloggers can add links to other Internet locations. Clicking a link sends readers to another place in the same blog, or to another site.

Labels Keywords are assigned by the blogger to categorize a post. Click a label to see other posts in this category.

Comments Clicking on this link allows visitors to read comments and add their own.

ID Entries include the name of the author and date the post was entered.

Creating a Blog

Keep these hints and strategies in mind to help you create an interesting and fair blog:

- Focus each blog entry on a single topic.

- Vary the length of your posts. Sometimes, all you need is a line or two to share a quick thought. Other posts will be much longer.

- Choose font colors and styles that can be read easily.

- Many people scan blogs rather than read them closely. You can make your main ideas pop out by using clear or clever headlines and boldfacing key terms.

- Give credit to other people's work and ideas. State the names of people whose ideas you are quoting or add a link to take readers to that person's blog or site.

- If you post comments, try to make them brief and polite.

Social Networking

Social networking means any interaction between members of an online community. People can exchange many different kinds of information, from text and voice messages to video images. Many social network communities allow users to create permanent pages that describe themselves. Users create home pages to express themselves, share ideas about their lives, and post messages to other members in the network. Each user is responsible for adding and updating the content on his or her profile page.

Here are some features you are likely to find on a social network profile:

Features of Profile Pages

- A **biographical description**, including photographs and artwork

- **Lists of favorite things**, such as books, movies, music, and fashions

- **Playable media** elements such as videos and sound recordings

- **Message boards**, or "walls," on which members of the community can exchange messages

Privacy in Social Networks

Social networks allow users to decide how open their profiles will be. Be sure to read introductory information carefully before you register at a new site. Once you have a personal profile page, monitor your privacy settings regularly. Remember that any information you post will be available to anyone in your network.

Users often post messages anonymously or using false names, or pseudonyms. People can also post using someone else's name. Judge all information on the net critically. Do not assume that you know who posted some information simply because you recognize the name of the post author. The rapid speed of communication on the Internet can make it easy to jump to conclusions—be careful to avoid this trap.

> You can create a social network page for an individual or a group, such as a school or special interest club. Many hosting sites do not charge to register, so you can also have fun by creating a page for a pet or a fictional character.

Tips for Sending Effective Messages

Technology makes it easy to share ideas quickly, but writing for the Internet poses some special challenges. The writing style for blogs and social networks is often very conversational. In blog posts and comments, instant messages, and e-mails, writers often express themselves very quickly, using relaxed language, short sentences, and abbreviations. However in a face-to-face conversation, we get a lot of information from a speaker's tone of voice and body language. On the Internet, those clues are missing. As a result, Internet writers often use italics or bracketed labels to indicate emotions. Another alternative is using emoticons—strings of characters that give visual clues to indicate emotion.

:-) **smile** *(happy)*   **:-(** **frown** *(unhappy)*   **;-)** **wink** *(light sarcasm)*

> *Use these strategies to communicate effectively when using technology:*
>
> ✔ *Before you click Send, **reread your message** to make sure that your tone is clear.*
>
> ✔ ***Do not jump to conclusions**—ask for clarification first. Make sure you really understand what someone is saying before you respond.*
>
> ✔ ***Use abbreviations** your reader will understand.*

Widgets and Feeds

A **widget** is a small application that performs a specific task. You might find widgets that give weather predictions, offer dictionary definitions or translations, provide entertainment such as games, or present a daily word, photograph, or quotation.

A **feed** is a special kind of widget. It displays headlines taken from the latest content on a specific media source. Clicking on the headline will take you to the full article. Many social network communities and other Web sites allow you to personalize your home page by adding widgets and feeds.

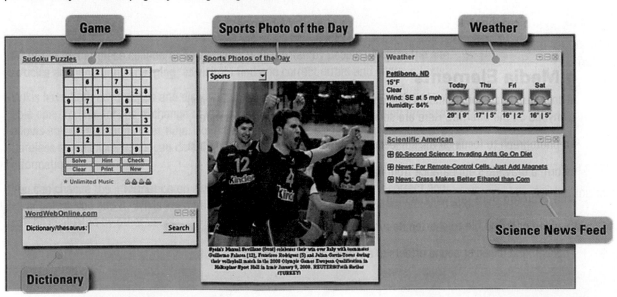

Multimedia Elements

One of the great advantages of communicating on the Internet is that you are not limited to using text only. When you create a Web profile or blog, you can share your ideas using a wide variety of media. In addition to widgets and feeds (see page R9), these media elements can make your Internet communication more entertaining and useful.

GRAPHICS	
Photographs	You can post photographs taken by digital cameras or scanned as files.
Illustrations	Artwork can be created using computer software. You can also use a scanner to post a digital image of a drawing or sketch.
Charts, Graphs, and Maps	Charts and graphs can make statistical information clear. Use spreadsheet software to create these elements. Use Internet sites to find maps of specific places.

VIDEO	
Live Action	Digital video can be recorded by a camera or recorded from another media source.
Animation	Animated videos can also be created using software.

AUDIO	
Music	Many social network communities make it easy to share your favorite music with people who visit your page.
Voice	Use a microphone to add your own voice to your Web page.

Editing Media Elements

You can use software to customize media elements. Open source software is free and available to anyone on the Internet. Here are some things you can do with software:

- **Crop** a photograph to focus on the subject or brighten an image that is too dark.
- **Transform** a drawing's appearance from flat to three-dimensional.
- **Insert** a "You Are Here" arrow on a map.
- **Edit** a video or sound file to shorten its running time.
- **Add** background music or sound effects to a video.

Podcasts

A **podcast** is a digital audio or video recording of a program that is made available on the Internet. Users can replay the podcast on a computer, or download it and replay it on a personal audio player. You might think of podcasts as radio or television programs that you create yourself. They can be embedded on a Web site or fed to a Web page through a podcast widget.

Creating an Effective Podcast

To make a podcast, you will need a recording device, such as a microphone or digital video camera, as well as editing software. Open source editing software is widely available and free of charge. Most audio podcasts are converted into the MP3 format. Here are some tips for creating a podcast that is clear and entertaining:

- **Listen to several podcasts by different authors** to get a feeling for the medium.

- **Make a list** of features and styles you like and also those you want to avoid.

- **Test your microphone** to find the best recording distance. Stand close enough to the microphone so that your voice sounds full, but not so close that you create an echo.

- **Create an outline** that shows your estimated timing for each element.

- **Be prepared** before you record. Rehearse, but do not create a script. Podcasts are best when they have a natural, easy flow.

- **Talk directly to your listeners**. Slow down enough so they can understand you.

- Use software to **edit your podcast before publishing it**. You can edit out mistakes or add additional elements.

Wikis

A **wiki** is a collaborative Web site that lets visitors create, add, remove, and edit content. The term comes from the Hawaiian phrase *wikiwiki*, which means "quick." Web users of a wiki are both the readers and the writers of the site. Some wikis are open to contributions from anyone. Others require visitors to register before they can edit the content. All of the text in these collaborative Web sites was written by people who use the site. Articles are constantly changing, as visitors find and correct errors and improve texts.

Wikis have both advantages and disadvantages as sources of information. They are valuable open forums for the exchange of ideas. The unique collaborative writing process allows entries to change over time. However, entries can also be modified incorrectly. Careless or malicious users can delete good content and add inappropriate or inaccurate information. Wikis may be useful for gathering background information, but should not be used as research resources.

You can change the information on a wiki, but be sure your information is correct and clear before you add it. Wikis keep track of all changes, so your work will be recorded and can be evaluated by other users.

WRITING FOR THE
Workplace

Writing is something many people do every day at work, school, or home. They write letters and reports, do research, plan meetings, and keep track of information in notes.

Writing for the Workplace shows you some models of the following forms of writing:

- **Note Cards**
- **Meeting Agenda**
- **Business Letter**
- **Friendly Letter**

Creating Note Cards

Whether you are working on a research report or gathering information for another purpose, it is helpful to keep your notes on individual cards or in note files on a computer. You will need to make sure that you note your sources on your cards. You can organize information many different ways, but it is most helpful to keep notes of one kind together.

> The **topic** is the main focus of the notes.

> You can name the **source**, as shown here, or refer to the source by number (e.g., Source 3) if you are using source cards.

Topic: Octopus

Source: PBS Web site Accessed 10/15/2010

http://www.pbs.org/wnet/nature/episodes/ the-octopus-show/ a-legend-of-the-deep/2014/

- Acrobatic and shy animals
- Can squeeze into very small spaces to hide or catch food
- Talented swimmers
- Can change color
- Live in all kinds of environments

> In the notes section focus on the ideas that are most important to your research. Note that these ideas may not always be the main ideas of the selection you are reading. You do not need to write in full sentences. However, you may want to use bullets to make your notes easier to read.

Writing a Meeting Agenda

When you have a meeting, it is helpful to use an agenda. An agenda tells what will be discussed in the meeting. It tells who is responsible for which topic. It also provides a guide for the amount of time to be spent on each topic.

Book Drive Project Meeting

Your meeting will need a **title** that explains the purpose of the meeting.

Saturday, February 6, 2010 2:00 P.M–6:00 P.M

You should also include the **date** and **time**.

Called by Daphne Farkis

This is the person who **called** the meeting. The person often, but not always, leads parts of the meeting.

Attendees: Bill Aldridge, Erika Cruz, Alexis Chang, Daphne Farkis, Alex Guitierrez, Tiffany Hopper, John Robinson, Sylvie Snopes

The **attendees** are all the people invited to the meeting.

The **time** provides a guide for how long a topic should be discussed.

This is the **item**, or **topic**, to be discussed.

The **owner** is the person who will lead each section of the meeting.

Time	Item	Owner
2:00 P.M–2:30 P.M	Welcome and introduction	Daphne
2:30 P.M–3:30 P.M	Overview of book drive process	Daphne
3:30 P.M–4:00 P.M	Discuss roles and responsibilities	Alexis, All
4:00 P.M–4:30 P.M	Break	All
4:30 P.M–5:00 P.M	Brainstorm session for flyer ideas	Erika, All
5:00 P.M–5:30 P.M	Next steps and deadlines	Daphne, All
5:30 P.M–6:00 P.M	Recap and adjournment	Daphne

Writing Business Letters

Business letters are often formal in tone and written for a specific business purpose. They generally follow one of several acceptable formats. In block format, all parts of the letter are at the left margin. All business letters, however, have the same parts: heading, inside address, salutation, body, closing, and signature.

The **heading** shows the writer's address and organization (if any).

The **inside address** indicates where the letter will be sent and the date.

A **salutation**, or **greeting**, is punctuated by a colon. When the specific addressee is not known, use a general greeting such as "To Whom It May Concern."

The **body** of the letter states the writer's purpose. In this case, the writer requests that the class participate in the book drive.

The **closing**, "Sincerely," is common, as are "Best regards," "Yours truly," and "Respectfully yours."

Oscar Diego
Community Book Drive
P.O. Box 34535
Middletown, NY 10941

February 10, 2010
Yin Wallenez
English Teacher
Marsden School
1515 Main River Drive
Middletown, NY 10940

Dear Ms. Wallenez:

We are writing to you to encourage you and your class to join in this year's Community Book Drive. We really appreciated your participation last year and hope you will join us again. As you know, the Community Book Drive gathers books for hundreds of children who otherwise could not afford them. Last year we gathered more than 1,500 books!

Participating this year is simple. Just nominate two members of your class to serve as the book drive leaders. They will post flyers about the book drive around the school and other community areas. They will also be responsible for letting the book drive team leaders know when the drop boxes at your school are getting full.

Please let me know if you are interested. I sure hope that your class will be able to make this year's drive as much of a success as the last! Thanks for your time and consideration.

Sincerely,

Oscar Diego

Oscar Diego • Co-Coordinator, Community Book Drive

Writing Friendly Letters

Friendly letters are less formal than business letters. You can use this form to write to a friend, a family member, or anyone with whom you'd like to communicate in a personal, friendly way. Like business letters, friendly letters have the following parts: heading, inside address, salutation, body, closing, and signature. The purpose of a friendly letter might be:

- to share news and feelings
- to send or answer an invitation
- to express thanks

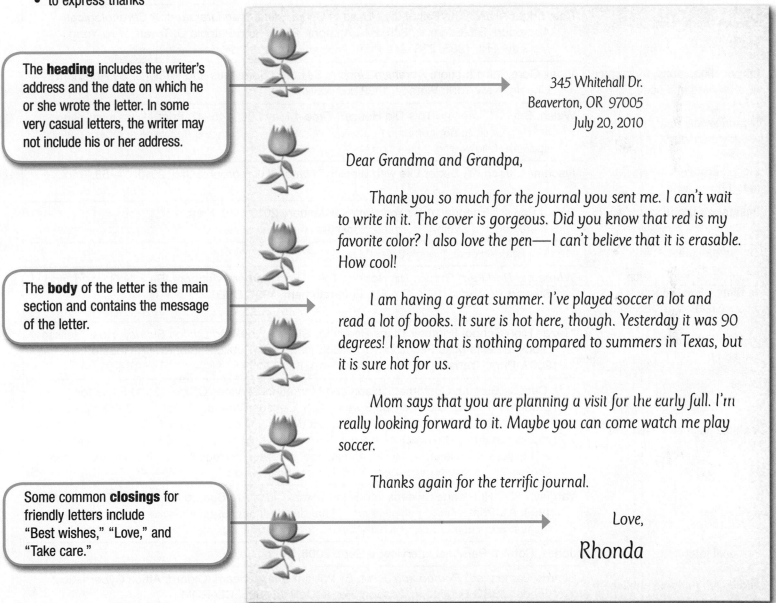

The **heading** includes the writer's address and the date on which he or she wrote the letter. In some very casual letters, the writer may not include his or her address.

The **body** of the letter is the main section and contains the message of the letter.

Some common **closings** for friendly letters include "Best wishes," "Love," and "Take care."

345 Whitehall Dr.
Beaverton, OR 97005
July 20, 2010

Dear Grandma and Grandpa,

Thank you so much for the journal you sent me. I can't wait to write in it. The cover is gorgeous. Did you know that red is my favorite color? I also love the pen—I can't believe that it is erasable. How cool!

I am having a great summer. I've played soccer a lot and read a lot of books. It sure is hot here, though. Yesterday it was 90 degrees! I know that is nothing compared to summers in Texas, but it is sure hot for us.

Mom says that you are planning a visit for the early fall. I'm really looking forward to it. Maybe you can come watch me play soccer.

Thanks again for the terrific journal.

Love,

Rhonda

MLA Style for Listing Sources

Book with one author	London, Jack. *White Fang.* Clayton, DE: Prestwick House, 2007. Print.
Book with two or three authors	Veit, Richard, and Christopher Gould. *Writing, Reading, and Research.* 8th ed. Boston: Wadsworth Cengage, 2009. Print.
Book prepared by an editor	Twain, Mark. *The Complete Essays of Mark Twain.* Ed. Charles Neider. New York: Da Capo, 2000. Print.
Book with more than three authors or editors	Donald, Robert B., et al. *Writing Clear Essays.* 3rd ed. Upper Saddle River, NJ: Prentice Hall, Inc., 1996. Print.
A single work from an anthology	Poe, Edgar Allan. "The Fall of the House of Usher." *American Literature: A Chronological Approach.* Ed. Edgar H. Schuster, Anthony Tovatt, and Patricia O. Tovatt. New York: McGraw-Hill, 1985. 233–247. Print. [Indicate pages for the entire selection.]
Introduction, foreward, preface, or afterward in a book	Vidal, Gore. Introduction. *Abraham Lincoln: Selected Speeches and Writings.* By Abraham Lincoln. New York: Vintage, 1992. xxi–xxvii. Print.
Signed article in a weekly magazine	Walsh, Brian. "Greening This Old House." *Time* 4 May 2009: 45–47. Print. [For a multi-page article that does not appear on consecutive pages, write only the first page number on which it appears, followed by a plus sign.]
Signed article in a monthly magazine	Fischman, Josh. "A Better Life with Bionics." *National Geographic* Jan. 2010: 34–53. Print.
Unsigned editorial or story	"Wind Power." Editorial. *New York Times* 9 January 2010: A18. Print. [If the editorial or story is signed, begin with the author's name.]
Signed pamphlet	[Treat the pamphlet as though it were a book.]
Audiovisual media, such as films, slide programs, videocassettes, DVDs	*Where the Red Fern Grows.* Dir. Norman Toker. Perf. James Whitmore, Beverly Garland, and Stewart Peterson. 1974. Sterling Entertainment, 1997. DVD.
Radio or TV broadcast transcript	"Texas High School Football Titans Ready for Clash." *Weekend Edition Sunday.* Host Melissa Block. Guests Mike Pesca and Tom Goldman. Natl. Public Radio. KUHF, Houston, 18 Dec. 2009. Print. Transcript.
A single page on a Web site	U.S. Census Bureau: Customer Liaison and Marketing Services Office. "State Facts for Students: Texas." *U.S. Census Bureau.* U.S. Census Bureau, 15 October 2009. Web. 1 November 2009. [Indicate the date of last update if known or use n.d. if not known. After the medium of publication, include the date you accessed the information. You do not need the URL unless it is the only way to find the page. If needed, include it in angled brackets at the end, i.e. <http://www.census.gov/schools/facts/texas.html >.]
Newspaper	Yardley, Jim. "Hurricane Sweeps into Rural Texas; Cities Are Spared." *New York Times* 23 Aug. 1999: A1. Print. [For a multipage article that does not appear on consecutive pages, write only the first page number on which it appears, followed by a plus sign.]
Personal interview	Jones, Robert. Personal interview. 4 Sept. 2006.
Audio with multiple publishers	Simms, James, ed. *Romeo and Juliet.* By William Shakespeare. Oxford: Attica Cybernetics; London: BBC Education; London: HarperCollins, 1995. CD-ROM.
Signed article from an encyclopedia	Askeland, Donald R. "Welding." *World Book Encyclopedia.* 1991 ed. Print. [For a well-known reference, you do not need to include the publisher information, only the edition and year, followed by the medium used.]

Commonly Misspelled Words

The list on this page presents words that cause problems for many people. Some of these words are spelled according to set rules, but others follow no specific rules. As you review this list, check to see how many of the words give you trouble in your own writing.

absence	benefit	conscience	excellent	library	prejudice
absolutely	bicycle	conscientious	exercise	license	previous
accidentally	bought	conscious	experience	lightning	probably
accurate	brief	continuous	explanation	likable	procedure
achievement	brilliant	convenience	extension	literature	proceed
affect	bulletin	coolly	extraordinary	mathematics	pronunciation
agreeable	bury	cooperate	familiar	maximum	realize
aisle	buses	correspondence	fascinating	minimum	really
all right	business	courageous	February	misspell	receipt
allowance	cafeteria	courteous	fiery	naturally	receive
analysis	calendar	criticism	financial	necessary	recognize
analyze	campaign	curiosity	foreign	neighbor	recommend
ancient	canceled	deceive	fourth	niece	rehearse
anniversary	candidate	decision	generally	ninety	repetition
answer	capital	defendant	genuine	noticeable	restaurant
anticipate	capitol	definitely	government	occasion	rhythm
anxiety	career	dependent	grammar	occasionally	sandwich
apologize	cashier	description	guidance	occur	schedule
appearance	category	desert	height	occurred	scissors
appreciate	ceiling	dessert	humorous	occurrence	theater
appropriate	certain	dining	immediately	opinion	truly
argument	changeable	disappointed	immigrant	opportunity	usage
athletic	characteristic	distinguish	independence	parallel	valuable
attendance	clothes	effect	independent	particularly	various
awkward	colonel	eighth	individual	personally	vegetable
bargain	column	embarrass	intelligence	persuade	weight
battery	commercial	enthusiastic	judgment	physician	weird
beautiful	commitment	envelope	knowledge	possibility	whale
beginning	condemn	environment	lawyer	precede	yield
believe	congratulate	especially	legible	preferable	

A

action (ak´shən) *n.* in a story or play, the events which are part of the plot

advantage (ad vant´ij) *n.* something that puts a person in a better position than others; a way in which one thing is better than another

analysis (ə nal´ə sis) *n.* the process of looking at something closely to understand its meaning, structure, or parts

analyze (an´ə līz) *v.* to look at something carefully to understand its meaning or structure

anticipate (an tis´ə pāt´) *v.* to expect or predict; to foresee and then be ready to deal with

argument (är´gyü mənt) *n.* a discussion (written or spoken) which aims to persuade; a set of statements putting forward and backing up an idea or position

audience (ô´dē əns) *n.* the readers of a book or other piece of writing; a group of listeners or viewers

authority (ə thôr´ə tē) *n.* a person or written work that is accepted as a source of reliable or expert information

C

cause (kôz) *n.* a person, object, or event that makes something happen

character (kar´ik tər) *n.* a person (or animal) who plays a part in the action of a story, play, or movie

chronological (krän´ə läj´i kəl) *adj.* described or arranged in the order of time, starting with what happened first

coherence (kō hir´ənts) *n.* the state of having ideas that are clear and logical

coherent (kō hir´ənt) *adj.* well-planned, clear, logical; holding together well

compare (kəm par´) *v.* to examine the differences and similarities between things

comparison (kəm par´ə sən) *n.* the act of comparing, examining the differences and similarities between two or more things

conclusions (kən klü´zhənz) *n.* opinions and ideas formed about something after careful study or thought

conflict (kän´flikt´) *n.* the struggle between people or opposing forces which creates the dramatic action in a play or story

connection (kə nek´shən) *n.* an event or thing that brings together people or ideas; a relationship between people and/or ideas

consequence (kän´si kwens´) *n.* the result, or outcome, of a previous action

consider (kən sid´ər) *v.* to take into account; to think about with care

contradict (kän´trə dikt´) *v.* to say something is wrong or not true

contrast (kən trast´) *v.* to compare in a way that shows differences

controversial (kän´trə vur´shəl) *adj.* something which is likely to stir up strong disagreement

convey (kən vā´) *v.* to make something (for example, an idea or a feeling) known to someone; to communicate

counter-argument (kount´ər är´gyü mənt) *n.* a reason against the original argument

D

demonstrate (dem´ən strāt´) *v.* to make a fact clear by giving proof or evidence

detail (dē´tāl´) *n.* a specific fact or piece of information about something

develop (di vel´əp) *v.* to explain or build an idea or example bit by bit

device (di vīs´) *n.* the use of words to gain a particular effect in a piece of writing

dialogue (dī´ə lôg´) *n.* a conversation between two or more people in a book, play, or movie

differentiate (dif´ər en´shē āt´) *v.* to notice differences in information

documentation (däk´yü mən tā´shən) *n.* the noting of sources to back up an idea or opinion

E

effect (e fekt´) *n.* the way that something changes because of a separate action

effective (e fekt´iv) *adj.* successful in getting the desired results

emotion (ē mō´shən) *n.* a feeling, such as love or joy; feelings and automatic responses, as opposed to logical thoughts and conclusions

evidence (ev´ə dəns) *n.* anything that gives proof or shows something to be true

external (ek stūr´nəl) *adj.* on the outside

extraneous (ek strā´nē əs) *adj.* not relevant, unnecessary; unrelated to the subject being discussed

F

factor (fak´tər) *n.* something that is one of the reasons for a particular result or outcome

fact (fakt) *n.* a piece of information that can be shown to be true

focus (fō´kəs) *n.* the main topic or most important point; the center of attention

formal (fôr´məl) *adj.* reflecting language that is traditional and correct, not casual

formatting (fôr´mat´ing) *adj.* related to the arrangement of text, images, and graphics on a page

G

genre (zhän´rə) *n.* a type of writing that contains certain features

H

hyperbole (hī pur´bə lē) *n.* over-the-top exaggeration

I

idiom (id´ē əm) *n.* an expression, made up of a group of words, where the meaning as a whole is different from what the words mean individually

image (im´ij) *n.* a word or phrase in a poem or other kind of writing which appeals to one or more of the five senses

imagery (im´ij rē) *n.* descriptive language that paints pictures in the mind or appeals to the senses

inconsistencies (in´kən sis´tən sēz) *n.* things that contradict each other

information (in´fər mā´shən) *n.* facts about a subject or topic

insight (in´sīt´) *n.* a useful, important, and deep understanding about a topic

internal (in tūr´nəl) *adj.* on the inside

introduce (in´trə düs) *v.* to present a person or information to another for the first time

introduction (in´trə duk´shən) *n.* the part at the beginning of a piece of writing which often tells what the rest will be about

J

judgment (juj´mənt) *n.* an opinion or conclusion formed after careful thought and evaluation

L

letter (let´ər) *n.* a written or printed message

line (līn) *n.* the direction of the action in a plot or story ("plot line" and "story line"); one row of words in a poem; one set of words spoken by an actor in a play or movie

literary (lit´ər ar´ē) *adj.* of or relating to books or other written material

logical (läj´i kəl) *adj.* clear and reasonable; based on logic

M

meter (mēt´ər) *n.* a poem's rhythmic pattern, made by the number of beats in each line

N

narrative (nar´ə tiv) *n.* a story, either fiction or nonfiction

note (nōt) *v.* to observe and/or mention

O

offensive (ə fens´iv) *adj.* upsetting, embarrassing, rude, hurtful or angering; aggressive, attacking

opinion (ə pin´yən) *n.* a belief or view that is not necessarily based on facts

oppose (ə pōz´) *v.* go against, disagree

organized (ôr´gə nīzd´) *adj.* the state of being in order

P

paraphrase (par´ə frāz´) *v.* to reword information into one's own words

personal (pūr´sən əl) *adj.* individual, relating to a particular person

personification (pər sän´ə fə kā´shən) *n.* a type of figurative language where animals or other non-humans are given human characteristics

plausible (plô´zə bəl) *adj.* likely to be true or valid

point of view (point uv vyü) *n.* the perspective from which a story is told; an attitude, position, standpoint, or way of looking at a situation; an opinion

position (pə zish´ən) *n.* a point of view or attitude toward something

profound (prō found´) *adj.* very deep, intense, or strong; full of insight

Q

quality (kwôl´ə tē) *n.* the degree of excellence of something

quotation (kwō tā´shən) *n.* a group of words copied exactly from a speech or piece of writing

R

reader-friendly (rēd´ər frend´lē) *adj.* easy for an audience to read and understand

research (rē´surch´) *v.* to carefully study information on a topic; *n.* the careful study of information on a topic

reasoning (rē´zən ing) *n.* the process of reaching a conclusion by looking at the facts

reflect (ri flekt´) *v.* to show, make apparent

resolution (rez´ə lü´shən) *n.* what happens to resolve the conflict in the plot of a story

rhetorical devices (ri tôr´i kəl di vī´səz) *n.* strategies and techniques, for example metaphor and hyperbole, used by writers to draw in or persuade readers

S

scheme (skēm) *n.* (for a poem) a design or ordered structure

sensory (sen´sər ē) *adj.* of or relating to the five senses

sequence (sē´kwəns) *n.* when the items in a group follow each other in a particular order

setting (set´ing) *n.* the time and place of the action in a story or other piece of writing

stanza (stan´zə) *n.* a group of lines of poetry, usually with a similar length and pattern, separated from other lines with spaces

strategy (strat´ə jē) *n.* in a piece of writing, a literary tactic or method (such as flashback or foreshadowing) used by the writer to achieve a certain goal or effect

structure (struk´chər) *n.* the way something is organized and put together; *v.* to put together according to a pattern or plan

style (stīl) *n.* a way of doing something; a way of writing

subject (sub´jekt) *n.* something that is discussed or studied; a topic

support (sə pôrt´) *v.* to hold up, to back

suspense (sə spens´) *n.* a feeling of anxiety and uncertainty about what will happen in a story or other piece of writing

sustain (sə stān´) *v.* to keep up, hold up; to affirm or support as true

symbol (sim´bəl) *n.* anything that stands for or represents something else

synthesize (sin´thə sīz´) *v.* to combine, to bring different parts together into a whole

T

technique (tek nēk´) *n.* a special way of doing something

theme (thēm) *n.* a central message, concern, or purpose in a literary work

thesis (thē´sis) *n.* an idea or theory that is stated and then discussed in a logical way

tone (tōn) *n.* a writer's attitude toward his or her subject

topic (täp´ik) *n.* a subject that is written about or discussed

transition (tran zish´ən) *n.* the change from one part, place, or idea to another; in writing, the change between sentences, paragraphs, and ideas

V

verse (vūrs) *n.* a group of lines that make a unit in a poem, a stanza; writing, such as poetry, that has a meter

viewpoint (vyü´point´) *n.* an attitude, position, standpoint, or way of looking at a situation

Spanish Glossary

A

action / acción *s.* en una historia u obra de teatro, los eventos que son parte del argumento

advantage / ventaja *s.* algo que le pone a alguien en una mejor posición que a otros; la forma en la que una cosa es mejor que otra

analysis / análisis *s.* el proceso de examinar algo detenidamente para entender su significado, su estructura o sus partes

analyze / analizar *v.* examinar algo detenidamente para entender su significado o estructura

anticipate / anticipar *v.* esperar o predecir; prever y estar preparado para tratar con algo

argument / argumento *s.* razonamiento (escrito o hablado) con el fin de persuadir; una serie de declaraciones que proponen o apoyan una idea o postura

audience / audiencia, público *s.* los lectores de un libro u otra obra escrita; un grupo de oyentes o espectadores

authority / autoridad *s.* una persona u obra escrita que es aceptada como una fuente de información fiable o experta

C

cause / causa *s.* una persona, objeto, o evento que hace que ocurra algo

character / personaje *s.* un individuo (humano o animal) que tiene un papel en la acción de un cuento, una obra de teatro o una película

chronological / cronológico *adj.* descrito o arreglado en el orden temporal, empezando con el evento que ocurrió primero

coherence / coherencia *s.* el estado de tener ideas claras y lógicas

coherent / coherente *adj.* bien planeado, claro, lógico; congruente

compare / comparar *v.* examinar las diferencias y semejanzas entre cosas

comparison / comparación *s.* el acto de comparar, examinar las diferencias y semejanzas entre dos más cosas

conclusions / conclusiones *s.* opiniones o ideas sobre una materia o deducción a que se ha llegado tras su estudio o análisi

conflict / conflicto *s.* la lucha entre personas o fuerzas opuestas que crea la acción dramática en una obra de teatro o un cuento

connection / conexión *s.* un evento o una cosa que une a las personas o ideas; una relación entre personas y/o ideas

consequence / consecuencia *s.* el resultado de una acción previa

consider / considerar *v.* tomar en cuenta; meditar sobre algo

contradict / contradecir *v.* decir algo que no es correcto o que no es verdad

contrast / contrastar *v.* comparar dos o más cosas para señalar las diferencias entre ellas

controversial / controvertido *adj.* algo que tiende a levantar diferencias de opiniones

convey / expresar *v.* darse a entender algo a alguien (por ejemplo una idea o sentimiento); comunicar

counter-argument / contraargumento *s.* una razón contra el argumento original

D

demonstrate / demostrar *v.* aclarar un hecho por dar pruebas o evidencia

detail / detalle *s.* un dato específico o información específica de algo

develop / desarrollar *v.* explicar o exponer poco a poco una idea o ejemplo

device / técnica (literaria) *s.* el uso de palabras para tener un efecto específico en una obra escrita

dialogue / diálogo *s.* una conversación entre dos personajes o más en un libro, obra de teatro o película

differentiate / diferenciar *v.* notar las diferencias

documentation / documentación *s.* la anotación de fuentes para apoyar una idea u opinión

E

effect / efecto *s.* la manera en la que algo cambia a causa de una acción separada

effective / efectivo, eficaz *adj.* exitoso en producir los resultados deseados

emotion / sentimiento *s.* una sensación emotiva como el amor o la alegría; sensaciones y respuestas automáticas, en contraste a los pensamientos y conclusiones lógicos

evidence / pruebas *s.* cualquier cosa que demuestre o indique que algo es cierto

external / externo *adj.* afuera de

extraneous / superfluo *adj.* irrelevante, innecesario, no relacionado al tema tratado

F

factor / factor *s.* algo que es una de las razones de un resultado determinado

fact / hecho *s.* un dato que se puede verificar

focus / foco, idea central *s.* el tema principal o la idea más importante; el centro de atención

formal / formal *adj.* que refleja lenguaje tradicional y correcto, no informal

formatting / formateo *s.* la colocación de texto, imágenes y gráficos en una página

G

genre / género *s.* una clase de escritura que tiene características específicas

H

hyperbole / hipérbole *s.* exageración excesiva

I

idiom / modismo *s.* una expresión compuesta de un grupo de palabras cuyo significado en conjunto es diferente de lo que significan las palabras individuales

image / imagen *s.* una palabra o frase en un poema u otra clase de escritura que atrae uno o más de los cinco sentidos

imagery / imágenes *s.* lenguaje descriptivo que crea dibujos en la mente o que atrae los sentidos

inconsistencies / inconsecuencias *s.* cosas que se contradicen

information / información *s.* datos sobre un asunto o tema

insight / perspicacia *s.* el profundo entendimiento útil e importante de un tema

internal / interno *adj.* dentro de

introduce / presentar *v.* dar a conocer a una persona o información por primera vez

introduction / introducción *s.* la parte inicial de una obra escrita que muchas veces cuenta de qué se trata el resto de la obra

J

judgment / juicio *s.* una opinión o conclusión formada después de una consideración y evaluación cuidadosa

L

letter /carta *s.* un mensaje escrito o impreso

line / línea, verso *s.* la dirección de la acción en un argumento o historia (por ejemplo, "plot line" y "story line" en inglés); una línea de palabras en un poema; un grupo de palabras habladas por un actor en una obra de teatro o película

literary / literario *adj.* perteneciente o relativo a los libros u otra materia escrita

logical / lógico *adj.* claro y razonable; basado en la lógica

M

meter / métrica *s.* el patrón rítmico de un poema, marcado por el tiempo y ritmo de cada verso

N

narrative / narrativa *s.* un cuento de ficción o no ficción

note / notar *v.* observar y/o mencionar

O

offensive / ofensivo *adj.* que provoca disgusto, vergüenza, daño o enfado; grosero, agresivo, combativo

opinion / opinión *s.* una creencia o perspectiva que no es necesariamente basada en los hechos

oppose / oponerse *v.* estar en contra, no estar de acuerdo

organized / organizado *adj.* que está ordenado

P

paraphrase / parafrasear *v.* formular información utilizando sus propias palabras

personal / personal *adj.* individual, relativo a una persona particular

personification / personificación *n.* un tipo de lenguaje figurado en el que los animales u otros seres no humanos tienen características humanas

plausible / creíble *adj.* con buena probabilidad de ser verdadero o válido

point of view / punto de vista *n.* la perspectiva de la cual se cuenta una historia; una actitud, postura, o manera de ver una situación; una opinión

position / postura *n.* el punto de vista o la actitud hacia algo

profound / profundo *adj.* muy intenso o fuerte; lleno de perspicacia

Q

quality / calidad *s.* el grado de excelencia de algo

quotation / cita *s.* un grupo de palabras copiadas exactamente de un discurso o texto

R

reasoning / razonamiento *s.* el proceso de llegar a una conclusión por examinar los hechos

reflect / reflejar *v.* mostrar, hacer aparente

research / investigar *v.* estudiar cuidadosamente la información sobre un tema; investigación s. el estudio cuidadoso de la información sobre un tema

resolution / resolución *s.* lo que ocurre para resolver el conflicto en el argumento de una historia

rhetorical devices / técnicas retóricas *s.* estrategias y técnicas, por ejemplo la metáfora y la hipérbole, utilizadas por los escritores para atraer o persuadir a los lectores

S

scheme / esquema *s.* (para un poema) un diseño o estructura ordenada

sensory / sensorial *adj.* perteneciente o relativo a los cinco sentidos

sequence / secuencia *s.* cuando una serie de eventos ocurre en un orden determinado

setting / escenario *s.* el lugar y el momento de la acción en un cuento u otra obra escrita

stanza / estrofa *s.* un grupo de líneas de poesía, normalmente con un patrón y extensión similar, separado por espacios de otras líneas

strategy / estrategia *s.* en un texto, una táctica o método literario (como el flashback o el presagio) empleado por el autor para lograr un objetivo o efecto específico

structure / estructura *s.* la manera en la que algo está organizado o compuesto; estructurar v. organizar o componer según un patrón o plan

style / estilo *s.* una manera de hacer algo; una forma de escribir

subject / tema *s.* algo de que se habla o que se estudia; un tema

support / apoyar *v.* sostener, respaldar

suspense / suspenso *s.* una sensación de ansiedad e incertidumbre sobre lo que va a pasar en una historia u otra obra escrita

sustain / sostener *v.* mantener, apoyar; afirmar o confirmar como verdadero

symbol / símbolo *s.* algo que representa o significa otra cosa

synthesize / sintetizar *v.* combinar, unir diferentes partes para formar una totalidad

T

technique / técnica *s.* una manera especial de hacer algo

theme / tema *s.* una idea, asunto, o propósito principal de una obra literaria

thesis / tesis *s.* una idea o teoría que se expone y que se discute de una manera lógica

tone / tono *s.* la actitud del autor hacia su tema o materia

topic / tema *s.* una idea de la cual se escribe y que se discute

transition / transición *s.* el cambio entre partes, lugares y conceptos; en la escritura, el cambio entre oraciones, párrafos e ideas

V

verse / verso *s.* un grupo de líneas que componen una unidad en un poema, una estrofa; texto, como la poesía, que tiene una métrica

viewpoint / punto de vista *s.* una actitud, postura, o manera de interpretar una situación

Meeting Agenda

Meeting Title: _____

Date: _____

Time: _____

Called by: _____

Attendees: _____

_____

Time	Item	Owner

Cause and Effect Chart

Cluster Diagram

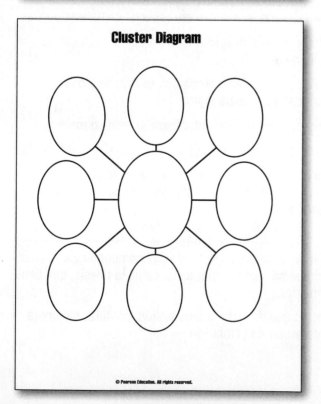

Five Ws Chart

Use these questions as you read, and write important details. Remember, you may not need to answer every question.

Who?

What?

When?

Where?

Why?

Writing Coach Online

Resource Go online for printable versions of these graphic organizers.

KWL Chart

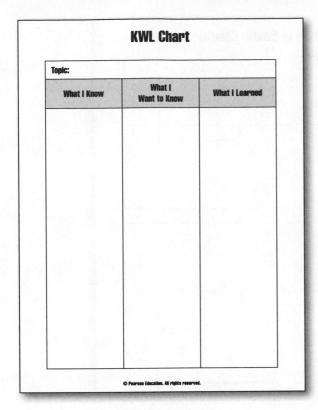

Topic:

What I Know	What I Want to Know	What I Learned

Main Idea and Details Web

Use these questions as you read, and write important details. Remember, you may not need to answer every question.

Meeting Notes

Topic

Decisions

Next Steps

Note Card

Topic:

Source:
-
-
-

Topic:

Source:
-
-
-

Problem and Solution Chart

Problem:

Details of Problem:

Solution 1:

Outcome:

Solution 2:

Outcome:

Solution 3:

Outcome:

Proposed Solution:

Series of Events Chart/Flowchart

Source Card

Source Number: _____

Source Name: _____

Kind of Source: _____

Author(s): _____

Editor (when applicable): _____

Publisher: _____

Publication Date: _____

Publication Location: _____

Other Information _____

Source Number: _____

Source Name: _____

Kind of Source: _____

Author(s): _____

Editor (when applicable): _____

Publisher: _____

Publication Date: _____

Publication Location: _____

Other Information _____

Outline

Topic   I. _____

   Subtopic   A. _____

      Supporting   1. _____
      details   2. _____
                 3. _____
                 4. _____

   Subtopic   B. _____

      Supporting   1. _____
      details   2. _____
                 3. _____
                 4. _____

Topic   II. _____

   Subtopic   A. _____

      Supporting   1. _____
      details   2. _____
                 3. _____
                 4. _____

   Subtopic   B. _____

      Supporting   1. _____
      details   2. _____
                 3. _____
                 4. _____

Steps in a Process Chart

Steps	Details
Step 1:	
Step 2:	
Step 3:	
Step 4:	
Step 5:	

Storyboard

Timeline

Venn Diagram

Graphic Organizer Handbook   **R27**

Listening and Speaking Handbook

Communication travels between people in many forms. You receive information by listening to others, and you convey information through speaking. The more developed these skills are, the more you will be able to communicate your ideas, as well as to comprehend the ideas of others.

If you improve your listening skills, it will become easier to focus your attention on classroom discussions and to identify important information more accurately. If you develop good speaking skills, you will be better prepared to contribute effectively in group discussions, to give formal presentations with more confidence, and to communicate your feelings and ideas to others more easily.

> This handbook will help you increase your ability in these two key areas of communication.

Listening

Different situations call for different types of listening. Learn more about the four main types of listening—critical, empathic, appreciative, and reflective—in the chart below.

Types of Listening		
Type	**How to Listen**	**Situations**
Critical	Listen for facts and supporting details to understand and evaluate the speaker's message.	Informative or persuasive speeches, class discussions, announcements
Empathic	Imagine yourself in the other person's position, and try to understand what he or she is thinking.	Conversations with friends or family
Appreciative	Identify and analyze aesthetic or artistic elements, such as character development, rhyme, imagery, and descriptive language.	Oral presentations of a poem, dramatic performances
Reflective	Ask questions to get information, and use the speaker's responses to form new questions.	Class or group discussions

Using Different Types of Questions

A speaker's ideas may not always be clear to you. You may need to ask questions to clarify your understanding. If you understand the different types of questions, you will be able to get the information you need.

- An **open-ended question** does not lead to a single, specific response. Use this question to open up a discussion: "What did you think of the piano recital?"

- A **closed question** leads to a specific response and must be answered with a yes or no: "Did you play a piece by Chopin at your recital?"

- A **factual question** is aimed at getting a particular piece of information and must be answered with facts: "How many years have you been playing the piano?"

Participating in a Group Discussion

In a group discussion, you openly discuss ideas and topics in an informal setting. The group discussions in which you participate will involve, for the most part, your classmates and focus on the subjects you are studying. To get the most out of a group discussion, you need to participate in it.

Use group discussions to express and to listen to ideas in an informal setting.

Communicate Effectively Think about the points you want to make, the order in which you want to make them, the words you will use to express them, and the examples that will support these points before you speak.

Ask Questions Asking questions can help you improve your comprehension of another speaker's ideas. It may also call attention to possible errors in another speaker's points.

Make Relevant Contributions Stay focused on the topic being discussed. Relate comments to your own experience and knowledge, and clearly connect them to your topic. It is important to listen to the points others make so you can build off their ideas. Work to share the connections you see. For example, say whether you agree or disagree, or tell the goup how your ideas connect.

Speaking

Giving a presentation or speech before an audience is generally recognized as public speaking. Effective speakers are well prepared and deliver speeches smoothly and with confidence.

Recognizing Different Kinds of Speeches

There are four main kinds of speeches: informative speeches, persuasive speeches, entertaining speeches, and extemporaneous speeches.

Consider the purpose and audience of your speech before deciding what kind of speech you will give.

- Give an **informative speech** to explain an idea, a process, an object, or an event.

- Give a **persuasive speech** to get your listeners to agree with your position or to take some action. Use formal English when speaking.

- Give an **entertaining speech** to offer your listeners something to enjoy or to amuse them. Use both informal and formal language.

- Give an **extemporaneous speech** when an impromptu occasion arises. It is an informal speech because you do not have a prepared manuscript.

Preparing and Presenting a Speech

If you are asked to deliver a speech, begin choosing a topic that you like or know well. Then, prepare your speech for your audience.

To prepare your speech, research your topic. Make an outline, and use numbered note cards.

Gather Information Use the library and other resources to gather reliable information and to find examples to support your ideas.

Organizing Information Organize your information by writing an outline of main ideas and major details. Then, when you deliver your speech, write the main ideas, major details, quotations, and facts on note cards.

When presenting your speech, use rhetorical forms of language and verbal and nonverbal strategies.

Use Rhetorical Language Repeat key words and phrases to identify your key points. Use active verbs and colorful adjectives to keep your speech interesting. Use parallel phrases to insert a sense of rhythm.

Use Verbal and Nonverbal Strategies Vary the pitch and tone of your voice, and the rate at which you speak. Speak loudly and emphasize key words or phrases. Avoid consistently reading your speech from your notes. Work to maintain eye contact with the audience. As you speak, connect with the audience by using gestures and facial expressions to emphasize key points.

Evaluating a Speech

Evaluating a speech gives you the chance to judge another speaker's skills. It also gives you the opportunity to review and improve your own methods for preparing and presenting a speech.

When you evaluate a speech, you help the speaker and yourself to learn from experience. Listed below are some questions you might ask yourself while evaluating another person's speech or one of your own speeches.

- Did the speaker introduce the topic clearly, develop it well, and conclude it effectively?

- Did the speaker support each main idea with appropriate details?

- Did the speaker approach the platform confidently and establish eye contact with the audience?

- Did the speaker's facial expressions, gestures, and movements appropriately reinforce the words spoken?

- Did the speaker vary the pitch of his or her voice and the rate of his or her speaking?

- Did the speaker enunciate all words clearly?

Listening Critically to a Speech

Hearing happens naturally as sounds reach your ears. Listening, or critical listening, requires that you understand and interpret these sounds.

Critical listening requires preparation, active involvement, and self-evaluation from the listener.

Learning the Listening Process Listening is interactive; the more you involve yourself in the listening process, the more you will understand.

Focus Your Attention Focus your attention on the speaker and block out all distractions—people, noises, and objects. Find out more about the subject that will be discussed beforehand.

Interpret the Information To interpret a speaker's message successfully, you need to identify and understand important information. You might consider listening for repeated words or phrases, pausing momentarily to memorize and/or write key statements, watching non-verbal signals, and combining this new information with what you already know.

Respond to the Speaker's Message Respond to the information you have heard by identifying the larger message of the speech, its most useful points, and your position on the topic.

Multimedia projects, 25
advertisement for story, 217
instructions, 266–267
poetry, 139
press conference script, 249
public action day, 191
research report, 264
sci-fi film trailer, 113

Multimedia resources, 232

Music, sharing, R10

Music titles. *See* Titles

Mystery stories, 11, 93

Myths, 12, 93

Negative words, avoiding double, 455, *456*

Newspaper articles, 17, 147

Nominative pronoun case, 502, *503*, 504, *507, 510*, 511

Non-count nouns, 295, *297*

Nonfiction narration, 9, 64–89
fiction versus, 91
forms of, 9–10, 67
See also Personal narratives

Note cards, R12, R25

Notebook, 4

Notes
Meeting, R25
for research reports, 234–235, 265

Nouns, 293, 294
as adjectives, 331, 332, *333*, 334, *336*
adjectives modifying, 326–327, *328*
after other nouns, 405
beginning sentences with, 442
classifications, 294
concrete, 294, *296*
conjunctions connecting, 356–357
count, 295, *297*
hyphens with compound, 590, *591*
infinitive phrase as, 412, *414*
non-count, 295, *297*
in pronoun-antecedent agreement, 527–529
pronouns before, 506
singular/plural, 514
apostrophes with possessive case for, 286, 595
types, 294–295, 296–297, 298, 299
verbs as, 411, 413
See also Abstract nouns; Collective nouns; Common nouns; Compound nouns; Possessive nouns; Predicate nouns; Proper nouns

Number
in pronoun-antecedent agreement, 527–529
in subject-verb agreement, 514

Numbers
commas in, 566, 567, *568*
hyphens in, 589, *591*

compound, 374, 375–376
indefinite pronouns as, 308–309
in questions, 378, 379
singular/plural, 514
unstated, 422, 494
of verbs
    nominative case for, 502, 504, *510*, 511
    in sentences, 368–369, 370
word order and finding, 377–378, 379, 380–381, *382*

Subject-verb agreement, 513, 526
collective nouns and, 518, 519
compound subjects and, 520–521, 523
indefinite pronouns and, 524–525, 526
in inverted sentences, 521–522, 523
in number, 514–516, 517
prepositions, prepositional phrases and, 214

Subjunctive mood, 494

Subordinate clauses, 415–416, 417
adjectival clauses as, 418
adverbial clauses as, 421
commas and, 556
forming sentences using, 49, 292, 425–426, 438, *440*
as fragments, 292, 415–416, *417*, 445–446
main versus, *428–430*
relative pronouns and, 306–307, 309, *310*
who and *whom* beginning, 511

Subordinating conjunctions, 357, *360–362*
in adverbial clauses, 421, 423
common, listed, 422
in complex sentences, 438
in subordinate clauses, 416

Suffixes, hyphens for, 589

Summaries, 224, 228, 234, 235, 240

Superlative forms, 534
of irregular modifiers, 538–539, 540
of regular modifiers, 535–536, 537
rules for using, 538–539, 540

Suspense, 103, 104

Syllables
hyphens dividing, 592–593, 594
modifiers with one or two, 535, 540
modifiers with three or more, 535, 540

Symbolism, 55

Symbols, in poetry, 129

Synthesizing information, 149, 155

T

Tables, 241

Tall tales, 12, 93

Taste, as sensory detail, 103

Technical newsletter, 166–167

Technology, 7, 39, 43, 52, 55
See also Media, writing for

TEKS (Texas Essential Knowledge and Skills), *R2–R5*

Television series titles. *See* Titles

Tense, 472, 480
See also Verbs

Texas Essential Knowledge and Skills (TEKS), *R2–R5*

Theme
in notes, 234, 265
in science fiction, 92, 102, 104, 108

for scripts, 24
See also Topics

Thesaurus, 39, 55, 273

Thesis/thesis statements
developing, 34, 53, 154
in persuasive essays, 172, 183
in research reports, 224, 226, 238–239, 244, 265
in responses to literature, 20
restating, 35, 53
for review of short stories, 200, 206
supporting, 35

Things. *See* Nouns

Thoughts, complete/incomplete
to show sudden break in, 605
using clauses, 415–416, 417
|using complements, 383–384, 385
using subjects/verbs, 292, 369, 370
See also Expressions; Fragments

Time (hours of day), *573*

Time management
research process and, 237
revising and, 36
writing process and, 5

Time periods, 615

Timeline, R27

Titles
of people, capitalization of, 622–623, *624*
of works
    capitalization of, 280, 625
    quotation marks in, 586, 588
    underlining/italics in, 586–587, 588

Tone, 24, 103, 117
See also Moods

in sentences, 369, 370
singular/plural, 515
subjects after
   agreement in, 521–522, 523
   for emphasis, 381, 382
   in questions, 378, 379
   for variety, 442, 443
substitutions for verb *walk*, 41
tenses, 471
   conjugating, 481–482, 485, 488, 489
   identifying, 480, 483, 487, *489*
   perfect, 82–83, *484–486*
   progressive, 82–83, 487, 488, *489*
   switching between, 284, 466
   using consistent, 82–83, 214–215, 284, 466, *467*
transitive, 314, 316
troublesome, 496–498, 499–500
unstated, in elliptical adverbial clause, 422
See also Action verbs; Compound verbs; Helping verbs; Linking verbs

Video, R10

Visual elements, 54

Vivid images, 81, 109, 135

Voice, 26–28, 57, 63
active, 490, 492, *493*
adding, to Web page, R10
in compare-and-contrast essays, 163
passive, 490, 491–492, 493
in personal narratives, 83
in persuasive essays, 172, 189
in poetry, 137
in research reports, 247
in review of short stories, 215
in science fiction, 111

Vowel sound, 329

W

Watching, finding ideas by, 3

Web page
adding voice to, R10
citation of, 236

Web safety, R6

White space, 54

Widgets, R9

Wikis, R11

Word choice, 27, 28, 58, 63
in compare-and-contrast essays, 163
in personal narratives, 83
in persuasive essays, 187, 189
in poetry, 137
in research reports, 247
in reviews of short stories, 215
in science fiction, 111

Word order
agreement in inverted, 521–522, 523
normal/inverted, 377–378, 379
reversing, for variety, 442, 443
rewording inverted
   to identify pronoun case, 511, 512
   to identify subject, 378–381, *382*

Words
commonly misspelled, R17
feelings through, 119
missing, 281
single, commas separating, 285
student's, 246
See also Specific types

Workplace writing, 22–23, 256–269
characteristics of, 257
forms of, 22, 257

Works Cited list, 228, 234, 236–237, 244

Writing
collaborative writing, **6,** 7
cooperative, 6
free, 4
to inform, 2, 251
objective versus subjective, 250
online tools for strengthening, 55
for persuasion, 2, 18–19
portfolio for, 7
Reader's Journal for, 7
reasons/purposes for, 2, 65, 197, 258
reflecting on, 7, 25, 47, 84, 112, 138, 248
types of, 3, 8–25, 53
See also Research writing; Workplace writing; specific forms and genres

Writing process, 26–47
comfortable environment for, 5
five steps in, 30
materials for, 5
for multimedia projects, 25
reasons for using, 31
rubrics in, 28–29
time management and, 5
working with others in, 6–7
See also Drafting; Editing; Organization; Planning; Prewriting; Publishing; Revising

Writing traits, 26–27, 48
for developing composition, 56–59
See also Conventions; Focus and coherence; Organization; Voice

Index of Authors and Titles

Acknowledgments

Grateful acknowledgment is made to the following for copyrighted material:

Carole Berglie, Literary Estate of May Swenson

"Southbound on the Freeway" by May Swenson from *Imaginary Gardens: American Poetry and Art for Young People*. Copyright © 1978 by May Swenson. Used by permission of The Literary Estate of May Swenson. All rights reserved.

Enslow Publishers, Inc.

From *Sandra Cisneros: Latina Writer and Activist* by Caryn Mirriam-Goldberg. Copyright © 1998 by Caryn Mirriam-Goldberg. Published by Enslow Publishers, Inc., Berkeley Heights, NJ. All rights reserved. Used by permission.

Neal Levin

"Baby Ate a Microchip" by Neal Levin previously published in *Rolling in the Aisles* (Meadowbrook Press). Copyright © 2004 Neal Levin. Used by permission.

Longman Publishing Group, A Division of Pearson Education, Inc.

"Writing in a Second Language" from *Writing: A Guide for College and Beyond (2nd Edition)* by Lester Faigley. Copyright © 2010 by Pearson Education. Used by permission.

National Council of Teachers of English (NCTE)

"Mistakes are a fact of Life: A National Comparative Study" by Andrea A. Lunsford and Karen J. Lunsford translated from *bcs. bedfordstmartins.com/lunsford/PDF/Lunsford_article_Mistakes. pdf*. Copyright © NCTE. Used by permission of National Council of Teachers of English (NCTE).

Naomi Shihab Nye

"The Rider" by Naomi Shihab Nye from *Invisible*. Copyright © 1998 by Naomi Shihab Nye. All rights reserved. Used by permission of the author.

Marian Reiner, Literary Agent

"December Leaves" by Kaye Starbird from *Don't Ever Cross A Crocodile*. Copyright © 1963, Copyright renewed © 1991 Kaye Starbird. Used by permission of Marian Reiner, Literary Agent.

Science News for Kids / Society for Science & the Public

"Brainy Bees Know Two from Three" by Liz Savage from *http:// www.sciencenewsforkids.org/articles/20090218/note3.asp*. Copyright © 2009 Society for Science & the Public. Used by permission of Science News.

Paul Zindel Revocable Trust c/o Curtis Brown, Ltd.

"My First Fistfight" by Paul Zindel. First published in *The Pigman and Me*, published by HarperCollins. Copyright © 1992 by Paul Zindel. Used by permission of Curtis Brown, Ltd.

Texas Education Agency

The *Texas Essential Knowledge and Skills for English Language Arts and Reading* reproduced by permission, Texas Education Agency, 1701 N. Congress Avenue, Austin, TX 78701

Note: Every effort has been made to locate the copyright owner of material reproduced in this component. Omissions brought to our attention will be corrected in subsequent editions.

Image Credits

Illustrations
   Robert Chouinard

All interior photos provided by Jupiter Images. Except

   64: © Barry Austin/age fotostock; 90: © Inti St Clair/age fotostock; 118: © Louis Brawley Louisey/age fotostock; 170: © Blend Images / SuperStock; 226, 228: Courtesy of The Library of Congress; 256: © Alistair Berg/ age fotostock.